BITTERSWEET GOODBYE

THE BLACK BARONS, THE GRAYS, AND THE 1948 NEGRO LEAGUE WORLD SERIES

EDITED BY FREDERICK C. BUSH AND BILL NOWLIN
ASSOCIATE EDITORS: CARL RIECHERS AND LEN LEVIN

Society for American Baseball Research, Inc.
Phoenix, AZ

Bittersweet Goodbye: The Black Barons, the Grays, and the 1948 Negro League World Series

Edited by Frederick C. Bush and Bill Nowlin
Associate editors: Carl Riechers and Len Levin

ISBN 978-1-943816-55-2
Ebook ISBN 978-1-943816-54-5

Cover and book design: Gilly Rosenthol

Front Cover Photographs: Spectators at a Negro League game (from the Withers Family Trust, Memphis, Tennessee) and Homestead Grays in action (from the National Baseball Hall of Fame, Cooperstown, New York).

Back Cover Images: Logos of the Birmingham Black Barons and Homestead Grays
(Courtesy of Charlie Fouché).

Society for American Baseball Research
Cronkite School at ASU
555 N. Central Ave. #416
Phoenix, AZ 85004
Phone: (602) 496-1460
Web: www.sabr.org
Facebook: Society for American Baseball Research
Twitter: @SABR

CONTENTS

CONTENTS

CONTENTS

PREFACE AND ACKNOWLEDGEMENTS

Love and appreciation for the game of baseball have been passed down from generation to generation for well over a century. In 2015, my oldest son Michael, who caught baseball fever from me at the youngest possible age, had just started second grade when he checked out a book from the library titled *The Journal of Biddy Owens* by Walter Dean Myers. Since it was written at a fourth-grade reading level, we sat down together to examine this fictionalized account of the Birmingham Black Barons. The events of the 1948 season were documented through the eyes of the title character, an imaginary teenager who serves as a part-time equipment manager and player for the Black Barons, to present both the Negro Leagues and the segregation in America that made them a necessity.

My son's favorite character/player in the book was Birmingham pitcher Bill Greason because of the position he played and the fact that he became a pastor in his post-baseball life. Michael wanted to know more about Greason, and I was curious as well, so I determined to write Greason's profile for the SABR Biography Project website. In the process of my research for the article, I was reminded that the 1948 World Series between Birmingham and the Homestead Grays had marked the end of an era as the Negro Leagues were in decline after Organized Baseball had begun to lure away their best players in the wake of Jackie Robinson's Brooklyn Dodgers debut in April 1947.

The decline (and eventual demise) of the Negro Leagues was considered a mixed blessing at the time. Although the integration of baseball certainly was a positive development, the Negro Leagues and many of their players began to fade into obscurity. I was certain that I was not the only person interested in the fate of the Negro League players of this era, and it seemed that the Birmingham and Homestead teams were logical representatives for an examination of the time period. The title of this book, *Bittersweet Goodbye*, is an acknowledgement of the paradox that the celebration of baseball's integration was mixed with sadness at the loss of the camaraderie among the black players who had to endure the tribulation of segregation; that camaraderie is on display in the letter by Willie Mays that opens this volume, which was written upon the occasion of his friend and former Black Barons teammate Jim Zapp's death in September 2016. The Negro Leagues also contributed greatly to African-American culture and pride during the dark days in which America was separate but not equal. This book provides a glimpse into baseball and its role in society as America entered a period of dramatic transition in race relations in the second half of the twentieth century.

The attempt to chronicle this period in black baseball poses a challenge due to the fact that even the major African-American newspapers of the day had turned their attention away from the Negro Leagues to the black players who had entered the major leagues during the 1947 and 1948 seasons. Such a reaction on the part of both the black press and black fans long had been predicted by both proponents and opponents of baseball's integration. Insofar as the games themselves are concerned, only brief articles and line scores (rather than box scores) are available for most games; thus, while this book was inspired by the last Negro League World Series in 1948, the primary focus of its content is on the players and the circumstances that surrounded them far more than the games themselves. The lack of detailed press coverage, the fact that not every player was a star with a lengthy career, and gaps in public records of that time (especially in regard to African-Americans) also have created a situation in which it is not possible to present the life of every single player as fully as we would like. The SABR researchers who have contributed player biographies and feature articles to this book have done utmost diligence to uncover every possible nugget of information that is currently available and, in many instances, new discoveries have been made and many of the players' lives and careers have been presented to a much greater extent than previously had been done.

This book would not have been possible without the involvement and support of Bill Nowlin, who fully embraced the idea and who generously agreed to be co-editor to guide me through the process of completing a SABR book project. In spite of the fact that he works simultaneously on numerous SABR books, as well as his own business and projects, Bill always answered my emails almost as soon as I had written them and always provided immediate assistance on every issue; his vast experience, knowledge, and network of connections brought the book to fruition, and I enjoyed working with him on this project.

The other members of our editorial team were Carl Riechers and Len Levin. Carl served as the fact-checker, which had to be an intimidating prospect when he joined this project since he knew that he would have to verify every fact and statistic in every article; the variations in statistics between different sources had to be almost maddening at times, but Carl never missed a discrepancy in players' records. As for Len, he has served as the copy editor for just about every SABR book that has been published, which speaks volumes about how well he does the job. No matter how well-written an article already may be, it is always improved after Len has put his finishing touches on it.

Many thanks are due to all of the SABR members who contributed their research and writing to this volume. The excitement often expressed when one of them uncovered previously unknown (or unavailable) information about the players of this bygone era confirmed my belief that the subject was of great interest to many individuals. Jeb Stewart, who contributed two biographies to this book, jokingly referred to "the collegiality of Type-A personalities" among SABR members in one of our email exchanges. Jeb's humorous observation was right on target, as the support

and cooperation among SABR members that was in evidence over the course of putting together this book was most gratifying.

There were numerous other individuals who also provided assistance, including players' family members who gave interviews and provided photos and documents and both SABR and non-SABR researchers and historians who provided assistance and information. The authors for this book have acknowledged individuals who assisted them in their respective articles.

Special thanks go to the following family members of players: James Zapp, Jr., who lives two small towns over from my mother and whom I now count as a friend; I was fortunate to have the opportunity to meet his father, former Black Baron Jim Zapp, just one month before he passed away. Kirk Bruce, Wilmer L. (Billy) Fields, Jr., and Artie Wilson, Jr., each of whom provided information in telephone conversations and were able, in some instances, to contribute documents and photos of their fathers. Carlis Robinson, the daughter of John Wright, who provided assistance to Niall Adler as he wrote her father's profile for this book. As it turns out, Carlis currently works in the same school district for which I taught when I first moved to Houston, and I hope to provide assistance to her effort to preserve her father's legacy.

Gratitude is also extended to Dr. Layton Revel of the Center for Negro League Baseball Research in Carrollton, Texas, and the Negro Southern League Museum in Birmingham, Alabama; Larry Wilhelm of the CNLBR, who helped to access photos from the CNLBR's website; Dr. Rob Ruck of the University of Pittsburgh's History Department, who has authored a trio of books about the Negro Leagues and baseball in Latin America and who put me in contact with Kirk Bruce; Dr. Raymond Doswell of the Negro Leagues Baseball Museum in Kansas City, Missouri; SABR Negro League Committee Chair Larry Lester, who contributed photos via his company Noir-Tech Research, Inc.; John Klima, author of *Willie's Boys*, who answered several questions for me and then offered to adapt material from his book to contribute his article about the signing of Willie Mays; SABR members Merritt Clifton, Art Black, William (Bill) Plott (author of *The Negro Southern League: A Baseball History, 1920-1951*), Kyle Eaton (for the valuable research he provided from the Memphis Public Library), Gary Ashwill (who maintains the Agate Type website, which is dedicated to Negro League baseball research), and Jay-Dell Mah (who maintains the Western Canada Baseball website and generously donated photos to this effort); Bob Retort of R.D. Retort Enterprises, who donated the use of several players' photos from his Negro League Legends postcard set (thanks to Barbara Retort as well); and Bryan Steverson, author of *Baseball: A Special Gift from God* for the information and photos of Bill Greason that he provided. Thanks to Dr. Denise "Dee" Lofton and Rosalind Withers of the Withers Family Trust of the Withers Collection Museum and Gallery in Memphis, Tennessee. Thanks to Emmet Nowlin for providing hyperlinks for most of the articles in the book. And thanks to Charlie Fouché for the team logos used on the back cover; they are from the Negro Leagues APBA game that he created.

If I have omitted anyone else who provided valuable input and assistance, I accept the responsibility for the oversight and offer my apologies here and now.

Lastly, thanks are due to my patient wife, Michelle, and my three sons—Michael, Andrew, and Daniel—who dealt with my obsession over this book and who were willing to concede the time that my research, writing, editing, and correspondence took away from them. I am pleased that they, too, often shared in the excitement of the new contacts and discoveries that were made over the past 18 months.

Frederick C. (Rick) Bush
May 2017

———————

I'd like to add just a few words. First of all, I would particularly like to express my appreciation to James Zapp Jr., who provided not only information but inspiration right from the outset of this project, and the opportunity to speak briefly with his father on the telephone.

It was a real pleasure working with Rick Bush on this book. He is as thorough a co-editor as I have ever worked with. We met for the first time at the Jerry Malloy Negro Leagues Conference in 2016, and that the book has been completed in record time—and thus is able to be published to coincide with the 2017 Malloy Conference—is a result of Rick's drive and attention to detail. His editorial hand has improved each and every article in this book.

Bill Nowlin
May 2017

LETTER FROM WILLIE MAYS IN COMMEMORATION OF JIM ZAPP

Jim Zapp, an outfielder with the 1948 Birmingham Black Barons, passed away on September 30, 2016 in Harker Heights, Texas, at the age of 92. His former teammate Willie Mays was unable to attend the funeral, but he wrote a letter in memory of his longtime friend to be read during the service. The letter shines a light on the remarkable bond that existed between these two men over the course of almost 70 years. Thanks to the generosity of James Zapp, Jr., the text of that letter is presented here.

Willie Howard Mays, Jr.

JAMES S. ZAPP, SR.

There's a famous photo of the Birmingham Black Barons team of 1948. Somebody got a shot of us in the tiny clubhouse after the game. There we all are grinning like kids on Christmas morning. We look so young. Someone described that photo to me by saying, "You guys exuded exhilaration and exhaustion!"

Amidst those impossibly thin, goofily thrilled, worn out victors is Jim Zapp. You can see him standing with us guys crowded around him after that 1948 Championship game that secured the Birmingham Black Barons' entry into that year's Negro League World Series. He is grinning too, almost sheepishly, as teammates rub his head and cheer his game-winning, Championship-clinching home run. He seems to be enduring the adulation as much as enjoying it. Not for him was the big show. That's just how he was – he didn't ask for much. He just quietly went about the business of doing his job.

It's almost easy to forget about somebody like that; you depend on them so much that they become part of the background, the landscape, the things you just know are there, but don't really think about. Sort of like a foundation or even a rulebook. Baseball has a lot of rules. You start picking them up when you're a kid – 3 bases, one home plate, 3 strikes, 3 outs, 9 innings. Later, you start getting the tougher stuff – ground rule doubles, balks, how and when to "deke" a guy. After a while, all those rules just sink in. They become your unseen guide; the language you use. You stop thinking about them. You just live baseball. All those rules are written down if you want to look them up, but you don't ever need to. You just know.

That's how Jim Zapp was for me. I call him "Zapp," so I mean no disrespect. He called me "Buck." We all had names. Piper Davis was our manager on the Barons. His real name wasn't Piper, but that's what we called him. Anyway, Zapp wasn't going to give a motivational speech before a game. He wasn't going to ask a lot of fool questions. He wasn't going to complain about the batting order. But, he was going to be the guy you counted on. He was going to play and he was going to hit and he was going to score. He was a ball player's ballplayer. And, he was my friend.

I remember when I first started with the Birmingham Black Barons, I was still in school and my dad wouldn't let me quit to play ball. So, I could only play on the weekends until school let out at the end of May. Many times the team bus would stop and pick me up along our old country dirt road as I walked toward the bus stop. One time, they passed me by!!! I ran like hell and hollered, "Hey, it's me!! Stop! It's me! Willie!!" After watching me run, panicked that I'd be left behind, the bus finally stopped so I could board. They were all laughing! They'd done it on purpose! Boy did Zapp roar at that one!!

You see, all the other guys were older than I was. They liked to tease me. Zapp always watched out for me though. He was like a big brother. I had to go to bed on time and I couldn't pick up any bad habits like drinking or smoking. I have a lot to be grateful for, and the biggest thanks goes to Zapp and the guys who gave me my start.

So, like I said, Zapp was always there. He watched over me. He taught me. He always came when I needed him. Even about 10 years ago when I had a job that demanded that I travel through the South. Zapp would meet up with me and come along. We went from Birmingham to Nashville to Atlanta – all kinds of places. He even came to visit me in Arizona at Spring Training one year. He brought some of his family and there's no denying a Zapp child – they are tall and broad-shouldered and strong!! Just like their dad!!

One time, Zapp joined me in LA at a dinner to raise funds for a baseball scouts organization. On that trip we had 5 Birmingham Black Baron players together again: Artie Wilson, Sammy C., Rev. William Greason, Zapp, and me. That's the last time we 5 were all together. Then several years later, Zapp flew with his wife Muffy to my 80th birthday party in San Francisco. He was part of the on-field ceremony with me and Greason. What a day that was!!

So, you see, like the Grand Canyon, the Empire State Building, the Mississippi River, the rio Grande, or Rickwood Field, Jim Zapp, for me, was dependably, firmly, always, always there. If you took a look, you saw grandeur, nobility, a formidable athlete. If you took the time to get to know him, you found a man of conviction, strength, humor, and heart. I couldn't have asked for a better friend. I can't believe it's time to say goodbye.

"Zapp,
 So long old pal!"

Your friend,

Willie Mays

LLOYD PEPPER BASSETT

By Frederick C. Bush

Lloyd Pepper Bassett made his name in Negro League baseball as the "Rocking-Chair Catcher." If calling a game and receiving pitches while sitting in a rocking chair seems like a gimmick, the reason is that it was one. Bassett began his professional career with the New Orleans Crescent Stars, and low attendance led him to suggest to the team's owner that he catch from a rocking chair. As Bassett later said, "I had to figure out a way to put some people in the park."[1] Bassett caught only occasional games from his rocker, but the gimmick worked, and he continued to use it after moving to Texas, where he played for the Austin Black Senators, the team that had started shortstop Willie "El Diablo" Wells on his path to the Hall of Fame in the 1920s. According to Negro League umpire Bob Motley, the rocker that Bassett used "was actually smaller than a standard rocking chair, which made it easy for me to see over it and call balls and strikes."[2]

Although Bassett used the gimmick that gave him his nickname throughout his playing days, he was far more than a mere sideshow: he was a premier backstop who was voted into eight East-West All-Star Games in seven different seasons (he played in both games in 1939) over the course of his career. In his memoirs, Motley extolled the catcher's abilities:

"A switch-hitting slugger, Bassett had an arm like a rifle and would sometimes mow down base stealers while sitting at the edge of the rocker. Most times, however, he would leap up from the chair and fire a bullet down to second, or pick off a runner loafing at first. If there was going to be a play at the plate, Bassett would kick that rocker out the way so fast you'd think he was kicking shit off his shoes. He'd quickly position himself to make the play. ... Bassett was really an outstanding catcher, truly one of the best in the league. If times had been different, there's no doubt in my mind that he would have found his way up to the majors."[3]

The paradox that the Negro Leagues had to exist due to segregation but were nonetheless often popular even with racially unenlightened white fans is perhaps best summed up in the words of one white Texan who asserted about Bassett, "I didn't care if I was the only white man in the stands. I was gonna see that nigger in the rocking chair."[4] Bassett's prime years were behind him by the time integration of Organized Baseball began, and he never did make it to the major leagues.

Lloyd Pepper Bassett was born in Baton Rouge, Louisiana, on August 5, 1910, to Cortez Bassett and Lillie Hatter.[5] No information about his parents is available, but it appears to have been important to them for their son to get an education as Bassett attended Reddy Street Elementary School and later graduated from McKinley High School.[6] Along the way, however, baseball got in young Bassett's blood and, as was the case with so many youths in his time, he honed his skills by playing ball on the local sandlots after school. The details of Bassett's early life have been lost to history, but he became a professional ballplayer at the age of 23 when he joined the New Orleans Crescent Stars in 1934.

After his debut with New Orleans and his travels through Texas with the Black Senators, the burly Bassett—he stood 6-feet-3 and weighed 220 pounds—caught on with the Homestead Grays in 1936. Playing time was sparse for Bassett that season, but he made the most of his opportunities by going 7-for-22 at the plate for a .318 batting average.[7] The press was complimentary, with one article asserting, "Pepper Bassett is the big league sensation behind the plate. ... [H]e has become one of the best catchers in the game today."[8]

In March 1937 Bassett was one piece of a major trade between the Grays and their crosstown rivals, the Pittsburgh Crawfords. Gus Greenlee, the Crawfords owner, who had funded his team via his numbers lottery and had barely avoided a conviction in 1934, was running low on money. Greenlee was unable to pay his

Lloyd Pepper Bassett in a Birmingham Black Barons uniform. Though he was widely-known for being "The Rocking-Chair Catcher," Bassett only used his rocker in non-league games that did not affect his teams' playoff chances. (*National Baseball Hall of Fame, Cooperstown, New York*)

stable full of star players any longer, and he began to unload them to other teams. This circumstance led to Greenlee's trading future Hall of Famers Josh Gibson and William "Judy" Johnson to the Grays in exchange for Bassett, Henry "Little Splo" Spearman, and $2,500, which was "reportedly the largest sum involved in a player deal in black baseball to date."[9]

Bassett never attained Gibson's level as a player, but he was an adequate replacement for the legend in 1937, batting .377 over the course of 18 Negro National League games for the Crawfords.[10] His performance was good enough to win him a starting spot in that year's East-West All-Star Game, and he was the leading vote-getter among catchers with a total of 41,463.[11] In the game, which was played before 25,000 fans at Chicago's Comiskey Park on August 8, Bassett went 0-for-3 with the bat. Perhaps to make up for this shortcoming, the *Pittsburgh Courier* was effusive about his defensive performance, stating, "Practically sitting on his heels, he swayed as he snatched the fast and slow ones as they came skipping across the plate, and then tossed 'em back without shifting his position."[12]

Bassett returned to the Crawfords in 1938, but his batting average dipped precipitously to .250 in 17 league games.[13] Greenlee attempted to turn Bassett into his main attraction and "had a multicolored rocker built" for Bassett to use in "selected nonleague games," from which he swore the catcher could "knock a gnat off a dwarf's ear at a hundred yards."[14] Greenlee's efforts were not enough to save the franchise. At the end of the season, his financial situation compelled him to disband the team, and he sent Bassett a letter to inform him that he was now a free agent; these "new circumstances left (Bassett) unable even to cash his final $53 check from the Crawfords."[15]

Bassett joined the Negro American League's Chicago American Giants for the 1939 season, where his batting average plummeted to .202 as he went only 21-for-113 in 30 league games.[16] His defensive prowess was such, however, that he was still selected to the West team for that year's two East-West All-Star Games. As he done in 1937, Bassett led all catchers with a total of 502,394 votes, which was second among all players to first baseman Ted Strong's tally of 508,327.[17] In the first game, played at Comiskey Park on August 6, Bassett caught the first four innings and took part in a double play behind the plate while going 0-for-2 with the bat. He repeated his 0-for-2 batting performance in the second All-Star Game, which was played at Yankee Stadium on August 27.

In 1940 Bassett became one of the many Negro Leaguers who jumped to the Mexican League, where he played for the Nuevo Laredo Tecolotes and batted .230 with eight home runs.[18] After his foray into Mexico, Bassett returned to the Chicago American Giants for the 1941 season. In spite of an abysmal .174 average in only eight league games, his popularity was such that he was once again the starting catcher for the West team in the July 21 All-Star Game at Comiskey Park. Once again the honor of playing in the game had to suffice as Bassett went 0-for-1 at the plate and allowed the East's second run of the game to score when he was charged with a passed ball in the first inning of the West's 8-3 loss.

In 1943 Bassett joined the barnstorming Ethiopian Clowns, a team with a name and a show-business flair that seemed suited to his rocking-chair routine. He continued to play for the team after it was relocated to Cincinnati in 1944 and became a member franchise of the Negro American League. Statistics for Bassett's two seasons with the Clowns are unavailable, but he added new forms of showmanship to his game that he continued to use throughout his career. Fellow catcher James Dudley, who played for the Baltimore Elite Giants, later remembered, "That guy [Bassett] lay down in the dirt like a little child playing. He'd tell the pitcher, 'Throw hard 'cause you can't throw bad.' It didn't make no difference where the ball went in that dirt, he got it."[19]

Dudley's reminiscence about Bassett's catching acumen was an example of how well the rocking-chair catcher had developed that aspect of his game. In fact, Bassett's focus on defense led to his contribution to the history of baseball equipment. According to Negro League historian Donn Rogosin:

> "[Bassett] found that the 1930-style catcher's mitt with its pillow-like design was unsatisfactory, particularly when a quick release was needed to get the runner stealing second. Experimenting, he gradually removed more and more of the padding, toughening up his hand in the process. Unknown to history, he helped create the 'squeezer' style of catcher's mitt."[20]

In light of Bassett's serious effort to be a first-rate backstop, it made sense for him to leave the Clowns, which he did when he signed with the NAL's Birmingham Black Barons in 1944. As a part-time starter, Bassett batted .212 for the powerful Birmingham squad, which won the NAL title and faced the Homestead Grays, one of his former teams, in the Negro League World Series that year. As fate would have it, however, Bassett and at least three other Black Barons—including Tommy Sampson, John Britton, and Leandy Young—were involved in a car accident in which a drunk driver hit their vehicle head-on. Sampson, who had been driving and who had suffered the worst injuries, recalled:

> "I got hurt the week before the [1944] World Series. I think we had played in Louisville, I believe, and we were on our way to Birmingham when we had the accident. I was out 'til that next spring. I was in the hospital, I think, almost

At the age of 44, Lloyd Pepper Bassett spent the final season of his 21-year career with the Detroit Stars in 1954. *(Withers Family Trust, Memphis, Tennessee)*

13 weeks. I had a broken leg, head busted, and everything."[21]

Though Bassett's injuries were minor compared to Sampson's, he also missed out on playing in the World Series, which Birmingham lost to Homestead in five games.

Bassett settled into his role as a platoon catcher with the Black Barons and stayed with the team through the 1950 season; after a year in Canada, he rejoined Birmingham for the 1952 season, his last with that franchise. Statistics are scarce for the 1945-47 seasons with Birmingham, but Bassett did make it to his first East-West All-Star Game with the Black Barons in 1947. He played in the second of the two All-Star Games, which was held on July 29 at the Polo Grounds in New York, and registered his first-ever hit in such a game as he went 1-for-2 with the bat. In the offseason after 1946 and 1947, Bassett also plied his trade—by all accounts sans rocking chair—in the Cuban Winter League.

In 1948 Bassett had his finest season with the Black Barons as he went 43-for-123 to post a .350 batting average. Once again he played in the second of that season's East-West Games on August 24 at Yankee Stadium; this time, he reverted to a 0-for-2 batting line in the contest.

At 38 years of age and with 14 years of professional experience, Bassett had also attained the status of grizzled veteran. Birmingham's youngest player, 17-year-old Hall of Fame-bound Willie Mays, learned a hard lesson from Bassett about the pecking order among players on one particular bus ride. According to Mays' biographer James S. Hirsch:

> "One night, over a long, bumpy road, (Mays) was jounced so badly that he moved to the front of the bus to sit with Bassett. ... Willie tried to get him to move, but he wouldn't. So Willie asked [manager Piper] Davis, sleeping nearby, for assistance, but Bassett opened his eyes and growled, 'You better get away from me.' He took a swing, missed, and hit an overhead rack. Willie retreated."[22]

Team chemistry was normally better, though some of the other veterans also were initially resentful of the youthful Mays, and the team won the NAL pennant. After defeating the Kansas City Monarchs in the NAL playoffs, they once again faced the Homestead Grays in what became the last Negro League World Series. This time around, Bassett got to play in the Series, though his fortunes were much the same as in the majority of his All-Star Game appearances: In Game One he was thrown out at the plate in the eighth inning of a game that the Black Barons lost, 3-2.[23] Birmingham again lost to Homestead in five games, just as it had in 1944; it was their third loss to the Pittsburgh-area squad in three World Series; they had also fallen in seven games in 1943.

The halcyon days of the Negro Leagues were past after 1948, due almost exclusively to the integration of Organized Baseball. Bassett was too old to merit consideration by either a minor-league or major-league team, so he remained with the Black Barons; he batted .295 in 1949 and .271 in 1950.[24] On August 20, 1950, at Comiskey Park, Bassett went 1-for-1 with a double in his final East-West All-Star Game as a Black Baron.. During his lengthy stint with Birmingham, Bassett was known for "a propensity for fancy clothes and fine ladies that matched his hitting prowess."[25] He also had become a fan favorite who, according to sportswriter Ellis Jones, was "one of the most popular players ever to wear the livery of the Black Barons."[26]

In spite of his popularity in Birmingham, the 1951 season found Bassett playing in his third different foreign country when he went north to join the Brandon Greys of Canada's ManDak (Manitoba-Dakota) League. Bassett may have been struck by the irony of playing for a team whose name, though spelled differently, was the same as that of the nemesis that had prevented him from being part of two Negro League championships, but it would become a sweet irony by the end of the season.

On June 28 Bassett won a game against the Elmwood team in dramatic but unusual fashion. Brandon trailed 6-5 in the bottom of the ninth inning and had two men on base when Bassett came to bat and belted what appeared to be a game-winning home run. The ball was "clearly heading out of the park, [but it] hit a guy wire and fell back onto the playing field. He was awarded a triple."[27] The hit still resulted in two RBIs that gave the Greys a 7-6 come-from-behind victory. For the season, Bassett batted .251 with 2 homers and 23 RBIs for Brandon.[28]

Bassett played a key role in Brandon's playoff fortunes as he doubled and scored the winning run in the 10th inning of a 2-1 victory over Carman on September 4. Ten days later he was behind the plate as Brandon defeated the Winnipeg Buffaloes, 5-3, to win the ManDak League's title.[29] After losing twice to the Negro League's Homestead *Grays*, Bassett finally had become a champion with the Brandon *Greys*.

In 1952 Bassett returned to the warmer climes of Birmingham, where he now split the catching duties with Otha Bailey. The rigors of catching were getting to be too much for Bassett's now 42-year-old body, and Bailey recalled, "He'd catch four and I'd catch five, but then if the game get real tight, I would come in as a defensive catcher 'cause I could move faster and get a lotta balls that he don't get 'cause he's big and kinda old, too. ... Later on, I was the startin' catcher."[30]

Clearly, Bassett's career was nearing its end. He began 1953 with the Philadelphia Stars but spent most of the season with the Memphis Red Sox. He had one last hurrah as a player when he took part in his eighth All-Star Game as the starting catcher for the West team. In the game, which was played at Comiskey Park on August 16, Bassett went 0-for-3 in the West's 5-1 triumph over the East. Bassett's final season was spent with the Detroit Stars in 1954.

Though Bassett's career has been documented fairly well, not much is known about his personal life. He did marry Exidena Johnson in April 1941, but the couple never had any children. When Bassett's playing career ended after the 1954 season, they ended up in California, where he worked as a janitor until he died on December 28, 1980, in Los Angeles.[31] Even his death remains shrouded in mystery, as former pitcher Bill Beverly once told an interviewer, "He's [Bassett] passed. There's two conflicting stories. One said he was killed in California with marked cards and another one said that he just passed."[32] Though Bassett is gone, the Rocking-Chair Catcher lives on in baseball lore.

NOTES

1 Donn Rogosin, *Invisible Men: Life in Baseball's Negro Leagues* (Lincoln: University of Nebraska Press, 1983), 143.

2 Bob Motley with Byron Motley, *Ruling Over Monarchs, Giants & Stars* (New York: Sports Publishing, 2012), 121.

3 Ibid.

4 Rogosin, 143.

5 Some well-known sources, including James A. Riley's *Biographical Encyclopedia of the Negro Leagues* and *The Negro Leagues Book* by Dick Clark and Larry Lester, give the year 1919 for Bassett's birth. However, Bassett's 1940 World War II draft registration form lists his birth year as 1910. Bassett also gave his full name as Lloyd Pepper Bassett, indicating that Pepper was his middle name rather than a nickname.

6 Lloyd Pepper Bassett file, National Baseball Hall of Fame, Cooperstown, New York. Thanks to Negro League historian Leslie Heaphy for providing information from Bassett's HOF file.

7 baseball-reference.com/register/player.cgi?id=basset000ll0, accessed February 3, 2017.

8 "Colored Teams to Appear at Riverside Park," *Portsmouth* (Ohio) *Times*, September 16, 1936: 8.

9 Neil Lanctot, *Negro League Baseball: The Rise and Ruin of a Black Institution* (Philadelphia: University of Pennsylvania Press, 2004), 61. The Grays got the short end of this trade as Johnson retired before playing a single game for the team and Gibson jumped the team during the 1937 season to play for the barnstorming Trujillo's All-Stars with Satchel Paige; see James A. Riley, *The Biographical Encyclopedia of the Negro Baseball Leagues* (New York: Carroll & Graf Publishers, Inc., 1994), 314, 445.

10 seamheads.com/NegroLgs/player.php?playerID=basse01pep, accessed February 3, 2017.

11 Larry Lester, *Black Baseball's National Showcase: The East-West All-Star Game, 1933-1953* (Lincoln: University of Nebraska Press, 2001), 106.

12 Lester, 104.

13 Seamheads.com.

14 Mark Ribowsky, *Josh Gibson: The Power and the Darkness* (Urbana: University of Illinois Press, 2004), 166.

15 Riley, 65.

16 Seamheads.com.

17 Lester, 139.

18 Riley, 66.

19 Brent Kelley, *The Negro Leagues Revisited: Conversations With 66 More Baseball Heroes* (Jefferson, North Carolina: McFarland & Company, Inc., 2000), 56.

20 Rogosin, 73.

21 Kelley, *The Negro Leagues Revisited*, 127. Accounts of this accident vary greatly among several different sources, and Sampson did not go into detail about the accident in his interview with Kelley. One discrepancy involves how many players were riding in Sampson's car. No one disputes that the four players named here were in the vehicle, but some accounts claim that Artie Wilson also was involved in the accident and that he suffered a sprained wrist: however, Wilson played in the World Series and batted .271. In an April 13, 2017 phone conversation with the author, Artie Wilson, Jr. confirmed that his father had not been involved in the accident. The second discrepancy involves the extent of Bassett's injuries, with some sources stating that he incurred only minor cuts and bruises while other sources claim that he suffered two broken ribs; since Bassett did not play in any of the five World Series games, the latter accounts appear more likely to be accurate. All sources agree that Britton suffered a thumb injury and Young a hip injury.

22 James S. Hirsch, *Willie Mays: The Life, the Legend* (New York: Scribner, 2010), 50-51.

23 "Grays Score First Win in World Series," *Afro-American*, October 2, 1948: 9.

24 negrosouthernleaguemuseumresearchcenter.org/Portals/0/Birmingham%20Black%20Barons/Statistics%20-%20Birmingham%20Black%20Barons.pdf, accessed February 3, 2017.

25 Tim Cary, "Slidin' and Ridin': At Home and on the Road with the 1948 Birmingham Black Barons," *Alabama Heritage*, Fall 1986: 26.

26 Ibid.

27 Barry Swanton and Jay-Dell Mah, *Black Baseball Players in Canada: A Biographical Dictionary, 1881-1960* (Jefferson, North Carolina: McFarland & Company, Inc., 2009), 26.

28 Ibid.

29 Ibid.

30 Brent Kelley, *Voices From the Negro Leagues: Conversations With 52 Baseball Standouts* (Jefferson, North Carolina: McFarland & Company, Inc., 1998), 280.

31 Lloyd Pepper Bassett file. As is the case with Bassett's birth year, a different death year is found in some sources. Baseball-Reference.com is one source that lists Bassett's death date as February 27, 1981; however, the state of California's Death Index shows that Bassett died on December 28, 1980.

32 Kelley, *Voices From the Negro Leagues*, 284.

HERMAN BELL

By Margaret M. Gripshover

I n his lifetime Herman Bell was a highly re-garded defensive catcher for the Birmingham Black Barons, but one who could not catch a break. His career in the Negro Leagues was marred by untimely injuries and complicated by unexpected happenstances and the harsh reality of being an African-American baseball player in the Jim Crow South. His story is not unlike that of other African-Americans who found their baseball footing in Birmingham's industrial leagues in the 1930s and 1940s and later gained entry into pro-fessional baseball through the Birmingham Black Barons of the Negro American League.

Herman Bell was born in Birmingham, Alabama, on April 18, 1915, the first of Henry and Mamie Lee Smith Bell's three children. A second son, Lucious Bell, was born in 1916. The youngest, daughter Marian (sometimes spelled "Marion" or "Mary"), was born in 1919. In 1915 the family lived with Herman's maternal grandparents, Anderson and Gertrude Smith, in East Birmingham. Henry Bell worked at cottonseed-oil mills alongside his father-in-law.

The Bell family's roots can be traced to 120 miles south-southeast of Birmingham, in Alabama's cot-ton-belt country. Herman's great-grandfather Joshua Bell was born into slavery around 1840, near Tuckers Store, a now-defunct community in southeastern Montgomery County. Evidence from the US Census population and slave schedules suggests that Joshua and his wife, Hester Ann Prince, were the property of Orsmond Robert Bell, a cotton-plantation owner and member of a prominent Alabama family. Joshua and Hester lived near Tuckers Corner even after Emancipation and the Civil War and continued to do so for the remainder of their lives. Their son George Bell, Herman Bell's grandfather, was born a slave in 1861. George worked in the cotton fields with his parents and siblings but by 1900 left the farm and headed north to Birmingham to seek work in an iron furnace.

George married Millie Warner in 1884, in Montgomery County. Millie, whose name also ap-pears in the record as Minnie, was born there in 1868. After they moved to Birmingham, George and Millie had at least four children—one daughter and three sons. Their eldest son, Henry Bell, born in 1894, was Herman Bell's father.

Herman Bell's mother, Mamie Lee Smith, was born in Georgia around 1898. Her parents, Anderson and Gertrude Bearden Smith, were born in Georgia, but were married in Birmingham. Anderson Smith was a laborer at a fertilizer factory and cottonseed-oil plants in East Birmingham. Anderson and Gertrude played an important role in Herman Bell's early years. Herman and his family lived in his maternal grand-parents' household throughout much of his early childhood.

After Anderson Smith's death, on March 2, 1920, at the age of 55, Herman and his family continued to live with his grandmother Gertrude Smith. The temporary stability of the Smith-Bell household was likely due to home-ownership, Henry Bell's paycheck from the oil mill, and Gertrude's work as a laundress.

In 1928, when Herman was 13 years old, for the first time in his young life he did not live in his grand-mother Smith's house. In fact, neither did Gertrude Smith. Household data from the 1930 Census il-lustrates Herman Bell's fractured family situation. His mother's marital status was listed as "widow" although her husband, Henry, was very much alive. Herman was 14 years old. Gertrude Smith was no longer a home-owner. Instead, the Bells rented a house for $25 per month in East Birmingham. In 1930 Mamie was the only wage earner in the household; she supplemented her meager income as a laundress by taking in two boarders.

Between 1930 and 1935, Henry Bell was in and out of the family picture. For several years he was not part of the household. In 1934, the family was briefly reunited, but the following year, when Herman was 10 years old, Henry was absent once more.

Henry Bell's frequent absences from the family household during the 1920s were likely due to marital problems rather than work obligations. Although one baseball historian asserts that Henry played for the Birmingham Black Barons,[1] a review of box scores and newspaper articles provides no evidence to support that assumption, and other Negro League histories do not corroborate this assertion. Further, Henry Bell did not work for ACIPCO or Stockham, two Industrial League training grounds for Black Barons players. This is not to say that Henry Bell did not play baseball—there is no evidence to support or refute that claim—but it is highly unlikely that Henry Bell ever wore a Black Barons uniform.

Herman Bell lived just a short walk from his first employer, Stockham Pipe and Valve Company, for whom he likely played his first organized baseball on the company's Industrial League team. On March 22, 1936, he married Lillie Harris, who lived across the street. Herman was 21 years old and Lillie was 20. Bell worked for Stockham Pipe before and after his marriage to Lillie and played baseball for the company's Birmingham Industrial League team; he later played for Stockham's archrival, the American Cast Iron Pipe Company (ACIPCO). As it turned out, Bell's baseball career lasted much longer than his marriage to Lillie. The 1940 Census provides some clues about their abbreviated marital life. In November 1939 Lillie gave birth to daughter Eva May Bell. By April 1940, Lillie and 6-month-old Eva May (also spelled "Eva Mae") moved out of the Bell household and never returned. The census gave Herman's marital status as "married, spouse not present." It noted that Herman was 25 years old, had one year of high school to his credit, and was a "catcher" employed as a "ball player."

In April 1940 when the census enumerator documented that Herman Bell was "absent" from the household, it was because he had already joined up with Hank Rigney's Toledo/Indianapolis Crawfords

of the Negro American League. He had embarked on a new life as a barnstorming baseball player, an adventure that lasted for more than a decade. The 1940 Census provides evidence that Herman Bell began his Negro League baseball career before he joined the Black Barons. Most biographical entries for Herman Bell state that his Negro League career began in 1943 with Birmingham, but clearly it began as early as 1940 with the Crawfords.

Bell had hitched his wagon to a circus in the form of Hank Rigney's Toledo Crawfords. The previous season was not financially successful for Rigney's Crawfords. He was punished by the Negro League for poaching players from the Homestead Grays and was not permitted to schedule games for the Crawfords until he paid a fine.[2] Rigney claimed that the league had conspired against him and blamed them for his red ink.[3] After being given the go-ahead for the 1940 season, Rigney ostensibly moved the team from Toledo to Indianapolis although the team more often than not was referred to in the press as the Toledo Crawfords.

In February Rigney entered into an agreement with Syd Pollock for the Crawfords to barnstorm with the Ethiopian Clowns with an "extraordinary sports carnival and baseball show."[4] In the center ring of the "sports carnival" was Olympic track star Jesse Owens, whom Rigney managed in the early 1940s. Owens and Rigney also were co-owners of the Toledo Crawfords, with Owens serving as the club's president.[5]

Rigney was also the business manager of the Toledo White Huts of the National Basketball League. He attracted some controversy in 1941 with his inclusion of two African-American players on the Toledo squad in what was otherwise an all-white league. In response to the scorn Rigney received, he blasted the press by saying, "Hell, I don't give a hang about their color. What I want to do is to win."[6]

Bell ended up as the catcher for the 1940s Toledo Crawfords after the previous season's starter, Tommy "Dixie" Dukes, decided to play in the Mexican leagues. Backup catcher Willie "Pee Wee" Spencer was a contract holdout, leaving the starting job open for rookie Bell. Spencer eventually rejoined the team, but he had lost his starting position as catcher to Bell.

If there had been any uncertainty surrounding who would serve as the Crawfords' backstop in 1940, there was even more confusion over the name of their new catcher. Some of the omissions and errors regarding Herman Bell's baseball career are linked to his name. Reporters covering the Crawfords at the start of the 1940 season referred to Herman as "James Bell" or "Steel Arm Bell." Bell's name was most likely changed to James based on confusion with a better-known Negro Leaguer, James "Cool Papa" Bell, who had played for the Pittsburgh Crawfords from 1933 to 1938. Cool Papa Bell played several positions with distinction in his long and illustrious career, but catcher was not one of them.

Herman Bell was referred to as Steel Arm Bell for the 1940 season with the Crawfords but not during his tenure with the Birmingham Black Barons. By all accounts, he earned his nickname through his excellent throwing skills, but it was also appropriate given his work in Birmingham's steel and iron manufacturing sector. The first use of this nickname was in the spring of 1940 when the local press touted Steel Arm Bell as a "catcher who can hit and throw"[7] before the Crawfords played the Monarchs at Monroe, Louisiana. Bell was last referred to as Steel Arm in 1942 when he played in a game featuring a Birmingham Industrial League all-star team versus the Atlanta Sunshine Stars.[8]

After one homestand, Bell and the Crawfords headed to Storm Lake, Iowa, for a game, at which Jesse Owens held a sprinting exhibition against Irwin Crotty, a former Notre Dame football star.[9] When the Crawfords headed back home, Rigney chose Owens and two Crawfords—pitcher Ernest "Spoon" Carter and Bell—as traveling companions in his car. The four had driven nearly 500 miles when they reached Elgin, Illinois, around noon on Saturday, June 8. Rigney was behind the wheel when his car stuck another vehicle that was entering the highway. Both cars were "heavily damaged" and Owens was taken to the hospital with "lacerations about the arms, head and face."[10] Bell, Carter, and Rigney were

also hurt but no report was given as to the extent of their injuries. Bell was out of the lineup for several weeks after what came to be the first of several misfortunes that beset his career in the 1940s. As Bell recuperated, Willie "Pee Wee" Spencer reclaimed the Crawfords' catcher's position.

The highlight of Bell's season with the 1940 Crawfords must have been the doubleheader he played against the Birmingham Black Barons at Rickwood Field on July 7. The game was billed as a "homecoming" for "two of the most valued members of the Crawfords, Herman 'Steel Arm' Bell, the league's deluxe catcher, and John 'Lefty' Smith, hard-hitting left fielder."[11] The *Chicago Defender* wrote, "Both of these boys formerly starred in the fast Birmingham Industrial league here and have a host of followers in this city who are anxious to see them for the first time in big league competition."[12]

After the 1940 Negro League season, Bell returned to Birmingham. He worked as a laborer at ACIPCO and played for its Industrial League team. It was not a happy homecoming because he and Lillie were still separated and would remain so until they divorced after his discharge from the US Army in 1944.

Bell continued as the starting catcher for the ACIPCO team through the summer of 1942. The squad was undefeated in league play and was viewed by some as the "best industrial league team of all time";[13] the Industrial League champions finished with a 49-1 record and Bell's batting average was .351.[14]

Bell joined the Birmingham Black Barons late in the 1943 season after the team had become short-handed in the catching department. Starting catcher Paul Hardy had been lost to the draft, which left the team with only 35-year-old John Huber, who had the lowest batting average on the team. The Black Barons were headed for a matchup with the Homestead Grays in the 1943 World Series but were in dire need of a backstop, which set the stage for Bell to join the team. If Bell thought his luck was changing, he was wrong. After just eight plate appearances, and on the eve of the 1943 World Series, he was injured and missed his chance to play in his first Negro League championship. After Bell was hurt, the

Black Barons found themselves in the World Series without a catcher. In an extraordinary concession by the Grays, the Black Barons were permitted to use the services of Ted "Double-Duty" Radcliffe, catcher and manager of the Chicago American Giants, for the duration of the series.[15] In an odd twist of fate, after granting permission for Birmingham to use Radcliffe, the Grays' own catcher, Josh Gibson, fell ill and was unable to play.[16] Gibson recovered in time to return to the Grays lineup and hit a grand-slam in the fifth game of the eight-game series. Bell would have to wait until 1948 to get another chance to play in a World Series for Birmingham.

World War II and the draft initially had created an opening for Bell on the Birmingham roster, but then the draft took him away. Bell reported for Army duty at Fort McClellan in Anniston, Alabama, on January 25, 1944 at age 29. Herman's civilian occupation fell under the category of "Athletes, sports instructors, and sports officials," and this line of work would persist during his military service. He played baseball at Fort Benning, Georgia, for the Reception Center Tigers. The Army team crossed bats with civilian and military teams, including the Atlanta Black Crackers and the Tuskegee Army Fliers. It was during a game with Tuskegee, on June 24, 1944, that Bell became a baseball casualty of the war when he broke his right leg sliding into second, and "was removed from the diamond by an ambulance" with speculation that he would probably be lost to the team for the season.[17]

But Bell returned to his catching duties in early August 1944 after a brief six-week recovery. In October the Black Barons were once again in a World Series against the Homestead Grays without him. The Grays won, four games to one.

Bell was discharged from the Army, on December 6, 1944. By the end of March 1945, Birmingham announced its lineup for the season, which included catchers Bell and Pepper Bassett.[18] Though Black Barons manager Winfield S. Welch maintained a positive outlook, not everyone outside of the organization was as enthusiastic. *Pittsburgh Courier* sportswriter Wendell Smith favored Cleveland over Birmingham for the Negro American League crown,

noting that the Black Barons had deficiencies in the "catching and infield departments."[19] In May the catching situation was still uncertain, and Bell platooned with Double Duty Radcliffe and Bassett. By June, only Bell and Bassett were sharing the catching duties.

On July 16 a Black Barons game in Cleveland to benefit a local community center was marred by a fight between Birmingham's second baseman, Lorenzo "Piper" Davis, and umpire Jimmy Johnson in which Davis broke the umpire's nose in front of 12,000 fans.[20] The brawl was just the beginning of the team's troubles. The Black Barons were criticized by Negro American League President Dr. J.B. Martin for splitting the squad into two teams; however, since no official league games were involved, no more than an admonishment was forthcoming. In Battle Creek, Michigan, on July 22, Bell and pitcher Jimmie Newberry were the only two regular Black Barons who took the field as part of a makeshift team for an exhibition game.[21] Fans had been expecting the full 1944 pennant-winning squad to appear, and Welch's mea culpa was that the team had lost players like Radcliffe to the Harlem Globetrotters and John Britton to the Mexican League.[22] The Battle Creek Clark Equipment team and the Lafayette Red Sox withheld travel expenses and Birmingham's share of the gate receipts, which, in the case of the Battle Creek game, would have totaled around $350.[23] A writer for the *Battle Creek Enquirer* mused, "It looks like there'll be plenty of meatless days for the Birmingham Black Barons of the Negro American league in the immediate future—and it won't all be because of the short of ration points."[24]

In early August the Black Barons and New York Black Yankees were scheduled to play a game at Knoxville, Tennessee. Bell was slated as the starting catcher.[25] But the Black Barons' bad luck followed them to Tennessee when the Black Yankees' bus broke down near Chattanooga and the game was canceled.[26] The result was another day without a paycheck for the team.

On September 8 the Black Barons played the Black Yankees in a two-day Labor Day holiday series that also featured games with the Cincinnati Clowns and the Philadelphia Stars. The games were played at Yankee Stadium before crowds of over 10,000. The Black Barons lost to the Black Yankees and were eliminated from the series finale, but they lost more than a game — they also lost Bell when he was "struck in the head by a New York batsman who swung late, the bat thudding against the catcher's temple as he crouched behind the plate."[27] That was Bell's last appearance for the Birmingham in 1945.

Off the field Bell had not fared much better; his marriage to Lillie Harris Bell finally ended in 1945. Bell did not remain a bachelor for long. On May 26, 1945, he married Mary Belle Cobb Boykin in Birmingham. Mary Belle Cobb was born in Bessemer, Alabama in 1919 and previously had been married to William Boykin with whom she had one son William Charles "Bo Pee" Boykin Jr., born in 1937.

When the 1946 Black Barons' season began, Bell found himself watching from the dugout while Pepper Bassett did the bulk of catching, especially in official Negro League games. Bell made only sporadic plate appearances, mostly in exhibition games during barnstorming tours. His fortunes began to change in mid-July when his batting average improved to .300 and he regained his status as the primary catcher; for the first time that year, it was Bell who started the first game of Negro League doubleheaders.

By the end of July, Bell's offensive production was getting noticed by sportswriters. In August, the Black Barons moved up in the standings and showed some of their old form but they could not catch up with Satchel Paige and the Kansas City Monarchs and finished in second place.

In 1947 baseball's spotlight shifted to Brooklyn, where National League Rookie of the Year Jackie Robinson was becoming a star. Negro League teams struggled to draw fans through the turnstiles and to attract supportive press coverage. The Black Barons announced that they would conduct their 1947 spring training in Orlando, Florida. Bell was included in the team's spring-training roster but Bassett was not; he and Newberry were in California "after playing winter baseball in Cuba and Mexico."[28] Manager Tommy

Sampson named Percy Howard as Bassett's replacement, but Howard did not graduate to Birmingham's regular-season roster.

By the time the Black Barons played their first exhibition games at Birmingham's Rickwood Field, Bell was not in the lineup because Bassett had made a late return and had resumed his role as the starting catcher. As in previous years, Bell was a slow starter and seemed to hit his stride later in the season, especially with his bat. It appears that Bell was replaced in the Birmingham lineup by backup catcher Earl Ashby, who also filled in at first base. Ashby had started his 1947 season with the Homestead Grays and was "loaned to the Black Barons" for the remainder of the year.[29] According to *Atlanta Daily World* sports columnist Emory O. Jackson, during spring training Bell was relegated to mentoring Birmingham's rookies, including pitcher and first baseman Alonzo Perry.[30]

When Birmingham opened the regular season at Rickwood with a 5-2 win over Kansas City on May 10, 1947, Bell was on the bench. The next day he shared catching duties with Ashby in the first game of a doubleheader against the Monarchs. An error-prone Birmingham nine lost both games. When the Barons and Monarchs met three days later on the road in Shreveport, a local sportswriter noted, "Undoubtedly, 'Pepper Bassett' of 'rocking chair fame' is the most colorful and capable in the negro [sic] major league … with William [sic] Bell as his understudy."[31] Not only was Herman Bell not getting any playing time or praise from the press, they could not even get his name right.

As had been the case the previous year, Bell began to get into the groove by midseason. In June he began to alternate starts with Bassett, and Ashby was no longer being used as the default backup. By the end of the month Bell was hitting a blazing .375, second on the team only to Piper Davis, who was batting .380.[32] The Black Barons were on fire and were leading the Negro American League with an overall batting average of .303.[33] But by August Bell's bat had cooled off and he was once again demoted to being Bassett's backup.

Bell's 1947 season with the Black Barons was a vast improvement over his fortunes in previous years in the Negro League. First, he did not suffer any major injuries as he had in 1940 (car accident), 1943 (unspecified injury), 1944 (broken leg), and 1945 (head trauma). In spite of his typical slow start to his season, Bell played in 26 league games and ranked third among Negro American League catchers with a .304 batting average and a .976 fielding average.[34]

Bell and Bassett returned to Birmingham in 1948, but Bell was now 33 years old and in the twilight of his playing days. The two catchers were described by columnist Ellis Jones as the Black Barons' "old guard," part of a group of "oldtimers" that also included Ed Steele and John Britton.[35]

In March 1948 the Black Barons held spring training at the historically black Alabama State Teachers College (now Alabama State University) in Montgomery. Filling out the roster with top-flight players was becoming more difficult for Negro League teams, so owners were forced to come up with some new staffing strategies. The Black Barons held tryouts for players attending Alabama A&M, Alabama State, Florida A&M, Grambling, Knoxville College, and Lane College.[36] Sharing spring training with collegians must have made some of the grizzled veterans like Bell feel particularly aged. However, it was not a youthful collegian who had the greatest impact on the Black Barons' 1948 season. Instead, it was a 17-year-old high schooler named Willie Mays.

During spring training, on April 11, Bell's mother, Mamie Lee Bell Smith, died in Birmingham at age 58. Bell was in Greenville, Mississippi, with the Black Barons for an exhibition game against the New York Cubans. To add to his grief, there would be no paycheck since the Cubans failed to show and 2,000 fans demanded a refund.[37]

The Black Barons opened the season against the Cleveland Buckeyes at Rickwood Field on May 1. Birmingham won the opener, 11-2, and took two of three games from Cleveland with Bell behind the plate for both wins. His career revival in early 1948 was noted by one sportswriter who said, "The youthful Bell has been doing the bulk of catching in the early games and his handling of pitchers, and his heavy stick work has been causing eyebrow lifting around the circuit."[38]

At the end of May, with Birmingham sitting atop the NAL standings, Bell found himself spending more time in the dugout; Bassett had a blazing .444 batting average in mid-June that assured him the starting catcher job. Bell, his role diminished, still contributed to the team's success and mentored younger players, including Willie Mays. Bell briefly took over the catching duties for the Black Barons when Bassett suffered a hand injury in July,[39] but as soon as Bassett recovered, Bell resumed his backup duties.

The Black Barons were pursuing their first NAL championship since 1944, and Bell did his part when called upon. He was not known as a power hitter, but he had a flair for providing the occasional base hit or sacrifice fly when called upon at a pivotal moment in a game. Such was the case when the Birmingham took a doubleheader from the Cleveland Buckeyes at Rickwood Field before a crowd of 9,000 on August 8.[40] Bell knocked a pinch-hit single to drive in two runs that lifted the Black Barons to a 4-3 victory.

The final weeks of the regular season proved costly for the Black Barons. They lost center fielder Norman "Bobby" Robinson to a broken ankle, though this injury resulted in Mays moving from left field to his natural position in center field. Player-manager Piper Davis was hobbled after being spiked, as was Bell.[41] Bell's injury came on September 10, the day before the playoffs were set to begin, as the Black Barons played the Chicago American Giants at Comiskey Park. With the Giants down two runs in the bottom of the ninth, Quincy "Big Train" Trouppe homered with the bases empty to narrow the margin to one run. Then, with the Giants' Chet Brewer on first, Big Jim McCurrine[42] grounded to second baseman Artie Wilson. Wilson was unable to get Brewer out at second so he threw to first. Wilson's throw to first baseman Joe Scott was too late to get McCurrine. Brewer rounded third and headed for home at "full tilt." When Bell applied the tag, the catcher's "foot was cut and he was forced to retire from the game."[43]

Bassett stepped in to replace Bell at that point. McCurrine later scored and tied the game, but the Black Barons answered with a run of their own in the top of the 10th inning and held on to win the game, 9-8. It was a satisfying win for Birmingham but a resolutely painful personal loss for Bell. Just as in 1943, when an injury had denied Bell the chance to play in the Negro Leagues World Series, a physical setback once again sent him back to the dugout.

The first two games of the seven-game NAL playoffs against the Kansas City Monarchs were played at Rickwood Field on September 11 and 12. Bassett was in the lineup and Bell was on the bench while Piper Davis did triple duty as manager, second baseman, and backup catcher.[44] Birmingham swept the first two games, with Bassett providing the winning RBI in Game Two, and the teams headed to Kansas City. After leading three games to two, the Black Barons needed the seventh game of the series to punch their ticket to the Negro League World Series, which they did when they won the deciding game, 5-1.

Bell did not play in any of the games against the Monarchs, and his leg injuries did not heal in time for him to appear in the regular lineup in the Negro League World Series, against the Homestead Grays. He did make one plate appearance as a pinch-hitter in the second game of the Series, hitting a run-producing double, but the "lumber-legged Bell" was pulled from the game for a pinch-runner.[45] The Black Barons lost the last Negro League World Series to the Grays in five games and, as in previous years, Bell returned to his life in East Birmingham after the season ended.

When spring training began in 1949, Bell was a 34-year-old catcher whose career was nearing its end due to an injury-worn body and the rapid decline of Negro League baseball. He and Bassett resumed their tag-team duties as the Black Barons' catchers. Bell started out well, but by the end of the season, his batting average was in the neighborhood of .200. He remained a sharp defensive player, but age had caught up to him and his diminished skills at the plate relegated him to backup duties for most of the season. There may have been a second contributing factor to Bell's declining performance: At the end of May he was batting .278,[46] but he suffered an injury to his right hand in early June,[47] and by early July, he was hitting just .240.[48]

In spite of Bell's subpar performance in 1949, when the final East-West All-Star Game lineups were announced, Bell was listed as the reserve catcher for the West. He replaced Earl Taborn, who had been signed by the New York Yankees in late July.[49] His selection was especially surprising given that he was hitting a paltry .207 at the time.[50] The East upset the heavily favored West, 4-0. Bell pinch-hit for Memphis shortstop Orlando Verona, but popped up in his first and only appearance in an All-Star Game.[51]

The Negro National League had folded after the 1948 season, so no World Series was slated for 1949. After the regular season concluded, the Black Barons and other Negro League teams engaged in a series of games throughout the South, including contests with Jackie Robinson's barnstorming All-Stars. After the last game was played, Bell returned home to Birmingham, where his widowed father still lived and worked at the cottonseed-oil mill. His younger brother Lucious was now married and he and his wife were part of the household. But his sister, Marian Bell Pearson Goodwin, had died on March 29, 1949, at the age of 29.

In March 1950 Bell was the starting catcher early in the season. He occasionally caught both games of a doubleheader as he did against the Indianapolis Clowns on April 16, one day after his 35th birthday.[52] By early May, however, the lineup pattern from previous years emerged and Bell fell back into his familiar role as the backup catcher. One positive event in Bell's life in 1950 was the arrival of his only son, Herman Bell Jr., who was born in Birmingham on June 21.

One of the Black Barons' most notable baseball achievements in 1950 took place in Knoxville, Tennessee. Arguably more important and longer lasting than anything else the Black Barons ever accomplished, it has gone largely unnoticed by sports historians. A benefit game between the Black Barons and Houston Eagles at Caswell Park in Knoxville was organized by Claude Walker of the Knoxville

City Recreation Bureau, a program developed for the city's African American population. Walker had played for the Knoxville Colored Giants in the 1920s and was one of the organizers of the new 1945 edition of the Negro Southern League.[53] The proceeds of the charity game were earmarked for what Walker claimed would be the first "Negro Little League team in the South."[54] Prior to the event, Walker said that the future of "Little League for Negro boys hangs in the balance at Caswell Park tonight."[55] The Black Barons returned to Caswell Park for a second benefit game in October against Luke Easter's "All-Stars" and added more funds to the Little League's coffers.

Today, Claude Walker Park Ballfields honor Walker's contributions to Knoxville sports history and the African American community. Bound up within Walker's legacy are Bell and the Birmingham Black Barons, who helped provide the seed money to create the first Little League team for African Americans in Tennessee and, most likely, the first such team in the South. It is also likely that the benefit game against Luke Easter's team was the last game Bell played in a Black Barons uniform.

In 1951 Bell was among the veterans who signed up for another tour of duty, but he did not play with the Black Barons beyond spring training at Alabama State College in Montgomery. Pepper Bassett continued with the team in 1951 along with two new backup catchers, Louis "Sea Boy" Gillis and Roy "Willie" Patterson.

After his playing days ended in 1951, Bell returned to East Birmingham. He did not return to factory work at ACIPCO or Stockham; his post-baseball occupation, according to Birmingham city directories, was as a janitor and warehouseman for the Kirby-Pierce Paint Company in North Birmingham.

Herman Bell died in Birmingham on September 27, 1970, at the age of 55. His wife, Mary Cobb Bell, died on December 26, 1985. Herman's brother Lucious, the last surviving Bell sibling, died in Milwaukee in 2007. Both Herman and Mary Bell were buried in Shadow Lawn Memorial Gardens in Birmingham. After Bell's death in 1970, his accomplishments—often overshadowed by the exploits of other Black Barons with better offensive skills and/or those who later played in the major leagues—were largely forgotten. He also had played much of his career at a time when press coverage of Negro League games was either absent or minimal, even in African-American newspapers. Bell did have one champion in the media, though: *Atlanta Daily World* columnist Othello Nelson "Chico" Renfro mentioned him often. Renfro had firsthand knowledge of Bell's baseball talents, having played shortstop in the Negro Leagues for the Monarchs, Buckeyes, and Clowns between 1945 and 1950, during Bell's tenure with the Black Barons.

In 1977 Renfro wrote a column in which he criticized New York Yankees catcher Thurman Munson's salary demands and included Bell among "the great catchers of the old Negro National and American League [who] could tie one hand behind their back and out catch Munson and when they came to bat they could untie the hand and blind fold them and they could out hit him."[56] A year later Renfro again referenced Bell, judging him to have been one of the best players on the 1942 ACIPCO team.[57] Renfro continued his high praise of Bell into the 1980s when he referred to the catcher as being "among the unsung heroes of the Negro Leagues."[58] When Negro League historian Brent Kelley interviewed Willie Young, a one-handed pitcher for the Black Barons in 1945, he asked, "Who was the best player you saw?" Young replied, "In my time? Herman Bell was the best catcher."[59]

NOTES

1   John Klima, *Willie's Boys: The 1948 Birmingham Black Barons, The Last Negro League World Series, and the Making of a Baseball Legend* (New York: Wiley, 2009), 127.

2   "East-West Game Aug. 18," *Chicago Defender*, March 2, 1940: 24.

3   Leslie A. Heaphy, *The Negro Leagues, 1869-1960* (Jefferson North Carolina: McFarland, 2003), 89.

4   "Ethiopian Clowns Eye Another Big Season," *Atlanta Daily World*, February 20, 1950: 5.

5   "Chicago at Indianapolis for a Double Header," *Chicago Defender*, May 25, 1940: 5.

6   Fay Young, "The Stuff Is Here," *Chicago Defender*, November 15, 1941: 22.

7   "Owens and Negro Clubs Coming Here," *Monroe Morning World*, April 14, 1940: 8.

8   "Birmingham, Sunshine Stars Play Two at BTWHS Today," *Atlanta Daily World*, August 30, 1942: 8.

9   "Jesse Owens Runs at Storm Lake Tonight," *Des Moines Register*, June 6, 1940: 16.

10   "Jesse Owens Injured in Elgin Crash," *DeKalb Daily Chronicle*, June 10, 1940: 7.

11   "Crawfords at Birmingham Sunday July 7," *Chicago Defender*, July 6, 1940: 23.

12   Ibid.

13   "American Cast Iron and Pipe (ACIPCO): ACIPCO Dominates the Birmingham Industrial League," Negro Southern League Museum Research Center, undated: 18.

14   Emory Jackson, "Birmingham ACIPCO Nine Lost 1 Game," *Chicago Defender*, October 24, 1942: 24.

15   "Sox Park Is Site of Negro Game Today," *Chicago Tribune*, September 26, 1943: A6.

16   Cum Posey, "Posey's Points," *Pittsburgh Courier*, October 2, 1943: 16.

17   "Reception Center Defeats Tuskegee," *Columbus Sunday Ledger-Enquirer*, June 25, 1944: 10.

18   "Cubans Play Barons Sunday," *Chicago Defender*, March 31, 1945: 7.

19   Wendell Smith, "The Sports Beat," *Pittsburgh Courier*, May 5, 1945: 12.

20   "Cleveland Group Demands Apology," *Pittsburgh Courier*, August 4, 1945: 12.

21   "Birmingham Barons' Actions Draw Fire of Unit President," *Battle Creek Enquirer*, July 29, 1945: 14.

22   Ibid.

23   "Black Barons Denied Gate Receipts Share," *Battle Creek Enquirer*, July 28, 1945: 8.

24   Ibid.

25   "Black Barons Play Yankees," *Knoxville News-Sentinel*, August 2, 1945: 16.

26   "Negro Battle Is Called Off," *Knoxville News-Sentinel*, August 3, 1945: 12.

27   "Black Yankees Win Two Games in Row in Stadium Tourney," *New York Amsterdam News*, September 8, 1945: 11A.

28   "B'ham Black Barons to Leave for Spring Training March 9," *Atlanta Daily World*, February 25, 1947: 5.

29   James A. Riley. *The Biographical Encyclopedia of the Negro Baseball Leagues* (New York: Carroll & Graf Publishers, 1994), 39.

30   Emory O. Jackson, "Hits and Bits," *Atlanta Daily World*, April 29, 1947: 5.

31   "Barons Who Play Monarchs, Second in 1947 Flag Race," *Shreveport Times*, May 12, 1947: 11.

32   "Black Barons Hard Hitters of the N.A.L.," *New York Amsterdam News*, June 28, 1947: 12.

33   Ibid.

34   Ellis Jones, "Art Wilson Cops League Batting Crown Honors," *Atlanta Daily World*, February 11, 1948: 5.

35   "Ellis Jones, Hits and Bits," *Atlanta Daily World*, April 1, 1948: 4.

36   "Birmingham to Try Out Collegians," *Pittsburgh Courier*, March 6, 1948: 17.

37   "Greenville Club to Seek Initial Pre-Season Win," *Greenville (Mississippi) Delta Democrat-Times*, April 12, 1948: 5.

38   "Black Barons Set to Face Famed Indianapolis Clowns May 16-18," *Atlanta Daily World*, May 14, 1948: 6.

39   "Barons, First Half Negro Champions, Here Thursday," *Newark Advocate*, July 20, 1948: 8.

40   "Barons Win Two From Cleveland," *Pittsburgh Courier*, August 14, 1948: 10.

41   Emory O. Jackson, "Hits and Bits," *Atlanta Daily World*, September 11, 1948: 5.

42   James "Big Jim" McCurrine's last name appears in some sources as McCurine.

43   "Black Barons Win, 9-8, Game From Chicago," *Chicago Defender*, September 11, 1948: 11.

44   "Birmingham Grabs First Two Games in Playoff Series," *Chicago Defender*, September 18, 1948: 11.

45   Klima, 180.

46   "Negro American League," *Atlanta Daily World*, June 1, 1949: 5.

47   "New York Cubans Lose Twice to First Place Black Barons," *Atlanta Daily World*, June 15, 1949: 5.

48   "Negro American League," *Atlanta Daily World*, July 6, 1949: 5.

49   "Yankees Purchase Two Players From Monarchs," *St. Louis Post-Dispatch*, July 29, 1949: 30.

50   "LaMarque and Porter Possible Starters for Annual East-West Baseball Classic," *Atlanta Daily World*, August 7, 1949: 7.

51   Marion E. Jackson, "East Upsets West 4-0 in 17th Annual Competition in Comiskey Park, Chicago," *Atlanta Daily World*, August 16, 1949: 5.

52   "Black Barons Stop Naptown Clowns Twice," *Pittsburgh Courier*, April 22, 1950: 23.

53   "The New Southern Negro League," *Macon (Georgia) Telegraph*, February 19, 1945: 8.

54   "Barons, Eagles to Clash for Little Loop Fund," *Knoxville News-Sentinel*, August 15, 1950: 14.

55   Ibid.

56   Chico Renfro, "This and That in Sports," *Atlanta Daily World*, January 27, 1977: 9.

57   Chico Renfro, "Let's Remember the Old 'Atlanta' Black Crackers," *Atlanta Daily World*, June 15, 1978: 8.

58   Chico Renfro, "Sports of the World," *Atlanta Daily World*, May 16, 1986: 5.

59   Brent P. Kelley, *I Will Never Forget: Interviews with 39 Former Negro League Players* (Jefferson, North Carolina: McFarland, 2003), 185.

JOHN BRITTON

By Bill Nowlin

John "Jack" Britton played professional baseball in four countries—the United States, Mexico, Canada, and Japan. He was even a pioneer in Japan, joining pitcher Jimmie Newberry as the first two African American ballplayers on a Japanese team. But he never had the opportunity to play in the major leagues.

Britton played in the Negro Leagues for more than 10 years, typically at third base. Unfortunately, we know far less than we would like to know regarding his life—not atypical for Negro League ballplayers.

He was born as John A. Britton Jr. in Mount Vernon, Georgia—the county seat of Montgomery County—on April 21, 1919. His father was, of course, John A. Britton. His mother is listed in Social Security Administration files as Tehnie Collins. Britton's death certificate gives her name as Tempie Collins.

How and when Britton got started playing baseball eludes us so far, but he is said to have begun in 1940 with the Minnesota Gophers, described as "a minor black team."[1] His play there was said to have impressed Abe Saperstein of the Gophers, who recommended him to Cincinnati's Ethiopian Clowns and to the Homestead Grays; he signed with the Clowns later in the year. Jim Riley writes, "While with the Clowns, he played shadow ball and engaged in a few of their comedy routines. The one best received by the fans involved his wig. He had a clean-shaven head, but wore a wig and, as part of a comedic routine, after a bad call by the umpire would take his hat off and throw it on the ground in mock anger while arguing the ump's call, and then would take his wig off and do the same with it. Then he would pick the wig and hat back up and put them on this head. The crowds loved it."[2]

John Britton batted left-handed but threw right-handed, stood 5-feet-8, and is listed at 160 pounds. And he had a shaved head.

Dick Clark and Larry Lester say he also played for the New Orleans-St. Louis Stars in 1940. Jim Riley has him with the Ethiopian Clowns from 1940 through 1942, though at least one news story had him still playing for the Gophers (though the geography had changed somewhat) along with Goose Tatum and others.[3] In March 1943 the *Macon* (Georgia) *Telegraph* reported that "Johnny Britton, hard-hitting third-sacker of the St. Paul-Milwaukee Gophers has been signed by the Clowns for this year."[4] Tatum and King Tut were both on the 1943 Clowns team and, along with pitcher Edward "Peanuts Nyasses" Davis, were said to form a "triumvirate of buffoons unequaled in baseball funology."[5]

In 1943 one unidentified author wrote, "Britton hit .389 for the 1943 Cincinnati Clowns and was traded to the Birmingham Black Barons for Hoss Walker. With Birmingham, Britton was a key player in the heart of the order, batting third for the next five years."[6] Jesse "Hoss" Walker had already been with the Black Barons since 1941, however, and played for Birmingham in the 1943 playoffs and World Series against Homestead, so one is left to wonder when the trade took place. Given the fluidity of player movement in those days, it is not at all impossible that Walker opened and closed the season with Birmingham but was traded to Cincinnati at some point during the season. Perhaps the trade was after the season. Newspaper articles in May and June of 1943 show Walker at shortstop for Birmingham and Britton with the Clowns.

When games were played, of course, in cities such as Dallas and New Orleans, newspapers noted, "Special sections will be provided for Negro and white fans" or "A large section of the Pel Stadium stands will be reserved for white patrons tonight."[7]

In 1944 John Britton played for the Barons and is shown with a .338 batting average in 68 plate appearances with one homer and 11 RBIs.[8] One suspects he played in more games than this, but records are unfortunately less than complete throughout Negro Leagues baseball. John Holway cited his average as .324, ranking him fifth among Negro American League batters.[9] Holway may well have been citing an unattributed summary record in Britton's Hall of Fame player file, which shows a .324 batting average over 259 at-bats in 65 games. The *New Orleans Times-Picayune* showed him at .327.[10] Artie Wilson led the team in hitting.

The Kansas City Monarchs had beaten the Homestead Grays in the 1942 Negro World Series. The Barons had finished second in the Negro American League in 1941 and 1942. Now in 1948, it was Birmingham's turn to take on the Grays, Negro National League champion for six consecutive years. The series went to the seventh game, but Homestead prevailed.

Both Wilson and Britton were among five Barons in an "auto smashup" just prior to the Series, but as of September 16 most were expected to play, though Tommy Sampson had a broken leg and hip.[11] Britton was in fact unable to play, due to a dislocated left hand, and both shortstop Wilson and catcher Lloyd "Pepper" Bassett were forced to miss action.[12]

Lester "Buck" Lockett filled in for Britton at third base. Homestead took the first three games, but Birmingham shut out the Grays 6-0 in Game Four behind the pitching of Johnny Huber. The Grays won in five games, and then the two teams continued to play each other in a series of exhibition games. Britton was active again with the touring Black Barons team, which made it to California in October. He was with the team during the preseason and as late as the end of April, but then departed, taking a sojourn to Mexico.

He played for the Azules de Veracruz (Veracruz Blues) in Mexico City, not in the coastal city of Veracruz. The owner of the team was Jorge Pasquel, himself a native of Veracruz. Signing Britton was far from an aberration. In 1940 alone, Pasquel had signed

13 Negro League players for the Blues. Author John Virtue reports that "Many fans dubbed the *Azules* the *Aquila Negra* because it was the Veracruz team with more black players than any other team in Mexico."[13] Veracruz at one time or another featured six future residents of Cooperstown: Cool Papa Bell, Ray Dandridge, Leon Day, Martin Dihigo, John Gibson, and Willie Wells. In 1942 Monte Irvin and Roy Campanella played baseball in Mexico, as did many others over the years. Willie Wells had managed the Azules in 1944, and Ray Dandridge was the manager when Britton played for the team in 1945.

With Dandridge playing third base and batting .366, Britton didn't get that much work. He played in 29 games for Veracruz, collecting 118 at-bats. He was

Third baseman John Britton (pictured here) and pitcher Jimmie Newberry, his former Black Barons teammate, became the first African-Americans to play in Japan after World War II when they joined the Hankyu Braves in 1952. (*Courtesy of Jay-Dell Mah/Western Canada Baseball*)

John Britton in the uniform of the Indianapolis Clowns in 1950; he also had spent time with the Ethiopian (Cincinnati) Clowns prior to joining the Black Barons in 1944. *(Withers Family Trust, Memphis, Tennessee)*

33-for-118, with four doubles and three triples as his extra-base hits. That gave him a .280 batting average and a .364 slugging percentage. He did not homer, but he scored 18 runs and drove in 10. He had a pair of stolen bases.[14]

Back with the Birmingham Black Barons, Britton appears to have gotten into 27 games in 1945, with a .333 batting average.[15]

Britton played very little in 1946 and 1947, according to currently available statistics, with only seven plate appearances in 1946 (he was 2-for-7 at the plate) and 28 in 1947 (with only 25 at-bats and a .160 batting average).

In 1948 Britton got into quite a few more games, with 141 plate appearances, 18 RBIs, and a .201 batting average. He played in the 1948 World Series against Homestead, walking and scoring the second Barons run in the eighth inning of their 3-2 loss in Game One. In Game Four's 14-1 loss, it was Britton who grounded out for the final out of the game.

Britton started the 1949 season at third base with the Barons. After 58 games, in mid-September,

Britton was batting .242. Final statistics have so far proven elusive. After the season Britton played on a Creole All-Stars team which played Jackie Robinson's Major League All-Stars in an October 16 game at Atlanta's Ponce de Leon Park. Don Newcombe pitched for the Major-League All-Stars and won, 15-4, but Britton was 2-for-4 in the game.[16]

Britton started the 1950 season with the Indianapolis Clowns and helped beat Birmingham in an April matchup, singling to drive in the first run of the game. In late May he was the lead man—scoring on the play—as the Clowns pulled off a triple play against the Barons during a Negro American League game in Chattanooga.[17]

By the end of May 1950, Britton had headed north of the border, to Canada, where he played very briefly for the Elmwood Giants, but primarily with the Winnipeg Buffalos.[18] Syd Pollock of the Indianapolis Clowns said Britton had jumped his NAL contract, but that he'd be willing to accept a cash settlement from the Buffalos.[19] In the May 27 game against the Brandon Greys, hitting into the wind, "John Britton, hard-slugging third sacker for the Buffs, powered a tremendous home run onto the roof of the Amphitheatre to open the seventh."[20] He also had two singles in the game, and was singled out by the *Winnipeg Free Press* for his fielding. He had a few three-hit games, on August 5 a triple and two doubles, and a four-hit game on the 24th. Barry Swanton in his book on the Mandak (Manitoba-Dakota) League reports that Britton batted .328 with the one home run and 26 RBIs. Jimmie Newberry and Leon Day both pitched for Winnipeg. The next year, 1951, Britton hit over .300 again, batting .310 with 3 homers and 40 RBIs for the Elmwood Giants. (Elmwood was a neighborhood in Winnipeg.)[21]

Having played in the United States, Mexico, and now Canada, what was Britton's next move?

On April 28, 1952, the occupation of Japan officially ended and Japan was again declared independent. That same day Bill Veeck and the St. Louis Browns sent Britton and pitcher Jim Newberry to the Hankyu Braves. The Associated Press story announcing the arrangement is somewhat amusing and informative and worth quoting at length:

Bill Veeck and his St. Louis Browns, who always welcome festive occasions, today marked the return of Japanese independence by sending two farm club ball players to Japanese professional baseball.

This marks the first time in history American ball players have been loaned to clubs outside the Continental United States.

Both of the lend-lease players are Negroes –third baseman John Britton, Jr., and pitcher James Newberry, a curve-balling right hander.

Final arrangements for sending the pair to Japan were completed by Abe Saperstein, owner-coach of the Harlem Globetrotters, and a stockholder in the new Brownies. Britton and Newberry were scheduled to leave Chicago late today for the plane hop to Japan.

They are on loan to the Hankyu Braves of the Japanese Pacific League. The club plays in Nishinomiya Stadium at Osaka, about 300 miles south of Tokyo.

They'll be the first Negro players in Japanese baseball.

Explaining the move timed with today's unveiling of an independent Japan, Veeck said: "As Japan gains its independence as the world's newest democracy, we of the St. Louis Browns are happy to aid the mutual relations between the United States and Japan by sending two of our American ball players to the Japanese pro leagues. In Japan, as well as in America, baseball is the national game, and we feel that this gesture on the part of American baseball will go a long way toward cementing good relations with the Japanese.[22]

A photo of Britton, Saperstein, and Newberry ran in *Jet* magazine on May 15.[23]

One might wonder why a Japanese team would be named the Braves. Before the Second World War,

the Hankyu baseball team was established in 1936 by Ichizo Kobayashi, the founder of Hankyu Railways Group. The team's name was "Hankyu-Gun" ("Gun" means military troop in Japanese), and this name went through until 1946. Perhaps needless to say, the idea of a baseball team bearing such a name was not appropriate in the immediate aftermath of the war.

In fact, all the teams were "-Gun" before the war's end, and the Supreme Commander for the Allied Powers suggested a change in name.

In 1947, perhaps with the Chicago Cubs in mind, the Hankyu team changed its name to the Hankyu Bears. As Tom Yamamoto explained, the team unfortunately went on a losing streak right at the start of the season and some felt the name was another poor association, since in financial circles a bear market indicates one of rapidly falling prices. They decided to appeal to the public for suggestions. The name Braves was selected and the person who had submitted the winning suggestion explained that he had had the Boston Braves team in mind.

The season was already under way when Britton and Newberry arrived. In their first game for Hankyu, at Korakuen Stadium on May 7, 1952, Britton was 2-for-4 with a triple against the Mainichi Orions. He tried to steal home, but was thrown out at the plate. Jimmie Newberry started and went five innings, but the game was lost, 3-2, the three runs attributed to Newberry's reliever, Yoshio Tempo. The winning pitcher for Mainichi was a Nikkei Nisei from Hawaii, Masato Morita. Britton, who wore number 8, was said to have made good defensive plays as the third baseman, backing up the pitcher and other infielders well.

Statistics show that Britton appeared in 78 games, batting .316 (seventh in Pacific League play) with 2 homers and 35 RBIs. We have learned since that foreigners arriving in Japan often have difficulty adjusting to Japanese pitching. Britton did so rather quickly and struck out only 12 times in 332 plate appearances.

Helping facilitate Britton's welcome was manager Shinji Hamasaki, who had seen African American baseball players in his youth, finding them very friendly during a 1927 barnstorming tour of Japan. It was apparently he who requested that Hankyu sign some of the black ballplayers.

Britton was sufficiently impressive that he was named to the All-Star team, the first foreign player named to an All-Star team. The Braves finished fifth in what was that year a seven-team league, and not having made the top four, their season ended before any postseason play. Britton and Newberry returned to America on September 25.

Britton returned to Japan on February 13, 1953, and played a full season for the Braves, batting .276 with 60 RBIs. Still an exceptionally good contact hitter, he struck out only 13 times in 448 plate appearances. Former Negro Leaguers Larry Raines and Rufus Gaines were also on the Braves in 1953. The Braves finished in second place. Manager Shinji Hamasaki resigned, having not won the championship.

The season over, Britton once more returned to the United States. His professional baseball career as a regular was over. He still cropped up from time to time playing baseball. In Springfield, Massachusetts, he is found in June 1954 playing with the Harlem Globetrotters baseball team (headlined by Satchel Paige, though Paige was a no-show for this game), beating the House of David team, 9-6, Britton's third-inning single having contributed to the win.[24]

After this point, Britton is not easily found in a search of online newspapers.

In June 1989 a reunion of Negro Leaguers was held in Atlanta and Britton was among them. An Associated Press photograph accompanied the story in some newspapers; the caption in the *Augusta Chronicle* read: "Former Brooklyn Dodgers pitcher Don Newcombe checks out dome of John Britton, who played for Birmingham Barons in Negro League."[25] Britton's bald dome reminds one of his shaved-head antics with the Ethiopian Clowns.

The last 12 years of his life he had lived in Chicago and worked as a freight loader for Lifschultz Freight Lines.

Britton was being treated for prostate cancer at Oak Forest Hospital in Bremen Township, Oak Forest, Cook County, Illinois, when he died on December 2, 1990, of an acute myocardial infarction.

Oak Forest is a city about 24 miles south/southwest of Chicago. He was survived by his wife, the former Louise Paige. He is buried at Oak Woods Cemetery on Chicago's South Side.

SOURCES

Many people were very helpful in gathering information for this biography. Baseball records had not recorded the place of his death or burial, but SABR member David J. Holmes secured his death certificate from the Cook County Clerk. Terry Bohn helped with leads and information on the Man-Dak League years of 1950 and 1951.

Very helpful as well were Tomotada "Tom" Yamamoto and Ichiro Shinohara of SABR's Tokyo Chapter, and Dr. Virgilio Partida, SABR member from Mexico, and Daigo Fujiwara of SABR Boston.

NOTES

1 baseball-reference.com/bullpen/John_Britton.

2 James A. Riley, *The Biographical Encyclopedia of the Negro Leagues* (New York: Carroll & Graf, 1994), 111. Riley is also the source for the Abe Saperstein story.

3 "Ace First Sacker With Colored Nine," *Daily Illinois State Journal* (Springfield, Illinois), July 15, 1942: 10.

4 "Cincinnati Clowns to Open Season," *Macon Telegraph*, March 29, 1943: 2.

5 "Clowns to Meet Monarchs Tonight," *Daily Illinois State Journal* (Springfield, Illinois), September 14, 1943: 11.

6 baseball-reference.com/bullpen/John_Britton.

7 See the *Dallas Morning News*, July 28, 1943: Section Two, 7, and the *New Orleans Times-Picayune*, April 27, 1943: 12.

8 John Holway, *The Complete Book of Baseball's Negro Leagues* (Fern Park, Florida: Hastings House, 2001), 406.

9 Holway, 413.

10 "Grays, Barons Meet Tuesday," *New Orleans Times-Picayune*, September 17, 1944: 24.

11 Ibid. See also John Klima, *Willie's Boys* (New York: John Wiley & Sons, 2009), 40.

12 "Black Barons Back at Top Strength," *New Orleans Times-Picayune*, March 31, 1945: 9.

13 John Virtue, *South of the Color Barrier: How Jorge Pasquel and the Mexican League Pushed Baseball Toward Racial Integration* (Jefferson, North Carolina: McFarland, 2008), 78.

14 Mexican League statistics are courtesy of SABR member Dr. Virgilio Partida, citing Pedro Treto-Cisneros, editor. *Enciclopedia del Biesbol Mexicano*, eighth edition (Mexico City, 2015).

15 The source for this is the unattributed player record in the National Baseball Hall of Fame.

16 Joel W. Smith, "Jackie Robinson All-Stars Beat Creoles Before 7,500," *Atlanta Daily World*, October 18, 1949: 5.

17 *Chicago Defender*, May 27, 1950: 19.

18 His first appearing with Elmwood is noted by Bob Moir, "Wells' Double Beats Carman in Tenth," *Winnipeg Free Press*, May 25, 1950: 16.

19 "Contract-jumpers in Loop?" *Brandon* (Manitoba) *Daily Sun*, June 23, 1950: 2.

20 Jim Reid, "Dropped Third Strike Gives Greys Win," *Brandon Daily Sun*, May 29, 1950: 2.

21 Barry Swanton, *The Mandak League: Haven for Former Negro League Ballplayers, 1950–1957* (Jefferson, North Carolina: McFarland, 2006), 79.

22 Associated Press, "Veeck Sets Precedence by Farming Pair to Jap Loop," *Morning Advocate* (Baton Rouge, Louisiana), April 29, 1952: 11. Rob Fitts comments: "The first African-American player to play professionally in Japan was actually Jimmy Bonna, who played in 7 games for the 1936 Dai Tokyo team. Although he hit .458 he did not stay with the team and had little impact on the history of Japanese baseball." Fitts' February 25, 2013, post is found at agatetype.typepad.com/agate_type/2013/02/early-black-ballplayers-in-japan.html.

23 *Jet*, May 15, 1952: 51.

24 Harold W. Robbins, "Satchel Paige Does Not Appear at Pynchon Park," *Springfield Republican*, June 27, 1954: 7.

25 Associated Press, "Negro League Greats Gather to Reminisce About Old Times," *Augusta* (Georgia) *Chronicle*, June 5, 1989: B5.

LORENZO "PIPER" DAVIS

By Jeb Stewart

On June 12, 1996, the Birmingham Barons returned to historic Rickwood Field after an eight-year absence for the first Rickwood Classic. Before the game with the Memphis Chicks, the team honored former Baron Walt Dropo and Birmingham baseball legend Lorenzo "Piper" Davis. As the capacity crowd of over 10,000 cheered Davis, he must have reflected on his life in the game. He had traveled from rural Alabama to the proving grounds of Birmingham's industrial leagues, and he had played baseball for 24 years in nearly every corner of the Americas, including the Negro American League, the Eastern, Mexican, Pacific Coast, and Texas Leagues, the Caribbean, and in countless barnstorming games. Piper Davis was a great player, a fine manager, and a scout for many years.

Lorenzo Davis was born on July 3, 1917, in tiny Piper, Alabama, a coal-mining camp about 40 miles south of Birmingham established along with the town of Coleanor by the Little Cahaba Coal Company.[1] He was the only child of John and Georgia Davis.[2] His father had steady work in the mines, often working long hours to provide for his family.[3] Lorenzo was a good student, particularly at math, where he was at the top of his class;[4] his father hoped his son could avoid a treacherous life in the mines.[5]

Lorenzo had an early interest in baseball. He followed the Southern Association's Birmingham Barons by listening to Bull Connor call their games on the radio.[6] He played baseball and basketball in elementary school; as a teenager, he distinguished himself as the best baseball player in his age group, which was known in his community as "the second nine."[7] He batted and threw right-handed, and he played so well that he accepted an invitation to play with the men on "the first nine"; recalling with pride, Piper said, "[s]o they put me over there. I was fourteen then. I've played first nine ever since."[8]

Because the local school ended in ninth grade, Lorenzo moved to Fairfield, Alabama, in the Birmingham metropolitan area, to live with his mother's family. There, he attended Fairfield Industrial High School, and met his future wife of nearly 60 years, Laura Perry.[9] He earned his lifelong nickname during a basketball game in which the students, not remembering his name but knowing his talent as a basketball player cheered, "We want Piper-Coleanor! We want Piper-Coleanor!"[10] Soon he was simply Piper, and he also became a star on the Tigers baseball team, where Willie Mays's father, Cat, was his teammate.[11]

Moving to Fairfield introduced Piper Davis to the Negro Leagues, as a number of clubs trained and barnstormed in the South.[12] After graduating from high school, he "wrote to the Philadelphia Stars for a tryout."[13] Because the Stars wanted him to pay for his own transportation expenses to Mississippi (agreeing to reimburse him only *if* he made the team), his father persuaded him not to go.[14]

Instead, Davis enrolled at Alabama State College in Montgomery on a partial basketball scholarship in 1934.[15] His father borrowed money from his employer to cover the remainder of his tuition.[16] During the second term, a strike at the mine made borrowing more tuition money untenable, and Davis withdrew from college.[17] He moved home and worked in the mines with his father until early 1936.[18] After an incident at work left a man dead, Davis lost his stomach for mining coal and quit.[19] The company payroll clerk would not pay him without an explanation from Davis, who told him, "[J]ust put on there, 'afraid of mines,'" which the clerk accepted as "a good enough reason."[20] Baseball beckoned once again.

In 1936 Davis signed a contract to play baseball with the Omaha Tigers for $91 a month,[21] nearly $1,600 a month in 2017 dollars.[22] The Tigers barnstormed from Memphis across the northern half of the Great Plains and into Washington state.[23] Considering the Depression Era economy, Davis's pay was decent for an 18-year-old, but also illusory.[24] He found the unending travel by bus, which was necessary to make a living as barnstorming ballplayer, to be "[t]oo much traveling and not enough money";[25] and he was happy he followed his parents' advice to always hold back enough money to return home.[26] Back in Fairfield, he got a job with the Tennessee Coal, Iron and Railroad Company (TCI) making $3-4 a day, and playing on a TCI baseball team.[27] When TCI laid him off in 1938, he signed with the Yakima (Washington) Indians.[28] The Indians were another barnstorming outfit and Davis spent the next year playing in games against teams from towns across the West; the Indians even toured with the famously long-bearded House of David for a couple of weeks.[29] However, he grew disenchanted with his pay, and returned to Fairfield in 1938.

On September 18, 1938, Davis married his high-school sweetheart, Laura Perry, who had waited for him during his baseball travels. He got a job with the American Cast Iron and Pipe Company (ACIPCO) in Birmingham, and played for the Pipemen, the company baseball team, from 1939 until early 1943.[30] ACIPCO's roster included future Black Barons Artie Wilson, Bill Powell, Ed Steele, and Sam Hairston.[31] With Davis manning first base, the Pipemen won the Birmingham Industrial League title five years in a row.[32] According to the research of Layton Revel, founder of the Center for Negro League Baseball Research, Davis hit an astounding .410 during his playing career with ACIPCO.[33]

By 1941 the Birmingham Black Barons had taken notice and tried to sign Davis, who weighed 188 pounds with a long 6-foot-3 frame. The following year, at age 24, he played in a few exhibition games with the Black Barons. While playing at Rickwood Field, he first faced Satchel Paige, who toyed with the youngster before striking him out on a fastball that he had difficulty even seeing.[34] Manager Winfield Welch finally persuaded Davis to leave ACIPCO permanently and sign with the Black Barons for the 1943 season. They offered him $300 per month plus $2

Perhaps no other player in the history of the Birmingham Black Barons embodied the franchise more than Lorenzo "Piper" Davis, whose nickname came from the tiny settlement of Piper, Alabama, where he was born. *(Withers Family Trust, Memphis, Tennessee)*

a day for meals. When Abe Saperstein, who acted as the Black Barons' business manager for owner Tom Hayes, found out that Davis could play basketball, he increased the monthly offer by $50 and Piper Davis became a two-sport star with the Black Barons and the Harlem Globetrotters.[35]

Davis played basketball with the Globetrotters for three straight winters, from 1943-44 to 1945-46, and later played with them briefly in the early 1950s.[36] Playing two professional sports year-round, along with the uncomfortably long bus rides, took a toll on his body.[37] During the summers the Black Barons rarely had a day off; while they often appeared at Rickwood on Sundays, the rest of their games were played on the road—from rural communities in Alabama and Mississippi to Northern cities like New York, Chicago, and Philadelphia—and always by bus.[38]

Davis once recalled, "I made both teams and for three years played both seasons with a week off in between to see my family. I quit when I found my legs shaking after a Globetrotters game at the end of the 1946 season."[39] From 1947 to 1956, he made a living during the winters by playing baseball in Puerto Rico (with the Mayaguez Indios, the Caguas Criollos, and the Ponce Leones), Venezuela, and the Dominican Republic. Winter baseball allowed him to bring his family along during the holidays.[40] In 1949, while he was the player-manager of the Ponce Leones, a fire broke out at a plant adjacent to the house the Davis family was renting, but he arrived in time to kick the door in and get everyone to safety.[41]

Davis also barnstormed during most offseasons, both with the Black Barons and with various bands of all-stars. In 1944 *The Sporting News* reported that the Black Barons defeated Augie Galan's major-league all-stars, 7-4.[42] The Black Barons won the California Winter League Championship that season.[43] Davis also barnstormed with Satchel Paige's All-Stars and faced Bob Feller's all-star squad.[44] In one game, Davis hit a home run off Eddie Lopat.[45] Although he had great respect for Bob Feller and his famed fastball, he believed Satchel threw harder: "Satchel was the best pitcher I ever faced, and the best I've seen."[46] He also credited Satchel as "[t]he only hero I looked up to. ..."[47]

Piper Davis was the Black Barons' most versatile player. He regularly played first base, second base, shortstop, and outfield from 1943 to 1949 before crowds at Rickwood Field that were often larger than those that attended the games of the Double-A Southern Association's Barons.[48] So great was his ability to adapt defensively that double-play partner Artie Wilson asserted, "[H]e was a superstar-type player like Pete Rose [and] could play any position and play it like he had been playing it all the time.[49] At the plate Davis shone as a hitting machine for the Black Barons. From 1945 to 1948, he terrorized opponents' pitching staffs while consistently posting batting averages well over .300.[50] The right-hander was a line-drive hitter with good power.[51] By 1945, Dodgers general manager Branch Rickey was aware

of Davis's strong performance, and considered offering him a contract;[52] he finally decided Davis was too old and instead signed Jackie Robinson, who was only 18 months younger.[53]

During Davis's tenure with Birmingham, the Black Barons would have rivaled the Kansas City Monarchs as the most dominant club of the era had it not been for the Homestead Grays. The Negro National League champion Grays defeated the Black Barons in the Negro World Series in 1943, 1944, and 1948. In the '43 World Series, Birmingham came closest to a title, narrowly losing to the Grays, four games to three. Davis lamented, "[W]e were short handed, but we carried them to the limit. We never did win a World Series."[54]

In 1945 Davis won election to the West squad for the East-West All-Star Game, but he missed the game after being suspended for shoving an umpire during an argument over a call.[55] From 1946 to 1949, Davis played in seven East-West All-Star Games as a second baseman and compiled a solid .308 batting average for the West in black baseball's premier biannual event.[56] He paced the West with two hits and a run batted in, and he also scored a run in the 1946 contest at Griffith Stadium.[57] The following year, at Comiskey Park, he had two more hits, including a double, walked, scored a run, and stole a base in the West's 5-2 win.[58] James Riley called him "a master of the double play";[59] the box scores from those seven All-Star Games agree, telling the story of Davis's stalwart defense: he participated in 11 double plays while committing no errors.[60]

In 1947 the Pittsburgh Pirates and Philadelphia Phillies were reportedly scouting Davis and his teammate Artie Wilson.[61] Later that summer, the St. Louis Browns purchased a 30-day option on Davis and requested that the Black Barons play him exclusively at first base.[62] The option expired in August, and Davis remained with the Black Barons. The initial explanation was that Black Barons owner Tom Hayes turned down the offer because the Browns wanted to send Davis to the Class-A Elmira Pioneers in New York, while Hayes believed he should go straight to St. Louis.[63] The Browns were the worst team in baseball and had nothing to lose by bringing Davis directly to the big leagues. They had already signed and released two black players from the Monarchs, Hank Thompson and Willard Brown, who had "struggled to adjust to the pitching and were treated poorly by their white teammates" in St. Louis.[64] That failed experiment surely affected general manager Bill DeWitt's decision to assign Davis to the minors. Later reports surfaced that the Browns also tried to have Davis take a pay cut of nearly 30 percent ($150 per month), which he refused.[65] DeWitt must have known that such an offer was unrealistic, if not insulting.

By 1948, the Black Barons named Davis, now 30, as player-manager. After batting .353 for the season,[66] he skippered Birmingham to a thrilling Negro American League Championship Series victory over Buck O'Neil's Monarchs before falling to the Grays in the last Negro Leagues World Series.[67] In the second game of the championship series against the Monarchs, Davis hit a ball over Rickwood's enormous scoreboard, which was "one of the longest balls in Rickwood history."[68] Davis had blended young stars Jimmy Zapp, Bill Greason, and Wiley Griggs with veterans Artie Wilson, Bill Powell, Jimmie Newberry, Jehosie Heard, Lloyd Bassett, Joe Scott, and Ed Steele to capture the NAL pennant. However, it was his discovery and signing of 17-year-old Willie Mays, who was playing for the Chattanooga Choo Choos in the Negro Southern League, which gave the Black Barons their youngest star.[69] Davis told the tale to Chris Fullerton, author of *Every Other Sunday:*

The story behind Willie Mays is that when I was in high school at Fairfield, I played with Willie Mays's daddy [Cat], before Willie was born. I had heard about Willie Mays.... We were in Chattanooga, and hotel reservations was rough for negroes, only one or two hotels, usually two. After our game in Chattanooga, Willie and them came into Chattanooga looking for rooms and that was the first time I'd seen him. I talked with him, didn't say nothing about joining us because I hadn't seen him play. I told him, "if you're

out playing ball for money, you can't play no kind of competition in high school next year." [Willie said], "I don't care. The next week we played in Atlanta, same thing. I said, "I see you're still out here." [Willie said], "Yeah, but I'm not going to play no more, the man messed with our money." I said, "Okay, if you want to play, and your daddy lets you play, have him call me Sunday morning at ten o'clock." His daddy called me and said, "if he wants to play, let him play." I said, "Okay, have him out at the ball park at twelve o'clock." Now, I needed an outfielder ... I started him off in the outfield just to see if he had a good arm ... so I put him in center field, and he handled that pretty good. That was my first year managing.[70]

Over the next two seasons, Davis took Mays under his wing and taught the phenom all he knew about the game.[71] He also carefully protected him from trouble off the field.[72] From the dugout he counseled Mays on how to spot a pitcher's tendencies and how to hit breaking balls, and he reminded him to always be patient at the plate.[73] Once, after Cleveland Buckeyes pitcher Chet Brewer struck him in the ribs with a fastball, Mays fell hard to the ground in pain.[74] Davis calmly walked to home plate and talked with Mays. He asked him if he could see first base. After Mays told him that he could, Davis instructed him to "get on up and get down there. When you get to first, steal second. When you get to second steal third. When you get to third, steal home."[75] After Davis's lessons, Willie Mays later found playing in the major leagues to be an easy task.[76] During his 1979 Hall of Fame induction speech, Mays credited both Piper Davis and Artie Wilson as being "very good teachers" to him.[77]

One of Davis's fondest memories during the 1948 season came against future major-league pitcher Joe Black, who was pitching for the Baltimore Elite Giants. In the first game of a series in Baltimore, the Black Barons trailed but loaded the bases in the ninth. With two outs, and needing only a hit to take the lead, Davis came to bat. He felt more than normal

SCRANTON ELECTRIC CITY BASEBALL CLUB, INC.

EASTERN LEAGUE
SCRANTON, PENNSYLVANIA

TELEPHONE: 4-8629
4-8620

1350 MONROE AVENUE

JAMES F. MURRAY, Pres., Gen. Mgr., Treas.
JACK DAVIS, Vice President

HIRAM W. MASON, Secretary
MIKE RYBA, Manager

August 13, 1949.

Thomas Hayes, Jr., President
The Birmingham Black Barons
680 S. Lauderdale Ave.,
Memphis, Tenn.

Dear Mr. Hayes:

      Mr. Joseph Cronin, General Manager of the Red Sox
called me today to tell me that he has arranged for the Scranton
Club to purchase the contract of Lorenzo Piper Davis.

      Enclosed you will find our check for $7,500.00
which is the amount Mr. Cronin says was agreed upon. Will you
please send us the necessary papers stating that we have purchased player Davis for the sum stipulated on the enclosed
check?

      Very truly yours,

      SCRANTON ELECTRIC CITY BASEBALL CLUB, INC.

      Jas. F. Murray,
      President.

M:r

Letter from the Scranton Miners, Class-A affiliate of the Boston Red Sox, confirming the purchase of Piper Davis' contract. Davis played only 15 games in Scranton before being released and returning to the Black Barons. (*Courtesy of Memphis Public Library*) pressure because scouts from the Boston Red Sox were watching, and Black struck him out to end the game. Davis got his revenge on Black the following night in front of the same scouts. He told Prentice Mills, "I wasn't going to let Black do it to me again. … He threw me a fastball, and I hit it pretty hard. I knew I had a base hit, but as I was coming around between first and second I saw the umpire signal a home run! I think that was the most memorable home run I ever hit."[78]

Bill Greason, a starting pitcher, was in his first season with the Black Barons in 1948. He won the pennant-clinching game against the Monarchs as well as the only game the Black Barons won in the World Series. Greason praised Davis as the greatest manager he played for and one of the finest men he knew. Davis insisted that the players dress well, avoid profanity, and carry themselves with dignity; he also demanded their maximum effort on the field. According to Greason, Davis "wanted us to be professionals on the field, and be gentlemen off the field; and we had one of the finest teams you would ever want to play with because of his kind of character."[79]

The statistical record of Davis's career with the Black Barons is not fully known due to sporadic record-keeping. Baseball-Reference.com credits Davis as an accomplished .293 hitter during his eight seasons in the Negro American League. However, Dr. Layton Revel, Executive Director for the Center for Negro League Baseball Research, determined that Davis had a .348 average during his career with the Black Barons.[80] Revel's conclusions are based on the Howe News Bureau's official statistics of the Negro American League, which were compiled at the time of each season.[81]

In July 1949 Davis was hitting .392 for the Black Barons and remained a "good big-league prospect" amid reports that the Cincinnati Reds were scouting him.[82] The Boston Red Sox passed on signing Willie Mays and inked Davis to a contract in 1950.[83] The Louisville Colonels and the Birmingham Barons were the Red Sox' top minor-league affiliates. The fact that the Barons were in the same city and even played in the same ballpark as Davis's Black Barons was a cruel footnote to his signing with the Red Sox organization since the Birmingham Barons could not be integrated due to Jim Crow laws.[84] Accordingly, Red Sox GM Joe Cronin assigned him to a Northern affiliate, the Class-A Scranton (Pennsylvania) Miners.[85] The Red Sox paid Davis $7,500 to sign, and agreed to pay him another $7,500 if he was still on the club after May 1.[86] Signing Davis might have been an odd decision because of the presence of slugger Walt Dropo,[87] Boston's first baseman, who won the American League Rookie of the Year award in 1950. Of course, Davis could have played any position.

The insensitive treatment Davis endured in Scranton extended from the locker room to the diamond. During one game with the Miners, a heckler yelled a racist insult as he stood at the plate. Davis responded with a home run. He walked over to the stands and said, "Take that!" as other fans cheered him.[88] Davis played just 15 games in Scranton. Although he was leading the Miners in batting average, runs batted in, and home runs, the Red Sox released him and avoided making the second payment, citing "economic conditions" as their excuse.[89] Years later, Davis told Chris Fullerton, "when Boston released me, that took all the joy out of it for me."[90]

After his release, Davis returned to Birmingham and batted .383 for the Black Barons.[91] Later in the '50 season he signed with Jalisco in the Mexican League.[92] There, he played with former Black Barons teammate Bill Greason for the first-place Charros.[93]

In 1951 another old teammate, Artie Wilson, who was playing with the Oakland Oaks in the Pacific Coast League, called Davis and told him that the Oaks wanted to sign him.[94] Though he was 33 years old when he first signed with Oakland, Davis played seven seasons in the PCL with the unaffiliated Oaks and later the Los Angeles Angels. Despite his advancing years, he posted a solid .288 batting average during his career in the PCL.

On June 12, 1951, Davis had one of his finest performances as a professional with four hits in four at-bats, including two home runs and a double, while driving in five runs to lead the Oaks to a win over San Diego.[95] Davis did not avoid controversy in the PCL, however. Late in July 1952, during a game against San Francisco, Seals pitcher Bill Boemler slapped Davis with a hard tag at home plate.[96] He took offense and punched Boemler twice, knocking him down. According to *The Sporting News*, "both clubs joined in a five-minute melee at home plate [but] none of the players was tossed out of the game after order was restored [because] … there would have been no one left to play."[97] White players on the Oaks had defended their black teammate in the fight, signaling that a real change was taking place in baseball; the Oaks players not only accepted Davis, they fought for him.[98] On the final day of the 1952 season, Oaks manager Mel Ott started Davis as his pitcher, and then played him for one inning at every position, as Oakland honored its talented star.[99] It was Ott's last day as a manager and he praised Davis, saying, "Piper Davis is the best all-around player I ever saw."[100] Davis batted .306 in '52, and hit .287 during his five seasons in Oakland.

After he turned 37, the Oaks traded Davis to the Los Angeles Angels, an affiliate of the Chicago Cubs. Despite batting .253 in 1955, he bounced back in the 1956 season to hit .316 as a part-time utility player for the first-place Angels. Art Clarkson, who later owned the Birmingham Barons, was a teenager living in Los Angeles that season. Clarkson was a fan of the Hollywood Stars who regularly attended their games; he disliked the Angels but remembered Davis as a star for the Los Angeles team.[101]

The Cubs sent Davis down to the Double-A Fort Worth Cats in 1957. According to the Cubs, "The idea was for Piper to help coach and instruct some of the younger players on the Cats while playing a utility role on the roster."[102] In his final season in professional baseball in 1958, Davis batted .282 for the first-place Cats as a 40-year-old.

Davis retired as a player and moved back to Birmingham. Initially, he worked for the Harlem Globetrotters again, "doing everything from coaching to driving the team bus during the 1958 and '59 seasons, and accompanied the team on a tour around the world in 1959."[103] He also returned to Rickwood Field as the manager of the Birmingham Black Barons for the 1959 season.[104] Under his leadership,

the team returned to a familiar position as it won the Negro American League Championship.[105] After that season, he never managed in professional baseball again. Davis explained, "The old Negro American League was about gone, really just an exhibition outfit by then, but I was glad to go back with the team one last time."[106] With Organized Baseball now integrated, the shrinking talent pool caused the Negro Leagues to wither and die within a few years.[107]

Davis worked for many years as the night auditor for Birmingham's A.G. Gaston Motel. The math skills he had evidenced early in life continued to serve him well, and he impressed the hotel's owner with his ability to keep the books.[108] For a time he also managed the Honey Bowl in Birmingham, a state-of-the-art bowling facility.[109] At Birmingham's Sardis Baptist Church, he served as a deacon, an usher, and a member of the choir.[110]

Piper Davis never strayed far from baseball, though. In 1960 he signed as a scout with the Detroit Tigers.[111] He was a player-coach for Stockham Valves from 1962 to 1964 and managed the industrial squad from 1965 to 1967.[112] He scouted for the major leagues' Central Scouting Bureau from 1968 to 1970.[113] In 1971 the St. Louis Cardinals hired him as a scout and he worked for the club until 1976.[114] He last scouted for the Montreal Expos from 1984 to '85.[115]

In 1981 Davis appeared at the Negro League reunion in Ashland, Kentucky. Always a teacher of the game, he happily demonstrated the fine nuances involved in a properly-turned double play.[116] Even at 64, while wearing an old glove, "he handled each throw so quickly that it appeared he was spearing the ball with his throwing hand."[117]

In 1985 Barons owner Art Clarkson organized an Old-Timers Game to celebrate the 75th anniversary of Rickwood Field.[118] Piper Davis managed one team and Ben Chapman (the former Phillies manager who had verbally assaulted Jackie Robinson in 1947) managed the other.[119] To his surprise, historian Allen Barra saw the two men "laughing and slapping each other on the back."[120]

Davis retired for good in 1986.[121] He was inducted into the Alabama Sports Hall of Fame in 1993,[122] and the Birmingham Barons recognized him as a special guest at the inaugural Rickwood Classic in 1996. The latter honor filled him with pride, although his daughter Faye insisted, "You would have never known it."[123] Kevin Scarbinsky documented the moment for the *Birmingham News*:

> During the pregame ceremonies, Davis stood near one end of the line of former players, Dropo near the other. When they introduced Davis, he stepped forward and tipped his cap. When they introduced Dropo, Davis stepped back, walked the length of the line and shook his hand. That's the way it should have been in 1948. Two players. One park. One team. Sometimes if you turn back the clock, you can help make up for lost time.[124]

After the game started, Piper and Faye began to leave Rickwood because the June weather had turned hot.[125] As they exited, she was struck by a foul ball on the leg, and the same ball still sits on her desk today.[126]

On May 21, 1997, Piper Davis died of a heart attack. At his funeral, Bill Greason, Jimmy Zapp, Lyman Bostock, Bill Powell, Joe Black, Sam Hairston, Rufus Beal, and Charlie Speights served as honorary pallbearers.[127] His wife, Laura, died on November 25, 2012. They are buried side-by-side in Birmingham's Elmwood Cemetery.

The community that gave Piper Davis his nickname is a mere memory, having been replaced by a marker that does not mention its most famous son. But Davis's legacy in baseball is preserved by his inclusion in the Alabama Sports Hall of Fame and the Birmingham Barons Hall of Fame.[128] Additionally, two books have been dedicated to him,[129] and an international youth baseball league bears his name.[130] Photographs of Piper Davis are displayed proudly throughout Rickwood Field, and the Rickwood Classic has been played annually for more than 20 years.

In reflecting upon the entirety of his baseball career, Davis modestly remarked, "I had some beautiful moments."[131] Barra put Davis's career in perspective when he noted that "most of the players and managers I talked to over the years thought Piper could have been a Hall of Famer himself."[132]

ACKNOWLEDGEMENTS

The author deeply appreciates Faye Davis and Rev. Bill Greason for allowing him to interview them for this chapter. In addition, David Brewer, the Operations Director of the Friends of Rickwood, and Dr. Layton Revel, the founder of the Center for Negro League Baseball Research, were both very helpful in providing the author with important research materials and suggestions.

NOTES

1 Theodore Rosengarten, "Reading the Hops: Recollections of Lorenzo Piper Davis and the Negro Baseball League," *Southern Exposure*, May 1977: 64.

2 John Klima, *Willie's Boys* (Hoboken, New Jersey: John Wiley & Sons, Inc., 2009), 8; "A Service of Worship Celebrating the Life of Deacon Lorenzo Davis 'Piper,' Saturday, May 24, 1997, Sardis Baptist Church, Birmingham.

3 Klima, 64.

4 Faye Davis, telephone interview with author, December 9, 2016; Piper Davis, interview with Chris Fullerton, Birmingham Public Library Digital Collection, March 8, 1993.

5 Rosengarten, 66.

6 Rosengarten, 65.

7 Rosengarten, 64.

8 Ibid.

9 Rosengarten, 66; Klima, 11.

10 Klima, 11; Rosengarten, 66; Faye Davis, telephone interview.

11 Klima, 12.

12 Rosengarten, 65-66.

13 Rosengarten, 66.

14 Ibid.

15 Ibid.

16 Rosengarten, 66; and Prentice Mills, "The Baron of Birmingham, An Interview with Lorenzo 'Piper' Davis," *Black Ball News*, Vol 1. No. 5, 1993: 4.

17 Ibid.; Rosengarten, 66; and Klima, 12.

18 Mills, 4; Rosengarten, 66; and Klima, 12.

19 Rosengarten, 67.

20 Ibid.

21 Ibid.

22 bls.gov/data/inflation_calculator.htm.

23 Rosengarten, 67-68.

24 Rosengarten, 68.

25 Ibid.

26 Mills, 5; Fullerton interview.

27 Rosengarten, 68; Dr. Layton Revel and Luis Munoz, *Forgotten Heroes: Lorenzo 'Piper' Davis* (Carrollton, Texas: Center for Negro Baseball Research, 2010), 1; Fullerton Interview.

28 Rosengarten, 68; Revel & Munoz, 1.

29 Rosengarten, 68; Mills, 5.

30 Rosengarten, 69; Revel & Munoz, 5.

31 Fullerton interview; Sam Hairston, interview with Ben Cook, Birmingham Public Library Digital Collection, June 16, 1995; Willie Powell, interview with Ben Cook, Birmingham Public Library Digital Collection, 1995; Mills, 7.

32 Revel & Munoz, 5.

33 Ibid.

34 Rosengarten, 74-75.

35 Rosengarten, 71.

36 Revel & Munoz, 28.

37 Ibid.; Shelley Smith, "Remembering Their Game," *Sports Illustrated*, June 6, 1992: 92.

38 Fullerton interview; Rosengarten, 71.

39 Smith.

40 Faye Davis, telephone interview with author.

41 Ibid.

42 "Major League Flashes," *The Sporting News*, October 26, 1944.

43 Revel & Munoz, 9-10.

44 Rosengarten, 75.

45 "Feller's Stars Cut Win Path to Coast," *The Sporting News*, October 22, 1947: 6.

46 Rosengarten, 75.

47 Fullerton interview.

48 Ibid.; Rosengarten, 71.

49 Bill Plott, "Piper Davis Was a Baseball Legend in Birmingham," *Birmingham News*, May 22, 1997: 8D.

50 Revel & Munoz, 14; James A. Riley, *The Biographical Encyclopedia of The Negro Baseball Leagues* (New York: Carroll & Graf Publishers, 2002), 218.

51 Rosengarten, 77.

52 Phil Dixon, *The Negro Baseball Leagues, A Photographic History* (Mattituck, New York: Amereon House, 1992), 270; Larry Powell, *Black Barons of Birmingham* (Jefferson. North Carolina: McFarland & Company, Inc., 2009), 170.

53 Chris Fullerton, *Every Other Sunday* (Birmingham, Alabama: R. Boozer Press, 1999), 92; Powell, 170; James S. Hirsch, *Willie Mays, The Life, the Legend* (New York: Scribner, 2010), 38.

54 Rosengarten, 71.

55 Mills, 8.

56 Larry Lester, *Black Baseball's National Showcase, The East-West All-Star Game*, 1933-1953 (Lincoln: University of Nebraska Press, 2001), 418.

57 Lester, 273.

58 Lester, 291-93.

59 James A. Riley, *Of Monarchs and Black Barons* (Jefferson. North Carolina: McFarland & Company, Inc., 2012), 194.

60 Lester, 274, 279, 295, 302, 313, 322, 336.

61 "Report Pirates, Phillies See Colored Stars," *Richmond Afro-American*, July 5, 1947.

62 Frederick Lieb, "Gates Rusting, Browns Rush in 2 Negro Players," *The Sporting News*, July 23, 1947, 20.

63 Revel & Munoz, 15 (citing the *Pittsburgh Courier*); "Offer to Davis Nixed as Browns' Option Ends," *Richmond Afro-American*, August 9, 1947.

64 Klima, 42.

65 "Series Sidebars," *Richmond Afro-American*, October 11, 1947.

66 Riley, *Of Monarchs and Black Barons*, 195.

67 Jeb Stewart, "Remembering the 1948 Birmingham Black Barons," *Rickwood Times*, Vol. 18, May 29, 2013: 2.

68 Tim Cary, "Slidin' and Ridin', At Home and on the Road With the 1948 Birmingham Black Barons," *Alabama Heritage*, Fall 1986: 31.

69 William Plott, *The Negro Southern League* (Jefferson, North Carolina: McFarland & Company, Inc., 2015), 178.

70 Chris Fullerton, *Every Other Sunday*.

71 Riley, *Of Monarchs and Black Barons*, 195-198.

72 Klima, 108-111.

73 achievement.org/achiever/willie-mays/#interview; Ben Cook, *Good Wood* (Birmingham, Alabama: R. Boozer Press, 2005), 68, Hirsch, 45.

74 Klima, 116-17.

75 Klima, 117; Hirsch, 46.

76 John Holway, "'They Made Me Survive,' Mays Says at a Reunion of Negro League Stars," *The Sporting News*, July 18, 1981.

77 Willie Mays's 1979 Hall of Fame Induction Speech, 21.

78 Willie Mays's 1979 Hall of Fame Induction Speech, 9-10.

79 Rev. Bill Greason, telephone interview with author, December 21, 2016.

80 Revel & Munoz, 14.

81 Dr. Layton Revel, telephone interview with author, February 14, 2017.

82 "The Future of Negroes in Big League Baseball," *Ebony*, May 1, 1949: 36; Oscar Ruhl, "From the Ruhl Book," *The Sporting News*, March 30, 1949: 15.

83 David Nevard and David Marrasco, "Who Was Piper Davis?" Buffalo Head Society (2001), 9. Reprinted in Bill Nowlin, ed., *Pumpsie and Progress: The Red Sox, Race and Redemption* (Burlington, Massachusetts: Rounder Books, 2010).

84 Nevard & Marrasco, 10.

85 Mills, 11.

86 Ibid.

87 Riley, 198-199.

88 Ibid.

89 Fullerton interview.

90 Ibid.

91 Russ Cowans, "'Go All the Way'; Rule of Hurlers With Monarchs," *The Sporting News*, May 31, 1950, 20; Revel & Munoz 14.

92 Revel & Munoz, 17.

93 Rev. Bill Greason, telephone interview with author; baseball-reference.com/register/league.cgi?id=e56ca649.

94 Mills, 11; Nevard and Marrasco, 11; Revel & Munoz, 17.

95 "Pacific Coast League," *The Sporting News*, June 27, 1951: 27-28.

96 John Old, "Loop Quakes With Fight and Protests," *The Sporting News*, August 6, 1952: 23.

97 Ibid.

98 Mills, 11-12.

99 Sam Schnitzer, "Boyd Clinched Bat Title on Final Day," *The Sporting News*, Oct. 1, 1949: 40-42.

100 Dave Kindred, "From Miner to Majors," *The Sporting News*, June 30, 1997: 6.

101 Art Clarkson, telephone interview with author, December 20, 2016.

102 Revel & Munoz, 19.

103 Mills, 12.

104 Ibid.

105 Marcel Hopson, "Black Barons, Memphis Divide, End Official NAL Season," *Birmingham World*, August 29, 1959.

106 Mills, 12.

107 Rosengarten, 78.

108 Faye Davis, telephone interview.

109 Ibid.; "Big Boom in Bowling," *Ebony*, September 1, 1962: 36.

110 "A Service of Worship Celebrating the Life of Deacon Lorenzo Davis 'Piper.'"

111 Watson Spoelstra, "Dykes Junks Rest Cure, Plants Fading Rocky Kaline in Garden, *The Sporting News*, June 29, 1969.

112 Faye Davis, telephone interview; Revel & Munoz, 29.

113 Revel & Munoz, 29.

114 Neal Russo, "Cards Told Shannon Is Out for Season," *The Sporting News*, February 27, 1971; Revel & Munoz, 29.

115 Revel & Munoz, 29.

116 Bruce Anderson, "Time Worth Remembering," *Sports Illustrated*, July 6, 1981: 46.

117 Ibid.

118 Art Clarkson, telephone interview.

119 Ibid.

120 Allan Barra, "Reconsidering the 'Alabama Flash,'" *Weld for Birmingham*, April 26, 2016: 4; Allan Barra, "What Really Happened to Ben Chapman, the Racist Baseball Player in *42*?," *The Atlantic*, April 15, 2013: 5.

121 Faye Davis, telephone interview.

122 ashof.org/index.php?src=directory&view=company&srctype=detail&refno=244&category=Baseball.

123 Faye Davis, telephone interview.

124 Kevin Scarbinsky, "Rickwood Makes Up for Lost Time," *Birmingham News*, June 13, 1996: 1-D.

125 Faye Davis, telephone interview.

126 Ibid.

127 "A Service of Worship Celebrating the Life of Deacon Lorenzo Davis 'Piper.'"

128 milb.com/content/page.jsp?ymd=20080505&content_id=41116562&sid=t247&vkey=team4.

129 Allan Barra, *Rickwood Field* (New York: W.W. Norton & Company, 2010); Klima.

130 piperdavisbaseball.org/our-history.

131 Fullerton interview.

132 Allan Barra, "What Really Happened to Ben Chapman, the Racist Baseball Player in *42*?"

BILL GREASON

By Frederick C. Bush

Jackie Robinson was the trailblazer who integrated major-league baseball in the 20th century. However, many other pioneering players were the first to integrate particular states or teams, and their proper acknowledgement took much longer. Bill Greason, a right-hander who began his baseball career with the Nashville Black Vols in 1947, is a case in point. As the first black minor-leaguer in the state of Oklahoma (in 1952) and the first black pitcher to play for the St. Louis Cardinals (in 1954), he was in the vanguard of baseball's racial integration.

Greason's major-league career consisted of only three appearances, but his contributions to baseball history should not be underestimated. Before his time with the Oklahoma City Indians, he had earned the Birmingham Black Barons' sole victory in their loss to the Homestead Grays in the 1948 Negro World Series. After his brief stint with the Cardinals, Greason played winter ball for Puerto Rico's Santurce Cangrejeros (Crabbers) in 1954-55. He teamed with two future Hall of Famers — Willie Mays and Roberto Clemente — to win the Caribbean Series championship. Another teammate, Don Zimmer, called it "probably the greatest winter league baseball club ever assembled."[1]

Greason's baseball career also intertwined with other experiences to create a compelling portrait of what life was like for an African-American man during segregation, as well as in its aftermath, in 20th-century America.

William Henry Greason was born on September 3, 1924 in Atlanta, Georgia, the middle child of James and Lizi Greason's five offspring; he had two older brothers, James Jr. and Willie, and two younger sisters, Jamie Mae and Louise. James Greason was a laborer and Lizi took in laundry for white families, which meant, in Bill Greason's words, that they "were poor folk."[2]

Greason grew up across the street from Dr. Martin Luther King, Jr. on Auburn Avenue — now known as the Sweet Auburn Historic District — a black neighborhood in segregated Atlanta. Both men graduated from Booker T. Washington High School, but they were not classmates as Greason was five years older than King; prior to attending Washington HS, Greason had also attended David T. Howard High School.

As a youth, Greason and his friends played pickup baseball games on sandlots, where his natural talent came to the fore. He confessed later in life, "I never dreamed that I would have been a baseball player. Nobody taught me how to play ... It was a gift."[3]

Though Greason had no baseball coach, he did have parents who taught him how to cope with life in the racially segregated South. They instructed him to respect all people — no matter their race — and told him not to worry about what other people might call him or think of him because of his color. Greason's mother said to him, "You are somebody. You are God's child. We are to treat each other with respect and to love each other."[4] Her edifying comments also instilled a belief in God that Greason called on during the horrors of battle in World War II and that helped lead to his eventual post-baseball vocation as a minister.

In 1943, Greason entered the United States Marine Corps and became one of the Montford Point Marines, black soldiers who underwent basic training at a segregated facility (Montford Point) in Camp Lejeune, North Carolina. Another member of that unit was Dan Bankhead, who became the first African-American pitcher in the majors with the Brooklyn Dodgers in 1947.

Greason served in the Pacific Theater and landed at Iwo Jima as part of the 66th Supply Platoon on the fourth day of the American invasion in 1945. He remembered, "Two of my best friends were killed on that island. I prayed and said, 'Lord, if you get me off this island, whatever you want me to do, I'll do it.'"[5] Greason survived and completed his tour in the USMC with 13 months as a member of the American occupation force in Japan, where he was stationed at Sasebo and Nagasaki after the United States had dropped an atomic bomb on the latter city.[6]

After being discharged from the Marines and returning stateside, Greason played quarterback in for two seasons (1946-47) for the Atlanta All-Stars, a semipro football team.[7] He embarked upon his career in professional baseball thanks to encouragement from Sammie Haynes, the manager of the Atlanta Black Crackers, who had been aware of Greason's pitching talent since his days of playing on Atlanta's sandlots. He spent the 1947 season with the Nashville Black Vols, for whom he posted a 12-4 record.[8] In 1948, he went to spring training with the Asheville Blues of the Negro Southern League and caught his first big break. The Blues played a game against the Birmingham Black Barons, and Greason so impressed Birmingham's catcher, Pepper Bassett, that he convinced legendary player/manager Lorenzo "Piper" Davis to acquire the young pitcher. According to Greason, "That [the game] was on a Monday night. Saturday morning I was in Birmingham. I don't know how they got me, they bought me or whatever, but in 1948 I was with the Barons."[9]

Birmingham had won Negro American League (NAL) pennants in 1943 and 1944 but had lost the Negro World Series to the powerful Homestead Grays both times. The 1948 team was the last great Black Barons squad, featuring four future major leaguers in Greason, 17-year-old Willie Mays, Jehosie Heard, and Artie Wilson. Jimmy Newberry and Bill Powell tied for the team lead with seven victories apiece, while Greason chipped in six wins during the league season. They won the NAL's first-half championship and defeated the second-half champion Kansas City Monarchs in the playoffs, with Greason starting and winning the final game to clinch a 4-3 series victory. The triumph set up a rematch against the Black Barons' old nemesis, the Negro National

League (NNL) champion Grays, in what turned out to be the last Negro League World Series ever played.

Homestead fielded future major leaguers of their own—including Luke Easter, Bob Thurman, and Luis Márquez—and they made short work of Birmingham, even without the advantage of a single home game.[10] The Grays took Game One in Kansas City by a 3-2 margin, and then defeated the Black Barons 5-3 at Birmingham's Rickwood Field to take a 2-0 series lead.

Greason earned the lone win for Birmingham at home in Game Three with both his arm and his bat. He entered the game in the eighth inning to relieve starter Alonzo Perry, who had allowed the Grays to tie the game at 3-3. In the bottom of the ninth, Greason hit a one-out single, advanced to second when John Britton walked, and scored the winning run as Willie Mays "hit through [pitcher Ted] Alexander's legs to center field."[11] It was the only bright moment for the Black Barons; the Grays won the next two games—in New Orleans and then back in Birmingham—to wrap up the championship.

In 1949, Greason was selected as one of Birmingham's representatives in the annual East-West All-Star Game, and he spun three shutout innings in the contest. The Black Barons experienced somewhat of a downturn, however, and he posted only a 7-12 record for the season.[12] The reversal of fortunes stemmed largely from the rapid rate of player defections to Organized Baseball that occurred after Jackie Robinson broke the color barrier in 1947. The Negro Leagues were losing all of their best talent, which caused a decline in the quality of play and a resultant decline in attendance. After the NNL was merged into the NAL in 1949, it became obvious that the Negro Leagues would not last much longer.

Nevertheless, Greason returned to the Black Barons in 1950 and posted a 9-6 record with a 2.41 ERA before moving south of the border to the Jalisco Charros of the Mexican League late in the summer.[13] In 14 games, he was 10-1, leading the league in winning percentage, while posting a 3.46 ERA. Jalisco made it to the Mexican League championship series but lost in six games to the Algodoneros de Unión

Pitcher Bill Greason, here wearing the cap of the Triple-A Rochester Red Wings (a St. Louis Cardinals affiliate), won Game Three of the 1948 Negro League World Series, Birmingham's lone victory against Homestead. (*National Baseball Hall of Fame, Cooperstown, New York*)

Laguna. After his first foray into Latin American baseball, Greason then joined the Cuban winter league's Marianao franchise in early 1951. In seven games, he was 2-2 with a 3.38 ERA.

Greason gained notice from Organized Baseball and was offered a tryout with the Pacific Coast League's Oakland Oaks in spring training of 1951. He arrived to Oakland's spring training camp late due to his playing in Cuba and, when he failed to make the team, the *Oakland Tribune* reported, "Sideliners believe that had Greason reported March 1, instead of two weeks late . . . he might still be with the Oaks."[14] Instead, the Oaks offered him a spot with their affiliate in Wenatchee, Washington, but Greason declined their offer and returned to Jalisco, where he said he

could make more money.[15] He was much less successful in Mexico this time around, though, going only 1-4 with a 7.94 ERA in seven games.

Greason left Jalisco early in the season and rejoined the Black Barons in Birmingham, where he quickly regained his form. Prior to a late-June exhibition game against the New Orleans Eagles, it was reported that "less than 48 hours after William Greason signed his 1951 contract with the Birmingham Black Barons he had pitched two winning games against the Kansas City Monarchs."[16] Greason had pitched five innings in relief in a 4-3 victory on a Saturday night and had followed up that performance with a 5-0 shutout in the first game of a doubleheader the next day. Entering the July 28 game against New Orleans, Birmingham had a 16-3 record in NAL games.[17]

In light of the good season the Black Barons and Greason were having, he was chagrined when was recalled to active military duty with the Marines later that summer. Greason was fortunate not to have to deploy overseas for another tour of combat, this time in the Korean War. He remembered, "I had a good camp commander. He said, 'That's a no-win war. You stay here. I'm going to have a baseball team.'"[18] During the time that Greason played ball for the Camp Lejeune ball club, he lost just once; in one game, he won a 1-0 decision over Brooklyn Dodgers ace Don Newcombe.[19]

Though the integration of both baseball and the armed forces was under way, Jim Crow still ruled in the South, and Greason once was prohibited from sitting with his teammates at a game in Florida. He remembered this incident as one of the few that angered him, saying, "I'm a Christian man, but I wasn't Christian at that moment. Something had to be said. That was awful."[20]

Greason received his second chance at a minor-league roster spot under most unusual circumstances. The story was that E. J. Humphries, owner of the Double-A Texas League's Oklahoma City Indians, called Greason after hearing about him from a Marine sergeant who had become stationed in Oklahoma.[21] He finally entered Organized Baseball when he signed a contract with Oklahoma City on July 28. Dave Hoskins, who had formerly pitched for the Homestead Grays from 1944 to 1946, had integrated the Texas League for the Dallas Eagles earlier that season, but Greason was the first black player in the state of Oklahoma, and the excitement was palpable for the city's black community. Russell Perry, an African-American youth who later became one of the city's civic leaders, remembered that, for him, "It was like Jackie Robinson was here . . . Everybody was very, very proud of him."[22]

As for Greason's reception throughout the Texas League, he declared that the hometown fans were kind and that Oklahoma City provided a good environment in general, though he did not socialize with any of the other Indians players—who were all white—outside of the ballpark. Things were different on the road though, and Greason recalled, "In other towns, they would give us a tough time. Me, at least. Same thing with Dave [Hoskins]. They'd call you names you never heard of."[23] He kept his composure—his anger in Florida had been an exception, not the rule—and eventually some of the fans began to relent. Greason has often retold the tale about a white woman in Beaumont who had made it her duty to torment him for two seasons, but who then approached him toward the end of 1953 and commended him for his grace under pressure.

On August 3, 1952, Hoskins and Greason matched up in what *The Sporting News* called "the novelty of the first all-Negro duel in Texas League history."[24] Though it may have been a "novelty" at the time, it was a harbinger of things to come as teams became aware of both the talent and the popularity of black ballplayers. As evidence of this, *The Sporting News* also made note of the fact that "more than 11,000 persons, over half of them Negroes, packed the park in Dallas to see the rare match."[25] Greason outdueled Hoskins that day to earn his second win in four days with the team as the Indians prevailed, 3-2. He not only started out of the gates quickly, but he ended up with a 9-1 record and a superb 2.14 ERA that made him a hot commodity.

After his breakout 1952, a bidding war for Greason began between several major-league teams, including the Yankees and the Red Sox, two teams that had yet to employ a black player. Humphries set a high price on his star pitcher's services. When asked what it would take to get Greason, he replied, "I might listen to something like $75,000, with a few players thrown in—and then I'd have to have the choice of what men I get."[26] He turned down $50,000 offers from both the Yankees and Red Sox, and it was suspected that he wanted "to use Greason for his box office value for one more season, then up the price to $100,000 for him next winter."[27]

Greason started slowly in 1953, endangering Humphries' plan; though he finished with a flourish and emerged with a 16-13 record, his ERA had increased to 3.61. After the season, the St. Louis Cardinals acquired Greason and Texas League batting leader Joe Frazier from the Indians in exchange for four players and $25,000 cash, which was considerably less than Humphries' original expectations.

Obtaining Greason was a change for the Cardinals under their new owner and president, August A. "Gussie" Busch, Jr., who had recently purchased the team from Fred Saigh, a staunch segregationist who had run afoul of baseball because of his conviction for tax evasion. St. Louis had been one of the cities that had made life most miserable for Jackie Robinson in 1947, but Busch was making changes and the Cardinals would soon be integrated. *The Sporting News* predicted as much when it reported that Greason was "likely to become the first Negro player ever to perform for the Cardinals."[28]

That distinction, however, went to first baseman Tom Alston, who began the 1954 season on the Cardinals' roster; Greason was called up in late May after starting 4-5 with the Triple-A Columbus (Ohio) Red Birds. His most impressive outing came at Kansas City on May 9, when he had a perfect game through six innings and a one-hitter through nine. He stayed in until the 15th, when he finally weakened and lost, 2-1.[29] After that game, he won three straight decisions to earn his May 28 callup to

St. Louis, which wanted him because the big club's pitching had been erratic.[30]

Greason soon found out that integration did not yet mean equality to the Cardinals' front office. When St. Louis forced him to take a pay cut from the $1,200 per month he had been making in Triple-A to $900 per month, his promotion turned out not to be the exhilarating moment he had anticipated. Greason protested the pay cut and was given a "take it or leave it" ultimatum that made him bitter and dejected. He said, "I tried to get there for years, and then when I got there, I didn't want to stay."[31]

Greason's already low spirits were not buoyed by the way Cardinals manager Eddie Stanky handled him, which was to remove him from games "faster than [he] could spew tobacco juice from his front teeth."[32] His major-league debut came on May 31, 1954 in the first game of a doubleheader against the Cubs at Wrigley Field. It was a brief start in which he surrendered five runs (all earned) and three homers—two by Hank Sauer and one by Ernie Banks—in three innings of a 14-4 rain-shortened (seven-inning) loss.

Greason's second start was on June 6 against the Phillies in St. Louis, and it went even worse. He surrendered a leadoff homer and walked the next two batters before being pulled by Stanky. Greason knew his days in St. Louis were numbered when Stanky's only words to him were, "Get the damn ball over the plate."[33] His premonition was correct as he made one final appearance on June 20 and pitched a scoreless inning of relief against the New York Giants, though he did allow a single and a walk, before being sent back to the minors. After never really being given a chance in the majors, Greason was relieved to return to Columbus, where he finished the 1954 season with a 10-13 record. The major leagues never beckoned again, but Greason's final tally of 0-1 with a 13.50 ERA for the Cardinals fails to define him as a ballplayer.

Following the 1954 season, Greason played his second season of winter ball for the Santurce Cangrejeros in Puerto Rico; his relationship with the team had started in 1953 and would last seven years. On the 1954 squad he was reunited with his former Black Barons teammates Artie Wilson and Willie Mays, who was already a star for the New York Giants. In addition to Mays in center field, Santurce had Roberto Clemente in right field. Greason combined with two other strong starters, Sam Jones and Rubén Gómez, to create a formidable pitching staff. The 1954-55 Cangrejeros were so powerful that the Puerto Rican media dubbed them the "Panic Squad" for the fear they instilled in their opponents. They "romped to the pennant, won the league finals, and captured the Caribbean Series."[34]

On the heels of his miserable experience with St. Louis and his subpar record for Columbus, Greason was happy to be in Puerto Rico and performed well for Santurce. He amassed a 7-2 record and won two games in the Caribbean Series, including the clincher. In his Game Two start against Panama, he also hit a home run to help his own cause. Later in life, Greason recalled, "It was great … one of the largest crowds I had ever pitched before. I remember the home run and winning, 2-1. There was a lot of excitement competing against Panama, Cuba, and Venezuela."[35] After the series-clinching victory over the Carta Vieja (Panama) Yankees on February 14, 1955, he was named to the series' All-Star team along with four of his teammates, which included future baseball lifer and Series MVP Don Zimmer.

The winters in Santurce were special to Greason. Though the team did not win another championship during his seasons there, he continued to shine. During his seven seasons with the Crabbers, he posted a record of 46-31 with a 2.99 ERA, striking out 372 batters in 701 innings.[36] The caliber of the Puerto Rican league was quite high then—it was generally regarded as just a shade below the majors.

The Cardinals still had Greason under contract, yet his performance in Puerto Rico had no impact upon his status with the franchise. In fact, in 1955, St. Louis dropped Greason to their Double-A affiliate. He found himself back in the Texas League, this time with the Houston Buffaloes, for whom he posted a 17-11 record, albeit with a 4.16 ERA. The

On May 31, 1954 Bill Greason became the St. Louis Cardinals' first African-American pitcher. Here, on September 21, 2014, he throws out the first pitch at Busch Stadium III prior to that evening's Cardinals game. (*Courtesy of Bryan Steverson*)

Texas League had continued to move forward with integration; Greason was now teamed with first baseman Bob Boyd, who, in 1954, had become the first black player in the Houston franchise's 66 years of existence. No matter their fortunes elsewhere, the two men were stars for the Buffs in 1955, as evidenced by games such as an 8-4 victory over the San Antonio Missions on June 24, in which Greason earned his fifth victory and Boyd hit a grand slam. Houston finished 86-75 and advanced to the Texas League championship series, which they lost to Shreveport.

Greason got a chance to play in another nation—the Dominican Republic—in January 1956. Santurce allowed him to join the Licey Tigres for a three-game playoff series to determine the other finalist for the Dominican league championship. In

Game One on January 25, Greason and Ron Kline of Águilas Cibaeñas engaged in a tremendous duel. Greason pitched 13 innings and Kline 14, and neither allowed a run. Águilas finally won in the 15th, 1-0.[37]

Greason returned to the Buffs in 1956 and had a 10-6 record before he was promoted back to Triple-A ball. He joined the Cardinals' affiliate in Rochester (New York), which became the final stop of his professional baseball career.

Greason was especially effective in Puerto Rico in the 1957-58 season. He was 12-6 with a 2.76 ERA and pitched 25 consecutive scoreless innings, a streak which was broken only after a start in which he had thrown 11 shutout innings.[38] His career with the Crabbers concluded the following winter.

43

At Rochester in 1958, Greason was teamed with another future Hall of Famer, Bob Gibson, who has noted that Greason "took him under his wing."[39] Now an elder statesman, Greason was used primarily as a reliever and compiled a 16-18 record in his time with the Red Wings, before being traded to a team in Charleston, West Virginia toward the end of 1959. After contract negotiations with Charleston fell through, Greason retired with a career minor-league record of 78-62.

Upon his retirement, Greason moved back to Birmingham, which was his wife's hometown. He had met his wife, Willie Otis, at Birmingham's Sixteenth Street Baptist Church, though the couple ended up being married by a Justice of the Peace in Mississippi in 1953.[40] Rev. and Mrs. Greason celebrated their 63rd anniversary in 2016; they have two adult daughters, two grandchildren, and six great-grandchildren.

Baseball was still in Greason's blood, and he pitched for an city-league team, Fairfield, with which he won a championship.[41] He also had the opportunity to play against Jackie Robinson when Robinson brought one of his barnstorming teams to town. He allowed only one hit in the game, prompting Robinson to joke with Greason, "They didn't come to see you. They came to see me."[42]

Greason worked for 14 years in Pizitz Department Store. However, he felt called to the ministry and enrolled at Birmingham Easonian Baptist Bible College; after earning a degree in religion, he also completed post-graduate work there and at Birmingham's Samford University. He had become a parishioner at the Sixteenth Street Baptist Church and, by 1963, was preaching there once a month.[43] The church had become a meeting point for civil rights activists—including Greason's childhood neighbor Dr. Martin Luther King, Jr.—and was launched into the national spotlight on September 15, 1963. On that Sunday, four members of the Ku Klux Klan planted a bomb at the church that killed four young girls and injured 22 others, an act of terrorism that King called "one of the most vicious and tragic crimes ever perpetrated against humanity."[44]

In a twist of fate, Greason was not in attendance at the church on the day of the bombing; he was in Tuscaloosa as part of an organization trying to get youths involved in organized baseball programs.[45] He does remember the paroxysm of violence that gripped Birmingham after the bombing, saying, "We were angry—of course we were because they were using fire hoses on people. Then they brought dogs in like we were animals or something. That would anger anybody!"[46]

Birmingham had a reputation as the most segregated city in the entire United States, and its complete and stubborn resistance to any efforts toward integration has been called "mindless defiance."[47] Bombings were so common in the city—there had been 41 since 1947[48]—that the city's critics had derisively dubbed it Bombingham. Never before had there been casualties, however, and the bombing of the Sixteenth Street Baptist Church gave impetus to passage of the Civil Rights Act of 1964.

Greason used his part-time pulpit to push for civil rights during those turbulent times, and he has continued to preach ever since. He started the New Hope Baptist Church in Bessemer, Alabama and, in 1971 he was installed as the pastor of Bethel Baptist Church of Berney Points in Birmingham.[49] More than 45 years later, he is the senior pastor of the same congregation at the age of 92; as of January 2017, he still preaches every Sunday even after battling two serious health issues in 2014.[50]

In addition to his pastoral duties, Greason works with a non-profit foundation he co-founded in 2007, the American Negro League Baseball Association. The organization's goal is to unite the remaining Negro League legends and to support a program called Project HELP—an acronym for History Entrepreneurs Leadership Program—which works "to leave a lasting legacy to the underprivileged children of the [Birmingham] community."[51] He has also put together a Museum of Legends, featuring notable community members as well as mementoes from his life in baseball, which is currently housed at Bethel Baptist Church. For his decades of community service, Greason was presented with a lifetime achievement award at the annual Alabama Black Achievement Awards Gala in 2011.

America has continued to grapple with its racial history, but in later life Greason also has received long-overdue recognition for his accomplishments prior to his ministerial career. On June 27, 2012, he was in Washington, D.C. as part of a group of 370 Montford Point Marines who received the Congressional Gold Medal, the nation's highest civilian honor. Two months later, on August 30, he was honored by the minor-league Oklahoma City Redhawks (now Dodgers) on the 60th anniversary of his breaking the color barrier in the state of Oklahoma. On September 21, 2014, the St. Louis Cardinals held a similar ceremony to commemorate the 60th anniversary of his debut as the franchise's first African-American pitcher.

Greason has said about his life's experiences, "I have no regrets. I thank God for the direction he led."[52] Far from simply having no regrets, he earned many reasons to be proud: as a U.S. Marine, pioneering baseball player, civil rights activist, pastor, husband, and father, Greason has become a quintessential American.

SOURCES

In addition to the sources cited in the endnotes, the author also consulted the following:

Figueredo, Jorge S. *Cuban Baseball: A Statistical History, 1878-1961* (Jefferson, North Carolina: McFarland & Co., 2003).

McNary, Kyle. *Black Baseball: A History of African-Americans & the National Game* (New York: Sterling Publishing Company, Inc.), 2003.

Treto Cisneros, Pedro, editor. *Enciclopedia del Béisbol Mexicano* (Mexico City: Revistas Deportivas, S.A. de C.V.: 11th edition, 2011).

Vance, Mike, editor, *Houston Baseball: The Early Years 1861-1961* (Houston: Bright Sky Press, 2014).

www.bethelbcbp.org

www.montfordpointmarines.com

Also, special thanks go out to the following:

Dr. Bill McCurdy and Mike Vance, fellow members of SABR-Houston's Larry Dierker Chapter, who responded to my inquiries about Bill Greason's time with the Houston Buffaloes. Their spirit of helpfulness is greatly appreciated.

Rory Costello, who took great interest in this biography and contributed both expert editing as well as his additional knowledge about Greason's time in the Caribbean when it was first written for SABR's Biography Project.

Bryan Steverson, author of *Baseball: A Special Gift from God* and a friend of Rev. Greason, who answered questions and was generous enough to offer his interview notes, which provided additional information that has resulted in a slightly expanded version of this article for this book.

NOTES

1   Thomas E. Van Hyning, *Puerto Rico's Winter League* (Jefferson, North Carolina: McFarland & Company, 1995), 216.

2   John Klima, *Willie's Boys: The 1948 Birmingham Black Barons, the Last Negro League World Series, and the Making of a Baseball Legend* (Hoboken, New Jersey: Wiley & Sons, Inc., 2009), 62.

3   KTVIDScruggs and CNN Wires, "Cardinals first African American pitcher honored with Living Legend Award," September 1, 2014, http://fox2now.com/2014/09/01/cardinals-first-african-american-pitcher-honored-with-living-legend-award/, accessed October 23, 2015.

4   Bryan Steverson, *Baseball: A Special Gift from God* (Bloomington, Indiana: Westbow Press, 2014), 238.

5   Nick Diunte, "Former Negro League pitcher Greason graciously shares his grand life story," February 25, 2013, http://www.examiner.com/article/former-negro-league-pitcher-greason-graciously-shares-his-grand-life-story, accessed October 23, 2015.

6   Larry Powell, *Black Barons of Birmingham: The South's Greatest Negro League Team And Its Players* (Jefferson, North Carolina: McFarland & Company, 2009), 172.

7   Bryan Steverson, Notes from Interviews and Conversations with Rev. Bill Greason, email from Bryan Steverson to this author, December 16, 2016.

8   Diunte, "Former Negro League pitcher Greason graciously shares his grand life story." Official statistics from Greason's season with the Nashville Black Vols are unavailable. Greason's win-loss record stems from his own recollection of his time with the Nashville team.

9   Ibid.

10 The Grays played their home games at either Pittsburgh's Forbes Field or Washington's Griffith Stadium; however, both stadiums were being used by their major-league tenants at the time of the1948 Negro World Series.

11 "Grays Hold 3-1 Lead in Series," *Afro-American*, October 9, 1948.

12 Negro Leagues Baseball Museum eMuseum, "William Greason," http://coe.k-state.edu/annex/nlbemuseum/history/players/greason.html, accessed October 23, 2015.

13   Powell, 174.

14   Emmons Byrne, "The Bull Pen," *Oakland Tribune*, April 3, 1951: 28.

15   "Pacific Coast League—Oakland," *The Sporting News*, April, 18, 1951: 30.

16   "Big Negro League Tilt at V.F.W. Stadium Tonight," *Sikeston* (Missouri) *Daily Standard*, June 28, 1951: 8.

17   Ibid.

18   Berry Tramel, "Oklahoma City's Jackie Robinson: When Bill Greason integrated baseball here," *The Oklahoman*, August 22, 2012, http://newsok.com/article/3703298, accessed October 23, 2015.

19   Larry Moffi and Jonathan Kronstadt, *Crossing the Line: Black Major Leaguers 1947-1959* (Lincoln, Nebraska: University of Nebraska Press, 1994), 111.

20   Derrick Goold, "Cards honor Greason, one of their trailblazers," *St. Louis Post-Dispatch*, September 21, 2014.

21   Al Hirshberg, "Bosox Bid for Negro Hill Star, Greason, Also Sought by Yanks," *The Sporting News*, December 24, 1952, 9.

22   Tramel, "Oklahoma City's Jackie Robinson: When Bill Greason integrated baseball here"

23   Ibid.

24   John Cronley, "Negro Duel Makes Lone Star History," *The Sporting News*, August 13, 1952, 31.

25   Ibid.

26   "Humphries Puts Price Tag at $75,000 Plus on Greason," *The Sporting News*, September 24, 1952: 27.

27   "Oklahoma City Turns Down $50,000 Offers for Greason," *The Sporting News*, January 28, 1953: 21.

28   Bob Broeg, "Cards, Reshuffling Hands, Get Texas Negro Ace in Deal," *The Sporting News*, October 21, 1953: 11.

29   "One-Hitter for Nine Frames, Greason Bows in 15th, 2-1," *The Sporting News*, May 19, 1954: 28.

30   Bob Broeg, "Ragged Pitching Grounds Rich-in-Hitting Redbirds," *The Sporting News*, June 2, 1954: 9.

31   Klima, *Willie's Boys*, 268.

32   Ibid.

33   Diunte, "Former Negro League pitcher Greason graciously shares his grand life story."

34   Thomas E. Van Hyning,, *The Santurce Crabbers: Sixty Seasons of Puerto Rican Winter League Baseball* (Jefferson, North Carolina: McFarland & Company, 1999), 63.

35   Van Hyning, *The Santurce Crabbers*, 70.

36   Van Hyning, *Puerto Rico's Winter League*, 253.

37   Lou Hernández, *The Rise of the Latin American Baseball Leagues, 1947-1961* (Jefferson, North Carolina: McFarland & Company, 2011), 52. "Hoy 25 de Enero…en Béisbol Invernal Dominicano," Lidom.com, January 25, 2014.

38   Moffi and Kronstadt, *Crossing the Line*: 111.

39   Goold, "Cards honor Greason, one of their trailblazers."

40   Steverson, Notes from Interviews and Conversations with Rev. Bill Greason.

41   Powell, 179.

42   Powell, *Black Barons of Birmingham*, 180.

43   Ibid.

44   David J. Krajicek, "Justice Story: Birmingham church bombing kills 4 innocent girls in racially motivated attack," *New York Daily News*, September 1, 2013.

45   Powell, *Black Barons of Birmingham*, 180.

46   KTVIDScruggs and CNN Wires, "Cardinals first African American pitcher honored with Living Legend Award"

47   Bruce Adelson, *Brushing Back Jim Crow: The Integration of Minor-League Baseball in the American South* (Charlottesville, Virginia: University Press of Virginia, 1999), 245.

48   Adelson, *Brushing Back Jim Crow*, 246.

49   Steverson, Notes from Interviews and Conversations with Rev. Bill Greason.

50   Ibid. Steverson noted that Greason had a pacemaker installed and had colon cancer surgery in 2014.

51   "American Negro League Baseball Association Project HELP," *Birmingham Times*, August 14, 2014, http://www.birminghamtimes.com/2014/08/american-negro-league-baseball-association-project-help, accessed November 2, 2015.

52   Tramel, "Oklahoma City's Jackie Robinson: When Bill Greason integrated baseball here."

WILEY GRIGGS

By William Dahlberg

Without war and baseball, it is likely Wiley Lee Griggs III might never have left Birmingham, Alabama. He was born to Wiley Griggs II and Fair Bell Griggs on March 24, 1925, in Union Springs, Alabama. The Griggs family moved sometime before 1930 to Birmingham, which, except for a few seasons with other teams, would be his home for the rest of his life. Both during and after his career, Griggs lived within a few miles of Rickwood Field, where he played with the Birmingham Black Barons during the waning years of the Negro Leagues.

During Griggs's youth, and into much of his adulthood, Birmingham was one of the most racially divided cities in the United States. Life was not easy under the confining limits of Jim Crow in the so called "Magic City." Neither of Wiley's parents had graduated from high school; his father completed the sixth grade, and his mother made it only through third grade. Wiley Griggs II worked in construction as a carpenter for many years, and the Griggs family lived in Titusville, which was one of several predominantly black industrial, working-class neighborhoods adjacent to the booming steel industry on which Birmingham was built.[1]

As a child, Griggs said, he grew up playing "rag ball" out in the streets with his older brother, Acie "Skeet" Griggs, and his younger brother, Bennie. Around the time he was 14, Wiley joined his first organized league, playing for the Ingalls Iron Works, which was located in Titusville close to his home.[2]

Wiley attended Parker High School, the only high school for African-Americans in Birmingham at the time. Parker was one of the largest all-black schools in the country with an enrollment of nearly 3,000 students.[3] Wiley dropped out of Parker before graduating, most likely to work full-time in one of the industrial plants. A few months after turning 18 during World War II, he enlisted in the US Army on September 28, 1943, and was sent to Fort Benning, Georgia, for basic training.[4] He served until after the war ended, being discharged on April 8, 1946.[5]

According to Griggs, in early 1948, Lorenzo "Piper" Davis extended an invitation to Griggs to attend the Black Barons' spring training. Griggs, who played primarily second base, was vying for the same position as Davis, who was a seasoned veteran. The *Birmingham World*, the largest African-American newspaper in Alabama, reported on the team's progress in spring training and took note of Griggs in an article headlined "Local Boy Fights," which declared, "Another newcomer, Wiley Lee Griggs, a Birmingham product, is battling for a slot on the Barons roster. Griggs has been handling the second base duties flawlessly in spring games and has surprised many with his stick work to date. He may hold on as a reserve. The would-be-Black Barons played last season with Chattanooga of Negro Southern League"[6]

The *World* continued to extol Griggs's abilities throughout the spring, at one point stating that "Wiley Griggs, another newcomer to the Ebony Barons, will hold down the keystone sack. Griggs has been playing ball all spring and is making a serious bid for regular duty with the Barons this year."[7] Shortly before training camp broke, the *World* reported that "another newcomer, Wiley Lee Griggs, has found himself fielding and hitting at a terrific clip to all but insure his presence with the Ebony Barons this season. Griggs … can play short, second, or third base and seems to be retained as the utility infielder in '48."[8]

During the 1948 season Griggs was given his nickname, "Diamond Jim," by Black Barons pitcher Alonzo Perry.[9] Over the course of that season, Griggs filled a backup role and played in only 14 out of 76 league games. He went 8-for-33 with the bat for a .242 average; he hit two doubles and scored six runs.

WILEY GRIGGS

Infielder Wiley "Diamond Jim" Griggs was a versatile backup/utility player for the 1948 Birmingham Black Barons, batting .242 in 14 league games for the NAL champions. (*Courtesy R. D. Retort Enterprises*)

Following his limited—but successful—1948 season, Griggs was initially listed as one of eight infielders on the preseason roster for the Black Barons in April of 1949.[10] Unfortunately, Griggs suffered an injury and was released by the Black Barons. He ended up playing the 1950 season with the Cleveland Buckeyes and Houston Eagles.[11] He remained a member of the Eagles after they moved to New Orleans, and played there in 1951. Griggs was selected to represent the Eagles in the annual East-West All-Star Game during his lone season in New Orleans. In the game, which was played on August 12 at Chicago's Comiskey Park, Griggs was hitless in his one at-bat for the East team as a pinch-

hitter.[12] Before long, however, Griggs was back in Birmingham, where he played the remainder of his career with the Black Barons.

Statistics are incomplete for many of the later seasons that Griggs played with the Black Barons. In 1956, Griggs played in at least 46 games with a 45-for-180 batting line that gave him a .250 average. Available statistics for 1958 show that he played in 31 games, going 17-for-108—a .157 batting average—with two doubles, one home run, and 11 runs scored.[13] Griggs hung up his spikes for good prior to the 1959 season.

Baseball and military service were both family affairs for the Griggses; both of Wiley's brothers also played professional baseball and served tours of duty during the war years. His younger brother, Bennie Lenton Griggs, pitched for the Birmingham All-Stars and several other Negro League teams after having first paid his dues in Birmingham's industrial leagues. Bennie spent 10 seasons in Canada (nonconsecutively) between 1949 and 1963, compiling an 82-41 record in his years north of the border.[14] He was drafted into the US Army during the Korean War in 1951 and was awarded a Purple Heart for being wounded in action.[15]

Wiley's older brother, Acie "Skeet" Griggs, played for the Black Barons, the Atlanta Black Crackers, and the New York Cubans in the late 1940s and 1950s after having served in the US Navy during World War II. In 1954, Acie and Bennie Griggs played together for the Saskatoon Gems of Canada's Saskatchewan Baseball League.[16]

In a 1995 interview, Ben Cook asked Griggs if traveling with the Barons had been simple compared to his travel with the Army during World War II. Griggs responded, "It was way better than a piece of cake!" Asked to reflect on his hitting, Griggs conceded, "I could hit, but not what you'd call one of the great hitters. No, I wasn't that. Hitting singles … fair."[17]

In the same interview, Griggs expressed his belief that even though the Negro Leagues were on the decline during his playing days, the ballplayers were still very good. When asked about the greatest pitcher he ever faced, he gave a familiar name: Satchel Paige. Griggs said of Paige's pinpoint control, "You could ask where you wanted it and he'd get it to you! It's up to you to hit it—if you can! I couldn't do nothing with him. I tell the truth about mine. Some could hit him, but I couldn't do anything about my part."[18] Griggs could not think of the best hitter he had seen—he emphasized that there were many good hitters in the league when he played and lamented that all the old-time hitters were likely "dead and gone on!"[19]

Griggs asserted that his favorite memory as a Black Baron was playing for the 1948 team, especially in the Negro American League playoff series against the Kansas City Monarchs and the final Negro Leagues World Series against the Homestead Grays. As to the end of his career, Griggs said he knew when it was time to retire. He recalled, "Well, I was getting old. One thing I was getting old—and I had a family, so I had to do a little better."[20] And do better he did. Griggs got a job with the Birmingham Water Works board, where he worked for 28 years until his retirement in 1987. He and his family were active members of St. Mark C.M.E. Church in Birmingham. Later in his life Wiley became a double amputee and was confined to a wheelchair.[21]

Griggs said that he kept in touch with some teammates after his playing career, occasionally speaking to them on the phone. He also made it out to Rickwood Field for various events. In a final reflection on his career, Griggs said, "We played for nothing, but still, we enjoyed it. We didn't mind playing. It was nice playing. I enjoyed myself. Wasn't making too much money, but yet still—that was my life. I loved baseball. I played baseball—and I don't have no regrets." He thought he had come along at just the right time to play professional baseball as he also observed that the level of play at the professional level was elevated in modern times, but kids did not seem to have as much of an interest in the game as they had once had.

Wiley Griggs III died on August 23, 1996, in Birmingham. He was buried in Elmwood Cemetery, a short distance from his home and Rickwood Field.

He was survived by his wife, Frances Griggs, and his children, Deborah Cunningham, Sharon E. Griggs, Wiley M. Griggs, Andrew Wright, and Adolphus Griggs.[22]

SOURCES

In addition to the sources listed in the notes below, the author also consulted Ancestry.com, Baseball-Reference.com, and the following:

Negro League Baseball eMuseum.

Negro League Baseball Players Association (nlbpa.com).

Powell, Larry. *Black Barons of Birmingham: The South's Greatest Negro League Team and Its Players* (Jefferson, North Carolina: McFarland & Company, Inc., 2009).

NOTES

1   According to the 1940 Census, the only income in the household was from Wiley Griggs Sr. of $560 for the year, well below the average median income of $956 at the time. Adjusted for inflation, it would mean that the Griggs family of five was surviving off of $9,600 in today's economy—surely a challenge no matter if you look at it in terms of 1940 or 2016.

2   "Wiley Griggs," Oral History Interview, Birmingham Public Library Digital Collections. bplonline.org/virtual/ContentDMSubjectBrowse.aspx?subject=Griggs%2C%20 Wiley, accessed January 13, 2017.

3   Parker High School United Alumni Association, parkeralumni.com/history.html, January 12, 2017. (Bill Bruton, who played for the Milwaukee Braves and Detroit Tigers also attended Parker High School. Given that Griggs and Bruton were both born in 1925, it is likely they were classmates or at the very least knew each other.)

4   US World War II Army Enlistment Records, 1938-1946.

5   US Department of Veteran Affairs BIRLS Death Files, 1850-2019.

6   "Black Barons Eye '48 Championship; Leave City for Exhibition Games," *Birmingham World*, April 6, 1948: 6.

7   "Black Barons, Clowns Set for Doubleheader Sunday," *Birmingham World*, April 16, 1948: 6.

8   "Black Barons Set to Meet Cleveland Buckeyes May 1, 'Griggs Shines,'" *Birmingham World*, April 23, 1948: 5.

9   Wiley Griggs, Oral History Interview.

10 "Barons Pilot Picks Squad of Players To Start '49 Season," *Indianapolis Recorder*, April 9, 1949: 11.

11 James A. Riley, *The Biographical Encyclopedia of the Negro Baseball Leagues* (New York: Carroll & Graf Publisher, Inc., 1994), 342. The Negro Southern League Museum lists Griggs on the Black Barons 1949 roster, but in their summary of statistics for the entire season, Griggs is nowhere to be found.

Given that there are no statistics for Griggs for any of the 1949 season with the Barons (or any other team), it seems likely that his injury—which Riley gives the only mention of that I could find—occurred early in the season, and was sever enough, that it kept him sidelined for quite a while.

12   Larry Lester, *Black Baseball's National Showcase: The East-West All-Star Game, 1933-1945* (Lincoln: University of Nebraska Press, 2002), 360, 408.

13   Rosters: Negro American League 1958-1962, cnlbr.org/Portals/0/Rosters/Rosters%20-%20Negro%20American%20League%20(1958-1962).pdf, accessed January 3, 2017.

14   Barry Swanton and Jay-Dell Mah, *Black Baseball Players in Canada: A Biographical Dictionary, 1881-1960* (Jefferson, North Carolina: McFarland & Company, Inc., 2009), 79.

15   "Bennie Lenton Griggs," attheplate.com/wcbl/profile_griggs_bennie.html, accessed February 2, 2017.

16   Swanton and Mah, 78.

17   Wiley Griggs, Oral History Interview.

18   Ibid.

19   Ibid.

20   Ibid.

21   Riley, 342.

22   Wiley Griggs, findagrave.com/cgi-bin/fg.cgi?page=gr&GSln=Griggs&GSfn=Wiley&GSbyrel=all&GSdyrel=all&GSst=3&GScntry=4&GSob=n&GRid=99229414&df=all& , accessed January 30, 2017.

JEHOSIE HEARD

By J.W. Stewart

Left-hander Jehosie Heard stepped onto a major-league mound for the first time on a chilly Chicago spring day in April 1954. As he walked out to the mound at Comiskey Park, Heard became the first African-American to play for the Baltimore Orioles. The team was in Chicago for a four-game series against the White Sox; both squads were at .500 after eight games.[1] On the previous day the Orioles had won 3-1 in a 10-inning game; however, when Heard stepped to the mound during the eighth on April 24, the Orioles were down 10-0. He was the third of four pitchers manager Jimmy Dykes would tap during the losing effort. Heard pitched a little more than an inning, giving up no hits or walks. The Orioles lost, 14-4, but Heard was happy with his first big-league performance and hoped he would remain with the team.[2] Heard's tenure with Baltimore would last only until June. Eight years of Negro League and minor-league development led to a short four months with the Orioles and then a return to the minors.

Jehosie Heard was born to John and Annie Heard on January 17, 1921, in the small community of High Shoals, Georgia. However, a 1920 census shows a one-year-old Jehovah Heard, the youngest of six children. For most of his career Heard would accumulate multiple variations on his name, thanks to misunderstandings. Jehosa, Josie, Jehova, and Hosea are all recorded in various news stories and records.

High Shoals, about 65 miles east of Atlanta, drew its existence and name from the High Shoals Manufacturing Company, a textile mill established during the 1840s.[3] Surrounding the mill were fields of cotton, one of which was owned by Heard's parents. However, shortly after Jehosie's birth, John moved his family to Birmingham in order to work at a stove and range factory. It was an auspicious move as the High Shoals mill burned down in 1928. The resultant eco-nomic calamity pushed the town of a few thousand down to a few hundred.[4]

The Heard family had avoided one calamity only to be subjected to a much more serious and personal one in 1924. Jehosie's father died of pneumonia on August 11, leaving Annie a widow at 29. She took a job as a cotton stripper to support her four young children. The oldest, Emma, returned home after marrying and worked as a laundress.[5] Jehosie was enrolled in Birmingham public schools in 1926 and attended the all-black Thomas School and later Parker High School, also a segregated school. Jehosie struggled in school. His attendance was spotty and in 1932 he failed five subjects in the first semester. In 1935 Jehosie had to repeat part of the seventh grade and then in 1937 part of the eighth, putting him far behind his peers. Teachers described him as "sly" and made a note of his "weak" attendance.[6] Jehosie entered Parker High in 1937 but did not finish the first semester. His poor academic performance, coupled with the financial pressures put on his mother as a single parent during the Depression, surely pushed Jehosie from school into the workforce.

Sometime before World War II, Annie was unable to work any longer, identified as disabled in census records. Her disability and the challenges of the Depression Era job market forced Jehosie and his mother to move in with a woman named Louise Battle and her younger daughter. Work was scarce for Jehosie, who found steady work for only three months out of the year in 1939. He worked as a gas station attendant in the winter of 1939-40, but lost this job in March of 1940.[7]

Heard enlisted in the US Army in October 1941 and became one of the many African-Americans who served in the military prior to the attack on Pearl Harbor. His war records were lost to the 1973 National Archives fire; however, according to author Larry Moffi, Jehosie was first exposed to baseball on

Pitcher Jehosie Heard made an appearance for the Birmingham Black Barons in Game Four of the 1948 Negro League World Series. In April 1954 he became the first African-American to play for the Baltimore Orioles. (*National Baseball Hall of Fame, Cooperstown, New York*)

an Army base during the war. Heard's family placed his introduction to baseball with his brother John. It is unlikely Heard was never exposed to baseball as a kid given the prominence of the Birmingham Black Barons in the local black community and the near ubiquity of baseball among young boys at the time. Given Heard's skill at pitching immediately after his release from the Army, it is likely he sharpened his pitching abilities during the war. By all accounts, Heard spent the war stateside.

Soon after Heard's release, the country was embroiled in a coal miners' strike, which had a serious effect on the job market in Birmingham. Heard played on the 24th Street Red Sox team before he asked Birmingham Black Barons manager Tommy Sampson for a job.[8] Sampson not only gave him a job, but made him the starting pitcher on opening day in May 1946. The Parker High School band, the school's principal, and local officials showed up to

start the season. Heard gave up eight hits and two earned runs while recording six strikeouts and surrendering four walks. He was even responsible for one of the runs that contributed to his team's 7-2 victory over the Cleveland Buckeyes, the 1945 Negro League champions.[9] It was a promising start for his three-year career with the Black Barons.

Only a smattering of references to Heard can be found for the 1946 season, though what has survived shows an impressive degree of skill given his rookie status, especially a one-hitter he pitched against the Chicago American Giants in Birmingham on August 4.[10] He pitched well enough to be invited to participate in an exhibition game at Comiskey Park on September 21. Players from the Chicago American Giants and Cleveland Buckeyes challenged members of the Black Barons and Memphis Red Sox in what was billed as a North vs. South game. Dan Bankhead, the All-Star pitcher from the Red Sox, started but Heard relieved him in the eighth inning after Bankhead was shelled for five runs the inning before. Heard gave up two more runs in the South's 8-3 loss.[11]

For 1947, only three games in which Heard pitched were recorded, and he was 2-1 in those contests. A victory over the Chicago American Giants on June 22 was followed by a loss to the Kansas City Monarchs on July 13. The highlight of 1947 occurred in September when Heard pitched "a one-hit shutout in the five inning nightcap" of a doubleheader against the Memphis Red Sox.[12]

In 1948 the Black Barons returned to the Negro League World Series, their third trip to the Series and Heard's first. Heard saw action in the fourth game of the World Series against the Homestead Grays. After the Barons lost two close games to start the series and won the third game in Birmingham, they suffered a humiliating 14-1 defeat in New Orleans on October 3. Heard, the second of four pitchers used by Birmingham that day, relieved Bill Greason until he himself was replaced on the mound by Jimmie Newberry; the Black Barons' quartet of hurlers gave up 19 hits and 14 runs to the Homestead Grays.[13] Two days later Birmingham lost the final game of the

Series, 10-6.[14] Despite having home-field advantage, with three of the five games played in Birmingham, the team was no match for the Grays' batters.

The next year the Memphis Red Sox purchased Heard's contract from the Barons.[15] Heard and his new teammates reported to Martin Stadium in Memphis on March 13 for the start of spring training. However, sometime between February and April, Heard found himself running spring-training drills for the newly minted Houston Eagles of the Negro American League. The venerable Newark Eagles, the 1946 Negro League champions, had been sold by Abe and Effa Manley and the new ownership moved the franchise to Houston, Texas, for the 1949 season.

Houston's spring training ended in early April and the team headed to Nashville for an exhibition series with the Baltimore Elite Giants.[16] Before leaving for Nashville, the Eagles played an exhibition game against Memphis, losing 6-5. Heard was one of three relievers used by Houston manager Reuben Jones.[17] The Memphis Red Sox and the Eagles met 15 times between Opening Day and June 11, with the Eagles taking eight of the games.[18]

In late July a victory by Heard against the Philadelphia Stars led catcher Leon Ruffin, the new Houston manager, to express his confidence that Heard and his other three star pitchers would "bring Houston the league pennant."[19] The Eagles did not win the pennant, though Heard continued to provide yeoman performances on the mound. In an August 28 contest against the Memphis Red Sox, he struck out 11 and allowed only six hits in a 3-0 shutout. He drove in the Eagles' first tally when he was hit by a pitch with the bases loaded.[20]

Heard remained with Houston for the 1950 season, but the team and the entire Negro League suffered from a drain of talent and that resulted in dwindling attendance. By June 16, Houston was in third place in the Negro American League West and Heard's appearances were leading to losses.[21] In June Houston sold two of its best players to the Brooklyn Dodgers and decided to move home games to Nashville due to low attendance in Houston.[22] Despite his losing record, Heard was recruited to pitch for an all-star

traveling team that battled a team of major-league stars, and a September 2 article in the *Chicago Defender* referred to him as the "ace of the club."[23] Through October, Heard traveled with and played against the likes of Monte Irvin, Don Newcombe, and Roy Campanella.

Because of the low attendance in 1950, the Eagles were moved to New Orleans in 1951. The New Orleans Eagles spent spring training in Hot Springs, Arkansas, and played exhibition games in Arkansas, Mississippi, and Louisiana.[24] Heard, now used as a starter rather than a reliever, lost his first game at Pelican Stadium in New Orleans, 10-8, giving up five hits and striking out only three.[25] But by the summer he was being referred to as an "outstanding southpaw" with his 13-4 record. The *Chicago Defender* declared Heard one of the "four ... top pitchers of the league" as it recorded the explosion of wins the Eagles were racking up.[26] The *Kansas City* (Kansas) *Plaindealer* reported Heard was being scouted by the White Sox and the St. Louis Browns.[27] Heard scored a victory against every team in the Negro American League on Sundays in the preceding months, earning him the moniker "Sunday pitcher."[28] In the 1951 All-Star voting, Heard came in second among pitchers to Theolic Smith, a 15-year veteran of the Chicago American Giants.[29] In the East-West All-Star Game, Smith started while Heard came to the mound in the sixth inning as the West's third reliever. Heard struck out three, gave up two hits, walked none, and allowed one run.[30] For the season he had a 16-5 record and a league-leading 149 strikeouts.[31] Heard had an impressive year on the mound, but in a rarity for pitchers, he also saw success at the plate.

Heard's batting skills were first credited in a news story on April 29, 1951. While it's not clear exactly how he hit during the second game of a doubleheader against the Baltimore Elite Giants, it must have been impressive enough to warrant the headline "Heard's Stickwork Gives Eagles Even Break in Bill."[32] Heard ended the 1951 season with the headline "Jehosie Heard Top NAL Batter" thanks to a .396 batting average. His average had been as high as .422 at mid-season.[33] Heard had 106 trips to the plate in 51 games with 42 hits, 4 doubles, 3 triples, and 7 RBIs. To keep Heard's hot bat in the game, the Eagles used him as an outfielder when he was not pitching.[34]

Heard's performance on the mound and at the plate drew the attention of the major leagues. Rogers Hornsby, who briefly managed the St. Louis Browns in 1952, reportedly said that "he liked everything about him except for his size."[35] (He was listed as 5-feet-7 and 155 pounds.) Still, the Browns purchased his contract and infielder Curley Williams's from the Eagles for an estimated $100,000 at the end of August.[36] After six years in the Negro American League, Jehosie Heard was headed to a world far from his Southern home.

In December of 1951, on the heels of his new baseball opportunity, Heard married Mildred Davis. The two had met sometime between 1946 and 1948 while Heard played for Birmingham. During a road series in Memphis, the young ballplayer was introduced to 20-year-old Mildred at Metropolitan Baptist Church. She hailed from a working-class family in Memphis, was a college graduate, and worked as a social worker for the City of Memphis.[37]

Heard was sent to the Portland Beavers in the winter of 1952 and reported to training camp in Riverside, California, in March. There he was described as "painfully bashful" but displayed a "dazzling variety of fast and slow curves" and a "'sneaking' fastball."[38] Heard was used in relief, and eventually was optioned to the Victoria Tyees in April.[39] The first report of his performance with Victoria came in a May 9 game between Victoria and Wenatchee where he closed out the game. Heard "whiffed the four batters he faced" to hold onto Victoria's 3-2 lead. *The Sporting News* called the 1⅓ innings "one of the most impressive mound performances of the season."[40] By the end of May, Heard had pitched 34 innings with 27 strikeouts and a 4-1 record.

The Tyees started June with a 33-15 record and a 3½-game lead over the Spokane Indians. On two days' rest on June 7, Heard pitched a 4-2 win over Lewiston, making him the Western International League's first eight-game winner. He gave up only one walk in the victory and collected on a steak-

dinner prize awarded to pitcher with fewer than two walks in a game. It was the second time Heard had collected on the prize.[41] A month later Heard had pitched 146 innings in 27 games with 117 strikeouts and had a 12-6 record.

Heard's first recorded no-hitter occurred on September 10, 1952. The four walks he surrendered to the Lewiston Broncs, along with three fielding errors behind him resulted in two runs allowed. The final score was 11-2. In addition to his performance on the mound, Heard scored three runs. He was struck in the head on his fifth appearance, tried to continue with the at-bat, but then acquiesced to suggestions that he get checked out.[42] Heard's 20-win season caused Portland to recall him after the September 10 game.[43] Due in large part to Heard's 2.94 ERA and 216 strikeouts, Victoria won the Western International League pennant.[44]

As Heard worked his way up through the minor leagues, he was recruited by the Leones del Caracas of the Venezuelan League. He and Mildred boarded a Pan American flight out of New York on October 7 and headed out of the United States for the first time, celebrating their first anniversary in Venezuela.[45]

Heard donned a Caracas jersey for the first time on October 17 before a crowd of over 30,000 on Opening Day for the Venezuelan League and was one of two relievers as Leones del Caracas defeated the Venezuela Patriots, 9-5. Back pain kept Heard on the bench until he came in as a reliever on November 10.[46] Heard grabbed his first win on November 16 against Vargas, relieving in the fifth inning and leading Caracas to a 4-2 victory in 10 innings.[47] By Christmas Eve Caracas was in first place and Heard was being consistently used as a reliever. Caracas dominated the Venezuelan league, but was outmatched in the Caribbean Series, losing five of six games. Heard relieved in two games, and started in another. All three were losses.[48]

Heard returned stateside and joined his new team, the Portland Beavers of the Pacific Coast League, in March. The first reports of his success on the mound appeared in April with the "143-pound Negro lefty" picking up right where he left off in 1952. On April

26 Heard gave up only one unearned run in an 8-1 victory over the Sacramento Solons.[49]

For the second year in a row, however, late July and August proved to be a difficult time for Heard. Through the last weeks of July and the first of August, he lost six times in seven starts.[50] He ended the season 16-12 with a 3.19 ERA, 85 strikeouts, and 92 walks. Portland finished fourth, a position the team held every year between 1950 and 1953.[51]

As soon as Portland's season ended, Heard was on a flight to South America to play for Caracas. His performance in Venezuela, where he also played for Magallanes that season, did not matter much; his stint with Portland had been impressive enough for the Orioles to purchase his contract for $20,000. The 1954 season was the first for the Orioles after the St. Louis Browns were relocated to Baltimore. Aside from his 1952 and 1953 win totals, the Orioles based their decision on scouting reports from as far back as his Negro American League All-Star Game performance in 1951.[52] Bill Greason, one of Heard's former Birmingham teammates, also attributed Heard's selection to his "soft spoken nature." According to Greason, teams looked for black players "who could handle the abuse without cracking" and could integrate teams with little disruption.[53]

Heard was one of 18 pitchers at spring training in Yuma, Arizona, in 1954.[54] The initial list of players slated for Yuma included Satchel Paige as well, though his age and disinterest in the Orioles ultimately led to Heard being the only African-American at spring training. The expectations were high for the "smallest player in the Baltimore camp."[55] A former Baltimore resident living in Hollywood who had a chance to see Heard play reported to the *Baltimore News Post* that Heard had a "good chance of being the rookie of the year."[56] The *Washington Post* concurred, stating that Heard "could be Baltimore's No. 1 left-handed pitcher."[57]

The Orioles won the Cactus League title with a 12-5 record over the Giants, Indians, and Chicago Cubs. Coming out of spring training, "only Jehosie Heard ... has given [manager Jimmy] Dykes cause for cheers in the southpaw department," wrote the *New York Times*.[58] As Opening Day approached, Heard settled into the role of reliever rather than starter. Pitching was a serious weight on Dykes's mind, the lack of solid starters negating the strong infield he put together. Surveying his team, Dykes described them as a "sixth-place outfit."[59]

The pessimism and gloom were largely contained to Dykes and sportswriters. Baltimoreans, on the other hand, was excited to see the return of the Orioles after 52 years without a major-league team. On a chilly Opening Day, April 15, half a million fans lined the streets to welcome them. More than 46,000, including Vice President Richard Nixon, packed Memorial Stadium to watch the home opener.[60] Heard told the *Baltimore Afro-American* that "the spirit here in Baltimore makes me proud I'm starting here," and added, "I can only hope I can help the club pay off these fans."[61]

Heard's debut game on April 24 was broadcast across the country as ABC's *Game of the Week*.[62] When he stepped to the mound in the eighth, the game was already out of hand; the Orioles were down 10-0. Heard pitched 1⅓ innings and gave up no hits or walks.

By Heard's second appearance, on May 28, the excitement of the April parade had waned and fans now occasionally booed pitchers.[63] Heard took the mound in the fifth inning of the first game of a doubleheader against the White Sox at Memorial Stadium with Chicago up 4-2. Heard held them for an inning, but gave up five hits and five runs in the sixth inning; four of the runs scored on a grand slam by Cass Michaels. The Orioles lost 11-6.[64]

On June 6 the Orioles optioned Heard back to the Portland Beavers, whose performance had suffered by his absence from their pitching staff. The *Afro-American* wrote that the Orioles felt Heard "was not fast enough for the major leagues," an assertion borne out in previous observations that he relied mostly on his curve.[65] Former teammate Greason observed, "He didn't have a fastball to go with those breaking balls, but he threw strikes."[66]

The *Afro-American* also cited a more salacious reason for the demotion. Heard's neighbors had reported a domestic disturbance in the Heard household on the weekend of May 15-16 that involved broken furniture and "blood smears." The paper found a record of a husband and wife matching Jehosie and Mildred's description seeking medical treatment on the night in question. The mystery couple gave a nonexistent address similar to the Heards'. On the night of the incident, Heard had complained of a "stomach ailment" and had not reported to the ballpark for the Orioles game.[67]

Adding to the mystery was the fact that Heard filed a missing-person report for his wife at 2 A.M. on June 9. According to the paper and the police report, Heard reported that his wife had left with "approximately $80 in cash and that there was a possibility she had gone to Washington to the home of relatives."[68] Heard later claimed it was a misunderstanding and that Mildred was in New York at her sister's home and had not expected him back from a road trip. Further intrigue was the result of a reference in Heard's missing-person report to a scar over Mildred's right eye. The medical records of the mystery couple from May 15-16 included a reference to a cut over the woman's right eye.[69]

Heard denied any notion of trouble in his marriage. Reports from teammates were conflicting, with some commenting on his "typical" wandering eye and carousing while others suggested that his drinking had caused him to miss team meetings.[70] The Orioles denied any knowledge of trouble in Heard's marriage or that anything other than baseball ability influenced their decision to release Heard; however, the team expressed bewilderment as to why Heard was not on his way to Portland, having "provided his transportation and paid him off in full."[71] Heard finally made his way back to the Portland Beavers and spent the next three years trying to make it back to the majors, though he never succeeded.

Heard struggled again during the late summer of 1954 and suffered a personal tragedy as well when on August 10 his mother died in Birmingham.

Heard was not giving up many runs in his scant number of innings, but Portland had lost confidence in his ability to start and produce solid performances on a consistent basis. On October 6, 1954, the Orioles ended Heard's option to Portland and officially traded him to the Beavers in exchange for Robert Alexander, a right-handed pitcher.[72]

After the end of the regular season, Heard joined a travelling group of Negro League All-Stars composed of players from the Negro American League and the minor leagues, but he did not fare well against the major leaguers whom they played

In January 1955 Portland traded Heard and infielder Rocky Krsnich to the Seattle Rainiers for former New York Giant Artie Wilson.[73] In Seattle, the lefty would be a part of what was termed "the best pitching staff in the [Pacific Coast League]" by *The Sporting News* and observers at Seattle's 1955 spring training in Palm Springs, California.[74]

Nonetheless, Seattle optioned Heard to the Charleston (West Virginia) Senators in July. There he accrued a 1-3 record and a 5.43 ERA.[75] During the first week of August, Charleston sent Heard to the fifth-place Tulsa Oilers in the Texas League. The league had desegregated in 1952 but by 1955 there were still only a few African-American players in the circuit.[76] By mid-August Heard had racked up three victories and had pitched 27 consecutive innings without giving up an earned run.[77]

The *Dallas Morning News's* characterization of Heard's pitching at the end of August was a far cry from the descriptions of newspapers a year or two earlier. He was described as throwing an "assortment of 'junk,'" a mixture of "slow and medium speed pitches." Tulsa finished the season tied for fourth with the Houston Buffaloes and Heard had a 6-2 record.[78] Tulsa and Houston played a tiebreaker to see which team entered the playoffs. Heard started the game and gave up six hits, one walk, and one run through eight innings. But he threw a wild pitch in the ninth that allowed a Houston runner to score for a 2-1 victory.[79]

After the season Heard again joined the Negro American League All-Stars who toured with the Major League All-Stars organized by Don Newcombe and Willie Mays. While the NAL All-Stars rarely won, Heard had moments of pitching success, retiring every batter in order between the 7th and 12th innings of an October 23 matchup.[80] In a game in mid-October, he gave up home runs to both Ernie Banks and Hank Aaron.[81]

Afterward Heard headed south of the border again for winter ball, this time ending up in the Dominican League. He started with the Tigres del Licey in Santo Domingo, earning at least one win, on November 19. However, he ended the season with the Estrellas Orientales in San Pedro de Macoris. The latter team cut Heard just before Christmas.[82]

Heard was back with Tulsa in March 1956, but he struggled on the mound the first few months. The Oilers traded Heard to the Havana Sugar Kings of the International League in July. He entered a team and country in the midst of revolutionary rumblings. Heard's performance with Havana continued as it had with Tulsa, an uneven mixture of solid pitching and tough outings. The Sugar Kings ended the season in sixth place, and Heard ended it with a 3-5 record.[83]

Heard returned to the barnstorming circuit in October, but quickly signed on with the Vanytor team in the Colombian Winter League. He posted a 7-7 record with a team contending for another championship. Heard ended the season as one of the better pitchers in the league, registering a 2.08 ERA over 139 innings.

The 1957 season was the last of Heard's baseball career. He was back with the Sugar Kings, but he pitched only one or two innings at a time and produced little. In the fall of 1957, he signed with Leon in the Nicaraguan League. His last recorded games included a 5-0 shutout and then a 1-0 loss, both against the Cinco Estrellas.[84]

Heard attempted to find a place on a team in 1958 but was unsuccessful. He returned home to Memphis but moved back to Birmingham sometime after 1960. In Birmingham he took a job operating a dye machine for the Avondale Mill, eventually rising to a supervisory position.[85] According to the *Baltimore Sun*, Heard was an "avid fisherman" and maintained a social network of former Negro League players in the years after he retired.[86]

According to a relative, Heard "was proud of [integrating the Orioles], but he never talked about it." Heard suffered a stroke sometime in the 1990s and moved into a nursing home. He died of cancer on November 18, 1999.[87]

NOTES

1   "Major League," *Chicago Tribune* April 24, 1954: 1.

2   Bob Luke, *Integrating the Orioles: Baseball and Race in Baltimore* (Jefferson, North Carolina: McFarland & Company, 2016), 24.

3   Steven Moffson, "High Shoals Historic District." National Register of Historic Places Inventory/Nomination Form. Historic Preservation Division, Georgia Department of Natural Resources, Atlanta, August 2006.

4   John Eisenberg, "O's Quiet Pioneer," *Baltimore Sun*, April 23, 2004: 1E.

5   1930 US Census, Precinct 46, Birmingham, Jefferson County, Alabama; p. 25, family 390, dwelling 370, lines 87-91; April 16, 1930.

6   Birmingham Independent School District, Jehosie Heard Cumulative Record for Elementary and High Schools.

7   1940 US Census, Precinct 46, Birmingham, Jefferson County, Alabama; p. 2, dwelling 18, lines 8-11; April 2, 1940.

8   Eisenberg.

9   "Buckeyes Lose to Birmingham: Black Barons Win Home Opener 7-2," *Chicago Defender* (National edition), May 18, 1946: 11.

10 "Birmingham and Chicago Divide," *Chicago Defender*, August 10, 1946: 11.

11 "Jessup Hurls North to Win," *Chicago Defender*, September 28, 1946: 11; Rory Costello, "Dan Bankhead," sabr.org/bioproj/person/62db6502 [accessed December 31, 2016].

12 "Memphis Loses Two to Barons," *Chicago Defender*, September 6, 1947: 11.

13 William Dismukes, "Homestead Grays Swamp Black Barons," *Chicago Defender*, October 9, 1948: 10.

14 "1948 Negro World Series," Baseball-Reference.com, baseball-reference.com/bullpen/1948_Negro_World_Series [accessed December 31, 2016].

15 "Heard to Memphis," *Chicago Defender*, February 19, 1949: 13.

16 "Eagles and Baltimore Play Easter," *Chicago Defender*, April 16, 1949: 14.

17 "Sox Beat Eagles 6-5," *Chicago Defender*, April 16, 1949: 2.

18 "Eagles Open 2nd Series vs. Red Sox," *Chicago Defender*, June 11, 1949: 16.

19 "Stars Schedule Double-Header for Thursday," *Chicago Defender*, August 13, 1949: 16; "Eagles Make First Trip to Kay Cee," *Chicago Defender*, August 6, 1949: 15.

20 "Houston Eagles Defeat Memphis Red Sox," *Chicago Defender*, September 3, 1949: 15.

21 Jerry Parker, "The Score Book" *Kansas City* (Kansas) *Plaindealer*, June 16, 1950: 4.

22 Russ J. Cowans, "Russ's Corner," *Chicago Defender*, July 8 1950: 16; "American League Announces Second Half of Baseball Schedule," *Kansas City Plaindealer*, June 16, 1950: 4.

23 "Red Sox Make Final Bid for 2nd Half Title," *Chicago Defender*, September 2, 1950: 18; "Major League Stars Open Southern Tour," *Chicago Defender*, October 14, 1950: 18.

24 "New Orleans Eagles in 1st Game April 14," *Chicago Defender*, April 14, 1951: 16.

25 "New Orleans Eagles Split Twin Bill Against Barons," *New Orleans Times Picayune*, April 16, 1951: 48.

26 "Eagles Blow Hot and Earn Title of Wonder Team," *Chicago Defender*, June 30 1951: 17.

27 "Monarchs to Meet New Orleans Eagles in Three Game Series," *Kansas City Plaindealer*, July 27, 1951: 4.

28 "Ford Rebuilds Strong Eagles Club Around Heard and Curley Williams," *Chicago Defender*, July 28, 1951: 18.

29 "Chicago Hurler Leads East-West Voting," *Chicago Defender*, July 28, 1951: 18.

30 "21,312 See East Beat West, 3-1 in Annual Chicago Classic," *Pittsburgh Courier*, August 18, 1951: 7.

31 "Jehosie Heard Top NAL Batter," *Chicago Defender*, September 8, 1951: 16.

32 "Heard's Stickwork Gives Eagles Even Break in Bill," *Times Picayune*, April 30, 1951: 27.

33 "Ford Rebuilds Strong Eagles Club Around Heard and Curley Williams," *Chicago Defender*, July 28, 1951: 18.

34 "Jehosie Heard Top NAL Batter," *Chicago Defender*, September 8, 1951: 16. A September 15, 1951, article in the *Chicago Defender* incorrectly lists Ed Steele as the batting champion with a .370 average, .026 lower than Heard's. It also lists 163 strikeouts instead of 149.

35 L.H. Gregory, "Beavers' Staff Bulwarked by Diminutive Lefty Heard," *The Sporting News*, August 5, 1953: 23.

36 Russ J. Cowans, "Russ's Corner," *Chicago Defender*, September 1, 1951: 16.

37 Ruth Jenkins, "Church Was 'Lovers Lane' for the Heards," *Baltimore Afro-American*, May 4, 1954: 10.

38 L.H. Gregory, "Beavers' Staff Bulwarked by Diminutive Lefty Heard," *The Sporting News*, August 5, 1953: 23.

39 "Deals of the Week Majors-Minors," *The Sporting News*, April 30, 1952: 36.

40 "Western International League," *The Sporting News*, May 21, 1952: 33.

41 "Western International League," *The Sporting News*, June 18, 1952: 34.

42 Jim Tang, "Heard Hurls First '52 Gem in W-I Loop for 20th Win," *The Sporting News*, September 17, 1952: 33.

43 "Deals of the Week Majors-Minors," *The Sporting News*, September 17, 1952: 40.

44 L.H. Gregory, "Beavers' Staff Bulwarked by Diminutive Lefty Heard," *The Sporting News*, August 5, 1953: 23.

45 The National Archives, Washington, D.C.: Series Title: Passenger and Crew Lists of Vessels and Airplanes Departing from New York, New York, 07/01/1948-12/31/1956; NAI Number: 3335533; Record Group Title: Records of the Immigration and Naturalization.

46 Antonio Lutz, "Magallanes' Hex on Caracas Tightens Venezuelan Race," *The Sporting News*, November 19, 1952: 24.

47 Antonio Lutz, "Magallanes Drop Two, Caracas in Venezuelan Lead," *The Sporting News*, November 26, 1952: 20.

48 Pedro Galiana, "Santurce Wins Six in Row to Notch Caribbean Series," *The Sporting News*, March 4, 1953: 25.

49 "Pacific Coast League," *The Sporting News*, May 6, 1953: 26.

50 "Pacific Coast League," *The Sporting News*, August 19, 1953: 34.

51 "Pacific Coast League," *The Sporting News*, September 23, 1953: 20, 26.

52 Hugh Trader Jr., "Ehlers Promised Initial Crack at Big Slugger," *The Sporting News*, December 23, 1953: 8.

53 Eisenberg.

54 "Orioles Will Take 44 to Training Camp," *Washington Post*, January 17, 1954: C2.

55 "Navy Lists Spring Drills," *Washington Post*, February 25, 1954: 19.

56 "Rodger H. Pippen, Sports Editor, says," *Baltimore News Post*, February 12, 1954: 32.

57 "Navy Lists Spring Drills."

58 Lou Hatter, "Orioles Return to Major Leagues Marked by Successful Spring," *New York Times*, March 28, 1954: S3.

59 Hugh Trader Jr., "Dykes Now Doubts Orioles Can Finish Higher Than Sixth," *The Sporting News*, April 14, 1954: 11.

60 Herb Heft, "Orioles Pick Coleman to Face Tigers," *Washington Post & Times Herald*, April 17, 1954: 13; Sam Lacy, "46,354 fans in Stadium for Orioles Opening Game," *Baltimore Afro-American*, April 17, 1954: 1; Herb Heft, "Baltimore Flips Lid—500,000 at parade, 46, 354 See Game," *The Sporting News*, April 21, 1954: 13.

61 Lacy.

62 "April 24 'Game of Week' to Show Chisox, Orioles," *The Sporting News*, April 21, 1954: 16.

63   Herb Heft, "Is Honeymoon Over? Fans Give the Bird to Wobbling Orioles," *The Sporting News*: June 9, 1954: 9.

64   "How They Stand," *The Sporting News*, June 9, 1954, 19; "Games of Friday May 28," *The Sporting News*, June 9, 1954: 19.

65   "Why the Orioles Released Heard," *Baltimore Afro-American*, June 12, 1954: 1.

66   Eisenberg

67   "Why the Orioles Released Heard."

68   Ibid.

69   Ibid.

70   John Klima, *Willie's Boys: The 1948 Birmingham Black Barons, The Last Negro League World Series, and the Making of a Baseball Legend* (Hoboken, New Jersey: John Wiley & Sons, 2009), 74; Eisenberg.

71   "Why the Orioles Released Heard."

72   "Orioles Obtain Pitcher," *Washington Post & Times Herald*, October 7, 1954: 29. Baseball-Reference.com shows him with a 3.22 ERA.

73   "Deals of the Week," *The Sporting News*, January 26, 1955: 28.

74   John B. Old, "4 Coast Teams Warm in Praise of Desert Sites," *The Sporting News*, March 16, 1955: 31-32.

75   "Deals of the Week," *The Sporting News* June 22, 1955, 24; "The 1955 Charleston Senators," Baseball-Reference.com, baseball-reference.com/register/team.cgi?id=2a0d00fb [accessed December 31, 2016].

76   Eisenberg.

77   "Dallas, Padres in Slump; Lead Narrows," *Sweetwater* (Texas) *Reporter*, August 16, 1955: 2; "Missions Lose Speed in Chase for Pennant," *Austin* (Texas) *American Statesman*, August 16, 1955: C2.

78   "TL Playoffs Open Wednesday Night," *Dallas Morning News*, September 7, 1955: 18.

79   "Buffs Nip Tulsa in Ninth," *Dallas Morning News*, September 8, 1955: 23.

80   "Jones Triple in 13th Wins Game," *New Orleans Times Picayune*, October 24, 1955: 27.

81   "Mays-Newk Gates in Dixie Dropping With Temperature," *The Sporting News*, October 26, 1955: 23.

82   "Dominican League," *The Sporting News* November 30, 1955, 34; "Dominican League," *The Sporting News*, December 28, 1955: 22; The National Archives, Washington, D.C.; Series Title: Passenger and Crew Lists of Vessels and Airplanes Arriving at Miami, Florida. NAI Number: 2771998; Record Group Title: Records of the Immigration and Naturalization Service.

83   "International League," *The Sporting News*, September 19, 1956: 30-31.

84   Emigdio Suarez, "U.S. Imports Put Bounce in Boers in Chase of Leon," *The Sporting News*, November 20, 1957: 25.

85   Eisenberg.

86   Ibid.

87   Ibid.

WILLIE MAYS

By John Saccoman

If somebody came up and hit .450, stole 100 bases, and performed a miracle in the field every day, I'd still look you right in the eye and tell you that Willie was better. He could do the five things you have to do to be a superstar: hit, hit with power, run, throw and field. And he had the other magic ingredient that turns a superstar into a super Superstar. Charisma. He lit up a room when he came in. He was a joy to be around.

— Leo Durocher, Mays's first major-league manager, in *Nice Guys Finish Last*[1]

Many contemporary players and writers agree with Leo Durocher's assessment of Willie Mays as the best all-around player in baseball history. Mike Lupica, longtime columnist for the *New York Daily News,* quoted the late Boston columnist George Frazier on the combination and star power of an athlete such as Mays. "That guy has some Willie Mays in him, the same way you used to say this singer or that had some Elvis in him."[2] Former teammate and manager Bill Rigney said about Mays, "All I can say is that he is the greatest player I ever saw, bar none."[3] In baseball's never-ending attempts to somehow order its gods, Mays is the only contender whose proponents rarely use statistics to make their case. It is as if Mays's 660 home runs and 3,283 hits somehow sell the man short, that his wonderful playing record is almost beside the point. With Mays it is not merely what he did—but *how he did it*. He scored more than 2,000 runs, nearly all of them, it would seem, after losing his cap flying around third base. He is credited with more than 7,000 outfield putouts, many exciting, some spectacular, a few breathtaking.

How do you measure that? An artist and a genius, for most of his 22 seasons in the big leagues, you simply could not keep your eyes off Willie Mays.

The great ballplayer's father, William Howard Mays, was named after William Howard Taft, who was the United States president when he was born in 1912. The elder Mays worked in the steel mills of Westfield, Alabama, outside Birmingham. Nicknamed Kitty-Kat or Cat, he was a semipro baseball player for the Westfield entry in the Tennessee Coal and Iron League. Cat's father, Willie's grandfather, Walter Mays, was a sharecropper and pitcher. Cat's wife, the former Anna Sattlewhite, was a high-school athlete who ran track and who led her basketball team to three consecutive state championships.[4]

Anna gave birth to the third-generation Mays ballplayer, Willie Howard Mays, on May 6, 1931. According to Charles Einstein, the author of several books with and about Mays, a former Birmingham Black Barons teammate once said of Willie Mays, "His momma had but one."[5] In truth, Anna died in 1953 giving birth to her 11th child, but that was long after she and Kitty Kat had split up and she was married to a man named Frank McMorris.

It has often been reported that Kitty Kat put a baseball in Willie's crib and that Willie learned to walk at six months, ambling toward a baseball sitting on a chair. Despite these stories, Mays claims that his father did not push him to be a ballplayer.

Willie stayed with his father after his parents separated. When he was 10 years old the family moved from a company-owned house in Westfield to Fairfield, another suburb of Birmingham. Cat was now a Pullman porter on the Birmingham-to-Detroit train and Willie was virtually raised by Anna's two young orphaned sisters, Aunt Sarah and Aunt Ernestine.

In Mays's several first-person retellings of his childhood, he never stressed childhood difficulties, but of course he had plenty of hardships growing up as an African-American in the Deep South during the Depression. He did assert that "there were times that I went to school without any shoes."[6] As was typical for poor families at this time, the Mays household included a friend of Cat's from the mills, "Uncle" Otis Brooks, as well as several cousins. However, with Cat back working in the mills for $2.60 a day, when there was work, and Ernestine working as a waitress, Willie recalled, "everyone pulled together."[7]

Willie attended Fairfield Industrial High School, where he was trained to be a cleaner or presser for a laundry. He starred as a football quarterback and averaged 20 points per game in basketball. The school did not have a baseball team, so he played second base and center field alongside his father on the Fairfield Industrial League team and the semipro Gray Sox. Needless to say, both teams were solely African-American, as were their opponents and their fans. These games drew as many as 6,000 fans.

Willie excelled in the Industrial League and, briefly in 1947, for a Negro minor-league team called the Chattanooga Choo-Choos, essentially a farm team for the Birmingham Black Barons of the Negro American League. When he turned 16, Cat introduced him to Piper Davis, the manager of the Black Barons. Davis became very influential in Mays's life. That was the year Jackie Robinson broke the color barrier with the Brooklyn Dodgers, but Mays asserts that the bigger breakthrough came in 1946, when Robinson broke into white baseball with the Montreal Royals in the Brooklyn Dodgers' farm system. Mays much later remarked, "Every time I look at my pocketbook, I see Jackie Robinson."[8]

Cat Mays, Piper Davis, and Willie's high-school principal insisted that Mays should graduate from high school, so he played only in the Black Barons' weekend home games until the school year was over. Ineligible to play high-school sports, he was by far the youngest player on the defending champions of the Negro American League.

Even at 16 years old, Mays played the outfield like a more experienced player. According to Piper Davis,

A teenage Willie Mays with the Birmingham Black Barons. Mays' father did not allow him to join the Black Barons full-time in 1948 until school was over at the end of May. (*Courtesy of Memphis Public Library*)

"Nobody ever saw anybody throw a ball from the outfield like him, or get rid of it so fast."[9]

In his first professional appearance, batting seventh and playing left field in the nightcap of a doubleheader at Birmingham's Rickwood Field (shared with the white Birmingham Barons of the Southern Association), Willie had two hits off Chet Brewer, whom he called "one of the best pitchers in the league."[10] He moved to center field when the regular, Bobby Robinson, broke his leg. Upon his recovery, Robinson found himself in left field.

According to the *Biographical Encyclopedia of the Negro Leagues*, Mays batted .262 with one home run and one stolen base in 28 games with the Black Barons. Mays recalled his first meeting with Satchel Paige: "[D]uring the first meeting with the legend, I got a double off Paige my very first time up. I stood on second, dusted myself off, feeling pretty good.

Paige walked toward me. 'That's it, kid.' ... My next three times up I went whoosh, whoosh, whoosh. ..."[11]

Even at the tender age of 17, Willie came up big in big spots. In the Negro American League playoff series against the Kansas City Monarchs, his two-out, bases-loaded single in the bottom of the 11th broke a 4-4 tie and gave the Black Barons a Game One victory. His double in the bottom of the ninth in Game Two drove in future Giants teammate Artie Wilson with the tying run that sent the contest into extra innings. Another ninth-inning double in Game Three seems to have preceded a game-winning homer by teammate Jimmy Zapp, but the details are sketchy. What is not sketchy is that the Black Barons won three consecutive one-run games before the series moved to Kansas City. Mays tripled and scored in a losing effort in Game Seven (there had been one rain-shortened tie) and made the final putout in the clincher.

Willie played in the final Negro League World Series in 1948 when the Black Barons lost to the Homestead Grays. In Game Three of the Series, he made two sparking defensive plays, chasing down a Bob Thurman fly in the fourth and gunning down Buck Leonard trying to go from first to third in the sixth. A scorching single through the box in the ninth drove in Bill Greason with the winning run for a 4-3 Birmingham victory. Leonard, a power-hitting first baseman on that Grays squad, had this scouting report on his 17-year-old opponent, "He could run and he could throw. He wasn't hitting so good, because at that time he couldn't hit a curveball."[12]

Mays had batted .311 in 75 games for the Black Barons in 1949, and he continued to tear the cover off the ball in 1950, starting the year batting .330 and slugging .547. With more major-league teams developing an interest in signing young black players, Mays was obviously attracting attention.

After the 1949 season Dodgers catcher Roy Campanella led a barnstorming team in the South. In a game between the barnstormers and the Black Barons, Mays threw Larry Doby out at the plate after catching a fly ball near the center-field fence. This impressed Campy, and he begged the Dodgers to send scouts down to sign Willie. The scouting report filed by Wid Matthews echoed Buck Leonard: "The kid can't hit the curveball."[13]

In a 1954 letter to Tim Cohane, the sports editor of *Look* magazine, Giants scout Eddie Montague stated that he was scouting the Black Barons first baseman, Alonzo Perry, for the Giants' Sioux City Single-A club, when Mays caught his eye. He said, "[T]his was the greatest young player I had ever seen in my life or my scouting career."[14]

Leo Durocher wrote in his book *Nice Guys Finish Last* that Montague reported. "[T]hey got a kid playing center field practically barefooted that's the best ballplayer I ever looked at. You better send somebody down there with a barrelful of money and grab this kid."[15]

Willie concludes in his autobiography, *Say Hey*: "Montague was in our little house in Fairfield, and I signed my first professional contract. Since I was a minor, my father signed too. ... I got a $4,000 signing bonus and a salary of $250 a month."[16]

Instead of Sioux City, Willie was sent to Trenton of the Class B Interstate League. Race played a role in that shift; Sioux City did not want a black player because there was an uproar over the recent burial of a Native American in a "Whites Only" cemetery there. Nevertheless, Mays thought the level of competition in the Interstate League was far below what he had seen with the Black Barons. "No league that included Satchel Paige and Josh Gibson was a Class B league," he said.[17]

Before he could leave Birmingham, Mays gave a friend some money to take his date to the prom. That taken care of, Mays played his first game in June in Hagerstown, Maryland, one of the league cities below the Mason-Dixon Line. His manager at Trenton, Chick Genovese, started him in center field.

In a 1996 interview with a nonprofit organization that recognizes achievers, Mays recalled: "I was the first black in that particular league. And we played in a town called Hagerstown, Maryland. I'll never forget this day, on a Friday. And they call you all kind of names there, 'nigger' this, and 'nigger' that. I said to myself ... 'Hey, whatever they call you, they can't touch you. Don't talk back.'"[18]

He also recalled staying at a blacks-only hotel across town from the team's hotel, and five of his new white teammates came to his room to check on him: "About two o'clock in the morning, three players came through the window, and they slept on the floor. One of my right fielders, Hank Rowland, one of the catchers, Herb Perelto, and another guy, Bob Easterwood, slept on the floor until about six o'clock in the morning."[19]

Mays experienced collapses from fatigue late in the year after several consecutive doubleheaders. He played all-out, running hard on the bases and in the field, and by his own admission "expended more energy than the average player on worrying and thinking."[20] He would collapse in similar fashion several times over the course of his career, but doctors never found a medical cause for it, according to Willie.

After going hitless in his first four games in Hagerstown, Willie wound up with 108 hits in 81 games, batting .353 with 55 RBIs. Clearly, he was ready for a higher level of competition.

In 1951 Mays trained with the Giants' top minor-league club, the Minneapolis Millers of the American Association. The major-league team trained in Lakeland, Florida, and their minor-league camp was in nearby Sanford. A game was arranged between the team's two top farm clubs, Minneapolis and Ottawa, because Leo Durocher wanted to see Mays play, though the Giants' hierarchy would not bring him to the major-league camp.

In the arranged match, Mays hit a double and a long home run. Durocher began lobbying for Mays to play for the big club immediately, but owner Horace Stoneham resisted. He said Mays was going into military service "any minute." Stoneham had his way and Willie began the season with Minneapolis as planned.

The New York Giants won two of their first three games but then lost 11 in a row, while Willie collected 12 hits in his first week with Minneapolis and played a spectacular center field. Durocher's pleading for

Mays intensified. Mays, unaware of this, played still better.

In May Minneapolis was in Sioux City to play an exhibition against the Giants' farm club there. The Millers had an offday, and Willie went to a movie theater. Between features, the house lights went on and the manager announced, "If Willie Mays is here, would he please immediately report to his manager at the hotel."[21]

Manager Tommy Heath informed Mays that he had been called up to the Giants. Willie's response: "Tell Leo I'm not coming."[22] Heath called, and Durocher laid into Mays on the phone. Mays told him that he didn't feel that he could hit big-league pitching. Durocher, speechless for perhaps the first time in his life, finally broke his silence and asked Mays what he was hitting. Mays answered, ".477." (He had a current 16-game hitting streak and a .799 slugging percentage, and was on a pace to score more than 150 runs and drive in 120.) Durocher asked, very quietly but with some scatological punctuation, "Do you think you can hit .250 for me?" Willie responded in the affirmative.[23] He was on the next plane to meet the team in Philadelphia. Stoneham bought an ad in the *Minneapolis Tribune* to assuage the local fans' outrage at losing their young star.

The Giants were 17-19, in fifth place, on May 25, the day Willie joined the team at Shibe Park. Durocher immediately installed the 20-year-old in center field. The Giants won all three of the games in Philadelphia, though Mays was hitless in his first 12 at-bats. Despite his batting woes, when the team returned to the Polo Grounds, Willie's first home game saw him batting third against the Boston Braves and their star southpaw Warren Spahn. In his first at-bat, he hit Spahn's offering atop the left-field roof for a home run, his first major-league hit.

After the homer, Mays went on a 0-for-13 slide, leaving him hitting .038 (1-for-26). At this point, in an often-told story, Willie sat in front of his locker, crying, after taking the collar again. Coaches Freddie Fitzsimmons and Herman Franks sent for Durocher. Mays again said he couldn't hit big-league pitching. Durocher replied, "As long as I'm the manager of the Giants, you are my center fielder. ... You are the best center fielder I've ever looked at."[24] Then he told Mays to hitch up his pants more to give himself a more favorable strike zone. Willie then went on a 14-for-33 tear.

For a 20-year-old from the Deep South, living in Manhattan could have been overwhelming. The Giants took good care of him, setting him up in the Harlem rooming house of David and Anna Goosby at St. Nicholas Avenue and 155th Street, not far from the Polo Grounds. Willie, still very much a big kid, ate many meals there and Anna washed his clothes. Neighbors often waited outside for Willie to arrive home.

Outfielder Monte Irvin, a Negro League veteran, was assigned as the rookie's roommate and protector. Mays recalled that Irvin looked after him like a big brother, throwing out phone messages from baseball "groupies" and meeting his dates before they went out.

His stickball-playing reputation was forged in those early days. As *New York Daily News* columnist David Hinckley wrote, "If you were a 14-year-old New York kid in the summer of 1931, you couldn't just round up some of your musical pals, knock on Irving Berlin's window and have Irv come out and write a few songs with you. If you were a 14-year-old aspiring vocalist in the summer of 1941, you couldn't just grab a couple of tenors, knock on Frank Sinatra's window and have Frank come join you for a round of harmony. If you were a 14-year-old kid in the summer of 1951, you couldn't just knock on Willie Mays' window at 9 o'clock in the morning and have Willie come out and play an hour of stickball with you. Well, actually, you could."[25] In fact, the games were followed by a trip to the soda shop—Mays's treat. As Hinckley wrote, this was not some publicity stunt; he actually played. On August 30, 1951, Willie hit two home runs in one game against the Pirates at the Polo Grounds, and then homered in a stickball game later that day.

Mays later recalled encounters with his old stickball teammates while he was working for Bally's Casino in Atlantic City in the 1980s and '90s. Someone might say, "Do you remember me? I'm one of the kids that you bought the ice cream for on 155th St. and St. Nicholas (Avenue)." Willie said that, on such occasions, a "smile comes to my face. ... That's a very, very good thing."[26]

In addition to his stickball exploits, Mays also babysat for Durocher's 6-year-old adopted son, Chris. It was not always clear who was babysitting whom. On road trips they would eat together, play catch, go to movies, and read comic books. Police in Cincinnati once stopped them to ask what a white child was doing with a black man. A call to Durocher cleared up the matter.

On the field, it did not take long for Mays's game to warrant superlatives. One of the many outstanding defensive plays of his rookie season came at Pittsburgh. Rocky Nelson hit a shot to deepest center field, and Mays tracked it down looking over his shoulder, but the ball hooked away from his glove. He caught the ball barehanded on the dead run. The Pirates' general manager, Branch Rickey, called it "the finest catch I have ever seen."[27]

Others would say that a double play he initiated against the Dodgers with a spectacular catch of Carl Furillo's slicing line drive and a whirling throw to nab Billy Cox at the plate preserving a tie, was the best. Dodgers manager Chuck Dressen said, "I'd like to see him do it again."[28]

The Giants were playing better, but the Dodgers were running away with the league. On August 11 the Giants were in second place, 13½ games behind the Dodgers, nine games further behind than when Mays joined the club. This deficit merely set the stage for the Giants' miraculous 37-7 stretch to catch the Dodgers, and Bobby Thomson's famous home run to win the best-of-three playoff. Willie was kneeling in the on-deck circle when Thomson hit his homer in the bottom of the ninth in Game Three, and by his own admission, was still frozen there as Thomson rounded second. The 20-year-old was on his way to the World Series.

A few days later Willie met his idol Joe DiMaggio during warm-ups as the Giants readied to face the Yankees, but the Giants were out of miracles and lost in six games. Willie batted .182 in his first World Series.

Mays had made good on his vow to hit .250, winning the NL Rookie of the Year award with 20 home runs, 68 RBIs, and a .274 batting average in 121 games. Durocher wrote, "Just to have him [Mays] on the club, you had 30 percent of the best of it before the ballgame started. In each generation, there are one or two players like that, men who are winning players because of their own ability and their own ... magnetism."[29]

On his return to the Jim Crow South after the season, the first place he visited was the Woolworth lunch counter where Aunt Ernestine worked. He ordered a glass of water while her back was turned, and when she saw who it was, she chided the Rookie of the Year, "Junior, you know colored can't sit down at the counter in here."[30]

Starting the 1952 season, Willie batted just .236 in 34 games before he was drafted into the Army, an obligation that would keep him out of the major leagues until 1954. Red Smith chronicled Mays's last game before his military call-up, in Brooklyn's Ebbets Field: "[T]here was a fine, loud cheer for Willie. This was in Brooklyn, mind you, where 'Giant' is the dirtiest word in the language."[31] At the time of his departure, the Giants were in first place, with a 2½-game lead over the Dodgers. The Giants promptly lost eight of ten and were never a factor in the pennant race.

The Army sent Willie to Fort Eustis, Virginia, and assigned him to play baseball for the most part. According to Mays, Durocher kept an eye on him from afar, chiding him when he stole a base with his team leading and sending him money from time to time. The August 13, 1953, edition of *Jet* magazine reported that Mays broke a bone in his foot sliding into third base in an Army game and would wear a cast for five weeks. Mays recalled that he also sprained his ankle in a basketball game, prompting another call from Durocher, telling him to stay off the court. During his time in the service, his mother, Anna, died, and Willie harbored some bitterness that he wasn't allowed to resume his playing career to support

all his half-brothers and -sisters, since his stepfather was unemployed.

Willie estimated that he played 180 games while in the service. When he returned to the Giants in the spring of 1954, he was a half-inch taller and ten pounds heavier, now 5-feet-11 and 180 pounds. When Mays showed up at the Giants' camp in Phoenix on March 1, the consensus among New York writers seemed to be, "Here comes the pennant," despite the Dodgers' 105 wins in 1953. *Newsweek* predicted in its April 5 issue that Mays could mean the difference between "the second division and the pennant in 1954."

This optimism is remarkable; how is it possible that one player could make up the 35 games and four places in the standings that the Giants finished behind the Dodgers? His major-league résumé up to that time, in 155 games, included a .266 batting average, .459 slugging percentage, and 24 home runs—an impressive start to a career, but nothing to make one think he could take a mediocre team past the Dodgers, a group that included Jackie Robinson, Duke Snider, and Roy Campanella. On the other hand, Willie had yet to celebrate his 23rd birthday.

Many were not impressed with Mays's numbers. In an article about Mays written after his retirement, Roger Angell of the *New Yorker* recalled a spring training wager with Cleveland columnist Whitey Lewis, who claimed that Mays would not bat .300 for the season. Angell also quoted Indians coach Red Kress saying that "Willie was flat-out overrated." Lewis sent a check for $20 on September 1—as Angell described it, "a lovely concession speech."[32]

In Mays's favor was this bottom-line statistic: In the 155 regular-season games for which he had been on the major-league roster (including the '51 playoff series with the Dodgers), the Giants' record was 107-48, a .690 winning percentage. Whether or not it was a coincidence, writers and teammates clearly associated Mays with winning.

Bobby Thomson, who played center field before Mays's arrival in 1951 and again while Willie was in the Army, was now expendable, and the Giants traded him to the Boston Braves for left-handed hurler Johnny Antonelli. Antonelli was just 24, and

The Giants were in fifth place in a tight race on May 22, but took over the top spot by June 15, and led by 5½ games at the All-Star break. Although the Dodgers hung tough all season, the Giants clinched the pennant in the final week and won by five games. Willie Mays was back in the World Series, this time as a certified star.

And batting champion. Going into the final day of the season, teammate Don Mueller was hitting a league-leading .3426, the Dodgers' Duke Snider .3425, and Willie .3422. Mays finished 3-for-4, Mueller 2-for-6, and Snider 0-for-3. After the games, Mays was batting .345, Mueller .342, and Snider .341. In addition to his batting title, Mays hit 41 home runs, drove in 110 runs, and led the league in triples (13) and slugging percentage (.667). To put this statistic into perspective, consider the period from 1931 through 1992, bracketed between two live-ball eras. In those 62 seasons, only two other National Leaguers bested Mays's slugging percentage: Stan Musial (.702 in 1948) and Henry Aaron (.669 in 1971). Willie also played in his first All-Star Game, and after the season, sportswriters named him the league's Most Valuable Player, at 23. He is the third youngest National Leaguer to receive the award.

But Mays's season was not over, and the legend-making was not over either.

On September 29, 1954, the Giants hosted the Indians in the first game of the World Series at the Polo Grounds, New York's Sal Maglie hooking up with Cleveland's Bob Lemon. With the score tied, 2-2, in the top of the eighth inning, the Indians put their first two runners on. Although Maglie had allowed just seven hits, Vic Wertz, the next batter, had already tripled and singled twice. Accordingly, Durocher brought in left-hander Don Liddle to face the left-handed-swinging Wertz. Wertz hit a 2-and-1 pitch, a shoulder-high fastball, to deep center field, directly over Mays's head. No matter. Willie sprinted directly away from the batter and ran it down in the deepest part of the park, catching it over his shoulder like a receiver taking a long pass from his quarterback. The film clip of this catch is one of baseball's most famous.

Former Birmingham Black Baron Willie Mays became a Hall of Famer, batting .302 with 3,283 hits, 660 home runs, 1,903 RBIs, and 338 stolen bases over a 22-year career with the Giants and Mets. (*National Baseball Hall of Fame, Cooperstown, New York*)

finished a solid 12-12 for Milwaukee in 1953. The Giants needed another starter, but few would have predicted that Antonelli would lead the league in ERA and win 21 games, one of the key reasons the Giants won 97 games and captured the pennant. The main reason was the center fielder, who became the player Leo Durocher confidently suggested that he would be.

Before the 1954 season, Durocher predicted a .300, 30-home-run season for Mays, and Willie reached the second of those milestones by midseason, playing the first half of the season on a home-run tear. Batting .326 and ahead of Ruth's 60-homer pace when he hit his 36th on July 28, Durocher asked him to stop trying for the fences and go for base hits for the good of the team. Willie hit only five more homers the rest of the year, but batted .379 down the stretch.

At least as impressive as the catch was what happened next: As Arnold Hano described it in *A Day in the Bleachers*: "[He] whirled and threw like some olden statue of a Greek javelin hurler. ... What an astonishing throw. ... This was the throw of a giant, the throw of a howitzer made human." Larry Doby had tagged up and made it to third; a man of Doby's baserunning ability could have conceivably advanced two bases tagging up on a ball hit that deeply in the spacious Polo Grounds. Meanwhile, as Hano described it, the other runner, Al Rosen, "scampered back to first."[33]

Liddle, having retired Wertz, was relieved by Marv Grissom after Cleveland manager Al Lopez sent up a right-handed hitter. Later, in the clubhouse, Liddle reportedly told Durocher, "Well, I got my man."[34]

Many observers believed that play was the defining moment in the Series. The catch clearly saved the first game, as the Giants prevailed, 5-2, in the tenth inning, and may have provided the momentum they needed to sweep heavily favored Cleveland in four games. The October 14, 1954, issue of *Jet* magazine quotes New York sportswriter   Dan Daniel as writing that all great catches "fade out of the book as the Mays classic moves to the top." Lopez called it "the best I ever saw."

Mays himself felt that other catches he made were better. For example, he mentions one in Ebbets Field in 1952 on a ball hit by Bobby Morgan. Willie remembered this catch in a 1996 interview:

"I made a catch in Ebbets Field, off of a guy by the name of Bobby Morgan. And it was in the seventh inning, two men on, [two out,] a ball was hit over the shortstop—over the line—over the shortstop. Now you've got to visualize this. Over the shortstop. I go and catch the ball in the air. I'm in the air like this, parallel. I catch the ball, I hit the fence. Ebbets Field was so short that if you run anywhere you're going to hit a fence. So I catch the fence, knock myself out. And the first guy that I saw—there were two guys—when I open my eyes, was Leo and Jackie. And I'm saying to myself, 'Why is Jackie out here?' Jackie came to see if I caught the ball, and Leo came to see about me. So I'm saying to myself, 'This guy is

thinking very cool.' I'm talking about Jackie now. He wasn't even on the field, he was in the dugout. Now this is my thinking, he may have a different reason. That was my best catch, I think. It was off of Bobby Morgan in Ebbets Field. I caught a lot of balls barehanded, which I felt was good, but that was my best catch, I think."[35]

Mays also recalled a catch he made in Trenton in 1950. He said that Lou Heyman of Wilmington hit a ball 405 feet to dead center and he caught it barehanded, bounced off the wall, and threw the ball all the way home on the fly.

All in all, 1954 was a fine season. There were more to come.

Back home in Birmingham, Willie's Aunt Sarah died in 1954. He continued to send a good portion of his salary, soon to be $25,000, to his ten half-siblings and to Cat and Aunt Ernestine. Whether it was from grief or the Alabama heat, Mays almost fainted at Sarah's funeral.

Between the 1954 and 1955 seasons, Willie played in the Puerto Rican League for the Santurce Crabbers, managed by Giants coach Herman Franks. He was in the same outfield as the young and relatively unknown Roberto Clemente, a daunting prospect for opposing pitchers and baserunners. Mays batted a league-leading .393 for the Crabbers, who won the Caribbean Series for Puerto Rico that year. Willie recounted that he played for the team as a favor to Franks and Giants owner Horace Stoneham, whose friend owned the team. However, Mays had grown tired after playing 250 games in ten months and took six weeks off to rest before the Giants' spring training in 1955.

The champion Giants fell to a disappointing third place in 1955, despite Mays's 51 home runs, 127 RBIs, and .319 average. Willie was the seventh player in baseball history to hit more than 50 homers in a season, and Durocher actually had told him to start trying for the fences, contradicting the instructions of the previous year. He also led the NL in triples and slugging average and was second in stolen bases with 24 in 28 attempts, a success rate of better than 85 percent.

Leo Durocher's personality and outspokenness, tolerated in the pennant-winning and world championship seasons, grew stale when the team finished in third place. The club announced that he would be replaced by former infielder Bill Rigney for 1956.

Durocher recalled the last game that he and Mays were on the same team. On the final day of the season, during a doubleheader against the Philadelphia Phillies in the Polo Grounds, Durocher called Willie into a small bathroom just off the dugout. Leo told him, "You are the best ballplayer I ever saw. ... I'm telling you this because I won't be back next season." Willie said, "But you won't be here to help me." Durocher said, "Willie Mays don't need help from anybody," and then kissed him on the cheek.[36]

Even at this early stage, Mays's throwing arm was recognized as the best in the game. The *New Yorker* wrote on July 10, 1954, that it took Willie three years to learn his famous basket catch, with his hands waist-high and the "gloved hand turned out." He said his Trenton manager, Genovese, first suggested it, and he perfected it while he was in the Army. Some considered it showboating, but Mays felt that it helped him keep his eye on the ball and position his feet to throw. Willie led the NL in outfield assists in 1955 with 23, and in double plays with 8.

Willie was widely recognized as the best all-around player in the National League during the 1950s. His defensive prowess and howitzer throwing arm were already established. After he won the batting title in 1954 and hit 51 homers in 1955, the highest total in the National League since Ralph Kiner's 54 in 1949, he led the league in steals four years in a row beginning in 1956. His 40 steals that year were the most in the majors since 1944. His four-year totals (40, 38, 31, 27) were punctuated by a 77 percent success rate.

On May 6, 1956, his 25th birthday, Mays stole four bases in a 5-4 Giants victory. The next year *New York Times* writer John Drebinger credited Mays with "returning" the stolen base to baseball and compared his baserunning derring-do to that of Ty Cobb. He wrote, "Perhaps, by reason of Willie's spark ... more players soon may be goaded into trying to bring back what was once one of baseball's most picturesque plays."[37]

The stolen base returned to prominence in no small part because of the emergence of players from the Negro Leagues, which showcased a style more suited to the Deadball Era, with much basestealing and "inside baseball." Meanwhile, the white major leagues played a more "station to station" style. During the years 1946-1960 the average team stole fewer than 40 bases per season, 75 percent less than in the Deadball Era.

Willie's impact on the game went beyond his on-field exploits. Baseball historian Jules Tygiel wrote that "Mays, with his indisputable excellence, convinced all but the most stalwart resisters to integration of the need to recruit African-Americans."[38]

In his memoir of 50-plus years in the game, Don Zimmer, a contemporary of Mays who began his career as a shortstop for the Brooklyn Dodgers (and also Mays's teammate on the Santurce team), summed up the prevailing opinion of Mays:

"In the National League in the 1950s, there were two opposing players who stood out over all the others — Stan Musial and Willie Mays. ... I've always said that Willie Mays was the best player I ever saw. ... [H]e could have been an All Star at any position."[39]

The 1956 season was marked by Willie's marriage to the former Marghuerite Wendell. She had been married twice before, once to a member of the singing group the Ink Spots. In 1958 Willie and Marguerite adopted a five-day-old baby whom they named Michael, but the marriage would be troubled.

On the field, Mays was slightly less brilliant in 1956, with "only" 36 home runs, 84 RBIs, and a .296 batting average, for a team that dropped to sixth place. The next season he increased his average to .333, while recording 35 home runs and 97 RBIs. Besides his stolen bases, Mays became the fourth player in the 20th century to amass 20 or more doubles, triples, and home runs in the same season. He also won the first of 12 consecutive Gold Gloves in that award's inaugural year.

During the 1957 season, the unemployed Leo Durocher publicly criticized the Giants and Rigney, while still praising his old center fielder. Willie recalled, "After the article came out, I had to apologize for Leo. I admit ... that there was a coolness between me and Rigney. We didn't give each other a chance."[40]

In their final home game at the Polo Grounds, on September 29, 1957 the Giants lost to the last-place Pirates, 9-1. Mays had two of the team's six hits. After the season the Giants left New York for San Francisco, while the Dodgers moved to Los Angeles, depriving New York of National League ball for the first time since 1882.

The new city did not exactly greet Mays with open arms. After Soviet leader Nikita Khrushchev was warmly received there, Frank Conniff of the Hearst newspapers commented, "San Francisco is the damnedest city I ever saw in my life. They cheer Khrushchev and boo Mays."[41]

Mays recalled that a real-estate broker withdrew his offer on a home because of pressure from other homeowners in the neighborhood. Mayor George Christopher apologized and offered to share his home with Willie and Marghuerite. In mid-November, they moved into the original house; almost immediately someone threw a brick through a window.

Much has been made of the city's less-than-warm reception. Charles Einstein suggested three factors: "Mays was the hated embodiment of New York. ... He had the temerity to play center field in Seals Stadium, where the native-born DiMaggio had played it in his minor-league days. Also, Mays was black. The brick that crashed through his window almost as soon as he moved in had to reflect at least one of these viewpoints, if not all three."[42]

Relations between Mays and manager Rigney continued to be strained, and Rigney did not help matters when he predicted to the San Francisco media before the 1958 season that Willie would break Babe Ruth's record of 60 home runs in a season. Mays didn't come close, and that, coupled with the ascendancy of rookie first baseman Orlando Cepeda, likely resulted in Cepeda's being voted the team's MVP by the fans. Here are their statistics for 1958:

Mays: 152 G, 29 HR, 96 RBI, .347 BA, 121 R
Cepeda: 148 G, 25 HR, 96 RBI, .312 BA, 88 R

Willie's explanation of Cepeda's victory in the fan vote: "The fans were disappointed that I hadn't hit 61 home runs, and Orlando was theirs from scratch."[43]

Cepeda's performance brought him the NL Rookie of the Year award. However, Mays's numbers, by some measures, were the best in the league. Willie led the league in runs scored and stolen bases while winning another Gold Glove. He almost won the batting title as well; going into the last game of the season, he was neck-and-neck with the eventual winner, Phillies Hall of Famer Richie Ashburn. Rigney batted Mays leadoff in the final game, hoping to give him more at-bats and a shot at the title. He went 3-for-5, including a double and a home run, but Ashburn finished 3-for-4 and wound up at .350.

Willie's 1958 was a streaky season; he was batting .400 by early June, followed by a .240 pace through August. A "nervous exhaustion," which troubled him occasionally throughout his career, was reappearing. He was so tired that during a road trip to Philadelphia he was admitted to a New York hospital and was told there was nothing physically wrong, but that he needed to rest.

In 1959 Willie had his first brushes with serious injury. In spring training, he cut his leg on Red Sox catcher Sammy White's shin guard, requiring 35 stitches and a two-week recuperation. With the team in first place in early August, Mays broke his right pinkie sliding back to first base after a long single. While he still hit 16 more homers the rest of the way, the Giants as a team tailed off, finishing in third place, four games behind the Los Angeles Dodgers, who went on to win the World Series. Mays hit 34 home runs and batted .313.

Chicago Cub Ernie Banks won back-to-back NL MVP awards in 1958 and 1959. Looking back, he said, "When I was in the Big Leagues, there was a tremendous amount of great ballplayers, but the guy who stood head and shoulders above them all was Willie Mays. He was so exciting—not only exciting to the fans, but to the teams he played with—the Giants—and against. He was just amazing."[44]

After struggling their final years in New York, the San Francisco Giants began to introduce a string of players who would form the core of one of the finest squads never to win a championship—the Giants of the 1960s. After Cepeda in 1958, Willie McCovey came up in 1959, winning the Giants their third Rookie of the Year award in nine years. Mays and McCovey would form as potent a left-right power duo as ever played together. They were joined by third baseman Jim Davenport, shortstop Jose Pagan, catcher Tom Haller, and second baseman Chuck Hiller, pitchers Juan Marichal and Gaylord Perry, and three outfielder brothers from the Dominican Republic, Felipe, Matty, and Jesus Alou.

The Giants sported a 902-704 record from 1960 to 1969; the most successful team of the '60s, the Baltimore Orioles, won 911 games. But San Francisco played in only one World Series, losing to the Yankees in 1962 in seven games. By way of comparison, the Los Angeles Dodgers, who finished 24½ games behind the Giants during the decade, won world championships in 1963 and 1965 behind star pitchers Sandy Koufax and Don Drysdale, and stolen-base king Maury Wills.

The problem with recounting Mays's career is that the great statistics begin to run together. Although he won two MVP awards, in 1954 and 1965, he could have won virtually any year in between as well, since he seemed to have the same season every year. He won a Gold Glove 12 times, though they didn't create the award until Mays's fifth season. He played in 24 All-Star Games, and these were not just token appearances — he started 18 games in center field, and 11 times played the entire game. By midcareer he was not merely a star player, but was often considered *the* star, the greatest player ever.

Felipe Alou, who played alongside Mays, played against such luminaries as Frank Robinson and Hank Aaron, and managed Barry Bonds, said, "[Mays] is number one, without a doubt. ... [A]nyone who played with him or against him would agree that he is the best."

The game that may have been Mays's greatest took place on April 30, 1961, against the Milwaukee

Braves at County Stadium in Milwaukee. The night before, Mays and roommate McCovey ate a midnight snack of room-service spare ribs. Mays experienced sharp stomach pains and called for team trainer Doc Bowman. When Willie arrived at the ballpark, he took batting practice but reported feeling very weak. Using teammate Joey Amalfitano's lighter bat, he homered in his first two at-bats against Lew Burdette. After lining out against Moe Drabowsky in the fifth inning, he hit another round-tripper off lefty Seth Morehead in the sixth. Finally, in the eighth inning, he hit his fourth home run of the day, off Don McMahon. He finished 4-for-5 with 8 RBIs and missed a chance for a fifth homer when the top of the ninth ended with him on deck. After the fourth homer, McCovey quipped, "How 'bout some more ribs?" [45]

Two months later, on June 29, Mays once again showed his all-around abilities in leading the Giants to a doubleheader sweep at Philadelphia. In the first game, he hit three homers, including the game-winner in the tenth inning of the first game, becoming the fourth player with three or more home runs twice in one season. In the nightcap Mays tripled and doubled, while also gunning down a runner at the plate in one of three double plays in which he would participate in the season. Overall, just another Mays season: 40 home runs, 123 RBIs, .308 batting average.

On January 31, 1962, Mays signed a contract for $90,000 for the coming season. Once again, 11 years after the "Shot Heard 'Round the World," the Giants and Dodgers tied for first place and, 3,000 miles west, Willie and Leo would again be involved in a "sudden death" series, this time with Durocher as the third-base coach for Los Angeles.

The pennant race turned on July 17, when the Dodgers' Sandy Koufax, 14-5 and leading the league in strikeouts and ERA, left his start with a circulatory problem in his finger—he would miss two months, and would be largely ineffective when he returned in late September. The Dodgers had a one-game lead when Koufax went down, but valiantly held on.

Mays had his own health woes. In the second inning of a September 12 game in Cincinnati, Mays, feeling hot and dizzy, fainted in the dugout. Revived by Doc Bowman, he was carried away on a stretcher and sent to a hospital. He was diagnosed with tension and exhaustion, and rest was prescribed. Manager and former teammate Alvin Dark insisted that Mays rest until he was ready to return, despite the pennant fight, and Willie missed three games In his first game back, Mays hit a three-run home run in Forbes Field off the Pirates' Elroy Face.

On the last day of the season, the Giants needed to beat the expansion Houston Colt .45s and hope the Dodgers lost to the Cardinals to force a tie. Batting in the eighth inning of a 1-1 tie, Mays hit his 47th home run to secure the 2-1 victory. In Los Angeles, the Dodgers cooperated by losing 1-0 to a Curt Simmons five-hitter.

In the first game of the best-of-three playoff series, Mays finished 3-3 with two home runs and a walk, pacing the Giants to an 8-0 victory. His 49 home runs gave him the major-league title for the first time since 1955; the two in the extra playoff games allowed him to pass Harmon Killebrew, who had 48 round-trippers.

The Giants lost the second game, 8-7, leaving 13 runners on base. Durocher, coaching for the Dodgers, reportedly wore the same T-shirt he wore in 1951 on the day of Thomson's homer. Willie finished 1-5, but gunned down Maury Wills at third base in the sixth inning.

In the clincher the Giants trailed 4-2 when the team came to bat in the top of the ninth. The team rallied for four runs on two singles, four walks, and an error. Mays's line-drive single off pitcher Ed Roebuck's glove was right in the middle of the inning, southpaw Billy Pierce retired the Dodgers 1-2-3 in the ninth, with Willie catching the final out.

The Giants and Yankees met in the World Series for the seventh time, but the first since the Giants moved west. The Yankees won in seven games. Mays was left on base carrying the winning run when Willie McCovey lined out to end the Series. Mays batted .250, scoring three runs, driving in one, and stealing one base.

After the World Series Willie checked into Mount Zion Hospital in San Francisco to see if there was a reason for his physical collapses. Three days of tests produced no conclusive diagnosis; however, Mays undeniably had a great deal on his plate at that time. Besides the pennant race, he was in the middle of a divorce from Marghuerite. She had filed a separate-maintenance suit in 1961 and the couple, deep in debt, nearly filed for bankruptcy. Arnold Hano wrote a story for *Sport* in August 1963, under the headline "Willie Mays: His Loneliness and Fulfillment." The Mays he presented was not satisfied with his life, and spent most of his evenings alone. He quoted Mays: "I'm lonely. I want to have a family of my own. I have a son and love him, but Michael lives with his mother in New York, and I get to see him only once or twice a year. I want a wife who will love me for myself, because I am Willie Mays, a person, not Willie Mays, a good ballplayer."[46]

On the field he was the same old Mays. In 1962 he managed 49 homers and 141 RBIs (the most in his career), and batted .304. He slugged .615 and stole 18 bases in 20 attempts. He just missed out on his second MVP award, losing one of history's closest ballots, 209-202, to Maury Wills.

Before the 1963 season, Mays got a raise to $105,000 ($5,000 more than Mickey Mantle), making him the highest-paid player in baseball. His health issues did not go away, however, and the strain continued to show. On a trip to Chicago, Mays broke down crying in his hotel room and had the shakes. Doc Bowman gave him sleeping pills and Alvin Dark brought Mays to his room to sleep that night.

Despite his troubles off the field, Willie maintained a high level of play. In the July 2 game against the Braves, he homered in the 16th inning, providing the only run in a 1-0 Giants win. Juan Marichal bested Warren Spahn. Both pitchers went the distance.

In the All-Star Game, Willie went 1-for-3, drove in two runs, scored two, and stole two bases in the 5-3 NL victory. He also made a spectacular running catch in the eighth inning, depriving Joe Pepitone of an extra-base hit. These efforts earned him the game's

MVP award, established the previous year. Mays also garnered the award in 1968, becoming the first player to win it twice.

The Giants wound up 11 games out of first in 1963, but no one could blame the center fielder: 157 G, 38 HR, 103 RBIs, .314 BA, and 115 R.

Alvin Dark clearly viewed Willie with great affection. Mays received a note shortly after Dark was named to manage the Giants in 1961: "Just a note to say that knowing you'll be playing for me is the greatest privilege and thrill any manager could ever hope to have."[47]

The Giants averaged 92 wins each year over Dark's four seasons as manager, and featured one of the most powerful offenses in NL history. However, the 1964 season would prove to be Dark's downfall and leave a blot on his reputation.

The controversy began in May when a quote from Dark appeared in a book by Jackie Robinson, *Baseball Has Done It*: "Older people in the South have taken care of the Negroes. They feel they have a responsibility to take care of them. That's my opinion of how things are."[48]

In an attempt to defend himself from media criticism, Dark expressed the view that he would play "nine colored players on the field at one time as long as they can win." However, he also expressed the view that integration was "being rushed too fast."[49]

A few days after the story broke, Dark called Mays into his office and named him the Giants' first captain since Dark himself had left the team as a player in 1956, and the first African-American captain in major-league history. Mays took responsibility for mediating between Dark and many of the Giants' Latin players, particularly Cepeda. In July the racial and ethnic tensions exploded when Dark was quoted by Stan Isaacs of the newspaper *Newsday*: "We have trouble [atrocious mistakes] because we have so many Spanish-speaking and Negro players on the team. They are just not able to perform up to the white ballplayer when it comes to mental alertness."[50]

Elsewhere in the article, Dark exempted his new captain from this opinion, but every black and Latin player met in Willie's hotel room in Pittsburgh to discuss the situation. According to an account in Charles Einstein's *Willie's Time*, Mays, ever the voice of reason, quelled a potential rebellion. He told the players that changing managers during the season had been disastrous in 1960 and it would be disastrous again. Likely working with some inside information from his friends in the Giants brain trust, including vice president Charles Feeney and coach Herman Franks, he also told the players that Dark would not be back the next season, and that, notwithstanding what the manager had said, all of them had gotten a fair shake from him. When Cepeda vowed, "I'm not going to play another game for that son of a bitch," Mays replied, "Don't let the rednecks make a hero out of him."[51] For his part, Willie did not speak to Dark for the remaining two months of the season, and beyond.[52]

In *Willie's Time*, Charles Einstein quoted Mays's real feelings about Dark from that meeting in the Pittsburgh hotel room. Willie said to his teammates:

"I know when [Dark] helped me and I know why. ... [H]e likes money. That preacher's talk that goes with it, he can shove up his ass. I'm telling you he helped me. And he's helped everybody here. I'm not playing Tom to him when I say that. He helps us because he wants to win, and he wants the money that goes with winning. Ain't nothing wrong with that."[53]

The Giants finished in fourth place, only three games back. Dark was fired on the last day of the season.

Herman Franks, a Durocher crony, was named manager for 1965, and Mays was given much latitude as a field general, almost an assistant manager. When asked why, Franks responded, "Because he knows more about those things than I do. You got any hard questions?"[54] The new manager also was a successful investor and helped Willie recover financially, steering him toward solid investments.

On the field, the Giants responded to the firing of Alvin Dark by contending for another pennant in 1965, losing to the Dodgers by just two games. Though Mays turned 34 that season, he hit a career-high 52 home runs, leading the NL in on-base percentage (for the first time) and slugging percentage.

Along the way, he won his second MVP award, 11 years after his first.

One of Mays's 52 homers was the 500th of his career, on September 13 in the Houston Astrodome, a 450-foot liner to center off Don Nottebart. He was only the fifth player to hit 500 home runs, following Babe Ruth, Jimmie Foxx, Mel Ott, and Ted Williams. No National Leaguer had hit 50 in a season since Mays in 1955.

The pennant race was marred by one of the ugliest incidents in baseball history. On August 22 the Giants' Juan Marichal had knocked down two Dodgers hitters early in the game when he came to bat to lead off the bottom of the third inning against Dodgers ace Sandy Koufax. After Dodgers catcher John Roseboro, in a bit of retaliation, whistled the ball past Marichal's ear on his return throw to Koufax, Marichal shouted at Roseboro. When the catcher started to get out of his crouch to go after him, the enraged Marichal hit Roseboro over the head with his bat. Naturally, both benches emptied. Mays ran from the dugout to Roseboro's aid and cradled Roseboro's head in his hands, with blood staining Mays's uniform and tears streaming down his face. After play resumed, the next two batters made out, two men walked, and Mays hit a three-run homer, one of his NL-record 17 round-trippers that month.

Roseboro's account of Willie's role in the incident is particularly telling. "I guess Mays was more of a ballplayer than he was a Giant," he wrote in his autobiography, *Glory Days With the Dodgers, and Other Days With Others*. "He was a sensitive guy, a good buddy, and he didn't like what his teammate had done to me. ... Mays may have been shook, but he hit his fourth homer of the four game series [after the incident]. ..."[55]

Marichal was suspended for eight days and fined $1,750. League President Warren Giles said Mays's conduct was "fine and decent. ... This man was an example of the best in any of us."[56] On later road trips that season, Willie received rousing ovations in Pittsburgh, Chicago, Philadelphia, and, of course, New York. In Los Angeles the Giants were booed lustily, but during his first at-bat, Mays received a

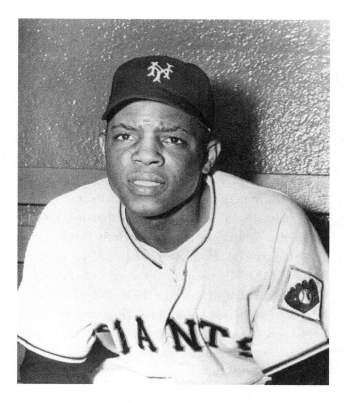

Willie Mays went from being a raw kid with the Birmingham Black Barons to "Say Hey Kid" superstar status with the New York Giants. (*National Baseball Hall of Fame, Cooperstown, New York*)

tremendous standing ovation, despite the rivalry and the pennant race.

Initially, the Giants went into a tailspin, going 4-8 in the first 12 games after the incident. Then they won 14 games in a row, and by September 16 they were in first place, 4½ games ahead of Los Angeles. But the Dodgers won 13 straight in late September to take the pennant by two games. Marichal, the Giants' best pitcher, finished the year with a 22-13 record, but likely missed two starts because of his suspension.

Mays's MVP seasons in 1954 and 1965 form excellent bookends for the story of his career. He was a perennial MVP contender, and many of those 12 seasons are indistinguishable from one another. The 1954 season was his first full year with the Giants, his first and only world championship and batting title, but his first of 13 consecutive seasons of 150 or more games, his first of 12 consecutive seasons of 100 or more runs scored, the first of five consecutive years of 400 or more outfield putouts, and the first of 20 consecutive years making the National League All-Star team. In addition, Willie led the league in slugging for the first of five times in his career. He led the league in on-base percentage for the first time in his career in 1965 (he would lead in that category once more), but the home run and slugging titles in 1965 would be his last.

The All-Star Game was considered Mays's greatest stage. He played in 24 midsummer classics, the most of any major leaguer. (Two All-Star Games were played each year from 1959 through 1962 to fatten the players' pension fund. Both Hank Aaron and Stan Musial also played in 24 All-Star Games.) Mays led the NL to an 18-6 record in his All-Star Game career, batting .307 in those contests, with 23 hits in 75 at-bats, two doubles, three triples, three home runs, and 20 runs scored. It is interesting to contrast these numbers with his postseason stats: In 25 career postseason games, he hit one homer, drove in 10 runs, and batted .247.

Mays enjoyed his last great season in 1966. He turned 35 that year and played in 152 games, hit 37 homers, drove in 103 runs, and scored 99, levels he would never reach again. He batted .288 (he would never top .300 the rest of his career) and captured his tenth straight Gold Glove, one for every season the award had existed. His 103 RBIs marked his eighth consecutive season with 100 or more, an NL record, although he never led the league in that category. In each of 12 seasons, 1954-1965, he had led the league in at least one major offensive category. For the rest of his career Mays topped the leader board only in walks and on-base percentage in 1971.

Mays continued his assault on the career home-run record, passing Ted Williams (521) in June 1966 and Jimmie Foxx (534) in August. The day after tying Foxx, Willie hit number 535 off the Cardinals' Ray Washburn, putting him in second place on the all-time list, 179 behind Babe Ruth. Mays recalled, "Until I actually got that 'close' at 535, I don't think I gauged how monumental his record was."[57]

The Giants remained in the race until the last day of the season. Along with his other accomplishments, Willie may have helped to prevent a large-scale race

riot. Rumors swirled about a potential riot in the predominantly black Hunter's Point section of San Francisco, and in an attempt to give the people something indoors to do, a game previously not on the TV schedule was added. Mays encouraged fans via radio ads to stay home and watch an important televised game from Atlanta. In *Willie's Time*, Charles Einstein wrote, "Mayor John Shelley told Horace Stoneham afterward that nothing else could have prevented all-out rioting and looting. ... The TV did it."[58]

The aging center fielder battled flu-like symptoms for much of 1967. In July he was hospitalized again for five days after leaving a game with fever and the shakes. He said he never felt strong the rest of the year. In an August contest, the Braves intentionally walked Jim Ray Hart to pitch to Mays. He hit a run-scoring single. At age 36, he finished with a .263 batting average and 22 home runs. Both figures were his lowest in any full season to that point.

In 1968, the "Year of the Pitcher," the NL won the All-Star Game, 1-0, with its 37-year-old leadoff batter scoring the only run, in the first inning. Mays was starting only because of an injury to Pete Rose. He singled, moved to second on an errant pickoff throw, got to third on a wild pitch, and scored on a double play. It was his last hit in All-Star competition, though he would bat at least once in every midsummer classic until his retirement. As mentioned previously, Willie received his second All-Star game MVP award for his efforts, a throwback to the "inside baseball" of his Negro League days.

Willie continued to approach milestones. He ended the 1968 season one steal shy of 300, 13 homers shy of 600, and 188 hits shy of 3,000. His numbers: 148 G, 23 HRs, 79 RBIs, .289 BA, and 84 R.

The 1969 season was frustrating for Mays; the Giants finished in second place for the fifth straight year, this time three games behind Atlanta. Manager Clyde King briefly experimented with Willie in the leadoff spot, a position foreign to him, as he had batted third almost exclusively for much of his career. He accepted this move as a team player would, but not before protesting to King that, at age 38, the duties of a leadoff hitter would have him, in his own words, "too tired" before the season was half over. He had other run-ins with King and, coupled with a knee injury, it made for an unhappy year. The Giants' brass might have agreed with Willie; King was fired after 42 games the next season.

The highlight of Mays's 1969 season may have come on September 22, when he became the second man to hit 600 career home runs, reaching the milestone and delivering the game-winning RBI in a pinch hitting appearance against San Diego's Mike Corkins. He also surpassed 300 stolen bases for his career.

Prior to the 1970 season, *The Sporting News* named Mays Player of the Decade for the 1960s. He started strong, hitting 19 home runs by the All-Star break. On July 18 Mays singled off Montreal pitcher Mike Wegener for his 3,000th career hit. Play was halted for a ceremony, attended by Monte Irvin, Carl Hubbell, and Stan Musial, the all-time NL hits leader at the time. All fans were given a free ticket to another game that season, and the Giants presented Willie's son, Michael, with a four-year college scholarship. Mays finished with 28 home runs and a .291 average, his best numbers since 1966. The team finished 16 games behind, in third place.

In 1971 Willie experienced a renaissance both professionally and personally. Manager Charlie Fox used him as an additional coach to instruct the outfielders. Fox said, "Willie Mays is the greatest player I saw or heard of."[59]

Mays hit his 629th career homer on the first pitch he saw on Opening Day. He hit home runs in the first four games of the season, the first time any player had done that. He had a .336 average at the end of May, 14 home runs by the All-Star break, and the Giants were in first place in the NL West for good by the end of April.

On May 6, his 40th birthday, Mays was honored at a banquet attended by such luminaries as Hank Aaron and Joe DiMaggio. Aaron once said that Mays was a greater ballplayer than he, although he saw himself as the stronger hitter. DiMaggio once told a young ballplayer to strive for perfection on the base-

ball field, and that, while that is impossible, Willie Mays came the closest. Commissioner Bowie Kuhn read a telegram from President Nixon that included a line that Willie was "proof that people over the age of 30 could be trusted."[60]

By this time Mays was reaching or eclipsing some milestone once a week. In the opener of a May 30 twin bill, he passed Musial to become the National League's all-time leading run scorer with 1,950, also hitting his 638th career homer in a 5-4 defeat of the Expos. On June 6 he hit his 22nd career extra-inning homer to lead the Giants to a 4-3 win over Philadelphia, earning the Giants a doubleheader split.

Helping the team any way he could, Mays worked the count more, leading the league in both walks and on-base percentage (.425). He played 84 games in center field and 48 at first base, to rest his legs. After he made several outstanding plays at first base in a game against the New York Mets, their manager, Gil Hodges, said, "I can't very well tell my players not to hit it to him. Wherever they hit it, he's there anyway."[61]

The Giants outlasted the Dodgers to win the Western Division by one game, but lost to the Pirates in the National League Championship Series. Mays hit his only postseason home run, a two-run blast off Bob Miller, in Game Two.

After the season Willie married Mae Louise Allen in Acapulco, after ten years of off-and-on dating. He originally got her phone number from Wilt Chamberlain.

The 1972 season began later than scheduled because of a player strike. While reticent in the past on commenting about controversial issues, he said this to the executive board of the union:

> I know it's hard being away from the game and our paychecks and our normal life. I love this game. It's been my whole life. But we made a decision … to stick together and until we're satisfied, we have to stay together. … [If] I have played my last game, it will be painful. But if we don't hang together, everything we've worked for will be lost.[62]

By now, Mays's salary was $160,000 a year, but he wanted a long-term contract from the Giants that would carry beyond his playing career. None was offered, and rumors began to surface that he would be traded. When the Giants reached Philadelphia in May 1972, New York sportswriter Red Foley informed him he would be traded to the Mets, though it took a few days to formalize the details. Willie would finish his career where he had started. He said, "When you come back to New York, you come back to paradise."[63] He was batting .184 after 19 games when he was traded to the Mets for minor-league pitcher Charlie Williams and $50,000. Horace Stoneham denied that any cash was included in the deal, and maintained that he was giving Willie a financial future that the Giants, one of only a handful of family-owned teams left in the majors, could not. Upon joining the Mets, Mays immediately received a contract that would pay him $175,000 per year for the rest of his career and, after he retired, $50,000 a year to coach for the club.

Mays's first game for the Mets was against the Giants, on May 14, 1972, Mother's Day, at Shea Stadium. In the fifth inning he homered to break a 4-4 tie, and the Mets won, 5-4. Having the all-time great on the roster did not make manager Yogi Berra's job any easier. The fans wanted to see Mays, but the manager, of course, had to put the best lineup on the field. As a part-time player, Willie was third on the club in batting average and second in slugging, despite having the worst numbers of his career to this point: 88 G, 8 HRs, 22 RBIs .250 BA, and 35 R. All eight of his round-trippers were with the Mets, and he played 11 of his 69 games as a Met in 1972 at first base.

In preparing for spring training of 1973, Willie had old friend Herman Franks watch him to see if anything was left in the tank. Franks told him he had one season left. When he had second thoughts about retirement in August, he consulted Franks, who told him to stick by his original decision.

He struggled at the start, hitting .118 in April, and did not drag his average over .200 until July 8. He informed the Mets he would retire at the end of the season, and that the club could announce it

in September. He had knee problems that required draining fluid, and favoring one leg caused problems with the other. He also had cracked ribs.

The team wasn't doing much better, settling in last place all of July and August. They finally escaped the cellar on August 31 but finished 20-8 after that and captured an extremely compressed division.

On September 25 the club had a Willie Mays Night. He resisted the honor initially for fear it would distract the team in the middle of a pennant race. After a one-hour ceremony, many gifts, and an outpouring of affection from the fans at Shea, he made his farewell speech:

"I hope that with my farewell tonight, you'll understand what I'm going through right now. Something that I never feared: that I were ever to quit baseball. But, as you know, there always comes a time for someone to get out. And I look at these kids over there, the way they are playing, and the way they are fighting for themselves, and it tells me one thing: Willie, say goodbye to America. Thank you very much."[64]

In the League Championship Series, he made his first appearance on the field as a peacemaker, not a player. In Game Three Reds left fielder Pete Rose's takeout slide into Mets shortstop Bud Harrelson ignited a brawl. Shea Stadium fans began heckling Rose in left field, and when a bottle flew from the stands toward him, Reds manager Sparky Anderson pulled his team off the field. The umpires threatened the Mets with a forfeit, so Mays, Berra, and Tom Seaver, among others, walked out to left and pleaded with the fans to let the game go on. The crowd settled down, and the Mets won, 9-2. Mays played only in the fifth and deciding game, but he made the most of the opportunity. He delivered a pinch-hit Baltimore chop single with the bases loaded in the home fifth, providing the game-winning RBI and later scoring an insurance run in the Mets' 7-2 victory.

The story of Mays misplaying two balls in center field in the second game of the World Series against the Oakland A's is always used when the topic is a star athlete who plays too long past his prime. Exhibit B might be Mays's ultimately harmless stumble on the basepaths in the same game. What is often forgotten is what happened in the 12th inning, when he duped A's catcher Ray Fosse into calling for a fastball, telling him, "Ray, it's tough to see the balls with that background. I hope he doesn't throw me any fastballs."[65] He bounced a Rollie Fingers fastball over the pitcher's head and into center to drive in the winning run.

Mays's last career hit in his next-to-last career at-bat provided the game-winning RBI in a World Series game. In the clubhouse watching the game on TV when Mays came to the plate, Mets pitcher and former Giants teammate Ray Sadecki said, "He has to get a hit. This game was invented for Willie Mays a hundred years ago."[66]

The Mets lost the Series in seven games. Many of his teammates lauded his impact. Tug McGraw: "I guess I learned as much from Willie Mays as anybody." Jerry Koosman: "He was still our best player. I begged him not to retire." Tom Seaver: "Many of the New York writers made him out as a load we had to carry, but, quite the contrary, he helped us *carry* the load we had all the way down through the season, especially the last month and a half, when we got hot and put it all together."[67]

Mays's post-career years were much less publicly eventful, of course. After retiring as an active player, Willie was a "goodwill" coach for the Mets, working with the young players, visiting farm teams, and appearing at booster-club dinners. He also did public-relations work for the Colgate-Palmolive company for 12 years.

In 1979 the Baseball Writers Association of America elected Mays to the Baseball Hall of Fame in his first year of eligibility. At his induction ceremony, he was eloquent and humble:

"What can I say? This country is made up of a great many things. You can grow up to be what you want. I chose baseball, and I loved every minute of it. I give you one word –love. It means dedication. You have to sacrifice many things to play baseball. I sacrificed a bad marriage and I sacrificed a good marriage. But I'm here today because baseball is my number one love."[68]

That fall he accepted a ten-year deal to do public-relations work for Bally's Casino in Atlantic City, to greet people and play golf, things he had done at the Dunes Hotel in Las Vegas for years. According to Mays, his agreement prohibited him from gambling within 100 miles of Bally's. Nevertheless, Commissioner Bowie Kuhn prohibited Mays and Yankees great Mickey Mantle, who had a similar job, from holding salaried positions with major-league clubs. While a number of owners, including the Yankees' George Steinbrenner and the Pirates' John Galbreath, had connections with horse racing, and despite the fact that Atlantic City did not (and does not) allow sports wagering, Kuhn forced two of the greatest names in baseball history to sever their ties with the game.

In 1981 *New York Daily News* writer Bill Madden interviewed Willie to mark his 50th birthday. Although saddened at his banishment, he was tending to his various business affairs, charitable efforts, and the Bally's job. Madden wrote: "And there was something about Willie Mays gave the fans more satisfaction than probably any other player of his time. Charisma is the way some other people would explain it. Mays has his own explanation as to why he is so beloved. "It's because I love people," he said. "You can't fool people. ... I loved what I was doing. ..."[69]

In March 1985, shortly after being named commissioner, Peter Ueberroth reinstated Mantle and Mays, saying, "They are two of the most beloved and admired athletes in the country today, and they belong in baseball."[70]

Giants general manager Al Rosen put Willie back in uniform as a spring-training instructor the next year. An All-Star third baseman for Cleveland in the 1950s, Rosen said, "From everything I ever witnessed, Mays was the finest player I ever saw. ... His presence is electric. ... [P]laying against him, you had the feeling you were playing against someone who was going to be the greatest of all time."[71]

At a ceremony in 1986 honoring Willie McCovey, Mays received a five-minute standing ovation from the Candlestick faithful. In his remarks to the crowd on his special day, McCovey paid homage to his longtime teammate, "Willie Mays, it was an honor to wear the same uniform you wore."[72]

The 1990s saw Willie lose three men who were great influences in his life. In 1991 Leo Durocher died, and in 1997 Piper Davis died. Both were father figures to him. Then Willie's natural father, Cat, died in 1999 at age 88. Willie had set Cat up in an apartment in Harlem in 1954 and moved him out to Oakland in 1958. However, it seemed that the greatest tragedy for Willie was Mae's diagnosis of Alzheimer's disease before she even turned 60.

In 2006, Willie Mays remained a part-time consultant for the Giants. A surrogate father to Barry Bonds, his godson, he gave his blessing when Bonds passed him for third place on the all-time home-run list in 2004.

And the accolades kept coming. Longtime baseball writer Ray Robinson said, "It's possible that no athlete in any sport can ever again mean to us what Willie Mays once meant." Despite their political differences, Presidents Bill Clinton, George Bush, and Barack Obama, baby boomers all, idolized him and desired contact with him. Clinton, a frequent golf partner of the Say Hey Kid, said, "When you see [Willie Mays] do something you admire, the image of that makes a mockery of all forms of bigotry."[73] Bush, who named Mays the commissioner of the White House T-ball league, said, "When I was growing up, I wanted to be the Willie Mays of my generation."[74] When President Obama was elected as the first African-American in the job, Willie sent him a note: "Dear Mr. President, Move on in. Your Friend, Willie Mays." Mays subsequently joined the President on Air Force One traveling to the 2009 All-Star Game.

When Peter Magowan, a Giants fan from the Polo Grounds days, purchased the team in 1993, one of his first acts was to give Willie Mays a lifetime contract to be a part of the Giants organization. On the occasion of Mays' 80th birthday in 2011, Daniel Brown of the San Jose Mercury News wrote, "Magowan was surprised a few years ago when Mays approached him about a contract extension. 'Willie, it's a lifetime contract. You know what that means, right?' Magowan said. 'I know what it means. I still want an extension,' Mays replied."[75]

Willie had requested the extra year to ensure that Mae would be cared for once he was gone. On April 19, 2013, Mae died of complications from her Alzheimer's disease.[76]

When The Sporting News polled fans to name the All-Century team for the 20th century, Willie placed second to Babe Ruth. He wrote the foreword for the book honoring the team: "It's a great honor to be named the No. 2 player in baseball history. ... I have the satisfaction of knowing that when they call my name, everybody knows me. If you'd asked me when I was 15 in Birmingham if all this could happen, there's no way I would have said yes."[77]

SOURCES

Astor, Gerald, The Baseball Hall of Fame 50th Anniversary Book (New York: Prentice Hall, 1988).

Durocher, Leo, Nice Guys Finish Last (New York: Pocket Books, 1975).

Einstein, Charles, Willie's Time: A Memoir (Carbondale: Southern Illinois University Press, 2004).

Elias Robert, ed., Baseball and the American Dream: Race, Class, Gender and the National Pastime (Armonk, New York: M.E. Sharpe, 2001).

Eskenazi, Gerald, The Lip: A Biography of Leo Durocher (New York: William Morrow and Company Inc., 1993).

Golenbock, Peter, 'Amazin': The Miraculous History of Baseball's Most Beloved Team (New York: St. Martin's Griffin, 2002).

Hirsch, James S., Willie Mays: The Life, the Legend (New York: Simon and Shuster, 2010).

Honig, Donald, The All Star Game (St. Louis: The Sporting News Publishing Company, 1987).

Kahn, Roger, The Era: 1947-1957, When the Yankees, the Giants and the Dodgers Ruled the World (New York: Ticknor and Fields, 1993).

Klima, John, Willie's Boys: The 1948 Birmingham Black Barons, the Last Negro League World Series, and the Making of a Baseball Legend (New York: John Wiley and Sons, Inc., 2009).

Mays, Willie, with Lou Sahadi, Say Hey: the Autobiography of Willie Mays (New York: Simon and Schuster, 1988).

Mays, Willie, as told to Charles Einstein, Willie Mays: My Life In and Out of Baseball (New York: E.P. Dutton & Co., Inc., 1966).

Museum of Living History, Academy of Achievement Interview with Willie Mays, February 19, 1996 (achievement.org)

Roseboro, John, *Glory Days With the Dodgers and Other Days With Others* (New York: Atheneum Publishing, 1978).

Rust, Art, *Get That Nigger Off the Field: An Oral History of Black Ballplayers From the Negro Leagues to the Present* (Los Angeles: Shadow Lawn Press, 1992).

The Sporting News, *The Sporting News Selects Baseball's Greatest Players: A Celebration of the 20th Century's Best* (St. Louis: The Sporting News Publishing Company, 1998.)

Thomson, Bobby, with Lee Heiman and Dan Gutman, *"The Giants Win the Pennant! The Giants Win the Pennant!"* (New York: Kensington Publishing Co., 1991).

Ward, Geoffrey C., and Ken Burns, *Baseball: An Illustrated History* (New York: Alfred A. Knopf, 1994).

Zimmer, Don, with Bill Madden, *The Zen of Zim* (New York: T. Dunne Books, 2004).

New York Daily News

New York Times

Newsweek

New Yorker

Saturday Evening Post

San Jose Mercury News

Sport magazine

Sports Illustrated

Jet magazine

achievement.org, Willie Mays interview, accessed December 31, 2013

gilhodges.com (accessed January 6, 2013)

blog.sfgate.com/giants/2013/04/19/willie-mays-wife-mae-dies-at-74/ (accessed January 6, 2013)_

Baseball-almanac.com (accessed January 6, 2014)

Retrosheet (retrosheet.org)

TV show, *The Sporting News 100*, interviewed by Bob Costas

Lee, Anthony, Seton Hall University librarian (personal communication)

NOTES

1   Durocher, *Nice Guys Finish Last*, 385.

2   Mike Lupica, *New York Daily News*, May 8, 2011

3   Hirsch, *Willie Mays: The Life, The Legend*, 257

4   Hirsch, 35.

5   Einstein, *Willie's Time*, 348.

6   Mays, *Say Hey*, 19.

7   Hirsch, 24.

8   Baseball-almanac.com.

9   Hirsch, 47.

10   Hirsch, 31.

11   Mays, *Say Hey*, 31-32.

12   Mays, *Say Hey*, 43.

13   Thomson, *"The Giants Win the Pennant,"* 107.

14   Mays, *My Life in and Out of Baseball*, 29.

15   Durocher, 271.

16   Mays, *Say Hey*, 45.

17   Mays, *My Life in and Out of Baseball*, 32.

18   Achievement.org.

19   Achievement.org.

20   Mays, *Say Hey*, 52.

21   Hirsch, 77.

22   Mays, *My Life in and Out of Baseball*, 85.

23   Hirsch, 78.

24   Durocher, 273.

25   David Hinckley, *New York Daily News*, October 1, 2003.

26   *The Sporting News 100*.

27   Mays, *Say Hey*, 83.

28   Hirsch, 125.

29   Durocher, 271.

30   Einstein, 65.

31   Red Smith, *New York Times*, May 29, 1952.

32   Roger Kahn, *The Era*, 320.

33   Einstein, 107.

34   Hirsch, 196.

35   Achievement.org.

36   Gerald Eskenazi, *The Lip*, 283.

37   John Drebinger, *New York Times*, May 24, 1957.

38   Elias, 183.

39   Zimmer, 162.

40   Mays, *Say Hey*, 142.

41   Einstein, 111.

42   Ibid.

43   Mays, *Say Hey*, 151.

44   Rust, 124.

45   Mays, *Say Hey*, 168.

46   Arnold Hano, *Sport*, August, 1963.

47   Mays, *My Life in and Out of Baseball*, 204.

48   Einstein, 201.

49   Mays, *Say Hey,* 209.

50   Mays, *Say Hey,* 215.

51   Mays, *Say Hey,* 210.

52   Hirsch, 421.

53   Einstein, 210-11.

54   Einstein, 316.

55   Roseboro, 8.

56   Einstein, 244.

57   Mays, *Say Hey,* 232.

58   Einstein, 253-54.

59   Einstein, 320.

60   Einstein, 321-22.

61   gilhodges.com.

62   Ward and Burns, 426.

63   Mays, *Say Hey,* 253.

64   Golenbock, 309.

65   Mays, *Say Hey,* 257.

66   Hirsch, 529.

67   Golenbock, 308.

68   Hirsch, 535-36.

69   Bill Madden, *New York Daily News,* May 7, 1981.

70   *Sports Illustrated,* March 25, 1985.

71   Mays, *Say Hey,* 274.

72   Astor, 272

73   Hirsch, 233.

74   George W. Bush, speech, July 30, 2006.

75   Daniel Brown, *San Jose Mercury News,* May 5, 2011

76   blog.sfgate.com/giants/2013/04/19/willie-mays-wife-mae-dies-at-74/

77   *The Sporting News Selects Baseball's Greatest Players.*

JAMES LEE "JIMMIE" NEWBERRY

By Jeb Stewart

James Lee "Jimmie" Newberry was a starting pitcher for the Birmingham Black Barons from 1942 to 1950. Most newspapers and historical sources refer to "Jimmy" as the diminutive of Newberry's first name. However, the best evidence, which includes two autographs, signed "Jimmie Newberry," is that he preferred to use the variant "Jimmie."[1]

Newberry was born on June 26, 1919, in Ruthven, a sawmill town in Wilcox County, Alabama.[2] He was the sixth of 10 children born to Will and Lula Newberry. Two of his brothers played professionally for the Chicago American Giants in 1947: An older brother, Henry, was a pitcher, and a younger brother, Richard, was an infielder.[3] Richard also played four seasons in the Northern League, where he consistently batted over .300.[4] Jimmie Newberry's nephew, James Lovejoy, credited Lula Newberry for the family's baseball talent, recalling that she was always a good hitter at family reunions.[5]

Will Newberry worked as a laborer at the sawmill and Lula worked as a tenant farmer.[6] By any measure, rural Wilcox County was one of the poorest counties in Alabama; only 10 years after Jimmie Newberry's birth, the Black Belt county's population had decreased by nearly 20 percent, from 31,080 to 24,880.[7] The lack of opportunity under the sharecropping-based economy caused the mass exodus of many black families during the Depression. The Newberrys left Wilcox County sometime between 1930 and 1935 after a family member had a dispute with a local store owner who threatened to involve the Ku Klux Klan.[8] The move would prove to be a good decision for the future of the family; modern Wilcox County's population has shrunk to slightly over 11,000, and it remains the poorest county in the state, if not the entire country.[9] Wilcox is one of two counties in Alabama without a federal highway, and the town of Ruthven no longer exists.[10]

The family settled in the north Birmingham neighborhood of Collegeville, where Will Newberry found work at the Birmingham Southern Railroad Company and later at the United States Pipe and Foundry Company.[11] Jimmie Newberry dropped out of school in the sixth grade and was playing baseball by the time he was 15 years old. He got a job with the Louisville & Nashville Railroad and pitched for the L&N Stars in the Birmingham Industrial League.[12]

At age 23, Newberry reportedly signed with the Birmingham Black Barons late in the 1942 season, although the details of his signing are unknown.[13] Not until 1943 did newspapers notice Newberry, who "won his pitching spurs in the local shop league."[14] In photographs, he had a youthful innocence, but with a mischievous grin, and sportswriters called him Schoolboy Newberry.[15] Late in his career with the Black Barons, an incredulous Newberry asked a reporter, "I wonder where they get that 'school boy' name from? I'm no school boy. I am a man."[16] If the press thought he was an innocent schoolboy, his teammates knew him better. They called the lanky right-handed pitcher Newt.[17]

That he was one of the harder drinking members of the Black Barons also belied the Schoolboy nickname. Newberry was a regular patron at Bob's Savoy on Fourth Avenue North in Birmingham, and he frequented clubs on the road whenever the team stayed in a hotel.[18] Manager Piper Davis, who did not drink, kept impressionable young Willie Mays away from Newberry off the field.[19] John Klima, author of *Willie's Boys*, documented Newberry's fondness for alcohol:

> Kick-ya-poo juice was the hardest whiskey a man could get, moonshine even, and Newberry drank the hard stuff until it lived up to its nickname and kicked him square in the ass. He would never turn down a free drink, either. [Teammate Bill] Greason

lost track of how many times he got his roommate out of trouble. ...[20]

On the field Newberry took his job seriously and could be counted on to take the ball when it was his turn to pitch. He stood just 5-feet-7 and weighed 170 pounds, but "had a rubber arm. [He could] pitch tonight, [and] relieve tomorrow.[21] Newberry "had more pitches than Satchel Paige," according to Black Barons shortstop Artie Wilson.[22] Greason fondly remembered him as one of the best-liked players on the squad, who used to entertain the other players by singing on the bus.[23] In his opinion, Newberry was also one of the top pitchers on the ballclub; he had a good fastball and a devastating curve that he could throw with the same pitching motion.[24] Davis, Newberry's manager in 1948 and 1949, went even further, citing Newberry as being "one of the *best* pitchers playin' in that league."[25]

Wilson described Newberry's array of pitches as including a "knuckleball, screwball, sinker, dipsy-doo—that was an overhand drop—and he had a good fastball too. [He] could make it run in, make it run out."[26] The dipsy-doo was Newberry's out pitch. Wilson remembered, "[E]very time he'd get two strikes on a guy, I'd holler from short, 'Time for the dipsy-doodle, Jim'—and that was all for that batter."[27] James Lovejoy, who saw his uncle pitch at Rickwood Field, described Newberry's curve:

> He threw a curveball you would not believe. Have you ever seen the Sandy Koufax curveball? He could throw it at Second Street and it came in at home plate. ... Nobody wanted to face Newt. He had a good fastball, but, buddy, that curve was mean. That was his pitch![28]

Newberry quickly became one of manager Winfield Welch's top pitchers on the Black Barons, and he posted a 3.22 earned-run average in 1944.[29] Birmingham won back-to-back Negro American League pennants in 1943 and 1944 but succumbed both times to the Homestead Grays in the Negro League World Series. During this period, the Black Barons had one of the most imposing pitching staffs

in the league, which one newspaper called "as great a hurling corps as the league has ever seen."[30] The *Birmingham World* credited Welch with developing Newberry and other local players "to stardom."[31] Despite Newberry's 3.06 earned-run average and 12-2 record, as reported contemporaneously by the *Los Angeles Times*, the Black Barons could manage only a frustrating second-place finish in 1945.[32]

Newberry also learned new tactics to use when his famed curve was not breaking. On a hot August day in Baltimore late in the 1945 campaign, the Elite Giants accused Newberry of cutting balls to increase the break in his pitches.[33] Welch "denied that his pitcher was resorting to such illegal tactics."[34] However, after the umpire replaced several scuffed balls with new ones, Vernon Greene, the Giants' business manager, presented "Welch with a total of 17 balls thrown out of the game by the umpire, which he charged showed definite signs of having been scratched by an object with sharp or rough edges."[35] Welch removed Newberry from the game. Catcher Roy Campanella later asserted, "[w]hen y'all don't cut it, it goes up against the fences,"[36] as he went 2-for-3 with a double.[37] Despite the accusations of ball cutting, Newberry's strong performance in 1945 earned him a raise the next year.[38]

Now 27, as Newberry entered the prime of his baseball career, he married gospel singer Willie May Thomas, a contralto with the popular Gospel Harmoneers, who were later renamed the Gospel Harmonettes.[39] Their marriage did not last long, although the specific details regarding their divorce are not available. On the field, the newspapers now identified Newberry as the headliner of the Black Barons staff, and he delivered an 11-6 record in 1946, although the Black Barons missed the postseason again.[40]

In 1947 Newberry met with success early in the year. In a spring exhibition game at Rickwood Field, he relieved Jehosie Heard, and scattered five hits in four scoreless innings of relief in shutting down the Cleveland Buckeyes, who always struggled to hit his repertoire of pitches.[41] In April Newberry struck out 11 batters to defeat the Black Barons' archnemesis, the Homestead Grays.[42] With a 5-2 record, he was selected to the West All-Star squad for the biannual East-West All-Star game in Chicago, though he did not play in the game.[43] After the Black Barons finished third in the Negro American League, Newberry barnstormed with the Kansas City Royals as they battled Bob Feller's All-Star team in the fall.[44]

Newberry posted the best statistical record of his career in 1948, which was arguably the Birmingham Black Barons' greatest season. Ellis Jones of the *Birmingham World* had forecast a pennant for Birmingham and expected a strong performance for Newberry, writing:

> Jimmie Newberry, for years the standard bearer of the Ebony Barons slabmen, has just returned from south-of-the border and will join his teammates upon their return from the Carolinas. Newberry won 5, lost 6, last year but is expected to show the form this year that ranked him as one of the game's greatest hurlers.[45]

The prediction was prescient. In late May Newberry struck out 10 in a close loss to Memphis.[46] By June, the newspapers were touting him as the "ace of the staff."[47] On July 31, with Pepper Bassett behind the plate, Newberry outdueled Cleveland's Vibert Clarke — who allowed only six hits — by throwing a no-hitter to defeat the Buckeyes, 4-0, in Dayton, Ohio.[48] (On the same day that the *Birmingham World* reported the no-hitter, Newberry grumbled that Birmingham's fans "ride me too much."[49]) The fans eventually must have appreciated him, since he led the squad in every major pitching category, finishing with a 14-5 record, 112 strikeouts in 157 innings, and a 2.18 earned-run average.[50] That performance helped the Black Barons clinch a playoff spot against the Kansas City Monarchs, who they defeated to win the Negro American League pennant.

Newberry was the natural choice to start Game One of the Negro League World Series against the Homestead Grays. He pitched well, throwing a complete game and striking out six, but gave up three runs in the second inning, which was enough for the

opportunistic Grays, and lost 3-2.[51] For the series, Newberry had a 2.31 earned-run average in 11⅔ innings pitched, but his efforts were not enough as the Grays won the series, four games to one.[52]

At the beginning of 1949, sportswriter Wendell Smith cited Newberry, now 29, as a Negro American League player who could be offered a major-league contract; however, he also noted that Newberry's age was working against him, since he would turn 30 during the season.[53] In May, as if to prove that his 1948 no-hitter was no fluke, Newberry threw another against the Buckeyes, who were now based in Louisville, Kentucky.[54] Before he could replicate his success of 1948, a vicious line drive broke his pitching arm in June.[55] The break was severe enough to end his season after only nine starts through which he had a 4-2 record.[56] By October, Newberry had recovered and appeared in an exhibition game for the Creole All-Stars against Jackie Robinson's All-Stars in Atlanta's Ponce De Leon Park.[57]

In the following year, Newberry's last as a Black Baron, both he and the team started fast. In late May he struck out 12 in a grueling 15-inning start for

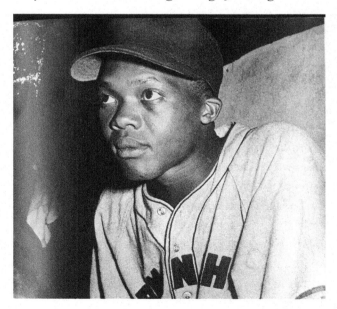

Jimmie Newberry was the ace of the 1948 Birmingham Black Barons' pitching staff, finishing 14-5 with a sparkling 2.18 ERA. He also spun a no-hitter against the Cleveland Buckeyes on July 31, 1948. *(Withers Family Trust, Memphis, Tennessee)*

Jimmie Newberry in 1959, when he attempted a comeback with the Lloydminster-North Battleford Combines of the Canadian-American League. Newberry's first stint in Canada had included winning the 1950 Manitoba-Dakota League championship with the Winnipeg Buffaloes. (*Courtesy of Jay-Dell Mah/Western Canada Baseball*)

Birmingham; the *Birmingham World* reported that he had also registered 21 strikeouts over his previous two games.[58] With Newberry recording an 8-3 record, the first-place Black Barons won 13 games in a row.[59] The only thing hotter was the team's bus, which caught fire in New York City on June 7, destroying the equipment and the players' belongings.[60] The bus fire was a fitting symbol for the end of the most competitive period for Birmingham in the Negro American League.

On June 20 the *Birmingham World* reported that Newberry had jumped the club during the New York City trip to join a Canadian team.[61] Details emerged over the next few days that he signed with

the Winnipeg Buffaloes of the Manitoba-Dakota (ManDak) Baseball League, who were raiding players from the Negro Leagues under manager Willie Wells.[62] Black Barons owner Tom Hayes later claimed he had advanced Newberry his salary before he left the team, a charge Newberry's nephew, James Lovejoy, disputes; Lovejoy maintains that Hayes was a skinflint, who refused to pay his star pitcher what he was worth.[63] Winnipeg offered Newberry an enticing salary, so he agreed to pitch in Canada, where he joined former Black Barons teammates Lyman Bostock, John Britton and Johnny Cowan. Hayes was furious and, in a futile gesture, suspended his star pitcher indefinitely.[64]

With the New York Giants' signing of Willie Mays announced only two weeks after Newberry left Birmingham, and Artie Wilson having already left for Oakland, the core of the Birmingham Black Barons was quickly disintegrating. By the end of the season, Piper Davis would be gone and the end of the era would be complete.

Newberry was soon dazzling batters in Canada with his wide variety of pitches.[65] The ManDak league also provided a chance for him to pitch on an all-black squad in an integrated league. In Canada life was easier for black players as there were no Jim Crow laws. Newberry and his teammates discovered a more egalitarian society, which offered them real freedoms. On the mound, he pitched well; he won his first start on June 17 while striking out 11 and won both games of a doubleheader on August 24.[66] He finished at 7-7 and pitched 14 complete games as the Buffaloes advanced to the ManDak championship series.[67] In the series, against the Brandon Greys, Newberry won two games and saved another, as Winnipeg won the league title.[68] Catcher Frazier "Slow" Robinson recalled that Newberry's dipsy-doodle curve remained effective and "drove batters nuts."[69]

In 1951 Newberry started 6-3 while pitching in 12 games for the Buffaloes.[70] His time in Canada was short-lived, however. Newberry's former manager, Winfield Welch, who was now the manager of the Chicago American Giants and a scout for Bill Veeck's

St. Louis Browns, began to follow the Buffaloes. In spite of the indefinite suspension imposed by Hayes, Welch signed Newberry to pitch for the American Giants and the pitcher returned to the United States. Marcel Hopson of the *Birmingham World* reported that Newberry expected to join Satchel Paige on the St. Louis Browns shortly, and happily added, "[i]t's great to know that Newberry is back in the fold."[71] Newberry finished with a 2-1 record for Chicago, but he did not join Paige on the Browns because Veeck had other plans for him.[72]

During the mid-1940s Abe Saperstein had been the Black Barons' business manager for Hayes. He liked Newberry and advanced his salary to him regularly.[73] By the early 1950s, Saperstein was a minority owner of the St. Louis Browns and a scout. In February of 1952, the Associated Press reported that Saperstein requested permission from owner Bill Veeck to reach a working relationship with a Japanese professional team for player development, an idea that Veeck approved despite some hesitation.[74] On April 28, 1952, the Browns announced the signing of Newberry and third baseman John Britton, who were training with the independent Thomasville Tomcats, and revealed that the pair was being loaned to the Hankyu Braves of the Japanese Pacific League. Newberry became the first black professional pitcher in Japan after World War II.[75]

Newberry soon discovered that "the Japanese players were smaller and made for a smaller strike zone. … [H]e had to work on his control and remember to keep the ball down."[76] This change made Newberry's results for Hankyu even more impressive. He finished with a record of 11-10 and an ERA of 3.23 in 206⅓ innings pitched and made the all-star team for the fifth-place Braves.[77] The switch-hitter also batted .288, which was the fifth highest average for Hankyu.[78]

Newberry was popular with Japanese fans, who welcomed him and Britton.[79] They were so well-liked that "about 1,000 fans escorted [them] to the plane to bid [them] farewell … when [they] left for the States."[80] Despite a successful campaign in Japan, the 33-year-old Newberry decided not to play a second season in Osaka because he wanted to win a spot

with the Browns.[81] He was unsuccessful in that endeavor, so he returned to Canada in 1953, playing for the Carman Cardinals and posted a 5-9 record while leading the league with 30 appearances.[82]

From 1954 to 1956, Newberry played for six independent professional teams in nearly every corner and region of Texas. His tour of Texas began near the southeast with the Bryan Indians, where he pitched in the Class-B Big State League from April until July 19, 1954. In June Newberry suffered probably the worst pitching performance of his career, against the Tyler Tigers, in which he gave up three home runs, three doubles, and 18 hits in a 13-1 loss; his dipsy-doodle curve clearly was not breaking that day, but his defense did not help either as the Indians committed seven errors.[83] Bryan's record was 32-65 and the team was mired in seventh place on July 19, when owner Arturo Gonzalez dealt Newberry and pitcher Roland Jones to the Abilene Blue Sox in north-central Texas.[84] Financial conditions forced Gonzalez to sell even more players.[85] The team was losing money as fast as it was losing games, and relocated to Del Rio the following week.[86] All things considered, Newberry had pitched well for Bryan and led the Indians in wins with a 9-10 record.[87]

Newberry's new team, the Abilene Blue Sox, played in the Class-C West Texas-New Mexico League and was in contention for a playoff spot when it purchased his contract from Bryan. Manager Jay Haney expressed confidence in his new pitchers, saying, "You can quote me on this. I believe that these two boys are just what we needed to not only keep us in the first division, but help us to overtake Pampa for first place by the end of the season."[88] Newberry met with mixed results as he finished 2-5 for Abilene.[89] He threw a three-hitter against the Lubbock Hubbers in early August but lost, 2-0.[90] On August 31 he threw a five-hitter and won an important game to get the Blue Sox close to a playoff berth.[91] The Blue Sox did end up making the playoffs, but they lost to the first-place Pampa Oilers in the Shaughnessy playoff format.[92]

In 1955 Newberry returned to the Class-B Big State League and signed with the Port Arthur Sea

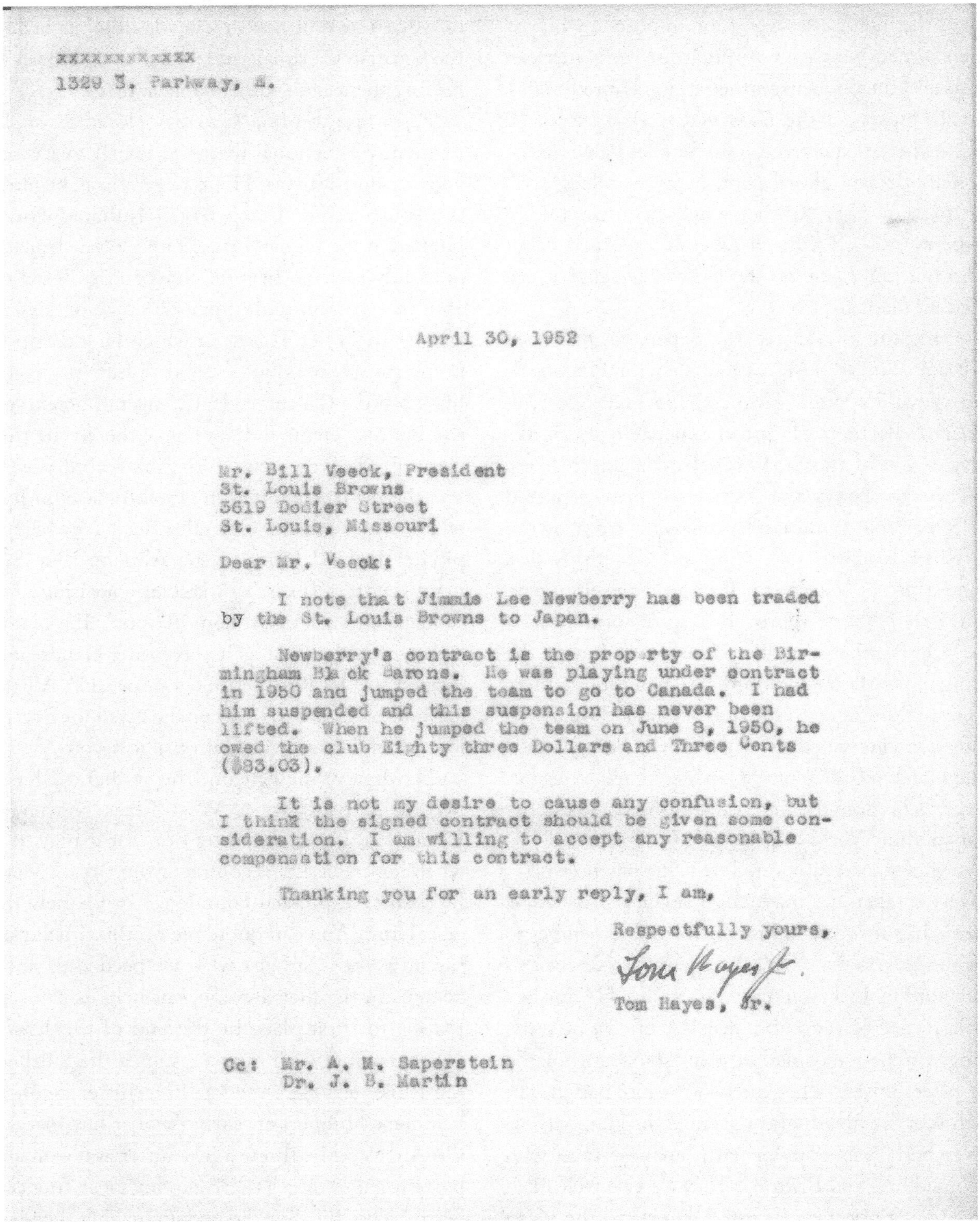

```
XXXXXXXXXXX
1329 S. Parkway, S.



                              April 30, 1952



    Mr. Bill Veeck, President
    St. Louis Browns
    3619 Dodier Street
    St. Louis, Missouri

    Dear Mr. Veeck:

         I note that Jimmie Lee Newberry has been traded
    by the St. Louis Browns to Japan.

         Newberry's contract is the property of the Bir-
    mingham Black Barons.  He was playing under contract
    in 1950 and jumped the team to go to Canada.  I had
    him suspended and this suspension has never been
    lifted.  When he jumped the team on June 8, 1950, he
    owed the club Eighty three Dollars and Three Cents
    ($83.03).

         It is not my desire to cause any confusion, but
    I think the signed contract should be given some con-
    sideration.  I am willing to accept any reasonable
    compensation for this contract.

         Thanking you for an early reply, I am,

                              Respectfully yours,

                              Tom Hayes, Jr.


    Cc:  Mr. A. M. Saperstein
         Dr. J. B. Martin
```

Jimmie Newberry jumped the Black Barons to join the Winnipeg Buffaloes in June 1950. When the St. Louis Browns signed Newberry in 1952, Birmingham owner Tom Hayes voiced his displeasure to Browns owner Bill Veeck. (*Courtesy of Memphis Public Library*)

Hawks on the Texas Gulf Coast, where he pitched primarily as a reliever.[93] In the spring he led the team with a 3-0 record and surrendered only a single unearned run in 22 innings.[94] His fortunes took a downturn, and he began to struggle to get outs after the league's hitters adjusted to his pitches. Newberry finished his stint at Port Arthur with a 6-4 record, allowing 69 earned runs for a 5.01 earned-run average while striking out 51 batters in 124 innings.[95] At the end of July, Port Arthur traded him to the Big Spring Cosden Cops of the Class-C Longhorn League.[96] Newberry's former Black Barons teammate Jim Zapp was sent by the Cosden Cops to the Sea Hawks, apparently as part of the deal.[97]

Newberry won a game in his first appearance for Big Spring and appeared in several games, but his complete statistics for the Cosden Cops are unavailable.[98] He spent less than three weeks with Big Spring before leaving West Texas for the Panhandle, after the Amarillo Gold Sox of the Class-C West Texas-New Mexico League obtained him.[99] Details regarding the acquisition are also lost to history.

Newberry faced his former team, the Abilene Blue Sox, in his first appearance for Amarillo. He relieved starter Dean Higgins and recorded the third out of an inning in a wild 15-14 victory over Jay Haney's squad.[100] Ten days later, Haney got his revenge as Newberry started against Abilene and lost, 4-2, though he pitched well and allowed no hits until the fourth inning.[101] Newberry finished the regular season with a 0-3 record for Amarillo; he allowed 31 runs and struck out 13 batters in just 23 innings pitched.[102] The Gold Sox finished in first place in the league but lost the championship series to the third-place Pampa Oilers, four games to one.[103] In the playoffs, Newberry pitched well in relief, shutting out the Pampa over 3⅔ innings in Game Three on September 17.[104] He also threw a scoreless inning of relief the following day as the Gold Sox won their only game of the series.[105]

Newberry's tour of Texas ended in the westernmost part of the state in 1956, when he pitched in a handful of games for the El Paso Texans of the Class-B Southwestern League in late April and early May.[106] In the last news story in which his name appeared, the 37-year-old battled until the end: "Newberry replaced McNeal on the mound for the Texans and was greeted by a single by Frank Kemper, which scored Cross. A double by Flores put men on first and third, but Newberry then retired the side on infield outs."[107] Details regarding Newberry's statistics and the circumstances of his departure from the Texans are not available.

Newberry did not play baseball professionally in 1957 and 1958. In 1959 he briefly attempted "a comeback with the Lloydminster-North Battleford Combines in the Canadian-American League, but saw action in only one game."[108]

After his baseball career ended, Newberry had no second career. He traveled the country and stayed with friends, mostly former ballplayers, including Al Smith and Joe Black. He always dressed well, wearing a suit with wing-tip shoes and a hat, and he liked to go to clubs. In Chicago he stayed with his sister, Minnie Newberry Lovejoy, and her son James for many years in the South Side.[109] When James Lovejoy coached Little League baseball, Newberry would sometimes help out by showing the kids how to throw the curve. Lovejoy remembered that Abe Saperstein was always generous to Newberry in the 1960s: "Abe Saperstein took care of my Uncle in Chicago. … [W]hen he needed money he would go see him, and Abe would say, 'Newt, what are you doing?' He said, 'Well, I'm trying to get by today,' and Abe Saperstein would give him money."[110] Later, when Bill Veeck bought the Chicago White Sox for the second time, he always gave Newberry tickets to games at Comiskey Park in the 1970s.[111]

Richard Newberry Jr., another nephew, also remembered his uncle with fondness: "He was a great guy. He came to visit us when I was a young boy. He was a bigger-than-life person. He could juggle. He could ride a bicycle backwards. And the things that he could do with a baseball were amazing."[112]

On June 23, 1983, two weeks after his 64th birthday, Jimmie Newberry died in Bremen Township, Illinois, of cardiac arrest brought on by chronic obstructive pulmonary disease. His death certificate appropriately identified his usual occupation as "Baseball Player."[113] He was cremated at Chicago's Oak Woods Cemetery.

On May 25, 1987, James Lovejoy drove to Comiskey Park to see the Chicago White Sox play the Kansas City Royals. As he walked up to the ticket booth, bought a ticket to the game, and entered the ballpark, none of the White Sox employees noticed the small container that he carried under his jacket. He sat in the lower stands on the first-base side near the foul pole in right field.[114] Bret Saberhagen, who had a good curveball, threw a six-hit complete game and struck out six batters as the Royals defeated the White Sox, 6-1.[115] The box score did not record the most significant event that day. During the game, whenever the fans rose to cheer, Lovejoy scattered Newberry's ashes into right field.[116] Jimmie Newberry, who once had scattered hits as a pitcher in what would become America's oldest baseball park (Rickwood Field), had his ashes scattered at what was then the oldest professional ballpark (Comiskey Park).

In 2016 the *Birmingham News* named the greatest athlete from each of Alabama's 67 counties. The paper credited Jimmie Newberry as the representative of Wilcox County, Alabama.[117]

ACKNOWLEDGEMENTS

The author is indebted to Frederick C. Bush for helping him to locate Jared Newberry, who helped him to contact Richard Newberry Jr. It was Richard Jr. who put the author in touch with James Lovejoy; the story of Jimmie Newberry's later life could not have been told without his help. At the 2013 Rickwood Classic, the minor-league Birmingham Barons commemorated the 1948 Birmingham Black Barons team. Jimmie Newberry, smiling broadly, appeared on the promotional poster for the event. The author is proud to have been able to share copies of the poster with the Newberry family.

NOTES

1   Alabama. Wilcox County. 1930 U.S. Census, population schedule. Digital images. Ancestry.com. February 12, 2017 ("Jimmie"). ancestry.com; Death Certificate for Jimmie Newberry, June 23, 1983, File No. 036274, Illinois Department of Public Records ("Jimmie"); a scorecard for the 1950 season created by the Birmingham Black Barons ("Jimmie"); and the Official Statistics compiled by the Howe News Bureau (Chicago) ("James" or "Jimmie"). The author is grateful to James Tate, who provided a copy of Jimmie Newberry's signature with a barnstorming team led by Willie Mays; in addition, while playing for the Winnipeg Buffaloes, Newberry signed an autograph, "Jimmie Newberry, Best Wishes."

2   Death Certificate for Jimmie Newberry, June 23, 1983, File No. 036274, Illinois Department of Public Records. Alabama. Wilcox County. 1930 U.S. Census.

3   Armand Peterson and Tom Tomashek, *Town Ball, The Glory Days of Minnesota Amateur Baseball* (Minneapolis: University of Minnesota Press, 2006), 290-292; Frank White, *They Played for the Love of the Game: Untold Stories of Black Baseball in Minnesota* (St. Paul: Minnesota Historical Society Press, 2016, Kindle Edition), 2033; James A. Riley, *The Biographical Encyclopedia of the Negro Baseball Leagues* (New York: Carroll & Graf Publishers, 1994), 581.

4   Riley, 581; Peterson and Tomashek, 290-292.

5   James Lovejoy, telephone interview with author, March 1, 2017.

6   Alabama. Wilcox County. 1930 U.S. Census.

7   census.gov/population/cencounts/al190090.txt.

8   James Lovejoy, telephone interview with author, February 15, 2017.

9   census.gov/quickfacts/table/PST045215/01131; Brendan Kirby, "4 Things To Know About Poverty in Wilcox County," AL.Com, February 16, 2014.

10   Virginia O. Foscue, *Place Names in Alabama* (Tuscaloosa: University of Alabama Press, 1989), 121; James Frederick Sulzby, *Historic Alabama Hotels and Resorts* (Tuscaloosa: University of Alabama Press, 1960), 259.

11   Alabama. Jefferson County. 1940 U.S. Census, population schedule. Digital images. Ancestry.com. February 14, 2017. ancestry.com; Lovejoy, telephone interview with author, February 15, 2017.

12   Riley, 581; Larry Powell, *Black Barons of Birmingham* (Jefferson. North Carolina: McFarland & Company, Inc., 2009), 87; Larry Powell, *Industrial Baseball Leagues in Alabama*, October 19, 2009, encyclopediaofalabama.org/article/h-2479.

13   Birmingham Black Barons, 1950 Scorecard; Powell, 87; Emory O. Jackson, "Hits and Bits," *Birmingham World*, May 27, 1949: 7.

14   "Barons Tame Giants, 2-0," *Birmingham World*, August 2, 1943: 4.

15   "Fighting Black Barons Primed for Battles With Eastern Foes," *Pittsburgh Courier*, September 4, 1943; "Black Barons Showing Much Class Here," *Birmingham World*, April 4, 1944: 5.

16   Emory O. Jackson, "Hits and Bits," *Birmingham World*, June 6, 1050: 4.

17   Rev. Bill Greason, telephone interview with author, February 10, 2017; Lovejoy, telephone interview with author, February 15, 2017.

18   Rev. Bill Greason, interview.

19   Riley, 581 John Klima, *Willie's Boys* (Hoboken, New Jersey: John Wiley & Sons, Inc., 2009), 108.

20   Klima, 109.

21   Stan Federman, "I Loved the Game," *Oregonian* (Portland), August 8, 1991.

22   robneyer.com/baseball-books/neyer-james-guide-to-pitchers/pitchers-l-to-r/.

23   Rev. Bill Greason, telephone interview with author, February 24, 2017.

24   Rev. Bill Greason, February 10 interview.

25   Brent Kelly, *Voices From the Negro Leagues: Conversations with 52 Baseball Standouts of the Period 1924-1960* (Jefferson, North Carolina: McFarland & Company, Inc., 1998), 131.

26   robneyer.com/baseball-books/neyer-james-guide-to-pitchers/pitchers-l-to-r/.

27   Federman, 3.

28   Lovejoy, telephone interview with author, February 15, 2017.

29   Official Negro American League Statistics for 1944, compiled by the Howe News Bureau (Chicago).

30   "Cubans Play Barons Sunday," *Chicago Defender*, March 31, 1945: 7.

31   "Picks Black Barons to Win Championship Again," *Birmingham World*, April 25, 1945: 6; Emory O. Jackson, "Hits and Bits," *Birmingham World*, July 3, 1945: 3.

32   Official Negro American League Statistics for 1945, compiled by the Howe News Bureau (Chicago); "Royals, Barons Meet Tonight," *Los Angeles Times*, October 31, 1945: A9.

33   "Elites, Charging Illegal Pitching, Beat Barons, 6-2," *Baltimore Afro-American*, August 18, 1945: 26.

34   Ibid.

35   Ibid.

36   Frazier Robinson, *Catching Dreams: My Life in the Negro Baseball Leagues* (Syracuse, New York: Syracuse University Press, 1999), 161.

37   "Elites, Charging Illegal Pitching, Beat Barons, 6-2."

38   Emory O. Jackson, "Hits and Bits," *Birmingham World*, January 22, 1946: 5.

39   Rev. Bill Greason, February 10 interview; James Lovejoy, telephone interview with author, March 1, 2017; Vladimir Bogdanov, Chris Woodstra, and Stephen T. Erlewine, editors, *All Music Guide to the Blues* (San Francisco: Backbeat Books, third edition, 2003), 121.

40   Riley, 581.

41   "Black Barons Defeat Cleveland Buckeyes," *Atlanta Daily World*, March 25, 1947: 5.

42   "Wild Hurling of Grays Enable Barons to Win," *Norfolk* (Virginia) *Journal and Guide*, April 26, 1947: 14.

43   Larry Lester, *Black Baseball's National Showcase, The East-West All-Star Game, 1933-1953* (Lincoln: University of Nebraska Press, 2001), 295.

44   "Royals, All-Stars in Doubleheader Sunday," *Los Angeles Sentinel*, October 16, 1947: 23; "Bob Feller's 9 in 2-1 Win Over Royals," *Norfolk Journal and Guide*, October 25, 1947: 14.

45   Ellis Jones, "Black Barons Eye '48 Championship; Leave City for Exhibition Games," *Birmingham World*, April 6, 1948: 5.

46   "Cleveland Rips Chi Twice; Memphis, Barons Split," *Pittsburgh Courier*, June 5, 1948: 15.

47   "Indianapolis Clowns to Meet B'ham Black Barons Today," *Atlanta Daily World*, June 24, 1948: 5.

48   Marion E. Jackson, "Sports of the World," *Atlanta Daily World*, August 3, 1948: 5; "Cleveland Buckeyes Defeated by Barons," *Atlanta Daily World*, August 4, 1948: 5; "Hurls No-Hitter," *Birmingham World*, August 6, 1948: 6.

49   Emory O. Jackson, "Hits and Bits," *Birmingham World*, August 6, 1948: 6.

50   Official Negro American League Statistics for 1948, compiled by the Howe News Bureau (Chicago).

51   Larry Lester and Dick Clark, "Day by Days for Pitchers—World Series," Negro League Researchers and Authors Group, 2004, 4. "Homestead Grays Defeat Black Barons 3 to 2," *Birmingham World*, September 28, 1948: 4.

52   Lester and Clark, 4.

53   "Few, If Any, Colored Stars Ready to Join Majors, Says Negro Scribe," *The Sporting News*, January 12, 1949: 13.

54   Emory O. Jackson, "Hits and Bits," *Birmingham World*, May 10, 1949: 2; "Cubans to Play Black Barons," *New York Times*, May 42, 1949: 36.

55   "New York Cubans Lose Twice to First Place Black Barons," *Atlanta Daily World*, June 15, 1949; Lovejoy, telephone interview with author, March 1, 2017.

56   "Black Barons Edge New York Cubans," *Pittsburgh Courier*, June 18, 1949; Official Negro American League Statistics for 1949, compiled by the Howe News Bureau (Chicago).

57   "Robinson's All-Stars to Play Here Sunday," *Atlanta Daily World*, October 12, 1949: 5; "Robinson, Campanella, Newcombe, Doby in 'All-Star Dream Game' at Poncey Park," *Atlanta Daily World*, October 16, 1949: 7.

58   "Barons, Memphis Play to 4-4 Tie," *Birmingham World*, June 2, 1950: 2.

59   "Mays' Big Bat Sparks Barons' Win Streak," *Pittsburgh Courier*, June 24, 1950; photo inset, *Birmingham World*, June 16,

1950; Black Barons Pitchers Record, *Birmingham World*, July 18, 1950: 4.

60 Marcel Hopson, "Hits and Bits," *Birmingham World*, June 23, 1950: 6.

61 Marcel Hopson, "Hits and Bits," *Birmingham World*, June 20, 1950: 3.

62 Robinson, 164-165.

63 Lovejoy, telephone interview with author, March 1, 2017.

64 Marcel Hopson, "Hits and Bits," *Birmingham World*, June 27, 1950: 6.

65 Marcel Hopson, "Hits and Bits," *Birmingham World*, June 30, 1950, 7.

66 Barry Swanton and Jay-Dell Mah, *Black Baseball Players in Canada: A Biographical Dictionary, 1881-1960* (Jefferson, North Carolina: McFarland & Company, Inc., 2009), 121.

67 Robinson, 170; Swanton and Mah, 121.

68 Swanton and Mah, 121.

69 Robinson, 170.

70 Swanton and Mah, 121.

71 Marcel Hopson, "Hits and Bits," *Birmingham World*, August 3, 1951: 6.

72 Statistics published in the *Baltimore Afro-American*, September 4, 1951: 16.

73 baseball-reference.com/bullpen/Jimmy_Newberry.

74 Ibid.

75 Gary Ashwill, "Early Black Ballplayers in Japan," agatetype. typepad.com/agate_type/2013/02/early-black-ballplayers-in-japan.html, accessed March 21, 2017.

76 Robinson, 171.

77 baseball-reference.com/register/league.cgi?id=5b45c99a; and http://www.baseball-reference.com/bullpen/Jimmy_Newberry.

78 baseball-reference.com/register/team.cgi?id=f7b7734f.

79 Robert K. Fitts, *Wally Yonamine: The Man Who Changed Japanese Baseball* (Lincoln: University of Nebraska Press, 2008), 119; Robinson, 171.

80 Fay Young, "Fay Says," *Chicago Defender*, February 14, 1953: 22.

81 "Caught on the Fly," *The Sporting News*, October 15, 1952: 38.

82 Swanton and Mah, 121.

83 "Indians Lose to Tyler in First Game of Series," *Bryan* (Texas) *Eagle*, June 7, 1954: 7.

84 "Baseball Standings," *Bryan Eagle*, July 20, 1954: 8; "Austin Widens Lead With 5 to 3 Win Over Indians," *Bryan Eagle*, July 20, 1954: 8.

85 Dave Campbell, "On Second Thought," *Waco News-Tribune*, July 24, 1954" 12.

86 "Bryan Indians May Be Moved," *Bryan Eagle*, July 11, 1954, 6; "Last Year of Pro Ball in Bryan," *Bryan Eagle*, July 11, 1954, 6; "Indians Granted Permission to Move Team to Del Rio," *Bryan Eagle*, July 25, 1954: 5.

87 "Redskins Records," *Bryan Eagle*, July 18, 1954: 6.

88 "Haney Confident New Hurlers will Click," *Abilene* (Texas) *Reporter-News*, July 23, 1954: 10-A.

89 "WT-NM AVERAGES," *Pampa* (Texas) *Daily News*, September 12, 1954: 7.

90 "Alonso After 19th Against Hubbers," *Abilene Reporter-News*, August 3, 1954: 6-A.

91 "Blue Sox Playoff Berth," *Pampa Daily News*, September 1, 1954: 7.

92 baseball-reference.com/bullpen/West_Texas-New_ Mexico_League.

93 "Sea Hawks Romp Past Texas City Texans 10 to 1," *Valley Morning Star* (Harlingen, Texas), April 21, 1955: 9; "Clippers Risk Lead Against Texas City," *Corpus Christi Caller Times*, April 27, 1955: 6-B.

94 "Ed Charles Leads Big State Hitters," *Corpus Christi Caller Times*, May 1, 1955: 13-B; "Big State League," *The Sporting News*, May 4, 1955: 35.

95 Individual Pitching Statistics, *Corpus Christi Caller-Times*, August 7, 1955: 25.

96 Jack Holden, "Sports Spotlight," *Abilene Reporter-News*, July 31, 1955: 2-D.

97 "Hawks Capture Pair, Leave BSL Cellar," *Waco News*, July 29, 1955: 13.

98 "Holden, 2-D; Odessa Takes 3-1 Win Over Cops to Break 12-Game Losing Skein," *Odessa American*, August 3, 1955, 8; Dick Clark and Larry Lester, *Records of the Negro League Players* (Cleveland, Ohio: SABR, 1994), 326-327.

99 "B-Sox Drop 15-14 Tilt," *Abilene Reporter News*, August 15, 1955: 2A.

100 Ibid.

101 Jack Holden, "5,000 Expected to See Santa Face Pampa at 8," *Abilene Reporter-News*, August 25, 1955: 2-B.

102 "WT-NM AVERAGES," *Abilene Reporter-News*, September 11, 1955: 4-D.

103 baseball-reference.com/bullpen/West_Texas-New_ Mexico_League.

104 Buck Francis, "Venable Goes Route; Fortin Pounds Pair of Homers," *Pampa Daily News*, September 18, 1955.

105 "Sox Edge Pampa in Playoff, 6-5," *Albuquerque Journal*, September 19, 1955: 15.

106 Clark and Lester, 326-327.

107 "Oilers Clip Texans, 7 to 3, Saturday," *Pampa Daily News*, May 6, 1956: 11.

108 Swanton and Mah, 121.

109 James Lovejoy, telephone interview with author, February 15, 2017.

110 Ibid.

111 Ibid.

112 Richard Newberry Jr., telephone interview with author, February 15, 2017.

113 Death Certificate for Jimmie Newberry, June 23, 1983, File No. 036274, Illinois Department of Public Records

114 James Lovejoy, telephone interview with author, February 15, 2017.

115 Mike Kiley, "Sox Find Home Unsweet Again, 6-Hitter Gives Saberhagen 8th Victory," *Chicago Tribune*, May 26, 1987: C1.

116 James Lovejoy, telephone interview with author, February 15, 2017.

117 al.com/sports/index.ssf/2016/12/whos_the_no_1_athlete_from_eac.html.

ALONZO PERRY

By Dennis D. Degenhardt

Alonzo Perry had a successful Negro League career primarily as a pitcher but also as a first baseman and outfielder, and even pitched in the last Negro League World Series. Although he had two brief stints in the minor leagues, he became a baseball star in Latin America while playing in the Dominican Republic and a superstar during his time in Mexico.

Alonzo Perry was born on April 14, 1923, in Birmingham, Alabama, to Homer Perry and Rosa Thomas. His middle name was Thomas.

At age 17, Perry entered the world of baseball, appearing on the Homestead Grays' 1940 roster, though statistics for his performance that year are unavailable. His professional career continued in the Negro Southern League, where he played for the Atlanta Black Crackers in 1945 and the Chattanooga Choo Choos to start the 1946 season.[1]

Perry's Negro League career took off later in 1946 when he returned to the Homestead Grays as a pitcher and posted a 2-2 won-lost record.[2] After seven games, he left the ballclub after a dispute with the team owner over money he had won gambling, finishing the season with his hometown Birmingham Black Barons of the Negro American League. He remained with the Black Barons through the 1950 season.[3] Though he continued to pitch through 1949, the strapping 6-foot-3 Perry's hitting ability led to his making his initial appearances as a first baseman in 1946; eventually he split his playing time between the mound, first base, and occasionally the outfield.

Perry had his best year to date in 1948, helping lead the Black Barons to the Negro League World Series for the first time since 1944. He won 10 of 12 decisions and batted .325 while playing almost daily. One of his teammates was a talented high-school student, Willie Mays, who was in the first of his three seasons with Birmingham. Because of Mays's youth, he had a different teammate watch over him every night,

and he couldn't go anywhere without a chaperone. The exceptions were two players, Jimmie Newberry and Alonzo Perry, who could not be trusted with watching the young Mays. As the baseball protégé said in *Say Hey,* "No one knew what they would get into after a game. They liked the ladies and like their beer."[4]

In what became the last the Negro League World Series, against the Homestead Grays, the only record of Perry playing was in Game Three, in which he was the Negro American League champions' starting pitcher at Birmingham's Rickwood Field. In Birmingham's lone victory in the series, Perry had a strong performance, maintaining a 3-1 lead until the eighth inning, when he gave up two runs that tied the game. He was relieved by Bill Greason, who halted the Grays' rally and scored the winning run in the bottom of the ninth inning on an RBI single by Mays.

The 1949 season was Perry's last as a starting pitcher in the Negro Leagues and was also his best as he finished with a 12-4 record with a 3.45 ERA. He also continued to play first base and the outfield. Manager Piper Davis also used his versatile pitcher-first baseman as an assistant coach because of his ability to steal the opposing team's signs.[5] However, Perry did not finish the 1949 season in Birmingham; he was sold to the Pacific Coast League's Oakland Oaks and had his first opportunity to prove himself in Organized Baseball at the Triple-A level. Black Barons owner Tom Hayes, who was selling off his top stars to fend off a financial crisis, received $5,000 for Perry.[6]

Perry had a short stay in Oakland, playing in only 12 games. The lanky pitcher-first baseman was used in much the same way as in Birmingham; he pitched in eight games, played two games at first base, and pinch-hit twice. On the mound, he made four starts, pitched a total of 33 innings, and lost his one decision.

Because of wildness, his 4.91 ERA was much higher than it had been as a Black Baron. The new Oak allowed more hits, 34, than innings pitched while both walking and striking out 20, and unleashing four wild pitches. His lackluster performance may have been a preview of the arm trouble that he developed after the season and which ended his pitching career. Perry's performance at the plate was not much better. In 15 at-bats, he managed only three hits (for a .200 batting average) and one RBI. The Oaks released him and he returned to the comfortable setting of Birmingham for the 1950 season.

After arm trouble ended his pitching career, Perry settled into being a full-time position player. He played primarily at first base but also strolled the outfield during the 1950 season, which was his last in the Negro Leagues. Playing in the field full-time suited him well; he displayed what became his forte: hitting. He batted .313 with 14 home runs and 64 RBIs. Perry was also named to the East-West All-Star Game, in which he started at first base and went 2-for-3.[7] (Only the Negro American League remained after the collapse of the Negro National League after the 1948 season, but the league's premier players continued to meet at Chicago's Comiskey Park and the participants were selected from the Eastern and Western divisions of the 10-team league.)

In 1950 Perry also became tied to a story about the "discovery" of Willie Mays. Over the years several variants of a story developed in which the Giants sent scout Eddie Montague to look at Perry because they needed a first baseman for their farm system; in doing so, he allegedly discovered Mays and signed both players.[8] However, James S. Hirsch's 2010 biography, *Willie Mays: The Life, The Legend*, which was authorized by Mays, had a different version. Although Montague was going to see Perry, Boston Braves scout Bill Maughn, a native of Alabama, who was unable to sign Mays because his front office did not agree with his assessment, told Montague to forget Perry and to "sign a young Negro player … with a great arm."[9] Montague knew that Perry wasn't his man and concentrated instead on getting Mays. He

Pitcher Alonzo Perry was 10-2 with the 1948 Black Barons. Later, as a slugging first baseman, he became a legend in Mexico and the Dominican Republic, where the Licey Tigres retired his number 5. (*Courtesy of Center for Negro League Baseball Research*)

ended up signing both players; with the veteran being assigned to Triple A for the 1951 season.

History has revealed all such stories to be apocryphal. The facts are that Giants owner Horace Stoneham and Black Barons owner Tom Hayes had reached an agreement in which Hayes would sell Mays's contract for $10,000, and Montague was dispatched to get Mays's signature on a contract. Montague's story about being in Birmingham solely to scout Perry was a smokescreen he used to prevent other scouts and teams from becoming savvy to the fact that the Giants already had Mays sewed up.[10]

Although Perry was originally designated to go to the San Francisco Seals of the Pacific Coast league for 1951, he was sold to the Syracuse Chiefs of the International League before the start of the season.

ALONSO PERRY

Alonzo Perry won the Puerto Rican League's 1948-49 championship with the Mayagüez Indios. Perry posted an 11-4 record with a 3.38 ERA and batted .303 with 9 homers and 64 RBIs. (*Courtesy of Jay-Dell Mah/Western Canada Baseball*)

At Syracuse he played in only nine games, going 5-for-18 (.278) with 3 RBIs before being released. The starting first baseman, Eddie Shokes, was hitting only .238 at the time, which made Perry's release a head-scratcher. It is possible that a defensive collision at first base in mid-May, in which the Chiefs pitcher was injured and the baserunner eventually scored the winning run, played a role.[11] In his short time with the team, Perry made history by becoming the first player to break the color line in Syracuse. Although Elston Howard was the first African-American to sign with the Chiefs, he went into the military and never played in Syracuse. Vic Power, who played the entire year with the team and faced the brunt of the abuse for being the first black Chief in 1951, was actually a dark-skinned Puerto Rican; thus, according to

the *Syracuse Herald Journal*, the honor goes to Perry, who played in only nine games.[12]

Like many former Negro Leaguers before him, Perry found another place willing to sign him so he could continue to play baseball in 1951. He first joined the Brandon Greys of the Man-Dak League, a Canadian league that became a refuge for Negro League ballplayers from the late 1940s to the middle 1950s. Displaying the hitting and power that would become his trademark wherever he played, the tall first baseman made quite the impression in his May 29 debut, clouting a home run, double, and two singles, with two walks, driving in three runs, and helping lead the Greys to an 8-6 victory over Elmwood. In a June 15 home rout of Carman, Perry slammed a homer that cleared the center-field fence and the avenue beyond. It was believed to be the first clout to clear the ballpark since 1933.[13] When he left the league after five weeks to play for more money in the Dominican Republic, he was hitting .389 with 28 hits, including five home runs. Perry also had two pitching appearances with no record.[14]

Perry's decision to play for the Licey Tigers of the Dominican Summer League was a great one; he thrived in Latin America, where he soon became a superstar. Licey's investment of a $1,500-per-month salary was quickly rewarded when Perry hit successfully in every game he played, a 25-game hitting streak that yielded a .400 average with 9 homers and 34 RBIs. His hot hitting carried over into the playoffs, and he delivered a hit in each of the seven games to stretch his streak to 32 games. He capped his 1951 season with a grand slam in the ninth inning of Game Seven to clinch the Summer League's championship for the Tigers.

Perry led the Tigers to another championship in 1953, and the new hero continued performing for Licey through 1954, the Summer League's last season before it converted to a winter league. For his four seasons with Licey, he batted .327 with a .592 slugging percentage while leading the league in home runs in 1951, 1952, and 1953; RBIs in 1952 and 1953; batting average in 1954; runs scored in 1954; and stolen bases in 1953.

Perry continued to play for Licey in the Winter League, starting with the 1954-55 season through 1958-59. The muscular slugger added another batting title (.332) in 1957-58 before finishing his Dominican career with the Estrellas Orientales in 1959-60. By the time he was through playing in the Dominican Republic, Perry held the league's career slugging record, .489, the second highest Licey Tigers career batting average at .317, and the fourth highest batting average in Dominican League history at .310. He also set Licey's career record with 45 home runs. The Tigers retired their star's number 5, and Perry, who was nicknamed "Su Majestad" (His Majesty) by the Dominican fans, received the ultimate honor when he was inducted posthumously into the Dominican Republic Sports Hall of Fame in 1995 for his "great merits as a baseball player."[15]

Winter ball was not new to Alonzo Perry when he joined Licey for the Dominican League's inaugural 1955-56 season; he had already played four seasons in the Puerto Rican Winter League. Like many black ballplayers, making a living on the diamond year-round was better money than the alternatives offered by the segregated American society of that time. In Puerto Rico Perry joined Artie Wilson's Mayagüez Indios, a team built around a core of Negro League players, which won the league's championship in the 1948-49 season. Perry, who was still pitching at the time, played a key role in the rotation by throwing 11 complete games and posting an 11-4 won-lost record; in 18 games his ERA was a respectable 3.38. Adding to his value was the fact that he was also one of the team's heavy hitters, belting nine home runs for a healthy .506 slugging percentage and knocking in 64 runs while batting .303.

Perry returned to Mayagüez in 1950-51. He could no longer pitch but had another solid year with the bat, hitting .333 with a .460 slugging percentage. In his last year with Mayagüez, 1951-52, he became the player-manager and continued to hit at a .323 clip, though his slugging percentage slipped to .442. Perry did not play winter ball in the following two years, but he returned to Puerto Rico with Ponce for the 1954-55 campaign after an opportunity to play for Martin Dihigo in the Mexican Winter League fell through. His season with Ponce turned out to be the worst of his career; he batted a meek .217 with only one homer while playing in 22 games.[16]

After the Dominican League changed to a winter format, Perry played summer ball in the Mexican League, where he had his greatest success and became a legend. In 1955, his first season with the Mexico City Red Devils, he thumped 21 homers and drove in 122 runs while batting .375, but he was just warming up. The 1956 season was the finest of his remarkable career as he led the Red Devils to the Mexican League championship and won the Triple Crown with 28 home runs, 118 RBIs, and a .392 batting average. As if that were not enough, he also topped the league in hits (177), doubles (33), triples (13), and runs scored (103).[17] The club's commanding record was 83-37 (a .692 winning percentage), and their first-year manager knew whom to credit for the successful season. *The Sporting News* wrote, "The domination of the Mexico City Reds in the pennant race south of the border represents a personal triumph for Manager Lazaro Salazar, who took over the club this season, but the Blue Prince would be the first to credit his success to the spectacular hitting of Alonzo Perry, the greatest slugger in the Mexican League since the days of the late Josh Gibson."[18] The comparison to the slugging prowess of Josh Gibson placed Alonzo Perry in the rarefied company of one of baseball's greatest sluggers.

Perry's Mexican moniker was "El Espiriton" (The Great or Honored One), and he continued to star with the Red Devils, leading the league in RBIs again in 1957. He retired after the 1959 season. During the last year in Mexico City, he suffered a broken finger that kept him out of the lineup for a time, but upon his return he resumed his power-hitting ways by punching four homers in two consecutive games.[19] Although he was a superstar, he was not untouchable and had his 1959 Cadillac seized by customs officials for failure to take the car out of Mexico before the expiration of the permit that allowed him to bring it into the country.[20] He finished the season with a .333 batting average that was second only to team-

Alonzo Perry and his son Alonzo Jr. The elder Perry played for Birmingham from mid-1946 through 1950; his son followed in his footsteps and played for the Black Barons in 1962. (*Courtesy of Center for Negro League Baseball Research*)

mate Al Pinkston's .369.[21] Mexico City finished the regular season in third place, but the Red Devils won the playoffs and placed the largest number of players (five) on the postseason all-star team, including first baseman Alonzo Perry.[22]

After the season, Perry remained in Mexico to be the player-manager for the Puebla Sweet Potatoes of the Vera Cruz Winter League. The skipper's only recorded pitching appearance after 1949 occurred in a Puebla game in 1959 in which three Puebla pitchers were shelled by the Cordoba Coffeemakers. Perry took the mound in the eighth inning with two runners on base and one out. He struck out the two hitters he faced to retire the side, then set down all three batters in order in the ninth to preserve a 9-7 victory.[23] Late in December, with the Sweet Potatoes in last place, sporting a 7-16 record, 9½ games off the pace, Perry stepped down as manager and was

replaced by Luis Molinero. He found it difficult to both manage and play.[24]

The Mexican League was struggling financially, so the Mexico City Reds, in an effort to save money, dumped salaries by releasing Perry and several other players. Perry quit baseball and retired.[25] However, it turned out that he was not yet done with Mexican League baseball after all. The Monterrey Sultanes brought him out of retirement for the 1962 championship run. El Espiriton had a successful comeback as he led Monterrey to a 77-53 record and the Mexican League title. In doing so, Perry led the League in RBIs (105) for the second time; he tied his rookie teammate, Hector Espino, on the last day of the season.[26] The strong first baseman also batted .316 and smacked 14 home runs. He returned for a final season in 1963 and went out in style by hitting for a .353 average with 17 homers and 90 RBIs. After the season, he retired again at age 40, finishing his

Mexican League career as one of its greatest hitters. As the player with the league's second highest career batting average (.355), he had become a legend in Mexico. He concluded his career south of the border with 1,107 hits, 128 home runs, and a .589 slugging percentage.

Negro League historians Dr. Layton Revel and Luis Munoz have speculated about why Perry never got an opportunity to play in the major leagues. First, he was making as much money playing south of the border as he would have earned in the major leagues. Second, playing in Latin America gave him status and celebrity without the racial discrimination he would have experienced in the United States; he did not have any issues with staying in the best hotels and eating at all restaurants. And finally, he may have fallen out of favor with Organized Baseball when he played in the Dominican League because it was considered an outlaw league.[27] James Riley cited additional reasons, stating, "Some scouts indicated that he lacked 'style' but his temperament and off-field activities might have been the real reason he was not signed by a major-league ballclub. He was often in trouble with the law, both while playing ball and after he retired from the diamond, and may have spent some 'hard time' as a result of his illegal activities."[28]

Away from baseball, Perry was married to Gladys Davis on March 21, 1942, in Birmingham. According to the marriage certificate, she was born in Phenix City, Alabama, on April 17, 1923, to Pastor Joe Davis and Viola Hawkins. Perry listed his birth year as 1922 on the license, thus adding a year to his age, perhaps in an effort to appear to be older than his bride. Alonzo and Gladys divorced in December 1951. Her obituary lists four children including Alonzo Jr. and Diane Perry Favors. Alonzo Perry Jr. followed in his father's footsteps and played first base for the Birmingham Black Barons in 1962 and with the Black Barons and Philadelphia Stars in 1963 and 1964 when they were barnstorming teams. Although he was a good hitter, he was not his father's equal. Junior, who was born on July 20, 1942, died at age 67 on September 23, 2009.

Perry died on October 13, 1982, at the age of 59. As Revel and Munoz have written, "When Alonzo Perry passed away … we lost one of the great black ballplayers of his era. Unfortunately most baseball fans in the United States never had the opportunity to see him play."[29]

Acknowledgment

Special thanks to SABR member Bill Mortell of Maryland, whose knowledge of Ancestry.com and research skills have proven invaluable in helping find information on Alonzo Perry.

NOTES

1   Dr. Layton Revel and Luis Munoz, *Forgotten Heroes Alonzo Perry*, Center for Negro League Research, 2009, cnlbr.org.

2   Ibid.

3   James A. Riley, *The Biographical Encyclopedia of the Negro League Baseball Leagues* (New York: Carroll & Graf Publishers, 1994), 620-621.

4   Willie Mays with Lou Sahadi, *Say Hey—The Autobiography of Willie Mays* (New York: Simon and Schuster, 1988), 39.

5   Larry Powell, *Black Barons of Birmingham: The South's Greatest Negro League Team and Its Players* (Jefferson, North Carolina: McFarland & Company, Inc., 2009), 149.

6   Powell, 56.

7   Revel and Munoz.

8   Willie Mays with Lou Sahadi, *Say Hey—The Autobiography of Willie Mays* (New York: Simon and Schuster, 1988), 44.

9   James S. Hirsch, *Willie Mays: The Life, The Legend* (New York: Scribner, 2010), 59-60.

10 John Klima, *Willie's Boys: The 1948 Birmingham Black Barons, the Last Negro League World Series, and the Making of a Baseball Legend* (Hoboken, New Jersey: John Wiley & Sons, Inc., 2009), 248-55.

11 Cy Kritzer, "International League," *The Sporting News*, May 16, 1951: 26.

12 Matt Michael, "Who Broke the Color Line for the Chiefs in 1951?," *Syracuse Herald Journal*, February 6, 1997

13 attheplate.com/wcbl/1951.

14 Ibid. I used the statistics from attheplate.com because of the detail it had on Perry's brief stay in Canada. But Revel and Munoz had a different batting average for Perry with him leading the league in hitting at .397 with 19 RBIs when he left. Like attheplate.com, they had him with five homers. It is possible the difference could be caused by what games they

recorded or missed at the end of his stay before he left for the Dominican Republic.

15 William F. McNeil, *Black Baseball Out of Season*, (Jefferson, North Carolina: McFarland & Company, Inc., 2007), 152

16 Revel and Munoz.

17 Riley, 620-621.

18 Miguel Calzadilla, "Mexican League," *The Sporting News*, August 22, 1956: 39.

19 Roberto Hernandez, "Mexican League," *The Sporting News*, July 29, 1959: 33.

20 Ibid.

21 Roberto Hernandez, "Mexican League," *The Sporting News*, September 16, 1959: 33.

22 Roberto Hernandez, "Mexican League," *The Sporting News*, October 21, 1959: 21.

23 Roberto Hernandez, "Mexican League," *The Sporting News*, December 9, 1959: 22

24 Roberto Hernandez, "Mexican League," *The Sporting News*, December 30, 1959: 25.

25 Johnny Janes, "Don't Quote Me," *San Antonio Express*, April 22, 1960: 1-B.

26 *The Sporting News*, August 25, 1962: 39.

27 Ibid.

28 Riley, 620-621.

29 Revel and Munoz.

NAT POLLARD

By Jay Hurd

The year was 1865, and the Civil War had ended. Northern and Southern states now faced the overwhelming task of rebuilding physical, political, cultural, and emotional infrastructure. Hundreds of thousands of human lives had been lost, physical resources depleted, and the ideal of hope challenged. The state of Alabama was not immune to the repercussions of war, and by the early twentieth century faced a failing agriculture—in particular, cotton production—and a struggling economy. Farm laborers, and others, in need of employment turned to the expanding coal, iron, steel, and limestone industries. Communities arose around the coal mines. Here families lived, worked, attended school and church, and found respite in recreational activities provided by the coal-mining companies. Baseball became one of the activities promoted by the companies and, appreciating the high level of play, it was not long before amateur and semipro industrial leagues appeared. Out of these leagues came players who would go on to careers—some long, some brief—with organized professional baseball in the Negro Leagues and the white major leagues. One of these players was pitcher Nat Pollard.

Nathaniel Hawthorne "Nat" Pollard[1] was born to Hubert and Cora (McKinney) Pollard on January 24, 1915. His birthplace, Alabama City—a "populated place" in the city of Gadsden—is approximately 65 miles northeast of Birmingham and 100 miles northeast of Piper, the mining community where his family lived and worked. Nat attended school in Piper until he was 15 years old and had completed his second year at the Piper-Coleanor High School. Nat showed athletic ability in basketball and baseball. In a path similar to that of Lorenzo "Piper" Davis, who also grew up in Piper, Nat's baseball skill drew the attention of industrial league teams, including the two top teams, American Cast and Pipe Company

(ACIPCO) and the Stockham Valve and Fittings Company. Nat played with each of these teams.[2] Although he is likely to have played other positions, his primary position was pitcher.

The 1940 US Federal Census shows that Nat lived with his wife, Josie (Moore) Pollard, in the "populated place" called Six Mile, in Bibb County—about 50 miles southwest of Birmingham and 10 miles to the southeast of Piper, where he worked in the coal mines. The census record indicates that he, Josie, Nathaniel (son, six months), and Sarah Hughes (niece, age 15) rented their home for $6 per month while he earned $680 per year as a laborer, based on 34 weeks of work. The records also show that Josie died that same year in September, at the age of 19. Nat continued to work and to play baseball.

In his book *Willie's Boys: The 1948 Birmingham Black Barons, the Last Negro League World Series, and the Making of a Baseball Legend*, John Klima refers to the term "hot box" as describing, in general, a difficult or delicate situation; a baseball player in a baserunning predicament; or, more specifically, the immense challenges of segregation and poverty.[3] Baseball became for some—black and white—the means out of the "hot box" of life in the coal mines. Author Chris Fullerton wrote that "[b]aseball was about the only aspect of industrial life in which black labor not only knew the score, but actually stood a chance of coming out on top."[4]

Pollard's industrial-league career appears to have begun with Stockham Valve and Fittings in 1940.[5] Although he was two years younger than Pollard, Piper Davis's name appears on the roster of the ACIPCO team as early as 1939 while Pollard's name does not appear until 1941; and on the 1942 ACIPCO roster, in one of the variations of the spelling of his first name, he is identified as Nate Pollard.[6] By 1942 Nat's pitching skill—his arm was "strengthened" by "years spent chucking coal ... to the point where it

Pitcher Nat Pollard, like many of his Black Barons teammates, got his start in Birmingham's industrial leagues. Though injured for much of 1948, he did appear in World Series Game Four against Homestead. (*Courtesy R. D. Retort Enterprises*)

matched his surly disposition"[7] — became more evident when he posted a team-best 20-1 record with 12 shutouts that season. His batting average, apparently never very high, was .256.[8] In 1943 he was a member of the ACIPCO team known as the "Best Industrial League team of all-time";[9] that team boasted a 28-0 league record and a 49-1 record overall. Nat again led his team in victories with a 16-0 record. A teammate, pitcher Earl Little, also was undefeated that year, posting a 13-0 record. Pollard and Little combined for the two wins, by scores of 9-5 and 8-2, needed to claim the 1943 Birmingham Industrial League title.

After the 1943 season with ACIPCO, Nat's name was added to the Birmingham Black Barons roster alongside those of ACIPCO teammates Piper Davis, Herman Bell, Ed Steele, Sam Hairston, and Artie Wilson. However, the United States had been in World War II since December 1941, and the need for additional military manpower led Nat to military service in 1944. His service time is known to be 1944-1945. One account says he served in the Army.[10] But three other sources, the Veterans Affairs Beneficiary Identification Records Locator Subsystem Death File,[11] a 2008 piece on a Lawson State College scholarship created in his honor,[12] and a book by David Finoli[13] all indicate that he served in the Navy with the rating of steward's mate 3rd class. As was typical of the time, a black man in the Navy often served as a steward (until 1943 known as a "mess attendant.")[14] Whether or not Pollard played baseball during his time in the military is not apparent, but he and his arm were ready for a 1946 return to Alabama and the Birmingham Black Barons. At the age of 31 he rejoined teammates Piper Davis, Ed Steele, Artie Wilson, and new manager Tommy Sampson.

Pollard, a right-handed pitcher known for his fine curveball, was 5-feet-10 and listed at 175 pounds. The 1946 season saw him win two games, with no losses. He pitched 22 innings, gave up 11 hits and 2 walks, and struck out 11. He had two complete games and gave up no runs.[15] In 1947 he returned to the Black Barons, still managed by Tommy Sampson. Pollard was the starting and losing pitcher for the Barons in the first game of the season, on May 4, 1947, vs. the Cleveland Buckeyes at League Park in Cleveland.[16] He pitched three complete games that season, winning two and losing one. In 44 innings of work Pollard gave up 47 hits and 22 runs, walked 10 and struck out 16.[17]

In 1947 Willie Mays, 16 years old, began play—appearing in weekend home games only—with the Black Barons. Piper Davis knew Mays's father, William Howard "Cat" Mays, and saw the enormous ability in Willie. Piper promised Cat that he would do whatever he could to help Willie develop his talent while insulating him from negative influences. Nat Pollard became one of Piper's resources in fulfilling his promise.[18] Nat, also known as "The Prophet"[19] due to his regular quoting of Scripture, often remained close to Mays to evade the carousing, womanizing, and drinking habits of other players. While the young Willie Mays contributed to a Negro American League pennant-winning season in 1948, Pollard was injured much of that year and not able to pitch. A photo from that season shows Pollard dressed for attendance at church and a baseball game at Birmingham's Rickwood Field. He appears in tie and fedora and is sitting despondently in the stands.[20] He played in only eight games that year, including an appearance in the fourth game of the World Series which the Barons lost to the Homestead Grays, 14-1. Pollard, William Greason (Game Three winner), Jehosie Heard, and Jimmy Newberry pitched in the loss to Wilmer Fields, giving up nine hits and eight runs. Pollard had only one plate appearance with no hits.[21] His team had failed to win the World Series, losing three games to one, but Nat's role as a positive influence and guiding hand for Mays was indispensable.

Nat again appears on the Black Barons roster in 1949, not as a pitcher, but as road secretary.[22] Perhaps his injury-plagued 1948 season, his age, and years as a laborer combined to keep his pitching appearances to a minimum through the 1949 and 1950 seasons. In 1950 his name does appear as the starting and winning pitcher in a game vs. the Greensboro Red Birds.[23] He surrendered eight hits and only one run and was relieved in the 10th inning by Bill Powell, who completed the game. In 1950 Pollard appeared in 13 games, surrendered 93 hits and 41 runs, walked 27, and struck out 41. He finished his season, and career, with a 7-3 record.[24]

Pollard was proud to play baseball and to be with the Black Barons. He said, "Your uniform was about the best thing you had and you thought you were something when you had it on. You looked good and the people were out there to see you, and that's what made you want to play."[25]

He performed on the pitcher's mound with competitive grace, pleased to be there when he could

Birmingham pitcher Nat Pollard (front right) was injured for much of the 1948 season, and his misery was evident as he became part of the crowd for a Sunday afternoon game at Rickwood Field. (*Courtesy of Memphis Public Library*)

and disappointed when he could not. Pollard was as happy for his teammates when they succeeded as he was for himself when he did well. When white scouts from the Boston Red Sox appeared at a Black Barons game in 1949, it was—as Piper Davis recalls—Nat who told him, "Hey, some scouts out here want to see you."[26] Pollard appears to have had the gift of positive encouragement all of his life as, on April 1, 2008, at Lawson State Community College in Birmingham, he received posthumous accolades from US Air Force Lieutenant Colonel Leernest Ruffin as a mentor for himself and other Birmingham natives.[27]

Nathaniel Pollard completed his Negro American League career playing with only one team, the Birmingham Black Barons. His name appears, again as Nate, on the Black Barons' 1962 roster.[28] After baseball "The Prophet" turned to the Christian ministry and attended Birmingham (Alabama) Baptist College and Samford University, a Christian university in Homewood, Alabama.

Nat Pollard died on November 23, 1996, in Dolomite, Alabama. A funeral service was conducted in Ensley, Alabama, on November 30 (his name spelled Nathanael), and he was buried in George Washington Carver Memorial Gardens in Birmingham.[29]

NOTES

1   Regarding Nat Pollard's name, variations in the spelling of his first name/nicknames include Nathaniel, Nathanel, Nathanael, Nat, Nate, NH, N.H.

2   Larry Powell, *The Birmingham Black Barons: The South's Greatest Team and Its Players* (Jefferson, North Carolina: McFarland and Company, Inc., Publishers, 2009), 95.

3   John Klima, *Willie's Boys: The 1948 Birmingham Black Barons, the Last Negro League World Series, and the Making of a Baseball Legend* (Hoboken, New Jersey: John Wiley & Sons, Inc., 2009), 9.

4   Chris Fullerton, "Industrial Ball," *Birmingham-Pittsburgh Traveler,* northbysouth.kenyon.edu/2000/baseball/Industrial%20ball.htm, last accessed October 10, 2016.

5   "NEGRO LEAGUE Player Register," *Center for Negro League Baseball Research,* cnlbr.org/Portals/0/Players%20Register/O-Q%202016-08.pdf, last accessed October 10, 2016.

6   "American Cast Iron and Pipe (ACIPCO)," *Negro Southern League Museum,* negrosouthernleaguemuseumresearchcenter.org/Portals/0/Birmingham%20Industrial%20League/ACIPCO.pdf, last accessed October 10, 2016.

7   Klima, 9.

8   "American Cast Iron and Pipe (ACIPCO)."

9   Ibid.

10   Gary Bedingfield, *Baseball in Wartime,* baseballinwartime.com/, last accessed October 10, 2016.

11   "N. Pollard in the US Department of Veterans Affairs BIRLS Death File, 1850-2010," *Ancestry.com,* search.ancestry.com/cgi-bin/sse.dll?indiv=try&db=VADeaths&h=8464299, last accessed October 10, 2016.

12   Geri Albright, "Lawson State Alumnus Establishes Scholarship," *Lawson State College News,* April 15, 2008, lawsonstate.edu/Articles/lawson_state_alumnus_establishes_scholarship.aspx, last accessed October10, 2016.

13   David Finoli, *For God and Country: World War II Baseball in the Major and Minor Leagues* (Jefferson, North Carolina: McFarland & Company, Inc., Publishers, 2002), 297.

14   *"Uniforms and Insignia United States," U.S. Navy, World War II Enlisted Rates: Messman/Steward Branch,* uniform-reference.net/insignia/usn/usn_ww2_enl_steward.html, last accessed October 10, 2016.

15   "Nat Pollard," Baseball Reference, *baseball-reference.com/register/player.cgi?id=pollar0oonat.* We realize that these statistics are most likely incomplete.

16   Christopher Hauser, *The Negro League Chronology: Events in Organized Black Baseball, 1920-1948* (Jefferson, North Carolina: McFarland & Company, Inc., Publishers, 2006), 156.

17   "Nat Pollard."

18   Klima, 110.

19   Klima, 109.

20   Klima, 86.

21   "Nat Pollard."

22   "Hot Off the Baseball Griddle, Piper Davis Picks Black Barons Squad," *Kansas Plain Dealer* (Kansas City, Kansas), April 8, 1949: Vol. .l51, Issue14, 4. genealogybank.com/doc/newspapers/image/v2%3A12ACD7C7734164EC%40GB3NEWS-12C5685637D7C2D8%402433015-12C568565D691550%403-12C568574BCB2270?folder=true&search_terms=pollard%7Cnathaniel, last accessed October 10, 2016.

23   "Barons Turn Back Red Birds," *Greensboro* (North Carolina) *Daily News* July 12, 1950: 13.

genealogybank.com/doc/newspapers/image/v2%3A11EA68DA9EC1533C%40GB3NEWS-149285534055F77C%402433475-1490845343924E83%4012-, last accessed October 10, 2016.

24   "Birmingham Black Barons: Negro National League 1929-1958," *Negro Southern Leagues Museum,* negrosouthernleaguemuseumresearchcenter.org/Portals/0/Birmingham%20Black%20Barons/Statistics%20-%20Birmingham%20Black%20Barons.pdf, last accessed October 12, 2016.

25   "Birmingham Black Barons: All-time Roster," *Barons.Com Official Site of the Birmingham Barons,* milb.com/content/page.jsp?ymd=20080419&content_id=41116560&sid=t247&vkey=team4, last accessed October 10, 2016.

26   Klima, 211.

27   Geri Albright, "Lawson State Alumnus Establishes Scholarship," *Lawson State College News,* April 15, 2008, http://www.lawsonstate.edu/Articles/lawson_state_alumnus_establishes_scholarship.aspx, last accessed October10, 2016.

28   "Rosters—Negro American League (1958-1962)," *Center for Negro League Baseball Research, http://www.cnlbr.org/Portals/0/Rosters/Rosters%20-%20Negro%20American%20League%20(1958-1962).pdf*

29   Leslie Heaphy, *The Negro Leagues 1869-1960* (Jefferson, North Carolina: McFarland & Company, Inc., Publishers, 2003), 340.

BILL POWELL

By Mark Panuthos and Frederick C. Bush

William H. Powell is not a household name like Jackie Robinson, Larry Doby, or Satchel Paige. He never matriculated into the majors, is not listed in the pantheon of Negro League greats, and failed to acquire a nickname other than Bill. He had a good fastball and claimed, "I was the hardest-throwing pitcher on the team" [Birmingham Black Barons], though he was not noted as a strikeout artist.[1] While statistical accounting in the Negro Leagues and in some minor leagues is notoriously sketchy — at times incomplete and often contradictory between sources –Powell is probably the most underrated, underappreciated, and least-known pitcher who may have won as many as 250 games over the course of his Negro League, minor-league, and winter-league careers.

In looking back on his lengthy career, Powell consistently maintained two narratives throughout his numerous interviews. The first was that, despite the rigors of bus travel through the segregated South in the mid-1940s and early 1950s, his memories of his times with the Black Barons were mostly positive. He recalled, "It was tough then, man: Segregation was bad." Some restaurants refused to serve him and his teammates but over the years they found others that would. They developed something of a network of "mom's restaurants." "If they knowed we was coming," he explained, they would send customers away, explaining that "We don't have any more food," and provide the Black Barons with "good, home-cooked food."[2] The other consistent theme was that he took great pride in his pitching acumen. He once noted, in all sincerity, that he "was the winningest pitcher just about everywhere" he went.[3]

William Henry "Bill" Powell was born on May 8, 1919, to Jim and Thelma Watson Powell in Comer, Georgia.[4] Little is known about his family, but they moved to Birmingham, Alabama, when he was 9

years old.[5] By age 15, Powell started to play baseball in a Birmingham YMCA League. At 17 he was playing semipro baseball for the Twenty-sixth Street Red Sox, and then he played for the well-known American Cast Iron Pipe Company (ACIPCO) team in Birmingham's Industrial League while working in the company's factory.[6]

As was the case with many baseball players in both white and black leagues, World War II took some years off Powell's career. In 1942 he was drafted into the US Army, and he served through the end of 1945. While in the military, Powell played for his unit's baseball team, presumably as a pitcher. After his discharge he returned to Birmingham and received offers to play baseball from several semipro and professional teams. Powell ultimately opted in favor of his hometown Black Barons, for whom he played from 1946 through 1950, when he had a falling-out with owner Tom Hayes.[7]

In his 1946 rookie season with the Black Barons, Powell is credited with posting a 4-5 mound ledger.[8] His performance in 1947 began to garner attention for the 6-foot-2-inch, 195-pound right-hander as he completed the Negro American League regular season with a perfect 7-0 record; Powell, who understandably also liked to count nonleague games in his total, claimed a total of 19 victories for the season.[9]

As the 1948 season began, the Black Barons had high hopes for claiming the NAL pennant, and Powell received the assignment to start the league opener against the defending champion Cleveland Buckeyes on May 1 in front of 8,000 frenzied fans at Birmingham's Rickwood Field. He did not disappoint as he pitched a complete game to earn the win in Birmingham's 11-2 triumph.[10]

Powell and the Black Barons were off and running. On May 16 he pitched seven-hit ball in a 5-0 shutout victory over the Indianapolis Clowns in Birmingham; the press noted, "It was the third league triumph and

BILL POWELL

Bill Powell in a Ponce (Puerto Rico) Leones uniform in 1949. He soon joined the Mayagüez Indios and earned the win in the first-ever game won by a Puerto Rican team in the Caribbean Series. (*Courtesy of Jay-Dell Mah/Western Canada Baseball*)

the first shutout for the lanky mound star who fanned eight Clowns."[11] Less than a week later, on May 20, he victimized the Clowns again, this time pitching no-hit ball for 6⅔ innings before settling for an 8-4 complete-game win at Victory Field in Indianapolis.[12]

By June, Powell had a 5-0 record that was tops among all NAL pitchers. Dating back to the previous season, he was 12-0 in league play over almost 1½ seasons, and the press began to extol his virtues:

"Big league material, Powell has speed, savvy, confidence in himself and his teammates. His swift breaking curve ball can be carefully delivered from many angles as his strikeout ball. His sole weakness is in bases on balls, arising from the fact that he is a 'spot' pitcher. Above all, Powell does not ruffle under

adverse conditions, for he is at his best with men on base."[13]

The Black Barons won the NAL's first-half championship. On July 20 they had a 42-16 record in league play and, according to the Howe News Bureau, were tops in the NAL in team hitting, team fielding, and team pitching.[14] At that point in the season, it was noted, "Bill Powell is the leading man in the pitching department with 10 wins and one loss."[15]

Birmingham's "leading man" was selected as the starting pitcher for the West team in the first of that season's two East-West All-Star Games, which was played at Chicago's Comiskey Park on August 22. Though two East-West Games were played some years—the second game in 1948 was held at Yankee Stadium on August 24—the Comiskey Park game was the highlight of every Negro League season and drew the largest crowds. In front of 42,099 spectators, Powell earned the win by pitching three scoreless innings in the West's 3-0 triumph; he allowed one hit, walked one batter, and uncorked a wild pitch while also registering two strikeouts.[16]

The Kansas City Monarchs won the NAL's second-half championship and faced the Black Barons to determine who would represent the league in the Negro League World Series. Powell, who had finished the season with an 11-3 record and a 3.81 ERA in league play, started two games in the hard-fought series.[17] In Game Three, played on September 15 at Martin Field in Memphis, Tennessee, Powell pitched a complete game and earned the victory when left fielder Jim Zapp hit a two-run homer in the bottom of the ninth inning to win the game, 4-3.[18]

Powell started the official Game Six—the September 20 game had been rained out, ruled a tie, and would not be made up—on September 22 at Kansas City's Blues Stadium. He took a 3-2 lead into the ninth inning but began to tire, allowing the first two Monarchs to reach base. Birmingham manager Piper Davis sent Jimmie Newberry to the mound in relief, a move that backfired when Hank Thompson clouted Newberry's first pitch for a three-run, game-winning homer that saddled Powell with the loss and tied the series at three games apiece. Birmingham claimed the NAL pennant with a 5-1 victory the next day and faced the Homestead Grays in what became the last Negro League World Series.

Powell started Game Two of the World Series on September 29 at Rickwood Field. The Black Barons struck first and gave their starter a quick 2-0 lead. Powell protected the lead until the top of the sixth inning, when the bottom fell out and he allowed all five Grays runs in what became a 5-3 loss. On October 5 Powell took the mound in Game Five at Rickwood Field with the Black Barons in need of a win to extend the series. The Grays struck for two runs in the first inning of what became a back-and-forth game. Powell lasted five innings and surrendered no additional runs, but the Grays prevailed, 10-6, in 10 innings to capture the championship.

The 1948 Negro League World Series provides a watershed moment in black baseball history; it was the last of its kind. Jackie Robinson's ascension into the majors in 1947 had initiated the pilfering of the best Negro League players by major- and minor-league franchises, which led to the Negro Leagues' eventual demise. Though he could not have known it at the time, Powell would go down in history as one of the two starting pitchers in the last-ever Negro League World Series game.

Although Birmingham did not win the World Series in 1948, it had been a successful season for the team and for Powell personally. Of the three Black Barons pitchers who registered more than 120 innings pitched in 1948, Powell finished second in wins (Newberry led with 14, though he pitched 12 more games), second in winning percentage at .786 (having pitched 10 more innings than Alonzo Perry, whose 10-2 record led all pitchers with an .833 percentage), and second in ERA at 3.81 (to Newberry's outstanding 2.18).[19]

The 1948 season was also the first of three that marked Powell and young Willie Mays as teammates on the Black Barons. A half-century later, Powell gave a humorous description of Mays while acknowledging him as the greatest player he had ever seen, saying, "Willie Mays. He's the best. I ain't never seen a ballplayer like that in my life. When he was comin'

up, a li'l ol' boy, his pants was too big for him, the bat was too heavy."[20] In spite of the fact that Mays did not look the part of a professional ballplayer at age 17 in 1948, Powell always told stories about how amazed he had been by Mays's speed in the outfield and his strong arm.

The Negro National League disbanded after the 1948 World Series, and the NAL absorbed four of the former NNL teams and realigned itself into two five-team divisions. The Black Barons played the 1949 season as members of the NAL's Western division, which was won by the Monarchs; Birmingham finished in third place with a 45-39 record.[21] Powell posted an 11-11 record with a 3.61 ERA and led the Black Barons staff in innings pitched (182) and strikeouts (124).

Though the 1949 season resulted in an average record for Powell on the field, he had a stellar off-field moment when he married Odessa Leon Perry on June 20. Powell later related the story of how the couple met:

> "She used to come to the ballpark with Piper's wife 'cause Piper was her brother-in-law, and when she came home from school breaks she watched me two years. I said, 'You been sittin' in that ballpark watchin' me for two years.' I said, 'What did you want with me out of all them fine doctors and lawyers?' She said, 'I don't know. I loved you.' We stayed together 47 years [until Odessa's death on June 28, 1997]."[22]

Powell also began to pitch in the winter leagues in 1949. He explained, "[I]f you're a good pitcher, they get you in the winter time to play overseas."[23] Powell first pitched for Puerto Rico's Ponce and Mayagüez teams in the 1948-49 season, registering a 7-6 record and 2.83 ERA.[24] In the inaugural Caribbean Series, in 1949, he earned the only win for Mayagüez and thereby recorded the first Caribbean Series win by a Puerto Rican team. In 1951, Powell pitched 3⅓ innings of one game for the Santurce Crabbers, which was enough to make him a participant on Puerto Rico's first Caribbean Series-winning team.[25] He also

Birmingham's Bill Powell was the starter for the West team in the All-Star Game at Comiskey Park on August 22, 1948. He pitched three scoreless innings to earn the win as the West prevailed 3-0. (*Noir-Tech Research, Inc.*)

pitched in the Cuban Winter League in 1949-50 (1-4, 5.03 ERA for Marianao) and 1952-53 (3-2, 3.86 ERA for Cienfuegos).[26]

In 1950, both Powell and the Black Barons team rebounded with fine seasons. Powell finished at 15-4 with a 3.00 ERA and again led the squad in innings pitched (162) and strikeouts (110).[27] The Black Barons' record in NAL play that year was 52-25-1, a .675 winning percentage, but the team finished second to the Monarchs in the NAL Western Division.[28] Powell had pitched well enough to be selected to participate in the East-West All-Star Game for the second time in his career. He returned to Comiskey Park for the August 20 game (there was only one that year) and again pitched three innings. This time, however, he pitched the final three innings, rather than the first three as he had in 1948, and allowed one run as his West team prevailed, 5-3. Another sign of the Negro Leagues' continuing decline was that only 24,614 fans

were in attendance in 1950, compared with the 42,099 who had been on hand at Comiskey Park in 1948.[29]

After his stellar 1950 campaign for the Black Barons, Powell got the attention of Organized Baseball but could not find a team. According to Powell, the Reds, the White Sox, and even the Dodgers all wanted him, but the major-league contract never came. "All of 'em was after me," he told interviewer Brent Kelley, "but I don't know, they just looked me over."[30] He ended up spending the next three years, 1951-53, playing for teams affiliated with the Chicago White Sox. In 1951 he signed a contract with the Sacramento Solons of the Triple-A Pacific Coast League, where he lost his only decision and was soon optioned to the Class-A Colorado Sky Sox, for whom he posted a 14-8 record with a 4.69 ERA and 157 strikeouts.[31]

Powell split the 1952 season between Toledo and Charleston of the Triple-A American Association.[32] It was a disastrous campaign in which he finished 5-15 with a 5.09 ERA.[33] Once again, however, he rebounded with a 14-9 record and 3.06 ERA for the Charleston Senators in 1953.[34] A game account of Charleston's 2-0 victory over the Indianapolis Indians on September 4 touted Powell's four-hit pitching "before the largest crowd [7,163] in the Senators' short American Association history."[35]

In 1954 Powell pitched well enough to get the attention of the Cincinnati Reds, who signed him to participate in their spring-training camp; however, he was optioned after spring training. Consequently, Powell split the 1954 season between the Triple-A International League's Toronto Maple Leafs and the Havana Sugar Kings, going a combined 10-8 for the season and posting a 4.23 ERA.[36] At Toronto, he played alongside Sam "Jet" Jethroe and pitched to Elston Howard, the first African-American to play for the New York Yankees. In 1955 Powell began the season with Havana, where he was 3-4 with a 5.28 ERA before returning to Charleston for a second stint there. He did not fare much better with the Senators, going 3-10 and 5.15 to give him a season totals of 6-14 and 5.19.[37]

Powell started the 1956 season with the same lack of success he had experienced the previous year, going 1-3 with a 5.74 ERA for the San Antonio Missions of the Double-A Texas League. He moved down to Class-A ball and finished the season with the Savannah Redlegs for whom he went 8-12 but with a much-improved 3.14 ERA.[38] Powell was still with Savannah at the outset of 1957, but he jumped the team to join the Nuevo Laredo Tecolotes of the Mexican League. He finished his sole season in Mexico with a 3-7 record and a 3.96 ERA.[39] The following season was the last in which Powell logged considerable playing time. He was 39 years old in 1958, when he posted a 7-8 record with a 3.70 ERA in 141 innings for the Class-A Knoxville Smokies.[40]

Powell made one appearance for the Class-A Asheville Tourists in 1959, but spent the majority of the year and all of 1960 away from Organized Baseball. In the fall of 1960, he was a member of a barnstorming team. On November 5 he was the winning pitcher as the American League Negro All-Stars defeated their National League counterparts, 7-6, at Spar Stadium in Shreveport, Louisiana. Powell gave up nine hits and all six runs in earning a complete-game victory.[41] In 1961 he attempted a comeback with the Class-A Charlotte Hornets, but after he posted a 1-1 record with a 5.62 ERA over 24 innings, his professional baseball career was over.[42]

Powell remained remarkably injury-free for most of his career, which is especially impressive given the fact that he pitched for 15 seasons. Given his total time in baseball and the fact that he sometimes played year-round, it is possible that Powell did in fact win 250 or more games. Had his early development not been hindered by three years of wartime service, he might have developed into a true major-league prospect. As it stands, Powell expressed that he never had any regrets about his career and would have done it all over again.[43]

Bill and Odessa Powell spent the remainder of their lives together in Birmingham. Powell adored his wife, saying, "She made me. You won't see two people married like we were. She was a teacher and I had no kind of formal education."[44] They never had children,

apparently because Odessa was unable to bear any, but Powell was pragmatic about that circumstance, revealing, "That use to hurt me so bad, but I found out there's thousands and thousands of women don't have children."[45]

After his baseball career ended, Powell found work as a sales representative for the Schlitz Brewing Company. He eventually retired from Schlitz as a sales supervisor in 1987.[46] Bill Powell died on August 21, 2004, and was buried beside his beloved Odessa in Birmingham's Elmwood Cemetery.

SOURCES

The game accounts of the 1948 NAL Playoffs and World Series were provided through the research done by SABR members Japheth Knopp and Rich Puerzer, who have written articles on those respective series, and from descriptions in John Klima's book *Willie's Boys: The 1948 Birmingham Black Barons, the Last Negro League World Series, and the Making of a Baseball Legend* (Hoboken, New Jersey: John Wiley & Sons, Inc., 2009).

NOTES

1   Brent Kelley, *The Negro Leagues Revisited: Conversations with 66 More Baseball Heroes* (Jefferson, North Carolina: McFarland, 2000), 219.

2   Kelley, 217.

3   Kelley, 216.

4   The year 1926 can be found listed as Powell's birth year in a number of sources; however, Powell's marriage certificate lists his age as 30 at the time of his marriage in June 1949. His obituary also gives 1919 as his birth year.

5   Larry Powell, *Black Barons of Birmingham: The South's Greatest Negro League Team and Its Players* (Jefferson, North Carolina: McFarland, 2009), 151. As is the case with Powell's birth year, there is also a discrepancy over his birthplace, with some sources listing it as West Birmingham, Alabama; however, Comer, Georgia, is given as his place of birth on his marriage certificate. His father, Jim Powell, had been born on July 5, 1888, in Georgia (where exactly is unknown) and died in July 1975 in Birmingham, Alabama. Bill Powell had at least one sibling, a sister named Mary Elizabeth, who was still living at the time of his death; it is unknown whether he had other siblings who preceded him in death.

6   Kelley, 215.

7   Ibid.

8   James A. Riley, *The Biographical Encyclopedia of the Negro Baseball Leagues* (New York: Carroll and Graf Publishers Inc., 1994), 640.

9 "Bill Powell Sparkling for Birmingham Club on Mound," *Pittsburgh Courier*, June 5, 1948: 15. The 7-0 record comes from the contemporaneous *Courier* article. Both James A. Riley and *The Negro Leagues Book*, edited by Dick Clark and Larry Lester (Cleveland: SABR, 1994), 329, give his record as 5-0.

10 "Birmingham Wins Opener Before 8,000," *Pittsburgh Courier*, May 8, 1948: 15.

11 "Birmingham Rolls Over Clowns Twice," *Pittsburgh Courier*, May 22, 1948: 14.

12 "Barons Protect Early Lead to Top Clowns," *Pittsburgh Courier*, May 21, 1948: 29.

13 Emory O. Jackson, "Bill Powell Rated Best Top Hurler in America," *Indianapolis Recorder*, June 5, 1948: 11.

14 "Barons, First Half Negro Champions, Here Thursday," *Newark (Ohio) Advocate*, July 20, 1948: 8.

15 Ibid.

16 Larry Lester, *Black Baseball's National Showcase: The East-West All-Star Game, 1933-1953* (Lincoln: University of Nebraska Press, 2001), 313.

17 Kelley, 220.

18 Two items are worth noting about this game: 1) It was held in Memphis because Rickwood Field was being used by the minor-league Birmingham Barons, and 2) After the passage of almost a half-century of time, Powell's memory of the game was a bit faulty. In his interview with Brent Kelley, he remembered the NAL playoff series as the World Series, the score of this game as 3-2, and this game as the clincher. He did remember correctly that the game was won on Zapp's home run in the bottom of the ninth. (See Kelley, 218).

19 "Birmingham Black Barons," The Negro Southern League Museum Research Center, negrosouthernleaguemuseumresearchcenter.org/Portals/0/Birmingham%20Black%20Barons/Statistics%20-%20Birmingham%20Black%20Barons.pdf, accessed November 19, 2016-March 11, 2017.

20 Ben Cook, "Willie Powell Interview," 1995, Birmingham Public Library Digital Collections, cdm16044.contentdm.oclc.org/cdm/ref/collection/p15099coll2/id/7, accessed March 11, 2017.

21 "League and Black Barons Team Standings," The Negro Southern League Museum Research Center, *negrosouthernleaguemuseumresearchcenter.org/Portals/0/Birmingham%20Black%20Barons/League%20and%20Black%20Barons%20Team%20Standings.pdf*, accessed March 11, 2017.

22 Kelley, 219. Bill and Odessa Powell were actually married for 48 years (June 20, 1949 — June 28, 1997).

23 Kelley, 216.

24 Riley, 640.

25 Jorge S. Figueredo, *Cuban Baseball: A Statistical History, 1878-1961* (Jefferson, North Carolina: McFarland, 2003), 346.

26 Figueredo, 327, 371.

27 "Birmingham Black Barons," The Negro Southern League Museum Research Center.

28 "League and Black Barons Team Standings," The Negro Southern League Museum Research Center.

29 Lester, 349.

30 Kelley, 217.

31 Kelley, 220.

32 Powell is listed on the Black Barons' 1952 roster in several sources—including Riley's and Kelley's books and the Negro Southern League Museum Research Center's website—but no verification for his return to the team for part of that season can be located. Powell himself said that he and owner Tom Hayes had a falling out in 1950 (see Kelley, 215), so it seems unlikely that he would have returned to the team. The only available statistics from 1952 show Powell to have been in the minor leagues that year.

33 "Bill Powell," Baseball-Reference.com, http://www.baseball-reference.com/register/player.fcgi?id=powello06wil, accessed March 11, 2017.

34 Ibid.

35 "Sens Blank Hoosiers," *Louisville (Kentucky) Courier-Journal*, September 4, 1953: 38.

36 "Bill Powell," Baseball-Reference.com.

37 Ibid.

38 Ibid.

39 Pedro Treto Cisneros, *The Mexican League: Comprehensive Player Statistics, 1937-2001* (Jefferson, North Carolina: McFarland, 2002), 477.

40 "Bill Powell," Baseball-Reference.com.

41 Bill Baker, "By 7-6 Count, American League Gets Nod in Exhibition Here, *Shreveport Times*, November 6, 1960: 50.

42 "Bill Powell," Baseball-Reference.com.

43 Cook, "Willie Powell Interview."

44 Kelley, 219.

45 Kelley, 220.

46 Powell, 153.

NORMAN "BOBBY" ROBINSON

By Bob LeMoine

Norman "Bobby" Robinson was the starting center fielder on the 1948 Birmingham Black Barons team that played in the last Negro League World Series. At least he was until an injury sidelined him. By the time he returned to action, he was moved to left field because a rookie and future baseball legend had replaced him in center. The Black Barons had two outfielders with blazing speed, but Robinson had a weak arm and could not hit for power like this young phenom who seemingly could do everything on the field. Norman Robinson has been forgotten to history; the achievements of Willie Mays are part of baseball lore. Both began playing during a time of segregation. When Jackie Robinson broke the color barrier, the 17-year-old Mays was destined for stardom, while the 35-year-old Robinson was winding down. However, for the two seasons in which they shared the outfield for Birmingham, it must have been a delight to watch them run.

"Norman could *run,*" remembered his brother Henry Frazier Robinson, who was called Frazier during his own Negro League career as a catcher. "He always seemed to know a way to get on base, and after he'd get on he was just like Cool Papa Bell. He was gonna be running. He was somebody that could get you two or three runs a game. Regardless. In any league."[1]

Norman Wayne "Bobby" Robinson was born on April Fools' Day, April 1, 1913, in Oklahoma City to the Rev. Henry and Corrine (Black) Robinson. Oklahoma had been a state less than six years when Norman was born, and Frazier recalled the state being a mixture of African Americans, Caucasians, and Cherokee, Creek, and Osage Native Americans.[2] "Oklahoma was kind of a wild place when I was a boy," Frazier recalled.[3] Many African Americans at the time moved their families from the segregated South to the more racially tolerant, though often law-less, Oklahoma.[4] Frazier had been born in Alabama three years prior to Norman, before the family settled in the Sooner State. Norman was the baby of the family, which also included older brothers Edward, Theophilus, and John, and sisters Maybelle and Estelle.[5] Frazier grew up hearing family stories of his paternal grandparents being freed slaves.

The family later moved to Okmulgee, Oklahoma, and the siblings grew up in a bungalow with little that resembled modern amenities. "It had an outhouse and pump out back," Frazier remembered. "Near the pump we had tubs and washboards for the washing and a clothesline to hang it all out on. We didn't have electric, either; we had oil lamps and lanterns. We finally got electric and city water and bathrooms put in when I was a teenager, but my entire childhood, we'd use an outhouse, go fetch water in back, do our homework by the light of an oil lamp, cook over a woodstove, and keep coal for the furnace. That's the way it was."[6] Norman, Frazier, and John took care of the family dogs, a fox terrier named Spot and a shepherd named Jack.

Henry Robinson was the pastor of a Baptist church and a strict disciplinarian who did not approve of his sons' love of baseball. "I don't think my father was proud of Norman and me playing baseball for a living," Frazier recalled. "It was kind of against his teaching. He saw baseball as a worldly thing, and he wanted us to follow in his footsteps. We tried to follow his beliefs as best we could, but we just couldn't let go of that baseball."[7] But the brothers knew their boundaries in regard to baseball and church attendance. "If my father ever found out that we had been playing baseball on a Sunday, why there'd be trouble when he got home from his revival [special church service] on Monday," Frazier wrote. "That's the way we grew up, under those kind of rules."[8] Although the brothers undoubtedly got into mischief as kids, "Norman didn't get in to too much trouble. ... I

1938 CHAMPION OF IOWA

E. HENNELEY G. NEARS R. LIGON C. MCLEMORE G. LIGON STREET P. MCDANIELS T. GIBSON

V.R. LIMMON OWNER

D. THOMAS   J. BROWN   C. JOHNSON   N. ROBINSON

MIDDLE ROW R. JONES B. MANSFIELD D. MCGOWN S. SMITH
MANAGER

Norman (Bobby) Robinson (front row, right) with the Texas Black Spiders in 1938. While with the Black Barons in 1948, Robinson suffered a broken leg and 17-year old Willie Mays took over center field. (*Courtesy of Jay-Dell Mah/Western Canada Baseball*)

can't recall anything bad he ever got into," Frazier surmised.[9]

While their father was busy writing sermons, Frazier and Norman learned baseball from kids in the neighborhood. Frazier remembered when he was 16 and "the boys in our neighborhood on the east side challenged a team of boys on the west side for a game. We had a lot of fun, and it became a regular thing. We would play for ten or twelve cases of Coke or something like that. We *loved* to play baseball."[10] The brothers also played baseball at Dunbar High School in Okmulgee, Frazier often catching and Norman in the outfield. Norman also ran track and excelled at the 100-yard dash. "Whatever sport Norman

participated in," Frazier boasted of his brother, "he would condition himself, keeping himself in shape, and play it. He was just a good athlete, that's what he was."[11] According to Frazier, Norman attended Langston University, a historically black institution in Langston, Oklahoma, and lettered in baseball, basketball, and football. (This was not mentioned by Norman in his Hall of Fame questionnaire.)

Norman Robinson played for the semipro San Angelo Black Sheepherders in 1938. The Black Sheepherders were "originally from San Angeles, Texas," wrote the *Emporia* (Kansas) *Gazette* when the team came to town, and they were "qualifying through the Kansas semipro tournament at Wichita for the National Semi-Pro baseball tourney because the Texas program bars colored teams."[12] The team was also called the Kansas City Black Sheepherders during its time in Kansas. The Sheepherders defeated Emporia 9-2 with a 14-hit attack, but Robinson, batting fifth and playing left field, went 0-for-4.[13]

Robinson also spent part of the 1938 season with the Mineola (Texas) Black Spiders, an independent barnstorming team. A box score in Iowa's *Rock Valley Bee* showed Robinson batting eighth and playing center field. He was not credited with an at-bat and the Spiders lost to Rock Valley, 8-3.[14]

Robinson and Frazier spent the winter back in Oklahoma. One day the phone rang. It was the Kansas City Monarchs, and they were looking for Norman. "My brother was an outstanding defensive center fielder," Frazier wrote, "with excellent speed, and he was an excellent switch hitter, so I wasn't surprised he got the call. So Norman caught a train to New Orleans to join the Monarchs in the spring of 1939."[15] Later, the Monarchs needed an extra catcher, and Frazier also joined the team.

The brothers did not actually join the fabled Monarchs team itself; they became members of the Satchel Paige All-Star team which was a barnstorming "B-Team" of the Monarchs. The barnstorming team was called the Travelers by team owners but Baby Monarchs by the players themselves. "The squad was a blend of young players on their way up and oldsters ready to retire," wrote Paige biographer Larry Tye. "The shortstop quit midseason to go back to teaching school and the first baseman kept threatening to leave. No one complained when the manager shot rabbits out of the window of their moving bus."[16] Having Paige in the team name was an attempt to draw on his fame as the team traveled the country, and Paige was prominent in advertisements in local newspapers.[17]

The Robinson brothers also rode from town to town in Paige's Chrysler. It was always an adventure riding with Paige behind the wheel. "Satchel was a terrible driver," Frazier recalled. "I couldn't stand his driving because I'd be scared he'd get us killed at any second. ... Satchel was liable to run into anything

at anytime."[18] When they would stop for the night, Paige and Norman were two polar opposites. Paige was known not to spare any expense on a good dinner and night on the town, while Norman would save 50 cents of his dollar-a-day meal money. "Norman was the sort of guy that would take big steps to save on shoe leather. Tight, *tight!*" Frazier jokingly remembered.[19]

To keep themselves distracted while Paige drove like a maniac, the brothers and teammate John Markham would sing songs, particularly "Blue Skies."[20] It would have been compelling to see ballplayers zip around the mountains of Montana while singing out of fear for their lives. Some of their games in Big Sky Country were recorded in local papers. The Helena (Montana) *Independent Record* devoted a lengthy column to describing these young Monarchs and their opponent, The House of David. "The fastest man in negro baseball, according to many," the columnist boasted about Norman Robinson. "He is a base-stealing fiend ... and already offered contracts by several negro major league teams."[21] The Monarchs won 12-6 and Robinson, batting sixth and playing center field, went 3-for-5 and scored twice.[22] On July 1 the All-Stars defeated a local team in Butte, Montana, 17-5, with Robinson registering four hits.[23] On another occasion in Butte, Frazier joined his brother on the field, catching and batting fifth with Norman batting seventh and playing in center field as the Monarchs won, 9-4.[24]

After the 1939 barnstorming tour, the Robinson brothers parted ways. Frazier stayed with the All-Stars; Norman refused because he despised manager Newt Joseph's tendency to cuss.[25] Norman moved to Baltimore to play with the Elite Giants, a club that included an 18-year old Roy Campanella. Robinson is mentioned in an April article in the *Pittsburgh Courier* as battling for the third outfield spot.[26] It was a neck-and-neck pennant race between the Elite Giants, winners of the Negro National League pennant in 1939, and the Homestead Grays, with both teams in a tie for first on August 10.[27] The Grays eventually won the championship, and Robinson spent the season mainly as a substitute outfielder. He also started some games for the Sparrows Point Giants in a community south of Baltimore. This team was owned by Dr. Joseph Thomas, who wanted to capitalize on the large Bethlehem Steel plant in the area.[28]

To make a living, Robinson also worked as a clerk at a shipyard in Baltimore. Frazier lived with Norman that winter and also worked at the shipyard. After a long day the brothers would get dates and head to the Edmondson Avenue Club, where they were entertained by stars like Billie Holiday, Louis Armstrong, Oscar Peterson, and Nat King Cole.[29] In the spring Frazier stayed in Baltimore despite being under contract with Kansas City, and both brothers played for Sparrows Point in 1941. Norman may have played at Sparrows Point in 1942 as well, but this is not clear.

Norman returned to the Elite Giants for the 1943-1944 seasons and was again a reserve outfielder; he batted .294 and .290 respectively in the two seasons. On August 8, 1944, Robinson had the misfortune to be in the outfield when Josh Gibson of the Homestead Grays pounded three triples, two of them over his head in left field.[30] In 1945 Robinson became an everyday player, splitting time between the outfield and third base. The September 15, 1945 issue of the *Brooklyn Daily Eagle* reported that he was third in the league in batting at .329.[31] He finished the season batting .361.[32]

In 1946 Robinson split the season with two teams on opposite coasts. He played again for Baltimore, batting .321,[33] but also went west and played for the Seattle Steelheads of the short-lived West Coast Baseball League. The Steelheads' team bus had engine trouble on the way to Jacksonville, Illinois, and their game against the Havana Las Palomas of Cuba started late. Fortunately, there were plenty of other scheduled events to fill the time. The Havana team performed a shadowball exhibition, a clown performed, and the legendary Jesse Owens gave a speech and later challenged the fastest Cuban players in a number of races. Exhausted after a 12-hour overnight bus ride from Indianapolis, Seattle lost 4-2. Robinson batted with the go-ahead run on base in the third inning and grounded out.[34]

Robinson spent part of the 1947 season with Baltimore, but later went south and played for the Birmingham Black Barons of the Negro American League. He played well in a doubleheader sweep over the Chicago American Giants, 3-0 and 2-0. "His fielding feats in both games and knocking the first runs in brought him the plaudits of the fans," wrote the *Pittsburgh Courier* of Robinson.[35] After the NAL season ended, he spent the winter of 1947 in the Cuban Winter League, playing for the Almendares Alacranes.[36]

Robinson was back with Birmingham in 1948 and contributed to a Memorial Day weekend series against the Kansas City Monarchs. In the Saturday night game, on a soggy field, Robinson's centerfield counterpart, Willard Brown, had three hits with two home runs and a double but Robinson made a "galloping catch" to rob him of another hit. Birmingham prevailed, 8-6. In Game One of the Sunday doubleheader, Robinson scored on a first-inning hit and Birmingham led 1-0. In the seventh, when Birmingham trailed 2-1, Robinson stroked a single and then watched pinch-hitter Alonzo Perry knock one out of Rickwood Field. Birmingham won in the bottom of the ninth, 4-3.[37] On a Saturday night in June, Robinson drove in the winning run in the 10th inning in a 13-12 victory. On June 30 he was batting .291.[38]

An injury to Robinson gave an opportunity for a 17-year-old high-school kid to play every day. "Norman had been playing an excellent center field for Birmingham and batting leadoff," Frazier remembered. "Norman was chasing a fly ball in the outfield, stepped in a hole, and broke his leg."[39] They say "the rest is history" and such is true considering this young budding star was Willie Mays.

Mays' recalled in his 1989 autobiography:

By June 1, 1948, when I was just a few weeks out of high school, I was the regular centerfielder. Norman Robinson, who was very fast, had broken his leg, and [manager] Piper Davis told me to take over. Even when Robinson came back later in the season, Piper kept me in center and played Robinson in left. Piper said Robinson was faster, but that I had a stronger arm. He liked to say, "Willie can go get it, and Willie can bring it back."[40]

Robinson returned to play later in the summer, but Mays had proven himself, combining speed and the throwing arm Robinson did not have. Mays was now the center fielder and Robinson moved to left. There are questions over when this injury happened and when Mays officially joined the Black Barons. James S. Hirsch, a Mays biographer, described Robinson's injury not as a broken leg but a broken ankle.[41] Author John Klima wrote that Mays was with the team in June but played only in nonleague games "against small-town teams far away" until he finished high school.[42] Mays made his official Negro American League debut, according to Klima, on July 4.[43]

Birmingham veterans, including Robinson, were not thrilled at first to see a new energetic kid on the field. Jimmy Zapp, the left fielder whom Mays was replacing in the lineup that day, even went into a profanity-laced tirade when he read the lineup card.[44] By July, after Robinson returned, the Black Barons had an outfield of speed in left and center. "If you were playing Birmingham," Frazier wrote, "you'd better hit to right or hit it out."[45] Robinson was featured in a *Newark* (Ohio) *Advocate* blurb when the Black Barons came to town. "He's a great centerfielder," the *Advocate* boasted, showing perhaps that Mays's rise wasn't as fast as he remembered.[46] As late as July 20 Mays was still being described as a "new utility outfielder."[47]

Robinson batted .299 for the 1948 season, in which the Black Barons defeated the Monarchs for the NAL pennant but lost the final Negro League World Series to the Negro National League's Homestead Grays.[48]

In 1949 Bill Maughn, a major-league scout, saw the speedy Robinson and Mays in the outfield and it was obvious that one was superior to the other. "The left fielder [Robinson] for Birmingham couldn't throw," Maughn said. "[Houston] had runners on first and second and it was the second inning. The next batter hit the ball off the scoreboard and the

left fielder got to it. The center fielder came running over yelling, 'Give it to me, give it to me,' and be-doggoned if the left fielder didn't shovel pass to him like a football player. The center fielder threw out the runner trying to go from first to third."[49]

In the middle of the 1949 season, on June 7, Robinson married Sarah Johnson. Perhaps enlivened by wedded bliss, he was batting a strong .342 for the Black Barons by early July[50] and finished at .312 (93-for-298) with 3 home runs and 54 RBIs.[51] In 1950 he again excelled at the plate, batting .309 (90-for-291) with 29 RBIs.[52]

In 1950 Robinson played in the All-Star Game in Chicago. In front of 23,312 fans, he drove in a run in the sixth inning to give the East a 2-0 lead in a game that they won, 3-1.[53] Robinson continued to play for Birmingham in 1952, and the *Huntsville* (Alabama) *Times* commented that he "is another slugger who gives the ball long rides."[54] By this time the Black Barons and the rest of the Negro Leagues were suffering after Jackie Robinson broke the color barrier of the once whites-only major leagues and many great Negro stars followed him into Organized Baseball. The Black Barons continued to field teams through the 1950s, but the glory years of the league had long since passed.

The 1952 season was Norman's last in Birmingham, and he joined Frazier in Canada. The Man-Dak League (Manitoba-Dakota) was attracting many former Negro League players. Norman and Frazier both played for the 1952 Brandon Greys, and Norman batted .276 with 27 RBIs. In 1953 Norman played for the Canadian Carman Cardinals, batting .325, which ranked him sixth in the league. He continued to play to the age of 41 in 1954, when he batted .244 for Carman, and thereafter retired.[55]

Frazier Robinson compared Norman's ferocious style of play to that of Ty Cobb, who often slid into bases with his spikes up and injured opposing players. "He had a reputation in the league where you'd get out of the way or you were going to be cut," Frazier wrote. "That's the way he played the game."[56] There would also be fierce competition when the Robinson brothers faced each other. "Norman was always hustling, always trying to get an edge, always looking to beat you, just like he had back when we were playing the House of David or when we were kids," Frazier recalled. On one occasion when Norman came to bat, he told Frazier, who was catching, that he was going to run when he got on base. Norman singled and "right away started dancing off first base," Frazier said. "He jumped up and left on the first pitch, and I threw him out by forty feet. They had it in the paper the next morning 'Brother Against Brother.' That's the way we played."[57]

After retiring from baseball, Robinson lived in Chicago for a while and often took road trips to visit Frazier, who resided in Cleveland. Later, Norman moved to California and worked for ARA Services, a food vending company. He developed bleeding ulcers which were bad enough that Frazier and his wife relocated to California in 1966 to be with him. Norman recovered and was able to secure a job for Frazier with ARA. Over the years, Satchel Paige came by for visits, and the trio would sing old songs while Satchel played his ukulele; on those occasions, Norman could sing without having to worry about Paige getting him killed in a car wreck.[58]

Norman Robinson died on March 26, 1984, in Los Angeles at the age of 70 with his wife, Sarah, and son, Norman Jr., by his side.

SOURCES

"Norman Robinson," Negro Leagues Baseball E-Museum. coe.k-state.edu/annex/nlbemuseum/history/players/robinsonno. html. Retrieved January 14, 2017.

Norman Robinson's questionnaire from the Giamatti Research Center at the Baseball Hall of Fame in Cooperstown, New York.

NOTES

1   Frazier Robinson and Paul Bauer, *Catching Dreams: My Life in the Negro Baseball Leagues* (Syracuse, New York: Syracuse University Press, 1999), 174.

2   Gerard Early, "Introduction: Freedom and Fate, Baseball and Race," in *Catching Dreams*, xix.

3   Early, xviii.

4   Early, xviii.

5   Robinson and Bauer, 2.

6   Robinson and Bauer, 3.

7   Robinson and Bauer, xix.

8   Robinson and Bauer, 2.

9   Robinson and Bauer, 6.

10   Robinson and Bauer, 6-7.

11   Robinson and Bauer, 7.

12   "Bakers to Play Fast Colored Team Friday," *Emporia* (Kansas) *Gazette*, June 30, 1938: 14.

13   "Bakers, Beaten by Texans, to Face Abilene," *Emporia Gazette*, July 2, 1938: 7.

14   "Texas Black Spiders 3-R.V. 8," *Rock Valley* (Iowa) *Bee*, July 1, 1938: 1.

15   Robinson and Bauer, 21.

16   Larry Tye, *Satchel: The Life and Times of an American Legend* (New York: Random House, 2009), 122-123.

17   Robinson and Bauer, 21.

18   Robinson and Bauer, 39-40.

19   Robinson and Bauer, 41.

20   Robinson and Bauer, 40.

21   "House of David and Kansas City Monarchs Play This Eve," *Helena* (Montana) *Independent Record*, June 28, 1939: 7.

22   "Monarchs Beat Davids 12-6 and Meet East Helena Today," *Helena Independent Record*, June 29, 1939: 8.

23   "Negro Stars Dazzle Fans, Local Rivals," *Montana Standard* (Butte), July 2, 1939: 18.

24   "Monarchs in 9-4 Victory Over Davids," *Montana Standard*, August 13, 1939: 18.

25   Robinson and Bauer, 51.

26   Cum Posey, "Posey's Points," *Pittsburgh Courier*, April 13, 1940: 16.

27   "Baseball Results," *Pittsburgh Courier*, August 10, 1940: 16.

28   Robinson and Bauer, 77.

29   Robinson and Bauer, 77-78.

30   "Large Crowd Sees Homestead Grays Beat Baltimore Elites 9-0," *Altoona* (Pennsylvania) *Tribune*, August 9, 1944: 6.

31   "Bushwicks Play Elite Giants Encore Pair at Dexter," *Brooklyn Daily Eagle*, September 15, 1945: 7.

32   Larry Powell, *Black Barons of Birmingham: The South's Greatest Negro League Team and Its Players* (Jefferson, North Carolina: McFarland & Company, Inc., 2009), 99.

33   Ibid. The average may be combined for both teams played for.

34   "Cuban Squad Defeats Seattle Steelheads; Jesse Owens Appears," *Jacksonville* (Illinois) *Daily Journal*, August 13, 1946: 6.

35   "Birmingham Beats Chicago, 3-0, 2-0," *Pittsburgh Courier*, June 7, 1947: 14.

36   Robinson and Bauer, 172.

37   John Klima, *Willie's Boys: The 1948 Birmingham Black Barons, the Last Negro League World Series, and the Making of a Baseball Legend* (Hoboken, New Jersey: John Wiley & Sons, 2009), 83-84.

38   Klima, 95.

39   Robinson and Bauer, 141.

40   Willie Mays and Lou Sahadi, *Say Hey: The Autobiography of Willie Mays* (New York: Pocket Books, 1989), 40.

41   James S. Hirsch, *Willie Mays: The Life, the Legend* (New York: Simon & Schuster, 2010), 45.

42   Klima, 94.

43   Klima, 95.

44   Klima, 96-97.

45   Robinson and Bauer, 141.

46   "Barons' Star," *Newark* (Ohio) *Advocate,* July 19, 1948: 8.

47   "Barons, First Half Negro Champions, Here Thursday," *Newark Advocate*, July 20, 1948: 8.

48   "Birmingham Black Barons. Negro American League. 1948," Negro Southern League Museum Research Center. negrosouthernleaguemuseumresearchcenter.org/Portals/0/Birmingham%20Black%20Barons/Statistics%20-%20Birmingham%20Black%20Barons.pdf. Retrieved January 8, 2017.

49   Klima, 195.

50   "Hot Oil Baseball Griddle," *Kansas City* (Kansas) *Plaindealer,* July 8, 1949: 4.

51   Negro Southern League Museum Research Center. negrosouthernleaguemuseumresearchcenter.org/Portals/0/Birmingham%20Black%20Barons/Statistics%20-%

52   Ibid.

53   Wendell Smith, "21,312 See East Beat West, 3-1, in Annual Chicago Classic," *Pittsburgh Courier*, August 18, 1951: 14.

54   "Barons and Stars to Play Tuesday," *Huntsville* (Alabama) *Times*, June 1, 1952: 18.

55   Barry Swanton and Jay-Dell Mah, *Black Baseball Players in Canada: A Biographical Dictionary, 1881-1960* (Jefferson, North Carolina: McFarland & Company, Inc., 2009), 145; Western Canada Baseball website: attheplate.com/wcbl/1954_2.html; attheplate.com/wcbl/1953_2.html. Date accessed January 17, 2017.

56   Robinson and Bauer, 34-35.

57   Robinson and Bauer, 137.

58   Robinson and Bauer, 192-196.

JOE SCOTT

By Charles F. Faber

Joe Scott's ancestors were probably kidnapped or purchased by slave traders in West Africa, survived the horrors of the Middle Passage, and were sold into slavery in North America. His great-grandmother Annie Scott, who was born a slave in South Carolina in January 1820, gained her freedom as a result of America's Civil War. She could neither read nor write, but she passed considerable intelligence, drive, and ambition down to her descendants. Annie's son Bearl became a farmer in Alabama; in turn, Bearl's son Elbert rented a farm in Louisiana and became successful enough to buy a home in Shreveport and own a shop.[1] Another generation later, Elbert's son Joe had some success in professional baseball, both in the Negro Leagues and with formerly all-white minor-league teams.

Joseph Scott was born on June 15, 1918, in or near Shreveport in Caddo Parish, Louisiana. He was the fifth child and eldest son among the nine children of Elbert and Addie (Caldwell) Scott. Neither parent had attended school beyond the seventh grade, but they insisted on a high-school education for all of their children at a time when the Census Bureau reported that only 17.7 percent of the total adult population and 3.2 percent of the nonwhite adult residents of Louisiana completed four years of high school.[2]

In the 1920 census Elbert Scott was identified as a renter and a farmer in rural Caddo Parish, and Addie was designated a farm laborer. By 1930 Elbert was working as a laborer in Shreveport, and the family resided on East 72nd Street. By 1940, Elbert was listed as a homeowner and a pipefitter in his own shop while Addie was a cook in a private household.

Joseph Scott graduated from Shreveport's Central High School, and began to play baseball with the Shreveport Black Sports in 1938. The following year he toured with the Texas Black Spiders; after the squad went bankrupt and disbanded in midseason, he joined the semipro Dunsiath Giants from North Dakota. After traveling through the Midwest and part of Canada with the Giants, he returned home to Shreveport, where he rejoined the Black Sports in 1940.[3]

Scott joined the US Army in 1941 and served with the 350th Field Artillery, which was attached to the 46th Brigade in the European Theater of World War II. His unit arrived in Normandy six days after the D-Day Invasion in 1944, and Scott found himself in Belgium at the end of the war. He attained the rank of staff sergeant by the time of his discharge in November 1945.[4]

After his stint in the Army, Scott played for the Los Angeles White Sox of the West Coast Baseball League, a Negro winter league. In 1946 he played for the Detroit Senators before being recruited to the Birmingham Black Barons by catcher Lloyd "Pepper" Bassett.

At Birmingham in 1947, Scott was a backup to first baseman Piper Davis, who hit .360 in 56 games for which statistics are available; thus, the rookie Scott was no threat to dislodge Davis from his position. Since Scott played sparingly, and since almost no box scores were provided in black newspapers in 1947, his statistics for the season are unavailable.[5]

This information is vital to the correct identification of the subject at hand due to the proliferation of Joe Scotts in the game. At least three men with that name played in the Negro Leagues during the 1930s or 1940s: 1) Willie Lee "Joe" Scott, a first baseman, who most notably batted .354 for the Indianapolis ABCs in 1932 and who played in the Negro major leagues from 1927 to 1938; 2) Joseph Burt Scott, an outfielder for the Memphis Red Sox from 1944 to 1949; and 3) Joe Scott of the Birmingham Black Barons, whom writers sometimes confuse with one of the other two players by that name.

In 1948 player-manager Davis moved himself to second base, but that did not open up first base for

Scott as Alonzo Perry became the starter at that position for games in which he was not the starting pitcher. Scott played primarily in the outfield, and available statistics show that he hit .196 in 68 of the club's 76 games with 3 home runs, 47 runs scored, and 40 runs batted in.[6] Perhaps due to his underwhelming statistics, Scott's role on the Black Barons is sometimes overlooked. Willie Mays, for example, devoted a chapter of his autobiography to his time with the Black Barons, but never once mentioned Joe Scott.[7] Mays's omission had to be disconcerting to Scott since the two of them had roomed together on the road in both the 1948 and 1949 seasons.[8]

Under Davis's leadership, the Black Barons won the NAL's first-half championship and defeated the second-half champion Kansas City Monarchs in the playoffs. In Game Two, Davis hit for the cycle while Mays garnered three hits to lead Birmingham to a hard-fought 6-5 victory. Though the Black Barons swept the series, each game was tightly contested: Games One through Three were each decided by one run while Game Four ended as a two-run decision.[9]

After dispatching the Monarchs, the Black Barons met the Homestead Grays in the 1948 Negro League World Series. Birmingham had faced the Grays, perennial champions of the Negro National League, in the championship series in 1943 and 1944, losing both times. Both clubs still had plenty of star power in 1948. The Grays had started four stars in the 1948 East-West All-Star Games—Luis Marquez, Luke Easter, future Hall of Famer Buck Leonard, and Wilmer Fields—while the Barons had been represented by Artie Wilson, Piper Davis, and Bill Powell, who was the winning pitcher in the first of that season's two All-Star Games which had been played at Chicago's Comiskey Park.

The usual procedure was, of course, for World Series games to be played on the home fields of the competing clubs; however, the Grays were unable to host games in the 1948 series. Homestead is a suburb of Pittsburgh, and the Grays played most of their home games there at Forbes Field while also using Washington's Griffith Stadium as a second home. As it happened, at the time of the 1948 Negro League

JOE SCOTT

Joe Scott's RBI-single in the second inning of Game One of the World Series gave Birmingham a quick 1-0 lead. It was not enough, however, as the Grays prevailed 3-2 at Kansas City's Municipal Stadium. *(Courtesy R. D. Retort Enterprises)*

World Series, both the Pirates and the Senators were occupying their home fields, so the Grays had to play the entire series on the road.

The Black Barons, on the other hand, shared venerable Rickwood Field with the Birmingham Barons of the still-segregated Southern Association. On September 29 the white Barons were wrapping up the Southern Association playoffs in Nashville. They were off on September 30 and in Fort Worth for a Dixie Series game on October 5, thus opening up Rickwood Field for use by the Black Barons on those dates.

In Game One at Kansas City's Blues Stadium on September 26, Joe Scott singled home Ed Steele in the second inning to give the Black Barons a 1-0 lead, but they were unable to hold it and lost, 3-2.[10] The series moved to Birmingham on September 29, but home-field advantage wasn't enough to pull the Barons through and they dropped a 5-3 decision and fell behind two games to none. On the next day, in Game Three, the Barons won their only victory of the series, sparked by the heroics of Mays and pitcher Bill Greason. Mays made two outstanding defensive plays and drove in the winning run, while Greason contributed both on the mound and at the plate. He relieved starting pitcher Alonzo Perry in the eighth inning, with the score tied 3-3, and shut out the Grays the rest of the way. In the bottom of the ninth, Greason hit a single, went to second on a walk to John Britton, and scored the winning run on a drive through the box by Mays for a 4-3 victory.[11]

The series moved to New Orleans for Game Four. On modern interstates the Crescent City is only about a six-hour drive from Birmingham. But in 1948 there were no interstate highways. The Black Barons' bus had to traverse US 11 as it wound its way through the countryside and the city streets of Meridian, Laurel, and Hattiesburg. The trip took most of a day, but there was a reward at the end. At the back of the bus station in New Orleans there was an eating place staffed with black cooks and black waitresses, who gave the ballplayers special service.[12]

Homestead pitcher Wilmer Fields almost missed his Game Five start. The day before the game, he was at home in Virginia to pick up his wife and son. He drove almost nonstop to New Orleans, taking only a brief nap by the side of the road in Mississippi, which was a dangerous thing for a black man to do in the Deep South of that era. When he arrived in the Crescent City, he said, "I was in such bad shape I was shaking."[13] Although he was fatigued after driving his car for 25 hours from Manassas, Virginia, to New Orleans, Fields' fastball baffled the Birmingham batters in his 14-1 triumph. Two days later the series returned to Birmingham's Rickwood Field, Where Fields relieved R.T. Walker in the 10th inning and shut down the Black Barons as the Grays won the championship, 10-6.

The 1948 Negro League World Series was the last of its kind as the NNL folded after the season. Too many black stars were now playing in Organized Baseball, and African-American fans were more interested in following the exploits of Jackie Robinson, Roy Campanella, Satchel Paige, and Larry Doby than they were in the Negro teams. A total of 72 players from the Negro Leagues went to the majors between 1947 and 1969, including at least seven who had played at one time or another with the Birmingham Black Barons.[14] Bill Greason, Jehosie "Jay" Heard, Willie Mays, and Artie Wilson were with the Black Barons in 1948. The others—Billy Harrell, John Kennedy, and Willie Smith—played for Birmingham at a later time. Though six of those seven players did not achieve success in the majors, Mays became one of the greatest players of all time.

Scott never made it to the major leagues. He retained his position at first base for the Black Barons in 1949, hitting .238 and appearing in a career-high 76 league games and an undocumented number of exhibition games on the barnstorming circuits. NAL salaries were so low that most players toured the country during the offseason to supplement their income, playing wherever and whenever crowds could be attracted. Some players made more money barnstorming than they earned in the entire regular season.

In the Jim Crow era, black ballplayers often had difficulty finding places to eat and sleep while on the road. Problems were not confined to barnstorming in the Deep South. Jack Marshall recalled, "In the Negro American League when we left Chicago to go to St. Louis and play, there was no place between here and St. Louis where we could stop and eat. … From St. Louis to Kansas City, same thing. So many times we would ride all night and not have anything to eat, because they wouldn't feed you."[15]

In 1950 Piper Davis was back at first base for Birmingham, so Scott sought employment elsewhere.[16] He ended up playing for Ted "Double Duty" Radcliffe with the Chicago American Giants, for whom he plied his trade at first base and in left field. He hit .226 in 39 games for the American Giants during his last season in baseball.[17] Although he had played in the 1948 Negro League World Series, he had never become a star; even his greatest claim to fame as Mays's roommate during their Black Barons days was largely forgotten

After baseball, Scott embarked upon a career with the railroads. He moved to Los Angeles, where he initially found employment with the Santa Fe Railroad. After a time he switched companies and went to work for Amtrak for 28 years until his retirement in 1979. He continued to live in Los Angeles up to his death—on January 12, 1997—at the age of 78.[18]

SOURCES

Thanks to Susan Campbell Lounsbury of the Southern Regional Education Board for providing information about the educational attainment of Louisiana residents. Other sources are identified in the Notes.

NOTES

1   Data about Minnie Scott and her descendants are taken from reports of the United States Census, 1900, 1910, 1920, 1930, and 1940.

2   US Census Bureau, Decennial Census of Population, 1940 to 2000, Table 11.

3   James A. Riley, *The Biographical Encyclopedia of the Negro Baseball Leagues* (New York: Carroll & Graf Publishers, Inc., 1994), 704.

4   Ibid. See also baseballinwartime.com/negro.htm.

5   John Holway, *The Complete Book of Baseball's Negro Leagues* (Fern Park, Florida: Hastings House, 2001), 445.

6   Dick Clark and Larry Lester. *The Negro Leagues Book* (Cleveland: SABR, 1994), 301.

7   Willie Mays with Lou Sahadi, *Say Hey* (New York: Simon and Schuster, 1988), 39.

8   Riley, 704.

9   cnlbr.org/Portals/0/RL/Negro%20League%20Play-Off%20Series%20(1940-1955).pdf, accessed July 15, 2016.

10 Blues Stadium had formerly been known as Muehlebach Field and would later be renamed Municipal Stadium.

11 "Grays Hold 3-1 Lead in Series," *Afro-American*, October 9, 1948.

12 Mays and Sahadi, 39-40.

13 John Klima, *Willie's Boys* (Hoboken, New Jersey: John Wiley & Sons), 184.

14 Clark and Lester, 144, 256-57. Prior to 1947, 13 players had appeared in both Negro League games and major-league games—Fleet Walker and his brother Weldy in 1884, and 11 light-skinned Cuban players from 1911 to 1929

15 Robert Peterson, *Only the Ball Was White* (New York: Oxford University Press, 1970), 154-155.

16 Davis would become the first African-American player signed by the Boston Red Sox during the 1950 season, but Scott had already departed for Chicago by that time.

17 Riley, 704.

18 Ibid.

ED STEELE

By Will Osgood

Edward D. Steele was an Alabama fixture through and through. He was born in Selma on August 8, 1916, to Ezekial Steele and Viola Dawson, about whom nothing is known except that they were apparently married. Steele made it through the 10th grade before he began his own career both as a laborer and baseball star, eventually making his name as an outfielder for one of the Negro Leagues' more successful franchises, the Birmingham Black Barons. The native Alabaman later settled in Birmingham, where he died in February 1974 at the youthful age of 57.

In his brief lifetime Steele made his presence felt in the baseball world. Though he was somewhat underappreciated as a player, he had an aura about him that made him an ideal fit as a manager, a position he filled quite well after his playing days came to an end.

Steele was known as Stainless Steele, though the nickname rarely shows up in contemporary publications. The play on words that involved both his last name and Birmingham's big industry became his sobriquet early in his career, and Steele embraced it.

Birmingham was indeed the Steel City of the South in the first half of the twentieth century. Much of the city's economy, from its dawning until after the Civil Rights era, was dependent upon steel processing and other warehouse-type industries. Many black ballplayers worked in the mines and steel mills by day and played their beloved game by night and on weekends.

Steele began his career as a player on the American Cast Iron Pipe Company (ACIPCO) team, which was the pre-eminent squad in Birmingham's Industrial League. Although not ACIPCO's intent, the company's team had so many outstanding players that it often ended up serving as a farm team for the Negro major-league teams, including the hometown Black Barons.

According to US Census data from 1940, it appears that Steele was joined in his household during those years by a wife, Glady Davis, who became Glady Steele. The couple had two daughters born a year apart, Elizabeth in 1930 and Ruby Lee in 1931. They lived in a rented house at 2405 18th Street in downtown Birmingham.

Steele was one of ACIPCO's better players, and Black Barons manager Winfield Scott Welch snatched him away in 1942. In his nine seasons playing with ACIPCO, Steele recorded a .363 batting average that included three seasons in which he hit better than .400.[1] In spite of his obvious talents, which included a strong arm and home-run power, Steele played sparingly in 1942 and 1943 before becoming a Black Barons regular in the 1944 season.

Available statistics show that Steele had nine plate appearances for the Black Barons in 1942, recording three hits and three RBIs while also walking once and scoring a run. Statistics for 1943 are even less complete, showing only five plate appearances in which he hit safely twice and drove in a run. Though his play was irregular in Welch's first two seasons at the helm of the Black Barons, he had the support of his former ACIPCO teammate and future manager, Piper Davis, who recommended Steele as the ideal right fielder for the Black Barons based on their roster composition and the fact that they played their home games at Rickwood Field.[2]

At 5-feet-10 and 195 pounds, Steele was for that time a beast of a man. Those who saw him said he was blessed with a barrel chest, broad shoulders, and Popeye-like arms that enabled him to throw cannon shots from the outfield. He could stand in the outfield, catch a ball flat-footed, and still throw a runner out who was trying to tag up. There are tales of Stainless throwing runners out by several steps with a throw that never even came close to scraping the dirt.[3]

Perhaps Steele's most important shot was fired in extra innings of Game Two of the 1948 Negro American League Championship Series. With the Black Barons tied with their nemesis, the Kansas City Monarchs, in the 10th inning, Steele's arm came to the rescue of relief pitcher Bill Greason.

The reliever was fading fast, having entered the contest in the top of the fifth inning just a day after pitching in relief in the series' inaugural game. With a Monarch on second base, Greason allowed a soft single to right field, where Stainless was loading up his cannon. In his book *Willie's Boys*, John Klima describes the play:

> "Ed Steele charged the ball and picked it up on a good hop. Steele's shot to pigtail Pepper Bassett never touched the turf. As Baker raced home, his eyes widened when he saw Pepper waiting on him. 'Edward Steele cut Baker down at the plate with a line peg for the most beautiful play of the game,' the *World* reported. Said Greason, 'Ed Steele had a great arm. I was glad he did.'"[4]

The Black Barons went on to win that important game, their second in a row, and eventually defeated the Monarchs to advance to the Negro League World Series against the Homestead Grays. Though they would end up losing the last such World Series ever to be played, Steele was a key cog who helped them to advance as far as they did in 1948.

In spite of the fact that Steele was known for his lethal throwing arm, he was not a premier defensive outfielder. Stainless often misplayed fly balls and line drives to the outfield, misjudging them or simply by being too slow to get the baseball.[5] Having Willie Mays by his side in center field made Steele's job easier in 1948. It did not matter if Steele was not fast enough to get to a ball hit to right-center, since that was Mays's territory anyway.

Though Piper Davis had initially recommended Steele to former manager Welch, he was now unhappy about Mays's uncanny ability to routinely mask Steele's slowfooted efforts in right field. As the Black Barons' new manager, Davis had no issue with Mays's

Outfielder Ed Steele was a key cog for the 1948 Birmingham Black Barons. As manager of the Detroit Stars, he led the 1956 squad to a 52-16 record and the Negro American League pennant. (*Courtesy of Center for Negro League Baseball Research*)

Houdini-like magic, but it did not sit well with him that Steele seemed to rely on the future major-league legend to make every play.[6]

Davis made his displeasure known to Steele, saying, "'The ball goes out to right-center,' Piper said to Steele. 'I hear, 'Come on, Willie!'"[7] In fairness to Steele, however, Davis leveled the same accusations against Jim Zapp, the Black Barons' left fielder in 1948. Though Davis appeared to believe that both players used Mays's amazing ability as an excuse or justification for relaxing in the outfield, it may simply have been a case of an eager 17-year-old trying to cover as much ground as possible in order to make a good impression on his manager.

While Steele may have had adventures in the outfield, at the plate he was known for having a power swing, which was a rarity in that period of baseball when most hitters were content to slash the ball through the hole or to try their luck by going back up the middle. Steele wanted to make his own hole by placing the ball over the wall in one fell swoop. Since Steele had the potential to go deep at any time, Davis inserted him into the lineup as the team's cleanup hitter.

Big Ed, the other nickname Steele went by, exemplified the premier slugger. During the incredible 1948 season, Steele and Davis held an impromptu home-run derby with the all-white Birmingham Barons' first baseman Walt Dropo.[8] It was a brash announcement on Davis's part that the Black Barons were better than their white counterparts.

When Steele was not hitting balls over the wall, he was either being hit by pitches (being hit was one of his claims to fame in the league)[9] or lining balls back up the box. Pitcher Bill "Fireball" Beverly once talked about Steele's batting acumen:

> They had a guy in Birmingham before I went there, Ed Steele. You can look him up. Steele was 'bout the best hitter I pitched against. He didn't only hit me, he hit other pitchers. I don't mean Texas leaguers — bloopers — a *line*! Everything he hit, you could hang clothes on it. Line drives. He hit one back through the box on me one time. I said, 'I'll get him out. I'll throw the ball on the outside corner, as hard as I can throw it.' He hit the ball right back up the center, hit me on the elbow and they thought he'd broke my elbow, but I shook it off and went on and finished the ballgame. He was one of the best hitters I faced.[10]

Steele's power was perhaps amplified by the fact that, despite being a right-handed thrower, he hit from the left side of the plate. With his unusual power, he could simply flick his wrists and line one out the opposite way to left field, since that the fence in that direction stood just 321 feet from home plate. Conversely, he could also turn on a ball and jar it out of the yard to right field, where the fence was a mere 332 feet away.[11] He did both with regularity.

Little is known today about who Stainless was as a person, but the legend of his hitting prowess lives on. He is often painted as a home-run masher. Other times he is seen as a consistent line-drive hitter. Available statistics show that Steele never hit below .300 in the Negro Leagues, which also happened to be his average in the 1948 NAL championship season.[12] Omitting 1946, for which statistics are sparse, Steele never had an on-base percentage below .400 while playing in the Negro Leagues.

In addition to hitting for average and being a home-run threat, Steele was also a doubles machine. In his first full season with the Black Barons, he tied Neil Robinson for second in the Negro American League in doubles with 12. Two years into his career, Steele was asked to tour the country with the Satchel Paige All-Stars. During that 1946 tour he reportedly went 1-for-4 in his plate appearances.[13] In 1947 he saw more action at the plate, going 4-for-16 against the Bob Feller and Ewell Blackwell All-Stars, but those numbers are unofficial. He played again for the All-Stars once more in 1948, and went 1-for-2.[14]

Before embarking on the traveling tour, Steele was also part of a rag-tag group of Negro League players, as well as one future major-league star, who challenged the Jackie Robinson All-Stars when they came to Birmingham. Piper Davis and Artie Wilson, two of the Black Barons' best players, had left town to play winter ball in Puerto Rico, but Steele was still in town and was the longest-tenured veteran of the players who made up the team that challenged Robinson and Roy Campanella. Among the others on the Birmingham squad were Jimmy "Schoolboy" Newberry, Lyman Bostock, and Willie Mays, who, as the story goes, had to skip a day of high school to play in the game.[15]

Despite playing with the Satchel Paige All Stars from 1946 to 1948, it took until 1950 for Steele to gain his first East-West All-Star Game selection. In the game he batted seventh and played left field for the West team, going 2-for-3 while also driving in a run. As typified his defensive reputation, however, he also made an error in the field.

One season later, Steele was one of the biggest stars in the then-disintegrating Negro major leagues as he led all Negro League players in the East-West Game with a total of 10,019 votes.[16] Playing in his second East-West All-Star Game in 1951, Steele hit fifth in the lineup and played right field, this time for the East squad. He was again a key contributor to an All-Star victory, as he tripled home a run and then scored on a double in the sixth inning, making him responsible for two of the East's three runs in the victory. The man who would have been the All-Star Game MVP if such awards had been handed out then finally caught the eye of major-league scouts.

In 1952 Steele split time between the Triple-A Hollywood Stars and Class-A Denver Bears, two minor-league affiliates of the Pittsburgh Pirates. He hit just .213 for the Stars, but his average improved slightly when he moved down to the Single-A club, where he hit .254.[17] Steele hit no home runs with Denver despite playing at the higher altitude; conversely, he played only 22 games for the Stars but hit two homers for that team.

Though Steele's minor-league career was short-lived—it lasted just that one year—and unsuccessful, it was a victory that Steele had the opportunity to play the game alongside whites in 1952. When he began playing full-time in the Negro Leagues with the Black Barons in 1944, that idea had seemed implausible. Even though Steele was probably as good as any player the Birmingham Barons had, he could not have played for the whites-only Birmingham team. Such were the conditions of that era, especially in the Jim Crow South.

Steele was not ready for his career to end after his brief stint in the minor leagues, so he spent parts of 1953 and 1954 in Canada with the Intercounty League's Galt Terriers. He rediscovered his power in 1953, and led the Intercounty League with 14 homers; however, no statistics are available for the 1954 season.[18]

Once his playing career was finally over, Steele returned to the United States in 1955 to manage the Detroit Stars, a Negro American League team with the same name as Detroit's original Negro League franchise that had experienced its most successful seasons in the 1920s after being founded as a charter member of the Negro National League in 1919.

Steele managed the Stars for four seasons, through 1958, and was quite successful as a manager. In the 1956 season he led his Stars team to a 52-16 record (.765) and a Negro American League title.[19] In all four seasons he managed the squad, he was elected manager for the East team in the East-West All-Star Game. He was 2-2 as a manager in those games, winning 11-5 in 1956 and 6-5 in 1958. The two losses were 2-0 in 1955 and 8-5 in 1957.[20]

Occasionally manager Steele would insert himself into the Stars' lineup. In 1958, his last season in baseball, he hit .273 with an impressive .591 slugging percentage. In that season the Stars were renamed the Clowns. The Clowns played a doubleheader in Yankee Stadium in the Bronx, the closest he or many Negro League players would ever come to the big leagues.

After his retirement from baseball, Steele returned to his adopted hometown of Birmingham and became a barber. His shop was located on 4th Street in the downtown section of the city.[21]

In later years Steele seemed to be ambivalent about his baseball career. When he was asked to fill out a questionnaire, along with many of his Negro League compatriots, "he seemed shocked that someone remembered him. Like many Negro League ballplayers, his personal history was washed out like a faded photograph."[22]

Though Steele has not been entirely lost to history, little information about him is known and his career has become an afterthought. Even in Birmingham, nary an Ed Steele-autographed baseball can be found at the city's new Negro Southern League Museum. One of the greatest sluggers in Birmingham Black Barons history is all but forgotten in the place where he lived so much of his life and died in February 1974.

Steele died at the relatively young age of 57 due to several health complications. Shortly before his death, he had responded in the aforementioned questionnaire, "I will send some photos when I find my scrapbook. They moved it around when I was in the hospital. … I have a glove and a bat with my name on it if you want it."[23]

All indications are that Steele was a calm, poised, and fun-loving gentleman throughout his lifetime. In nearly every available photo of him, he sports a smile or a poised neutral gaze. Steele fit the description of his former roommate, Piper Davis, as a religious man. If so, it is a pleasant description to summarize the life of a man who remains largely unknown.

NOTES

1   Dr. Layton Revel and Luis Munoz, *Forgotten Heroes: Edward "Big Ed" Steele* (Birmingham: Center for Negro League Baseball Research, 2012), 24.

2   John Klima, *Willie's Boys: The 1948 Birmingham Black Barons, the Last Negro League World Series, and the Making of a Baseball Legend* (Hoboken, New Jersey: John Wiley & Sons, Inc., 2009), 39.

3   Klima, 159.

4   Ibid.

5   Klima, 165, 171.

6   Klima, 152.

7   Ibid.

8   Klima, 121.

9   James A. Riley, *The Biographical Encyclopedia of the Negro Baseball Leagues* (New York: Carroll & Graf Publishers, Inc., 1994), 740.

10 Brent Kelley, *Voices From the Negro Leagues: Conversations with 52 Baseball Standouts* (Jefferson, North Carolina: McFarland & Company, Inc., 1998), 286.

11 "Rickwood Field," baseballpilgrimages.com/rickwood.html, December 29, 2016.

12 Revel and Munoz, 24.

13 Revel and Munoz, 25.

14 Revel and Munoz, 12.

15 Allen Barra, *Rickwood Field: A Century in America's Oldest Ballpark* (New York: W.W. Norton & Company, 2010), 159.

16 Larry Lester, *Black Baseball's National Showcase: The East-West All Star Game, 1933-1953* (Lincoln, Nebraska: University of Nebraska Press, 2001), 354.

17 Riley, 741.

18 Barry Swanton and Jay-Dell Mah, *Black Baseball Players in Canada: A Bibliographical Dictionary, 1881-1960* (Jefferson, North Carolina: McFarland & Company, Inc., 2009), 155.

19 Revel and Munoz, 17.

20 Ibid.

21 Revel and Munoz, 19.

22 Klima, 269.

23 Ibid.

BOB VEALE

By Joseph Gerard

Bob Veale was one of the hardest-throwing and most intimidating strikeout pitchers in the National League from 1962 through 1972. The bespectacled left-hander stood 6-feet-6 inches tall and weighed 212 pounds—the combination of size, arm strength, and questionable vision made him an imposing figure on the mound and one of the most difficult pitchers to hit in his era. During his tenure with the Pittsburgh Pirates, Veale struck out 1,652 batters, second only to Bob Friend for the team record. He led the National League with 250 strikeouts in 1964, edging out Bob Gibson, and struck out a career-high 276 in 1965, only to finish a distant second to Sandy Koufax. He won a world championship ring with the Pirates in 1971, and on September 1 of that year he played in the first major-league game started by an all-minority lineup, entering the game in relief. He was sold to the Boston Red Sox in 1972, and pitched for them for three seasons. He finished with 120 wins and a career ERA of 3.07, better than the league average, and a strikeouts-per-nine-innings ratio of 7.96, which as of 2014 was a Pirates team record.

Robert Andrew Veale was born on October 28, 1935, in Birmingham, Alabama, to Robert Andrew Veale Sr. and Ollie Belle (Ushry) Veale, the second of their 14 children, and one of their largest—he came into the world at 13 pounds, 4 ounces. His father pitched for a short time for the Homestead Grays of the Negro National League. He worked for the Tennessee Coal and Iron Company, a subsidiary of US Steel that was Birmingham's largest employer at the time. Young Veale played on the sandlots of Birmingham with both blacks and whites. "We didn't know we were breaking segregation laws," he said. "We just thought we were playing baseball. I had white friends, kids I played ball with all the time. We weren't thinking about integrating anything. We were just playing ball."[1] As a youngster he excelled in both baseball and basketball. Winfield Welch, manager of the Birmingham Black Barons of the Negro American League from 1942 to 1945 and coach of the Harlem Globetrotters, wanted young Veale for his traveling basketball team, but Veale's father would not agree to it.

At 12 Veale played for the 24th Street Red Sox in the Birmingham Industrial League, and worked the concession stand at Rickwood Field, home to the Black Barons and the Birmingham Barons of the Southern Association. "I used to run change around to the different concession stands, anything to make a coin," he said.[2] Veale used to chase foul balls and home runs at Rickwood and then sell the balls back to the Black Barons or the visiting team. Eventually player-manager Piper Davis made him the batboy and let him pitch batting practice regularly. "I used to pitch batting practice for the white Barons and come back and do the same for the Black Barons," Veale said. "When the game started I went to the concession stands and did the things I normally did."[3]

On some summer days in 1948, however, Veale got closer to the action; Davis would let him pitch for the Black Barons—featuring 17-year-old Willie Mays in the outfield—in league games, appearances that, because he was a minor, were covered up and never made it to the record books.[4] By 1950 Mays had been signed by the Giants and was on his way to the major leagues, and Veale—burning with ambition to get out of Birmingham—wanted to pitch against him one day. Hustling for money by hanging around the Negro Leagues no longer held its appeal. "You go someplace, they gonna give you a dollar to play and a dollar for meal money," Veale said. "But a growing kid need more than that."[5]

The Black Barons had a longstanding rivalry with the Kansas City Monarchs, and Monarchs manager Buck O'Neil had seen Veale pitch at Rickwood Field. While Veale attended Holy Family High School in

Twelve-year old Bob Veale was a batboy for the 1948 Birmingham Black Barons. Sixteen years later he led the National League with 250 strikeouts while pitching for the Pittsburgh Pirates. (*National Baseball Hall of Fame, Cooperstown, New York*)

the Ensley neighborhood. Monarchs owner Tom Baird repeatedly tried to sign Veale for his team. After the integration of the sport, Baird had realized that the future of baseball for an owner of a Negro League team was channeling talent to Organized Baseball. He wrote to the Veale family in November 1954 and again in June 1955, after Veale left Birmingham to attend Benedictine College in Atchison, Kansas, on an athletic scholarship. In the second letter, Baird suggested that the father and son had agreed that Bob would sign with the Monarchs during a conversation with O'Neil in May of 1955. The Veales felt they were being coerced. "Buck O'Neil and all those guys were demagogues," Veale said. "They were out for their own personal gain, one way or another, for financial and prestigious gain, or whatever they were

seeking at the expense of others. I didn't think it was too businesslike or too compassionate."[6]

Veale played baseball and basketball in college, and by 1958, when he was a senior, he was well known to scouts. In May of that year he was invited to try out for the Cardinals in St. Louis. Unbeknownst to the host team, Pirates scout Tuffie Hashem was in attendance early that day, and watched Veale warm up. Buddy Hancken, the Pirates' scout in Birmingham, who had been following Veale for years, seconded Hashem's recommendation, and Veale auditioned for general manager Joe Brown and pitching coach Bill Burwell at Wrigley Field in Chicago, where the Pirates were playing. They signed Veale that day.

At the age of 22, Veale was dispatched to San Jose of the Class C-California League. About the same time the team was transferred to Las Vegas. In 17 games (eight starts), he was 2-6 with an earned-run average of 5.43. The following year at Wilson of the Class-B Carolina League, he became a starting pitcher. In 147 innings he gave only one home run and led the league with 187 strikeouts. On July 23, 1959, he pitched a 2-0 no-hitter against Raleigh. He completed the year with a 12-5 record and an ERA of 3.49, and was advanced three levels to Columbus of the Triple-A International League for the 1960 season.

During his time in North Carolina, Veale experienced the worst treatment of his career as a result of the racism that was prevalent in the South during the period. While the harassment was constant, Veale did not let it bother him. "To me, it was just funny," he said. "I grew up in Alabama and got used to hearing stuff like that. It was just another stepping stone to success, I guess. Those remarks just made you work harder to achieve the goals that you had in sight."[7]

Veale spent three seasons with Columbus. In 1960 he led the league in walks allowed, with 119 in 172 innings. He won 10 of 19 decisions and finished with an ERA of 3.51. Veale established himself as a genuine prospect the following year. In 201 innings he struck out a league-leading and team-record 208 batters, and cut his walks down to 92.

The Pirates were suitably impressed, and invited Veale to spring training in Fort Myers, Florida, in 1961. While the white players stayed at the Bradford Hotel, the black players were placed with host families in the black neighborhood. Veale grew up with segregation, and he did not dispute the circumstances. In some ways, he preferred staying with the Evans family in Fort Myers. "Boy, you'd have the finest cooks you'd ever want to meet," he said. "We ate much better than the white players at the Bradford Hotel. I couldn't wait to leave the ballpark and get home and eat dinner."8 Sent back to Columbus, he won 14 games and lost 11 with a 2.55 ERA and only 92 walks in 201 innings pitched.

Veale stuck with the Pirates in 1962 and made his major-league debut on April 16, starting against the Chicago Cubs at Wrigley Field. He lasted only 2 1/3 innings, allowing three earned runs on six hits and three walks. He got his first win in his next start, on April 26 in Pittsburgh when he pitched a complete game to defeat the New York Mets, 4-3, and give the Pirates their record-tying 10th consecutive victory to start the season. Veale failed to make it through the fourth inning in his next two starts, and was moved to the bullpen, where he pitched four times through May 25, when he was sent back to Columbus. On August 10 he set an International League record for the most strikeouts in a game, 22 against the Buffalo Bisons. Veale didn't get the win; he was lifted for a pinch-hitter in the top of the 10th inning. He suffered an even worse fate on September 3, when he pitched a one-hitter against Jacksonville and struck out 15, only to lose 2-1. After winning eight games and striking out 179 in 134 innings, Veale and his good friend Willie Stargell were called up to the Pirates in September. On September 20 against the Cincinnati Reds, he pitched into the seventh inning in a 4-3 win. He followed that with a three-hit win over Milwaukee on the 28th, and earned his first save two days later.

Manager Danny Murtaugh began the 1963 season intending to use Veale out of the bullpen, preferably to face only one left-handed batter or in a mop-up role. After his first two appearances, Veale appeared in 10 games before a stretch of 15 straight Pirates losses, despite an ERA of 0.70 in relief. On August 25 the Pirates put Veale back in the starting rotation. He shut out the Phillies for seven innings, but the Pirates lost in the 11th when Johnny Callison hit a two-run home run off Elroy Face. Veale was sensational in September; in six starts, he threw three complete games, two of them shutouts, and finished with an ERA of 1.20 for the month.

Veale made his first start in 1964 against the Chicago Cubs, allowing four earned runs over seven innings in an 8-4 loss. He earned his first victory of the year two starts later with a complete game against the Mets. On the evening of June 7 against the Houston Colt .45's, he needed only seven innings to strike out 12 batters, tying the team record for most strikeouts in a nine-inning game set by Babe Adams in 1909. He not only failed to record the record-breaking strikeout, but he also lost the Pirates' 3-1 lead in the final frame, as the Colt .45's tied the game on two-strike hits by both Mike White and Walter Bond. "Yes, I knew I had tied the record," Veale said. "But I'm angry at myself for not finishing. It was all my fault."9

Two starts later, on June 16, Veale duplicated his feat, striking out 12 New York Mets in a complete-game, 6-4 victory. Adams' record finally fell on September 22 when Veale fanned 15 Milwaukee Braves, but it was not a happy occasion as he pitched a complete game only to lose 2-0.

Veale definitely paid attention to his strikeouts. Heading into the last day of the 1964 season, he had 245, and felt he was comfortably ahead of Bob Gibson for the league title. In the clubhouse he heard Harry Caray announce on the radio that Gibson was warming up in the bullpen for St. Louis against the Mets in New York. Veale requested three innings of work, and recorded five strikeouts, for a total of 250. Had he not pitched, he would have finished in a tie with Gibson. He concluded the season with a record of 18-12 and an ERA of 2.74. He reportedly received the largest pay increase of the team for the next season.

In 1965 Veale finished with a record of 17-12 and an ERA of 2.84. He pushed his strikeouts to 276, the most in the modern era by a Pirate. Led by Veale on the mound and Stargell and Roberto Clemente at the plate, the Pirates finished with a record of 90-72, good enough for third place in the National League, seven games behind the pennant-winning Los Angeles Dodgers.

One of the highlights of Veale's campaign took place on June 1 in Pittsburgh, when he pitched a five-hit shutout of the Philadelphia Phillies to give the Pirates their 12th straight victory, while striking out 16 batters to break his own team record. The game was interrupted twice for long periods due to rain, forcing Veale to warm up on three separate occasions. "I watched him warm up three times," said Phillies pitcher Chris Short, "and I swear he got faster every time."[10] On September 19, 1966, Veale pitched a 10-inning, one-hit shutout against the Phillies in Pittsburgh, striking out 12 batters. "It had to be the best game I ever pitched in the majors," he said. "I never had a one-hitter before and never felt as confident in my pitches."[11]

With an outfield consisting of Willie Stargell, Roberto Clemente, and Matty Alou, the Pirates made a serious run at the National League pennant in 1966, finishing with a record of 92-70 that left them only three games behind the Los Angeles Dodgers. Despite a sore back that flared up from time to time, Veale was a workhorse once again, starting 37 games and finishing 12 while posting a 16-12 record and an ERA of 3.02. One of his best efforts came on June 19, 1966 when he pitched an 11-inning complete game against the Atlanta Braves, allowing only five hits while striking out nine. "No man should lose if he can pitch the way Veale did that day," said Stargell, who won the game with a home run in the final inning. "Why, I could see the blue flame rising from his fastball way out in left field."[12] The game fell on Father's Day, leading Veale to speak of his father after his performance. "My dad would have been proud of me had he been there to see the game," he said.[13]

In 1967 Veale started fast, winning his first six starts and seven of his first eight. Accolades from opposing hitters continued to pile up, with predictions of a 20-win season. "Over the first four innings

in his second game against us, Veale was faster than I've ever seen Koufax," said Lou Brock.[14] But by the end of a campaign that saw the Pirates finish a disappointing 81-81, Veale once again had 16 victories, but with an elevated ERA of 3.64 and only six complete games.

During the 1968 season, the nagging injuries to his back and shoulder gave way to a more serious elbow problem. After a shutout against the Cardinals in which he struck out 13 batters, Veale admitted to having pitched through elbow pain throughout the game. "My elbow was hurting me all through the game," he said. "I wanted to get out of each inning in a hurry. I don't believe in overpowering the batter anymore. I find when I try to cut loose I feel a dull ache in my elbow."[15]

Despite the injury, 1968 was a good season for the left-handed ace, but the numbers support the change he was forced to adopt. Both his strikeout and walk rates were significantly reduced, suggesting that Veale was attempting to pitch to contact more often. The Pirates finished at 80-82 for the year - Veale's own record of 13-14 was a reflection of the disappointing campaign.

Over the next two seasons, Veale maintained his usual workload of 200-plus innings, and the Pirates won 88 and 89 games respectively, but he finished with a losing record in both years. His ERA rose to 3.92 in 1970, and prior to the 1971 campaign there were rumors that the Pirates were looking to trade him. Danny Murtaugh, who returned to manage the club in 1970, instead switched Veale to the bullpen.

The 1971 season turned to be one of the greatest in the history of the franchise. Under Danny Murtaugh, the Pirates won the Eastern Division title with 97 victories, then defeated the San Francisco Giants three games to one in the NLCS. In an epic World Series, the Pirates defeated the Baltimore Orioles in seven games.

Veale pitched in 37 games out the bullpen, but despite finishing with a record of 6-0, his ERA was a very high 6.99. He did come on strong in September as the Pirates made their push for the division title, allowing only one run and two hits in his last 7⅔ innings. He made only one postseason appearance, however, in Game Two of the World Series. He faced five batters, allowing two inherited runners to score on two walks and one hit, as the Orioles won, 11-3.

On September 1, 1971, the Pirates became the first major-league team to start a lineup of all minorities. Veale entered the game in the third inning in relief of starter Dock Ellis, and struck out the only batter he faced. Many of the players on the team realized what was about to take place when they first saw the lineup card, while others didn't realize what was happening until the game was under way. At one point, Dave Cash exclaimed to Al Oliver, "Scoop, we got all brothers out there!"[16] Rather than cause dissension, the event brought an already friendly, loose bunch of players even closer together. "I think it was a great thing that happened there," said Bob Robertson, who was replaced by Al Oliver in the starting lineup of the historic game. "That was the type of ballclub we had. It didn't make a difference if you were black, yellow, green, purple, whatever. We got along fine. We enjoyed each other's company. We had a lot of respect for one another. I thought that was a great evening, to see that."[17]

While the 1971 season ended with a World Series ring, Veale, now 36 years old, realized that his time with the Pirates was probably nearing the end. Still, the team protected him on the 40-man roster. "I'd like to stay in Pittsburgh," he said. "But if I don't, I won't quit. I still think I can help some club. Why is it that so many people feel you're through when you pass 35?"[18]

Veale pitched well in his first three outings to begin the 1972 season, but was hit hard in his next two appearances, and the Pirates, needing a roster spot, placed him on waivers. On May 10 he was released. "I knew it was coming," he said. "I always wondered how it would feel, the moment like this. It's kinda harsh, you know."[19] Manager Bill Virdon delivered the message. "It wasn't an easy thing to do," he said. "Everybody liked Bob. He was a good man around a ballclub. Never a problem. Veale wasn't that kind of a person."[20]

Veale cleared waivers and agreed to accept an assignment to the Pirates' Triple-A farm club in Charleston. He appeared in 17 games for the Charlies, including 12 starts, and finished with a 2.82 ERA and 76 strikeouts in 83 innings of work. On September 1, upon the recommendation of Danny Murtaugh, the Boston Red Sox signed Veale. He made his first appearance in the American League on September 10, and pitched extremely well, allowing only two hits and no runs in eight innings. The Red Sox pennant run fell short, but the club would bring him back in 1973.

Veale married his high-school sweetheart, Eredean Sanders of Graysville, Alabama, in February of 1973. He married later in life than many of his teammates; while he never made much of it, he had been waiting until he helped all 13 of his siblings attend college. Veale pointed out the problem of mixing baseball and marriage: "You've got to have a real fine, tolerant wife—one who understands the problems of baseball. If you're not fortunate enough to get the right one, she can pull you down. But, thank God, I've got the right one."[21]

Veale had a comeback season for the Red Sox, making 32 relief appearances and earning 11 saves. At the end of the year, the team released him but invited him to return to spring training in 1974 on a minor-league contract. Under the rule in place at the time, Veale could not be added to the Red Sox 25-man roster until May 15, so he began the season with Triple-A Pawtucket. There he pitched as well as served as a coach. While warming up on the night before he was scheduled to rejoin the Red Sox, he heard a pop in his shoulder and experienced enough pain that he could not lift his left arm the following morning.

The Red Sox training staff worked on Veale's arm throughout the year, and he was able to appear in 18 games. But as the season progressed, he was used sparingly, pitching only 13 innings, with an ERA of 5.54. His last major-league appearance came on September 8 against the Milwaukee Brewers. Once the season was over, he made it known that he would like to stay in baseball as a coach or minor-league instructor, and while he had to sit out the 1975 season, he was hired in 1976 by the Atlanta Braves as a minor-league pitching instructor.

On his way to the Braves' West Palm Beach spring training camp in February of 1977, Veale drove his car into a canal when he became drowsy from medication he had taken for the flu. "Believe me, I'm lucky," he said. "Two feet either side of where I went into and I'd have hit a concrete culvert head-on."[22] Despite his scare, Veale enjoyed his new job. "I love it," he said. "Actually, it's more challenging than playing. There's great satisfaction in being in a position to move young fellows up to the major leagues. That's what life is all about."[23]

Veale went on to work for New York Yankees in the same capacity, and in 1983 he was hired as pitching coach of the Utica Blue Sox, an independent team playing in the affiliated New York-Penn League. On "Bob Veale Day," the Blue Sox celebrated his career, and Willie Stargell flew in for the occasion. Stargell commented, "There are givers and there are takers in the world. Bob Veale is a giver."[24]

Veale had always maintained his offseason home in Birmingham, and after his retirement from baseball he returned there to stay. At the age of 58, Veale stayed connected to his baseball roots by working as a groundskeeper at Rickwood Field two days a week. He played an important role in preserving the storied old ballpark he played in as a child.

Veale was always well-liked by his teammates and trusted by his managers. Danny Murtaugh selected him to be his enforcer. "Anytime anyone got in trouble, I had to go get 'em," said Veale. Murtaugh would send me because he knew I would bring them back."[25]

Considering that he was perennially among the league leaders in walks, and was perhaps the hardest throwing left-handed pitcher in baseball, hitters were naturally reluctant to dig in against Veale. Manny Sanguillen said, "Lou Brock was a little scared of Veale sometimes because Bob was nearsighted and would take off his glasses and pitch anyway. Willie McCovey, too. One day, Bob took those glasses off and threw the ball 100 miles per hour at McCovey. I

asked Veale what happened, and he said, 'My glasses were too wet, and I wanted to show him I could throw a strike without my glasses.' That pitch was ten feet high."[26]

As fearsome as he was on the mound, Veale did not have a mean streak. "He can throw the ball through a brick wall, but everybody knew that he was a gentle giant," said teammate Gene Clines. "If Veale would knock you down, it had to be a mistake. He didn't want to hurt anybody."[27]

Veale did not begrudge current players the high salaries they achieved after he left baseball. "I should have been born in 1955 instead of 1935," he was quoted as saying in 2002. "But I don't dwell on anything like that. It's the foam at the bottom of the spillway. It's water over the dam. Veale had one more claim to fame; it was rumored that he was the originator of the famous baseball oxymoron, "Good pitching can stop good hitting every time ... and vice versa." Author Allen Barra once approached Veale at Rickwood Field, where Veale was consulting on the production of the film *Cobb*. "I asked him, 'Mr. Veale, are you the one who said 'Good ...' He cut me off with 'Yes, I am.'"[28]

When he was a young boy facing adversity, Veale often remembered the words of his father. "My daddy said, 'If you got what it takes, everything will work out.'"[29] His ambition had been to follow Willie Mays to the big leagues. When he achieved his goal, he was named to two National League All-Star teams, in 1965 and 1966. Willie Mays led off both games for his team. "That was good advice from my daddy, said Veale."[30]

In 2016 Bob Veale, 78 years old, still resided in Birmingham with his wife, Eredean. In 2006, he was inducted into the Alabama Sports Hall of Fame.

SOURCES

In addition to the sources cited in the Notes, the author also relied upon the following:

Bird, John T., *The Bill Mazeroski Story* (Birmingham, Alabama: Esmerelda Press, 1995).

Hall, Donald, *Dock Ellis in the Country of Baseball* (New York: Touchstone Books, 1989).

Markusen, Bruce, *The Team That Changed Baseball: Roberto Clemente and the 1971 Pittsburgh Pirates* (Yardley, Pennsylvania: Westholme Publishing, 2006).

Powell, Larry, *The Black Barons of Birmingham: The South's Greatest Negro League Team and Its Players* (Jefferson, North Carolina: McFarland & Company, 2009).

NOTES

1   Allen Barra, *Rickwood Field: A Century in America's Oldest Ballpark* (New York: W.W. Norton, 2014), 140.

2   John Klima, *Willie's Boys: The 1948 Birmingham Black Barons, The Last Negro League World Series, and the Making of a Baseball Legend* (Hoboken, New Jersey: Wiley Publishing, 2009), 70.

3   Klima, 71.

4   This would mean that the 12-year-old Veale was pitching in the Negro Leagues. Author Klima quotes Veale as saying that he pitched batting practice for the Barons, but there is no suggestion in *Willie's Boys* that Veale pitched in a league game. —Eds.

5   Klima, 84.

6   Ibid.

7   Frank Garland, *Willie Stargell: A Life in Baseball* (Jefferson, North Carolina: McFarland & Company, 2013), 41.

8   Ibid.

9   Les Biederman, "Tying SO Record Hard to Swallow for Veale," *Pittsburgh Press*, June 8, 1964.

10   Mark Mulvoy, "Baseball's Week," *Sports Illustrated*, June 14, 1965.

11   Les Biederman, "Bob Veale," *Pittsburgh Press*, October 2, 1965.

12   Les Biederman, "Blue Flame Trails Each Veale Pitch," *Pittsburgh Press*, July 9, 1966.

13   Ibid.

14   Les Biederman, "Veale Ignores an Aching Back—Buc Lefty Making Hitters Moan," *The Sporting News*, May 27, 1967.

15   Les Biederman, "Smokeless Bob Veale a Puzzle to Redbirds," *Pittsburgh Press*, June 1, 1968.

16   Bruce Markusen, "Remembering the All-Black Lineup," *Bruce Markusen's Cooperstown Confidential* (blog), September 1, 2006 (8:50 a.m.), bruce.mlblogs.com/2006/09/01/remembering-the-all-black-lineup/.

17   Markusen.

18   Charley Feeney, "There's Still Life at 36 for Veale in Pirate Bullpen," *Pittsburgh Post-Gazette*, December 4, 1971.

19   Pat Livingston, "Bob Veale the Pirate: A Memory," *Pittsburgh Press*, May 4, 1972.

20   Livingston, "Bob Veale the Pirate."

21   Fred Ciampa, "Veale Another Coup for O'Donnell," *Boston Herald*, April 22, 1973.

22   Pat Livingston, "Bang, Veale's Back!," *Pittsburgh Press*, March 4, 1977.

23   Ibid.

24   Scott Pitoniak, "Stargell, Veale Renew a Longtime Friendship," *Daily Press* [Utica, New York], 1983.

25   Garland, 69.

26   Bird, 216.

27   Hall, 33.

28   Allan Barra, "My Most Favorable Baseball Moments," *Salon*, July 26, 2002.

29   Klima, 85

30   Ibid..

SAMUEL C. WILLIAMS

By Bob LeMoine

Sam Williams was born in a small, poor town in segregated Alabama, served his country in World War II, played in the last Negro League World Series, and then pitched for minor-league teams from California to Canada and from Mexico to the Dominican Republic. "It didn't matter who I pitched against, I was going to pitch my game," Williams said. "If you hit me, you hit me, but I figured I was going to get you out. I figured you had one chance to get a hit, and I had nine chances to get you out. That's the way I approached pitching."[1] Known for his smiles and happy-go-lucky attitude, Williams was simply grateful for the opportunity to play the game he loved despite receiving neither wealth nor fame because of the color of his skin. "We all loved the game," he said. "We weren't playin' for the money because we wasn't makin' no money."[2]

Samuel Clarence "Sammy C" Williams was born on October 13, 1922, in Ketona in Jefferson County, Alabama, about seven miles north of Birmingham. Now incorporated into the city of Tarrant, Ketona was the site of Jefferson County's poorhouse. "The place name came to mean not a suburb of northeastern Alabama, but a place where indigents disappeared into oblivion," wrote historian Wayne Flynt. "Only the most calamitous set of circumstances—illiteracy, indigence, illness, and lack of family—brought one to such a destination."[3]

Williams was born to Jake and Sylvia (Johnson) Williams. By the 1930 census, the couple had apparently divorced and Sylvia had married Roosevelt Ferguson (spelled "Feurgeson" on the census form), a laborer in a steel mill. The other children were Warren, Marvelene, and Rosetta. Also at the residence were Sylvia's parents, Sam and Florence Johnson. Sam worked at a rock quarry. The family owned their own home, valued at $1,800. At the 1940 census the residence was listed as a farm in Ketona valued at $600.

Roosevelt, now listed as "Robert," was making $390 a year as a coal miner. Neither of Sylvia's parents had finished more than three years of school; Robert had only finished the eighth grade and Sylvia the seventh. Sammy graduated from Hooper High School, possibly the first of his family to complete school.

Baseball was part of Sammy's life early on. "When I was a kid we used to play in the fields with little neighborhood teams," he reminisced.[4] After graduating from high school, he went into the military during World War II and served in the US Army Air Forces from 1943 to 1946. "When I was in the service, I drove heavy equipment and the driver [would] get tired and I'd relieve him and give him some rest," Williams said.[5] He met his future wife, Frances, while stationed in Pueblo, Colorado. They were married in New Mexico in 1943.[6] Williams also played service baseball.

When the couple returned to Alabama, Williams got a job in a steel mill. He played for the Clow Pipe Shop team, a pipe manufacturing plant that fielded a team in Birmingham's Industrial League. The baseball teams were segregated; plant owners financed both black and white teams in an attempt to reach both demographics of fans. "Birmingham had a lot of companies there that sponsored baseball and they had a good city league," Williams remembered. "At one time, you could go to Birmingham and pick up any kind of a good ballplayer that you'd want to, but the thing about it is, the fellas didn't want to leave. They was workin' for those plants and they didn't wanna leave."[7] Clow Pipe won the city championship in 1946, and that winter played a game against the Birmingham Black Barons of the Negro American League. Williams impressively pitched all nine innings in the 2-1 loss and Black Barons manager Tommy Sampson and player Artie Wilson visited him the next day. They offered him a contract, but Williams was hesitant. "I'd never been out of Birmingham, except for my time in the Army," the young pitcher said. "I wasn't sure that I wanted to go." Wilson promised, "I'll take care of you," and Williams spent the next four seasons pitching for Birmingham.[8]

Williams spent his rookie season of 1947 being a spot starter and relief pitcher for the Black Barons, pitching mostly in nonleague games. "It was all right with me," he said. "That was good experience for me."[9] Williams made $300 a year for Birmingham.[10] He also learned how to master control of his pitching from pitcher Chet Brewer, who taught him about pitch placement. Williams had arrived with an arm that could blow fastballs by hitters in the Industrial League, but he would have to learn new pitching mechanics when facing the more talented batters in the Negro Leagues. "Chet told me that I was wild in the strike zone," Williams said. "I'd never heard that before."[11] Brewer encouraged Williams to throw to different spots of a player's body—belt buckle, knee-cap, etc.—while playing catch. "After I got it down, I figured I was on my way," Williams said. He was now hitting the corners of the plate when pitching.[12]

Williams displayed his talent in a game in New Haven, Connecticut, shutting out a local team called the Sailors, 2-0. "That game really gave the Barons an idea of what they had," Williams remembered.[13] Late in the 1947 season, he went the distance in a 7-4 win over the Memphis Red Sox in which he scattered nine hits.[14]

Williams remembered the long, grueling bus rides. "We traveled for a week without sleepin' in a bed. We would play here tonight and we'd be on the road goin' to the next town to play." But he had a fondness for those days. "We were a very close group of fellas. There was no animosity or nothin'. We were just like a bunch of brothers. Under the conditions that we were travelin'— buses and changin' clothes in buses at the ballpark—everybody pitched in, nobody grumbled. All we wanted to do was play ball. That was the highlight of my career, them bus rides."[15] When the bus driver was tired, Williams would replace him behind the wheel.

SAM WILLIAMS

Pitcher Sammy C. Williams posted a 6-3 record and a 3.21 ERA in league play for the 1948 Birmingham Black Barons. Here he is shown during his time with the Eugene (Oregon) Emeralds in 1955. (*Eugene Register-Guard, April 24, 1955*)

The 1948 season was a memorable one. The Black Barons had a strong pitching staff and Williams was 4-1 by the end of July.[16] He finished 6-3 with a 3.21 ERA in 12 league games and the Black Barons went to the playoffs. He started Game Six of the Negro American League championship series. Birmingham led the Kansas City Monarchs three games to one (with one game a tie). Williams had scattered eight hits over eight innings as he took the mound in the bottom of the ninth inning with Birmingham leading, 4-3, three outs away from the pennant. He retired the first batter, but then Earl Taborn singled. Kansas City manager Buck O'Neil sent up pitcher Hilton Smith, a good hitter to pinch-hit. Williams, tiring, tried unsuccessfully to sneak a fastball by Smith, who ripped a double to right field, sending Taborn to third. Williams walked Herb Souell to load the bases.

Birmingham manager Artie Wilson jogged out to the mound to talk to Williams. He had no other pitching options at that point and the dangerous lefty Hank Thompson was coming up. His only hope was a double-play ball or a fly ball to Willie Mays, who had the strongest arm in the outfield. Thompson lined an opposite-field single to left in front of Jim Zapp, who had the weakest arm in the outfield. Taborn scored and O'Neil, coaching third base, waved home Smith, who scored the winning run and kept Kansas City alive in the series. Williams and the Black Barons walked off the field in despair, but it would be short-lived as they finished off the Monarchs and won the series.[17] They lost the final Negro League World Series to the Homestead Grays.

In 1949 Williams went 8-6 for the Black Barons with a 3.21 ERA in 21 games. After the season he played against a Jackie Robinson-led touring team.[18] In 1950 he was 13-7 for Birmingham with a 3.81 ERA in 22 games. The Negro Leagues were facing tough financial times as owners saw a shortage of talent, money, and attendance. Star players followed Robinson to the major leagues after he broke the color barrier. Other players went north to play in Canada, while still others, like Williams, went south to play in Mexico. "Down there," Williams recalled, "a baseball player was a god at that time. You were a big-time celebrity in Mexico. We were treated real well. The pay was more. This is why I chose to go to Mexico, because we could make more money down there."[19] Williams said decades later that he had made $600 to $900 a month playing in Mexico.[20]

Williams pitched the 1951 season for the Jalisco, Mexico, club, going 5-10 with a 3.97 ERA.[21] The 1952 season was a busy one for him. Williams went 9-5 for Jalisco, and also 8-3 for San Domingo.[22] He later returned to the Black Barons and, in July, was sent to the Brandon Greys of the ManDak (Manitoba-Dakota) League. "Williams is highly recommended by several players now with the Greys," wrote the *Brandon Daily Sun*.[23] He pitched in 16 innings for the Greys, going 1-2.[24] Williams went the distance with a three-hitter in a 9-0 win over Winnipeg in the Winnipeg Tournament, which Brandon won.[25] He entered in the fourth inning of Game One of the ManDak semifinal playoff series against Minot. Brandon was trailing 5-1 and Williams finished the game, giving up five hits and two runs in a 7-2 loss.[26] Brandon was swept, and Williams's time in Canada was over. He made a quick trip south and played briefly for the Tigres del Licey team in Santo Domingo, Dominican Republic.

In 1953 Williams was signed by the Oklahoma City Indians (Double-A Texas League), which had been integrated by his former Black Barons teammate, pitcher Bill Greason, the previous season. A new Oklahoma City teammate remarked, "Oh, you're Sad Sam from Birmingham," and the nickname stuck.[27] Williams was told by a white player on the team that he was the best pitcher on the staff, but they already had a black player and couldn't have two.[28] It was common practice at the time, at both the major- and minor-league levels, for teams to have a limit on the number of black players on the roster. Williams and his black teammate, most likely Greason, actually had to call a black cab driver at the train station because white drivers refused to give them a ride.[29] Williams was in Oklahoma City during spring training, then was sent to the Pampa (Texas) Oilers of the Class-C West Texas-New Mexico League.[30] He pitched well right from the start for the Oilers, giving up only six hits in a 12-4 "virtually invincible" win over Clovis on April 26.[31] On May 1, Williams carried a shutout into the ninth against Albuquerque, but "the negro mound artist weakened," in the words of the *Albuquerque Journal*, and gave up four runs, yet held on for the 7-4 win.[32] In early June, Williams was leading the Pampa pitching staff with an 8-2 record.[33] On July 4 he won both games of a doubleheader, defeating Abilene 7-3 and 9-0, to bring his record to 15-5.[34] He had extra motivation during the game, as he faced racial slurs from a fan in the stands. "It made me a better person and a much better ballplayer," Williams said.[35]

Williams had 19 wins when he pitched for the South in the All-Star game on July 23. The South lost 7-3, but many in attendance were rolling in the aisles watching a Williams at-bat against pitcher Eddie Locke. Williams worked the count to 3-and-2 and then fouled off several pitches. After each foul Williams would playfully yell at Locke something like "throw dat ball in here and ah'll ware it out!"[36] Several fans remarked that the exchange, ending in a strikeout, was worth the price of admission. Though Williams won 26 games, Pampa did not qualify for the playoffs.[37] Williams was voted the league's Rookie of the Year.[38]

"I was famous for breaking these color lines," Williams said.[39] He was the only nonwhite player on the Pampa team and found the African-American community there (which lived in a section of town near the railroad tracks where there were no sidewalks) warm and receptive. There were black-owned hotels and restaurants in town, which was a new experience for him. Williams had often stayed in homes of prominent black families while his white teammates stayed in a hotel.[40] On one occasion, in Plainview, Texas, Williams slept in the boiler room of the hotel while his white teammates slept in their rooms.

Williams spent the early part of the 1954 season with Oklahoma City, but returned to Pampa after falling to 0-3. He won a doubleheader on June 1 against Lubbock, starting the first game and relieving in the second.[41] He shut out Albuquerque on six hits and used his bat to drive in the go-ahead run in a doubleheader sweep on August 5.[42] Williams homered in a 4-0 win over Plainview on September 5, gaining his 16th win and propelling Pampa into first place.[43] He finished the regular season 15-10. He guided Pampa to an 8-1 win over Abilene in the opening game of the playoffs.[44] After Game Three, the team bus was in an accident, and Williams was hospitalized with numbness in his left arm and bruises on his head.[45] He returned to pitch Game Six, eliminating Abilene with a 17-3 shellacking.[46] In the

league championship series, Williams defeated Clovis 6-3 in Game Three, giving Pampa a 2-1 series lead.[47] Pampa later won the series.[48] Williams played winter ball that year for the Spur Cola team in Panama.[49]

In January 1955, Williams was acquired by the Eugene, Oregon, team of the Class-B Northwest League.[50] The team and the league itself were in its first year of organization. His age was reported as 26 years, not his actual 32, so there were rumors that three major-league clubs were interested in acquiring him.[51] Williams became popular with teammates and fans early on. "He is a happy-go-lucky sort of fellow who keeps his teammates in good humor," wrote the *Eugene Register-Guard,* which would soon refer to him as Smilin' Sam. He impressed his new team during batting practice when he smashed a home run into the left-field stands "and kept strutting until Bobby Doerr put three somewhat farther into the stands." Doerr, the former star for the Boston Red Sox and was later inducted into the Hall of Fame, was now a retired cattle rancher in Oregon who was an executive with the Eugene club.[52]

Williams threw a three-hit shutout against Spokane on July 2.[53] He finished 9-7 with a 3.42 ERA in 25 games, only 12 being starts. In dramatic fashion, Eugene rallied from four runs down in the ninth inning of Game Six to stun Salem in the Northwest League championship series. Williams, who had entered the game with two outs in the eighth, struck out Harvey Koepf to end the game and "the entire Eugene dugout erupted and the fielders rushed in to mob Smilin' Sam," wrote the *Register-Guard.* "The dressing room was a bedlam—not because the players collect $13.86 as their winning share, but because they had won a championship—and will soon be heading home."[54] Williams' got the pennant-winning victory with his 1⅓ innings of scoreless relief.

Williams recalled another memorable moment from his time in Eugene, but it did not occur in a game. Max Patkin, who called himself the Clown Prince of Baseball, was in town to put on one of his performances. Patkin would hang upside down in front of a wall or backstop and swing away at pitches thrown to him, more often than not making contact.

Patkin asked to face the pitcher with the best control and manager Cliff Dapper recruited Williams, saying he was "the best control pitcher we got." Williams laughed at the memory years later. "I got a kick out of it. He used to put on a good show."[55]

Williams spent the winter in Eugene working as a gas-pipe inspector.[56] In January 1956 he was traded to San Jose of the Class-C California League.[57] Williams won his first three starts[58] and had another strong season: 15-9 with a 3.10 ERA in 203 innings pitched with 52 walks and 121 strikeouts.[59] He also batted .354 in 79 at-bats. Williams had trouble trying to find a black barber shop in town, and even more difficulty with housing discrimination. He often found that the home he and Frances were interested in buying would become unavailable when their race was discovered.[60] After renting for 13 years, the Williamses were finally able to purchase a home in San Jose in 1972.[61]

Williams returned to Mexico for the 1957 and '58 seasons, going 8-8 for Veracruz in 1957 and 9-11 for Poza Rica in 1958. He held out during spring training in 1959 when he wanted to sign with the Mexico City Reds, but Poza Rica didn't want to release him. When he asked for a raise, Poza Rica refused, and Williams failed to report. The boss of the minor leagues, George Trautman, suspended him for a year, and that was the end of Williams's career. Frances had already been urging him to retire and spend more time with his children, Sam Jr. and Sharon. The suspension all but decided the issue for him.[62]

Williams got a job driving a bus in San Jose for the Valley Transit Authority. He thought this would be a temporary job, but found that the job fit his personality perfectly. "I liked it because of the people," he said. "The people were friendly and nice to me and I'm a fella that likes to laugh and talk and I just got a kick out of it." He retired from the job in the early 1980s after 25 years,[63] and Frances retired as a sales clerk.[64] In January 2007, nearly 60 years after playing together in the last Negro League World Series, the last surviving members of the Birmingham Black Barons gathered in Beverly Hills, California. The occasion was the annual Professional Scouts Foundation dinner. Mays, the most famous Black Baron of them all, honored his four living teammates: Williams, Greason, Zapp and Wilson. Mays made sure those gathered at the dinner knew he was only an American legend because of his teammates. "What they did for me, I'll never forget," Mays said. "Those four guys knew I could play baseball, and even though they were older than I was, they would say to me, 'You have a better chance of getting to the big leagues than we do, and we want to make sure you get there.' I want to give them as much credit as I possibly can."[65]

Samuel and Frances had been married over 60 years by the time of her death in 2005. Samuel died two years later, on August 8, 2007, at the age of 84. He was survived by his two children. He and Frances are buried in Pueblo, Colorado.[66]

Williams said baseball was "the best job I ever had in my life. I wouldn't take nothin' for the experience. You meet a lot of nice people, you get a chance to see the world and some of the country, and the value that you get from meetin' people you can't put no price on. It's an education."[67]

SOURCES

In addition to the sources listed in the Notes, the author also benefited from the following:

"1952 ManDak League," in *Western Canada Baseball*. attheplate.com/wcbl/1952_20i.html. Retrieved March 14, 2017.

"1952 ManDak League Playoffs," in *Western Canada Baseball*. attheplate.com/wcbl/1952_20h.html. Retrieved March 14, 2017.

Powell, Larry. "Industrial Baseball Leagues in Alabama," *Encyclopedia of Alabama*. Retrieved March 10, 2017. encyclopediaofalabama.org/article/h-2479.

San Jose (California) Public Library.

Special thanks to Lorraine Denise Grant for research assistance.

NOTES

1   Larry Powell, *Black Barons of Birmingham: The South's Greatest Negro League Team and Its Players* (Jefferson, North Carolina: McFarland, 2009), 161.

2   Brent Kelley, *I Will Never Forget: Interviews With 39 Former Negro League Players* (Jefferson, North Carolina: McFarland, 2003), 177.

3   Wayne Flynt, *Poor but Proud: Alabama's Poor Whites* (Tuscaloosa, Alabama: University of Alabama Press, 2001), 186.

4   Kelley, 175.

5   Powell, 160.

6   Lorraine Denise Grant, "Ex-Negro League Player Sam Williams Never Strikes Out!" *Exodus*, October 12-November 11, 1993: 8.

7   Ibid.

8   Powell, 159.

9   Ibid.

10   Ibid.

11   Ibid.

12   Ibid.

13   Ibid.

14   "Black Barons Stop Memphis Sox, 7-4," *Arkansas Democrat* (Little Rock), September 19, 1947: 17.

15   Kelley, 177.

16   "Winning Hurlers Pace Birmingham," *Lexington (Kentucky) Leader*, July 30, 1948: 5.

17   John Klima, *Willie's Boys: The 1948 Birmingham Black Barons, the Last Negro League World Series, and the Making of a Baseball Legend* (Hoboken, New Jersey: John Wiley & Sons, Inc., 2009), 167-169.

18   Powell, 160.

19   Kelley, 175.

20   Grant, 8.

21   The *Pampa Daily News* (June 7, 1953) claims Williams pitched for Birmingham in 1951, going 18-8.

22   "Meet the Oilers," *Pampa (Texas) Daily News*, June 7, 1953: 10.

23   "New Pitcher and Catcher to Bolster Roster of Greys," *Brandon Daily Sun*, July 14, 1952: 2.

24   "1952 Statistics," *Western Canada Baseball*. attheplate.com/wcbl/1952_2.html. Retrieved March 14, 2017.

25   "Brandon Greys Thump Giants and Edge Carman Cards to Win Winnipeg Tournament," *Brandon Daily Sun*, August 5, 1952: 3.

26   "Minot Mallards Win Semi-Final Opener," *Brandon Daily Sun*, August 19, 1952: 3.

27   "Meet the Oilers."

28   Grant, 8.

29   Grant, 9.

30   "Oilers Sign Two More; Play Hubs Tonight," *Pampa Daily News*, April 9, 1953: 12.

31   "Oilers Dump Pioneers, 12-4," *Pampa Daily News*, April 27, 1953: 5.

32   "Williams Stops Late Uprising," *Albuquerque Journal*, May 2, 1953: 13.

33   "Meet the Oilers."

34   "Iron Man Williams Halts B-Sox Twice," *Abilene (Texas) Reporter-News*, July 5, 1953: 44.

35   Grant, 9.

36   Buck Francis, "Press Box Views," *Pampa Daily News*, July 24, 1953: 7.

37   "B-Sox Clip Hubs, Dukes Clinch Tie for 1st Place," *Abilene Reporter-News*, September 7, 1953: 6. Sources including baseball-reference.com credit Williams with 25 wins.

38   "Sam Williams Rookie of Year," *Clovis (New Mexico) News Journal*, August 30, 1953: 8.

39   Grant, 9.

40   Grant, 8.

41   "Hubbers Continue Plunge With Double Loss at Pampa," *Lubbock (Texas) Morning Avalanche*, June 2, 1954: 14.

42   "Pampa Slames Dukes Twice," *Abilene Reporter-News*, August 5, 1954: 24.

43   "Oilers Trip Ponies; Take Over 1st Place," *Pampa Daily News*, September 6, 1954: 10.

44   Buck Francis, "Oilers Take Playoff Lead; Thump Abilene Blue Sox, 8-1," *Pampa Daily News*, September 12, 1954: 7.

45   "4 Oilers Injured in Wreck," *Pampa Daily News*, September 14, 1954: 1.

46   Jack Holden, "Blue Sox Close Season with Loss," *Abilene Reporter-News*, September 18, 1954: 2.

47   "Pampa Staggers Clovis, Takes WT-NM Series Lead," *Lubbock Morning Avalanche*, September 21, 1954: 17.

48   Buck Francis, "Oilers Bring WT-NM Flag Back to Pampa," *Pampa Daily News*, September 24, 1954: 7.

49   Buck Francis, "Press Box Views," *Pampa Daily News*, December 23, 1954: 6.

50   Joe Kelly, "Between the Lines," *Lubbock Evening Journal*, January 20, 1955: 18.

51   "Dapper, Williams of Emeralds at Portland Training," *Eugene (Oregon) Register-Guard*, March 4, 1955: 15.

52   Dick Strite, "Highclimber," *Eugene Register-Guard*, April 17, 1955: 27.

53   "Emeralds Beat Spokane Twice," *Eugene Register-Guard*, July 3, 1955: 12.

54   Dick Strite, "Emeralds Claim Northwest Crown," *Eugene Register-Guard*, September 13, 1955: 18.

55   Kelley, 176.

56   Dick Strite, "Highclimber," *Eugene Register-Guard*, April 15, 1956: 13.

57   "Williams Sold to San Jose," *Eugene Register-Guard*, January 13, 1956: 13.

58   "3rd Win Notched by Sam Williams," *Eugene Register-Guard*, May 24, 1956: 38.

59   Dick Strite, "Highclimber," *Eugene Register-Guard*, September 28, 1956: 14.

60   Grant, 9.

61   Ibid.

62   Kelley, 176, 178.

63   Kelley, 179; sources differ on whether Williams drove a bus until 1982, 1983, or 1984. Williams claimed he drove for the company 25 years, which following his career would have been 1959-1984. His obituary says he drove 30 years for the company, and other sources say he retired in 1982 or 1983.

64   Grant, 9.

65   Mel Antonen, "Holes, Questions Dot Pitching Staffs," *USA Today*, January 5, 2007.

66   "Samuel C. Williams," obituary retrieved March 14, 2017. legacy.com/obituaries/mercurynews/obituary. aspx?n=samuel-c-williams&pid=92508546; "Frances Elizabeth Williams," obituary retrieved March 14, 2017. legacy.com/obituaries/mercurynews/obituary.aspx?n=frances-elizabeth-williams&pid=15816701

67   Kelley, 179.

ARTIE WILSON

By Rob Neyer

Artie Wilson's career makes just the barest impression in the old *Baseball Encyclopedia*: 19 games and 24 plate appearances spread across five weeks in the spring of 1951. But both before and after that short stint with the famously fated '51 Giants, Wilson ranked for years as one of the biggest stars in *two* big-time leagues, and is forever remembered by big-time baseball fans in both the Deep South and the Pacific Northwest.

Arthur Lee Wilson was born near Birmingham, Alabama, in the fall of 1920, just a couple of weeks after the Cincinnati Reds finished off the Black Sox in the World Series.[1] We don't know much about Wilson's childhood. By the late 1930s, though, he was working in a Birmingham factory. In 1939 he suffered an accident that might easily have cost him a sterling baseball career almost before it began. "I was cleaning up the machine shop," Wilson later recalled. "I happened to be standing close by a machine and then a long piece of iron got hooked and was vibrating in the saw. I tried to grab it but I didn't know what happened. I ran across to the warehouse station and I needed someone to turn off that machine. I didn't know my thumb was [gone] until I pulled the glove off. I pulled out my thumb, which got caught up in that glove."[2]

More than a half-century later, Wilson recalled using a golf ball as a rehab tool. "I carried that golf ball all the time," he said in 1997. "My thumb got strong and I never missed it. The only thing was that when I threw, I had a natural sinker."[3]

Wilson reportedly didn't miss a single day of work. Or a baseball game, either. In those years, the Birmingham Black Barons played the area's best baseball. But just a rung below was the Industrial League, with all-black teams representing local factories and steel mills. Before the 1944 season, Barons shortstop Piper Davis told the owner about an even better

shortstop. Just a few months later, having signed with the Barons, Wilson earned a spot in the starting lineup for the Negro American League in the East-West All-Star Game, black baseball's annual soiree held at Chicago's Comiskey Park. He missed out in 1945—Jackie Robinson got the spot instead—but was again the West's starting shortstop from 1946 through '48. In the latter season, Wilson was credited for many years with a .402 batting average in 76 games; today, some consider him the last .400 hitter in a "major" league (a claim bolstered only by further research showing him with a .428 average that season, in approximately 40 official league games).

The story of how Wilson wound up as property of the New York Yankees has been told in different ways in different places, but Neil Lanctot's version in *Negro League Baseball: The Rise and Ruin of a Black Institution* seems the most reliable.

In the winter after the '48 season, the Yankees offered Black Barons owner Tom Hayes the going rate: $5,000 for Wilson's rights, with another $5,000 if he was still with the Yankees in June. Hayes telegraphed his acceptance, but later reneged when Bill Veeck's Indians offered more; Wilson, too, reportedly wasn't thrilled about going to the Yankees and taking a significant pay cut from his Barons salary. So on the 9th or 10th of February, with Bill Veeck having flown to Puerto Rico for the occasion, Wilson signed a contract with the Indians. "Our scouts say he is the best prospect in the Negro Leagues today," Veeck told reporters. "Better, even, than Larry Doby."[4]

"I've hit major league pitching before," Wilson said. "I think I can hit it again. ... It's going to be like going to school all over again. I know I have a lot—an awful lot—to learn. But again, I think I can do it."[5] After the '46 season, Wilson had joined Satchel Paige's All-Stars in a barnstorming tour around the Eastern half of the United States, with Bob Feller's All-Stars providing the competition, and

Shortstop Artie Wilson hit .402 for the 1948 Birmingham Black Barons and won the Negro American League batting title. (*John W. Mosley Photograph Collection, Temple University*)

the black and white players mingled freely. "I talked with all of them," Wilson told me in 2004. "Phil Rizzuto said, 'If I had an arm like yours, I'd play for a hundred years.' We went out there to beat 'em, the major leaguers. And they wanted to win. They didn't want no black players beating them."

The Yankees didn't have any real interest in Wilson, but they certainly didn't want Veeck to have him, either. Immediately after the news broke about

Wilson's new contract, general manager George Weiss issued a statement: "There are so many angles to this affair which must be studied, that the Yankees offer no comment at this time other than to say Cleveland has acted unethically if not in direct violation with baseball law." For his part, Wilson said during spring training, "New York made me an offer. I didn't accept it. Cleveland came along with another offer. I liked it. I accepted it and signed. That's all there is to it."

Ah, but the Yankees lodged a formal complaint. Meanwhile, Wilson reportedly enjoyed spring training with the Tribe. "They treated me like a king," he said many years later. "I thought I could play shortstop until I came to that camp. I learned the most from [Joe] Gordon. He told me I had to learn to play the hitters, watch the catcher's signals and take a step before the ball was hit."[6]

However much he learned, Wilson had almost no chance of breaking into the Indians' lineup. Not with manager Lou Boudreau manning shortstop, perennial All-Star Ken Keltner at third base, and future Hall of Famer Joe Gordon at second base. Before spring training ended, Wilson was optioned to the Indians' farm club in the Pacific Coast League, leading Dan Daniel to write, "Wilson has been sent to San Diego, and never will make the major leagues. Not so long ago Veeck said he would not trade Wilson for Phil Rizzuto."[7]

On May 13 the Office of the Commissioner handed down Decision No. 26, regarding the disposition of both Wilson and Luis Marquez (also the subject of a dispute between Veeck and Weiss). In what must have seemed a brilliant balancing act, Commissioner Albert "Happy" Chandler gave Marquez to the Indians and Wilson to the Yankees; more specifically, Wilson was "awarded to the Newark International League Club."[8]

Wilson was immediately transferred from the San Diego club—with whom the Indians had a working relationship—in the Pacific Coast League to the Yankees' Newark affiliate in the International League. But Wilson never went to Newark. Instead he stayed in the Pacific Coast League, thanks to a deal with the Oakland Oaks. Still in his prime, Wilson batted .348 overall and captured his second batting title in two years.

When Wilson arrived in Oakland, there weren't any other black players and he was told he'd have to room alone. According to one story, Billy Martin said, "He's got a roomie now. I'll room with him."[9]

"We were close," Wilson said in 1993 about Martin. "We'd go hear music together, everything. And we stayed in touch."[10]

But while Martin would soon join the Yankees, Wilson would not. First Boudreau had blocked Wilson, and now Rizzuto (plus the Yankees' deeply held organizational prejudices). So 1950 was just more of the same, as Wilson batted .311 in 196 games with the Oaks. That May the *New York Age*, a black newspaper, reported that while the Yankees still owned Wilson's rights, "Art would rather quit baseball than play with the Bombers who tried their best to get rid of him last year. ... He's on the Coast playing with the Oakland team and making a boatload of loot."[11]

After the season, though, it looked as though Artie would finally get his shot in the majors, when the New York Giants acquired him from Oakland in a six-player, $125,000 deal. Asked for comment, Bobby Hofman, Wilson's erstwhile double-play partner with the Oaks, allowed that Wilson was solid rather than flashy on the field. But off the field? "He collects those silly looking golf caps, all colors," Hofman said. "He doesn't play golf at all, he just wears the damn caps. Must have 40 of them, at least." For his part, Wilson would admit owning only seven or eight: "I just like to wear 'em."[12]

A couple of weeks before Opening Day, Giants manager Leo Durocher was asked to name the spring's biggest development. His response: "This fellow Wilson. In my book he has been terrific and I don't see how I'm going to keep him out of the lineup. He can play second, short, or third; he can play the outfield, and don't be surprised if one of these days you see him on first base. A fellow who can field and hit the way he can is going to take somebody's job, make no mistake about that."[13] He'd also reportedly claimed that only three National League

shortstops—the Giants' own Alvin Dark, along with Granny Hamner and PeeWee Reese—could beat out Wilson in a fair match.[14]

As expected, though, Wilson opened the season on the Giants' bench. His third game action—like the first two, as a pinch-hitter in a game the Giants were losing—came against the Dodgers, who just happened to be managed by Chuck Dressen, Wilson's manager with Oakland in both 1949 and '50. Dressen probably had seen Wilson play more games against tough competition than anyone else, and he trotted out that knowledge against the Giants, ordering what the *New York World-Telegram's* Joe King described as "a shift which probably had never before been seen in the big leagues... shifting three of his infielders to the left side of second base, and pulling in his right fielder, Carl Furillo, to play second. He left right field wide open, undefended, and right field in Harlem roams 460 feet from the plate before it turns toward center."[15]

Alas, Wilson couldn't take advantage of the shift, tapping weakly to pitcher Don Newcombe. According to King, Dressen hadn't invented the shift; "Lefty O'Doul of the San Francisco Seals had worked it on Wilson frequently," and Wilson's only home run in 1950 came when he hit the ball against the shift.

In fact, Wilson had been facing extreme shifts since early in his Organized Baseball career. Back in 1950, the following item appeared in *Pacific Coast Baseball News*:

"Li'l Artie has done more than expected of him since he joined the Oaks from the Padres. ... His play at short has been so remarkable defensively the Oaks pace all other teams in double-plays. His scrappiness has earned him the admiration of his teammates, the respect of his foes. Yet, with his skills and years of experience, he still possesses the eagerness to learn and is often out during the day with skipper Charley Dressen trying to improve his fielding and hitting when a night game is slated. He's the fire in the Oakland wheel that keeps it rolling so fast toward first place. *And even the adoption of the 'Williams' shift hasn't stopped his flurry of base-hits.* The lad runs, hits, fields superbly —what more does one need to be the outstanding player of the year[?]"[16]

Wilson finally started a game on April 26, going 1-for-3 with a walk while spelling Eddie Stanky at second base. On May 6 he started at shortstop in the second game of a doubleheader, going 1-for-4. While he would get into 10 more games with the Giants, he wouldn't start again. His last hit came on May 12 when he singled home Bobby Thomson in a losing effort against the Phillies. In the stands that afternoon: General Douglas MacArthur, dressed in mufti and attending his first major-league game since 1935.[17]

Back in 1948, Wilson's last season with the Barons, one of his teammates was a 17-year-old outfielder named Willie Mays. In the spring of '51, Mays was batting .477 for the Giants' Minneapolis farm team. It was time. But with Mays coming up, somebody had to go down. It was Willie's old Birmingham mentor.

Tommy Sampson, who played with and managed Wilson in Birmingham, attributed Wilson's short stint in the majors to his extreme hitting style. "You know the reason why?" Sampson told interviewer Brent Kelley. "He couldn't hit the ball to right field. That was his problem. You throw the ball and he's gonna hit it to left field anyway, or he's gonna hit it to shortstop. He was always running away from the plate; he hit running. That's the reason why he didn't stay up."[18]

Meanwhile, Monte Irvin offered a couple of reasons for the demotion: "Although nobody wants to admit it," Irvin wrote in his memoir, "there was an unwritten quota system at the time that limited the number of black players on a ballclub. But Durocher was going to send Artie down anyway because Leo thought it was simply outrageous that he couldn't pull the ball. If he had been getting base hits, it might have been different. ... Wilson had never pulled the ball before and couldn't in the majors. ..."[19]

Yes, keeping Wilson would have given the Giants five black players: Wilson, Mays, Irvin, third baseman Hank Thompson, and backup catcher Ray Noble. It's been said that owner Horace Stoneham simply didn't want more than four black players on the club. As a practical matter, most teams with black players preferred an even number, because it was felt, however ridiculously, that a black player must have a black roommate. And it was two per room.

Of course, it was also true that Wilson's manager hadn't found much use for him. When Mays was promoted, Wilson had started only two games, pinch-hit in 11 more, and collected just four hits (all singles) in 22 at-bats.

And as Wilson would later say, "Leo had two people that he could option out — Ray Noble or myself. But we already had an agreement that if he wasn't going to play me, he was going to send me to Oakland's minor-league affiliate in the Pacific Coast League because I can't sit on the bench and just do nothing; I've got to play."[20]

Initially the Giants sent Wilson to Ottawa in the International League. But after just a few days (and two games) with that club, he was shifted to Minneapolis. And after a few weeks there, it was back to Oakland. According to one source, Oaks owner Brick Laws called Giants owner Horace Stoneham and pleaded for Wilson, because otherwise the Oaks just wouldn't draw any fans. Oakland's fans presented a large floral arrangement upon Wilson's return to the city, and the club drew more than 23,000 fans for his first three games. And after a doubleheader against the San Francisco Seals that season, manager Lefty O'Doul said, "You don't see shortstop being played better by anybody than you saw it today. I spent a few years in the majors, but I never saw anything like the exhibition Wilson staged."[21]

After the season the Cardinals and other National League clubs reportedly inquired with the Giants about acquiring second baseman Eddie Stanky to serve as player-manager. It says something about Artie Wilson's declining stock that, in the event Stanky did leave, Wilson was merely listed among lesser lights Bob Hofman, Davey Williams, and Rudy Rufer as candidates to replace him in the Giants' lineup.[22] In the event, the Giants did trade Stanky to the Cardinals, and Williams took over at second base. In fact, just before Stanky was officially dispatched, the Giants sold Wilson to the Pacific Coast League's Seattle Rainiers.[23]

Wilson's stock had obviously fallen, not surprising considering his .255 batting average in 81 games with the Oaks. But with the Rainiers he rediscovered his batting stroke, topping .300 in each of his three seasons in Seattle. In '53, Wilson became the Rainiers' everyday second baseman, and would play mostly that position for the rest of his career. In 1955 he joined the PCL's Portland Beavers, where one of his teammates was outfielder Ed Mickelson. In Mickelson's memoir, he wrote,

"Artie kept us alive with his infectious, positive spirit, saying, 'Never fear, Artie's here!'

… Artie's forte was a line drive over the third baseman's head, just inside the left field line. Even though he was a left-handed hitter, the defense bunched him to the left, but he would still manage to drop the ball the opposite way, safely down the left field line for a base hit. …

"Artie, whom I guessed to be either a shade over or under 40, could still run, display an average arm, hit PCL pitching for over a .300 average and, perhaps most importantly, display a love and zest for the game that was unmatched by most. God! How I would have loved to have seen Artie Wilson play in his youth."[24]

According to one source, Wilson became known in the Coast League as "the Birmingham Gentleman."[25] He returned to Seattle for most of 1956 and all of '57, struggling in the latter season. Still only 36, Wilson seemed finished. But in 1962, after four seasons out of baseball, he made a brief and unsuccessful comeback, batting .186 over 39 games in the Class-A Northwest League and the Triple-A PCL (with Portland again). After which he really was finished in the game.

Very late in his life, Wilson's youthful skills would be acknowledged once more. At a 2006 gala in Beverly Hills, Willie Mays honored his four living Birmingham Barons teammates: Bill Greason, Stephen Zapp, Sammy Williams, and Artie Wilson. "What they did for me," Mays said before the dinner, "I'll never forget. … I want to give them as much credit as I can."[26] A few months later, Wilson threw out the first pitch at a Yankees-Mariners game in Seattle. And around the same time, the *ESPN*

Artie Wilson, shown here in the uniform of the Triple-A Pacific Coast League's Oakland Oaks, was known to be as good a fielder at shortstop as he was a hitter. (*National Baseball Hall of Fame, Cooperstown, New York*)

Baseball Encyclopedia retroactively named Wilson the Negro American League's Most Valuable Player in 1944.[27]

At times in his career, Wilson had been listed as 5-feet-11 and 170 or even 175 pounds. But late in his life he would say, "I never weighed 175 pounds. I weigh 162 pounds, what I've always weighed. And I'm only 5-feet-10."[28]

On October 31, 2010, just three days after his 90th birthday, Artie Wilson died in Portland. Until nearly the end, Wilson had kept going to work at a Portland-area Ford dealership where he'd been employed for decades. "I can't sit down," he said in 1997. "There's nothing to do at home."[29]

He was survived by his wife, Dorothy, whom he'd wed back in 1949. They had two children, Zoe and Arthur Lee Wilson II. Known as Artie Jr., the latter starred in basketball at the University of Hawaii, and for some years worked in broadcasting and real estate. The elder Wilson also had a daughter from an earlier marriage, and departed with four grandchildren and nine great-grandchildren.[30]

NOTES

1   His birthdate was October 28, 1920, and he was apparently born in Jefferson County, near Birmingham Alabama.

2   John Klima, *Willie's Boys: The 1948 Birmingham Black Barons, the Last Negro League World Series, and the Making of a Baseball Legend* (Hoboken, New Jersey: John Wiley & Sons, 2009), 37-38.

3   Bob Dolgan, "He could always hit," Cleveland *Plain Dealer*, August 26, 1997.

4   Ed McAuley, "Indians sign Birmingham Negro shortstop," *Cleveland News*, February 10, 1949.

5   Associated Press, "Gordon of Indians ends holdout for salary believed near $40,000," *New York Times*, March 8, 1949.

6   Dolgan, "He could always hit."

7   Dan Daniel, "Dan's Dope," *New York World-Telegram*, April 30, 1949.

8   Baseball, Office of the Commissioner, May 13, 1949.

9   Dolgan, "He could always hit."

10 Filip Bondy, "Story of a different color," *New York Daily News*, September 16, 1993.

11 *New York Age*, May 20, 1950.

12 Bill Roeder, "Wilson sets his cap on steady Giant duty," *New York World-Telegram and Sun*, March 7, 1951.

13 John Drebinger, "Wilson, versatile Negro player, slated for regular Giant berth," *New York Times*, April 3, 1951.

14 Bill Roeder, "Oakland supplies flag edge," *New York World-Telegram and Sun*, March 26, 1951.

15 Joe King, "At least, Leo can't call Chuck shiftless," *New York World-Telegram and Sun*, April 21, 1951.

16 "Noren, Wilson clash for "rookie" honors with amazing play," *Pacific Coast Baseball News*, September 10, 1949.

17 Louis Effrat, "Konstanty scores," *New York Times*, May 13, 1951.

18 Brent Kelley, *The Negro Leagues Revisited: Conversations with 66 More Baseball Heroes* (Jefferson, North Carolina: McFarland & Co., 2000), 125.

19 James A. Riley and Monte Irvin, *Nice Guys Finish First* (New York: Carroll & Graf, 1996), 142-143.

20 Ross Forman, "Negro League great Artie Wilson profiled," *Sports Collectors Digest*, January 29, 1993.

21 Larry Moffi and Jonathan Kronstandt, *Crossing the Line: Black Major Leaguers, 1947-1959* (Iowa City: University of Iowa Press, 1996), 68-69.

22 James P. Dawson, "Cards rebuffed in bid for Stanky," *New York Times*, November 29, 1951.

23 John Drebinger, "Lanier and Diering slated for Giants," *New York Times*, December 11, 1951.

24 Ed Mickelson, *Out of the Park: Memoir of a Minor League Baseball All-Star* (Jefferson, North Carolina: McFarland & Co., 2007), 168-169.

25 Matt Schudel, "Hit .400 in baseball's Negro Leagues," *Washington Post*, December 15, 2010.

26 *USA Today*, January 5, 2006.

27 Larry Blakely, "Last of the .400 hitters," *Chicago Sports Weekly*, September 12, 2007.

28 Filip Bondy. "Story of a different color," *New York Daily News*, September 16, 1993.

29 Dolgan, "He could always hit."

30 Bruce Weber, "Artie Wilson, 90, shortstop who was mentor to Willie Mays," *New York Times*, November 8, 2010.

JIM ZAPP

By Bill Nowlin

Jim "Zipper" Zapp played a big role in getting the Birmingham Black Barons to the 1948 World Series against the Homestead Grays. It was a season that had seen a young rookie named Willie Mays spell him in the second game of a doubleheader. Zapp was a big right-handed outfielder, standing 6-feet-2 or -3 and listed between 215 and 230-some pounds. He went on to play several more years before leaving the game.

In one sense, though, leaving the game was something Zapp did with some frequency. Looking back years later, he said that probably the one thing that held him back the most was that he kept quitting teams—and yet when he left he felt it was because he was standing up for fair treatment. He got branded as temperamental. "They called it temperamental," he told interviewer Brent Kelley, "but I didn't call it temperamental. If I didn't think the owners was treating me right, I'd quit, ask for my release, or whatever, as long as they didn't give me my money. Sometimes they did not."[1]

Nashville, Tennessee, was the birthplace of James Stephen Zapp on April 18, 1924.[2] Because of the racial mores of the day, his family history is a little difficult to understand. His father, Burt, was a baker by trade. Jim Zapp was born to a white man and a black woman. As James Zapp Jr. explained late in 2015, "My granddad was of German-English descent. My grandma was black. My dad was born in what you call 'out of wedlock' because back in those days white guys could not be with black women."[3] Jim's birth mother was Ardina Jordan and his birth father was Thomas Burton Zapp—Burt Zapp.[4]

The 1910 census says that Burt Zapp's father, Henry (a locomotive engineer, born to two German parents), came from Indiana, and his mother, Helen (Burton) Zapp, known also as Nellie, came from England.[5] Burt was born in June 1876.

The 1900 census shows Zapp working in Nashville and living with his wife, Ellen, and the head of the household, Green Simpson (perhaps Ellen's mother.) He was employed as a baker for the County Asylum.[6] The 1910 census has him living with a 7-year-old daughter, Katie A. Zapp. He's listed in the 1920 census as divorced, a native of Indiana, living with his daughter, Katie Wilian, 16, and her daughter, Ellen, who was 15 months old.

When Jim Zapp was born he was assigned the surname of his mother, Jordan. As James Jr. explained, back then "society was never told who the white father was, therefore, my dad and his siblings' birth certificates have no father named. My granddad was white. I've got pictures of him. He was white as snow. "[7]

Later, and sometime before he joined the Navy, Jim elected to take the last name of his father and became James Stephen Zapp. James Jr. added, "My dad's father was very bold and did inform society the children were his." His willingness to be so bold may have influenced Jim Zapp's willingness to stand up for himself when he felt he was not getting a fair shake.

Burt had a brother and a sister. James Jr. further explained that Kate was not Burt's daughter, but the daughter of his wife. Burt Zapp seems to have raised four children: Katie, Richmond, Jim, and Jennie.

Come 1940, "Birt" Zapp was listed as a roomer in the house of Audine (Ardina) Jordan, a widow. He was still working as a baker, and living with Richmond, an office clerk at a state park, and the younger James and Jennie. James, 15 at the time, was listed as a "new worker." Jennie was 13 and without an occupation.

Jim went into military service during World War II, early—in 1942, and that's said to be where he first truly got involved with baseball. He was a boatswain's mate 2nd class in the US Navy and was stationed in

Outfielder Jim Zapp who later in life asserted that the highlight of his baseball career had been playing for the 1948 Birmingham Black Barons against the Kansas City Monarchs in that season's NAL playoff series. (*Courtesy R. D. Retort Enterprises*)

Hawaii at Pearl Harbor. There he started playing ball for the Aiea Naval Barracks team — first the all-black team "and then joined the barracks' integrated team. He also played at Manana Barracks in Hawaii."[8]

Indeed, it may have been Zapp who integrated the team: "One day we were playing and the manager for the white team was watching us play. I was playing third base at the time. His name was Edgar "Special Delivery" Jones. He was an All-American football player from the University of Pittsburgh. ... He saw us play and he integrated the white team at that time. He took me and the first baseman ... Andy Ashford."[9]

Zapp's team won back-to-back titles in 1943 and 1944.[10] Before the war was over, Zapp had been trans-

ferred back to the States in April 1945, and played baseball for the Navy at Staten Island, New York, that summer.[11] He was one of two black players on the team, playing for manager Larry Napp, who later umpired over 3,600 American League games from 1951-74. Among those he had played with or against were Johnny Mize, Joe DiMaggio, Phil Rizzuto, and Pee Wee Reese.[12]

Apparently later in the year Zapp is also said to have been "signed by 'Fat Puppy' Green to join the Baltimore Elite Giants winter season," playing on weekends as a part-timer. In 1946 he "returned to Nashville to complete a season with the Nashville Cubs."[13]

In 1947, he said, he was traded to the Atlanta Black Crackers and played with them for about half the season. He hit 11 homers for Atlanta in the time he was with them, and so had to some extent proven his abilities.[14] But Jim told Kelley that when the team went to New York to play, where his mother and sister were living, "I quit the team right there because of the owner of the Atlanta Black Crackers; you had to almost *fight* him to get your money."[15]

Back in Nashville, he said, "I was uptown one day, standing in front of a nightclub, and a fella from the Memphis Red Sox, T. Brown, was coming through Nashville and he saw me. He said, 'I heard you quit playing baseball.' I said, 'Yeah, I'm giving it up. I can't stand it no more.' He said, 'Would you go back to playing if I recommend you to the Birmingham Black Barons?' I told him, 'Yeah, I'd go to the Black Barons.'"[16]

John Klima writes that Zapp had "a tan complexion that allowed him to pass in many social circles. He also learned that being light-skinned sometimes meant exclusion from both groups. This hurt and haunted him throughout his early years, but he found complete acceptance in black baseball."[17]

Zapp joined Birmingham during spring training at Alabama State University in Montgomery and played left field for manager Piper Davis. Davis had Ed Steele play in right field, with Norman Robinson in center. Rookie Willie Mays joined the team after school got out and would sometimes sub for Zapp in left during the second game of doubleheaders, but when Robinson broke his leg later in the season, Mays was brought in to play center. He hadn't yet developed the hitting skill and power that he would, but his fielding was strong enough to keep him in the spot—and when Robinson returned, Mays was moved to left field, leaving Zapp the odd man out for a while. Years later, Zapp very graciously said of Mays, "Here we thought we was the ones makin' him better, but it was the other way around."[18]

He was brought back in time to play a key role in the 1948 playoffs. "The highlight of my career was in 1948 when I was playing with the Birmingham Black Barons against the Kansas City Monarchs."[19] The two teams had matched up well and gone into Game Five of the league championship series. The Monarchs were up by a run, 3-2, but Zapp homered in the bottom of the ninth to tie the game.[20] Another run followed and the Black Barons held a one-game edge in the playoffs. They won the Negro American League pennant and went on to battle against the Homestead Grays in that year's World Series.

After the season, he quit again. There was a barnstorming tour put together, the Indianapolis Clowns against a team playing with Roy Campanella and Jackie Robinson. "They picked all the boys from Birmingham to go with Jackie Robinson and Campanella and they put me with the Clowns. I got upset again, so I told them just to give me my release. And they did, they gave me my release. That's probably one of the biggest mistakes I ever made in my life."[21]

That there might have been opportunities now that major-league baseball had begun to be integrated didn't seem to matter. Zapp told John Klima, "When [Brooklyn] signed Jackie, my attitude didn't even change. I didn't even think about going to the majors. I just kept on doing the same things I was doing. ... I just could not believe I would have the same chance."[22]

And the release apparently resulted in his effectively being blacklisted by Tom Hayes of the Black Barons. "Piper always used to say I was the biggest fool he had ever seen," Zapp said. "He said, 'You quit a championship team over a few dollars.'"[23]

Zapp played semipro ball in the Nashville area for the next couple of years—in 1949 for the Morocco Stars and in 1950 for the Nashville Stars. Jim Riley reports that he returned to the Baltimore Elite Giants "in the latter part of the 1950 season ... and remained with them in 1951."

During that 1951 season, Zapp was said to have been "playing the best ball of his entire career," but when he was not selected to the midseason East-West All-Star Game, he "immediately became disgruntled and left the team right there on the spot."[24] As he put it, "Here's another quitting deal. I was playing for a man by the name of Sue Bridgeforth, who bought the team. In midseason they had the East-West Game. I should have been in the East-West Game unanimous, but they took me off the team and replaced me with somebody else, so I quit the team and went on to New York. That was my best there in Negro league baseball. It was politics."[25] He added, "I said I'd never play in the Negro leagues again, which I didn't. Well, I played a few more games with them in '54, but I went out to Big Springs, Texas."

It was in 1952 that Zapp entered Organized Baseball by signing with the Paris (Illinois) Lakers of the Class-D Mississippi-Ohio River Valley League. The 1951 Lakers had won the flag with ease, finishing 15 games ahead of the second-place Centralia Zeros. In 1952 Danville won, by two games over Paris. SABR's Minor League Database shows teammate Clint "Butch" McCord with a .392 average and 15 homers, with Zapp playing in 122 games, homering 20 times, and batting .330.[26] Zapp's 136 RBIs led the league; years later, memory was that he still held the league record.[27]

Probably the most spectacular win for the team was the June 11 road victory over Centralia, 15-6, with Paris scoring every one of its runs in the fourth inning. Pitcher Herb Heiserer hit a grand slam in the inning and once the bases got loaded again, Zapp hit one too.[28] Zapp was named as the league's all-star left fielder.[29]

Zapp said, however, "Something happened during the season that they didn't like about my personal life, so they gave me an unconditional release during the winter."[30] This time it wasn't Zapp electing to leave. The team released him because he was dating a white woman. They could have sold his contract to a major-league team but instead they released him outright, which prevented him from catching on with a major-league team.[31]

Burt Zapp died on January 29, 1953.

Riley's biography of Jim Zapp perhaps helps explain his 1953 season. "His temperament, which had also always contributed to problems while he was playing, continued to plague him after leaving the Negro Leagues. In his second season in the Mississippi-Ohio Valley League he began with Danville, but played only briefly before joining Lincoln in the Western League, also for a brief time."[32] Zapp admitted as much: "Great temperament is not something I always had. I was very temperamental."[33] SABR's database shows him with 11 games for the Danville (Illinois) Dans (with a .286 batting average) and three games (one hit in seven at-bats) for the Class-A Lincoln Chiefs.

After spring training at Corpus Christi, Texas, in 1954, Zapp remained in Corpus Christi for a brief time —"for three or four days and Corpus Christi came up with the idea that they weren't ready for a black ballplayer yet so they optioned me to Odessa, Texas. … I inquired about Odessa from some of the guys in a barber shop and they said, 'Man, you don't want to go to Odessa. That's nothing but sandstorms, tumbleweeds, and rattlesnakes.' So I took my train fare and instead of going to Odessa I came back to Nashville."[34] He quit. "All of the trades, uprooting, and traveling had taken their toll. Jim had decided it was time to pack it in. He headed home to Tennessee."[35] There he took a job, but had second thoughts and contacted Odessa. Too late. They'd found someone else. But they did refer him to owner Robert "Pepper" Martin of the Big Springs (Texas) Broncs. Martin bought his contract for 1954, and Zapp hit a home run to center field in his first at-bat for San Angelo. He homered again his first game in San Angelo itself.

Because the area was segregated, Martin found him a room in a black private home.[36]

Zapp played the 1954 and 1955 seasons in Big Spring, two full and productive years in the Class-C Longhorn League. His 32 homers led the team in 1954; Zapp drove in 86 runs and hit for a .290 batting average. The Big Spring Broncs finished fifth in the eight-team league. Though the 32 homers were quite an accomplishment, this was the year that Roswell's Joe Bauman hit more than twice as many—72. Bauman drove in 224 runs. Zapp may have hit more, but he played in only 90 games. In the last month of the season, he had returned to the Negro American League to play both for the Elite Giants and the Black Barons.[37]

In 1955 the team changed its name to the Big Spring Cosden Cops, and finished seventh. Zapp hit 29 homers, batting .311. (Bauman hit 46.) Zapp was with Big Springs for 89 games, then played his last 39 games in organized ball for the Class-B Port Arthur Sea Hawks (Big State League), batting for a .287 average with eight home runs.

The team wanted to cut Zapp's salary, which he did not accept so they sold his rights to the Cleveland Indians. That is when he decided to retire. James added an aside, "His normal playing weight was 210 but he told my brother Richmond that he started drinking a lot of beer and picked up weight to about 230."[38] Zapp decided to leave baseball and took a position in Big Spring in 1956 as a civilian sports director with the US Air Force. "He was the athletic director at Webb Air Force Base," said James Jr. "He did that until 1977. The Air Force base closed in '77 and he transferred to Fort Rucker, Alabama, and was the athletic director at Fort Rucker until he retired. I want to say he fully retired in 1982. From that point on, he just lived the rest of his life in retirement."

Zapp did qualify for a pension. There's a bit of a story there, too, James Jr. explains. "My dad had turned in the affidavit with all his information and he got a letter back from Major League Baseball and they turned him down. I was still in the Army and I went there to visit and he showed me the letter and showed me the affidavit and I said, 'Well, Daddy, the dates on here are wrong. That's why they turned it down. You don't have the right dates on here. You didn't have enough time, based on these dates.'

"I called up a guy at Major League Baseball—I can't even remember his name—and I told him the dates were wrong. 'I'll tell you when my dad played. As a matter of fact, I have a book in my house that my dad gave each one of us years ago that this guy wrote on Negro Leagues baseball, and it has pictures and dates and everything.' I said, 'I will send you that book because I actually have two of them. He said, 'Well, I'll send it back.' I said, 'No, no, you keep it. Maybe you can use it to find out about other players.' I sent him that book and about two weeks later he called me and said, 'Your dad's approved. He will receive a check.' To this date, he still receives that $833.33 every month. It's called *Pictorial Negro Leagues Legend Album* by Robert D. Retort."

"In addition" to simply enjoying his retirement, Jim Zapp said, "I coached youth baseball and umpired for 20 years."[39] He attended a number of Negro Leagues reunions of one sort or another, and Jim and his wife frequently went to spring training in St. Petersburg. On Christmas Day 2016, James Zapp Jr.—who himself was still active umpiring high-school baseball—recalled a story about his father:

"My dad was one of the best umpires in west Texas in the 70's. He traveled quite a bit to umpire games and always made it to our baseball games no matter how far he had to drive to arrive at mine and my brother's games.

"One night Dad was on the road umpiring; the next day was a Saturday, and my brother and I had a game in Odessa which was 45 miles from Big Spring. He didn't come home Friday night, telling us that he would see us in Odessa. When we arrived, he came to hug and kiss us after we got off of the bus. Then he disappeared. We were in the dugout after warmups, and the umpires entered the field. One of them was my dad. He had never called any of our games. One of the umpires

originally scheduled to call our game had to cancel and my dad was asked to replace him. We were shocked to see Dad calling the first game of a doubleheader behind the plate.

"When I came to bat the first time, I hit a bomb that probably sailed 375 feet on the fly. The field had no fence so the outfielder quickly ran the ball down and held me to a triple. When I came to bat again two innings later, I was hit by a pitch on the first pitch. No one thought much of it until I came to bat two innings later and was once again hit by the first pitch. When the pitcher hit me the second time, I started toward the pitcher's mound. Dad knew what was going on before I could take one full step toward the mound and aggressively said to me, 'Whooooooa, boy.' (Knowing Dad and all that he taught us about respecting the game of baseball, I immediately stopped with tears of anger in my eyes and headed to first base. After that game my dad told me how proud he was of me. I guess I was not as temperamental as my dad was."[40]

Jim Zapp had four children. Born first, in November 1950, was James Earl Arnell. He later married Viola Elizabeth Webb and they had three children: Jenniffer Rhenee Zapp-Chaviest (b. September 24, 1954), James Stephen Zapp Jr. (b. May 1, 1957), and Richmond Christopher Zapp (b. August 6, 1958). All three children pursued careers in the military, and all three retired in the very same year, 2003.

James Jr. says: "I retired after 26 years in the Army. My rank was sergeant major (E9) and I was the senior medical NCO for III Corps and Fort Hood. I was a paratrooper with time in the 82nd Airborne and the Special Warfare Center at Fort Bragg. I was a paratrooper medic. I did NBC—nuclear, biological, chemical warfare. I was with the Special Forces for a while, until I broke my back on a parachute jump. I did a little bit of everything in 26 years. My sister retired from the Navy after 21 years after being involuntary extended for 2½ years due to 9/11. She retired as a first class petty officer (E6), with her job encompassing all aspects of aviation maintenance administration. Her duty stations, both sea duty and shore duty, spanned from Florida, Virginia, Maryland, and Texas. She also served overseas with numerous aircraft patrol squadrons, the USS John C. Stennis, and the USS Theodore Roosevelt [both aircraft carriers]. My brother retired after 23 years as a chief petty officer (E7) and was an independent duty corpsman. He served on three ships, several shore-duty commands, two overseas commands (Japan and Italy), and one tour with the US Marine Corps. His deployments aboard ship took him to Canada, Mexico, Bahamas, England, Denmark, Russia, Spain, Italy, Portugal, Philippines, Korea, Japan, Hong Kong, Thailand, and Australia. He also deployed in country to Latvia and Haiti. His last duty station was Pearl Harbor where our dad served during WWII. All of us served in Desert Storm and Desert Shield. I was also involved with deployments to Somalia and Bosnia, just short deployments. "[41]

Jim's wife, Viola, passed away in 1982 and he remarried Ehria "Muffy" Acklen — her former husband, Teddy Acklen, had owned a semipro team that Jim Zapp had played for, the Del Morocco All Stars. "Everyone knew him as Uncle Teddy," said James Jr. "As kids that is even what we called him. My dad also ran the numbers for him to make extra money." The Del Morocco itself was a "plush dinner club … owned by Theodore 'Uncle Teddy' Acklen, a remarkable self-made man who scrambled up from the streets to one day play host to Jackie Robinson and Roy Campanella."[42]

Ehria died in 2013. "That's when I went to Nashville," James Jr. said. "At Muffy's death we realized that he had Alzheimer's and I went to Nashville to pick him up. I got guardianship of him and brought him here." Here being Harker Heights, Texas.

In 2014 it looked as though Jim was dying. The word went out to leave him in peace.

But in 2015, another chapter of Jim Zapp's life was unfolded and it took an unexpected turn. First, it had seemed as though he was gone, but then he came back to life.

Son James Zapp Jr. brought his father to his home in Texas from his dad's home in Nashville. Jim was no longer able to take care of himself. James says. "When I brought my dad back here … I had redone my house and turned my office into his bedroom. My goal was to keep him here, but after about seven weeks, I realized my dad needed round-the-clock care and I couldn't give it to him. He could not take care of himself at all. His memory span was about two minutes. He would get upset when I left. I was either going to school or going to umpire and every time I would walk out the door he would be upset at me. He would be mad at me because I was leaving. He did not want the nurse. He wanted me."

It became difficult, and untenable. James found accommodation for him in a senior citizens home only about five minutes away from his own place. "He is in the area that requires 24 hours care. When I first put him there, my dad was still partly there. He complained to me, 'James, I shouldn't be here. I'm not crazy like these people.' Some of them were pretty bad.

"They were worried about him escaping. I said, 'He is not going anywhere. He doesn't even know where he's at. He even told me, "James, I'm not going anywhere. I don't even know where I'm at."' He knew he couldn't walk out of this place because he wouldn't know where to go." This was in May 2013.

At a certain point, Jim was diagnosed with stage four Alzheimer's disease. The staff at the facility also experienced some problems with Jim. He'd get upset, as Alzheimer's patients usually do. Around June 2014, the staff increased the medications. Jim had reported some pain and the medications addressed it.

Then his condition appeared to deteriorate. "Every time we went to see my dad, he looked like he was comatose. He couldn't stay awake more than 10 seconds and he would go back to sleep. They had him in one of these type wheelchairs where he was laying back and he couldn't get up. He couldn't feed himself. He couldn't talk. Nothing. This went on for six months, and basically my dad was nonexistent. We thought he was going. He was gone. He was basically gone."

Until that point, Jim had routinely signed auto-graphs by mail for those who would write in and request one. That became impossible. Around this time, SABR member Nick Diunte posted a letter from James Jr. on Nick's Baseball Happenings web-site. The letter was dated January 8, 2015. It began: "Thank you for contacting me in reference to my father autographing your card. Unfortunately my father is in the final stages of Alzheimer's, has as-pirations pneumonia, and is not expected to live to reach his 91st birthday." He added, "My father has been with me since March 2013 after losing his wife of twenty-seven years. He celebrated his ninetieth birthday on 18 April 2014. He was diagnosed with Alzheimer's six years ago and has gradually lost his short term and much of his long term memory. He has lived a great life."

Clearly, James Jr. didn't think his father was going to survive another three months, until his birthday in April 2015. But he did. In his own way, Jim Zapp fought on.

Fortunately, both James and his brother Richmond were medical professionals themselves. As anyone would, they believed the doctors at the senior home were doing what needed to be done—until one day James decided to question it. "I thought, 'This is odd. They're giving him all these drugs. Painkillers … for what pain, I do not know. They're giving him a lot of stuff. They were giving his anti-anxiety pills, clonaz-epam. And sleeping pills.'

"I got a hair on my butt one day and decided, 'You know what, I'm going to call a meeting with these people and I'm taking him off all the drugs. I'm going to tell the doctor not to give him another prescribed drug, period.'"

On September 7, 2015, they had that meeting, James with the doctor, the head nurse, the social worker, and the dietician. "I had a meeting with all of them, and I basically sat there and I told them, 'Hey, you are not to give my dad any more prescribed medicine at all, without my permission. You can't give him anything. Not even an aspirin.'

"They looked at me and said, 'What? Including the allopurinol?' He was taking allopurinol for gout.

Jim Zapp with the Big Springs (Texas) Broncs of the Class-C Longhorn League in 1954. He hit 32 home runs in only 90 games with the Broncs before returning to the Negro American League. (*Courtesy of James Zapp, Jr.*)

I told them, 'Look, my dad is almost 92 years old. We both know that when you get gout, it has to basically just run its course. If he gets gout, you guys call me and I'll come down here and I'll look at him and I'll talk to him and if he's in enough pain, I'll let you give him pain medicine. Otherwise, you guys are not allowed to give him anything.'

"One of the nurses asked, 'So, you mean to tell us if we call you at 2 in the morning, you're going to come down here?' I said, 'Look, I'm retired. I don't work. The only I thing I do is I umpire baseball. And if I'm not there, I will call my daughter who lives with me and is 19 and still going to college and I will tell her to go down there and look at her granddad. There's always going to be someone here.'

"So they took him off the medicine. They quit giving him any medicine at all."

Jim left Texas for Colorado for a couple of weeks and he was in for a shock when he returned. He went to the home, for another visit.

"We couldn't find my dad. We're like, 'Where's he at?' We finally look up and here comes my dad, in a regular wheelchair, with his feet walking and rolling down the hall. I stand in front of him and he looks up and he sees me, and he recognizes me!"

It had been over a year. "Over a year! My daughter Jayda was with me. He recognized my daughter. I immediately contacted my brother and my sister and said, 'You guys aren't going to believe this.' I took a video with my phone. I said, 'You guys are not going to believe this.' I sent them the video. My sister was in tears."

In January 2016 Richmond visited from Seattle. "He went down there to see my dad and he came back to my house and he said he couldn't believe it. He said, 'It's like he went backwards three years.'"

Overmedication is known to be a common problem in such facilities. "He was having some pain problems and they gave him pain medicine and they never took him off of it. I guess one thing led to another and they kept giving him more medicine. They gave him the anti-anxiety pills to help him sleep. They basically had been drugging my dad up, to stop from having to deal with him. I even called an attorney. I was going to sue them. My thought process is that they were drugging my dad to keep from having to do anything with him. The attorney said it's too hard to prove."

Did the nurse ever call at 2 A.M. due to pain? "They told me they would call me if he was ever in any pain. That was September. It's now almost February and they have called me one time when they said he was in pain and that was like a month ago. It was like at midnight. So I got up and I drove down there and my dad was asleep when I got there. I woke him up and he saw me and he says, 'Hey, Baby.' He always called us Baby. I said, 'Daddy, are you in

any pain?' He goes, 'No, you woke me up.' 'OK, good night.' I gave him a kiss and I walked out. So all this pain medicine they were giving him, he was not in any pain."[43]

In any given facility, there are almost bound to be a certain number of people who are overmedicated. A lot of families would never question it. Some family members aren't able to visit very often. Most would not have the medical background to even begin to understand the possibilities. Though every situation is different, the Zapp family's experience offers a lesson that may prove of some help to other families.[44]

More than five months after being taken off all medication, Jim Zapp was effectively brought back to life, where he could recognize his children and granddaughter.

More than six months later, this author had the opportunity to speak with Jim Zapp briefly over the telephone on March 27, 2016. It wasn't the time to pose difficult questions that might have taxed a memory afflicted by Alzheimer's, but Jim introduced himself by name and recalled briefly playing for the Barons and in Hawaii with the Navy. Hopefully, it may have offered him a little bit of good in the moment to converse about some good times.

James knew it was never easy for his father. "It's been a long road with my dad, but it's sad. It's very sad. My dad was always so spirited. There was never a day in my dad's life when we were kids that he did not give us a hug and tell us he loved us. A hug and a kiss, and an 'I love you.' Every day. I try to do the same thing with my kids, and it seems to work."[45]

Jim Zapp passed away on September 30, 2016. His funeral was held on October 6 and he was buried in the Nashville National Cemetery. He was survived by his children—James S. Zapp, Jr., Richmond C. Zapp, Jenniffer Chaviest, and James Arnell and wife Arnetta—and by grandchildren Martice Chaviest, Jenniffer Zapp, Marilyn Zapp, James S. Zapp III, Jayda Zapp, and Theress Arnell, as well as great-grandchildren Fiona Hastings, Liam Hastings, and Nethanial Chaviest. The family requested that, in lieu of flowers, memorial donations be made to the Say Hey Foundation in Menlo Park, California, a foundation set up to help fulfill the dream of his old Birmingham Black Barons teammate Willie Mays, the dream of "giving every child a chance, by offering underprivileged youth positive opportunities and safer communities."[46]

SOURCES

In addition to the sources cited in the notes, the author would like to offer thanks to Jim Zapp's three children—Jenniffer, James, and Richmond—each of whom read through the manuscript and offered suggestions for improvement.

NOTES

1   Brent Kelley, *The Negro Leagues Revisited* (Jefferson, North Carolina: McFarland, 2000), 198.

2   James Riley in his *Biographical Encyclopedia of the Negro Baseball Leagues* places Zapp's birth at Elyria, Ohio, but available census information uniformly places him as native of Tennessee.

3   Author interview with James Zapp, December 30, 2015.

4   Mr. Zapp's name was spelled Bud in the 1900 census, Bert in the 1910 census, Burt in 1920, and Birt in 1940. In the 1905 Nashville City Directory, he is listed as T. Burton Zapp, residing at 511 Garfield.

5   The 1880 census, however, says she was a Hoosier as well, born to two parents from England. Henry and Helen lived in Terre Haute at the time and had four children: Harry, Nina, Thomas Burton, and Cora.

6   From at least 1900 to 1947, Burt Zapp was a baker. The Nashville city directories of 1905 and 1908 both specify his work for the County Asylum.

7   Email from James Zapp Jr., January 4, 2016.

8   baseballinwartime.com/negro.htm.

9   Kelley, 197. After the war, Edgar Jones played five seasons in the NFL, one game in 1945 for the Chicago Bears and then 43 games for Paul Brown and the Cleveland Browns from 1946-49. He was a halfback and defensive back and scored 18 touchdowns for the Browns. See pro-football-reference.com/players/J/JoneEd21.htm.

10 James Riley, *Biographical Encyclopedia of the Negro Baseball Leagues* (New York: Carroll & Graf, 1994), 893.

11 baseballinwartime.com/BIWNewsletterVol7No37July2015.pdf.

12 Kelley, 200.

13 Both the Elite Giants and Cubs information comes from baseballinlivingcolor.com/player.php?card=160. Zapp told Kelley of playing weekends for the Baltimore Elite Giants.

14 James Riley, 893.

15 Kelley, 198.

16 Kelley, 198-99.

17 John Klima, *Willie's Boys* (New York: John Wiley & Son), 2009), 57-58.

18 Klima, 183.

19 *NLBM Legacy 2000 Players' Reunion Alumni Book* (Kansas City, Missouri: Negro Leagues Baseball Museum, Inc., 2000).

20 Zapp remembered this as in Game Three, and the score as 2-1, him homering with a man on to win the game, 3-2. See Kelley, 199. He said that then the two teams went to Kansas City, where the Barons lost three games in a row, bringing it to a decisive Game Seven, which Bill Greason won, 4-1, for Birmingham.

21 Kelley, 199.

22 Klima, 58.

23 Klima, 193.

24 baseballinlivingcolor.com/player.php?card=160.

25 Kelley, 201.

26 See also Lloyd Johnson and Miles Wolff, eds., *Encyclopedia of Minor League Baseball* (Durham, North Carolina: Baseball America, 2007), 464.

27 *NLBM Legacy 2000 Players' Reunion Alumni Book.*

28 "Canton Loses to Hannibal; Paris 'Afire,'" *Peoria Journal-Star*, June 12, 1952: 38.

29 "MOV Loop Names All-Star Squad," *Peoria Journal-Star*, September 19, 1952: 24.

30 Kelley, 200.

31 Email from James Zapp Jr., January 17, 2016.

32 Riley, 893-894.

33 Klima, 97, 152.

34 Kelley, 201.

35 baseballinlivingcolor.com/player.php?card=160.

36 Kelley, 201.

37 Riley, 894.

38 E-mail from James Zapp Jr., January 17, 2016.

39 *NLBM Legacy 2000 Players' Reunion Alumni Book.*

40 James Zapp Jr., e-mail to Rick Bush, December 25, 2016.

41 Author interview with James Zapp Jr., December 30, 2015; email from James Zapp Jr., January 4, 2016.

42 Daniel Cooper, "The Long History of Nashville Rhythm & Blues," *Nashville Scene*, December 12, 1996.

43 Author interview with James Zapp, January 27, 2016.

44 The medications Jim Zapp had been placed on were: Donepezil, 5mg. marketed under the trade name Aricept, is a medication used in the palliative treatment of Alzheimer's disease.

Risperdal (risperidone) is an antipsychotic medicine.
Clonazepam, sold under the brand name Klonopin among others, is a medication used to prevent and treat seizures, panic disorder, and the movement disorder known as akathisia. It is a tranquilizer of the benzodiazepine class.

Allopurinol reduces the production of uric acid in the body.
Metoprolol Tartrate 25 MG is used with or without other medications to treat high blood pressure (hypertension). Lowering high blood pressure helps prevent strokes, heart attacks, and kidney problems. This medication is also used to treat chest pain (angina) and to improve survival after a heart attack.

Donepezil is used to improve cognition and behavior of people with Alzheimer's, but does not slow the progression of or cure the disease. Common side effects include loss of appetite, gastrointestinal upset, diarrhea, difficulty sleeping, vomiting, and muscle cramping.

Risperidone works by changing the effects of chemicals in the brain. Risperdal is used to treat schizophrenia and symptoms of bipolar disorder (manic depression). Risperdal is also used in autistic children to treat symptoms of irritability. Side effects: Drowsiness, dizziness, lightheadedness, drooling, nausea, weight gain, or tiredness may occur.

Common side effects of clonazepam include sleepiness, poor coordination, and agitation. It may increase risk of suicide. Long-term use may result in tolerance, dependence, and withdrawal symptoms if stopped.

Uric acid buildup can lead to gout or kidney stones.
Allopurinol is used to treat gout or kidney stones, and to decrease levels of uric acid in people who are receiving cancer treatment.

Side effects of Metoprolol Tartrate: Drowsiness, dizziness, tiredness, diarrhea, and slow heartbeat may occur. Decreased sexual ability has been reported rarely. To reduce the risk of dizziness and lightheadedness, get up slowly when rising from a sitting or lying position. This drug may reduce blood flow to the hands and feet, causing them to feel cold. Smoking may worsen this effect. Dress warmly and avoid tobacco use. Jim Zapp was never a smoker, had never had a heart attack, but did experience continuous coldness in his hands and feet.

45   Author interview with James Zapp, January 27, 2016.

46   http://www.sayheyfoundation.com/

TOM HAYES

By James Forr

Tom Hayes is a footnote in baseball history. To the extent that he is remembered at all, it is for selling 19-year-old Willie Mays to the New York Giants and setting him on his path to immortality. However, in his time, this shrewd, gruff man was a towering figure, a pioneer whose impact in the black community spread far beyond baseball.

Hayes' father, Thomas Sr., was nothing if not determined. Born outside Richmond, Virginia, in 1868, he moved with his family to Tennessee as a child and toiled on the family farm until moving to Memphis, Tennessee, at age 16. He worked there as a porter for a decade before being bitten by the entrepreneurial bug.

That bite was particularly nasty. Hayes opened three grocery stores, all of which failed. Then he opened a barbershop, despite having no experience as barber. That enterprise apparently went as well as one might expect. After a stint as a traveling salesman, Hayes made yet another stab at running a grocery store. Then some good fortune finally came his way, although not in the way that he had planned. In the spring of 1902, after the death of a local undertaker, a friend persuaded Hayes to go into the funeral business. Again, he had no experience in the field, but he did have $1,400 in capital and a large storage shed next his store that could serve as a makeshift mortuary.[1]

It may have sounded like a harebrained notion, but in fact Hayes had stumbled onto one of the few paths to prosperity open to African-Americans in the pre-civil-rights South. A proper funeral was particularly important to blacks, who feared the ignominy of a burial in a pauper's grave. Moreover, when it came to the African-American community, white funeral directors tended to the dead with the same disregard they had for the living. To illustrate the point, a black funeral director in Raleigh, North Carolina, told the tale of a white counterpart showing up at the home of a black family that had suffered a loss, hoisting the coffin onto the porch, and then refusing to help the family lay the body inside. "We don't do anything about putting bodies in the coffin," he sneered.[2] On the day of the service, the man reserved his best horses for a white family, leaving the black family to transport the casket to the cemetery with mules. As Hayes put it to a gathering of the National Negro Business League, "The white undertaker doesn't know the wants of our people and really does not care."[3]

Thomas's son, Thomas Henry Hayes Jr., was born on November 20, 1902. When he was a teenager, his father and his mother, Florence, purchased a stately turn-of-the-century home on South Lauderdale Street in Memphis and remodeled it, making space for his funeral business on the ground floor while the family lived upstairs. In later years, the Hayeses installed a fountain and a fish pond in front, in which neighborhood children would frolic on warm days. T.H. Hayes & Sons Funeral Home would operate out of this location for more than 90 years, becoming the oldest black-owned business in the city.

The younger Hayes attended several institutions of higher learning—Atlanta University, Lincoln University in Missouri, and the University of Illinois—before returning to manage the funeral home in the mid-1920s. He ran it along with his brother, Taylor, and Taylor's wife, Frances, who learned the ins and outs of the profession quickly and became a driving force behind the business until her death at the age of 103 in 2010. "Everybody who was anybody, we buried them," she said.[4] In addition to his role in the family business, Taylor was president of the National Funeral Directors and Morticians Association and coached football at LeMoyne, a historically black college in Memphis.

In February 1929 Hayes married 17-year-old Helen Meadow, an intelligent, independent young woman

Memphis funeral home director Tom Hayes bought the Birmingham Black Barons after the 1939 season. His franchise competed with the Kansas City Monarchs for preeminence in the Negro American League throughout the 1940s. *(Withers Family Trust, Memphis, Tennessee)*

who became a highly admired community figure in her own right. She graduated from LeMoyne in 1934 and earned a master's degree in economics from Northwestern University, making her one of the first African-Americans in Memphis to complete an advanced degree. She taught at the Alonzo Locke Elementary School for 24 years, was one of the founders of the Vance Avenue Branch YWCA, and was active in the local chapter of the NAACP before she died of lung cancer in 1990.[5] She and her husband raised two daughters.

Hayes's father boasted business interests far and wide. He owned a copper mine in Arizona, was part-owner of a coal company in Oklahoma, had a stake in at least two life-insurance firms, and was vice president of a bank. Tom Jr. did not fall far from the tree. He was a natural businessman, good with numbers, and exceedingly competitive, and the sheer breadth of his interests was extraordinary. His grandson, Wesley

Groves, called him a "jack of all trades."[6] Hayes helped organize a number of firms that primarily served black customers, including the Memphis Mortgage Company and Mutual Federal Savings and Loan. He helped create the Union Protective Life Insurance Company in 1933 and functioned in various capacities for that firm until its sale in 1980. Hayes had a hand in buses, hotels, restaurants and nightclubs, and even a brand of flour that he named Helen Ann Flour, after his daughter. "It was a lot of weird things going on," she said with a chuckle years later.[7]

Outside of Memphis, Hayes was most widely recognized as the owner of baseball's Birmingham Black Barons during their heyday in the 1940s. Through the 1920s and '30s, the Black Barons bounced among the Negro Southern League (essentially the minor-league circuit) and the Negro American and National Leagues. Satchel Paige was the star of the Negro National League team that won a second-half pennant in 1927. The Great Depression wrecked the club's finances and forced it to drop back to the Negro Southern League in 1931. After an ill-fated return to the Negro American League, the Black Barons temporarily ceased operations in 1939. That offseason Hayes, seeing an opportunity to buy low, swooped in and purchased the franchise at the winter meetings of the Negro American League in Chicago. He vowed, "Nothing will be left unturned in order to give Birmingham a good club."[8]

Hayes was horizontally integrated, in a sense. His portfolio included the Rush Hotel in Birmingham, which catered to a predominantly black clientele and where visiting teams would stay when they came to town. He also owned the buses that the Black Barons used on road trips. Eddie Glennon, the amicable general manager of the white Birmingham Barons of the Southern Association, liked and respected Hayes. The two men had a deal that enabled the Black Barons to use Rickwood Field on Sundays or when the white ballclub was on the road, in exchange for a percentage of the gate receipts.

Hayes's business partner was the short, fast-talking, and perpetually rumpled Abe Saperstein, impresario of basketball's Harlem Globetrotters. Saperstein's experience and connections enabled him to book the Black Barons in major venues, including Yankee Stadium, freeing them from the grueling tedium of constant barnstorming through backwater outposts. Hayes, meanwhile, handled most of the salary negotiations and player signings. It was a partnership that worked out well for everyone involved. Several players, including Basketball Hall of Famer Reece "Goose" Tatum, did double duty, playing for the Black Barons in the summer and the Globetrotters in the winter.

Hayes got right to it, hiring peripatetic manager Candy Jim Taylor, who had spent three years at the helm of the Chicago American Giants. He also signed talented rookies Dan Bankhead and Lyman Bostock, who would help form the backbone of the Black Barons through much of the decade. Outside the lines, Hayes did whatever he could do to lure fans to Rickwood Field. Among his promotions that first summer were a bathing-suit contest and a showdown that featured Olympic sprinter Jesse Owens racing against a motorcycle.[9]

It all paid off nicely. The Barons captured Negro American League pennants in 1942, '43, and '48, although they lost to the Homestead Grays in the Negro League World Series each time. Game day in Birmingham was like a holiday. "We drew more people in Birmingham than any city in the country," asserted catcher Ted "Double Duty" Radcliffe. "That's one of the best baseball towns in the world. ... Every Sunday was a sellout."[10]

Hayes was not a man to be trifled with. He was stern and physically imposing, especially as he aged and put on weight. (His grandson described him as "D-shaped."[11]) Although his players generally respected him as a businessman, he was hardly a beloved figure. "He was alright so long as you understood one thing," Piper Davis cautioned. "If he told you the sun was going to rise in the west, you better be facing China."[12]

Hayes took care of players who kept their mouths shut and did their jobs. Those who vocalized very much displeasure or disagreement soon found their

way to a new home. For instance, before the 1947 season the players met with Hayes to demand an increase in their per diem from $2 to $3. Their spokesman, Lyman Bostock, said to Hayes, "As of now, we're not askin' that, but when that time come, we expect to get three dollars." As Bostock recalled with a sardonic laugh, "Hayes said, 'Ah, I see Bostock is your spokesman.' Nobody said nothin'. I got the message. I was traded to Chicago."[13] Toward the end of that season Hayes had a running dispute with manager Tommy Sampson over the way Sampson allocated playing time. After Sampson missed a few games with appendicitis, Hayes docked him $125, which was the end of it for Sampson, who said, "I told him to take his job and stick it."[14] Jim Zapp was insulted when, after the 1948 season, Hayes left him off a barnstorming team that was traveling with the Jackie Robinson All-Stars. In a huff, Zapp asked for his release. Hayes did him one better by essentially blackballing him from the Negro American League for a year.

The Black Barons were strictly an investment for Hayes. He was not a huge baseball fan and his only tenuous connection with the sport had been through a funeral home softball team. Nonetheless, he wanted to see that investment in action from time to time, so he purchased a private plane. Still a novice pilot, Hayes hired a World War II veteran named U.L. Gooch to assist him on his flights.

Gooch would go on to a notable career in aviation and in the Kansas State Senate, but at the time he was a young man looking for a job, and flying around the country with a well-heeled, well-connected fellow like Tom Hayes had its appeal. Gooch recalled that the man knew how to wield his influence. "He was a guy who could call somebody at our destination, and they'd have a suite ready for us at the hotel and also a room for me. Somebody would even meet us at the airport and take us." Hayes took care of Gooch in other ways, too. "Tom was liberal and liked to have fun. ... Just the fact that I was his co-pilot gave me status. Tom would always see that I had a good time, too. Girls always converge on athletes and an even more select group rises up to the management, and my proximity to Tom allowed me to enjoy some companionship. It was an exciting summer."[15]

Hayes's most notable signing was that of Willie Mays, whom he plucked from the Birmingham Industrial League on the recommendation of Piper Davis, at age 17. The two agreed to a contract of $250 per month on July 4, 1948, and Mays became a fixture in the lineup almost immediately.[16] As Mays was entering, however, many of the best Negro Leaguers were exiting. Jackie Robinson had broken the color barrier in 1947, and Negro League owners found themselves selling off their most talented players.

Over the next few years Hayes frequently quarreled with major-league owners who he thought were trying to give him the shaft. The ugliest spat pitted Hayes against the New York Yankees in a battle over shortstop Artie Wilson.

Wilson, like Mays, had come out of the Birmingham Industrial League. He signed in 1944 and rapidly earned a reputation as the best shortstop in the Negro Leagues, a smooth defender with great speed who won consecutive batting titles in 1947 and '48. New York Yankees scout Tom Greenwade approached Wilson about making the jump to Newark, the Yankees' International League affiliate. Wilson demurred; the money was not right. But Greenwade floated stories in the press which declared that Hayes had agreed to sell Wilson for $10,000 and that the star infielder would be in Newark at the start of the 1949 season.

According to John Klima, author of *Willie's Boys*, there is no evidence anywhere that Hayes formally agreed to anything, but the story took on a life of its own. Hayes claimed that Wilson wanted to return to Birmingham rather than make less money in Newark, so that settled it as far as he was concerned. "How do they expect him to sign when no money has been posted or paid?" Hayes said.[17]

With the sale to the Yankees apparently resolved, Hayes asked Saperstein to broker a deal with Cleveland, which also had expressed interest in Wilson. And what a deal it was. Indians owner Bill Veeck offered the highest amount ever paid for a Negro League player—$10,000 to Hayes and

Saperstein plus a $5,000 major-league contract for Wilson. When Wilson found out he exclaimed, "This is the greatest day of my life."[18]

But not so fast. The Yankees insisted they had a deal in place with Hayes and asked Commissioner Happy Chandler to intervene. The commissioner's office launched a slapdash investigation, never bothering to speak to Hayes or Wilson, and subsequently awarded Wilson to the Yankees. New York already had an established shortstop in Phil Rizzuto, so they turned around and sold Wilson at a profit to the Oakland Oaks of the Pacific Coast League.

Meanwhile, Hayes had to return $15,000—representing Wilson's contract fee and signing bonus—to the Indians. It was money he did not have because he was still waiting for his $10,000 from the Yankees. Chandler's ruling came down in May. The Yankees failed to send Hayes a check for the Wilson purchase until August 31.

Around this same time, Hayes also was in a state of high dudgeon at James Murray, owner of the Boston Red Sox affiliate in Scranton, whom he suspected of trying to ace him out of $7,500, half the price the Red Sox had agreed to pay for the rights to Piper Davis.[19] However, it was the Wilson mess that left Hayes particularly embarrassed and furious. He felt that the Yankees and the major-league establishment had shown him disrespect and he was determined to save face.

Never an easy man to negotiate with, Hayes became nearly impossible, at least as white owners saw it. He insisted on top dollar for his players and insisted on dealing directly with team executives, not just scouts. His players sometimes felt they were sacrificed on the altar of Hayes's pride. Hayes reportedly shot down more than one solid offer for his ace right-hander, Bill Powell, who grew resentful. "Tom Hayes wouldn't sell us. We got messed around. I could've been in the majors."[20] Pitcher Bill Greason felt Hayes genuinely wanted the best for his players, but business was business. "He was interested in protecting his property," according to Greason.[21]

Hayes's smoldering bitterness toward the Yankees made the prospect of selling Willie Mays to their

Black Barons owner Tom Hayes shows off his team's bus at the entrance to Birmingham's Rickwood Field, where his franchise played its home games. (*Courtesy of Memphis Public Library*)

National League rivals, the New York Giants, particularly appealing. Hayes failed to sign Mays to a contract in 1950, possibly, as author Neil Lanctot speculates, to avoid the burden of a season-long financial commitment in the face of dwindling attendance. New York agreed to pay $10,000 for the rights to the Black Barons star—even though legally the Giants probably didn't owe Hayes anything. That was certainly the position of Mays' father. "Why should Mr. Hayes get anything?" he wondered. "I ain't signed no contract with Mr. Hayes. Willie ain't signed no contract with Mr. Hayes."[22] However, the way Giants owner Horace Stoneham figured it, $10,000 plus a courteous, respectful telegram—from one successful businessman to another—was worth it to placate the querulous Black Barons owner and reduce the likelihood of a lawsuit.

The exodus of talent to Organized Baseball watered down fan interest and quickly made it in an increasingly hard slog for Negro League owners. Hayes could see as early as 1949 that, as he put it, "[t]he golden era has passed. Teams that are to survive must retrench and proceed with caution."[23] Those Sunday Black Barons games, once almost like a social event, drew increasingly sparse crowds and Hayes had to limit his club's travel just to make payroll.

By the end of the 1951 season, Hayes had had enough and announced that the Black Barons were for sale. "If some local group in Birmingham would be interested in keeping the team here in Birmingham, they can contact me before I make a move to transfer," he declared. "I feel that a group of Birmingham owners could make a success of the venture. It has been a profitable one for me up to the present year."[24] He found no takers and put another $2,000 into the club to keep it operating in 1952 before selling it to the owner of the Baltimore Elite Giants, Sou Bridgeforth, who combined the two teams and dissolved the Elite Giants.

Although Hayes ended up justifiably bitter toward the baseball establishment, he was proud of his involvement with the Black Barons and remained on good terms with Saperstein. The men got together in Memphis in 1965, when the Globetrotters were in town, and Saperstein followed up with a warm letter noting, "Would appreciate a periodic note … so that both of us know each other is well."[25] In another note to his old partner, Saperstein looked back fondly on their time together. "They were rough, tough days … but we were young, Tom, and could take most anything. It was a real hard push but there is a real sense of satisfaction in getting a job done."[26]

After leaving baseball, Hayes remained a prominent figure in Memphis, not only through his involvement with the funeral home and other businesses but also through his civic duties. He led a drive to install air-conditioning on city buses and served on the Memphis Transit Authority from 1966-70; he was instrumental in the push to hire the first black bus drivers. He was a member of the Metropolitan Baptist Church for 50 years and a longtime trustee. Metropolitan Baptist is located in the heart of a vibrant African-American neighborhood now known as Soulsville USA and which was home to Stax Records, a label whose roster included stars like Otis Redding and Booker T and the MGs.

The church played a key role in the civil-rights movement—it was a home for meetings of the NAACP and hosted Dr. Martin Luther King Jr. as a guest speaker. Dr. Reginald Porter, who grew up in the church and later became its pastor, remembers that era as a difficult and terrifying time. "Your neighborhood was a great place but then once you go outside the neighborhood and into white areas or Downtown then it [was] literally dangerous for you." However, men like Tom Hayes served as a beacon in that darkness. "Having examples of people who have been able to succeed and can encourage you to attempt great things was helpful."[27]

Hayes struggled with poor health in his later years. His death from a heart attack in 1982, at the age of 79, was cause for mourning throughout Memphis, par-

ticularly in the African-American community. After his sister-in-law died, the funeral home closed its doors and construction crews razed the 111-year-old house in 2011. One community leader said the loss of the historic funeral home demonstrated a "lack of foresight and appreciation for history."[28] However, Hayes's legacy in his hometown and his impact on baseball history endure.

NOTES

1   Green Polonius Hamilton, *Beacon Lights of the Race* (Memphis: E.H. Clarke & Brother, 1911), 438-443.

2   Suzanne E. Smith, *To Serve the Living: Funeral Directors and the African American Way of Death* (Boston: The Belknap Press of Harvard University Press, 2010), 56.

3   Smith, 56-57.

4   Quoted in Vance Lauderdale, "Crews Demolish Hayes Funeral Home—Oldest African-American Business in Memphis," *Memphis Magazine*, July 19, 2011, memphismagazine.com/ask-vance/crews-demolish-hayes-funeral-home-oldest-african-american-business-in-memphis/ (accessed October 10, 2016).

5   Program for funeral service for Helen Meadow, Box 1, Folder 9, T.H. Hayes Collection, Memphis Shelby Public Library & Information Center.

6   Wesley Groves, telephone interview with author, November 21, 2016.

7   Helen Hayes Groves, telephone interview with author, November 21, 2016.

8   "Jim Taylor, Manager Black Barons, Here," undated article, Box 1, Scrapbook 1, Hayes Collection, Memphis Shelby Public Library & Information Center.

9   "Baron's Bathing Beauty Contest Has Fans All Agog," *Birmingham World*, July 19, 1940, Box 1, Scrapbook 1, T.H. Hayes Collection, Memphis Shelby Public Library & Information Center; James Purdy, "Memphis Red Sox Split Twin Bill with Birmingham Barons," *Birmingham World*, July 20, 1940, Box 1, Scrapbook 1, T.H. Hayes Collection, Memphis Shelby Public Library & Information Center.

10 John Holway, *Voices from the Great Black Baseball League* (Mineola, New York: Dover Publications, 1975), 182.

11 Wesley Groves.

12 Charles Einstein, *Willie's Time: Baseball's Golden Age* (Carbondale, Illinois: Southern Illinois University Press, 2004), 299.

13 Brent Kelley, *Voices from the Negro Leagues: Conversations with 52 Baseball Standouts* (Jefferson, North Carolina: McFarland & Company, 2005), 65.

14 Brent Kelley, *The Negro Leagues Revisited: Conversations with 66 More Baseball Heroes* (Jefferson, North Carolina: McFarland & Company 2010), 127.

15 U.L. Gooch, "Rip," with Glen Sharp, *Black Horizons: One Aviator's Experience in the Post-Tuskegee Era* (Wichita, Kansas: Aviation Business Consultants, 2006), 81-82.

16 Copy of Willie Mays Contract, Negro American league of Prof Baseball Clubs Uniform Player Contract, Box 1, Folder 3, T.H. Hayes Collection, Memphis Shelby Public Library & Information Center.

17 John Klima, *The 1948 Birmingham Black Barons, The Last Negro League World Series, and the Making of a Baseball Legend* (Hoboken, New Jersey: Wiley), 228.

18 Ibid.

19 James Murray to Thomas Hayes, August 13, 1949, Box 1, Folder 4, T.H. Hayes Collection, Memphis Shelby Public Library & Information Center; Thomas Hayes to James Murray, August 23, 1949, Box 1, Folder 4, T.H. Hayes Collection, Memphis Shelby Public Library & Information Center.

20 Larry Powell, *Black Barons of Birmingham: The South's Greatest Negro League Team and Its Players* (Jefferson, North Carolina: McFarland, 2009), 152.

21 Klima, 226.

22 Einstein, 303.

23 Quoted in Neil Lanctot, *Negro League Baseball: The Rise and Ruin of a Black Institution* (Philadelphia: University of Pennsylvania Press, 2004), 342.

24 "Hayes Gives Up, Puts Black Barons on Sale," *Pittsburgh Courier,* October 6, 1951.

25 Abe Saperstein to Thomas Hayes, April 1, 1965, Box 1, Folder 8, T.H. Hayes Collection, Memphis Shelby Public Library & Information Center.

26 Abe Saperstein to Thomas Hayes, April 21, 1965, Box 1, Folder 8, T.H. Hayes Collection, Memphis Shelby Public Library & Information Center.

27 Lance Wiedower, "Metropolitan Baptist Church Has Long Soulsville USA History," *High Ground News,* March 9, 2016, highgroundnews.com/features/MetropolitanChurch.aspx (accessed January 18, 2017).

28 David Connolly, "Minister LaSimba Gray Pursues Building for Preserving African-American History," *Memphis Commercial-Appeal,* May 15, 2012, commercialappeal.com/news/minister-lasimba-gray-pursues-building-for-preserving-african-american-history-ep-385925924-329410551.html (accessed February 5, 2017).

ABE SAPERSTEIN

By Norm King

Some music is so well known that you can listen to it in a dark room and immediately associate it with an event. The tooting of a calliope immediately brings to mind the circus or a merry-go-round. "The Wedding March" lets passersby outside a church know that some guy's bachelorhood just bit the dust. And the whistling of "Sweet Georgia Brown" is a sure sign that the Harlem Globetrotters are in town performing their basketball wizardry and pasting the Washington Generals yet again.

The famous Globetrotters were founded in 1927 in Chicago by one 5-foot-5 Abe Saperstein, who not only founded the Clown Princes of Basketball, but also played a role much larger than his size in Negro League baseball.[1]

Abraham M. Saperstein was born on July 4, 1902, in London, England, as the eldest of eight children to Louis Saperstein, a tailor, and his wife, Anna. In 1907 Anna and the children arrived in a predominantly German and Irish neighborhood on Chicago's North Side to join up with Louis, who had moved there earlier to get established. Living in that area affected the direction he took in life.

"My dad and his family were the only Jewish family in the area that I'm aware of," said Abe's son Jerry. "I think that was a benefit because he constantly, I think, had to prove himself, try a little harder, work a little harder. And he did."[2]

Abe played baseball and basketball and ran track at Chicago's Lake View High School. But even as a teenager he displayed the gift for promotion that would mark his later career. "He was more or less a promoter and wanted to start a basketball team," recalled his sister Leah. "When he was in school, he worked for a Mr. Schiller, a florist, delivering flowers. When he started his first team, Abe approached Schiller with a promotional idea; if Schiller would sponsor the team, the team would advertise his busi-ness on the backs of their jerseys. Schiller agreed. Abe gathered five fellows, and they played basketball at various field houses."[3]

The exploits of Saperstein's Schiller-sponsored squad are unknown, but the experience gave Saperstein an idea of what he wanted to do in life. After one year of college at the University of Illinois, Saperstein quit and became a supervisor in the Chicago-area parks system. He went to work at a park on the city's South Side, where he saw gifted African-American athletes for the first time. "This was a revelation to him," said Jerry. "He felt that this is what he wanted to do, and what he wanted to do was assemble a great basketball team."[4]

In 1926 Saperstein met the members of a semipro team called the Savoy Five, a group of black basket-ball players whom the Savoy Hotel management had hired to play as a means of attracting young people to dance in the hotel's ballroom. That experiment lasted a month before the team was fired because they were not bringing in large enough crowds. But Saperstein offered to become the team's manager and had his father design uniforms for them with "New York" stitched on the front; he believed that it would be easier to book them for games if people thought they had come all the way from Manhattan to play.

The team was an on-court success from the start, winning 100 out of their first 105 games against local Midwest teams. Saperstein noticed that the people at-tending the games were more interested in his players' skin color than in their playing ability, because many of the people in the towns where they played had never seen an African-American before. To promote the fact that the players were black, and to impart the impression that they were much-traveled, Saperstein named them the Harlem Globetrotters. "When they arrived, they must have looked fairly exotic; there were not a lot of blacks west of Chicago in a lot of these smaller towns" said *New York Times* sports columnist George Vecsey. "Most white Americans never saw blacks."[5]

In addition to managing and coaching the team, Saperstein also served as chauffeur, driving his players to their games in his Model T Ford. His car did not have any heat, which made the traveling in the harsh conditions of Midwest winters even more uncomfortable. They played seven nights a week, often earning as little as $25, which Saperstein split rather unevenly. He gave one share to each of his five players and kept two for himself.

Whether fair or not, Saperstein at least provided his players with an income during the depths of the Depression. He also got to see firsthand the racism that his players were forced to endure, especially in the Jim Crow South, where "separate but equal" ruled the day. He had to find places for his players to eat and sleep; while some places had facilities for black people, not all did, and not just in the South. In one Nebraska town, for example, the players were forced to sleep in a jail.[6]

The Globetrotters played a different brand of basketball than all-white teams. Caucasian teams played rigidly, passing the ball around five times before shooting. Saperstein's men played a more freewheeling style, dunking the ball rather than relying solely on the set shot all the time. The team was much better than its opposition and often won by wide margins, so Saperstein began introducing some razzle-dazzle into their playing style. Fans laughed at the Globetrotters' trick passes and other antics, which made the games more entertaining and increased the team's popularity. This was especially important when white fans were watching their teams losing by a wide margin to a team of black players. "It was one thing to play a black team. ... It was another thing to get your tail whipped," said sportswriter Frank Deford. "If the Globetrotters could amuse people, [then] that got their foot in the door."[7]

Barnstorming was not the exclusive domain of the Globetrotters in the 1930s—it was not even unique to basketball. Baseball also had teams that traveled around the United States and Canada (the Globetrotters played in Canada as well) eking out

livings playing against local squads. Over time, Saperstein developed into a top-flight promoter and built up many contacts in the media and among other promoters. He began working as a booking agent for an independent barnstorming baseball team that operated under different names, including the Miami Giants and the Miami Ethiopian Clowns.[8] He became friends with a vaudeville promoter named Syd Pollock, who became part-owner of the Clowns in 1936 and sole owner in 1939.

By 1937, Saperstein looked to purchase a barnstorming team of his own. One such team was the Zulu Cannibal Giants, formed by former Negro Leagues pitcher Charlie Henry in 1934 in Louisville, Kentucky. The Giants played in grass skirts and had "African" names such as Wahoo, Taklooi, and Moki, and had some excellent players, including the legendary John "Buck" O'Neil, who played with the team in 1937. His name with the Giants was Limpopo.

Henry decided to sell the team that same year. Details are murky as to whom he sold it to, as it seems Saperstein was not the only buyer. Other purchasers included Pollock and a Kentucky Colonel named Charles B. Franklin. "In fact, history does not provide a complete list of those who contributed to the Charlie Henry retirement fund buying the Zulu Cannibal Giants," wrote Pollock's son Alan.[9]

Saperstein also became the booking agent for teams in the Negro American League when they barnstormed to supplement the money they made during their league schedules. He used his connections with these leagues and his access to the media to handle the publicity for the Negro Leagues' East-West All-Star Game. Roy Sparrow, an employee of Pittsburgh Crawfords owner and Negro National League President Gus Greenlee, came up with the idea for the East-West game and Greenlee organized it until 1939. Saperstein handled publicity for the event, and received 5 percent of the gate for his efforts until 1941.

Increasingly, Saperstein, Pollock, and other Jewish promoters and owners faced anti-Semitic hostility for their involvement in Negro League baseball. Effa Manley, co-owner of the Newark Eagles, "promised

Promoter par excellence Abe Saperstein, for a time also co-owner of the Black Barons, and primary owner Tom Hayes (at right) turned Birmingham into one of the NAL's premier franchises of the 1940s. (*Courtesy of Memphis Public Library*)

in 1941 that 'these Jews would be stopped in their tracks' if she or her husband were made [Negro National] league chairman … ."[10]

Many of the players, on the other hand, were pleased to be involved with Saperstein. Sug Cornelius "touted Abe Saperstein's publicity and administrative skills."[11] Ted "Double Duty" Radcliffe gave Saperstein the highest praise, saying, "He was the greatest friend to the colored athlete of anybody I know today. He's the greatest man in the history of Negroes, for helping Negroes. He got 'em up."[12]

Saperstein's opponents tried unsuccessfully to stop him. At a meeting between the NNL and NAL owners on June 26, 1941, Alex Pompez, who owned the New York Cubans, and Homestead Grays owner Cum Posey opposed having Saperstein handle the publicity with the "white" media for the East-West Game because they felt he was a negative influence on Negro baseball. According to the *Pittsburgh*

Courier, a major African-American newspaper of the time, "This contention was based on the fact that Saperstein was ridiculing Negro baseball, Negro players and the race in general by aiding in the booking of the E. Clowns, a group of colored players who travel over the U.S. with their faces painted to represent mythical natives of the African jungles."[13]

The criticism did not prevent Saperstein from increasing his involvement in Negro League baseball. He was heavily involved in promoting the Birmingham Black Barons of the NAL, a team he co-owned with Tom Hayes, a black funeral-home operator from Memphis, Tennessee. The two men worked well together, leading the Black Barons franchise through the greatest period in its history.

Saperstein's connections brought the Black Barons exposure they would not otherwise have enjoyed because he could get them to play in venues where Hayes could not. Saperstein was also able to gain publicity for the team beyond the black press in such newspapers as the *Chicago Tribune, Cincinnati Enquirer,* and *New York Times.*

"He'd book us where Tom Hayes couldn't get us booked," said Radcliffe. "He'd book us in those big four-team doubleheaders in Yankee Stadium. Every time the Yankees would leave, Birmingham would be in Yankee Stadium with twenty-five to thirty thousand people."[14]

Saperstein was also responsible for bringing Winfield Welch in to manage the team. Welch had been the road manager for the Globetrotters and was a one of Saperstein's trusted business associates. Under Welch the team won back-to-back NAL pennants, in 1943 and 1944. They won a third pennant under Piper Davis in 1948, but in all three seasons they lost the Negro League World Series to the NNL's Homestead Grays.

Saperstein's baseball activities complemented his operation of the Globetrotters. The team grew in popularity after Saperstein signed Reece "Goose" Tatum, whom he had discovered playing first base for the Black Barons in 1941. Tatum was as much a comedian as a ballplayer, performing such antics as kneeling in prayer before going up to bat and catching throws at first base behind his back.[15] He devised comedy routines that became Globetrotters staples, was crowned the Clown Prince of Basketball, and played for the Globetrotters for 15 years.

In 1942 Saperstein and Pollack joined forces to create the Negro Major Baseball League of America (NMBLA) which included the Baltimore Black Sox, Boston Royal Giants, Chicago Brown Bombers, Cincinnati Ethiopian Clowns (Pollock's barnstorming team that was originally from Miami), Detroit Black Sox, and the Minneapolis-St. Paul Gophers. NNL Secretary Cum Posey roundly condemned the league's formation and Saperstein's role in it, via the *Pittsburgh Courier*, in which he had a regular column. "As we analyze it, we would first call it 'Abe' Saperstein's Protective Association," Posey wrote. "It [the new league] is a personal threat of Saperstein directed toward his former associates of the Negro American League. Saperstein realized he was on the way out of organized Negro baseball. He is out to keep control of the independent ball parks of the middle west."[16]

Courier columnist Wendell Smith did not attack Saperstein personally, but was critical of the new league:

"I have nothing against Mr. Saperstein in his baseball promotions. I know him and think he is sincere and honest. But I do object to the league he has organized and tried to peddle as one on par with the Negro American and National Leagues. Mr. Saperstein would have us believe that that the Negro Major League *(sic)* is something we should be proud of and anxious to support. Well, we're not proud of it, nor are we anxious to support it. And the same goes for Mr. Pollock's Ethiopian Clowns (alias Cincinnati Clowns.)"[17]

The NMBLA lasted only one season. Pollack wanted the stability of regularly scheduled games, so he moved his franchise over to the Negro American League for the 1943 season, dropping "Ethiopian" from the team's name because it was insulting to the black population. The club moved to Indianapolis in 1944.

Saperstein tried to forge another Negro major league on the Pacific Coast in 1946. On the surface, it seemed a promising idea. While the black population was relatively low prior to World War II, African-Americans had flocked to Seattle, Portland, and other Pacific cities to take up war jobs. Pacific Coast cities also had stadiums that could be used when Organized Baseball's Pacific Coast League teams were on the road. In addition to being league president, Saperstein owned the Seattle Steelheads. The Steelheads were originally the Cincinnati Crescents, one of Saperstein's barnstorming teams, and he moved the team to Seattle as one of the new league's six franchises. Track and field legend Jesse Owens owned the Portland Rose Buds. Other franchises included the Los Angeles White Sox, Oakland Larks, Fresno Tigers, and San Francisco Sea Lions.

Everything sounded good in theory, but when reality hit, it hit hard. Sources differ on how long the league lasted, but the teams played only 30 games of their 110-game schedule before the league folded because of poor attendance, a lack of financing, and difficulty in accessing ballparks. After the circuit's demise, Saperstein turned his club into a barnstorming team. He changed the squad's name back to the Cincinnati Crescents but later changed it to the Harlem Globetrotters, even though they originated even farther from Harlem than the basketball team did. Some players, such as Goose Tatum, played for both the basketball and baseball teams.

As for the Harlem Globetrotters basketball team, they were reaching new heights in popularity with the war's end. They were so well-known that Saperstein and Max Winter, general manager of the National Basketball League champion Minneapolis Lakers, met to arrange an exhibition game between the two clubs at the Chicago Stadium on February 19, 1948.[18] More than 17,800 fans turned out for the contest, which the Globetrotters won 61-59 on a buzzer-beating basket by Ermer Robinson.[19] That contest went a long way toward integrating the NBA, which drafted its first black players in 1950.

The integration of Organized Baseball had begun four years earlier, when the Brooklyn Dodgers assigned Jackie Robinson to their Montreal Royals farm club in the Triple-A International League. Robinson's success opened the floodgates for other black athletes to play in the major leagues. Saperstein saw integration as another business opportunity.

In fact, Saperstein came up with a new twist on an old venture. He had booked legendary Negro League and barnstorming pitcher Satchel Paige onto various teams for years. Their association went back to 1933, when Saperstein booked Paige to play with an integrated team in Bismarck, North Dakota. The Bismarck team was owned by Neil Churchill, who also owned a basketball team that had played against the Globetrotters. Saperstein also acted as booking agent for Paige when Bill Veeck bought his services for the Cleveland Indians in 1948. According to Neil Lanctot in his book, *Negro League Baseball: The Rise and Ruin of a Black Institution*, the transaction cost Veeck $30,000, including $5,000 for the Monarchs, $15,000 for Saperstein, and a $10,000 bonus for Paige.[20]

Paige wasn't the only player Veeck signed for Cleveland on Saperstein's recommendation. Others included first baseman Luke Easter, who averaged 29 home runs and 100 RBIs in three seasons with the Tribe, and infielder-outfielder Orestes "Minnie" Miñoso, who had a long and successful major-league career.

Saperstein participated in another first in 1952, when he negotiated baseball's first lend-lease program. He arranged for two black St. Louis Browns minor leaguers, third baseman John Britton Jr. and pitcher James Newberry, to be loaned to the Hankyu Braves of the Japanese Pacific League. The arrangement was historic; it marked the first time that American baseball players were loaned to a team outside of North America. It also signified the end of the American occupation of Japan after World War II.

While the integration of major-league baseball sounded the death knell for the Negro Leagues, the same was not the case for the Globetrotters basketball team. The same year that blacks began to play in the NBA, the Globetrotters finally lived up to their name, making their first overseas trip in May 1950;

they played 73 games in nine European and North African countries over a three-month period. The trip was successful financially and diplomatically as well. "In addition to playing games, the teams [the Globetrotters and the squad that served as their opposition, the "American All-Stars"] also conducted basketball clinics and taught basic skills," wrote Damion Thomas. "The success of the trip was evident in the American consulate report that acknowledged "the unusually wide and deep impression of open friendship both inter-racially and inter-nationally" suggested by the Globetrotters' and American All-Stars' good sportsmanship."[21]

In the midst of the Cold War, Saperstein worked directly with the State Department to use the Globetrotters as a propaganda tool to demonstrate the superiority of the American way of life. During the team's 1951 World Tour, the American high commissioner in West Berlin, John J. McCloy, met with Saperstein after seeing the Globetrotters play in Frankfurt and asked him to have the team play in West Berlin. The game was played on August 22 at exactly the same time that Communist-controlled East Berlin was hosting a festival for two million young people that the State Department feared would incorporate anti-American propaganda into its activities.

The State Department saw the Globetrotters as a means by which to counter Communist assertions that about the poor treatment African-Americans suffered in the United States, and Saperstein was only too willing to comply. In a book (or propaganda piece, depending on one's perspective) about the team's 1952 World Tour by Dave Zinkoff, Saperstein wrote in the foreword, "The Communist argument is that the American Negro is exploited and held in bondage. The Globetrotters, without saying a word, refuted much of that by living at the best hotels and behaving in the manner of educated men."[22]

The NBA had struggled in its early years, but it was on better financial footing by the late 1950s. Saperstein applied for a franchise for Chicago but was refused.[23] Instead, the league awarded one to a Chicago businessman named Dave Trager. This turn of events prompted Saperstein to start a new circuit, the American Basketball League, with eight franchises (including one in Chicago) and with Saperstein as commissioner. It was a sign of Saperstein's power in the world of professional basketball that it was his league's franchise and not the established NBA's new team that got to play in the city's cavernous and lucrative Chicago Stadium. He told Stadium owner Arthur Wirtz that the Globetrotters would not play there if the NBA team did. The Packers, as they became known, ended up in a venue called the International Amphitheatre near the Chicago Stockyards, which was hardly the best location.[24] The ABL lasted only 1½ seasons; however, in that time, it introduced the wider free-throw lane in use today as well as the three-point shot. It also gave the American sports world future New York Yankees owner George Steinbrenner, whose Cleveland Pipers team won the league's only championship.

After the ABL's demise, Saperstein focused solely on the Globetrotters. The team continued to travel around the world, visiting 87 countries and logging more than 5 million miles. His last connection to baseball was including Paige in some of the team's comedy routines.

Saperstein died of a heart ailment on March 15, 1966, at age 63. By the time of his death, the Globetrotters had gone from traipsing around in an unheated Model T to appearing in front of royalty around the world. In terms of his baseball involvement, his connections brought black baseball teams to venues such as New York's Yankee Stadium and Chicago's Wrigley Field, where they might not otherwise have played. He was survived by his wife, Sylvia; son, Gerry; and daughter, Eloise.

SOURCES

Special thanks to Raymond Doswell, Ed.D., VP/curator, Negro Leagues Baseball Museum, and Jack Anderson, SABR member, Montreal, Quebec.

In addition to the sources cited in the Notes, the author also consulted:

Afe.easia.columbia.edu.

Alpert, Rebecca T. *Out of Left Field: Jews and Black Baseball* (New York: Oxford University Press, 2011).

Baseballhall.org.

Chicago Tribune.

Heaphy, Leslie A. *The Negro Leagues 1869-1960* (Jefferson, North Carolina, and London: McFarland & Company, 2003).

Hoophall.com.

Jewishsports.net.

Klima, John. *Willie's Boys: The 1948 Birmingham Black Barons, the Last Negro World Series and the Making of a Baseball Legend* (Hoboken: John Wiley & Sons, 2009).

Mohl, Raymond A. "Clowning Around: The Miami Ethiopian Clowns and Cultural Conflict in Black Baseball," *Tequesta* no. 62 (2002): 40-67.

McKenna, Brian. *Alex Pompez.* SABR BioProject: sabr.org/bioproj/person/acbbad4d.

Nelson, Murray R. *Abe Saperstein and the American Basketball League 1960-1963: The Upstarts Who Shot for Three and Lost to the NBA* (Jefferson, North Carolina, and London: McFarland& Company, 2013).

Milb.com.

Peterson, Robert. *Only the Ball Was White: A History of Legendary Black Players and All-Black Professional Teams* (New York: Oxford University Press, 1970).

St. Louis Post-Dispatch.

Thornley, Stew. *Basketball's Original Dynasty: The History of the Lakers* (Minneapolis: Nodin Press, 1989).

Tye, Larry. *Satchel: The Life and Times of an American Legend* (New York: Random House, 2009).

Wisconsin Jewish Chronicle.

NOTES

1 Saperstein's biography on the International Jewish Sports Hall of Fame website lists him at this height, while a profile of him in the March 3, 1995, edition of the *Chicago Tribune* has him at 5-feet-3.

2 Biography Channel, "The Harlem Globetrotters (Volume 2 of 5)," 12:23, January 15, 2011, youtube.com/watch?v=xPh5eJNNMqg.

3 Beatrice Michaels Shapiro, "No-Lose Situation: Whether It Was as a Team Owner, Coach or Promoter, Harlem Globetrotters Founder Abe Saperstein Always Had a Game Plan," *Chicago Tribune*, March 3, 1995.

4 Ibid.

5 Biography channel, "The Harlem Globetrotters (Volume 1 of 5)."

6 Ibid.

7 Ibid.

8 The team eventually moved to Indianapolis to become the legendary Indianapolis Clowns. Future major-league home-run king Hank Aaron played for the Clowns in 1952.

9 Alan J. Pollock (James A. Riley, editor), *Barnstorming to Heaven: Syd Pollock and His Great Black Teams* (Tuscaloosa: The University of Alabama Press, 2006), 84.

10 Neil Lanctot, *Negro League Baseball: The Rise and Ruin of a Black Institution*, (Philadelphia: University of Pennsylvania Press, 2004), 114.

11 Ibid.

12 John Holway, *Voices from the Great Black Baseball Leagues* (Mineola, New York: Dover Publications Inc., 1975), 182.

13 "Moguls Agree on Inter-Loop Games: July 27 Set as Date of East-West Game," *Pittsburgh Courier*, June 28, 1941: 17.

14 Holway, 182.

15 Encyclopediaofarkansas.net.

16 Cum Posey, "Posey's Points," *Pittsburgh Courier*, April 4, 1942: 16.

17 Wendell Smith, "Smitty's Sports-Spurts," *Pittsburgh Courier*, May 16, 1942: 17.

18 The National Basketball League merged with the Basketball Association of America in 1949 to form the National Basketball Association.

19 The two teams played again one year later. The Globetrotters won 49-45 on February 28, 1949, in Chicago, but lost 68-53 to the Lakers two weeks later. The two clubs met five times after that between 1950 and 1958, with the Lakers winning each time.

20 Lanctot, 336.

21 Damion L. Thomas, *Globetrotting: African American Athletes and Cold War Politics*, (Champaign: University of Illinois Press, 2012), 45.

22 Thomas, 49.

23 An article in the December 24, 2011, edition of the *New York Times* stated that Saperstein had wanted the Los Angeles franchise; however, since Chicago was his base of operations, it is more likely that he had wanted his team to be located in the Windy City.

24 The Chicago NBA franchise was known as the Packers in its first season and as the Chicago Zephyrs in its second. The stockyard stench ultimately proved to be too much to bear; the team moved to Baltimore (renamed the Bullets) for its third campaign.

RICKWOOD FIELD

By Clarence Watkins

The history of Rickwood Field is a story worth telling and retelling. Its origins are compelling as is the story of its evolution throughout its 77-year existence as a functional minor-league baseball park. Perhaps of greater interest is the story of how it has survived the past 23 years as an obsolete old ballpark. Rickwood Field today stands as a relic from the past, a historical structure that has become a living museum and a symbol for all the other bygone minor-league baseball parks that were unable to survive the ravages of time.

To completely appreciate the story of Rickwood Field, it is important to understand the beginnings of the city of Birmingham, Alabama. Birmingham was not a typical Southern city, being founded neither on the bluffs of a great river nor at the mouth of one. Birmingham came into existence after the Civil War when two railroad lines crossed in an area where there were rich deposits of coal and iron ore. It is a city of the New South, a term used by Atlanta journalist Henry Grady to describe Southern cities as an untapped resource to build new industries. In 1885 Grady was instrumental in forming the first professional baseball league in the South, the Southern League, to entice Northern industrialists. Southern cities had theaters, libraries, schools, and now baseball to entertain a new class of industrial workers.[1]

In 1877 Joseph Harvey Woodward came to Birmingham from West Virginia to take advantage of the coal and iron resources and to build an iron furnace much like the one his family operated. Joseph was also preparing his son Rick to follow in his footsteps. Rick had attended Sewanee College and then was sent to the Massachusetts Institute of Technology to finish his education. For Rick, being a catcher on the Sewanee baseball team was far more important than math and science. While attending MIT, he got a taste of the professional game in Boston. By the time he returned home, Birmingham was a member of the new Southern Association Baseball League that had been formed in 1901. While learning the family business, Rick enjoyed managing the company baseball team, which was part of an industrial league that provided entertainment and exercise for employees. In 1909 Woodward Iron played for the league championship. During the game several players approached Rick with demands for better pay and benefits, threatening to lose the game if they were not met. He did not give in to their demands and Woodward Iron lost the championship. Rick was finished with industrial league baseball, but within a few months he negotiated the purchase of the local minor-league team, the Barons, and made plans to build a new ballpark.

In April 1909 Rick traveled to Philadelphia to see the opening of Shibe Park, one of only five concrete and steel baseball stadiums in the major leagues. He had begun to plan his new ballpark even before he had purchased the Barons and intended it to reflect the latest technology in stadium construction. He sought advice from major-league owners Connie Mack and Barney Dreyfuss, and Mack even came to Birmingham to assist Rick in laying out his new park. The initial budget was for $25,000, but it soon grew to $75,000.[2] Construction began in the spring of 1910 with a completion date set for August 18.

On the morning of August 18, workers were still completing the last-minute details to finish the ballpark. The game that was to be played there that day was more than just a ballgame; it was the social event of the year for Birmingham. City workers were given the afternoon off as were most downtown retail workers so that they could attend the game. Mayor Jimmy Jones and any other politician who wanted to be seen attended the game. Rick Woodward's father even came to see what all the "nonsense" was about. Apparently Mr. Woodward was pleased with his

The original front entry to Rickwood Field with a notice for an upcoming Black Barons game. The Black Barons leased the field when its regular tenants, the Double-A Southern League's Barons, were on the road. (*Courtesy of Friends of Rickwood*)

son's accomplishments because he paid off all the outstanding debt from the construction.[3] By 2:30 P.M. streetcars were delivering fans to the park for the 3:30 pregame ceremony that would precede the 4:00 game. The stands and bleachers had a capacity of 5,000 but the crowd—accurately counted by the turnstiles—swelled to over 10,000. Fans lined the outfield wall from the third-base line to the right-field corner, and a new Southern League attendance record was set.

As the pregame ceremonies began, Rick Woodward appeared on the field in a full player's uniform to throw out the actual first pitch of the game. Shortly before the game began, the Barons' star pitcher, Harry Coveleski and outfielder Bob Messenger almost came to blows in front of the Barons dugout. The fans loved it. Coveleski was in rare form and between innings he performed pugilistic antics for the crowd. The game itself almost seemed anticlimactic; it was a low-scoring affair, not

uncommon at a time when the bunt was considered a big weapon of the offense. Trailing by a run in the ninth inning, the Barons use three bunts, a hit batsman, and a fielder's choice to win the game, 3-2. For several days the newspapers sang the praises of Rickwood Field. Even the name Rickwood was the idea of local fans, who had participated in a contest to name the new venue. The newspapers spoke of Rickwood adding to the aura of the "Magic City." It would be 15 years before the other Southern League teams built ballparks comparable to Rickwood. No one could have imagined that Rickwood would still be standing more than a hundred years later.

For Rickwood Field and the Barons, two league championships came quickly in 1912 and 1914; however, after that, mediocrity set in. By the mid-1920s, sports in general began experiencing a golden age as Babe Ruth, Jack Dempsey, and Bobby Jones dominated the front pages of newspapers. Woodward Iron was booming alongside the rest of the national economy, and Rick Woodward was ready to spend whatever it took to bring the Barons back to the top. Longtime manager Carlton Molesworth was fired and several different managers took the Barons' reins before a proven winner, Johnny Dobbs, was hired in 1926.

The ballpark was now over 15 years old and it, too, needed a makeover. During the winter of 1927-28, Rickwood Field received a major renovation that cost over $125,000, almost double the cost of the original park. The primary improvements included three iconic additions that remain the signature features of the park: A new scoreboard was added in left field, the bleachers were covered down the right-field line with a section of seats that wrapped around the foul line, and a new mission-style front entrance completed the park. From 1928 through 1931, Rick Woodward regularly purchased the contracts of proven major-league players to fill the needs of his team, and the Barons won three league championships.

After that period of success, the impact of the Great Depression hit the iron industry and minor-league baseball, and Woodward's major concern was keeping his iron works from going under. Toward the end of the Depression, employees of Woodward Iron were paid in company scrip which was good only at the company store.[4] By 1938 Woodward was ready to sell the team and his personal creation, Rickwood Field. Ed Norton of Birmingham bought the team, but he sold it to the Cincinnati Reds two years later, and the Barons became part of their minor-league farm system. In 1941 Cincinnati made one major change to Rickwood when they installed a new, wooden outfield wall that was located well inside the old, concrete outer wall. The hope was that more home runs would excite fans and increase attendance.

As a Reds affiliate, the Barons roster now included future major leaguers like an immature Joe Nuxhall, who was sent to Birmingham after his major-league debut in 1943. Nuxhall had let the fanfare of his short time in the majors go to his head, and it would take him six years to make it back to Cincinnati. The Reds ownership decided to sell the Barons and Rickwood Field back to another Birmingham man in 1946. Gus

Jebeles, a restaurant owner, bought the team and intended to bring it back to the Barons of the golden age that he remembered from his days as a boy growing up in Birmingham.

In July 1943 the Barons had founded their team's Hall of Fame and 40 players from the past had been part of its inaugural class. Large photographs of each player were hung in the concourse. For each year after, two players would be enshrined.

In his daily column, the *Birmingham News'* Zipp Newman listed several firsts for the Barons and Rickwood Field. Along with the team Hall of Fame, Rickwood was the first park to install ceiling fans and to the outfield walls free of advertising, while the Barons were the first team to have players wear numbers on the backs of their jerseys.[5]

In the mid- to late 1940s the Birmingham Black Barons regularly ran ads in Barons scorecards. The one-third-page ads stated, "When the Barons are away, See the Black Barons play." A list of future Black Barons games was included at the bottom. The ads speak at least to an amicable business relationship between the two teams, and no such ads appeared in the programs of the teams in other Southern League cities.

For Rickwood Field, Birmingham baseball in 1948 was truly a magical year. The servicemen had returned from the war, and baseball was experiencing a golden age throughout the United States. Even though the Barons finished in third place, they still posted an all-time attendance record. The third-place finish was enough to get in the playoffs, and the team got hot and rode their energized play all the way to the Southern League championship. Meanwhile, the Black Barons, managed by Lorenzo "Piper" Davis, won the Negro American League pennant over the Kansas City Monarchs and played the Homestead Grays in the last Negro League World Series. Three of the World Series' five games were played at Rickwood Field. But soon both the Barons and Black Barons experienced steady declines, albeit for different reasons.

The Black Barons, like all other Negro League teams, eventually folded after the integration of

Fans lined up to see the Black Barons play at Rickwood Field in Birmingham, Alabama. The Black Barons – who competed in the 1943, 1944, and 1948 Negro League World Series – were always a big draw. (*Courtesy of Memphis Public Library*)

Organized Baseball had robbed the leagues of their best talent and the majority of their fans. The fate of the minor-league Barons was also tied to race issues. After 1961 the Southern Association had lost three teams, and plans by Mayor Jimmy Jones of Birmingham to enforce the city ordinance that prohibited whites and blacks from playing sports together left owner Albert Belcher no other choice but to disband the team. Birmingham and Rickwood Field endured two years without any baseball. In 1964 the South Atlantic League was reorganized into the new Southern League and baseball returned to Rickwood Field. Whites and blacks played on the same team for the first time, and reporters from the North came to Rickwood to witness Birmingham's first integrated game. The crowd acted respectfully and simply enjoyed having baseball back, thus turning the game into a non-event for the press.[6]

The Barons played again in 1965, but new owner Charlie Finley moved the team to Mobile, Alabama, for the 1966 season. The team returned to Birmingham in 1967, but was now called the Birmingham A's. Although baseball was back in Birmingham, Rickwood Field was on the decline. The wooden outfield walls were replaced by a chain-link fence and the iconic left-field scoreboard was taken down. Attendance also declined, finally reaching a low of 25,000 by the end of 1975. In 1976 Finley moved the team to Chattanooga, Tennessee, and this time it took five years for professional baseball to return to Birmingham.

In 1978 Rickwood Field became the home of the University of Alabama at Birmingham's baseball team. The new team was coached by legendary major-league manager Harry "The Hat" Walker. During this time, most of the lower-level wooden seats were removed, and fans now sat on the concrete risers. A new addition to the park was a metal batting building that was constructed down the left-field side. Other than those two changes, very little was being done to keep the old park in shape. However, a small group of

Birmingham baseball fans wanted to see professional baseball back at Rickwood.

Dr. Jack Levin led a group that planned to purchase the struggling Montgomery Rebels team. An experienced person was needed to manage such a difficult undertaking, and many locals did not believe that the task could be accomplished. In 1980 John Forney, Alabama's football announcer, went to Memphis to interview Art Clarkson, the general manager of the Memphis Chicks who had done an outstanding job of reviving minor-league baseball in Memphis. Forney asked him to visit Birmingham and Rickwood Field to see if he would be interested in revitalizing baseball in another Southern city. When Clarkson came to Rickwood Field, he had to climb over the eight-foot chain-link fence to get into the park.[7] He saw that a lot of work needed to be done, but he also imagined the site as a living baseball museum. Clarkson decided that it was a challenge he could not turn down, and he struck a deal that brought back the Birmingham Barons in 1981. Many observers thought the rundown neighborhood around Rickwood would keep large numbers of fans away, but Clarkson showed them they would come. The Barons were a success in every way and won Southern League championships in 1983 and 1987.

After several years, Clarkson realized that there were limits to how far he could take the Barons at Rickwood Field. Once again the old ballpark faced the possibility of being deserted. Clarkson examined proposals from several Birmingham-area cities and decided to move the team to Hoover, Alabama, which planned to have a new ballpark ready for the 1988 season. The franchise's relocation appeared to spell the end of professional baseball at Rickwood Field. The City of Birmingham took over the ownership of Rickwood Field and offices for the city schools' athletic department were moved there; it was also decided that high-school baseball games between city schools would be played at Rickwood. During the summer, city school buses were parked inside the fenced-in area down the left-field line while old, city-owned cars could be seen parked in the lots around the park. It was a sad situation for the former palace

of Southern baseball. The only ray of hope was that the park was still intact and, therefore, might someday be resurrected.

In 1992 five local men—Tom Crosby, Terry Slaughter, Coke Matthews, Alan Farr, and Bill Cather — who had attended games at Rickwood Field in their youths formed an organization to save the venerable ballpark.[8] By now, Rickwood had fallen into disrepair, and improvements made in the 1980s to make it usable for minor-league baseball had aged to make the park look even worse. The new organization, named The Friends of Rickwood, had a monumental task ahead of it, and something was needed to jump-start the renovation project.

In 1993 filmmaker Ron Shelton came to Birmingham to scout out a site where he could film the baseball scenes for his new movie about the life of Ty Cobb, and he chose Rickwood Field. The repairs and improvements the film crew made to the venue brought the ballpark back to life. The publicity from the film brought together others interested in seeing the ballpark saved, with the idea of completely restoring Rickwood. Soon after the movie *Cobb* was completed, HBO came to Rickwood Field to film a movie about Satchel Paige, Josh Gibson, and Jackie Robinson that was titled *Soul of the Game*. ESPN followed suit and came to the ballpark to film commercials. The destruction of old Comiskey Park in Chicago made Rickwood Field the oldest professional baseball park in the nation, and it was now the place to be. Baseball groups soon began to rent the park for games.

In 1996 the first annual Rickwood Classic was played at the ballpark. The Birmingham Barons returned to play one game a year, and each Classic had a theme for which the teams wore period uniforms. Retired Barons players were invited back to be honored, and fans were encouraged to wear vintage clothes to complete the time-travel experience. For fans, one of the highlights of the day is to be able to go out onto the field after the game and stand on the mound where Dizzy Dean stood, or patrol the outfield where a 17-year-old Willie Mays played. The ballpark has indeed become a living museum.

Author's Note / April 2017

On April 8, 2017, after an inspection by city engineers had revealed structural issues that made the park unsafe, the city of Birmingham announced that Rickwood Field would be closed to the public while repairs are made to the facility. Unfortunately, the temporary shutdown of America's oldest ballpark occurred less than six weeks prior to the annual Rickwood Classic; the May 31, 2017 game was moved to Regions Field, the regular home of the Double-A Birmingham Barons. The Friends of Rickwood organization expends considerable time and effort in preparing for the annual event, and attending the Rickwood Classic is on many baseball fans' bucket lists. After the initial shock of having to move the 2017 Classic wore off, it became clear that the repairs were a positive development since they were necessary to make the stands safe for fans and to ensure that Rickwood Field will endure. Once the repairs have been completed, there will be a renewed appreciation for the park. For the Friends of Rickwood and fans alike, the 2018 Classic will be like a reunion with a long-lost friend, a reunion that will continue to take place for generations to come.

NOTES

1   Timothy Whitt, *Bases Loaded With History* (Birmingham: A.H. Cather Publishing, 1995), 13.

2   Allen Barra, *Rickwood Field, A Century in America's Oldest Ballpark* (New York: W.W. Norton & Co., 2010), 33.

3   Zipp Newman and Frank McGowan, *The House of Barons* (Birmingham: Cathers Brothers Publishing Co., 1950), 39-40.

4   Author interview with Allan Harvey Woodward III, grandson of Rickwood Field builder, A.H. Woodward, September 2016.

5   Zipp Newman, "Dusting 'Em Off," *Birmingham News*, July 13, 1943.

6   Author interview with Bob Scranton, traveling secretary for the Birmingham Barons in the 1950s and former part-owner of the Barons 1980s, several interviews from 1999 to 2008.

7   Author interview with Art Clarkson, former general manager and owner of the Birmingham Barons, November 11, 2016.

8   Author interviews with Tom Crosby, Allan Farr, and Bill Cather, board members of the Friends of Rickwood, October 28, 2016.

TED ALEXANDER

By Rob Neyer

Ted "Red" Alexander was born Theodore Roosevelt Alexander in Spartanburg, South Carolina, on September 15, 1912. His parents, Joseph (b. ~1871) and Lela (b. ~1875), were farmers. According to census records, Theodore was still there in 1930, the year he turned 18. It is probably safe to assume that he was a talented young ballplayer both before and after that year, but no proof of that exists until 1936, when Alexander began his professional baseball career with the Miami Clowns; the following season, he moved halfway across the United States to play for Chicago's Palmer House Stars.[1] Alexander stayed on the move, spending 1938 with the Negro American League's Indianapolis ABC's and at least part of 1939 with the barnstorming Satchel Paige's All-Stars, a "B team" of the Kansas City Monarchs. Paige, who had been injured, wasn't deemed healthy enough to pitch for the real Monarchs, but was still a big drawing card, and his "Baby Monarchs" spent most of their time touring the western part of America.[2] Alexander had a front-row seat as Paige somehow recovered from his injury to pitch brilliantly for another 20-plus years.

According to historian James A. Riley—who describes the 5-foot-10 right-hander as "an average pitcher with the standard three-pitch (fastball, curve, and change of pace) repertory"[3]—Alexander also pitched for the New York Black Yankees in 1939, the Cleveland Bears in 1939 and 1940, and perhaps the Newark Eagles as well; however, no statistics are available from his stints with those clubs. He pitched for the Chicago American Giants in 1941, but neither Riley nor any other reference has anything to say about Alexander's work in 1942.

In 1943 and 1944 Alexander, now in his early 30s, finally pitched for the big-league Kansas City Monarchs. There was a war on, of course, and in 1944 Alexander found himself in the US Army. More spe-cifically, for at least a spell he was stationed at Camp Breckenridge, Kentucky, where a chance meeting with a young black lieutenant who was waiting for his medical discharge might well be responsible for having utterly changed the course of baseball history.

It is a story that Jackie Robinson would tell, albeit with slightly different details, in both of his post-career memoirs. In the earlier version, from 1960, Robinson recalled:

> "I was walking across the camp recreation field when a baseball arched high into the sky and was carried toward me by a strong breeze. As it hit the ground and bounced toward me I leaned over and scooped it up with one hand. I saw a player running in my direction so I pegged a perfect strike to him. As it plopped into his glove he shouted, 'Nice throw!'"

After watching for a bit, Robinson struck up a conversation with the player, complimenting him on his curveballs. "He said he had heard of me as a football player and a track man," Robinson recalled, "but not as a baseball player. Then he explained that he pitched for the Kansas City Monarchs ... and that the team needed good players. He suggested that I write if I thought I could make the grade. I wrote."[4]

Robinson did not identify this Monarchs pitcher in 1960. But in his later autobiography, published in 1972, he identified him as "a brother named Alexander."[5]

Considering that baseball was not considered one of Jackie's best sports—a big star in both football and basketball at UCLA, he'd batted just .097 in his only baseball season, way back in 1940—it was hardly inevitable that Robinson would one day find his place in professional baseball. In fact, if his memoir is to be believed, it seems highly likely that major-league

Ted Alexander was on the losing end of the 1946 Negro League World Series with the Kansas City Monarchs. In 1948 he split his two World Series decisions as the Homestead Grays triumphed over Birmingham. (*Courtesy of Jay-Dell Mah/Western Canada Baseball*)

history would today look quite a bit different, absent that chance meeting at Fort Breckenridge.

Meanwhile, Alexander's biggest chance might have come in the fall of 1946 — at roughly the same moment that Robinson's Montreal Royals were winning the Little World Series — when his Monarchs squared off against the Newark Eagles in black baseball's World Series. Between them, the two powerhouse squads featured four future Hall of Famers in Satchel Paige, Monte Irvin, Larry Doby, and Leon Day; plus three future major leaguers, Willard Brown, Hank Thompson, and Connie Johnson. All those stars attracted the scouts, but Alexander garnered attention, too, as he started Game Four in Kansas City. It was not a stellar outing, and he gave way to Paige in the top of the sixth, trailing 4-1 in what would become an 8-1 Monarchs loss. Alexander pitched better out of the bullpen in Game Six, though that contest resulted in another Kansas City loss by a 9-7

score. Newark ended up taking the championship in a hard-fought seven-game series.

Alexander returned to the Monarchs in 1947, but the following season he joined the Homestead Grays. In the fall of 1948 he was back in the Negro League World Series, as the Grays squared off against the Birmingham Black Barons for black baseball's championship for the third time in six years. Alexander earned the win as the Grays triumphed, 3-2, in Game One in Kansas City. In Game Three, however, he was victimized by 17-year-old Willie Mays in Homestead's only loss in the series, at Birmingham's Rickwood Field. With the game tied, 3-3, in the bottom of the ninth, Alexander retired Birmingham's leadoff batter, Jim Zapp, but then surrendered a single to relief pitcher Bill Greason. He then induced a fly out from Artie Wilson but walked the fourth batter of the inning, Johnny Britton. Up to the plate came Mays, who "hit through Alexander's legs to centerfield," driving home Greason with the winning run.[6] Though Alexander took the loss in Game Three, he and the Grays earned the championship as they topped the Black Barons in five games. That winter the Negro National League folded, which left the Grays to operate as an independent, barnstorming club.

After the demise of the NNL, Alexander played for at least four different teams in 1949, eventually ending up as a member of the barnstorming New Orleans Creoles. His itinerant existence continued when he went north in 1950 to ply his trade in Canada with the London Majors of Ontario's Intercounty League. Alexander, who was listed at 185 pounds at the outset of his career, now weighed 220, which created an unusual dilemma as he began the season in London. According to the team's manager, Dan Mendham, "He was real heavy and the Majors didn't have a uniform big enough to fit him. That's why he started the season in his Homestead Grays outfit."[7]

Alexander spent all of 1950 with the majors and returned to the team in 1951; the highlight of second season in Canada was a 10-inning, two-hit shutout he pitched in London's 1-0 victory over Guelph.[8] After a brief stint with the Brandon Greys of the ManDak League in 1952, his baseball career was over.

According to his obituary, in the late '40s Alexander began to work at Electric Boat in Groton, Connecticut, as a "submarine technician," and retired from the company in 1977.[9] He later lived in Perth Amboy, New Jersey, and East Orange, New Jersey, where he died on March 6, 1999, at the age of 86. He is buried in the Brooklyn C.M.E. Church Cemetery in Chesnee, South Carolina.

NOTES

[1] Barry Swanton and Jay-Dell Mah, *Black Baseball Players in Canada: A Biographical Dictionary, 1881–1960* (Jefferson, North Carolina: McFarland & Company, Inc., 2009), 16.

[2] Larry Lester and Sammy J. Miller, *Black Baseball in Kansas City* (Charleston, South Carolina: Arcadia Publishing, 2000), 42.

[3] James A. Riley, *The Biographical Encyclopedia of the Negro Baseball Leagues* (New York: Carroll & Graf Publishers, 1994), 29.

[4] Carl T. Rowan with Jack R. Robinson, *Wait Till Next Year: The Life Story of Jackie Robinson* (New York: Random House, 1960), 93-94.

[5] Jackie Robinson as told to Alfred Duckett, *I Never Had It Made* (New York: G.P. Putnam's Sons, 1972), 35.

[6] "Grays Hold 3-1 Lead in Series," *Afro-American*, October 8, 1948: 8.

[7] Swanton and Mah, 16.

[8] Ibid.

[9] The obituary is unfortunately from an unknown newspaper.

SAM BANKHEAD

By Dave Wilkie

Hall of Famer and Negro League legend Judy Johnson called Sam Bankhead "one of the greatest outfielders we had."[1] Wilmer "Red" Fields, ace pitcher and 1948 World Series-winning Homestead Grays teammate, said, "He was the greatest team player I ever saw."[2] Blessed with a cannon for an arm, a penchant for clutch hitting, and the ability to play every position on the field, Sam enjoyed a 20-year-plus career playing with some of the most storied teams in baseball history. Left-handed slugger and All-Star Bob Harvey had this to say about Sam's throwing prowess: "He had a beautiful arm. Nobody tagged up at third and scored on a fly. He'd throw you out from the warning track."[3]

Samuel Howard Bankhead was most likely born on September 18, 1910, in Sulligent, Alabama.[4] His father, Garnett Bankhead Sr., labored in the coal mines and played first base in the Cotton Belt League, while his mother, Arie Armstrong, gave birth to five boys and two girls. Sam worked alongside his father loading coal until baseball led him to a better life.

All four of Bankhead's younger brothers played in the Negro Leagues. Fred was a slick-fielding second baseman from 1936 to 1948, making an All-Star appearance in 1942. Garnett played for three seasons from 1947 to 1949, including a short stint on the 1948 champion Homestead Grays with his brother Sam as manager. Joe had the shortest career, taking the mound a few times with the 1948 Birmingham Black Barons, and Dan became the first black pitcher in major-league history when he took the mound on August 26, 1947. for the Brooklyn Dodgers. Dan also hit a home run in his first major-league at-bat, but his success was short-lived; he was out of the majors by 1951.

Sam Bankhead punched his ticket out of the coal mines and into his Negro League career in 1929 with the Birmingham Black Barons, but he did not get much playing time as an 18-year-old rookie. From 1930 to 1932 he bounced around with Birmingham and the Louisville Black Caps until he finally found a home and a starting position with the Nashville Elite Giants.

In 1933 Negro League baseball introduced its inaugural East-West All-Star Game, which has been called "the pinnacle of any Negro League season," and described as "an All-Star game and a World Series all wrapped in one spectacle."[5] The annual games were so popular and star-studded that many observers, including Negro League historian Larry Lester, have credited them with helping to integrate Organized Baseball. Bankhead, as he often did in high-pressure situations, shined in these contests. A nine-time all-star at five different positions, Sam had 12 hits in 31 at-bats with 7 runs, 4 RBIs, and 2 stolen bases. He is also credited with scoring the first run in an East-West All-Star Game. Coincidentally, the National and American Leagues also debuted the major-league All-Star Game in 1933, but by the early 1940s it was often being outdrawn by its Negro League counterpart.[6]

After a solid season in 1934, his last with the Nashville Elite Giants, Bankhead moved on to one of the greatest teams in Negro League history, the Pittsburgh Crawfords. The 1935 Crawfords squad included future Hall of Famers Josh Gibson, Oscar Charleston, Judy Johnson, and Cool Papa Bell. Mark Koenig, shortstop for the 1927 New York Yankees, compared the '35 Crawfords favorably to his legendary World Series-winning team.[7] Bankhead made a seamless transition into this team of superstars, hitting .298 and playing a starring role as one of the Raindrop Rangers, a trio of speedy outfielders with Sam playing alongside Bell and Jimmie Crutchfield. Fanciful legend had it that the three players were so fast that they could keep a field dry by catching the raindrops before they hit the ground.[8] The Crawfords capped off their magical season with a hard-fought seven-game victory over the New York Cubans in the Negro League World Series. Bankhead had a solid Series with seven hits, including a clutch single, stolen base, and run scored that gave Pittsburgh the lead in the seventh inning of the seventh game.[9]

The Crawfords began a steady decline in 1936. Bankhead had an off-year, hitting just .204. Though the Crawfords still ended up winning the Negro National League championship, no agreement could be reached with the Negro American League to play a World Series that year. After the season Gus Greenlee, owner of the Crawfords and creator of the East-West All-Star Game, was forced to cut payroll and players due to his involvement in racketeering. The Crawfords hung on through the 1938 season, but they were a mere shell of the team that dominated Negro League baseball from 1932 to 1936.

In 1937 Greenlee's misfortunes turned into a boon for Crawfords players Bankhead, Bell, Gibson, and Satchel Paige, as they were all recruited to play in the Dominican Republic for dictator Rafael Trujillo's Dragones team. Trujillo, a corrupt and violent leader, paid exorbitant salaries to these players in order to field a winning team to gain favor in the coming election. His two political opponents also fielded highly competitive teams made up largely of players raided from Negro League squads. The pressure on the Trujillo players was such that they felt that winning the championship was a life-or-death endeavor. The team would often be locked up at night to ensure that they would be in tip-top shape for the next day's game.[10]

Bankhead posted a .309 batting average with 21 hits in 68 at-bats, but it was Gibson's .453 average and Paige's 8-2 record that led the Dragones to the championship game against San Pedro de Macoris. In that game Bankhead had the most dramatic at-bat of his career. The Dragones were trailing 5-4 in the seventh inning against Negro League All-Star pitcher Chet Brewer when Bankhead strode to the plate with Bell on first base. Bell recalled:

"Brewer knew Bankhead was a great clutch hitter and tried to be careful with him. Too

careful. The count went to three and one. Brewer came in with some smoke, but he got it high. I thought Bankhead would drive the pitch, but he had a big cut and fouled it back. Then he connected on the three-two pitch. He was a line-drive hitter, and this one went way over the left field fence. We were pretty happy."[11]

Paige retired the final six batters, five on strikeouts, to ensure the victory. "I guess we helped Trujillo stay in office," claimed Bell,[12] but the players could not get out of the Dominican Republic fast enough.

Bankhead, like many other Negro League players, treated baseball like a year-round job, and the winter of 1937 found him playing for the Santa Clara Leopards in Cuba. This turned out to be one of his finest seasons as he led the league in several categories, including a .366 batting average, 89 hits, 5 triples,

Though Dan Bankhead is better-known because he was MLB's first African-American pitcher in 1947, his brother Sam — a shortstop (pictured here) — had a Negro League career worthy of consideration for the Hall of Fame. (*National Baseball Hall of Fame, Cooperstown, New York*)

and 47 runs scored.[13] The Leopards finished with a 44-18 record and stood in first place in the final league standings.[14]

The year 1937 proved to be a busy one for Bankhead as he also married Helen M. Hall on February 25. The two had a daughter, Brenda, in 1939, and a son, Anthony, in 1941. Anthony was diagnosed with colon cancer in 1970 and died at the age of 29. Brenda's fate is unknown, and Helen died on October 10, 1985 in Pittsburgh.

Bankhead was known as Hall of Famer Josh Gibson's best friend and confidant.[15] Josh Gibson Jr. had this to say about their friendship: "I know that as far back as I can remember, Sammy was a constant. I don't think they were inseparable, 'cause my father didn't get that close to nobody. But they clicked out of mutual respect."[16] Unfortunately the two were also known for their legendary drinking prowess. Stories of drinking contests that lasted long into the night, drinking on buses, between double-headers, and sometimes even during games, can be found in every Gibson biography and article where Bankhead is mentioned. In 1947 Bankhead was managing in Caracas, Venezuela, when he received a telegram announcing Gibson's death. All-Star catcher, Bill "Ready" Cash was there and had this to say: "Bankhead went out that night, got drunk, came in and tore up everything in his room. They had to send him home."[17]

Bankhead mended fences with Gus Greenlee in time to join the Pittsburgh Crawfords for the 1938 season. Greenlee had been upset that many of his star players had been lured to the Dominican Republic and had chosen money over loyalty. The Crawfords lacked star power that year as Gibson headed to the Homestead Grays while Bell and Paige played in the Mexican League. The Crawfords finished in fourth place with a 24-16 league record that placed them 4½ games behind Gibson's first-place Grays.

The year 1939 marked the end of the great Pittsburgh Crawfords franchise, as Greenlee Field was demolished and replaced with housing projects.[18] Bankhead started the season with the relocated but short-lived Toledo Crawfords; however, he quickly jumped to the Homestead Grays to play second base with his old friend Josh Gibson. Bankhead hit a solid .292, as the Grays won the Negro National League pennant, but lost the Negro League World Series to future Hall of Fame catcher Roy Campanella and his Baltimore Elite Giants. Bankhead went 7-for-23 in the series for a .304 batting average.

Throughout the 1930s and 1940s, the integration of black players into Organized Baseball was a hot topic for both black and white sportswriters. Bankhead's name often came up in such discussions. In 1936 William G. Nunn, city editor for the *Pittsburgh Courier*, wrote, "We don't believe the majors can produce three outfielders with the all-around ability of 'Cool Papa,' Bill Wright or Bankhead."[19] Two years later white sportswriter Jimmy Powers of the *New York Daily News* wrote about seven Negro League players who would guarantee the New York Giants a pennant and included Bankhead as his starting center fielder.[20] Even white superstar players like Honus Wagner, Dizzy Dean, and Paul Waner went to bat for integration, but their cries fell on the deaf ears of antiquated thinkers like Washington Senators owner Calvin Griffith, Philadelphia Athletics owner Connie Mack, and Commissioner Kenesaw Mountain Landis.[21] Sadly, the window of time closed on Negro baseball legends like Gibson, Leonard, Bell, Bankhead, and many others.

In the decade preceding Jackie Robinson's arrival in the major leagues, more than 100 players from the Negro Leagues played in Mexico.[22] Mexican business mogul and multimillionaire Jorge Pasquel was a big reason why. Pasquel, a strong and fearless leader,[23] wanted to turn the Mexican League into baseball's third major league. He lured dozens of black players south of the border by offering them salaries that were two to four times greater than what they were making in the States.

In 1940 Bankhead signed with the Monterrey Carta Blanco, playing shortstop and leading the league in stolen bases with 32. He had 122 hits in 384 at-bats for a .315 average, but his team finished the year nine games behind Pasquel's championship club, the Vera Cruz Azules.[24] The Azules fielded one of the most impressive lineups in baseball history with Bell, Gibson, Ray Dandridge, Leon Day, Martin Dihigo, and Willie Wells, each of whom eventually received enshrinement in Cooperstown.

Bankhead signed with Monterrey again in 1941, which turned out to be career year for him as he tore up the league with 142 hits in 405 at-bats for a stellar .351 average. He hit 8 home runs, scored 74 times, stole 19 bases, and drove home 85 runs.[25] In spite of Bankhead's batting prowess, the Monterrey team finished in last place with a 43-59 record, 24 games behind the repeating champion Azules.[26]

At the conclusion of the 1941 Mexican League season, All-Star catcher Quincy Trouppe formed a barnstorming team that played throughout the United States. The team was called the Mexican League All Stars and included the familiar names of Bell, Dandridge, Wells, Gibson, and Bankhead. The team won all 10 of its games before disbanding for lack of financial support.[27] The well-traveled Bankhead then finished off the year by playing for the Ponce Leones in Puerto Rico.

Bankhead returned to the Negro Leagues with the Homestead Grays in 1942. Garnett Blair, pitcher for the Grays, said:

"Sam Bankhead to me was an outstanding player. He played shortstop and he would go behind third to get it and throw you out waist high across the diamond. He could not only play short, he could play second, third, he could play outfield, he could pitch, and he could catch. He was all around, so anytime I was pitching I said if that ball goes to Sam Bankhead, fine. There's nothing wrong with that, let it go there because if he got his glove on it, he was going to throw you out."[28]

Bankhead batted .283 while playing shortstop for the first-place Grays. On July 21, 1942, the *Mansfield (Ohio) News Journal* credited the Grays with a 79-4 record that included exhibition games.[29] The team reached the Negro League World Series but was quickly dismantled by Paige and the Kansas City Monarchs in five games.[30]

All the stars aligned for the Homestead Grays and Sam Bankhead in 1943, as the Grays finished the year with a 44-15 league record. Bankhead was second in the batting title race with an otherworldly .483 average.[31] The Grays won a hard-fought eight-game Negro League World Series against the Birmingham Black Barons.[32] With the Grays trailing 4-2 and two outs in the eighth inning, Bankhead delivered a clutch single to drive in what turned out to be the Series-winning runs.[33]

In what must have seemed like a foregone conclusion to the rest of the league, the Homestead Grays easily finished in first place in 1944 and 1945. Bankhead hit .345 in 1944 but slumped to .262 in 1945. The 1944 team once again met the Black Barons in the World Series and easily dispatched them in five games this time. Bankhead went 7-for-18 (.388) in the Series. The 1945 Series was a different story for the Grays as they were swept by future major leaguer Sam Jethroe and the Cleveland Buckeyes. In keeping with his subpar 1945 season, Bankhead had an uncharacteristically bad Series: 1-for-16 (.063).

The 1946 and 1947 seasons were both disappointments for the proud Homestead Grays. The 1946 team fell to third place with a losing record of 27-28, with Bankhead hitting .265. The 1947 squad finished in second place with a more respectable 38-27 record but Bankhead's average dipped to an anemic .246. A Grays team composed of aging veterans, Jackie Robinson's integration of major-league baseball, and the tragic death of Josh Gibson on January 20, 1947, seemed to spell the beginning of the end for the Homestead Grays.

The 1948 season turned out to be a last hurrah for both the Homestead Grays and the NNL. The press was paying far less attention to the Negro Leagues by this point, but it is known that the Grays defeated the Baltimore Elite Giants in the NNL playoffs and met the Birmingham Black Barons in the Negro League World Series for the third time in six years. The Black Barons had knocked off a strong Kansas City Monarchs team in the NAL playoffs and featured a 17-year-old legend in the making, Willie Mays.

Bankhead helped lead the Grays to a five-game championship victory. After the series ended, the NNL disbanded, which meant that the 1948 Negro League World Series had been the last of its kind.

The Homestead Grays still fielded teams for the 1949 and 1950 seasons, with Bankhead staying on as player-manager. By all accounts these teams were highly competitive, with newspapers reporting records of 97-15 and 64-8 for the 1949 and 1950 seasons respectively.[35] In 11 box scores found from the 1950 season, an aging Bankhead banged out 18 hits in 45 at-bats.[36] The decline of the Negro Leagues continued apace, however, and the Grays folded after the 1950 season.

After Josh Gibson's death in 1947, Sam became a surrogate father for 16-year-old Josh Gibson Jr., who played second base and third base for Bankhead's 1949 and 1950 Grays teams; however, Josh Jr. could not escape his father's enormous shadow. In 1951 Sam took Josh Jr. with him north of the border to play in the Class-C Canadian Provincial League for the Pittsburgh Pirates-affiliated Farnham Pirates. Canada was where Bankhead attained one of baseball's most underappreciated milestones by becoming the first black manager for a mostly white professional baseball team. Josh Jr. did not fare as well: While playing for Farnham, he broke his ankle sliding into second base, effectively ending his baseball career.

After spending the 1951 season in Canada, Sam and Josh Jr. returned home to the Hill District in Pittsburgh and took jobs working side by side for the Pittsburgh Sanitation Department. Josh Jr. had this to say about their experience together: "I worked with him. I listened to him still, like playin' baseball. He was one of the smartest guys 'cause he read all the time."[37]

Bankhead's post-baseball life has led to speculation, most notably by Negro League historian John Holway,[38] that the character Troy Maxson, from August Wilson's Pulitzer Prize-winning play *Fences* was based on Sam. Like Bankhead, Maxson was a bitter ex-Negro League star who worked on a garbage truck in Pittsburgh's Hill District. Bankhead was bitter that he never got the chance to play in baseball's major leagues,[39] and he refused to go to baseball games in his later years, even missing the chance to see his younger brother, Dan, pitch for the Brooklyn Dodgers. In a 1971 interview, Bankhead had this to say about major-league baseball: "After I quit, I never went to see a game again. I am not jealous, but I cannot be a fan."[40] Sam preferred to stay close to home, playing cards with his buddies, endlessly talking about the old days, and—most of all—drinking. Bankhead's brother Fred died in 1972, and his youngest brother, Dan, died in 1976, events that made Sam lean on the bottle even more heavily than before. While the exact circumstances of Sam Bankhead's death are not known, it is known that he was shot in the head and killed on the night of July 24, 1976.[41] Whether he was shot by a friend after an argument in a downtown hotel, or shot in self-defense by a co-worker at the William Penn Hotel in downtown Pittsburgh, one thing is certain: Negro League legend Sam Bankhead's life came to an unceremonious end at the age of 65.

In 2005 the *Washington Post* honored Negro League legend Ted "Double Duty" Radcliffe upon the occasion of his 102nd birthday and asked him, "What player do you think of when you think of the Negro Leagues?" Radcliffe responded, "Bankhead. He was a great player."[42] Indeed, Bankhead had been picked as the first-team utility player as early as 1952 in a *Pittsburgh Courier* poll that named the all-time Negro League All-Stars.[43] He was universally respected as a player and manager and continually rose to the occasion when playing with and against the greatest players in Negro League history.

Bankhead would have made a tremendous major-leaguer. By all accounts he was an exceptional fielder, a speed demon on the basepaths, and a skilled batsman, as his lifetime .289 batting average attests.[44] If nonleague statistics are included, then his average shoots up to well above .300. Bankhead is also credited with a .301 average against white major leaguers in barnstorming games.[45]

As of January 2017, there have been 220 major-league players elected to baseball's Hall of Fame. Negro League players have been grossly underrepresented, with only 35 players honored with plaques thus far. When examining the scope of his entire career, it is not hard to envision a place for Sam Bankhead in the hallowed halls of Cooperstown.

SOURCES

All statistics, unless otherwise noted, are from:

Holway, John B. *The Complete Book of Baseball's Negro Leagues: The Other Half of Baseball History* (Fern Park, Florida: Hastings House Publishers, 2001).

NOTES

1   John B. Holway, *Black Giants* (Springfield, Virginia: Lord Fairfax Press, 2010), 92.

2   Ibid.

3   Ibid.

4   Conflicting sources have Bankhead being born on September 18, 1905, in Empire, Alabama, but the 1910 birthdate shows up on both the US Social Security Death Index and on his gravestone in Sharpsburg, Pennsylvania.

5   Larry Lester, *Black Baseball's National Showcase* (Lincoln: University of Nebraska Press, 2001), 1.

6   Ibid.

7   Jim Bankes, *The Pittsburgh Crawfords* (Jefferson, North Carolina: McFarland & Company, Inc., Publishers, 2001), 148.

8   Lester, 88.

9   John B. Holway, *The Complete Book of Baseball's Negro Leagues: The Other Half of Baseball History* (Fern Park, Florida: Hastings House Publishers, 2001), 321.

10   Holway, John B., *Josh and Satch: The Life and Times of Josh Gibson and Satchel Paige* (New York: Meckler Publishing, 1991), 90.

11   Bankes, 110.

12   Ibid.

13   Dr. Layton Revel and Luis Munoz, *Forgotten Heroes: Samuel "Sam" Bankhead* (Carrollton, Texas: Center for Negro League Research, 2011), 23.

14   Ibid.

15   Brad Snyder, *Beyond the Shadow of the Senators* (New York: McGraw-Hill, 2003), 171, 274.

16   Mark Ribowsky, *The Power and the Darkness: The Life of Josh Gibson in the Shadows of the Game* (New York: Simon and Schuster, 1996), 164.

17   Brent Kelley, *Voices From the Negro Leagues: Conversations With 52 Baseball Standouts* (Jefferson, North Carolina: McFarland & Company, Inc., Publishers, 1998), 145.

18   Holway, *The Complete Book of Baseball's Negro Leagues,* 356.

19   Lester, 89.

20   Lester, 109-110.

21   Holway, *Josh and Satch,* 151-155.

22   John Virtue, *South of the Color Barrier* (Jefferson, North Carolina: McFarland & Company, Inc., Publishers, 2008), 11.

23   Virtue, 12.

24   Virtue, 85.

25   Revel and Munoz, 11.

26   Ibid.

27   Revel and Munoz, 12.

28   Larry Lester and Sammy J. Miller, *Black Baseball in Pittsburgh* (Charleston, South Carolina: Arcadia Publishing, 2001), 75.

29   Revel and Munoz, 12.

30   Holway, *The Complete Book of Baseball's Negro Leagues,* 398-399.

31   Tetelo Vargas of the New York Cubans hit .484.

32   Game Two ended in a tie.

33   Holway, *Josh and Satch,* 171.

35   Revel and Munoz,19.

36   Ibid. 19.

37   Brent Kelley, *The Negro Leagues Revisited: Conversations With 66 More Baseball Heroes* (Jefferson, North Carolina: McFarland & Company, Inc., Publishers, 2000), 258.

38   Holway, *Black Giants,* 92.

39   August Wilson, *Fences* (New York: Plume, 1986).

40   Holway, *Black Giants,* 97.

41   Ibid.

42   "Ex-Washington Player Goes Back a Few Years," *Washington Post,* April 12, 2005. washingtonpost.com/archive/sports/2005/04/12/ex-washington-player-goes-back-a-few-years/4a2faf00-9223-4718-b46c-e1b8e0213a6b/?utm_term=.66be349249e0. Accessed December 31, 2016.

43   James A. Riley, *The Biographical Encyclopedia of the Negro Baseball Leagues* (New York: Carroll & Graff Publishers, Inc., 1994), 52.

44   Holway, *Black Giants,* 99.

45   Holway, *Black Giants,* 101.

HOMESTEAD'S "LEFTY" BELL AND THE CHALLENGE OF NEGRO LEAGUE RESEARCH

By Frederick C. Bush

A pitcher whom the *Pittsburgh Post-Gazette* first identified as Charles "Lefty" Bell posted a 3-0 record for the Homestead Grays in 1948. The fact that Bell's first name was likely James, rather than Charles, is only the first obstacle in attempting to identify this player, whose life and career provide a prime example of the difficulties that are encountered in researching the Negro Leagues. According to the *Post-Gazette*, the Grays signed Bell in April 1948 after he had "won 27 and lost one, while pitching for the Laketon, Fla., club last season."[1] The city of Laketon is in Indiana; thus, the team Bell pitched for was based in Lakeland, Florida.

Compounding the difficulty in determining the identity of this pitcher is the fact that he was most often identified by the press simply as "Lefty" Bell. Additionally, conflicting information about Bell exists in the few available sources that mention him at all. Both James Riley's *Biographical Encyclopedia* and Dick Clark and Larry Lester's *The Negro Leagues Book* list a pitcher named Charles "Lefty" Bell as having played for the Grays in 1948.[2] The fact that his first name is given as Charles likely stems from the *Post-Gazette*'s article. Riley asserts that Bell "was a second-line pitcher ... but fashioned a perfect 3-0 record."[3]

A pitcher named Charles "Lefty" Bell also is listed on baseball-reference.com, where it is alleged that he was born in Lakeland, Florida, in some unknown year. However, this player is listed on the roster of the 1929 Memphis Red Sox and split his time between Memphis and the Chicago American Giants in 1930.[4] In light of those listings, two questions remain: Why does B-R.com not list this Bell on the roster of the

1948 Grays, and where did he spend the years between 1930 and 1946?

Further confusion arises from the fact that B-R.com, while not listing Charles Bell on Homestead's roster, does list a 50-year-old pitcher named William Bell on the roster of the 1948 Grays.[5] This pitcher has been identified as William Bell Sr. of Lavaca County, Texas, whose Negro League career spanned the years 1923-37 and 1948; his pitching line on B-R.com shows a 0-0 record in only 3⅓ innings pitched for Homestead in 1948. However, according to Riley, William Sr. was a member of the Homestead Grays in 1932 and "his last appearance in black baseball was as a manager of the [Newark] Eagles in 1948."[6] The differences in first name and statistics indicate that Charles "Lefty" Bell and William Bell Sr. have not accidentally been conflated into one and the same player.[7]

The Charles "Lefty" Bell who pitched for the Homestead Grays may have been a Mississippi native, and his true first name most likely was James. What may be the earliest mention of Bell in print appears in a news account of a game between the House of David team of Santiago, Cuba, and the Wechsler High Black Cats at Traction Park in Meridian, Mississippi, on April 29, 1931. Wechsler High's coach started a pitcher identified as "Jas. (Lefty) Bell," who allowed three runners to score when he made a wild pitch with the bases loaded in the game, which Wechsler lost, 8-6.[8] The Mississippi location and the year 1931 match up well with what little is known about "Lefty" Bell, though the abbreviation "Jas." for "James" indicates a different first name. While it is possible that there could have been both a James "Lefty" Bell and Charles "Lefty" Bell within short proximity of one another in Mississippi, such a scenario is improbable. More likely, in a time in which misspellings and typographical errors pervaded newspapers, is that "Jas." accidentally became "Chas." when Bell was signed by the Grays in 1948.

The likelihood that Wechsler High's James "Lefty" Bell was the player who eventually joined the Homestead Grays in 1948 stems from the fact that a player who was referred to simply as Lefty Bell began to pitch semipro ball in Mississippi at some point in the early to mid-1930s. A 1934 press account touted Lefty Bell and Baby Face Green, "two of the best semi-pro pitching stars [who] hooked up" in a 1-0 pitchers' duel in which Bell's Laurel Big "M" Black Cats defeated the Colored "Y" Tigers.[9] The following season, Lefty Bell was again in fine form as he led the Laurel Black Cats' staff in their attempt to win the Mississippi state title over the Meridian Giants. In two separate 10-inning, 1-0 victories over Meridian, he struck out 14 and 18 batters.[10] Bell continued to pitch for Laurel through at least 1938, but it is not certain where he might have played the next two seasons.

In April 1941 it was reported that the "Mobile Black Shippers [would] be strengthened for the occasion [of a doubleheader against the Ethiopian Clowns] by the addition of Lefty Bell of Laurel, Miss., and both Tommie Lee and Bill Tate, St. Louis."[11] However, whether or not Bell was simply on loan to Mobile, or had signed with the team was unclear. Bell may have led an itinerant existence that season, as he also spent time with the Reidsville, North Carolina, Black Luckies. On June 9, in Reidsville's 9-7 victory over the appallingly-named South Boston Spooks, "Lefty Bell did the mound duties for the Luckies and struck out 13 Spooks."[12]

Where Bell spent the years 1942-46, or how and when he ended up with the Lakeland team in the Florida State League is a mystery. Coverage of the league's games was sparse and inconsistent, but an August 23, 1947, news article—with Bell's last name misspelled as "Bill"—hints at Lefty's sustained pitching acumen. The *Palm Beach Post* reported, "Lakeland's Tigers used timely hitting and effective southpaw pitching by Bill to trim the local Yankees, 6

to 2, in a Florida State Negro Baseball League game at Wright Field Friday night."[13] Bell lost a shutout with two outs in the ninth inning but still earned the win in Lakeland's triumph. Whatever Bell's record may have been in 1947, he was certainly a known commodity prior to the 27-1 season attributed to him by the *Pittsburgh Post-Gazette*. In April 1946 the *Atlanta Daily World* had reported that the Birmingham Black Barons had not "had any success trying to get 'Lefty' Bell, billed as a good slab prospect, away from his Mississippi home."[14]

If pitching closer to home was important to him, it seems odd that Bell signed with the Homestead franchise—which played its home games in Pittsburgh and Washington—after not having signed with the much closer Birmingham franchise in 1946. Nonetheless, the first mention of a southpaw named Charles Bell occurs in the April 29 issue of the *Post-Gazette*. It is not far-fetched to suppose that since Bell was usually referred to simply as "Lefty," a reporter who had seen his first name abbreviated "Jas." may have remembered "Chas." and inadvertently changed Bell's first name to Charles. Errors in player names were not uncommon; for example, the April 10 edition of the *Pittsburgh Courier* reported that the Grays had acquired a new Cuban catcher named Ramon Sosa, whose actual first name turned out to be Victoriano.[15]

The Pittsburgh newspapers also appear to have embellished the new Grays previous accomplishments, though it is entirely possible that they were victims of misinformation spread by the Grays' front office in an attempt to make its new signees appear to be star acquisitions. The April 10 *Courier* article claimed that Sosa had been "recently obtained from the Mariaona [sic] team, a member of the Cuban Winter League," and that he had "won the Cuban Batting Championship in 1946."[16] In truth, Victoriano Sosa had spent his only season in Cuban baseball, which was 1946, with the Cerro team in Cuba's new Summer League, and there is no evidence that he had won the league's batting championship.[17] It is not a stretch to believe that Charles Bell's reported 27-1 record with Lakeland in 1947 may also have reflected hyperbole.

In any case, by July 17, 1948, Homestead's new southpaw was named as "Charles (Lefty) Bell" in an article printed prior to a start he was scheduled to make against the Philadelphia Stars at Wilmington Park in Delaware. In that article Bell was touted as "one of the greatest pitching finds in Negro baseball," who was "making his Wilmington debut for the Grays."[18] However, it appears unlikely that Bell pitched against the Stars that day; for reason(s) unknown, his stint with Homestead ended abruptly.

On Wednesday, July 21, 1948, the *Atlanta Daily World* reported that the Atlanta Black Crackers had defeated the Jacksonville Eagles, 2-1, three days earlier—on Sunday, July 18—"behind the stellar three-hit pitching of Lefty Bell, colorful southpaw who formerly tossed the pellet for the Homestead Grays of the Negro National League."[19]

On July 29 it was reported that "Lefty Bell, formerly with the Homestead Grays, will pitch for Atlanta" in a game between the Black Crackers and the Asheville Blues at McCormick Field in Asheville, North Carolina.[20] There still was no explanation as to why the Grays had parted ways with their so-called pitching sensation or how he had come to join the Atlanta team. From this point forward, Bell was again referred to simply as Lefty Bell—there is no further mention of the first name Charles, nor any mention of the name James—and he proceeded to win 15 games as the ace of the Atlanta staff in 1948.[21]

As late as September 2, the *Atlanta Daily World* referred to "Husky 'Lefty' Bell, southpaw sensation," who was going to take the mound for Atlanta against the Raleigh (North Carolina) Tigers.[22] Yet the *Daily World* never mentioned by which unusual manner a "second-line pitcher" for the Grays of the Negro National League, one of black baseball's two major leagues, had become a star for the Black Crackers of the Negro Southern League, a somewhat lower-level professional circuit.

The Black Crackers franchise encountered financial troubles, briefly moved to Detroit for part of the 1949 season, and then returned to the Negro Southern League as the Atlanta Brown Crackers in 1950. In advance of the new Atlanta franchise's May 14 game against the New Orleans Creoles, the *Daily World* ran a preview of the team and its key performers, which included a pitcher named James Bell (sans the nickname "Lefty" however).[23] Interestingly, the *Daily World* mentioned that the Brown Crackers had spent spring training in Lakeland, Florida.

Presumably, the Brown Crackers' James Bell was Lefty Bell; however, that would mean that the mystery man's identity has finally been solved. James Bell was selected as a Negro Southern League All-Star in 1950, and the *Daily World* listed the roster of the NSL All-Star team prior to its game against the Memphis Red Sox in July. James Bell was listed there as a right-hander.[24] Although this could well have been a misprint—Bell's name is found immediately below a left-hander, John Diamond of the New Orleans Creoles—it leaves open the possibility that this could have been a different James Bell.

One thing is certain: If "Jas." (Lefty) Bell of Meridian, Mississippi, who pitched for Wechsler High School in 1931, was indeed "Charles" (Lefty) Bell—which seems to be the most likely scenario—then he obviously was not the pitcher who played for Memphis and Chicago in 1929-30.[25] Thus, there remains the question: Who was the player supposedly named Charles "Lefty" Bell who pitched for Memphis and Chicago? The answer to that query may never be found.

The answers to most questions about James "Lefty" Bell's identity also remain elusive, showing how quickly a man's life can be erased from the annals of history. The lone fact about Bell that has not been obscured is that he was a pitcher of some renown in certain circles of the Negro Leagues. As late as 1986, Samuel Malone, Bell's manager with the Laurel Black Cats, asserted:

"Lefty Bell was the best left-hander I ever saw. He beat Satchel Paige one time 1-0. He had five pitches and mastered them all, including the knuckleball. I saw Warren Spahn and Whitey Ford pitch, but I'd take Bell. He was that good."[26]

In spite of such accolades, Lefty Bell remains almost as great a mystery as the Yeti or the Loch Ness Monster, rising suddenly out of the mists of time and quickly disappearing again before he can be fully grasped.

ACKNOWLEDGEMENT

The author thanks fellow researcher Margaret Gripshover, who unearthed the material about Lefty Bell's semipro days in Mississippi as well as the first article found that reported Bell's move from the Homestead Grays to the Atlanta Black Crackers in July 1948. The latter fact indicates that Bell was no longer a member of the Grays at the time of the World Series against the Birmingham Black Barons.

NOTES

1   "Grays Launch League Season," *Pittsburgh Post-Gazette*, April 29, 1948: 18.

2   James A. Riley, *The Biographical Encyclopedia of the Negro Baseball Leagues* (New York: Carroll & Graf Publishers, Inc., 1994), 71; Dick Clark and Larry Lester, *The Negro Leagues Book* (Cleveland: Society for American Baseball Research, 1994), 145, 171.

3   Riley, 71.

4   Charles "Lefty" Bell, baseball-reference.com/register/player. cgi?id=bell—006cha, accessed January 13, 2017.

5   1948 Homestead Grays, baseball-reference.com/register/team. cgi?id=113d8785, accessed January 13, 2017.

6   Riley, 75.

7   William Bell Sr. was a right-hander, which is another reason he could not be confused with Charles "Lefty" Bell. William "Lefty" Bell Jr. did not join the Negro Leagues until 1949, his first season with the Kansas City Monarchs; he pitched for Kansas City through the 1954 season and also spent part of 1950 with the Birmingham Black Barons.

8   "High School Sports: Wechsler Loses to Cubans," *Chicago Defender* (National Edition), May 2, 1931: 8.

9   "Laurel Black Cats Win Hot Baseball Set," *Chicago Defender* (National Edition), September 22, 1934: 17.

10 "Mississippi Nines Battle: State Title is Prize as Meridian, Laurel Play," *Chicago Defender* (National Edition), September 21, 1935: 15.

11 "Showboat Thomas Day on April 27th for Mobile Fans," *Chicago Defender* (National Edition), April 26, 1941: 22.

12 "Black Luckies Lose to Danville; Win Two Other Games," *Norfolk* (Virginia) *Journal and Guide*, June 21, 1941: 13.

13 "Homer in 9th Robs Lakeland of Shutout," *Palm Beach Post* (West Palm Beach, Florida), August 23, 1947: 5. The news article gives no indication as to the city of origin of the Yankees team that opposed the Tigers that night.

14 "Hits and Bits: Pitching Problems," *Atlanta Daily World*, April 30, 1946: 4.

15 "Pittsburgh Opener Set for April 29; Outfield Has Power," *Pittsburgh Courier*, April 10, 1948: 15.

16 Ibid.

17 Jorge S. Figueredo, *Cuban Baseball: A Statistical History, 1878-1961* (Jefferson, North Carolina: McFarland & Company, Inc., 2003), 272-73.

18 "Homestead Grays Tangle With Philadelphia Stars," *Wilmington* (Delaware) *Morning News*, July 17, 1948: 10.

19 "Crax Climb in Upper Division by Topping Eagles, 8-0, 2-1," *Atlanta Daily World*, July 21, 1948: 5.

20 "Blues Clash with Atlanta Here Tonight," *Asheville* (North Carolina) *Citizen-Times*, July 29, 1948: 17.

21 Leslie Heaphy, "The Atlanta Black Crackers," sabr.org/research/atlanta-black-crackers, accessed January 13, 2017.

22 "Black Crackers Gird for Blazing Battle With Raleigh Tigers," *Atlanta Daily World*, September 2, 1948: 5.

23 "Atlanta Brown Crackers Play New Orleans Creoles, Sunday," *Atlanta Daily World*, May 9, 1950: 5.

24 "Memphis Red Sox to Play All-Stars Here," *Atlanta Daily World*, July 9, 1950: 7.

25 There was another left-handed pitcher in the Negro Leagues named James Bell, who eventually was elected to the National Baseball Hall of Fame. However, James Thomas "Cool Papa" Bell of Starkville, Mississippi, began his career in 1922 and switched from being a "lefty" pitcher to a center fielder whose speed became legendary. Cool Papa Bell had a brother named Fred who pitched for several different Negro League teams over the course of his career. Fred Bell, who was a southpaw, was nicknamed Lefty.

26 Rick Cleveland, " 'Blinkum' had his heyday before color lines broke," *Clarion-Ledger* (Jackson, Mississippi), October 25, 1986: 43.

GARNETT BLAIR

By Bill Nowlin

Right-handed pitcher Garnett Blair had the opportunity to play for a hometown team. In a better world, it wasn't the one he might have pitched for. Racial segregation stood in the way of that.

Blair attended Pittsburgh's Langley High School, a member of the Class of February 1940. The school itself is an impressive one architecturally, and is on the National Register of Historic Places. He was 4-0 for Clark High in 1938, moving over to Langley in 1939. The Langley baseball team was the 1939 city champion team in Pittsburgh. Photography in the school yearbook suggests Blair was the only black player on the team, but he was one of two standout pitchers. The yearbook in general shows that this was a well-integrated school, and the notations next to student photos were kind to all. The photograph of him informs us today that his nickname was Tiny (he stood 6-feet-4 and is listed as weighing 215 pounds) and the write-up reads:

We know he's a star in the field of sports;
His character's got the swellest report.

Blair played basketball, baseball, and football, as well as serving as vice president of Consumer's Education. His standout moment in high school was the no-hitter he threw against Carrick High on May 11, 1940. Blair struck out 15 Carrick batters that day.

As yearbooks often do, there were remarks predicting what students would be doing 10 years hence—in 1950. Blair was foreseen as "star pitcher" for the Pittsburgh Pirates.

This was, of course, a remarkable notion, given that there would not be a black player for any of the major-league teams until Jackie Robinson broke the "color barrier" in 1947. Yet Blair's fellow students at Langley had no problem seeing him as pitching for the Pirates. In actuality, the Pirates themselves did not integrate until Curt Roberts joined the team in April 1954.

Blair did play professional baseball in Pittsburgh, but it was for the Homestead Grays of the Negro National League, for whom he played five seasons. His high-school record notwithstanding, Jim Riley says he was "discovered by the Homestead Grays playing sandlot ball with the Pittsburgh Monarchs."[1] He wasn't exactly a secret, though. The Pittsburgh Courier ran a three-column headline proclaiming, "Garnett Blair, Point Scoring Ace Of Pittsburgh High Schools, Turns Attention To Baseball."[2] Blair was 6-feet-3, 187 pounds at the time, "a fine-looking, curly-haired, 17-year-old colored boy who plays basket, baseball, and football equally well and thinks nothing of the brilliant records he has made in each of the three major sports during his sensational high school athletic career."[3]

Prior to his stint with the Grays, Blair had pitched for three seasons for the Pittsburgh Monarchs, a strong local team that reeled off 22 consecutive wins in 1941, with Blair noted as "still pitching like an ace."[4]

Garnett E. Blair was born on July 31, 1921, in East Carnegie, a neighborhood of Pittsburgh just about five or six miles southwest of the city center. His father, Edward Blair, came from Milledgeville, Georgia, where he had worked as a laborer in a tailor shop. He married fellow Georgian Celestine Brown on December 30, 1918, and the couple moved to Pittsburgh, where they lived on Copley Way. Edward's parents had been Moses Blair, a laborer in a brickyard, and Earnest Blair, a washerwoman for a private family.

Private family work was what Edward did after coming to Pittsburgh. He is listed in the 1930 census as a janitor for a private family, and in 1940 as a caretaker on a private estate. The couple raised five boys and one daughter. Garnett was the second-eldest. The youngest was Lonnie, who also played baseball for Homestead.

After high school, Blair went on to begin studies at Virginia Union University, a historically black university in Richmond, where he played center on the basketball team, the Panthers, in 1942. That December Blair enlisted in the US Army at Fort Meade, Maryland. He was in military service for more than three years, mustered out on February 17, 1946, at Indiantown Gap, Pennsylvania. Because of his talent in baseball, he worked in special services, playing some ball to provide morale-building entertainment for other military personnel. He returned to Virginia Union after the war, and ultimately graduated with a bachelor of science degree in commerce in 1949.

During his tour of duty in the Army, Pfc. Garnett Blair married Ruth Odessa Brown in January 1945. She was also a graduate of Virginia Union University.

Negro Leagues records are unfortunately quite incomplete, but Blair does appear to have started one game pitching for Homestead in 1942, without a decision (and also without a base hit in four at-bats.) In 12 innings pitched, he is reported to have given up 12 hits and five runs.

It was not uncommon for servicemen stationed stateside to have time to appear in occasional baseball games, and that appears to have been the case with Blair. He was stationed at Perry Point, Maryland, and pitched in Washington on weekends for Homestead when he could.[5] The Grays played "home games" both in Pittsburgh and in Washington, DC. Records available on Baseball-Reference.com show him pitching in (and winning) one game, working seven innings for the 1944 Grays. John Holway shows him as 2-0. Both agree he was 8-1 in 1945, starting nine games, striking out 35 while only walking nine. He's shown as 0-1 in two starts for Homestead in 1946, after having "turned up with a sore arm."[6] Though on the Opening Day roster, he doesn't appear to have pitched at all in 1947, and then 0-1 again in his only game in 1948. Jim Riley says he was 3-2 in 1948.

Buck Leonard said that Blair "had been a promising young pitcher. He went into the Army and never was the same when he came out. He hurt his arm and couldn't throw like he had before, so he quit baseball

and started playing basketball."[7] Blair's son, Douglas, understands it to have been a rotator-cuff injury to his right shoulder; doctors had wanted to operate, but with only a prognosis of a 50 percent chance of success. His father declined and took injections for pain for many years.[8]

Blair continued to play center for Virginia Union basketball in 1947 and 1948. (At the time, his amateur standing in basketball was not compromised by his having played professionally in another sport.) He was said to have also "made the Caribbean baseball circuit."[9] Douglas Blair says that a couple of his teammates played winter ball in the Caribbean but that his father "went back to college, the Virginia Union University in Richmond."[10]

In June 1948, Blair is also seen pitching for the Richmond Giants, in one game beating the Greensboro Red Wings with a two-hitter on June

Garnett Blair posted a 3-2 record as a pitcher with his hometown Homestead Grays in 1948. Blair had been a promising young pitcher, but a rotator cuff injury hindered his pitching career. (*Courtesy R. D. Retort Enterprises*)

Garnett Blair (at right) with fellow Grays' hurlers Wilmer Fields (left) and Bob Thurman. Blair's younger brother, Lonnie, joined the Grays in 1949 as a pitcher and second baseman. (*Noir–Tech Research, Inc.*)

6.[11] Blair also worked as baseball coach for Virginia Union University, while wrapping up his studies. He was also a member of the Joseph T. Hill Philosophy Club, the NAACP, and the Varsity Club, and played intramural sports.

Back with the new Negro American Association's Washington Homestead Grays in the early part of 1949, Blair was joined briefly by his younger brother Lonnie, who had finished up his school term and was signed by Homestead, reporting for duty on June 12.[12]

Jim Riley shows Lonnie Blair as pitching and playing second base for the Grays, writing that he "joined the Homestead Grays in 1947 while still in high school but was not on the traveling squad, and pitched mostly in exhibition games. After the demise of the Negro National League following the 1948 season, he stayed with the Grays for two more seasons while they played as an independent ballclub, sometimes 'passing' because of his light complexion to buy food for the team as they traveled throughout the South. Earning a salary of $300 per month with the Grays, he declined a tryout with the Cleveland Indians, and after the Grays broke up in 1950, he joined the Air Force."[13]

The two brothers overlapped briefly on the Grays.[14] Just shortly after the time Lonnie joined the new Grays in 1949 (Josh Gibson Jr. was also on the team as a utility player), Garnett Blair moved to work for the Richmond Giants. He won the second game of the August 7 doubleheader against the Washington Hilldales, 3-2, but lost a real heartbreaker, a 1-0 game that ran for 13 innings on September 17.

After his June 1949 graduation, Blair became the baseball coach at Manassas (Virginia) Regional High School.[15] He pitched for Richmond in 1950 and part of 1951 as well, but he then retired with a sore arm. In 1953 he was signed to pitch for the Richmond Colts, becoming the first black ballplayer on the team. Colts owner Eddie Mooers announced on April 8 that the Colts were considering adding a Negro player to the team. He chose not to present a name but said the man he had in mind was 6-4, weighed 225 pounds, and hailed from Richmond. Blair acknowledged he had been contacted by Mooers and would try to get himself into condition. "I think I'll be able to win in the Piedmont League," he said, "if my arm doesn't pain me."[16] He was working with the Binga Community Center at the time.

Blair made the Colts and opened the season with them, but he figured so little in actual play that he does not appear in final team stats. He pitched four scoreless innings against Binghamton on April 19 but apparently could not continue. Riley says he appeared in two games without a decision.

The travel did a number on Blair's arm. "Sitting with his arms crossed on rickety old buses that bounced along on bad roads for hours at a time took a toll on Blair's body," wrote Mike Harris of the *Richmond Times-Dispatch*. "Teams would often play doubleheaders on Friday, Saturday, and Sunday, in different cities. Even if the Grays were 'home,' there was travel because the team split its home games between Forbes Field in Pittsburgh and Griffith Stadium. For a while, the team was known as the

Washington Homestead Grays. Blair recalled one weekend where the team played a late doubleheader on Friday in Pittsburgh. It then got on the bus for Washington and arrived just in time to change clothes and go out and play two more games. After that doubleheader, the team got back on the bus and headed to Chicago for two more games.

"Eating, sleeping, even going to the bathroom was a chore on the road because blacks were still not allowed in many places. 'I remember once someone needing to use the bathroom and we had to drive through Richmond all the way to Fredericksburg before we could find a place,' Blair said. 'Nowadays, people wouldn't stand for that, of course. But we put up with it then, overlooked a lot of things we probably shouldn't have, because we wanted to play baseball. You had to conform, go on and do it. That's what we did.'"[17]

Blair later took up a position coaching and working in the special-education department of Richmond's Booker T. Washington Junior High School, where he served for nine or 10 years into the late 1960s. Subsequently, he spent 25 years as a special-education teacher at the Richmond Career Education Center. Blair also worked for many years officiating in both high-school and college basketball.[18]

Ruth Brown Blair became the first black policewoman in Richmond, serving from December 1949 to December 1966. "She was a detective," said the Blairs' son, Douglas.[19]

On September 10, 1988, Blair was honored along with 1948 Homestead Grays teammates at a 40th reunion hosted by the Pittsburgh Pirates. Joining him were Clarence Bruce, Wilmer Fields, Buck Leonard, and Willie Pope. He was also honored in an Upper Deck Heroes of Baseball tribute to the Negro Leagues at Philadelphia's Veterans Stadium on August 10, 1991. It was nice to be remembered so many years after his playing days, he told Harris, but he did wonder if the interest was genuine or if it was due to "cash to be made in the growing collectors market." Blair, who was already suffering from the colon cancer that took his life, said, "It is never too late to correct something that should have been done

years ago. But I do sometimes wonder what took so long and why is it happening now?" He had started to get requests for autographs in the mail, as many as 20 a week. After going more than 40 years without recognition of this sort, "All of a sudden, here is come, boom, like a flood. It is all I can do to keep up with it. Prior to that, you never heard one word about black baseball."[20]

Looking back on those days, he said, "You know, a lot of what we went through wasn't very pleasant. Back then it was because I was traveling and seeing the world. We were had, we really were, in a lot of ways. But we wanted to play baseball. That's as high as a black man could go to play baseball at that time. We got two dollars a day to eat on. We wanted $2.50. Today, players strike over that kind of thing. We didn't get that extra 50 cents. We kept on playing. We wanted to play ball. Besides, at $450 a month, I was making more than my father ever made."[21]

Blair told Harris he couldn't recall ever losing more than one game, but the problem in pinning that down later was the lack of accurate records: "They just weren't kept." He ascribed that more to his teammates' offense than his own pitching. "I've said it before, I'll say it again: If you could hold a team to seven, eight, nine runs, you could win a game with the Grays. They were that good. I didn't have many 1-0 games. Most of 'em were blowouts. If anybody could pitch at all, they could win there.

> "I only lost one game that I know of, 2-1 to the Philadelphia Stars at Griffith Stadium in Washington, D.C. It was on a Sunday. That's what I say. Somebody else wants to say something else, I'm not going to dispute 'em.

> "I have no idea how many games I won, no idea. I couldn't tell you to save my life. I do know I never had a home run hit off me in the eight years I played baseball."[22]

In later years, Blair was occasionally welcomed at events honoring former Negro Leagues players. His son Douglas says he held good memories of his time playing baseball. "We heard so much as kids, and thought maybe there was a little yeast in the stories, but later on they made some movies like *Bingo Long and the Traveling All-Stars*." He recalled buying his father the video of the 1976 film *The Bingo Long Traveling All-Stars & Motor Kings*. It had a little Hollywood stuff, but a lot of that was based on the Homestead Grays. Some of that was a little dramatized, but for the most part [he thought it was accurate.] They did some barnstorming. One story he liked to tell, they came to Richmond and play a game on a Friday, and then go south to another town called Colonial Heights. The story was that they'd give you a ticket if you were going one mile an hour over the speed limit. They stopped the bus and the man said, 'How much is the ticket?' and they said $100. 'Well, here's $200 because we're coming back Sunday.' So they gave him $200. You think that money ever made it to the court?"[23]

The main regret Douglas recalls his father expressing was when the commissioner of baseball cracked down on the barnstorming tours that often pitted Negro Leagues players against teams led by major leaguers such as Dizzy Dean. It spared the embarrassment to major-league ball that occurred when Negro Leagues teams beat some of the best in baseball. "That's what it was," says Douglas. "Dizzy Dean was one of the best pitchers in baseball. It wasn't like these were third-string guys."

Blair died of colon cancer at Johnston-Willis Hospital in Richmond on January 12, 1996, survived by his wife, Ruth Brown Blair, and described as "a retired educator and former pitcher in the Negro National League." Also surviving were the couple's three sons, Garnett Blair Jr., Douglas, and William. The three played Little League baseball when they were young. Garnett Jr. retired from the Virginia Employment Commission, Douglas sold life insurance for 37 years, and William works in the automobile business.

In 2008, Garnett Blair was honored with induction into the Virginia Union University Hall of Fame.

SOURCES

In addition to the sources noted in this biography, the author also accessed Blair's player file from the National Baseball Hall of Fame, the *Encyclopedia of Minor League Baseball*, Baseball-Reference.com, and the SABR Minor Leagues Database, accessed online at Baseball-Reference.com. Thanks to Douglas Blair, to Michael J. Szvetitz of the *Richmond Times Dispatch*, and to Selicia Gregory Allen of Virginia Union University.

NOTES

1   James A. Riley, *The Biographical Encyclopedia of the Negro Baseball Leagues* (New York: Carroll & Graf, 1994), 88.

2   "Garnett Blair, Point Scoring Ace Of Pittsburgh High Schools, Turns Attention To Baseball," *Pittsburgh Courier*, March 11, 1939: 13.

3   Ibid.

4   Robert Hughey, "Monarchs Qualify for City Series," *Pittsburgh Courier*, August 30, 1941: 16.

5   "Former Pitcher G.E. Blair Dies at 74," *Richmond Times Dispatch*, January 14, 1996: B3.

6   R. Earl Johnson, "The Sports Whirl," *Pittsburgh Courier*, June 1, 1946: 25.

7   Buck Leonard with James A. Riley, *Buck Leonard: The Black Lou Gehrig, An Autobiography* (New York: Carroll & Graf, 1995), 162.

8   Letter from Douglas Blair Jr. to author, June 21, 2016.

9   "Negro Hurler May Sign With Colts," *Richmond Times Dispatch*, April 9, 1953: 24. Wherever he may have played, he is not listed in the standard sources as having played professional baseball in Cuba.

10   Author interview with Douglas Blair on March 17, 2016.

11   "Giants Divide With Red Wings; Blair Star," *Richmond Times Dispatch*, June 7, 1948: 16.

12   "Grays Hope to Clinch First-Half Flag Today," *Washington Evening Star*, June 12, 1949: 44.

13   James A. Riley, 89. Riley says that Blair worked as a meatcutter in the Pittsburgh area after completing his military service.

14   See for instance the *Beckley* (West Virginia) *Post-Herald*, June 24, 1949: 12.

15   "Smith's Stars Whip Giants by 1-0 in 13th," *Richmond Times Dispatch*, September 18, 1949: 70.

16   "Negro Hurler May Sign With Colts."

17   Mike Harris, "Limelight at Last," *Richmond Times-Dispatch*, August 29, 1993.

18   Letter from Douglas Blair Jr.

19   Douglas Blair interview.

20   Mike Harris.

21   Ibid.

22   Ibid.

23   Douglas Blair interview.

ROBERT (BOB) BOSTON

By Bill Johnson

The 1948 Negro National League season was played on the cusp of a tectonic shift in the structure of Organized Baseball, as many black players were signed by clubs in the major and minor leagues. The 1948 iteration of the Homestead Grays, after two years of sub-.500 play and with a roster that no longer included immortals like Cool Papa Bell, Josh Gibson, and Ted Radcliffe was more of an amalgamation of veteran players, with the average age on the roster being almost 31 years old. That stipulated, this was no minor-league squad, either. With a lineup that included future Hall of Famer Buck Leonard, as well as several future major-league players, the 1948 Grays were a substantially better team than they had been for the previous two seasons. The *Pittsburgh Courier* reported a Grays victory over a South Carolina squad in the first exhibition game that spring, and noted that Homestead's new third baseman was "Bob Boston, big Ohio star, (who) played at third and out of five times at bat got one hit, a long line drive into right field and a walk."[1] Boston, the paper later noted in a report from spring training in Daytona Beach, Florida, was a "young star from East Liverpool, Ohio," and at 6-feet-4 and 205 pounds appeared to "have the inside track for third base this season since Howard Easterling left the hot corner. Boston led the East Liverpool City League in fielding and batting last year, and has made quite an impression on Manager Vic Harris."[2] The 1948 season would prove to be Bob Boston's only year in professional baseball, but he filled an important regular-season spot on the final Negro League World Series champion squad.

On July 4, 1918, Ed and Bernice "Burma" (Evans) Boston welcomed Robert Lee, their sixth and last child, into the world in Dearing, Georgia, a small community just west of Augusta.[3] Boston's parents were extraordinarily hard-working people who,

by available accounts, raised their family well.[4] Ed had emigrated from Nova Scotia, Canada, as a boy, and worked as a sawmill laborer at Culpepper & Company in McDuffie County. He died shortly after Robert's birth, at the young age of 26 or 27.[5] His even younger widow, called "Burma" by family and friends, had married Ed at the age of 14 and now was left to both raise and provide for her children on her own. Working out of their rented house in Rome, Georgia, she labored as a laundress just to keep a roof over their heads and a little bit of food on the table. The burden was incredible, and she died two days before Christmas in 1934.

Robert, the youngest child, was only 16 and was not yet ready to move out on his own. A neighbor took Boston in, and he took a job as a laborer at a local quarry. Like so many youths of that time, irrespective of race, he had developed a deep affection for baseball and filled his free hours with any games he could find. Boston later moved to Gadsden, Alabama, to take a job with the Goodyear Tire and Rubber Company. According to Mark F. Twyford:

> "The rubber company fielded two teams, one for whites and the other for blacks. An applicant's baseball abilities often played a deciding role in the outcome of the hiring process, and those employees who played for the company's teams were given more desirable jobs and had to work fewer hours each week than those who did not play. Boston's job required him to work only two days a week. The remainder of his work week was spent playing baseball."[6]

The young player reputedly took the field with several semipro teams in the area, largely as a way to supplement his meager income. In 1940, he married fellow Georgian Lucy Hachett. Boston continued a life of work and play without much money until

1943; on March 26 of that year, he reported to Fort Benning, Georgia, and enlisted in the US Army. Lucy moved to East Liverpool, Ohio, to stay with her sister while Robert was away. Boston remained on active duty through the end of World War II, but he was not finally discharged until 1946. He had obviously been a solid soldier, as he was a technician fifth grade (the modern equivalent would be an E-3) when he departed. Upon his release from active duty, Boston left the South for good, moving to Ohio to rejoin Lucy and taking a $300-a-month job at Crucible Steel in nearby Midland, Pennsylvania.

At Midland he naturally joined the company baseball team, with whom he played against numerous industrial-league players and teams. Boston distinguished himself in every aspect of the game: Not only was he well regarded as a powerful hitter and fast runner, he also pitched at least one no-hitter and struck out 16 batters in a game. It was his bat, though, that made outsiders pay attention. Clarence Huffman, manager of the Golden Star Dairy team in the East Liverpool City League, invited Boston to try out for his team.[7] When Boston accepted a roster spot, he became the only black player in the league.

In his first season at the higher level, Boston batted a reported .560 while leading Golden Star to the city championship. It was that renown that led the Homestead Grays to offer him a $500-a-month contract to play for them in 1948. Boston roomed with Luke Easter, a player with whom he drew favorable comparisons, and played well, as did the entire Grays team. In one evening game, he ran into a light pole at full speed while chasing down a foul ball and shattered part of his arm in the collision. Doctors told the Grays that Boston needed complete rest in order for his arm to heal properly, but Harris had his prized third baseman in the lineup as soon as the open wound on his arm had closed.

A few games after his return to the diamond, Boston attempted to throw out a runner who had grounded to third, but his arm would not go forward. Twyford noted that the rookie just dropped his glove and walked off the field; he exited both the game and Negro League baseball.[8] The career-ending injury de-prived Boston of the opportunity to prove his mettle with the Grays; had he been able to do so, he may even have had a shot at joining a team in Organized Baseball, since integration of the major and minor leagues was now under way. Boston was also deprived of the chance to play in the last Negro League World Series, as the Grays won the NNL championship and went on to defeat the NAL champion Birmingham Black Barons four games to one in that landmark series.

After the abrupt end to his stint with the Grays, Boston returned to Crucible Steel and worked there until his retirement in 1980. Eventually his arm healed well enough that he was able to resume playing for local baseball teams. Between 1948 and 1951 he was part of two East Liverpool City League championships with Golden Star Dairy, and he dominated most of the statistical categories. He also played first base on a team in an East Liverpool fast-pitch softball league. After 1951, now in his early to mid-30s, Bob Boston retired from baseball entirely, but continued to play softball until the late 1950s.

After Boston retired from Crucible Steel, he and Lucy relocated across Ohio to the Dayton area. Lucy died in 1993, and Bob was eventually admitted to long-term care at the Dayton Veterans Administration hospital. At 1:30 A.M. on July 2, 2002, Robert Boston died.[9] He and Lucy are buried together at the VA cemetery in Dayton.

SOURCES

In addition to the sources listed in the Notes, the author also consulted the following:

Ancestry.com.

Baseball-Reference.com.

Riley, James A. *The Biographical Encyclopedia of the Negro Baseball Leagues* (New York: Carroll & Graf Publishers, Inc., 1994).

NOTES

1 "Grays Curb Bats fo*(sic)*Spartansburg Sluggers, Win First Game 9 to 4," *Pittsburgh Courier*, April 3, 1948.

2 "Pittsburgh Opener Set for April 29; Outfield Has Power," *Pittsburgh Courier*, April 10, 1948.

3 It is not uncommon for records of the day (and particularly Negro birth, death, and marriage records) to be incomplete,

especially in the Southern United States a mere generation after the end of Reconstruction. There are several competing accounts of the details of Boston's birth. James A. Riley's *Biographical Encyclopedia of the Negro Leagues* and Boston's player listing at baseball-reference.com both give his birthdate as July 4, 1922, and his birthplace as Gaston, Alabama. Boston's biographer on the East Liverpool (Ohio) Historical Society's website is confident that Boston was indeed born on July 4, but in 1919 instead of 1922, and in Rome, Georgia, rather than Gaston, Alabama. Official census, Social Security, and other records variously list his birth date as either July 3, 4, or 13 in 1918, or July 4, 1919. His military discharge information used the July 4, 1918 date; thus, for the sake of consistency, that is the date that will be assumed to be correct in this biography. Additionally, based on the weight of documentation available onAncestry.com, it is most likely that Boston was actually delivered in Dearing, Georgia, rather than Rome, Georgia, or Gaston, Alabama.

4   Mark F. Twyford, "Blastin' Bob Boston: East Liverpool's Link to the Negro Baseball League," eastliverpoolhistoricalsociety. org/Bobboston.htm, accessed June 21, 2016. This essay first appeared in the *20th Anniversary Tri-State Pottery Festival Plater Turner's Handbook*, published in June 1987. Twyford relied on personal knowledge of the subject coupled with very thorough research to write his article about Robert Boston. To the greatest extent possible, the information used from that source has been corroborated by other, independent sources.

5   Ed Boston certified on his 1917 draft registration form that he had been born in 1891, but he was unaware of the exact date of his birth; he was also illiterate and was unable to sign his name on the form. (Source: US Draft Registration Form for Ed Boston, dated June 1917).

6   Ibid,

7   Ibid.

8   Ibid.

9   *Dayton Daily News*, July 7, 2002: B5.

CLARENCE BRUCE

By Frederick C. Bush

Clarence Bruce belongs to the majority of Negro League players who toiled in relative obscurity and whose stories can never be told in their entirety. Though the Negro Leagues became a subject for research in the late 1980s, the focus tended to be on the superstars who already had gained belated induction into National Baseball Hall of Fame as well as the other players who observers thought belonged in that hallowed institution. In addition to having to overcome the preoccupation with star players, baseball historians who attempted to chronicle the Negro Leagues were confronted with the fact that press coverage of the games was inconsistent at best and became an afterthought after Jackie Robinson broke Organized Baseball's color barrier in 1947.

Early works about the Negro Leagues provided only the most cursory introductions for many of the players. In *The Biographical Encyclopedia of the Negro Baseball Leagues*, James Riley describes Bruce as "a mediocre hitter without significant power … [who] was also an average defensive player."[1] The single biographical paragraph and its few accompanying statistical snippets provide an incomplete portrait of a man whose life, like the lives of players from all leagues in all eras, was far more complex.

Clarence Bruce the baseball player was actually Clarence Bruce Jr., and he was born on September 26, 1924, in Pittsburgh, the first of six children born to Clarence and Blanche Bruce. Clarence Sr. made his living as a headwaiter at the Roosevelt Hotel Downtown in Pittsburgh. Whenever he could, he attended games of both of the city's successful Negro League franchises, the Pittsburgh Crawfords and the Homestead Grays. He often took his namesake son to games with him, thus giving Clarence Jr. the thrill of seeing future Hall of Famers like Josh Gibson, James "Cool Papa" Bell, and Satchel Paige ply their trades in the primes of their careers.[2]

In an era when baseball was truly the national pastime, Bruce was no different from any other boy; he spent a good deal of his youth playing sandlot baseball in Pittsburgh. Though he enjoyed baseball, his education was important and, after graduating from Westinghouse High School, he enrolled in the University of Pittsburgh. His college career was brief, lasting about a year, because he was drafted into the US Army in 1943 as World War II continued to rage.

Bruce took part in the Allied invasion of Normandy in June 1944 that turned the tide of the war against Nazi Germany. Interestingly, his own family was unaware of his role in the war until they obtained his complete military record after his death,[3] a circumstance that may or may not be attributable to the fact that Bruce no doubt experienced many of the horrors of war that soldiers often do not care to recount.

Bruce was discharged from the Army in 1945, shortly after the end of the war, and he began his professional baseball career with the Brooklyn Brown Dodgers of the United States League in 1946. The USL, a third major Negro league that began play in 1945, was the brainchild of former Pittsburgh Crawfords owner Gus Greenlee. In order to lend credence to the endeavor, Greenlee struck a deal with Brooklyn Dodgers general manager Branch Rickey, who prompted the move of the USL's Hilldale franchise to Brooklyn. Immediately, the Brown Dodgers became the league's best-known franchise, and they gained additional publicity by hiring Negro League legend Oscar Charleston as their manager, though Charleston was gone before the end of the team's inaugural season.

The belief at the time was that Rickey was using the USL as a vehicle to allow him to evaluate African-American players for the Brooklyn Dodgers under the guise of merely scouting them for the Brown Dodgers. There is considerable doubt among modern baseball historians that this was Rickey's true purpose (though Rickey sought to confirm it years afterward[4]), especially since he withdrew from active participation in the USL when it became apparent that the Brown Dodgers were a failure. Rickey blamed the franchise's lack of viability on the team's owner/operator, Joe Hall, who Rickey said had "no idea of promotional work" with the result that the team "did not draw at all."[5]

The documentation of many Negro League players' careers is such a difficult task that Bruce still does not appear on the 1946 Brown Dodgers' roster in many of the currently available resources.[6] However, clear evidence for his being part of the team exists in the form of an old newspaper photograph with a handwritten caption that identifies Peewee Bruce

and Sonny Woods,[7] who are wearing Brooklyn jerseys while sitting in a dugout during a game. The photo has been preserved thanks to Blanche Bruce who, fulfilling the role of the proud mother, kept a scrapbook of her son's baseball career that contains photos, a player contract, letters, and newspaper clippings from 1946 through 1953. Clarence Bruce spent only one season with the Brown Dodgers (for which no statistics are currently available) as the USL folded after the 1946 campaign.

The USL's demise turned out to be a blessing in disguise for Bruce, who signed with the Homestead Grays of the Negro National League in 1947. This gave him the opportunity to play at least some of his games in his hometown of Pittsburgh. His player contract shows that Bruce was paid $300 per month

Homestead Grays infielders pose at Forbes Field in 1948. L-R: Luis Márquez, Buck Leonard, Charles Gary, Clarence Bruce, and Sam Bankhead. Márquez soon moved to the outfield and Bruce became the regular second baseman. (*Courtesy of Kirk Bruce*)

Negro National League of Professional Baseball Clubs

UNIFORM PLAYER'S CONTRACT

Parties

The Homestead Grays Baseball Club

herein called the Club, and *Clarence* Bruce

of Pittsburgh, Penna. , herein called the Player.

Recital

The Club is a member of the Negro National League of Professional Baseball Clubs. As such, and jointly with the other members of the League, it is a party to the Negro National League Constitution and to agreements and rules with the Negro American League of Professional Baseball Clubs and its constituent clubs. The purpose of these agreements and rules is to insure to the public wholesome and high-class professional baseball. by defining the relations between Club and Player, between club and club, and between league and league.

Agreement

In view of the facts above recited the parties agree as follows:

Employment

1. The Club hereby employs the Player to render skilled service as a baseball player in connection with all games of the Club during the year 194 7 including the Club's training season, the Club's exhibition games, the Club's playing season, any all-star games and the Negro World Series (or any other official series in which the Club may participate and in any receipts of which the players may be entitled to share) ; and the Player covenants that he will perform with diligence and fidelity and service stated and such duties as may be required of him in such employment.

Salary

2. For the service aforesaid the Club will pay the Player a salary of $ 300.00 per month from May 1 to Sept 15 , as follows:

In semi-monthly installments after the commencement of the playing season on the 1 and 15 day of each month covered by this contract, unless the Player is "abroad" with the Club for the purpose of playing games, in which event the amount then due shall be paid on the first week-day after the return "home" of the Club, the terms "*home*" and "*abroad*" meaning respectively *at* and *away from* the city in which the Club has its baseball field.

If the player is in the service of the Club for part of the month only, he shall receive such proportion of the salary above mentioned, as the number of days of his actual employment bears to the number of days in said month.

Loyalty

3. The Player will faithfully serve the Club or any other Club to which, in conformity with the agreements above recited, this contract may be assigned, and pledges himself to the American public to conform to the high standards of personal conduct, of fair play and good sportsmanship.

Service

4. (a) The player agrees that, while under contract or reservation, he will not play baseball (except post-season games as hereinafter stated) otherwise than for the Club or a Club assignee hereof ; that he will not engage in professional boxing or wrestling ; and that, except with the written consent of the Club or its assignee, he will not engage in any game or exhibition of football, basketball, hockey or other athletic sport.

Post-season Games

(b) The Player agrees that, while under contract or reservation, he will not play in any post-season baseball games except in conformity with the Negro Major League Rules, or with or against an ineligible player or team.

Assignment

5. (a) In case of assignment of this contract to another Club, the Player shall promptly report to the assignee club; accrued salary shall be payable when he so reports; and each successive assignee shall become liable to the Player for his salary during his term of service with such assignee, and the Club shall not be liable therefor. If the player fails to report as above specified, he shall not be entitled to salary after the date he receives notice of assignment.

Termination

(b) This contract may be terminated at any time by the Club or any assignee upon five days' written notice to the Player.

Regulations

6. The Player accepts as part of this contract the Regulations printed on the third page hereof, and also such reasonable modifications of them and such other reasonable regulations as the Club may announce from time to time.

Clarence Bruce's 1947 contract with the Homestead Grays. The Grays franchise was still a member of the Negro National League at the time, but the NNL would go out of business following the 1948 season. (*Courtesy of Kirk Bruce*) from May 1 to September 15 of that year, which was no meager sum for the average Negro League player of the 1940s.[8]

The Grays alternated home games between their true home in Pittsburgh, where they most often played at Forbes Field,[9] and their second "home" in Washington, D.C., where they rented Griffith Stadium. It was not unusual for the Grays to play a day game at one home field and then ride the team bus to play a night game at their alternate home. When they were on the road, the Grays players—like all Negro Leaguers—either had to stay at African-American hotels or with black host families. The former arrangement resulted in as many players being crammed into as few rooms as possible, while the latter one created difficulty with transportation since players were spread out among families that did not always live near one another.

In spite of such less than ideal travel conditions, Bruce was elated to be playing for the Grays. His son Kirk Bruce recalled his father's fond description of road trips, saying, "They would all pile into a couple of hotel rooms. Sometimes they would have some cheese and crackers and something to drink, and they thought they were living large [because they were] playing professional baseball."[10]

Bruce took great pride in being a professional Negro League player. The fact that the 1947 Grays roster was filled with stars like Luke Easter, Buck Leonard, and Luis Márquez demonstrates why Bruce once declared, "We didn't just play and think we were inferior. We thought we were great ballplayers and I think we walked with that air. … We knew we were great players. And the fans knew it. I think the white fans knew it."[11] In fact, far from feeling inferior, Bruce believed that the American and National Leagues [of Organized Baseball] were not the true major leagues because they did not have Negro players in them.[12]

The 22-year-old Bruce saw limited action in his first season with Homestead, during which he was, according to Riley, a part-time starter who batted .246.[13] In their landmark *The Negro Leagues Book*, Dick Clark and Larry Lester list the same batting average

and fill in a 34-for-138 batting line that included four doubles and three home runs.[14]

In 1948, his second season with the Grays, Bruce became the starting second baseman after Marquez was moved to center field.[15] In an era in which line scores largely replaced box scores for Negro League press coverage, the only available statistics show Bruce with a 3-for-25 batting line for a .120 BA.[16] Once again, such a minute sample cannot accurately reflect his usual level of play since he was the regular second baseman for that year's championship squad.[17]

Homestead, a powerhouse franchise through most of its existence, had won both the 1943 and 1944 Negro League World Series. The 1948 squad aimed at a third title in six years and was powerful enough to instill fear into the National League tenants of Forbes Field, the Pittsburgh Pirates. In 1988 Bruce retold the story of a Grays-Pirates game that never came to pass:

> "We were supposed to play the Pirates in an exhibition (in 1948), but some of their players came to watch us against the New York Black Yankees. Buck Leonard hit a home run over the roof in right field, Luke Easter hit one off the façade in right and Bob Thurman one over the 447-foot mark. We heard after that the Pirates didn't want to play us."[18]

Bruce and his Grays teammates rounded into playoff form in a doubleheader on Sunday, September 12, at which a crowd of 6,000— a far cry from the 35,000-plus the Grays often drew in the Negro Leagues' heyday—gathered at Griffith Stadium to bid farewell to retiring first baseman Buck Leonard. Leonard received tributes and gifts between victories over the Indianapolis Clowns (8-3) and Kansas City Monarchs (6-1), with Bruce contributing an RBI double in the second inning of the nightcap.[19] Bruce maintained a lifelong friendship with Leonard, a future Hall of Famer who was lauded for "his gentlemanly qualities on and off the field and his inspirational leadership as captain of the Grays."[20]

Homestead clinched the NNL's second-half championship and faced off against the first-half

CLEVELAND INDIANS
Farm System Training Base

P. O. BOX 1311
DAYTONA BEACH, FLORIDA

February 17, 1953

Mr. Clarence Bruce, Jr.
7344 Hermitage Street
Pittsburgh 8, Pennsylvania

Dear Mr. Bruce:

We have your letter of February 11th inquiring as to the procedure for a tryout with our organization.

Although Harry Simpson, who is here at our Daytona Beach base, recommended you very highly, we feel that it would be necessary that you be signed by one of our scouts or, if you would prefer, wait until May 1st when we return to Cleveland at which time we would be happy to give you a trial at Cleveland Stadium. We have a standing rule that no free agents not under contract be allowed to take part in our training activities at Daytona Beach.

Please write us again if you are still interested after May 1st.

Sincerely yours,

Laddie R. Placek

Laddie Placek
Director of Scouts

LP:ag

"The World's Most Famous Beach"

Letter from Cleveland Indians scouting director Laddie Placek outlining how Bruce could receive a tryout with the franchise. Note that former Negro Leaguer turned major leaguer Harry "Suitcase" Simpson had recommended Bruce. (*Courtesy of Kirk Bruce*) champion Baltimore Elite Giants, providing Bruce with the opportunity to participate in a playoff series that had an ending unmatched by any series in any league in the history of baseball. The Grays won the first two games, 6-0 and 5-3, and they turned a 4-4 tie into a 7-4 lead in top of the ninth inning of Game Three on September 17. It was then that Baltimore's 11:15 P.M. curfew became a factor. The Elite Giants, believing that the entire ninth inning would have to be replayed if it went past 11:15, began to stall the game by refusing to get Grays batters out.[21] At first, their tactic appeared to work as Game Three was indeed suspended and, before it was concluded, Game Four—an 11-3 Baltimore win—was played on September 19.

The next day, September 20, the Grays pulled off the oddity of a three-game sweep in spite of a Game Four loss, owing to a decision made by Rev. John H. Johnson, the NNL's president. Johnson applied a league rule that any inning begun before 11:00 P.M. had to be completed (even if it lasted past the 11:15 curfew) and "ruled [the Elite Giants' stalling] was unsportsmanlike and therefore grounds for the game to be forfeited to the Grays, 9-0."[22]

In such manner the Grays advanced to the World Series, where they met a familiar opponent in the Birmingham Black Barons, the very team they had victimized for their 1943 and 1944 championships. The third time around resulted in the same outcome as the Grays won the Series in five games. Their only loss came in Game Three when Birmingham's 17-year-old center fielder, Willie Mays, knocked a one-out single in the bottom of the ninth that scored Bill Greason from second base for a 4-3 victory. Clarence Bruce, ever proud of his time with the Grays, made sure to mention often that he had played against Mays—a future Hall of Famer who lit the major leagues on fire—back in the days before most of the American public had heard of him.[23]

The Negro Leagues were on the decline, however, and the NNL folded after the 1948 season. The Grays joined the Negro American Association in 1949, played as an independent club in 1950, and then disbanded in May 1951. As a result of these changes to

Homestead's fortunes, Bruce and three Grays teammates made an exodus to Canada in 1949, where they joined the Farnham (Quebec) Pirates of the Provincial League; Eudie Napier, Tom "Big Train" Parker, and Willie Pope were the other Grays on that season's Farnham squad. In 1951, another of Bruce's Homestead teammates, Sam Bankhead, became the first African-American manager of a predominantly white team at Farnham, but Bruce was no longer with the team that year. Statistics for Provincial League teams of that era are as scarce as for the Negro Leagues, and the only available statistics for Bruce show him batting .222 (12-for-54) in 14 games with Farnham in 1950. It was his last season to play professional baseball.

Once his baseball career was over, Bruce returned to Pittsburgh and settled into life as a family man. He married Marguerite Cole in 1952 and spent 35 years working as a clerk for the US Post Office and its successor, the US Postal Service; the couple had a son, Kirk, and a daughter, Jennifer. Prior to beginning his career with the post office, Bruce had one last flirtation with professional baseball in the form of a tryout offer from the Cleveland Indians. Harry "Suitcase" Simpson, who had been Bruce's opponent as a member of the NNL's Philadelphia Stars in 1947-48, was now an Indians player and had recommended Bruce. The team told Bruce it "would be happy to give [him] a trial at Cleveland Stadium"[24] Bruce did not make the Indians team in 1953, and his son Kirk is unsure if his father ever went to Cleveland for the tryout at all.

Bruce took up golf and often played at The Dandy Duffer, an African-American golf club, where he honed his skills well enough to become a driving-range instructor. He passed his athleticism down to Kirk and Jennifer, who both played basketball at the University of Pittsburgh, and he became a fixture at his college-age children's games. Kirk was a starting point guard from 1971 to 1975 and helped lead the 1974 team to a 25-4 record; as of 2016, he was an associate athletic director at Pitt. According to Kirk, though, Jennifer was the true star of the family; she became

Pitt basketball's all-time leading scorer—male or female—during her playing career at the university.[25]

In August 1986 Bruce had the opportunity to don a Pittsburgh Pirates uniform before a game at Three Rivers Stadium as part of a promotion by television station KDKA. The clock turned back more than 35 years as he fielded grounders and took batting practice. Bruce enthusiastically declared, "Oh, it felt good, I tell you. I hit 'em good. Almost jerked one out of there. I showed 'em."[26]

Two years later—on September 10, 1988—Bruce received an even greater honor and thrill as the Pirates raised a Homestead Grays flag over Three Rivers Stadium to commemorate the 1948 Grays championship. Bruce spoke on behalf of his former team and 18 other former Negro Leaguers were honored—a group that included Cool Papa Bell, Buck Leonard, and Monte Irvin—each receiving a medallion. Bruce told the fans, "We've waited and waited and waited to finally be recognized,"[27] and emphasized the importance of that evening's celebration when he said, "That means the Grays are a legend. That means we haven't been forgotten."[28]

On January 23, 1990, Bruce died in Pittsburgh at 65. Joan Bruce Griffin summed up her brother's life and baseball career by saying, "He never complained. He loved baseball. He would have played it for nothing if they would have just let him."[29]

SOURCES

The author wishes to express his gratitude to Kirk Bruce for taking the time to tell his father's story and for providing valuable artifacts in the form of scanned photos, letters, and his father's 1947 player contract with the Homestead Grays.

Thanks also to Dr. Rob Ruck, a University of Pittsburgh history professor and the author of several books about the Negro and Latin leagues, for pointing this author in the direction of his Pitt co-worker Kirk Bruce.

NOTES

1   James A. Riley, *The Biographical Encyclopedia of the Negro Baseball Leagues* (New York: Carroll & Graf Publishers, Inc., 1994), 129.

2   Kirk Bruce, telephone interview with the author, January 18, 2016.

3   Kirk Bruce interview.

4   Neil Lanctot, *Negro League Baseball: The Rise and Ruin of a Black Institution* (Philadelphia: University of Pennsylvania Press, 2004), 451.

5   Ibid.

6   The Center for Negro League Baseball Research correctly lists Clarence Bruce as a member of the 1946 Brooklyn Brown Dodgers and lists him as playing shortstop. (The roster can be viewed at cnlbr.org.)

7   Sonny Woods has been identified as pitcher Sam Woods. His nickname, according to the CNLBR, was Buddy, which indicates that Mrs. Blanche Bruce may have documented Woods's nickname incorrectly in her scrapbook. Kirk Bruce provided the author with a scanned copy of the photo, which unfortunately is too faded and grainy to reproduce well.

8   Newark Eagles co-owner Effa Manley said, "In those days $500 a month wasn't a bad salary for a ballplayer, a real good player like [Monte] Irvin." Irvin became a Hall of Famer so his salary was higher than the norm, but $300 per month was still a good salary for the average ballplayer. For the full interview with Manley, see John Holway, *Voices From the Great Black Baseball Leagues* (Mineola, New York: Dover Publications Inc., 1975). Manley's quote can be found on page 320 of Holway's book.

9   Though the Grays played the majority of their Pittsburgh games at Forbes Field, they played at many other ballparks in the Pittsburgh area as well. In May 1948, while Forbes Field was being resodded, the Grays played at West Field in Munhall. ("Grays to Play Games on Munhall Field," *Pittsburgh Post-Gazette*, May 10, 1948).

10 Kirk Bruce interview.

11 Lawrence D. Hogan, *Shades of Glory* (Washington: National Geographic, 2006), 305.

12 Kirk Bruce interview.

13 Riley, 129.

14 Dick Clark and Larry Lester, eds., *The Negro Leagues Book* (Cleveland: Society for American Baseball Research, 1994), 270. As a demonstration of the difficulty in determining Negro League players' statistics, baseball-reference.com lists Bruce as going 10-for-37 for a .270 batting average in 1947; these statistics perhaps include only league games. (See baseball-reference.com/register/player.cgi?id=bruce-001cla).

15 Riley, 129.

16 "Clarence Bruce," baseball-reference.com/register/player.cgi?id=bruce-001cla, accessed February 26, 2016.

17 Riley's *Biographical Encyclopedia* states that Bruce had a .255 batting average for the 1948 season; however, no specific statistics are provided, and it is unclear how many games or at-bats that average encompasses. In *The Negro Leagues Book*, Clark and Lester give no statistics for Bruce for 1948, emphasizing once more the difficulty in reconstructing the careers of Negro League players.

18 Alan Robinson, "THE NEGRO LEAGUE: Blacks Were Relegated to Their Own Hotels, Own Sides of Town and Played Baseball for Little Money, Recognition," *Los Angeles Times*, September 18, 1988. (Homestead's Bob Thurman related the same story, with slightly less detail, in Hogan, *Shades of Glory*, 305).

19 "6,000 Fans Pay Tribute to Grays' Buck Leonard," *Afro-American*, September 18, 1948.

20 Ibid.

21 Bob Luke, *The Baltimore Elite Giants* (Baltimore: The Johns Hopkins University Press, 2009), 2.

22 Ibid.

23 Kirk Bruce interview.

24 Laddie Placek, letter to Clarence Bruce, February 17, 1953. Kirk Bruce provided a scanned copy of this letter, which was typed on stationery that contains the logo and address of the Cleveland Indians' spring-training complex in Daytona Beach, Florida. Placek was Cleveland's director of scouts at that time.

25 Jennifer Bruce has since been supplanted by Lorri Johnson as the University of Pittsburgh's all-time scoring leader in basketball.

26 Byron Smialek, "Clarence Bruce Made the Best of His Only Opportunity," *Washington* (Pennsylvania) *Observer-Reporter*, January, 27, 1990.

27 Jimmy Dunn, "He Realized a Dream by Playing for Grays," *Pittsburgh Post-Gazette*, March 20, 1997.

28 "Clarence Bruce, Was Homestead Grays Player" [obituary], *Pittsburgh Post-Gazette*, January 25, 1990.

29 Byron Smialek, "When the Line Was Crossed," *Washington* (Pennsylvania) *Observer-Reporter*, April 8, 1997.

LUTHER "SHANTY" CLIFFORD

By Richard Bogovich

uther Clifford grew up in an atypical town for the Depression-era United States, a suburban melting pot largely free from racial tensions. What's more, he could draw inspiration from noteworthy ancestors dating back to the early days of the Civil War. His baseball career may not have been as remarkable, but there's little reason to think that he was anything other than comfortable with that.

Luther Franklin Clifford Jr. was born on January 16, 1924, in Clairton, Pennsylvania, less than 15 miles south of Pittsburgh and the site of a steel mill.[1] He was the only child of Luther Clifford Sr. and his wife, Effie, based on the family's 1930 census listing (and with no evidence to the contrary). Young Luther was listed as Franklin in that census and was commonly called by his middle name at least through high school.[2]

Luther Sr. worked at the mill's coke works. He was born on January 20, 1888, in Piedmont, West Virginia, and had five younger siblings, according to both the 1900 and 1910 censuses.[3] His parents were the former Elizabeth Ann Stephens and pioneering schoolteacher James Henson Clifford. James's older half-brother, John Robert Clifford, was the first African-American lawyer in West Virginia and a crusading newspaper publisher.[4]

In the 1910 census Luther Sr. was still living in West Virginia though newly married, to the former Isabella (or simply Isabell) Elizabeth Daugherty.[5] In 1911 Luther's brother Clyde was living within 20 miles of Clairton, in Irwin, where he ultimately lived for decades. A man named Luther Clifford was also in Irwin that year, as mentioned by a newspaper columnist reporting from there: "The fast colored team of Irwin defeated the McKeesport Colored Giants for the second time in a closely contested game by the score of 14 to 12," Gertrude Simpson wrote for the *Pittsburgh Courier*. "The Irwin battery featured

Clifford having 17 strike outs." She also mentioned an H.L. Johnson of the Irwin team, and it was unlikely mere coincidence that later in her column she named Luther Clifford and Harrison Johnson among five local men with "class" who seemed "to be the only real sports of the burg."[6] Of course, it's not a given that Luther was the pitcher named Clifford; it could have been Clyde, for one.

According to Luther Sr.'s draft registration card in 1917, he was married (though it doesn't say to whom), a child was part of the household, and he was working for a steel works. The 1930 census indicates that he and Effie were married around 1922. Also living in Clairton by 1930 were Luther's brother and sister-in-law, James Ward and Maude (sometimes Maud) Clifford, plus their children.

Effie Clifford was born on October 10, 1888, in Shirleysburg, Pennsylvania, after sister Pearl (who died of tuberculosis in 1919) and brother Ira. Effie and Ira remained close, and in the 1930 census she and the two Luthers were next door to Ira's household. Pearl, Ira, and Effie were the children of the former Lucy Bulger and Franklin Barnes. Her paternal grandfather, James Barnes, was a private in the Union Army during the Civil War.[7]

A resident four years younger than Luther provided insights about the Clairton of Luther Jr.'s youth many years later. "It was an interesting community," said Walter Cooper, in part because "there was not a rigid pattern of housing discrimination."

"The nonwhite population was approximately (10 to 12) percent," noted Cooper, who became the first African-American to earn a Ph.D. in chemistry at the University of Rochester in 1956. "We had neighbors from Italy, Hungary, Poland, Russia, Czechoslovakia. So as a youngster, I lived in a multi-ethnic, multicultural community. People being different—it never bothered me. We had harmonious relations with most of our neighbors. ... During the Depression years, we were poor, but on occasions we fed the poor across racial lines."[8]

One exception to such harmony was during the 1939-40 school year, while Luther was a high-school junior. "Colored pupils of the eighth grade of the junior high school returned from school … and told their parents that they were being separated from white pupils of the same class and placed in a room to themselves," reported the *Pittsburgh Courier*. "Several honor students were included among those so treated." After initial inertia, leaders undid that segregation. Though "Clairton colored citizens witnessed three days of the fanciest 'buck-passing' on record," the paper wryly wrote, after many complaints "school board members went into action quickly, with the result that colored students were back in their regular rooms" that same week.[9]

Overall, Dr. Cooper said, "in the school itself, there was no pattern of discrimination and I think, by and large, the students got along very well with one another."[10]

Luther Jr. was a three-sport athlete at the high school, and its 1941 yearbook noted that he was one of the senior lettermen in basketball. "Lumbering Franklin Clifford was considered the best offensive center in the section," the yearbook asserted. He was also a force to be reckoned with on the gridiron. "Big 'Ham' Clifford smiles through his classes. But on the football field, his slow moving ways cease," the yearbook enthused. "There he turns up the field in mad charges. He made the varsity in his senior year." Track and field was Luther's third sport, particularly discus and shot put.[11]

Luther's name popped up on area sports pages during high school. In one preview of a football game during his senior year he was listed in Clairton's starting lineup as a 185-pound fullback.[12] He closed out his high-school athletic career with a few shot-put and discus victories in April and May of 1941. He even set a new local record by heaving a shot 47 feet, 10½ inches.[13]

Happy high-school experiences were offset in Luther Jr.'s family. For one, his maternal grandmother, Lucy, died at the start of his sophomore year.

She had been living with them at the time of her death.[14] His other grandmother had died in 1911, and his grandfathers also had died long before he was born; Franklin Barnes died months before Effie's first birthday, and James Henson Clifford died in 1901, around the time Luther Sr. was 13 years old.

By the time Luther Jr. was halfway through high school his father was also out of the picture: Luther Sr. had left the household by the time of the 1940 census. At that point Effie and her son were living with her brother Ira. In fact, in the 1940 census there is a Luther Clifford who boarded with a family named Myrick in Washington, D.C. His age, race, and birthplace on that page, combined with the World War II draft registration card in his name filed during 1942, are all consistent with his being Luther Sr.[15] The census page also indicates that he had lived in Washington for five years, which would have been before his son started attending Clairton High. In any case, during the summer of 1942 Effie formally filed for divorce from Luther Sr.[16] That was about two months after her brother Ira died.

Luther Franklin Clifford Jr. entered the military on October 30, 1943, at Fort Meade, Maryland, and served in the Army Air Corps until March 1, 1946. At some point he married the former Sarah Thomas, and when he submitted a veterans benefits application in March of 1950 he listed a son, Ira Franklin Clifford, apparently 21 months old—which would put his birth in mid-1948.[17]

That was the year when Luther joined the Homestead Grays—and he was no longer called Franklin by sportswriters. He wasn't with the Grays at the beginning of their season, based on box scores and game previews. One of the first newspaper articles about the Grays that mentioned him said that he had previously played for Clairton's CIO (labor union) team.[18] In mid-May, one area newspaper reported on the start of the baseball season for Clairton's team in the United Steel Workers of America League: "It seemed in the seventh inning that Monessen was going to go run crazy but Bill Clifford, a catcher by profession, went to the mound and limited the outburst to one run." That paper also included a box score, in which Clairton's lineup had surnames matching those of Luther's teammates in his high-school yearbook and basketball box scores back then.[19] Thus, "Bill Clifford" might very well have been Luther.

With the Grays on June 11, Clifford made an immediate impact against the New York Black Yankees in a game played in New Castle, Pennsylvania, 50 miles northwest of Pittsburgh. He wasn't the starting catcher, but it appears that he had already driven in at least one run with a hit when he came up with the score tied 8-8. "The fans got a thrill in the eighth inning as Clifford, a new catcher with the Grays making his first appearance … blasted a tremendous homer over the left center field fence," reported the local paper. The Grays held on to win, 10-8, before 2,400 fans.[20]

Clifford didn't see much action in those early weeks, but when the *Chicago Defender* published Negro National League statistics in early July, he was listed as having 4 hits in 8 at-bats. Meanwhile, the Grays led the standings with a record of 22-11.[21]

A noteworthy exhibition game early in Clifford's career was played on July 3 in Charleroi, about 20 miles south of Clairton, between the Grays and Pie Traynor's Charleroi All-Stars. Harold "Pie" Traynor had played his entire major-league career with the Pittsburgh Pirates, managed them from 1934 to '39, and had been voted into the National Baseball Hall of Fame earlier in 1948. A preview of the game noted that both Bobby Gaston and Clifford were competing as backups at catcher to Euthumn Napier.[22] Still, the box score for the game shows that Clifford started and batted seventh. He went 1-for-5, drove in two runs and, at least as importantly, caught a shutout as the Grays won, 9-0. It was reportedly their 59th win in 61 exhibition games that season.[23]

In the Negro National League pennant race, Clifford contributed again toward the end of August. The Grays regained first place by edging the Philadelphia Stars, 4-3, thanks to homers by Luke Easter, Buck Leonard, and Clifford.[24] Clifford also got into at least two NNL championship games against the Baltimore Elite Giants in mid-September, and reportedly even pitched in the first match.[25] There is an absence of evidence of Clifford's having played in that final Negro World Series victory over the Birmingham Black Barons, but his first season still had its moments.

After the NNL disbanded at the end of November, there was some supposition that the Grays wouldn't continue. Meanwhile, the Negro American League imposed order on the competition to sign NNL players. In mid-February of 1949 the NAL unveiled a "distribution plan for players who formerly played with the now defunct Homestead Grays, Newark Eagles and New York Yankees." Luther Clifford was assigned to the Louisville (previously Cleveland) Buckeyes along with Grays pitchers Tom Parker and John Wright.[26] That ended up having no bearing on Clifford because the Grays continued to play as a member of the short-lived Negro American Association and then for one last season as a barnstorming team. It would be understandable if veteran players on the Grays found all this unnerving. Alas, Luther Clifford already had enough turmoil in his life at that point. Before the end of March 1949, he filed for divorce from Sarah. It was finalized three years later.[27]

In mid-May of 1949, one newspaper's preview of an early game for the Grays reported Clifford's weight as 230 pounds.[28] That was 45 more than when he finished playing high-school football. More significantly, two other papers later in the month said that with the release of Euthumn Napier, Clifford was to be the starting catcher for the Grays. Napier had gone to a minor league in Canada to continue his career.[29]

One season after facing a team led by a Pittsburgh Pirates legend, Clifford caught for the Grays in another such game. This time the Grays were facing the legendary Honus Wagner. On May 18 the Grays beat the Honus Wagner Stars in Carnegie, Pennsylvania, just southwest of Pittsburgh.[30]

Other highlights for the season included a performance that may have caused some déjà vu. Against the Black Yankees in New Castle, the foe and site of his memorable debut about a year earlier, Clifford homered in the sixth inning with Wilmer Fields on base to provide the game's decisive blow.[31] Another noteworthy game for Clifford took place about a month later, before 2,300 fans in Lima, Ohio, against the House of David team from Benton Harbor, Michigan. In beating that memorable team 15-5, Clifford led the way with four hits, including a triple and double.[32]

Not quite qualifying as a highlight was the *Washington Post*'s preview of a mid-August game against the Indianapolis Clowns in which there may have been an attempt to cement a nickname for Clifford: While mentioning him in the same breath as Buck Leonard, and Red Fields, the un-named sportswriter referred to him as Baby instead of Luther.[33]

The biggest news of Clifford's season occurred in September, when he joined the Kansas City Monarchs of the Negro American League. In July the Monarchs sold outfielder Bob Thurman and catcher Earl Taborn to the Newark farm team of the New York Yankees, and Luther Clifford was eventually brought in to help fill Taborn's shoes. He joined the Monarchs during a pennant race and faced at least two NAL opponents multiple times.

During the first week of September Clifford got into at least three games of a series against the New York Cubans. In one of those games he batted fifth and went 2-for-4.[34] He also played in games that month against the Indianapolis Clowns. He received some recognition for a key contribution in one of them, when he batted after Elston Howard (later the first African-American to play for the Yankees), who had walked, and drove him in with a long triple.[35] The Monarchs qualified for the NAL playoffs, but team owner Tom Baird quickly announced that the team wouldn't participate, saying that it was too depleted after the departure of Thurman, Taborn, and others. "The failure of the league to insist on Kansas City living up to its obligation is a definite violation of the baseball law," wrote Wendell Smith, the sports editor of the *Pittsburgh Courier*. "But from all indications, nothing will be done about it."[36] Smith was correct, and the Chicago American Giants replaced the

Monarchs as the Western team in the championship series against the Baltimore Elite Giants.

One source of stability for Luther Clifford throughout the 1940s may have been where he called home. His address was 146 Lincoln Way in Clairton on the application for veterans benefits that he filed in March of 1950. Though he left the section about his father blank, he listed his mother at the same address. She in turn had given their address as almost the same, 149 Lincoln Way, when she signed her mother's death certificate back in 1938.

Since his roots were in the greater Pittsburgh area, Clifford went from the Monarchs back to the Homestead Grays for 1950. The Negro American Association was no more, so the Grays were solely a barnstorming team. A preview of a mid-April game against the New York Black Yankees in North Carolina may have been the first time that the nickname used frequently for Clifford later in the decade appeared in print: Shanty.[37] The box score for a game during the first week of May showed that he played right field (going 2-for-4), and a newspaper article a few days later named him as one of the team's four outfielders.[38] That was presumably because catcher Euthumn Napier had also rejoined the Grays, though Clifford did see some action behind the plate in May and following months.[39]

On July 1 Clifford was listed as the center fielder in a box score of an exhibition game in which he faced legendary pitcher Satchel Paige. The Grays played the Raleigh Clippers in Charleston, West Virginia, and Paige pitched three innings. Clifford went 0-for-5, so he didn't get a hit off Paige.[40] A few days later a newspaper reported that the Grays had already compiled a record of 64 wins, 8 losses, and a tie, and that 7 of those victories were over the Paige All-Stars, for which Satchel typically pitched at least three innings.[41] Thus, Clifford may have batted against Paige in more than one game.

Late in July the Grays made a trip to Canada that would change Clifford's life forever. The big story from the game itself, which the Grays won 18-8, was that Josh Gibson Jr. was hit in the head by a pitched ball and suffered what was called "a slight concussion." The game was a benefit for the Shriners' Crippled Children's Hospital Fund, so goodwill between the teams was apparently assumed and reports of the incident didn't suggest any intent by the pitcher. The significance for Clifford was that the game was against the Brantford Red Sox,[42] a team he soon joined, in a city where he lived most of the rest of his life.

On August 3, 1950, Clifford was reportedly the pitcher for the Grays against the New York Black Yankees at Charleston, West Virginia. The Grays won handily, 11-4.[43] Clifford's name showed up a few more times in the following weeks, but his appearances dwindled by September. About three weeks into September it was reported that former Grays pitcher Dan Bankhead, who still had a few games left with the Brooklyn Dodgers, would tour with the Grays after the major leagues' regular season ended. Games were scheduled at least three weeks into October, but newspaper coverage was minimal.[44] The Grays were disbanded in 1951. By then, ownership of the club had passed from Cum Posey's widow, Ethel, and Rufus Jackson to Posey's older brother Seward, called See. It was See who reportedly persuaded Ontario's Brantford club to sign Clifford as well as Wilmer Fields.[45] Many years later, one sportswriter asserted that Clifford and Fields were paid $1,000 per month.[46]

Brantford, where hockey legend Wayne Gretzky was born a decade later, belonged to a semipro league in which players were compensated very well. Clifford seemed to fit right in, as indicated by a special community event in mid-June, a baseball school for younger local players. "Three members of the Brantford Red Sox, top team in the Senior Intercounty loop, were on hand to act as instructors," wrote an area newspaper. "Catcher Luther 'Shanty' Clifford, southpaw pitcher Alf Gavey and centre fielder Jerry Wilson put the boys through their paces in a three-hour session, which should benefit the players considerably."[47] The Red Sox ultimately won the Intercounty League pennant that season, though the London Majors prevailed in the playoffs.

However comfortable Clifford may have been in Brantford, for 1952 the 28-year-old accepted an opportunity enjoyed by many American players in that era: to play ball in the Caribbean. In his case, it was the Dominican Republic. The season began there on April 26, and the league consisted of four teams.[48] On April 1 Clifford departed from New York for San Juan, Puerto Rico, along with Gread McKinnis, Robert Griffith, and Otto Miller.[49] McKinnis and Griffith had been well-known pitchers in the Negro Leagues. The other passenger was likely the infielder for the Indianapolis Clowns in the summer of 1951, Otto "Buddy" Miller, who reportedly had played for the New York Black Yankees before the Clowns.[50] Clifford, Griffith, and McKinnis were all on the Estrellas Orientales, and Clifford even served as manager at one point.[51] Presumably the highlight for Clifford was a game in which he hit three home runs. A photo of him shaking the hand of a coach while circling the bases after one of those blows was published in 2004.[52]

By mid-July Clifford traveled back to Canada, though this time he went to Brandon, Manitoba, where a team was partway into the third season of the independent Manitoba-Dakota (ManDak) League. The player-manager for the Brandon Greys was Willie Wells, whose long career in the Negro Leagues led to his election to the National Baseball Hall of Fame in 1997. Upon reporting, the local paper noted that Clifford weighed 246 pounds and stood 6-feet-2-inches tall.[53]

At the beginning of the next month Clifford certainly made an impression among local sports fans. He jump-started his team's scoring in one game with a second-inning triple, but it was his defense that was praised in the newspaper. He picked runners off second base twice and added a difficult catch of a pop foul near the screen. Within the week Clifford had a two-homer game for the Greys, and those swats helped him reach 11 RBIs in his first 11 games.[54]

Howard "Krug" Crawford of the *Brandon Daily Sun* speculated that early on the Greys were looking to Clifford to generate such power often. Clifford sensed that, and challenged that thinking. "If it's home runs you want, I'm not your man," he volunteered. "Down where I [have] just come from (Santo Domingo) they expected me to hit a homer every time up. That's why I left." He had been back in Clairton for only a few hours when he received an urgent call from Brandon. "My mother had my shirts out on the line, and so I had to come fast (he flew) with only what I got." Crawford called Clifford "one of the best assets the Greys have right now." He noted that Clifford had "been hitting the fences with some of his blows," but he praised Clifford's defense in particular: "He's got a great throwing arm and he gets the ball away easily. And he's one of the best catchers of looping foul balls we've seen around here for some time."[55] Though the Greys may have been looking to Clifford for big blasts, he ended up topping their hitters with a .330 batting average.[56]

During the first few months of 1953 there were conflicting accounts of the next chapter in Clifford's baseball career. In January the Brantford Red Sox were reportedly expecting Clifford to rejoin them. A report in Toronto's *Globe and Mail* noted that he and Wilmer Fields had already been "the first African American battery" in the Intercounty League's history, and in 1953 the Red Sox were anticipating the league's *biggest* battery: 250-pound Clifford and 6-foot-9 John Alexander Gee, who pitched six years for the Pittsburgh Pirates and New York Giants from 1939 to 1946.[57] Conversely, in early April the *Brandon Daily Sun* twice reported that Clifford was among a few players expected to join Willie Wells in Chicago for a bus trip to Baton Rouge, Louisiana, for some preseason exhibition games before returning to Brandon in early May.[58]

In actuality, Clifford's spring training took place in Waycross, Georgia, at the minor-league camp of the Braves as that franchise was transitioning from Boston to Milwaukee. In late March the *Pittsburgh Courier* reported this fact, though in the context of Clifford being under contract with the Indianapolis Clowns—making him a teammate of Toni Stone, the first woman signed to a Negro American League contract. The *Courier*'s preview of Indy's season didn't explain why Clifford was working out in Waycross

instead of prepping with other members of the Clowns.[59]

In any case, on March 21 the *Waycross Journal-Herald* listed lineups for the first intrasquad games at the camp and Clifford was named as an alternate catcher.[60] A week later the paper listed players for a game that night between Class-B Evansville and Class-A Jacksonville. Clifford was one of the two catchers for the former, while Henry Aaron was listed as a second baseman for the latter.[61] Conditions in the South were rough for African-American players at the time; however, though Aaron experienced racism during his initial car ride to the camp, his treatment on the grounds was relatively enlightened for the time.[62]

In short order Aaron's team left the camp to head south to Jacksonville. Luther Clifford remained in Waycross, and one week into April he was the starting catcher for Evansville in a loss to the Class-B Eau Claire Bears. In at least two subsequent games he played for the Bears and in a contest against Evansville Clifford had two hits, but in mid-April it was reported that he had been cut by Eau Claire.[63] By mid-May he rejoined the Brantford Red Sox, as noted in the *Brandon Daily Sun*, with a hint of disappointment.[64] The remainder of his baseball career was spent in Ontario.

In 1953 another Negro Leagues player began an even stronger association with the Brantford Red Sox than Clifford's: Jimmy "Seabiscuit" Wilkes. His nickname implied that he was as speedy as the famous racehorse of that name. "If you think Jimmy's fast now, you should have seen him in his prime," Clifford told a *Brantford Expositor* sportswriter.[65] Despite such imported talent, Brantford didn't win the regular season or the playoffs the next few seasons.

Highlights for Clifford in the mid-1950s included a game against the London Majors in June of 1954 when he homered twice in the eighth inning. A few weeks later he squared off against the team that signed him in early 1953, the Indianapolis Clowns, before a full ballpark of more than 6,000 fans.[66] He won the league's batting title in 1956 with a .377 average. That achievement was undercut by the death of his mother on August 7. His return to Clairton for the funeral was noted in the *Pittsburgh Courier,* which described him as appearing "physically fit."[67]

For 1957 the Brantford and London clubs left the Intercounty League to join the new Great Lakes-Niagara District League. Clifford was the player-manager for the Red Sox.[68] Even in a new league the Red Sox were unable to find late- or postseason success. The new league folded after that single year and Brantford rejoined the Intercounty League, but Clifford signed with the Galt Terriers instead, for whom he was an all-star first baseman in 1958. He also came very close to winning the playoffs for Galt at home. The Terriers led the St. Thomas Elgins three games to two and the sixth game was knotted at 3-3 after seven innings. Clifford hit a 370-foot homer in the eighth, after which his team needed to shut down the Elgins for just three more outs. Instead, Galt gave up seven runs and lost the seventh game as well.[69]

Shanty Clifford overcame what a Toronto newspaper called "a minor back operation" to sign with Galt again for 1959.[70] That year he was finally on a pennant winner again, though the Terriers lost in the playoffs to Brantford.

Relatively little was reported about Luther Clifford's life after that, though in 1962, at least, one Pennsylvania newspaper noted that he visited his son Ira that summer in Mount Pleasant, about 30 miles southeast of Clairton.[71] His memory has been kept alive by some baseball enthusiasts, such as lifelong Brantford resident Jim Huff, who reminisced about Wilkes and Clifford on a local company's website. "Shanty Clifford worked with my dad at the school board—those guys were legends," he wrote.[72] Huff elaborated further:

> Shanty worked with my Dad at the Brant County Board of Education as a school janitor in the 1960s and 70s and that is when I first met him, although I had seen him play many times. My Dad introduced me to him but of course, I was already familiar with Shanty. ... We did talk all baseball (what else would you want to talk to Shanty about anyway) and he did say working for the

Board was the first full time job he ever had, because all he did was travel to play ball. The way he talked I think he was very happy with his occupation as a professional ball player. I will always remember shaking his hand, he had the hands of a catcher, big strong hands and "crooked fingers"—he looked like a ballplayer top to bottom.[73]

At the age of 55, Luther Clifford had the pleasure of marrying a local widow in Brantford, Lorraine Saunders, on September 28, 1979. Attendants were one of her daughters, Diane Davis, and a Paul Christopher.[74] Alas, Clifford's final years were marked by a long struggle with Alzheimer's disease.[75] It presumably had taken hold no later than 1987, because an author writing about him for a book interviewed just Lorraine instead.[76]

Luther Franklin Clifford died on May 4, 1990, at the age of 66. His obituary in the *Brantford Expositor* listed Lorraine and her five adult children among his loved ones, but also his son, Ira, and wife, Carla, in Pittsburgh and his aunt Maude back in Clairton. Thus, despite the decades he spent in Canada, he obviously still had enough contact with kin back in Pennsylvania for Lorraine to have noted that at the time of his passing. He was buried at Mount Hope Cemetery in Brantford. The obituary, which called him Shanty, mentioned that he "was supervisor at Brant County Board of Education for many years [and] an avid golfer at Arrowdale Golf Course." As might be expected, it also noted his time with the Homestead Grays in the Negro National League, the Brantford Red Sox, and the Galt Terriers.[77]

NOTES

1   According to Veteran Compensation Application Files, WWII, 1950-1966, for Pennsylvania, accessible via Ancestry.com. The steel mill was originally Carnegie Steel Co.

2   Though he may have typically been called by his middle name, in 1927 he might have been the Luther Clifford awarded first prize among 2- and 3-year-olds during Negro Health Week at the YWCA in nearby McKeesport. See "McKeesport, PA," *Pittsburgh Courier,* April 16, 1927: 9.

3   According to his federal Draft, Enlistment and Service registration cards for both World Wars, accessible via Ancestry.com.

4   According to Rosemary Clifford McDaniel, "The Early History of the Clifford Family of Maryland, Virginia/West Virginia, Pennsylvania and Ohio: Descendants of Isaac Clifford, The Patriarch," 2004, available at henryburke1010. tripod.com/lettsettlementreunion/id34.html. In 1898 John Robert Clifford won a landmark civil-rights case before the West Virginia Supreme Court for another teacher in Tucker County, in Williams v. Board of Education. In 2009 John Robert Clifford was among a dozen early civil-rights figures honored by a series of stamps by the US Postal Service.

5   Their marriage record is available at wvculture.org/vrr/ va_mcdetail.aspx?Id=11266551.

6   Gertrude Simpson, "Irwin, Pa.," *Pittsburgh Courier*, June 24, 1911: 2. For an early mention of a Clyde Clifford of Irwin, see Nellie V. Hackney, "Greensburg," *Pittsburgh Courier*, December 9, 1911: 2.

7   These details about Effie and her family are from federal censuses and documents accessible via Ancestry.com, including her entry in the Social Security Applications and Claims Index, several death certificates, and her grandfather's Record of Burial of Veteran on file with Pennsylvania's Department of Military Affairs, which lists him as having served in Company B, "8th Regt. P.V."

8   See Elaine Spaull, "The Magnificent Life of Dr. Walter Cooper," *Post* (Rochester, New York), March/April 2014, and Dr. Cooper's overlapping memories in the oral history transcript from 2008 at rbscp.lib.rochester.edu/rbfs-Cooper.

9   "School Segregation in Clairton Quickly Nipped," *Pittsburgh Courier*, September 23, 1939: 2.

10 See Note 8. Dr. Cooper made his own contribution to undoing discrimination at the high school just a few years after Luther graduated: "In 1943, when I was a sophomore at Clairton High School in Pennsylvania, the football squad was 30 percent African-American. So my sister Thelma and a few of the other African-American girls wanted to be cheerleaders. The unspoken rule in the physical education department was that black girls could not be cheerleaders. The football squad had won its first four games. Prior to the fifth game against our rival, I gathered the black football players and said, 'We're going to boycott practice in protest against this unwritten rule.' I talked it over with my mother, and she said it was the right thing to do. She said, 'I'll make some cookies and such for the athletes as they gather.' So in school on Monday, we boycotted practice. On Tuesday, you could hear the football coach bellowing up and down the corridor: 'What do they want? Give it to them!' We never met with the director of the physical ed department, but four black girls—my sister Thelma Cooper, and Ruby Sears, Hortense Gordon and Jane Moore—all ended up cheerleaders."

11 *Clairtonian Yearbook*, Clairton High School (Clairton, Pennsylvania), 1941, quoting from pages 57 and 54, respectively.

12 "Changed 'Cat Team Opens Away Season With Clairton," *Monongahela* (Pennsylvania) *Daily Republican*, September 27, 1940: 2.

13 "Mounties' Track Team Tops Clairton," *Pittsburgh Press*, April 17, 1941: 16; "Uniontown High Wins Track Meet," *Pittsburgh Press*, May 3, 1941: 8. See also *Pittsburgh Post-Gazette*, May 9, 1941: 18.

14 According to the death certificate for Lucy Barnes, accessible via Ancestry.com, on which her home address was 149 Lincoln Way in Clairton at the time of her passing, on August 25, 1938. The certificate was signed by Mrs. Effie Clifford, whose address was the same.

15 See Note 3.

16 "Divorce Libels Filed," *Pittsburgh Press*, August 6, 1942: 20.

17 See Pennsylvania's Veteran Compensation Application Files for WWII, 1950-1966, accessible via Ancestry.com. The military branch wasn't identified but his obituary in the *Brantford Expositor*— see Note 74—specified the Army Air Corps.

18 "Grays Break Even in Two With Cubans," *New York Amsterdam News*, July 3, 1948: 27.

19 "Monessen Triumphs in Opening USW Tilt," *Monessen* (Pennsylvania) *Daily Independent,* May 17, 1948: 5.

20 "2,400 Fans See Grays Nip Yanks," *New Castle* (Pennsylvania) *News,* June 12, 1948: 13.

21 *Chicago Defender,* July 3, 1948: 10.

22 "Grays, All-Stars Await Big Clash," *Charleroi* (Pennsylvania) *Mail,* July 2, 1948: 7.

23 "Homestead Grays Top Stars, 9-0" *Charleroi Mail,* July 6, 1948: 7.

24 "Grays Regain League Lead, Nip Philly Stars, 4 to 3," *New Castle News,* August 28, 1948: 12.

25 "Grays Win Over Baltimore, 6-0," *Pittsburgh Post-Gazette*, September 15, 1948: 20. See also Sam Lacy, "Grays Take First 2 in NNL Playoff Series," *Baltimore Afro-American*, September 18, 1948: 14.

26 "AL Teams Draft Stars of Clubs Calling It Quits," *Pittsburgh Courier*, February 19, 1949: 11.

27 "Divorce Proceedings," *Pittsburgh Post-Gazette*, March 29, 1949: 10; "Divorce Proceedings," *Pittsburgh Post-Gazette*, March 7, 1952: 11.

28 "Grays Open Local Baseball Season Sunday," *Indianapolis Recorder,* May 14, 1949: 11.

29 "Grays Strengthen Club With 3 New Players," *Baltimore Afro-American*, May 21, 1949: section 2, page 13; "Grays Sign 3 New Players, Meet Richmond Sunday," *Washington Post*, May 28, 1949: 10.

30 "Grays Defeat Stars," *Pittsburgh Post-Gazette*, May 19, 1949, 19.

31 "Homestead Grays Defeat Yankees," *New Castle News*, June 29, 1949: 18.

32 "2,300 See Grays Beat House of David," *Lima News* (Ohio), July 26, 1949: 12.

33 "Clowns Meet Grays Tonight," *Washington Post*, August 12, 1949: 27.

34 Clifford was catcher in one box score of a doubleheader covered by the *Kansas City Times*, September 6, 1949: 20. His 2-for-4 game was documented by the box score accompanying "4 Double Plays Feature Negro Big Leaguer Game," *Chillicothe* (Missouri) *Constitution Tribune*, September 9, 1949: 5. See also the *Kansas City Star*, September 8, 1949.

35 For examples, see one box score of a doubleheader covered by the *Kansas City Times*, September 12, 1949: 14. Clifford's triple behind Elston Howard was reported in "Baseball Season Ends," *Kansas City* (Kansas) *Plain Dealer*, September 23, 1949: 4. See also *Kansas City Star*, September 18, 1949.

36 Wendell Smith, "Kansas City Quits Play-Off Series," *Pittsburgh Courier*, September 17, 1949: 22.

37 "N.Y. Black Yankees to Meet Homestead Grays Thursday, April 13," *Carolina Times* (Durham, North Carolina), April 8, 1950: 4.

38 „Bushwicks Split in Official Opener," *Brooklyn Eagle*, May 8, 1950: 13; Art Carter, "From the Bench," *Baltimore Afro-American*, May 13, 1950: 28.

39 For examples, see the box score accompanying "Hustlers Lose to Homestead Grays, 7 to 3," *Frederick* (Maryland) *News*, May 23, 1950: 13, and the one in the *New Castle News*, June 22, 1950: 28.

40 "Clippers Lose Doubleheader Over Week-End," *Beckley* (West Virginia) *Post-Herald*, July 3, 1950: 6.

41 "Merchants Meet Homestead Grays in Exhibition Here Monday Night," *Greenville* (Pennsylvania) *Record-Argus*, July 8, 1950: 5.

42 "Gibson Jr. Gets Beaned," *Pittsburgh Courier*, August 5, 1950: 24. Accounts of the game in two Pittsburgh papers are vague about the date, but the beaning was also mentioned four days earlier, putting it in July. See Dan McGibbeny, "Josh Gibson Jr. Follows Footsteps of Famous Father as Grays' Slugger," *Pittsburgh Post-Gazette*, August 1, 1950: 12.

43 "17-Hit Gray Attack Buries Black Yanks by 11-4 in Slugfest," *Charleston* (West Virginia) *Gazette*, August 4, 1950: 13.

44 "Bankhead to Tour With Homestead Grays," *Pittsburgh Courier*, September 23, 1950: 8; for examples of specific games scheduled, see "Bushwick Games Rained Out," *New York Times*, October 9, 1950: 7, and "Homestead Grays Play Tuesday in North Gulfport," *Biloxi* (Mississippi) *Daily Herald*, October 23, 1950: 10.

45 Ted Beare, "A Man for All Seasons," *Brantford* (Ontario) *Expositor*, August 12, 2008. Available at brantfordexpositor.ca/2008/08/12/a-man-for-all-seasons.

46 George Hayes, "Just a Shell of What It Was," *Woodstock* (Ontario) *Daily Sentinel-Review*, July 10, 1981: 5.

47 "Baseball School Is Big Success," *Simcoe* (Ontario) *Reformer*, June 18, 1951: 6.

48 "Dominican Season Opens," *The Sporting News*, May 7, 1952: 39.

49 U.S., Departing Passenger and Crew Lists, 1914-1965, accessible via Ancestry.com.

50 "Ball Belters to Display Wares in Big Negro Tilt at Stadium," *Sikeston* (Missouri) *Daily Standard*, September 5, 1951: 8.

51 Bienvenido Rojas, "1952, Refuerzos Ganaron los Lideratos Ofensivos," *Diario Libre* (Santo Domingo, Dominican Republic), September 1, 2015: 35.

52 William Humber, *A Sporting Chance: Achievements of African-Canadian Athletes* (Toronto: Natural Heritage Books, 2004), 57.

53 "Greys Suffer Eighth Straight Home Loss," *Brandon* (Manitoba) *Daily Sun*, July 15, 1952: 2.

54 "Greys Hit Peak Form to Win Third Straight and Move to Within Striking Distance," *Brandon Daily Sun*, August 2, 1952: 2; "8-Run Rally Gives Cards 12-11 Victory," *Winnipeg* (Manitoba) *Free Press*, August 6, 1952: 21. "Clarence King in Second Place in Mandak Batting Race," *Brandon Daily Sun*, August 8, 1952: 2.

55 H.L. Crawford, "Here and There in Sports," *Brandon Daily Sun*, August 14, 1952: 2.

56 "Joe Mitchell and Skeeter Watkins Topped the League in Offensive, Defensive Play," *Brandon Daily Sun*, September 18, 1952: 2.

57 "Biggest Battery in IC Planned by Brant Hose," *Globe and Mail* (Toronto), January 27, 1953: 18.

58 "Bus Leaves Thursday to Pick up Greys," *Brandon Daily Sun*, April 1, 1953: 6; "Greys Assemble Today in Baton Rouge Camp," *Brandon Daily Sun*, April 6, 1953: 6.

59 "Two Stars to Rejoin Indianapolis," *Pittsburgh Courier*, March 28, 1953: 16.

60 "Braves' Initial Intra-Squad Contests Set This Week End," *Waycross* (Georgia) *Journal-Herald*, March 21, 1953: 2.

61 "Jacksonville and Evansville Play Exhibition Here Tonight," *Waycross Journal-Herald*, March 28, 1953: 2. On the same page two days later the paper reported that Evansville beat Jacksonville, 5-2, but little detail was provided and there wasn't even a line score.

62 Daniel Papillon and Bill Young, "The Red Clay of Waycross: Minor-League Spring Training in Georgia With the Milwaukee Braves," *The National Pastime: Baseball in the Peach State*, 2010: 123. This SABR journal article is available at sabr.

org/research/red-clay-waycross-minor-league-spring-training-georgia-milwaukee-braves.

63 "Braves Top Evansville Second Time, 5-4," *Hagerstown* (Maryland) *Morning Herald,* April 9, 1953: 23. "Eau Claire Bears Beat Quebec, 7-6," *Eau Claire* (Wisconsin) *Leader,* April 12, 1953: 10. "Bears Top Evansville 12-10; Carr Seeks Two," *Eau Claire Daily Telegram,* April 14, 1953: 12. "Quebec Wins 8-3 as Bears Falter," *Eau Claire Leader,* April 16, 1953: 16.

64 Jim Reid, "Sport Scripts," *Brandon Daily Sun,* May 16, 1953: 6.

65 For the Negro Leagues Baseball Museum profile of Wilkes, see coe.k-state.edu/annex/nlbemuseum/history/players/wilkes. html. For an overview of his life in Brantford, including the quote by Clifford, see Ted Beare, "Red Sox Star Loved City," *Brantford Expositor,* August 12, 2008.

66 "Clifford's Bat Booms as Sox Rout London for Fisher's 4th Win," *Toronto Daily Star*, June 10, 1954: 28; "Clowns, Kaycees Play in Chi, N.Y.," *New York Age*, July 3, 1954: 21.

67 "Things to Talk About," *Pittsburgh Courier*, August 18, 1956: A9.

68 For example, see "Hamilton Finally Slips to Third, London Wins," *Toronto Daily Star*, July 22, 1957: 14.

69 "St. Thomas and Galt in Sawoff Tuesday," *Toronto Daily Star*, September 22, 1958: 21.

70 "Slugger Clifford Back With Galt," *Toronto Daily Star*, May 7, 1959: 45. This article confirmed that he had been an Intercounty League all-star.

71 "Personal Mention," *Daily Courier* (Connellsville, Pennsylvania), August 15, 1962: 13.

72 See *brantfordhomes.com/brantford-red-sox/.*

73 Email exchange between James B. Huff and author, October 17, 2016.

74 See the short marital announcement, "302 Marriages," *Brantford Expositor,* October 11, 1979: 37.

75 See his obituary, "Clifford, Luther Franklin (Shanty)," *Brantford Expositor,* May 4, 1990: D1.

76 Humber, 138.

77 See Note 74.

LUKE EASTER

By Justin Murphy

I've seen a lot of powerful hitters in my time but for sheer ability to knock a ball great distances, I've never seen anybody better than Easter—and I'm not excepting Babe Ruth. - Del Baker[1]

Luscious "Luke" Easter was born August 4, 1915 at 8:15 PM in Jonestown, Mississippi. During his playing career and later in life, Easter would equivocate on his birth date. Indians general manager Hank Greenberg once said, "no one knows how old Luke really is. No one, that is, but Luke himself, and sometimes I'm not sure that he knows."[2] He first claimed to have been born August 4, 1921 in St. Louis, Missouri, then changed to the same date in 1913 and 1914. On August 17, 1963, during one of a series of Luke Easter Days at Rochester's Silver Stadium, Red Wings club president Morrie Silver offered Easter $10 for every year of his age, prompting Luke to announce that "my baseball age is 42, but my real age is 52," placing his birth in 1911 (and netting him $520). The 1915 date is substantiated by a birth certificate, census research, and Easter's Social Security application, as well as an inscription in the Easter family Bible.[3]

Luke was the fifth of 10 children born to James and Maude Easter. At the time of Luke's death in 1979, he still had six surviving siblings: brothers Robert, Julius (J.C.), and Wilbert, and sisters Minnie (married name Blanks), Ruby (Hayes), and Izell (Tillis).[4] Two other siblings died young. His father, who had attended the Tuskegee Institute and who, like his son, cut an imposing figure at 6-foot-1, 210 pounds, was a farmer in Jonestown, a town of 400, but in 1919 the family relocated to St. Louis, where James' brother found him work shoveling sand in a glass factory. Maude died of tuberculosis in 1922, when Luke was 7. Luke attended St. Louis public schools, and went to the same high school as fellow Negro Leaguer Quincy Trouppe, three years his elder. Luke dropped out, however, after the ninth grade, and spent his time playing ball. J.C. Easter relates that he and Luke used to play with a broomstick and bottletops.[5]

Luke was powerful; the only dislike I had for him, whenever we played, he used to beat the owner out of his money while we were on the road… they played knock rummy. They used to cheat each other and Luke used to beat him. We prayed that we could get paid before Luke got to see [owner Cum] Posey. - Ray Brown[6]

Easter first took part in organized baseball in 1937, when he played outfield and first base and batted cleanup for the St. Louis Titanium Giants. The Giants were sponsored by the American Titanium Company. Easter and the other players worked for the company year-round, but were given time off to play ball. The St. Louis Stars had previously been the top black team in the city, having succeeded the St. Louis Giants in 1922, and they won three Negro National League championships between 1928 and 1931. After 1931, however, the league was dissolved, and the Stars with it. In their absence, the Titanium Giants had become an elite club, defeating six Negro American League teams in exhibitions in 1940 and regularly winning 90 percent of their games. Indeed, when an attempt was made in 1937 to re-establish the St. Louis Stars under different management in the new Negro American League, the experiment lasted only two years, largely due to competition with the Giants. Luke's teammates in St. Louis included Sam Jethroe, Jesse Askew, and Herb Bracken. Askew once said that "Easter was unlucky in not getting an earlier shot at the Negro Leagues, primarily because he played poorly in exhibitions against teams like the Kansas City Monarchs."[7]

In 1941, Easter and several teammates were traveling in Jethroe's car to a road game. The car crashed, and Easter suffered a broken ankle.[8] This ended his 1941 season, and the Giants were disbanded the following year. Later in his career, Luke would deny having played baseball before 1946, claiming instead that he'd only played softball, a claim that some have labeled mythmaking.

By the beginning of 1942, World War II had broken out, and Easter, like many players, was drafted into the war effort. The National Archives and Records Administration lists him as being inducted on June 22, 1942, and stationing at Fort Leonard Wood, Missouri. He spent 13 months in the army before being discharged on July 3, 1943 because of his ankle injury.[9] He later found work in a "war chemical plant" in Chicago in the summer of 1945.[10]

At the end of 1945, with the war over, he spoke with "Candy" Jim Taylor, manager of the Chicago American Giants. Taylor directed him to Abe Saperstein, who was a major baseball promoter before founding the Harlem Globetrotters. Saperstein was starting a new team, the Cincinnati Crescents, and he invited Easter to join it.[11] The Crescents did not succeed in gaining admission into the Negro American League, and instead spent the 1946 season barnstorming across the country, competing against many Negro League teams. Statistics are not widely available for the 1946 Crescents, but the March 30, 1949 *Sporting News* reported that Easter had batted .415 with 152 RBIs; it has also been said that Easter hit 74 home runs, although that number is not verified. He also hit one of his more famous home runs, a ball that reached the center-field bleachers of the Polo Grounds in New York against the Cubans. As teammate Bob Thurman said, "he hit it halfway up the stands, about 500 feet. The thing about it—it was a line drive."[12]

As he was throughout his career, Easter was a fan favorite in Cincinnati, and in 1947, Easter was signed to the Homestead Grays for a reported $1100 a month, making him one of the highest paid players on the team.[13] The Grays sought a replacement in the lineup and at the box office for Josh Gibson, who'd died of a stroke the previous winter. In fact, Buck O'Neil writes that "we [i.e. the Negro Leagues] wanted to get Luke

away from the St. Louis Stars [sic] long before he went to the Grays, but he didn't want to leave home. He had a pretty good job there as a security guard."[14] The team already featured Hall of Fame slugger Buck Leonard; outfielder Bob Thurman, who would later play five seasons with the Cincinnati Reds; pitcher John 'Needle Nose' Wright, who later signed a minor-league deal with the Brooklyn Dodgers; and Wilmer Fields, who pitched and played third base, and who won eight MVP awards in different leagues in his career. In 219 at-bats in 1947, Easter hit 10 home runs and held a .311 batting average, while playing the outfield (since Leonard was at first base). The following year he recorded a batting average of .363, and his 13 homers tied him with teammate Leonard for the league lead (Leonard also took home the batting title that season, with a .395 average). He also led the NNL with 62 RBIs. Most impressively, in only 58 games, the 6-foot-4, 240-pound Easter legged out

As a rookie with the Grays in 1947, Luke Easter batted .311 in league competition and .382 overall. In 1950, his first full (rookie) season with the Cleveland Indians, he hit .280 with 28 homers. (*National Baseball Hall of Fame, Cooperstown, New York*)

a career-high eight triples, helping the Grays to a Negro League World Series championship. After the season, he was chosen to play in the 1948 East-West All-Star Game. The year 1948 also saw Luke's marriage to 24-year-old Virgil Lowe, a Cleveland native. Some sources claim that Virgil was his third wife, yet there is no reference to any other wives in any of the available documents.[15] He and Virgil would remain married until Luke's death, 31 years later.

Meanwhile, Easter had also been playing winter ball in Puerto Rico, Venezuela, and Hawaii for the prior three years.[16] Statistics for these seasons are difficult to come by, but over three years playing for Mayagüez in Puerto Rico, he amassed 48 home runs, 145 RBIs, and a .330 batting average, leading the league in home runs each season.[17] His best season was 1948-49, when he was named MVP, batting .402 as the team won the championship. Easter also later played for Hermosillo of the Mexican Pacific Coast League in 1954-55, leading the league with 20 homers, and for Caguas in Puerto Rico in the winters of 1955-56, leading the league in home runs at the age of 41, and in 1956-57.[18]

He was awesome…I was amazed by his strength and power. - Frank Robinson[19]

Had Luke come up to the big leagues as a young man, there's no telling what numbers he would have had. - Al Rosen[20]

By 1949, major-league baseball was slowly becoming integrated, and Bill Veeck signed Easter to a contract with the defending champion Cleveland Indians on February 19.[21] The Indians already featured Larry Doby, the first black player in the American League, as well as Satchel Paige. Easter, who had told Veeck that he was 27, was first assigned to Cleveland's Pacific Coast League affiliate in San Diego. He was only the second black player to appear in the PCL, but he assured San Diego president Bill Starr that "everybody likes me when I hit the ball."[22] That spring, however, he injured his right knee in an on-field collision, then had the same kneecap broken by a pitch. Despite the injury, he played on to packed crowds, with fans

flocking to the park to see him hit. Researcher Rick Swaine claims that the average attendance in his first 10 games was over 34,000; Goodrich reports, perhaps more realistically, that the total attendance of his first 17 games, home and away, was a record 101,492. Some clubs were even obliged to sell standing room only tickets in the outfield when San Diego came to town. In one three-game stand in Los Angeles, Easter hit six home runs, and fights broke out at the gates as fans clamored to watch him hit. Frank Finch, writing in *The Sporting News*, reported that the crowds to see him take batting practice were equaled only by those that turned out to see Stan Musial, Ted Williams, and Ernie Lombardi.[23] On the field, however, Easter did have to deal with racial discrimination. Some suggested that the pitch which had broken his knee in the spring had been intentional, and in a game against Portland, pitcher Ad Liska threw at him repeatedly in a single at-bat, including two that sailed behind the batter. Easter responded in his next at-bat with a 450-foot shot to dead center that, apocryphally, narrowly missed Liska's head on its way out of the park.[24]

The Padres, also featuring former major leaguer Max West and future major leaguers Al Rosen and Minnie Minoso, ended up in the championship series for the year. By the end of June, however, the pain in Easter's broken right knee had become insurmountable, and the Indians had him undergo surgery. Only six weeks later, still hobbled, he joined the Indians, making his major-league debut on August 11. According to *The Sporting News*, PCL owners estimated a loss of over $200,000 in revenue for the league after his departure[25], and the Indians were forced to part with the popular Allie Clark in order to make room for him on the roster. Easter became the 11th black player in MLB history. Bob Feller was the winning pitcher that day as the Indians defeated the White Sox, 6-5, in a game that lasted nearly four hours. Easter played in 21 games in 1949 and hit just .222 with no home runs. Bill Veeck, as he was wont to do, had created a great deal of publicity for Easter, and Cleveland fans did not take well to his early struggles. *The Sporting News* named him "the most booed player in the history of Cleveland Stadium." Tris Speaker pointed to the racial tension of the era, saying, "the poor guy came up under the worst possible conditions... [he] had nothing to do with the condition that made him the target of the boo birds."[26] Easter replied that "I hear them and I don't hear them...if I hit, they'll like me. If I don't hit, I don't deserve to be in the lineup."

Spring 1950 found Easter embroiled in a competition for the starting first base job with popular veteran Mickey Vernon. He performed well in spring training, leading the team with a .333 average and batting in 14 runs. Perhaps his most memorable shot, however, was an out: in a game between the Indians and the Browns, St. Louis pitcher Ned Garver thrust his glove in the way of an Easter line drive and was knocked off his feet by its momentum.[27] Despite the strong spring, however, Vernon started the year at first, with Easter in the outfield. Still slowed from his knee surgery, Easter's struggles at the plate continued early on, as did the booing, until May 6, when he blasted his first home run, off of Allie Reynolds of the Yankees. He went on to post a .280 batting average that year, with 28 home runs and 107 RBIs. Particularly noteworthy was a 477-foot home run he hit into the second deck in right field at Municipal Stadium on June 23, 1950 off Joe Haynes of the Senators, said to be the longest ball ever hit there.[28] He also was able to finish the season playing first base, as Mickey Vernon was traded to Washington to accommodate him. And, as was inevitable, by the end of the year Easter had won over the hostile Cleveland crowds with his powerful swing and his endearing demeanor. He was a regular unannounced spectator at local sandlot games, and signed endless autographs for the children who came to watch him play. On the field, though, Easter's struggle for acceptance continued, as he led the league in HBP.

Again in 1951, Easter was injured early, this time tearing a tendon in his left knee, but despite missing 26 games on the season managed 27 home runs and 103 RBIs, both team highs. The year was also significant for Easter due to the replacement of manager Lou Boudreau with Al Lopez, who had little use for

immobile infielders—or, according to researcher Rick Swaine, for black players in general. Easter, riddled with injuries and illness as well as deteriorating vision, started extremely poorly for the 1952 Indians, and was demoted to Triple-A Indianapolis after hitting just .208 through 63 appearances. In Indianapolis, however, he caught fire, hitting .340 with six home runs and 12 RBIs in only 50 at-bats. He was quickly brought back to Cleveland, and he stayed hot for the rest of the season, hitting 20 homers in the second half of the season. At the end of the year he was named the American League's Most Outstanding Player by *The Sporting News*. Hank Greenberg marveled, "his comeback is the most amazing thing I've ever seen. Six weeks ago...the snap in his swing was gone completely. They thought he'd never come back."[29]

Easter signed a contract for $20,000 at the beginning of the 1953 season and had high hopes of replicating his 1952 success. Unfortunately, he was struck by a pitch in the fourth game of the season, breaking a bone in his left foot. The injury hobbled him for the remainder of the season, and he was only able to appear in 68 games. He was released on October 1, but was invited back to spring training the following year, when he was again slowed, this time by an infection in his toe. He had six pinch-hit at-bats for Cleveland before being optioned to the minor leagues when the club had to make its final roster cuts in early May. His final big-league appearance came on May 4. Easter was initially bitter at being demoted, but ended up playing very well. He played 56 games with the Padres and 66 with Ottawa, batting .348 in his time in Canada. Between Ottawa and San Diego he managed to hit 28 home runs, but was released by the Indians after the season.

When kids quit on me, I'll quit, too. - Luke Easter[30]

Buffalo fans have always worshipped their sport heroes, but few have ever attained the near mythical status accorded to Bisons great Luke Easter. - plaque in the Greater Buffalo Sports Hall of Fame

Despite his success in the majors, Luke Easter inarguably received his greatest acclaim and adulation as a minor leaguer. Just as he had in St. Louis, Cincinnati, San Diego, and Cleveland, Easter became a local legend with his home run hitting and his likeable personality. He started with the Charleston (West Virginia) Senators of the American Association, where he tied for third in the league in home runs with 30. The following year, Easter signed a $7,500 contract with the newly independent Buffalo Bisons of the International League. Buffalo had just declined to renew their contract with the Detroit Tigers and were struggling with community ownership. The signing of Easter, the first black player on the team since Frank Grant in 1888, was their first important acquisition, and he did not disappoint.[31] Although the 1956 Bisons finished 21 1/2 games out of first, Easter hit .306 and led the league with 35 homers and 106 RBIs. More importantly, he helped capture the city's interest for the game with countless public appearances, a crucial task for a community-owned team.[32] He played even better in 1957, hitting 40 home runs for the Bisons, who by this time had signed a player development contract with the Kansas City Athletics. Among those 40 home runs was one which has become perhaps the most famous of all of Big Luke's famous blasts, hit in Buffalo. Buffalo baseball historian Joe Overfeld tells the story in *100 Seasons of Buffalo Baseball*:

The explosion occurred on the evening of June 14, 1957. It was mild and windless, and there was a trace of haze in the air. In the fourth inning of the second game of the evening's double-header, Columbus left-hander Bob Kuzava delivered what he later called "a perfect pitch"—a knee-high fastball on the outside of the plate. Easter swung, timed the pitch perfectly and sent it soaring high and deep to center field. As the ball disappeared into the haze, there was a mighty roar from the crowd as many fans realized at once what had happened: Luke Easter had just become the first batter ever to hit a ball over the centerfield scoreboard. As Easter completed his lumbering home run trot, dead-pan all the way, the cheering and ap-

plause reached decibel levels never previously attained in the old park.[33]

The center field fence at Buffalo's Offermann Stadium was 400 feet from home plate, and the scoreboard towered 60 feet in the air. The ball had traveled in an arc of approximately 550 feet. It concluded by crashing triumphantly through the window of Irene Luedke, who lived across the street from the stadium, and who "thought for sure someone had dropped an atom bomb on the roof."[34] After the game, Easter boldly predicted, "If my legs hold out, I'll do it again," and incredibly enough, he did, just two months later. Offermann Stadium saw its last game in 1960, and Easter went down in the history as the only man ever to clear that scoreboard—having accomplished it twice.

Easter played his third year with Buffalo in 1958, hitting 38 homers and driving in 109. After the season, however, the Bisons signed an agreement with the Philadelphia Phillies, who had important plans for prospect Francisco Herrera. Herrera, a big, right-handed first baseman, made Easter expendable. Several weeks into the 1959 season, on May 14, Easter was sold to the Rochester Red Wings for $100.[35] He responded by paying tribute to the fans of Buffalo, before making the 75-mile trip down the interstate to Rochester, where the last chapter of his baseball career was to play out.

In the remainder of the 1959 season, Easter managed to hit 22 home runs and drive in 76 runs. He followed with 14 home runs in 1960, 10 in 1961, 15 in 1962, and 6 in 1963, his last full season. By this point, Easter was practically immobile, although he would not suffer any further injuries after leaving the Indians in 1953. Even as his hitting faltered, however, he managed to become perhaps the most popular player in Red Wings history. Long-time Rochester writer George Beahon wrote, "foul weather or fair, he never denied an autograph. During those years, after I filed stories from the press box to the morning paper, I would see Luke still around the clubhouse or the parking lot, signing his name and making friends for the franchise."[36] Luke Easter Night in 1960 drew over 8,000 fans, who saw Luke receive "a color television set, fishing equipment, a $300 wrist watch with diamond numerals, a movie camera, luggage, and even a frozen turkey and five pounds of sausage."[37] In fact, Easter had started his own Luke Easter Sausage Company several years prior, and would regularly make gifts to his teammates in appreciation of strong performances.

Easter appeared in 10 games as a pinch-hitter in 1964 before finally deciding to hang up his cleats, 27 years after his debut with the St. Louis Titanium Giants and 15 years after breaking into the majors as a 34-year-old rookie. He remained with Rochester for the remainder of the season as a coach; major leaguers Boog Powell, Curt Blefary, and Pete Ward all credited Easter with helping in their development.[38] After the 1964 season, Luke moved back to Cleveland with his wife, Virgil.[39] Aside from a short coaching stint with the Indians in 1969, necessary to qualify for pension benefits, he would never work in baseball again.[40]

Even after he stopped playing, he would dream about baseball, and he'd be shaking, shaking shaking. I'd say, 'Luke, what's wrong?' He'd say, 'Nothin', I was just runnin'.' I could always tell when it was spring training because that's where Luke's dreams were. - Virgil Easter[41]

After returning to Cleveland, Easter immediately set to work again, though no longer in baseball. Former Negro Leaguer Frazier Robinson, in his autobiography, writes about having often gone to a cafe that Luke had opened in Cleveland called The Majestic Blue Room. He recalls that "he had a lot of jazz acts at his club, and it was a pretty popular place in Cleveland."[42] He also took a full-time job polishing airplane parts for TRW. Though he worked the night shift, he soon gained the confidence of his co-workers and was named chief steward of the Aircraft Workers Alliance.

It was in his capacity as union steward that Easter, in typical selfless fashion, came to his tragic end. He often cashed paychecks for fellow employees who could not make it to the bank. On March 29, 1979, he was carrying a small handgun for self-protection,

though at other times he procured a police escort.[43] Easter stepped out of a Cleveland Trust Company branch in Euclid, Ohio at 9:00 AM, carrying a bag full of cash. His *New York Times* obituary from March 30, 1979 reports that he had $5,000 in the bag, while Daniel Cattau gives $45,000. In either case, he was accosted by two gunman in the parking lot at East 360th St. and Euclid Ave. One of them was a former TRW employee who knew about the arrangement Luke had with his co-workers. They demanded the money from him. When he refused, they shot him several times in the chest; the *New York Times* obituary says that it was "a sawed-off shotgun and a .38-caliber revolver," while Cattau cites a .357 Magnum. The gunmen were captured after a high-speed car chase, their pockets filled with the stolen cash.[44] Easter was dead on arrival at the hospital.

On April 3, 1979, the baseball fans in Cleveland poured en masse into Mt. Sinai Baptist Church to pay their last respects to the legendary man. More than 4,000 people filed by the casket, and over 1,000 attended the funeral ceremony itself. Former teammates Bob Cain and Mike Garcia were pallbearers; ex-Indians Al Rosen and Bob Lemon, while longtime Cleveland sportswriter Hal Lebovitz and Indians team president Gabe Paul were among those serving as honorary pallbearers. Following the service, Easter was interred at Highland Park Cemetery. Besides his wife Virgil, survivors included six siblings, and six children (sons Terry Lee, Luke Jr., Travis, and George, and daughters Nana and Marla), two of whom (George and Marla) he and Virgil had adopted. He also had three grandchildren at the time of his death.[45]

Easter has been posthumously honored by many of the organizations to which he contributed as a player. He was a charter member of the Rochester Red Wings Hall of Fame in 1989 and also became a member of the Greater Buffalo Sports Hall of Fame in 1997. In Cleveland, a local ballpark was renamed in his honor, and a statue of him stands in front of it today. His wife Virgil became the first vice president of the Cleveland Baseball Federation,[46] of which Luke had earlier been chairman.[47] The most lasting impression of Luke Easter, however, lives in the minds of the countless fans who saw him club pitches far into the night, for whom he signed autographs, with whom he laughed, and whom he inspired with his infectious enthusiasm and unwavering kindness.

Luke was a great big, easy going, devil-may-care, jolly, hail fellow well met kind of guy who took a ribbing and dished it out. - Al Rosen[48]

You, Mr. Inspector, are face-to-face with the greatest home run hitter since Babe Ruth...there is no one alive who can hit a ball for distance with Luke Easter. - Buffalo teammate Joe Astroth, addressing an airport customs inspector in Havana[49]

Nearly everyone who ever saw Luke Easter play has a story about a seemingly impossible home run that he hit. Many, such as his colossal shots in the Polo Grounds in New York, Municipal Stadium in Cleveland, and Offermann Stadium in Buffalo, have become part and parcel of baseball mythology. Any attempt to recount Easter's life, however, should place the most emphasis on the impressions he made upon the people who had the pleasure of meeting him, no matter how briefly. He was adored by teammates and fans in every city he played in, even as one of the first black players in the PCL, the major leagues and in the International League. His demeanor was always positive, and he refused to be discouraged by the racism he often encountered. Joseph Thomas Moore, in his biography of Larry Doby, reports that the two players often had different ideas on how to breach the color issue: "they were as different from each other as Doby and [Satchel] Paige had been. While Doby was totally serious on the field, Easter relaxed and enjoyed his new status...as a big leaguer." Luke once told Doby, "Look, Larry, you fight just half the world and leave the other half to me."[50]

Away from the stadium, Luke was a partier and a gambler, a clotheshorse and a lover of fine food and cigars. Kevin Nelson has an apt description of Easter in *The Story of California Baseball*:

Everything about Easter was big—his home runs, his personality, his luxury Buick automobile. He liked for his teammate Artie Wilson to act as chauffeur and let him sit in the back seat so that when he was driving around town people would think a big shot was passing by. A woman who knew him (and there were more than a few of those) described his free-spending, party-loving personality as "flamboyant."[51]

Luke was a serious card-shark, quickly winning back large sums for teammates on the road when the need arose.[52] He was also an impeccable dresser who took especial care to keep his shoes shined and his pants pressed. James Goodrich reports in a 1950 interview that, "though Luke is an exceptionally large man, he eats only normal meals. His special appetite is for cereals and vegetable dishes." He also enjoyed going to watch gangster movies and listening to jazz[53]; Jim Fridley recalls Luke introducing him to Louis Armstrong.[54]

His social life aside, however, it is difficult to sum up the admiration and affection that Luke inspired in those who saw him play or shook his hand during his long baseball career. Minnie Minoso once recalled, "he was such a nice man. I didn't speak good English, so he'd take me to restaurants and other places and translate for me."[55] Buffalo historian Joe Overfeld recalls that when Easter died, "for many it was as though the life of a member of the family had been suddenly and tragically snuffed out."[56] Easter always had time for an autograph, a handshake, a photograph, or a smile. He was once fined at a minor-league game in Minneapolis for opening the gates to the stadium to let in children who couldn't afford tickets.[57] One often hears Easter compared to Babe Ruth. The comparison goes farther than their similar power at the plate—like Ruth, Easter had the ability to relate to all who watched him play, at home or on the road. It is with this intense enthusiasm and caring in mind that one can best understand the great baseball life of Luke Easter.

SOURCES

In addition to the sources cited in the Notes, the author also consulted:

Buffalo Bisons, www.bisons.com

Rochester Red Wings, www.redwingsbaseball.com

www.baseball-almanac.com

www.baseballthinkfactory.org

The National Archives, Washington, D.C.

NOTES

1   James Goodrich, "Luke Easter, King of Swat?" *Negro Digest*, August, 1950.

2   Rick Swaine, *The Black Stars Who Made Baseball Whole* (Jefferson, North Carolina: McFarland & Co. Publishers, 2006), 77.

3   *Sports Illustrated* April 9. 1979; Daniel Cattau, "So, Maybe There Really is Such a Thing as 'the Natural'," *Smithsonian*, August 1991, 117-127.

4   All listed as survivors on the program from Easter's memorial service. Obituary from Luke Easter's memorial service, Mt. Sinai Baptist Church, April 3, 1979, online at www.redwings-baseball.com.

5   Cattau.

6   Brent Kelley, *Voices from the Negro Leagues* (Jefferson, North Carolina: McFarland & Co. Publishers, 1998), 268.

7   Cattau.

8   Swaine, who denies that Jethroe was driving with Easter at the time (p. 68), has his dates confused.

9   Cattau, who interviewed several of Easter's family members, claims that he worked in Portland, Oregon in a shipyard for the duration of the war. It is clear at any rate that he played no baseball between 1942 and 1945.

10   Goodrich.

11   Goodrich tells an apocryphal-sounding tale in which Easter is first turned down by Taylor, who dismisses him as "too big and too awkward." Easter then earns a spot on a semipro team by convincing the desperate, short-handed manager that he's actually "a better pitcher than a first baseman," pitches against and defeats Taylor's Giants in an exhibition, and hits three home runs instead of the two he had promised.

12   Cattau.

13   Frazier "Slow" Robinson and Paul Bauer. *Catching Dreams: My Life in the Negro Baseball Leagues* (Syracuse, New York: Syracuse University Press, 1999). 121.

14   Buck O'Neil, Steve Wulf, & David Conrads. *I Was Right on Time* (New York: Simon & Schuster, 1997), 51.

15   Virgil's obituary from May 1, 2001, lists a stepson Terry Sr., who was named as a son in Luke's obituary. Her obituary also mentions son Gerald Sr., not named in Luke's obituary. Gerald is, however, mentioned in Cattau's article as Luke's son, so this

may have been an accidental omission. *Cleveland Plain-Dealer*, May 1, 2001.

16   *The Sporting News*, March 30, 1949.

17   Pat Doyle, "Luke Easter: Myth, Legend, Superstar," *Baseball Almanac*, September 2003.

18   See Peter C. Bjarkman, *Baseball with a Latin Beat* (Jefferson, North Carolina: McFarland & Co. Publishers, 1994), and Danny Peary (ed.), *We Played the Game* (New York: Hyperion Press, 1994), 348.

19   Cattau.

20   Ibid.

21   Buck Leonard reports, "We sold Easter to the Cleveland Indians for $10,000. They were going to pay another $5,000 if he went to the majors. But when he went to the majors, Luke wanted the other $5,000 himself. He had an argument with the Homestead Grays' management. At that time Rufus Jackson was dead and his wife was in charge. Luke said he wasn't going if he didn't get the $5,000, but they got together on something and Luke went." John Holway, John. *Voices from the Great Black Baseball Leagues* (New York: Dodd, Mead & Co., 1975), 271.

22   Swaine, 79.

23   *The Sporting News*, March 30, 1949.

24   Goodrich.

25   *The Sporting News*, August 24, 1949.

26   Cattau.

27   Goodrich.

28   Russell Schneider, *Tales from the Tribe Dugout* (Champaign, Illinois: Sports Publishing LLC, 2002), 51.

29   Cattau.

30   Ibid.

31   Joe Overfeld, *The 100 Seasons of Buffalo Baseball* (Kenmore, New York: Partner's Press, 1985), 150.

32   Swaine, 82.

33   Overfeld, 151.

34   *Sports Illustrated*, July 15, 1957.

35   Jim Mandelaro and Scott Pitoniak, *Silver Seasons: The Story of the Rochester Red Wings* (Syracuse, New York: Syracuse University Press, 1996), 114.

36   Ibid.

37   *Sports Illustrated*, July 14, 1960.

38   Mandelaro & Pitoniak, 114; Swaine, 83.

39   In fact, it is not entirely clear whether Luke spent 1965-66 in Rochester or in Cleveland. His obituary from the March 30, 1979 *New York Times* mentions that he had worked at his job in Cleveland for "about fifteen years," i.e. since 1964. The obituary

from his memorial service, however, says that he returned to Cleveland in 1966.

40   *The Sporting News*, March 1, 1969: 20. Easter was with the Indians from February 13 to September 20, 1969 (as mentioned in *The Sporting News*, October 4, 1969). The March article also notes a prior commitment he had as part of a job with the computer company Thompson Ramo Woolridge, also in Cleveland.

41   Cattau.

42   Robinson, 188. This may be the Majestic Hotel, which stood at East 55th and Central Avenue. Joe Mosbrook describes it as "Cleveland's primary African-American hotel." The Majestic had featured a jazz room since 1931. See Joe Mosbrook, "Jazzed in Cleveland," pt. 49. January 3, 2000. www.cleveland.oh.us/ wmv_news/jazz49.htm

43   Cattau.

44   Ibid.

45   Obituary from Luke Easter's memorial service.

46   When she died at the age of 77, Virgil had eight grandchildren and a great-grandchild. Obituary of Virgil Easter, *Cleveland Plain-Dealer*, May 1, 2001.

47   Obituary from Luke Easter memorial service.

48   Joseph Thomas Moore, *Pride Against Prejudice: the Biography of Larry Doby* (New York: Praeger Press, 1988), 92.

49   Cattau.

50   Moore, 92.

51   Kevin Nelson, *The Story of California Baseball* (San Francisco: California Historical Society Press, 2004), 240.

52   Cattau.

53   Goodrich.

54   Peary, 199.

55   Ibid., 101.

56   Overfeld, 150.

57   Cattau.

CLARENCE EVANS

By Dennis D. Degenhardt

Clarence Evans was a product of the District of Columbia's school system, where he was a successful pitcher at Washington's Armstrong High School. On May 25, 1937, the *Washington Post* reported that Evans pitched a one-hit, 12-0 shutout in a big win over Cardozo High of the South Atlantic Colored League, striking a blow in the defense of Armstrong's "colored inter-high school baseball championship."[1] In going the distance, he also fanned 14 Cardozo batters. In 1938 he again hurled a 12-0 shutout while striking out 10 hitters against Bates High School at Annapolis, Maryland.[2]

As a native of the D.C. area, Evans had to be familiar with the Washington Homestead Grays, one of the Negro Leagues' powerhouse franchises, which used Griffith Stadium as one of their two primary home fields (with their other home stadium being Pittsburgh's Forbes Field). The Grays finished their 1948 home season with a doubleheader on Sunday, September 5, 1948, at Griffith Stadium on Buck Leonard Day, celebrating Leonard's having spent 15 years with Homestead.[3] With 6,000 fans in attendance, the team and fans honored their longtime captain and first baseman. They proceeded to win both games against two different teams, outlasting the Indianapolis Clowns 8-4 in the first game and defeating the Kansas City Monarchs 6-1 in the nightcap.

In the opener, the Grays threw Clarence Evans against the Clowns in what became his only appearance for the eventual 1948 Negro League World Series champions. The "product of the Washington scholastic ranks"[4] was the winning pitcher, allowing four runs on nine hits in 7⅔ innings pitched. He surrendered four walks while striking out only one batter. At the plate, he was hitless in three at-bats. Evans had likely come to the Grays' attention by word of mouth or by the process of scouting the local

area's talent. Since his only appearance for the Grays took place in his hometown on the last weekend of the season, he may have been a replacement player or may have been auditioning for the team with an eye toward securing a roster spot for the following season.

Evans did indeed remain with the Grays for part of the 1949 season when the team joined the Negro American Association. He was listed as one of the hurlers by the *Baltimore Afro-American* in a June 4, 1949, article, but he did not finish the season with the team, and was not included in later articles. No record exists of his accomplishments that season.

Nevertheless, the 1949 season was not Evans' last campaign in professional Negro baseball. He was a member of the Washington Royals in 1951, the franchise that became the first Negro team to play in the City Series.[5] The team's best pitcher, Oswald Stewart Jr., the son of the team's manager, won most of their games, but the team also had a clever knuckleballer, Clarence Evans.[6]

After his time with the Royals, Evans disappeared into history as mysteriously as he had come out of it. So little information about Evans exits that neither accurate birth records nor any death record can be located.

Author's Note

Clarence Evans has been one of the most elusive players to attempt to research. We know neither the date of his birth nor of his probable death, and very little of his life in between. An attempt to reach the basics through Ancestry.com resulted in over one million entries. We know too little about his life to significantly narrow the search terms. Thanks to SABR member Bill Mortell for his expert help in this regard. We each found several candidates who might be Evans, but nothing pointed back to what we know about baseball, high school, or the teams he played on.

NOTES

1   "Armstrong High's Nine Defeats Cardozo, 12-0," *Washington Post*, May 25, 1937: 17.

2   "Armstrong High Defeats Bates," *Washington Post*, April 30, 1938: X18.

3   "Buck Marks 15th Year by Winning," *New York Amsterdam News*, September 11, 1948: 15.

4   *Baltimore Afro-American*, September 11, 1948.

5   Brian Bell Jr., "On the Sandlots," *Washington Evening Star*, August 5, 1951: 37.

6   Ibid.

WILMER FIELDS

By Frederick C. Bush

Josh Gibson has often been called "the black Babe Ruth" since he, like the Sultan of Swat, was his league's most-feared home run hitter, but Wilmer Fields — Gibson's teammate during four of his seasons with the Homestead Grays — had much more in common with the Babe than Gibson did. On the surface, this truth is not readily apparent; in fact, they initially appear to be polar opposites. Ruth's parents abandoned him to an orphanage/reform school, whereas Fields grew up in a loving home; Ruth's reckless hedonism contrasted with Fields' gentler, Christian demeanor; and Ruth became the savior of major-league baseball while Fields never played in a single major-league game. However, a look at their career paths and statistics shows that they were two of a kind: star players with the rare ability to pitch and to hit with equal acumen.[1]

As a pitcher for the Boston Red Sox, Ruth was a two-time 20-game winner and led the American League with a 1.75 ERA in 1916. He had a 94-46 career record (89-46 with Boston), and he also set a record by pitching 29⅔ consecutive scoreless innings in World Series play.[2] After he was sold to the New York Yankees and converted into an outfielder, he became baseball's first true power hitter, finishing his career with a batting average of .342 and smashing the total of 714 home runs and 2,214 RBIs for which he is best known. Ruth led the American League in home runs 12 times and won a batting title when he hit .378 in 1924. Surprisingly, he won only one Most Valuable Player Award, in 1923.[3] World Series championships, on the other hand, were plentiful for the Babe as he helped to lead his teams to seven titles (three with Boston and four with New York).

In comparison, Fields notched a 102-26 record in eight seasons as a pitcher for the Homestead Grays (1940-42, 1946-50). In addition to his Negro League totals, he posted career won-lost marks of 38-7 in

Canada, 11-1 with the semipro Fort Wayne Allen Dairymen, 28-15 in Puerto Rico, 6-2 in Venezuela, and 5-2 in the Dominican Republic for a composite pitching record of 190-53. Though he was primarily a pitcher with the Grays, Fields also learned to play third base and the outfield, and there was no fall-off in his performance at the plate or in the field. He had a .425 batting average for the Oshawa (Ontario) Merchants in 1955 and, in his final season of 1958, hit .392 as an outfielder for the Mexico City Red Devils. Fields won a total of six MVP awards in four different leagues: the Puerto Rican Winter League, the Intercounty (Canada) League (three times), the Venezuelan Winter League, and the Colombian Winter League. He also won the Negro League World Series with Homestead in 1948, and he helped lead Fort Wayne, representing the United States, to the Global World Series title in 1956. It could be argued that the only thing that Fields does not yet have in common with Ruth as a player is membership in the National Baseball Hall of Fame.

Wilmer Leon Fields was born on August 2, 1922, in Manassas, Virginia, to Albert and Mabel Fields. He was one of five children, along with his older brothers Morris, Marvin, and Oliver, and his younger sister, Evelyn. Albert Fields made a living by working in a lumber yard for 33 years, and he saved enough money to send all five of his children to college; their finances were helped by the small family farm they tended, which ensured that there was always plenty of food on their table.

Fields's earliest baseball experiences involved playing against his family and neighbors. He credited sibling rivalry with helping him to hone his skills from an early age, saying, "I had three older brothers that I used to compete against every day ... and I tried to play as good as they were playing."[4] Though he already was aware that the limitations imposed upon blacks in segregated America would keep him out

Pitcher Wilmer Fields won Game Four of the 1948 Negro League World Series for the Homestead Grays. He also won a total of six MVP awards in four different leagues in Canada and Latin America. (*National Baseball Hall of Fame, Cooperstown, New York*)

of the major leagues, he also knew about the Negro Leagues and he confessed that, by the age of 8, "I used to get on my knees and pray to God to give me the ability to play professional black baseball."[5] Fields evinced natural talent, and at the age of 10 he and his father played in a game together on the Manassas town team, an experience he described in his autobiography, *My Life in the Negro Leagues*, as one of his most cherished memories.

Fields played on his high school's baseball team, though their games were few, and became a regular member of the town team. When the Manassas team disbanded before his senior year, all four Fields brothers ended up playing for the Fairfax, Virginia, team. Fairfax's management arranged a tryout with the Homestead Grays for Wilmer, and he pitched

well enough in a game against a semipro team that he was offered a contract. At the age of 17, he left Manassas to embark upon his career in professional Negro baseball. Mabel Fields sent her son into the world with a Bible to strengthen him. Fields took the message to heart throughout his life and admitted, during that first year, "I even played baseball with that Bible. I'd wrap it up in a sock and stick it in my pants pocket."[6]

The Grays used Fields sparingly in 1940, as a youngster who was still learning the ropes, and he put up a 2-1 record for Homestead's fourth consecutive Negro National League title squad. That fall Fields was offered a football scholarship, and he enrolled at the Virginia State College for Negroes in Ettrick, Virginia, where he played quarterback.[7] During his freshman year, he was not allowed to participate in conference games because he had already played professional ball, even though it had been baseball rather than football; Fields was happy that the rule was changed by his sophomore season. At the end of his freshman year, Fields received a surprise—and his classmates' admiration—in the form of a package that contained a reward for being a member of the Grays: It was a baseball-shaped radio with "National Negro World Champions 1940" inscribed on it.[8] Initially, he continued to study and to play football during the Grays' offseason, but he ended up completing only his first two years of college as baseball stardom beckoned.

Having shown his mettle, Fields became a regular member of Homestead's starting rotation in 1941. He had a 13-5 record that season, which he followed up with a 15-3 mark in 1942 as the Grays won the NNL championship again in both years. Though Homestead was a suburb of Pittsburgh, the Grays actually had two homes: They played most of their Pittsburgh games at Forbes Field and they played the remainder of their "home" games at Griffith Stadium in Washington.[9] Since they were at home in two cities, played league road games, and were in demand for exhibition games all over the country, the Grays were most often on the go. The constant bus travel helped to mold the players into a close-knit squad and combined with the talent of the team's players to turn them into the Negro Leagues' pre-eminent juggernaut of the 1930s and 1940s.

Travel did have its downside for black players in the Jim Crow-era United States as the team never could be sure where they might be able to buy food or gas for their bus. Fields had a light enough complexion that he could pass for a white man—Ted "Double Duty" Radcliffe jokingly called him "the man who integrated the Homestead Grays"[10]—and he retold one particular incident that occurred on the road:

> "We were traveling through Mississippi. ... We stopped at a general store. ... I went in there and there was a bar there and about 13 men sitting at the bar. I told the manager I wanted a couple of sandwiches. ... I looked up and here come R.T. [pitcher Robert Walker] walking through the door. ... and [he] said, 'Hey, Chinky! Get me a couple of sandwiches!' The manager looked at me and looked at him. He said, 'You with him?' I said, 'Yeah, I'm with him.' He said, 'Get out of here.'"[11]

Fields' nickname, Chinky, had its origins in the Grays' camaraderie that he valued so much. He explained that a "chinkpin" was a brown and yellow-colored nut with a fuzzy covering and that he was wearing a black and gray jacket at practice one day when future Hall of Famer Buck Leonard told him, "Fields, you look just like a 'Chinkypin.'"[12] The nickname stuck and was even passed down to Fields' oldest son, Marvin.

Fields had become a star with the Grays, but World War II put his career on hold when he was drafted into the US Army in 1943. He went through basic and technical training at Camp Plauche, Louisiana, before being sent to New York, from where he was shipped to Liverpool, England.[13] Fields was fortunate not to be involved in combat, but he did become so seriously ill at one point that he was sent to Paris to recover in a hospital. A short time after Fields recovered, a first sergeant put together

a baseball game on a former battlefield and was so impressed by Fields that he wanted him join his company that was headed for Japan now that the war in Europe had ended. Good fortune again smiled upon Fields as Japan surrendered before he could be shipped out to the Pacific.

After he returned stateside, Fields completed his military service at Camp Plauche. While in Louisiana for the second time, he met his future wife, Audrey Roche, in New Orleans. They were married at Gretna, Louisiana, in May 1946 before Fields left for Fort Meade, Maryland, to be discharged from the Army. They would go on to raise three children—son Marvin, daughter Maridel, and son Wilmer Jr. (Billy)—over the course of a marriage that spanned 58 years.

During Fields's absence, the Homestead Grays had won three additional NNL titles and had defeated the Birmingham Black Barons in both the 1943 and 1944 Negro League World Series. Fields rejoined the team in 1946 and pitched as though he had never been gone at all—he had a 16-1 record—though the team failed to win the NNL. In his final start that season, an exhibition game against a barnstorming team, Fields dueled against Johnny Vander Meer, who was best known for pitching consecutive no-hitters for the Cincinnati Reds in 1938. In a low-hit, high-strikeout game by both of the pitchers, Vander Meer and his squad prevailed by a 1-0 score. In spite of this tough end to the 1946 season, Fields had pitched so well during the year that he had received the first of six offers from major-league teams that desired his services. The Brooklyn Dodgers had offered Fields a contract to play for the Montreal Royals, their Triple-A affiliate, for which Jackie Robinson played during 1946, his first season in Organized Baseball. Fields turned down the offer.[14]

Fields's talent continued to be noticed and, as the integration of baseball progressed, he received numerous contract offers; however, he turned them all down. Over the next several years, he declined offers from the New York Yankees (1948), Washington Senators (1949), Philadelphia Athletics (1951), St. Louis Browns (1952), and Detroit Tigers (1955). In his autobiography, Fields provided the rationale for what seemed to many people to be a peculiar decision. He explained that he was earning more money by playing in the Negro Leagues and, later, Canada and the Latin winter leagues than most major-league ballplayers were paid; it simply made more sense for him to earn as much money as he could to support his family. His son Billy Fields said another factor was that he was more comfortable having his family travel with him in Canada, as well as the Latin American countries in which he played, than throughout the still-segregated United States.[15]

Instead of joining a team in Organized Baseball, Fields remained with the Grays and posted a 56-16 record from 1947 through 1950. The 1948 season was his most memorable with Homestead as he was a member of the franchise's last championship squad. The team still had players like Sam Bankhead, Luke Easter, and Buck Leonard, and Fields went 13-5 during the season. He was selected to play in the annual East-West All-Star Game for the first time and took part in the August 22 contest at Comiskey Park in Chicago.[16] Fields pitched to his usual standard in front of the 42,099 fans who had gathered to witness Negro baseball's most popular annual event. According to the *Pittsburgh Courier*'s Bill Nunn, "The best form shown by an Eastern pitcher was that of Wilbur [Wilmer] Fields, the Grays' big right hander, who didn't allow a run in the three innings he worked."[17] Fields had done his part—he had allowed one hit, issued one walk, and struck out two batters from the fourth through sixth innings—but the West had prevailed 3-0.[18] Though pitching in the All-Star Game had been an exciting honor, Fields's biggest game of the 1948 season was yet to come in the Negro League World Series.

First, though, the second-half NNL champion Grays had to overcome the first-half champion Baltimore Elite Giants, which they did in convincing—and somewhat bizarre—fashion. After winning the first two games, the Grays turned a 4-4 tie into a 7-4 lead in top of the ninth inning of Game Three on September 17. In the process, the city of Baltimore's 11:15 P.M. curfew passed, and the Elite

Giants—believing that the entire ninth inning would have to be replayed if it went past 11:15—began to stall the game by refusing to get Grays batters out.[19] At first, their tactic appeared to work as Game Three was indeed suspended and, before it was concluded, Game Four—an 11-3 Baltimore win—was played on September 19.

On September 20 the Grays pulled off the oddity of a three-game sweep in spite of a Game Four loss, owing to a decision made by the NNL's president, Rev. John H. Johnson. He applied a league rule that said any inning begun before 11:00 P.M. had to be completed (even if it lasted past the 11:15 P.M. curfew) and "ruled [the Elite Giants' stalling] was unsportsmanlike and therefore grounds for the game to be forfeited to the Grays, 9-0."[20]

Now that the Grays had advanced to the Negro League World Series to face their old adversaries, the Birmingham Black Barons, they encountered a new problem: They were unable to use either of their home fields—Forbes Field or Griffith Stadium—because both venues were occupied by their major-league owners, the Pittsburgh Pirates and Washington Senators. Thus, Game One, a Grays' victory, was played in Kansas City on September 26 before the series shifted to Birmingham.[21]

Fields missed Homestead's Game Two win and Game Three loss in Birmingham as he had driven to Virginia to pick up his family so that he could take them to see his Game Four start in New Orleans on October 3. He drove for 27 hours, taking only a half-hour nap along the way, in order to make it to Game Four on time.[22] Former Negro League pitcher William "Dizzy" Dismukes, covering the game for the *Chicago Defender*, reported that the Grays "hammered everything the four Birmingham Black Barons pitchers dished up ... and slaughtered the Negro American League champions."[23] Fields, however, was masterful for the Grays in the 14-1 romp that gave Homestead a 3-to-1 lead in the series. He recalled, "I was in such bad shape I was shaking. My ball didn't run or move like other people's balls move, but that day I was in such bad shape it was moving—just like a slider."[24] Afterward, Birmingham's Artie Wilson said to Fields, "I didn't know you could pitch like that," to which he replied, "I didn't know either."[25]

Two days later, back in Birmingham, Fields relieved R. T. Walker late in Game Five. The Grays then scored four runs in the 10th inning to win the game, 10-6, and clinched the title over the Black Barons and their budding young star, 17-year-old Willie Mays. Homestead's triumph was the last glorious gasp of the rapidly declining Negro Leagues. Coverage of the series had been sparse, as even the black press focused more on the roles Larry Doby and Satchel Paige were playing for the Cleveland Indians in the major-league World Series. Attendance at the games had also been low. Fields explained, "We agreed to play it down South in AA stadiums instead of our usual major league parks. We only drew about four or five thousand spectators to these ballparks and that was a disaster."[26]

The integration of Organized Baseball had sent the Negro Leagues into decline as their member teams began to lose most of their best players to major- and minor-league baseball. The NNL folded after the 1948 season, meaning that the days of Negro League World Series play were at an end. The Grays joined the Negro American Association in 1949, played as an independent club in 1950, and then disbanded in May 1951.

The demise of the Grays meant that Fields would have to play elsewhere and, eschewing the major leagues, he turned to Latin America and Canada. He had already been playing winter-league ball in Puerto Rico since the 1947-48 season; he found the commonwealth's avid fans and lack of segregation greatly to his liking. After Fields and his wife, Audrey, had survived their first-ever airplane trip to San Juan, he settled right in. He was named Player of the Week twice in 1947-48 and reporters dubbed him "Wilmer Fields the Great."[27]

Fields returned to Puerto Rico for the 1948-49 season, now playing for Mayaguez, and won the first of his MVP awards. He was 10-4 on the mound and batted .332 with 11 home runs and 88 RBIs. He also played in the first Caribbean World Series, in 1949, as Mayaguez represented Puerto Rico in a four-

country field that also included Venezuela, Cuba, and Panama. Cuba's heavily favored Almendares Alacranes (Scorpions) won the inaugural series, which was played in their home country. Chuck Connors, who became famous as TV's *The Rifleman* in the 1950s, was a member of the Cuban team; he batted .409 with five RBIs and five runs scored, and tied for the series lead with four stolen bases. Though Connors had a great series, he may have had an off game when Cuba played against Puerto Rico since Fields observed, "He chose the right profession when he decided on acting."[28]

Fields was back in Mayaguez for the 1949-50 season, at the end of which he played in the second Caribbean World Series; this time the series was

Wilmer Fields was a member of four pennant-winning Homestead Grays squads. Later in life, as president of the Negro League Baseball Players Association, he spearheaded the effort to gain pensions for former Negro League players. (*Courtesy R. D. Retort Enterprises*)

played in Puerto Rico and was won by Panama's Carta Vieja Yankees. Fields' playing days in Puerto Rico came to an abrupt end during the 1950-51 season. The Puerto Rican Nationalist Party had begun a series of violent uprisings on October 30, as a push for Puerto Rico to gain independence from the United States, and the Fields family made its way to San Juan and off the island as quickly as possible. He finished the 1950-51 season with Maracaibo in the Venezuelan League.

After the winter season, Fields became one of the many former Negro League players to head north to Canada. In 1951, he played for the Brantford (Ontario) Red Sox of the Intercounty League, where he won his second career MVP award after compiling a 9-1 record and a .382 batting average, and leading the league in hits, home runs, and RBIs.[29] Fields enjoyed his time in Canada and considered it a second home thanks to the wholehearted acceptance he and his family felt while living there.

In order to earn a living as a professional baseball player, Fields had to play year-round, so he returned to Venezuela for the 1951-52 winter season. He played for Caracas, where one of his teammates was Chicago White Sox shortstop Chico Carrasquel, who was only the third Venezuelan major leaguer; his uncle Alex Carrasquel, who had pitched for the Washington Senators in 1939, had been the first. Fields did not pitch for Caracas, but he won his third MVP award by batting .348 with 8 homers and 45 RBIs. He played in his third and final Caribbean Series for Caracas in 1952, but Cuba's Habana Leones (Lions) won the championship in Panama that year.

In the spring of 1952 Fields returned to Canada under what he considered to be less than favorable circumstances. He still loved the country, but he was not happy that he was forced to play for the Toronto Maple Leafs of the International League. In 1951 he had been contacted by Jack Kent Cooke, Toronto's new owner, who would later gain greater notoriety as the owner of the NFL's Washington Redskins. Cooke had not been able to sign Fields at that time, but he finally made Fields a compelling offer while he was in Caracas in 1952: A $5,000 signing bonus, a major-

league contract, and the assurance that Cooke would pay for Audrey Fields to travel on all road trips. Fields accepted Cooke's offer by way of a telegram, not knowing that such a response constituted a binding contract. At the conclusion of the Venezuelan season, Fields had a change of heart about playing for Cooke, but Cooke would not release him from his contract.

In addition to the fact that he was unhappy at having to play for Toronto, Fields also had an unpleasant racial incident occur while he was with the team for spring training in Florida. Though this was 1952 and baseball was in the midst of integration, tolerance for blacks in the South was still low, and he unintentionally angered a white clubhouse attendant by calling him "Horse" while asking for a chair; according to Fields, "When I was playing in the black leagues, we used to call each other Horse."[30] The attendant never brought a chair; the next time Fields saw him, as he exited the clubhouse, the man was sitting on his pickup truck and holding a shotgun. What happened next made a lasting impression upon Fields, and he often cited this incident as an example of what black players had to endure:

> "I was about 25 or 30 yards away from him. There were some wires I had to go under and some blackbirds were setting on 'em. Man, he blasted away and knocked one of the blackbirds off of there and it fell down in front of me. I just kept walking. ... I never told anybody for a long time 'cause if I told my wife, she'd say, 'Let's go home.'"[31]

Fields did not go home. He fulfilled his obligation to Cooke, but his lone season with the Triple-A Maple Leafs was interrupted for six weeks when he suffered a broken wrist; he finished the 1952 campaign in Toronto with a .291 batting average.

After that, Fields bounced back and forth between Canada and Latin America over the next few seasons. He played the 1952-53 winter season in Venezuela, but he moved to the Dominican Republic in 1953-54. He played three games a week for San Pedro de Macoris for which he received $3,000 per month in salary and expenses, which constituted the highest pay of his baseball career.[32] After that, Fields spent two seasons in Colombia, where he won the sixth and final league MVP award of his career in the 1955-56 season. Fields was well-respected by every owner he played for—with the obvious exception of Cooke—and he was offered the managing job in Colombia after his second season in the country. In an example of the far-reaching effects of discrimination, Fields turned down the job because, as the only black American on the team, he was concerned that "there might have been a letdown from some of the other imports" as he recalled "some of the white imports not appreciating us eating at the same table as their families."[33]

In between his Latin excursions, Fields spent the 1953-55 summer seasons in Canada, though he was out from under his contract with Cooke's Toronto team. He spent 1953 with the Brandon Greys of the Manitoba-Dakota League, where he batted .356. On July 24 he hit a grand slam and totaled six RBIs in leading the Greys to a 13-5 victory over the Winnipeg Royals.[34] In 1954 Fields returned to Brantford, where he pitched his way to a 9-3 record while hitting at a .379 clip. The following season, he played for the Oshawa Merchants and improved his record to 8-0 while raising his batting average to .425.[35] As a true double-threat on the mound and at the plate, he again won the Intercounty League MVP award in both the 1954 and 1955 seasons.

On the heels of his final two successful seasons in Canada, Fields briefly played with the Indianapolis Clowns in 1956. The *Baltimore Afro-American* heralded his signing that May, proclaiming, "Fields, former star of the Homestead Grays, is still in his late twenties, one of the most dangerous and best hitters to come along since the days of Josh Gibson."[36] The *Afro-American* had shaved some years off Fields' age—he was 33 now—and had failed to note that he had been Gibson's teammate at one time. The Clowns were "not a high-quality ballclub" anymore, and it was obvious that little attention was paid to the vestiges of the Negro Leagues.[37] It seemed odd that Fields would join Indianapolis at all since, in the past, many Negro League players had taken umbrage

at the team's clowning, believing that it demeaned all of Negro baseball. His time with the Clowns, now primarily a barnstorming team, was brief and merited only one mention in his autobiography in which he recalled that the team's travel accommodations were so poor that he had slept in a YMCA once.

Fields soon joined a different franchise in Indiana, the Fort Wayne Allen Dairymen of the semipro Michigan-Indiana League. Fort Wayne had participated in numerous Global World Series, organized by the National Baseball Congress (NBC), and had won four consecutive championships from 1947 to 1950; with Fields on the team, they would win one more, in 1956.[38] Fort Wayne first had to win the US National Semipro Tournament in Wichita, Kansas, since the winner would represent the United States at the Global World Series in Milwaukee. Though the Texas Alpine Cowboys, who had the Brooklyn Dodgers' 1955 World Series MVP Johnny Podres on their team, were the favorites, the Allen Dairymen emerged as tournament champions.[39]

In Milwaukee, Fort Wayne made it to the championship game, against Hawaii.[40] In the first inning Fields hit a single to drive in his teammate John Kennedy for a quick 1-0 lead. It turned out to be the only run the Dairymen needed, though they added another in the seventh, as Pete Olsen spun a shutout to clinch the title.[41] Afterward, Fields was named to the tournament's "All-World" team.[42]

In 1957 Fields returned to Fort Wayne and again led the Dairymen to the NBC's tournament final in Wichita, but this time around they lost to the Sinton (Texas) Oilers; though he had played for the runner-up, Fields still was named the tourney MVP. He then played for the Sinton squad in the Global World Series as the United States tried to defend its championship in what was billed as "non-professional baseball's biggest tournament."[43] Fields and Clint Hartung, a former New York Giants pitcher and outfielder from 1947 to 1952, were the stars for the US team. In the first round, against Colombia, Hartung hit a 10th-inning RBI single that Fields followed with a two-run homer to give the US team a 6-3 victory.[44] Though the Oilers had advanced, they

Wilmer Fields turned down contract offers from six major-league franchises to play in Canada and Latin America, where he could earn more money. He was inducted into the Caribbean Baseball Hall of Fame in 2001. (*Courtesy of Jay-Dell Mah/Western Canada Baseball*)

would not secure a third consecutive championship for the United States. In fact, after suffering their first loss, against Japan, they "suffered the ignominy of the mercy rule as their game [against Canada] was shortened to seven innings by the score of 8-0."[45] It was small consolation that Fields, Hartung, and two of their teammates were named to the all-tournament team.

Though Fields had still performed well, his career was nearing its end. He played for St. Joes in the Michigan League in 1957, spent part of 1958 with the Yankton Terrys of South Dakota's Basin League,[46] and finished 1958 with the Mexico City Red Devils. Though he had batted .392 for Mexico City, he was now 36 years old and chose to retire from baseball.

Fields settled his family in his hometown of Manassas; they moved into a ranch house that was only two doors down from the house in which he grew up and where he learned to play baseball.[47] Initially, he worked as a bricklayer's helper; however, he soon found more satisfying work as a counselor for alcoholics for the District of Columbia Department of Corrections. Fields also worked at Lorton Reformatory, a D.C. prison in nearby Virginia, where he organized baseball games between inmates and students from the Prince William County School District.[48]

Family was of greatest importance to Fields throughout his life, and he coached his son Billy's youth baseball teams in the 1970s. In fact, Billy appeared set to follow in his father's footsteps when he unexpectedly received an offer from the Detroit Tigers as he prepared to enter college in 1978. According to Billy Fields, the Tigers offered to pay his college expenses and he would have attended their Florida training camp in the summers until he graduated, whereupon he would have been assigned to the minor leagues. As it turned out, however, the Tigers wanted to convert Billy from a pitcher into a first baseman or outfielder, so he chose to accept a basketball scholarship to Providence College instead.[49]

In time, the Negro Leagues began to be rediscovered by researchers and fans alike, and Fields appeared in various ceremonies at which the Homestead Grays were honored. On September 10, 1988, he was one of 11 Negro League players honored by the Pittsburgh Pirates who commemorated the 40th anniversary of the Grays' last championship prior to that evening's game. Five years later, on August 29, 1993, Fields was in attendance when the Pirates raised banners to honor both the Pittsburgh Crawfords and Homestead Grays; the flags would continue to fly alongside the Pirates' own championship banners at Three Rivers Stadium. In between the two Pittsburgh ceremonies, Fields attended a Negro League players' reunion in August 1991 that was hosted by the National Baseball Hall of Fame in Cooperstown, New York. He enjoyed the occasion immensely, joking that "It's always interesting when you go to a reunion and you can talk with all the guys, and nobody can tell a lie."[50]

Negro American Association of Professional Baseball Clubs

Uniform Player's Contract

724

Parties

The **HOMESTEAD GRAYS BASEBALL CLUB**

herein called the Club, and **WILMER FIELDS**

of _____, herein called the Player.

Recital

The Club is a member of the Negro American Association of Professional Baseball Clubs. As such, and jointly with the other members of the League, it is a party to the Negro American Association Constitution and to agreements and rules. The purpose of these agreements and rules is to insure to the public wholesome and high-class professional baseball by defining the relations between Club and Player, between club and club, and between league and league.

Agreement

In view of the facts above recited the parties agree as follows:

Employment

1. The Club hereby employs the Player to render skilled service as a baseball player in connection with all games of the Club during the year 1949 194 including the Club's training season, the Club's exhibition games, the Club's playing season, any all-star games, (or any other official series in which the Club may participate and in any receipts of which the player may be entitled to share); and the Player convenants that he will perform with diligence and fidelity and service stated and such duties as may be required of him in such employment.

Salary

2. For the service aforesaid the Club will pay the Player a salary of $ 450.00

per month **** to _____, as follows:

for 4½ Months

In semi-monthly installments after the commencement of the playing season on the 1st and

16th day of each month covered by this contract, unless the Player is "abroad" with the Club for the purpose of playing games, in which event the amount then due shall be paid the first weekday after the return "home" of the Club, the terms "home" and "abroad" meaning respectively at and away from the city in which the Club has its baseball field.

If the player is in the service of the Club for part of the month only, he shall receive such proportion of the salary above mentioned, as the number of days of his actual employment bears to the number of days in said month.

Loyalty

3. The Player will faithfully serve the Club or any other Club to which, in conformity with the agreements above recited, this contract may be assigned, and pledges himself to the American Public to conform to high standards of personal conduct of fair play and good sportsmanship.

Service

4. (a) The player agrees that, while under contract or reservation, he will not play baseball (except post-season games as hereinafter stated) otherwise than for the Club, or a Club assignee hereof; that he will not engage in professional boxing or wrestling; and that, except with the written consent of the Club or its assignee, he will not engage in any game or exhibition of football, basketball, hockey or other athletic sport.

Post-season Games

(b) The Player agrees that, while under contract or reservation, he will not play in any post-season baseball games except in conformity with the Negro American Association Rules, or with or against an ineligible player or team.

Assignment

5. (a) In case of assignment of this contract to another Club, the Player shall promptly report to the assignee club; accrued salary shall be payable when he so reports; and each successive assignee shall become liable to the Player for his salary during his term of service with such assignee, and the Club shall not be liable therefor. If the player fails to report as above specified, he shall not be entitled to salary after the date he receives notice of assignment.

Termination

(b) This contract may be terminated at any time by the Club or by any assignee upon five day's written notice to the player.

Regulations

6. The Player accepts as part of this contract the Regulations printed on the third page hereof, and also such reasonable modifications of them and such other reasonable regulations as the Club may announce from time to time.

Wilmer Fields' 1949 contract with the Homestead Grays (of the Negro American Association). His $450 per month salary paled in comparison to the $3,000 per month he received during the 1953-54 Dominican Republic winter season. (*Courtesy of Billy Fields*)

Fields became such a ubiquitous presence at Negro League events that his peers elected him president of the Negro League Baseball Players Association in 1994. Though he had not desired to serve as the organization's leader, after he received 67 percent of the vote, he said, "I couldn't turn my back on those people. ... I'm working every day—almost—on projects, trying to get something started."[51] Fields promoted the legacy of the Negro Leagues wherever he could, primarily through lectures at schools and community events. He also worked tirelessly to try to gain medical and pension benefits for former Negro League players, a venture at which he had some measure of success.[52] A short time prior to Fields' death, Commissioner Bud Selig had announced that Major League Baseball would pay in excess of $1 million in pension money to 27 former Negro Leaguers.[53]

Wilmer Fields died on June 4, 2004, in Manassas.[54] His legacy is secure, yet he is not one of the Negro League legends enshrined in the National Baseball Hall of Fame. When Negro League historian Brent Kelley asked Fields point-blank if he thought he should be in the Hall, Fields answered:

> "If the rest of the black ballplayers are in, I should be. Yes, they were outstanding players in their positions, but I played three positions. ... See, any time you play over ten years in Latin American countries in winter time, somebody gave you respect. You had to do something here in the States in order for them to notice you so that you could play winter baseball."[55]

In light of Fields' superlative career, it seems reasonable to conclude that he has not been enshrined in the Hall of Fame due to arguments that incorporate such logic as 1) Fields' feats are not the equal of Ruth's in scope because he never played in the major leagues, and 2) his accomplishments do not parallel Gibson's because, unlike Gibson, he did not play the vast majority of his Grays' career during the Negro Leagues' heyday. Nevertheless, it is a fact that Fields competed against top black, white, and Latin competition at various times, and he excelled wherever he played.

Though Fields believed he belonged in the Hall of Fame, he was not bitter about his exclusion, saying, "I asked the Lord for something [his baseball career] and He gave it to me. I'm thankful."[56]

In his foreword to Fields' autobiography, Negro League historian John Holway cited a story Fields told him about a home run he hit for Mexico City in 1958, his final season. Fields claimed to have hit a ball out of the Red Devils' stadium farther than anyone before him and ended his tale by telling Holway, "I wish you had seen that one."[57] Fields is a member of other Halls of Fame in places where people did see him. In 2001 he became only the third American player—following Willard Brown and George Brunet—inducted into the Caribbean Baseball Hall of Fame. In 2006 he was posthumously selected as an inaugural member of the Black Hockey and Sports Hall of Fame in Dartmouth, Nova Scotia, Canada. Perhaps someday a plaque depicting Fields will be seen in Cooperstown alongside those of Ruth and Gibson.

Author's Note:

There are a number of conflicting accounts in regard to certain events in Fields's life and his statistical record. One problem in particular is that statistics for Negro League players are notorious for being incomplete or, at other times, inaccurate. Every effort was made to consult as many different sources as possible in order to reconcile the conflicting events and statistical records and to arrive at an accurate representation of both; nevertheless, Fields's career record may well be incomplete. The difficulty in attempting to determine what happened 60 or more years ago is best exemplified by the fact that even Wilmer Fields himself made certain errors as he tried to recall all of his life's experiences while writing his autobiography in 1992; in one instance, he stated that he had played for Brantford in 1955, though game recaps and box scores clearly indicate that he had played for Oshawa. (Both teams were in the Intercounty League.) The author welcomes any and all corrections that may result from further information coming to light through future research. Frankly, it is to be hoped that more information about the Negro Leagues and their players will be rescued from obscurity to provide a fuller portrait of the past.

SOURCES

The author wishes to express his gratitude to Billy Fields for taking the time to discuss his father's life and career and for providing valuable artifacts in the form of scanned photos and documents.

In addition to the sources provided in the Notes, the author also consulted the following:

Baseball-Reference.com (*baseball-reference.com*).

Center for Negro League Baseball Research (*cnlbr.org*).

Treto Cisneros, Pedro, *The Mexican League: Comprehensive Player Statistics, 1937-2001* (Jefferson, North Carolina: McFarland & Co., Inc., 2002).

Clark, Dick, and Larry Lester. *The Negro Leagues Book* (Cleveland: SABR, 1994).

Klima. John. *Willie's Boys: The 1948 Birmingham Black Barons, the Last Negro League World Series, and the Making of a Baseball Legend* (Hoboken, New Jersey: John Wiley & Sons Inc., 2009).

Lanctot, Neil. *Negro League Baseball: The Rise and Ruin of a Black Institution* (Philadelphia: University of Pennsylvania Press, 2004).

Lester, Larry. "Wilmer Leon Fields: The Gentle Giant," *thenation-alpastimemuseum.com/article/wilmer-leon-fields-gentle-giant*, accessed March 7, 2016.

McNary, Kyle. *Black Baseball: A History of African-Americans & the National Game* (New York: Sterling Publishing Company, Inc., 2003).

Negro League Baseball Players Association (*nlbpa.com*).

Negro Leagues Baseball Museum eMuseum, "Wilmer Fields," *coe.k-state.edu/annex/nlbemuseum/history/players/fields.html*, accessed March 7, 2016.

Peterson, Robert. *Only the Ball Was White* (New York: Oxford University Press, 1970).

Pittsburgh Post-Gazette

Snyder, Brad. *Beyond the Shadow of the Senators: The Untold Story of the Homestead Grays and the Integration of Baseball* (Chicago: McGraw Hill, 2003).

Western Canada Baseball (*attheplate.com*).

NOTES

1   Two additional Negro League players bear mention here since they also excelled both on the mound and in the field: Martin Dihigo (1905-71) and Ted "Double Duty" Radcliffe (1902-2005). Dihigo, a Cuban, was primarily a pitcher over the course of his career from 1923 to 1945, but he also played all of the infield and outfield positions and wielded a dangerous bat; he played in the Negro, Cuban, and Mexican Leagues and was inducted posthumously into the National Baseball Hall of Fame in 1977. Radcliffe, whose career spanned the years 1928 to 1950, was a pitcher, catcher, and later also a manager; he earned his nickname, Double Duty, because he often pitched the first game of doubleheaders and caught the second game. Dihigo, Radcliffe, and Wilmer Fields never played in the major leagues, but all three players were dual threats, the likes of which have rarely been seen in any league. Though Dihigo is rightfully enshrined in the Hall of Fame, as of 2016, Radcliffe and Fields have not been inducted.

2   New York Yankees pitcher Whitey Ford broke Ruth's record in 1961 and extended his scoreless streak in World Series play to 33⅔ innings in the 1962 World Series.

3   There was no American League MVP award in 1929, though Ruth would have been a top candidate if there had been: He batted .345 with a league-leading 46 home runs and 154 RBIs.

4   Brent Kelley, *Voices From the Negro Leagues: Conversations With 52 Baseball Standouts* (Jefferson, North Carolina: McFarland & Company, Inc., 1998), 107.

5   Ibid.

6   Wilmer Fields, *My Life in the Negro Leagues: An Autobiography*, reissue with a new introduction (McLean, Virginia: Miniver Press, 2013), 3.

7   The institution is now named Virginia State University.

8   Fields, 7.

9   Since the Grays played half of their home schedule at Griffith Stadium, they also became known as the Washington Homestead Grays.

10   John Holway, "Foreword" in Fields's *My Life in the Negro Leagues*, x.

11   Kelley, 106.

12   Fields, 20. Fields was also known by the nickname Red; however, it is clear from his autobiography that the nickname he was best known by was Chinky. It should also be noted that the name of the tree that produces the nuts Fields described is the chinquapin; the pronunciations *chinkpin* and *chinkypin* are forms of dialect.

13   Camp Plauche was also known by the name Camp Harahan.

14   Former Homestead Grays ace John Wright, one of Fields's teammates, became the second black player signed by the Brooklyn Dodgers in 1946. He had a brief stint with the Montreal Royals, where he was Jackie Robinson's roommate; however, he made only two appearances with the team before he was sent to Three Rivers of the Canadian-American League. He returned to the Grays for the 1947 and 1948 seasons. See James A. Riley, *The Biographical Encyclopedia of the Negro Baseball Leagues* (New York: Carroll & Graf Publishers, Inc., 1994), 883.

15   Wilmer L. (Billy) Fields Jr., telephone interview with the author, June 5, 2016.

16 The second East-West All-Star Game was played on August 24, 1948, at Yankee Stadium. Fields did not play in the second game.

17 Larry Lester, *Black Baseball's National Showcase: The East-West All-Star Game, 1933-1953* (Lincoln: University of Nebraska Press, 2001), 309.

18 Lester, 313.

19 Bob Luke, *The Baltimore Elite Giants* (Baltimore: The Johns Hopkins University Press, 2009), 2.

20 Ibid.

21 Some sources erroneously list Memphis, Tennessee, as the site for Game Two. According to the *Birmingham Age Herald*, Game Two was played at Birmingham's Rickwood Field. (This information was provided by Dr. Richard J. Puerzer, a SABR member and researcher/author, in an email to this author dated May 25, 2016). John Klima, author of *Willie's Boys*, stated that he had discussed game articles with Rev. Bill Greason, the Birmingham Black Barons pitcher who won Game Three, and that he also had confirmed that Game Two took place in Birmingham (per an email from Klima to this author dated December 17, 2015).

22 Kelley, 103.

23 William Dismukes, "Homestead Grays Swamp Black Barons, 14-1," *Chicago Defender*, October 9, 1948.

24 Kelley, 103.

25 Ibid.

26 Christopher D. Fullerton, *Every Other Sunday* (Birmingham: R. Boozer Press, 1999), 90.

27 Fields, 33.

28 Fields, 36.

29 Barry Swanton and Jay-Dell Mah, *Black Baseball Players in Canada: A Biographical Dictionary, 1881-1960* (Jefferson, North Carolina: McFarland and Company, Inc., 2009), 65.

30 Kelley, 106.

31 Ibid. Fields recounted the same episode in his autobiography, albeit with less detail.

32 Fields, 43.

33 Fields, 59.

34 Swanton and Mah, 66. Some sources list Fields as playing for Brantford in 1953, but Swanton's and Mah's research shows that he played for Brandon; perhaps the similarity of the city names has created the common error.

35 Ibid. Fields, after the passage of almost four decades of time, wrote that he had played for Brantford in 1955; however, Swanton and Mah again cite game capsules in their book that show he had been with Oshawa in the Intercounty League.

36 "Clowns, Yanks Set Mark; Wilmer Fields to Return," *Baltimore Afro-American*, May 15, 1956.

37 Riley, 407.

38 The earlier Fort Wayne championship teams were named the Capeharts.

39 Bob Buege, "Global World Series: 1955-57," sabr.org/research/global-world-series-1955-57, accessed March 7, 2016.

40 To eliminate any confusion, it must be remembered that Hawaii did not become a state until August 21, 1959.

41 Ibid.

42 Swanton and Mah, 66.

43 "Hartung Ace in U.S. Win," *Milwaukee Sentinel*, September 14, 1957.

44 Ibid.

45 Buege, "Global World Series: 1955-57."

46 Swanton and Mah, 66. This well-researched book is the only source that lists Fields with the Yankton team.

47 Peter Vilbig, "Cooperstown to Recognize Black Players," *Hendersonville* (North Carolina) *Times News*, August 5, 1991.

48 Adam Bernstein, "Wilmer Fields, Negro Leagues Player and D.C. Counselor, Dies at 81," *Washington Post*, June 21, 2004. It should be noted that Manassas, Fields' hometown, is the county seat of Prince William County, which is why Fields chose youths from that area to play in the baseball games he organized.

49 Billy Fields interview. Billy had been completely unaware that he was being scouted until the evening that the Detroit Tigers scout, whose name he no longer remembers, came to visit the Fields home to make the team's offer. Though he was worried that his father might be disappointed by his decision not to pursue a potential baseball career, Wilmer Sr. was happy that Billy was getting a college education, no matter which sport he chose to play.

50 Vilbig, "Cooperstown to Recognize Black Players."

51 Kelley, 107.

52 Billy Fields noted that his father often received calls from individuals who claimed to have played for one Negro League team or another at one time or another, and Wilmer Sr. then had to undertake the task of attempting to verify the legitimacy of the claim. Fields wanted every player who was entitled to benefits to get them, but he also wanted to be sure that no impostors received undue compensation.

53 Lacy Lusk, "Wilmer Fields: A Legend of Stability," *Manassas Journal Messenger*, June 19, 2004. Lusk also pointed out that, previously, pension money had been given only to Negro Leaguers who had spent at least one day in the major leagues. Of course, this stipulation had been impossible for Negro Leaguers to meet prior to Jackie Robinson's breaking the color barrier in 1947.

54 Fields had been preceded in death by his daughter, Maridel, in 1996. His son Marvin died in 2015. As of the writing of this biography in June 2016, he is still survived by his widow, Audrey, and son, Billy.

55 Kelley, 103-4.

56 Kelley, 108.

57 Holway, "Foreword," xii.

ERVIN FOWLKES

By David Forrester

Ervin Fowlkes was born in Lake Charles, Louisiana, on January 18, 1922, and grew up in the Brownsville section of that humid city on the banks of the Calcasieu River.[1] He was the seventh-born of Richard and Rosa Fowlkes' 10 children. Richard and Rosa were both natives of southeastern Louisiana, although Richard's paternal line traces back to slavery and sharecropping in Nottoway County, Virginia.[2]

Ervin's younger brother, Samuel, left a larger mark in baseball history. Sam is thought to be the first black player to break the Louisiana baseball color line when he pitched for the Lake Charles Lakers in 1952. Both Ervin and Sam played for prominent Negro League teams in the years after World War II.

Ervin enlisted in the US Army in December 1942 and served through the end of 1945, attaining the rank of corporal. That following season he appeared with his brother on the roster for the 1946 Boston Blues of Branch Rickey's ephemeral United States League.[3] Sam was a pitcher and Ervin was a shortstop. The team played most of its games in the West and in New York, principally at Brooklyn's Ebbets Field. In fact, former Blues pitcher Robert Scott said that he didn't remember ever playing in Boston.[4] The Blues disbanded, along with the rest of the short-lived league, before the season was over.

In 1947 Ervin played shortstop and sometimes second base with the barnstorming Detroit Senators for the majority of the season. He appears to have joined the team only after it was involved in a bus crash on May 24 in which six of the team's players were injured.[5] The *Cincinnati Enquirer* provided a more detailed account of the crash in its June 18, 1947, edition:

"[…] a bus occupied by the Detroit Senators, Negro baseball team, crashed into a garage. … [Walter] Burch, who was driving the bus, en route to Cincinnati for a series of games, turned into the opposite side of the road in rounding the "Big Bend" on the Dixie Highway when the brakes on the bus failed, police said. Several of the players were injured."[6]

The *Enquirer* made no mention of the seriousness of the injuries. However, it did report that Edward and Rosella Kroiss, the owners of the property into which the bus had crashed, had filed a $500 lawsuit against Senators owner Abe Saperstein, Burch, and the Dependable Motors Company. Prior to the crash, there is no record of Fowlkes playing for the Senators; his name appears for the first time in an article and box score from a May 29 game against the Havana Las Palomas at Cincinnati's Fans Field; thus, it is possible that he was signed to replace one of the players who was injured in the bus crash.[7]

It is unclear where Sam spent 1947, but he pitched for the Kansas City Monarchs and the Chicago American Giants in 1948. Though Sam became the better-known player of the two Fowlkes brothers, it was Ervin who played on the team that made it to the last Negro League World Series as a member of the 1948 Homestead Grays. The 5-foot-7, 170-pound Fowlkes was a part-time shortstop for that championship squad. He has been described as "a good fielder but light hitter who usually batted in the eighth spot in the lineup."[8] His role was limited, and available statistics—which likely are incomplete—list him as having only 12 at-bats that season.[9]

Sam went on to play for several more seasons with the Monarchs; Western Canadian teams from Delisle and Saskatoon; the Lake Charles Lakers; and the Roswell and Clovis, New Mexico, teams. However, no accounts of Ervin playing baseball after 1948 have appeared. He went on to live in Kansas City, Missouri, where he married Ardella Cook in December 1957. Ervin and Ardella remained in Kansas City, raising a son and daughter while he worked as a branch manager for the S.A. Maxwell wall-covering company. Ervin was actively involved with his Baptist church and local Masonic club until his death on December 3, 1994, at age 72. He was buried at Leavenworth National Cemetery.

NOTES

1   Some sources, including baseball-reference.com, list Fowlkes with a birth year of 1924; however, his official military record lists his year of birth as 1922. As to the spelling of Fowlkes' name, he can be found listed most frequently with his first name spelled Erwin, though he is sometimes also listed as Irwin. His last name has been given alternately as Foulkes or Folkes. Census records show that his given birth name was Ervin Fowlkes.

2   "The Louisiana Jackie, Part 1" from Home Plate Don't Move blog—homeplatedontmove.wordpress.com/2014/04/15/the-louisiana-jackie-part-1/, confirmed via US Census records.

3   Center for Negro League Baseball Research, cnlbr.org/Portals/0/Rosters/Rosters%20-%20United%20States%20League%20(1945-1946).pdf.

4   Chris Lamb, "Did Branch Rickey Sign Jackie Robinson to Right a 40-Year Wrong?," *Black Ball: A Negro Leagues Journal*, Vol. 6: 17.

5   "Twin Bill at Reds' Park Today. Detroit Outfit to Play Despite Accident—Las Palomas, Crescents Also Billed," *Cincinnati Enquirer*, May 25, 1947: 36.

6   "Chicagoans Named in Bus Crash Suit," *Cincinnati Enquirer*, June 18, 1947: 18. Abe Saperstein, perhaps best known as the owner of the Harlem Globetrotters basketball team, was also a former co-owner of the Birmingham Black Barons. Winfield S. Welch, the Senators' manager in 1947, had been the Black Barons' manager and had scouted much of the Birmingham squad's talent while Saperstein co-owned the team. There is some irony in the fact that Fowlkes ended up playing for the Homestead Grays in 1948, since the Grays defeated the Black Barons—Saperstein's and Welch's former team—in that final Negro League World Series.

7   "Detroit Nine Beats Havana Crew, 8-3," *Decatur* (Illinois) *Daily Review*, May 30, 1947: 15. In what appears to have been an ongoing problem for Fowlkes, his name is misspelled as "Irvin Fowlics" in this news article.

8   James A. Riley, *The Biographical Encyclopedia of the Negro Baseball Leagues* (New York: Carroll & Graf Publishers, Inc., 1994), 295.

9   baseball-reference.com/register/player.cgi?id=fowlkeoooerw.

CHARLES GARY

By Chris Rainey

When longtime third baseman and fan favorite Howard Easterling left the Homestead (Washington) Grays after the 1947 season, the team signed a promising young player named Bob Boston to replace him. Boston had played in East Liverpool, Ohio, in 1947 and had a reputation as a slugger. The Grays went to spring training on March 25, 1948, in Daytona Beach; exhibition games started a few days later and Boston saw plenty of playing time at third base. That all changed after the Grays played the Florida Black Cats. Charles Gary, the Cats' third baseman, made quite an impression, and the Grays signed him in mid-April just in time for a swing through Florida, Baton Rouge, and New Orleans.[1]

Gary was a Navy veteran who had settled in Daytona Beach after his service. One of seven children, he was born on June 1, 1920, in Selma, Alabama, to George Murray and Cora Gary. The family moved to Mobile, where Gary attended high school before working in retail. During World War II he enlisted in the Navy. His rank was seaman first class and he spent time in the Philippines. What military action he saw is uncertain, but he did get the occasional chance to play baseball, often in integrated games.

Gary was mustered out at the Jacksonville Naval Base in Florida. After his service he worked in Daytona. In January 1947 the Florida State Negro League, which had begun play in 1945, was incorporated, and Gary played shortstop for the Daytona (aka Florida) Black Cats. The *Pittsburgh Courier* reported that he led the league in hitting in 1947 with a .408 average.

Gary stood 6 feet tall and weighed 180 pounds.[2] A right-handed thrower, he began his career as a switch-hitter.[3] The Grays opened league play on May 2 with Red Fields at third base, but after that Gary saw the majority of playing time at the hot corner.

Boston was relegated to pinch-hitting and outfield appearances.

The Grays featured future Hall of Famer Buck Leonard, Luke Easter, and Bob Thurman. With talent like that in the lineup, Gary found himself batting seventh or eighth. The Grays led the Negro National League pennant race in mid-June, but the Baltimore Elite Giants surged to take the first-half pennant. In the second half the Grays rallied and earned a spot in the playoffs. Gary contributed a .279 batting average to help the Grays win what proved to be their final pennant.[4]

Gary's finest performance in 1948 came in an August 18 exhibition game in Benton Harbor,

Charles Gary, who at one time was stationed in the Philippines during World War II, strikes a pose in his Navy uniform. In 1948, he joined the Homestead Grays. (*Courtesy of Lyndon Gary*)

Navy veteran Charles Gary (top row, third from right) also played baseball during his time in the service before joining the Homestead Grays in 1948. (*Courtesy of Lyndon Gary*)

Michigan. Before the game the *Benton Harbor News-Palladium* had labeled him the Grays' "sensational new rookie third baseman."[5] Gary responded with a 3-for-5 day and scored twice in a 16-7 win over the Benton Harbor Buds, though he tarnished the performance slightly by committing two errors. In the playoffs the Grays swept the Elite Giants before taking on Birmingham in what became the final Negro League World Series. Statistics for Gary in the playoff games have been lost, but the Grays defeated Birmingham in five games to clinch the title against the Black Barons and their 17-year-old rookie sensation Willie Mays.[6]

The Negro National League folded after the 1948 season, but the Grays played ball for two more seasons. Gary stayed with the team in 1949 and 1950. Vic Harris left the team and Sam Bankhead assumed the manager's role; with the managerial change, Gary

frequently found himself batting second in the order. Josh Gibson Jr. joined the Grays for their last two seasons. Because the young Gibson was a natural infielder, Gary would occasionally play outfield while Gibson played third. Box scores of games are sparse, making collection of meaningful statistics impossible.

George Murray, who had worked as a laborer, died in 1949. Gary's mother, Cora, moved to Daytona Beach after George's death. Cora had been a farm laborer in her 20s, but she no longer worked outside the home. Charles provided for her after the move to Florida.

The Grays called it quits in the spring of 1951. Gary returned to Daytona Beach after three seasons of never-ending bus rides, dwindling crowds, and dwindling paychecks. He met a recent divorcee, Alfreda Moore, in 1952 and fell in love; however, Gary's first love was baseball, and he was not ready to end his career quite yet. He returned to the Florida State Negro League. In 1953 the Regina Caps of the Saskatchewan League trained in Florida. The Caps, an all-black team, were managed by former Grays player Jim Williams. The exact circumstances of Gary's joining the Caps are unknown, but when Regina headed north on a barnstorming tour with the House of David, Gary was playing outfield. Regina also added Gary's friend and teammate Hiram Marshall, who played third base, outfield, and catcher.

The Saskatchewan League, which was not part of Organized Baseball, had four teams. The Saskatoon franchise had a working agreement with the Havana Sugar Kings and the bulk of the lineup was Cubans who had quite a shock when their opener was snowed out.[7] The Moose Jaw Maples were made up of recruits from the Oakland-San Francisco area and semipros from the United States and Canada. Some of the Californians left because of the weather, while others did not have the talent to compete. Departed players were replaced with castoffs from other teams. North Battleford had a roster made up of a few US-born players, notably slugger Bob Herron, and quite a few Canadians.

In another oddity, the league played a crossover schedule with the Mandak (Manitoba and North Dakota) League. This blended schedule was far from perfect. On June 12 the Caps played the Carman Cardinals. It was the Caps' sixth game in four days and they were forced to use a catcher and an infielder as their pitchers on the way to a 9-6 loss. Gary had three hits for the Caps, and Lyman Bostock Sr. paced the Cardinals attack.[8]

Gary and Marshall provided powerful offense for the Caps. Gary gave up being a switch-hitter and batted left-handed, and he emerged as one of the best hitters in the league. He collected four hits and a walk in the league opener at Regina on May 15, won the May 23 game with a triple, and scampered around the bases for an inside-the-park homer on June 6. He topped all those efforts with a 5-for-5 day on July 7 in which he drove in four runs and scored two as Regina routed Saskatoon, 24-7; he continued to torment Saskatoon with two hits and two RBIs on July

31 and three hits in a 6-4 Regina win on August 15.[9] He batted .322 for the season, placing in the league's top 10, and scored 35 runs. Marshall took the league batting title with a .353 mark. The Caps finished third and took on Saskatoon in the playoffs, which they lost four games to two.

Gary and Alfreda welcomed their first child in 1953, daughter Vernetta. They also were raising Alfreda's son, Lewis, from her first marriage. Gary was a fun-loving and caring person and wanted very much to marry Alfreda, but she had concerns about his baseball travel and still harbored bitter memories of her first marriage. The couple welcomed Charles Jr. in 1955 and Kathy in 1958. Finally, both grandmothers stepped in and pushed for a formal wedding that took place in April 1959. In the 1960s they welcomed sons Alton and Lyndon to the family. Alfreda had been quite an athlete in her youth and the children inherited their parents' athletic abilities.

Gary worked as a property manager and caretaker in vacation-oriented Daytona Beach. He and his wife were longtime members of the Mount Zion A.M.E. Church. He played baseball locally until he broke an arm in the early 1960s. When Gary died on June 4, 2011, he left behind Alfreda and five children (Charles Jr. had passed away) plus seven grandchildren and four great-grandchildren. His obituary mentioned how pleased he was to have lived to see an African-American president; the America of his old age was certainly different than the one of the Jim Crow South into which he had been born.[10] He was interred in Jacksonville National Cemetery.

SOURCES

I am indebted to Gary's son, Lyndon (Spanky), and daughter, Kathy, for a telephone interview on May 31, 2016. A second interview was conducted on August 15 with Gary's oldest daughter, Vernetta. A March 22, 1920, birth date is often associated with Charles (most notably by Social Security), but the children cited military records that list the June 1 date. The family recognizes June 1 as his birthday.

NOTES

1   "Pick Up Pitcher, Shortstop in Florida," *Pittsburgh Courier*, April 17, 1948: 13.

2   Conflicting heights and weights can be found for Charles Gary. James Riley's *Biographical Encyclopedia of the Negro Baseball Leagues* lists Gary as standing 5-feet-9-inches tall and weighing 170 pounds; however, the June 27, 1949, edition of the *Altoona Tribune* contains an article that lists Charles Gary at 6 feet and 180 pounds and his teammate Robert Richardson at 5-feet-9-inches and 170 pounds. It is entirely possible that Riley inadvertently attributed Richardson's height and weight to Gary. Additionally, Lyndon Gary has verified that his father stood 6 feet tall and has estimated that he weighed 180 pounds.

3   "Negro Teams List Starters for Night Tilt," *Altoona Tribune*, June 27, 1949: 9.

4   James A. Riley, *The Biographical Encyclopedia of the Negro Baseball Leagues* (New York: Carroll & Graf, 1994), 308.

5   *The News-Palladium* (Benton Harbor, Michigan), August 17, 1948: 8.

6   By 1948 box scores for Negro League games had been largely replaced by line scores, even in the African-American newspapers of the day. Box scores for each of the Grays-Black Barons World Series games are unavailable.

7   attheplate.com. This is a marvelous website for information on baseball in Western Canada.

8   Ibid.

9   Barry Swanton and Jay-Dell Mah, *Black Baseball Players in Canada: A Biographical Dictionary, 1881-1960* (Jefferson, North Carolina: McFarland and Company, Inc., 2009), 69.

10 *Daytona Beach News-vJournal* online obituary.

ROBERT GASTON

by Chris Rainey

With the clarity of hindsight it seems appropriate that an action photograph of Robert Gaston by noted African-American photographer Charles "Teenie" Harris shows what looks like Gaston launching a home run. As the backup to Josh Gibson and teammate of Buck Leonard, Gaston certainly saw his share of home runs. Gibson abandoned the Homestead Grays in 1940 and 1941, leaving Gaston as the main catcher. In that role, Gaston slammed two homers and drove in three runs in the seventh inning against the Baltimore Elite Giants on May 10, 1941. Ray Brown and Buck Leonard also homered in the 10-run rally that gave the Grays a 13-10 win.

Robert R. Gaston was born on March 19, 1910, to John and Corine Gaston in Chattanooga, Tennessee.[1] His father worked as a driver at that time, but the family joined the Northern migration and moved to the Homestead area of Pittsburgh, where John found work in a steel mill. The couple divorced in the late 1920s. Gaston's mother moved in with her sister and brother-in-law, Carrie and Charles Frye, and worked as the cook for a family. Gaston dropped out of high school after two years and by 1930 was working as a laborer and living in a rooming house in Homestead.

Gaston showed a talent for baseball and, since he was a local resident, it was natural that the Grays would take a look. Gaston's earliest box score appears in April 1932, when he saw action against the Detroit Wolves.[2] In the game he split time with Spoony Palm behind the plate. No Negro National League existed in 1932, and the Grays traveled the country playing all comers. Bill Perkins, Mack Eggleston, and Tom Young saw the bulk of the catching action, especially against top talent. A youngster like Gaston was used sparingly while he learned the game.

In 1933 Homestead joined the revamped Negro National League but dropped out after 20 games. Ted "Double Duty" Radcliffe was the team's number-one receiver. Gaston was given plenty of playing time in exhibitions but had only a few appearances in league games. His notable league appearance occurred on May 31 when he played left field in a 13-1 loss to the Pittsburgh Crawfords and Satchel Paige. His appearances read like a road map of Western Pennsylvania and Eastern Ohio with stops in McKeesport, Corapolis, Kittaning, Greensburg, and Warren, to name a few. In 1934 the Grays continued as an independent franchise with Fred "Tex" Burnett as the top catcher. Indications are that Gaston was Grays property, but no box scores were located that show him in action.[3]

The 1935 Grays rejoined the NNL and went to Wilson, South Carolina, for spring training. They had Burnett and Gaston under contract, but Burnett joined the Brooklyn Eagles and Tommy Dukes came in to share catching duties. Gaston started hot in the exhibition season with a home run against the Newark Dodgers. He followed that up with a double and triple on April 20 in Dayton, Ohio, against the Ducks of the Middle Atlantic League. When the season began he and Dukes frequently split innings in the games with one of them starting and the other entering the game as a replacement in the fourth or fifth inning; this arrangement gave Gaston experience. In important match-ups, Dukes played the whole game. An interesting sidelight to the season was that fans were invited to vote for their favorite players in advance of the All-Star game with results published in African-American newspapers like the *Pittsburgh Courier*. Gaston was enough of a fan favorite that he garnered 1,100 votes, more than some starters. (Dukes had more than 6,000 votes.)

Because Gaston saw limited playing time, it was difficult for him to gain the savvy necessary to be a top-flight catcher. That inexperience, coupled with an arm injury that limited his throwing, led the Grays to drop him after the season. After giving the arm time to heal, he joined the Edgar Thomson baseball team in Braddock, Pennsylvania, in 1937. That squad was a high-powered semipro team that enabled Gaston to refine his catching skills, strengthen his arm, and improve his accuracy on throws. He also increased his power statistics at bat.[4] In his absence, the Grays added Josh Gibson as their catcher.

Gaston rejoined the Grays in 1939. At 6-feet-1 and 185 pounds, he was referred to by one paper as porky. Fortunately that did not become his nickname; it had always been Rab Roy. In fact, in an April 1932 article, he is called by his nickname and nothing more.[5] Gathering data on Negro League games is an ongoing process. At the time of this writing Baseball-Reference credits Gaston with only two games in 1939. Seamheads.com lists him with four games and 11 plate appearances. However, a search of Pittsburgh newspapers found that he saw action in both ends of doubleheaders on June 10, 11, and 16, and August 10 and 12 against league opponents. In some cases Gibson was in left field; other times he was not in the lineup.[6] Besides Gibson, Gaston split the catching duties with Henry Turner and others. According to *Courier* writer Robert Hughey, Gaston had a batting average over .300 and "cut down many a run … with his accurate heaves."[7]

Josh Gibson chose to go to the Mexican League for a reported $800 a month in 1940-41. By contrast, Gaston listed his wages for 1939 at $800 in the 1940 census. Gaston took over as the Grays' number-one catcher. He handled the pitching staff of Ray Brown, Wilmer Fields, Edsall Walker, and Tom Roberts expertly. He hit .218 with an on-base percentage of .331.[8] The Grays finished in first place with a 28-13 record.[9] Elijah Miller, a Grays batboy, suggested that Gaston had become a superior defensive catcher to Gibson though nowhere close as a hitter.[10] Teammates Howard Easterling and Buck Leonard started in the 1940 East-West game played at Comiskey Park. Owner Cum Posey somehow arranged for eight other Grays, including Gaston, to be in the dugout. There were only five substitutions made by the East squad; of the extra Grays only Ray Brown saw action.[11]

In 1941 manager Vic Harris was concerned that Gaston was "a good prospect, but needs more experience. If we can find an experienced catcher everything will be alright."[12] No veteran was located and Gaston held the number-one spot with Ameal Brooks and Spoony Palm providing backup. Opening the year with his power display, he went on to have 17 runs batted in and 4 homers to go with his .272 average. Most of his career he hit in the eighth spot, but on occasion in 1941 he moved up to seventh.

The Grays were easy winners of the first half in 1941, but played only .500 the second half. Some of the blame for the dropoff landed on outfielder David Whatley, shortstop Chester Williams, and Gaston "for failing to keep in shape during the season."[13] The Grays welcomed back Gibson and Sam Bankhead in 1942. They took the NNL pennant, but fell victim to Satchel Paige and the Kansas City Monarchs in the Negro World Series.

In 1943 the Grays again reached the World Series. Gaston's sole appearance came in Game Three. Gibson had the day off, and Gaston opened the scoring with a single to plate Sam Bankhead; he then scored on an outfield error. The Grays eventually won 4-3 in extra innings over Birmingham and went on to claim the championship.

Some of the Grays, like Ray Brown and Vic Harris, took jobs in the defense industry during the war years. Gaston and Whatley enlisted in the Army after the 1943 season. Their service was short-lived because "the effects of old injuries received in sports contests made it necessary for the Army to send them home."[14]

Gaston saw less and less action in 1944 and 1945. In 1946 Ted Radcliffe and Eudie Napier replaced Gibson, leaving no room for Gaston. He played a few games with the Brooklyn Brown Dodgers before returning to the Grays in 1947. He saw limited action, but on August 22 against the New York Cubans he did record the only career stolen base currently on his record. The 1948 season opened with an exhibition in Spartanburg, South Carolina. Gaston caught and Napier played right field. During the season Gaston played sparingly, usually in the second game of doubleheaders. He remained with the Grays until 1949, when his playing days ended.

As with so many of the Negro League players, Gaston disappeared from sight after his playing days, little is known except that he stayed in the Homestead neighborhood. He is listed in the 1940 census as married, but was living in a rooming house without his spouse. Further information about his family life was unavailable. Unlike some of his peers, Gaston never went to Mexico or the Caribbean in the winters to play ball; instead, he would find work as a laborer. No doubt he found work in the mills and shops around Homestead.

There is a contradiction in what Robert Gaston the man was like. Somewhere a story started that he might have killed a man. When the Negro Leagues became a topic of numerous books in the 1980s and 1990s, this story found its way into print. James Riley went so far as to report that Gaston was considered "evil."[15] This depiction is in sharp contrast to contemporary newspaperman Robert Hughey's description of Gaston as "shy and unassuming."[16]

Former Grays batboy Elijah "Lucky" Miller considered Gaston his best friend on the team and would sit with him during the games. *Pittsburgh Post-Gazette* writer Kevin Kirkland did interviews with Miller from 2004 to 2010 and wrote a children's book, *Lucky Bats*, based upon Miller's memories. From his discussions with Miller, Kirkland had difficulty believing the negative depiction of Gaston. He suggested that Miller, a longtime usher at the Second Baptist Church, would not have associated with Gaston had he been truly evil.[17] At the age of 93 years, Miller showed his affection for Gaston by visiting him shortly before the player's death.

After years in obscurity, Gaston was one of six players invited in 1993 to attend a celebration in Pittsburgh that placed banners honoring the Grays and Crawfords. The following year he took part in Pittsburgh's bicentennial celebration. At an event called Founder's Fest, inner-city high-school baseball players re-created a game between the Crawfords and the Grays. Gaston made an appearance to help bring the past alive.

Gaston was residing in a Pittsburgh nursing home when he died on February 11, 2000. He is buried in Greenwood Cemetery, northeast of downtown Pittsburgh across the Allegheny River.

SOURCES

In addition to the sources cited in the Notes, the author also consulted:

Ancestry.com.

The Afro-American (Baltimore).

Altoona (Pennsylvania) *Tribune*.

Canton (Ohio) *Repository*.

Chicago Defender.

NOTES

1   There is some speculation that Gaston was born in 1913, not 1910.

2   *Pittsburgh Courier*, April 23, 1932: 16.

3   *Pittsburgh Courier*, March 16, 1935: 14. Gaston was listed as a team member, i.e., holdover from 1934.

4   Robert Hughey, "Grays Pin Catching Hopes on Bob Gaston," *Pittsburgh Courier*, April 19, 1941: 17.

5   *Pittsburgh Courier*, April 16, 1932: 15.

6   Box scores and line scores came from *Pittsburgh Press and Pittsburgh Courier*. Seamheads.com appears to have stats from about 60 percent of the 54-game schedule.

7   Hughey.

8   seamheads.com, accessed April 24, 2016.

9   Dick Clark and Larry Lester eds., *The Negro Leagues Book* (Cleveland: SABR, 1994), 161.

10 *Pittsburgh Post-Gazette*, August 11, 2006: 29.

11 *Pittsburgh Press*, August 19, 1940: 19.

12 *Pittsburgh Courier*, April 5, 1941: 17.

13 *Pittsburgh Courier*, March 21, 1942: 16.

14 *Pittsburgh Courier*, February 5, 1944: 16.

15 James A. Riley, *The Biographical Encyclopedia of the Negro Leagues* (New York: Carroll & Graf Publishers, 1994), 309.

16 Hughey.

17 Based upon email exchanges and a telephone interview on March 15, 2016, with Kevin Kirkland.

CECIL KAISER

By Brian Baughan

Cecil Kaiser earned the respect of his Negro League peers during a career that included seasons with the Homestead Grays and Pittsburgh Crawfords, all-star appearances, a stint with a well-known barnstorming team, and one especially strong Winter League performance. The southpaw had two different nicknames that spoke of his prowess on the mound: "Minute Man," a reference to the short length of time it took Kaiser to strike a batter out, and "Aspirin Tablet Man," for his deceptive pitches that made the ball look like an aspirin pill.

During Kaiser's heyday, in the late 1940s and early 1950s, he was not quite a household name, but his stature grew in succeeding years. His longevity certainly played a role: He lived to the ripe age of 94 and, during those final decades of his life, he attained the status of "Living Legend," enjoying visibility at various Negro League commemorative events. Tributes came not just from the few players still alive to share personal reflections, but also from students of the game who were eager to publicly appreciate the veterans of the Negro Leagues' twilight era. When Kaiser died in 2011, many obituaries dubbed him "the oldest living Negro leaguer" at the moment of his passing, a claim that was not easy to corroborate but that nonetheless conveyed the significance of his place in baseball history.[1]

Kaiser enjoyed a career of remarkable breadth. His talent and passion for the game won him stints with more than two dozen teams in eight countries in North and Central America. Even after retiring from organized ball in 1952, he managed to keep returning to the mound, first by playing in industrial leagues and later for old-timer teams.[2]

Cecil Kaiser was born on June 27, 1916, in New York City.[3] He was denied a relationship with his parents: His mother, a washwoman, died in childbirth, and he never knew his father.[4] He was raised instead by his grandmother Cornelia and grandfather Henry "Bud" Kaiser, a railroad worker. At some point, Bud's job required the family to resettle in Wythefield, Virginia, but before he left New York, Cecil received a serious dose of inspiration by watching Babe Ruth and Lou Gehrig play baseball at Yankee Stadium.[5]

Kaiser, a left-handed hitter, was not a pitcher originally. During the early 1930s he first played in the outfield, getting chances to compete in various sandlot leagues. His first stop was Welch, West Virginia, playing for the Welch's All-Stars, and for the next three years he remained in the state while playing on the Bishop Street Liners, the Gary Grays, and the Kimball West Sox.[6] By 1938 Kaiser had graduated to a higher level of play, having moved to Pontiac, Michigan, where he landed a spot with the Pontiac Big Six, a world-champion softball team. That same year he started playing with the Pittsburgh Crawfords. Manager Candy Jim Taylor was beset by an injury-plagued rotation and figured he might as well give Kaiser a shot as a starting pitcher. Comfortable in the outfield, the young player took the ball with trepidation but then proceeded to throw a complete-game victory. That fateful game sealed his place on the mound for good.[7]

Though Kaiser had now been converted into a pitcher, that stellar start with the Crawfords curiously did not lead to a permanent spot in Pittsburgh's starting rotation. From 1939 to 1945 he played on multiple Detroit-based teams, including the Detroit Stars and the Motor City Giants. During this time, he also married Margaret Bernice Cole. Little information is available about the marriage save for a 1940 census record revealing that the husband and wife lived with her family in Pontiac, Michigan. Their daughter, Beatrice Mae, was born in December 1940, and two years later their son, Robert Cecil, entered the world. Michigan records of a divorce between Kaiser and Cole indicate that the marriage lasted 10 years.

The year 1942 marked Kaiser's first trip south to play winter-league ball in Latin America. It became an annual ritual for the pitcher. After that first season in Tampico, Mexico, he played four consecutive seasons in Cuba. Meanwhile, during this stretch, he compiled a few highlight performances for various teams in the United States. Although career summaries of Kaiser do not list him as ever having played for the Toledo Cubs, a July 1943 story in the *Cincinnati Enquirer* identified him as one of the team's star players. By that point in the season he had "a no-hitter and several one- and two-hit performances" already under his belt.[8] The following season he struck out 17 batters in his first start of the season for the Motor City Giants.[9]

That successful start and others set the stage for Kaiser's first call-up to the Negro National League with the Homestead Grays, where he joined a squad that featured some of the league's greats, including Sam Bankhead, Cool Papa Bell, and Josh Gibson, though he did not get to enjoy their company for long. By year's end he was back with the Crawfords, which meant he missed the opportunity to play in that year's Negro League World Series between the Grays and the Birmingham Black Barons. Nonetheless, his memories of his time with the Crawfords, and particularly of owner Gus Greenlee, were positive. "The best guy in major-league baseball was Gus Greenlee," he recalled years later. "You didn't have to want for nothing. If you needed something, call him, and he would be there."[10]

By this point Kaiser, having reached the highest level available at the time to black ballplayers, began to "play the circle," as he called it, finding work whenever and wherever he could. "As soon as the scene was over [in the summer], I'd play in South America," he said. The Winter Leagues offered significant incentives, starting with compensation. While Kaiser made a pittance of $700 per month as a member of the Homestead Grays, he recalled making as much as $3,000 per week plus expenses in Latin America. Of course, the fact that the Latin American leagues were not segregated was another clear advantage to him and other Negro Leaguers. "It was better play-

ing in the Latin countries. Wasn't no segregation," he remembered. "Over here, you could run into a lot of trouble."[11]

In 1947 Kaiser returned to the Homestead Grays. One of his teammates was first baseman Luke Easter, on whom Kaiser must have made a strong impression, because he later would be selected for the barnstorming Luke Easter's All Stars. In 1948 Kaiser started but did not finish the season with the

Cecil Kaiser began 1948 with the Homestead Grays but moved to the Detroit Wolves prior to the World Series. In 2008, his hometown Detroit Tigers selected him in MLB's honorary Negro League player draft. (*National Baseball Hall of Fame, Cooperstown, New York*)

One of Cecil Kaiser's nicknames was "Aspirin Tablet Man," because one of his pitches looked as small an aspirin pill by the time it reached the plate. (*Noir-Tech Research, Inc.*)

Grays, instead moving to the Detroit Wolves. Once again he missed a chance to play in the World Series at season's end, and this time grab a title to boot. It also meant missing the final World Series the Negro League ever held.

Although the season concluded with that particular disappointment, the following year Kaiser was rewarded for his perseverance. First, he scored an invitation to play for the South team in the 11th Annual North-South All-Star Game, held in New Orleans.[12] There, a run-in with the law before the game nearly kept Kaiser from playing, as he revealed in an interview nearly 60 years later. En route to his hotel, a taxi driver had tried to overcharge him to the tune of $60. Kaiser flatly refused to pay the fee, only offering the cabbie a dollar before proceeding to his hotel.

Soon after, he was taken to jail, as the arresting officers were unsympathetic to his account of the cab ride. Kaiser used the phone call permitted him to reach out to Allen Page, the "promoter extraordinaire" behind the North-South game.[13] "Mr. Page, I won't be able to play tomorrow because I'm in jail," the pitcher lamented. It was a strategic play on Kaiser's part: He knew that Page had a vested interest in having all his players available and that he was a known commodity with significant pull. The policemen immediately sensed the trouble they could be in if they proceeded. "No, you don't have to do that," they told Kaiser, promptly ending the phone call. "Take this guy back uptown," the commanding officer ordered.[14]

After the North-South game, Kaiser concluded his "all-star" year that fall by joining his Grays teammate, Luke Easter, and other Negro League elites for a barnstorming tour. Luke Easter's All Stars played all over the country, with several games scheduled against Bob Feller's All Stars, including one at Wrigley Field.[15]

For Kaiser the tour represented the chance for him and his teammates to prove they could hold their own against the white players. "Our best teams could play with anyone, anytime, anyplace, and you know what? The white players knew it. They respected us," he said. He valued that respect during the tour, even as he and other black players suffered daily discrimination, including having to wait outside a restaurant that refused them entry while the white players dined inside. "The white guys didn't like it," Kaiser recalled. "They didn't think it was fair, but the higher-ups said it had to be that way. We just lived with it. We knew up front what was happening."[16]

When winter came, Kaiser was playing in Latin America once again. The 1949-50 season was the apex of the southpaw's career. Signed with the Caguas/Guayama Criollos in Puerto Rico, he ended the season with an ERA of 1.68, the best among the league's pitchers.[17] He also compiled a 13-2 record, and it was with that 13th win that the Criollos clinched the pennant.[18] In the final tie-breaking game of the Caribbean World Series, the Criollos lost to Carta Vieja from Panama.[19]

It was convenient that Kaiser was excelling in the Winter Leagues because back in the States the decline of the Negro Leagues spelled job insecurity.

He was enrolled in a draft that was set up after the dismantling of the National Negro League, with the remaining teams given a shot at the players still eligible to play. The Indianapolis Clowns drew Kaiser's name, but he declined their offer to play, instead deciding to return to the Winter Leagues.[20] In 1951 he added Canada to the circuits he covered as a professional player by playing for the Farnham Pirates of the Quebec Provincial League. He rounded out the pitching rotation but also occasionally filled in as an outfielder, thus picking up where he had started his career. The following year he played in the much warmer environs of Tampa in the Florida International League. It was there that he officially ended his US professional career.[21]

After Kaiser moved back to Detroit, the Industrial League beckoned. Starting in 1953, he found work at the Ford Motor Company and a roster spot on its baseball team, the Ford All Stars. At the time this was a common career move for ex-Negro Leaguers, especially the older players, like Kaiser, who were still in demand. "If you were a ballplayer, all you had to do was carry a wrench in your back pocket, walk around the plant a few hours a day and play games a few times a week," he remembered to the *Detroit Free Press*.[22] He stayed with the Ford All Stars until 1961, which marked his longest tenure with any team dating back to his sandlot beginnings.

For the next two decades, Kaiser largely remained out of the public eye. He married again, to Barbara Jean Treasvant, on November 6, 1971, and they went on to have four children together.[23] He eventually left Ford and found a position as a deliveryman and maintenance worker for the Goodwill Printing Company, in the Detroit suburb of Ferndale.[24] The most loyal of workers, he would keep that same job until 2009, the year the company closed down.

Kaiser was nowhere close to hanging up his spikes for good, however. He continued to find playing opportunities, including games for charity. A photograph in a 1982 issue of the *Detroit Free Press* captured the pitcher during one such game, looking spry on the mound for a player in his mid-60s.[25] He even was documented playing as late as 1990, the year he

turned 74 and filled a spot on the Miller High Life Old-Timers' team.

That same year, Michigan Governor James Blanchard presented Kaiser with a commendation, recognizing him as a Living Legend of Negro Baseball.[26] It was the first of many honors bestowed on Kaiser. In 2003, MLB's Detroit Tigers invited him to their first Negro League celebration weekend. It became an annual tradition, and Kaiser played a regular role in the festivities.

A few years later, Kaiser became one of 30 retired Negro League players drafted by Major League Baseball for honorary purposes. In the draft, which was the brainchild of Hall of Famer Dave Winfield, each team selected one player. Kaiser, as the hometown favorite of Detroit, went to the Tigers. A postdraft summary of the 30 selections dubbed Kaiser the "quintessential barnstormer."[27]

Kaiser died on February 14, 2011. After suffering a fall in his home in Southfield, Michigan, he was taken to the hospital, where his heart stopped.

Less than a month before he passed, he had once again been the special guest at a Negro League event, likely the final one he attended. On the importance of Kaiser's presence that day, Louis Manley, cofounder of the Michigan Chapter of Negro League Players, voiced a sentiment held by many fans: "[Kaiser] is living history. Just meeting him is part of keeping alive the legacy of what the Negro League accomplished."[28]

NOTES

1   Rob Neyer, "Cecil Kaiser, Oldest Living Negro Leaguer, Dies," SB Nation, February 15, 2011, sbnation.com/ mlb/2011/2/15/1995313/cecil-kaiser-oldest-living-negro-leaguer-dies, accessed December 31, 2016. Neyer shared some skepticism about the claim because "there were a lot of guys who played in the Negro Leagues for just a moment, and have been largely forgotten. Not to mention the many different definitions of 'Negro Leagues.'"

2   James A. Riley, "Cecil Kaiser," *The Biographical Encyclopedia of the Negro Baseball Leagues* (New York: Carroll & Graf Publishers, 1994), 455.

3   It should be noted that according to a few sources, including the player himself, Kaiser was born in 1918. Most sources, however, including his obituary, suggest he was born in 1916. Cecil Kaiser, video interview by Negro Leagues Baseball Museum,

Inc., February 22, 2007; Associated Press, "Negro Leagues Hurler Cecil Kaiser Dies," ESPN.com, February 14, 2011, espn.com/mlb/news/story?id=6121692, accessed December 31, 2016.

4   Kaiser, NLBM interview, February 22, 2007.

5   Ibid.

6   "Players Register: I-L," Center for Negro League Baseball Research website, cnlbr.org/Portals/0/Players%20Register/I-L%202016-08.pdf, p. 214, accessed December 31, 2016.

7   Riley, 455.

8   "Toledo Club to Oppose Homestead, *Cincinnati Enquirer,* July 20, 1943: 14.

9   "Giants' Star Faces Crawfords," *Detroit Free Press,* May 21, 1944: 14.

10   Kaiser, NLBM interview, February 22, 2007.

11   Ibid. For the sake of complete accuracy, the following points should be noted in regard to the $3,000-per-week salary figure given by Kaiser: 1) In order to accurately quote the interview, Kaiser's exact words have been included in the text of this article; 2) In spite of Kaiser's assertion, the figure must have been $3,000 per month as no player earned $3,000 per week; it is highly probable that Kaiser simply misspoke when he said "week" rather than "month."

12   "Players Register: I-L," CNLBR website, 215.

13   Ryan Whirty, "Negro Leagues All-Stars Were a Big Hit in the Big Easy in 1939," *New Orleans Times-Picayune,* September 30, 2009.

14   Kaiser, NLBM interview, February 22, 2007.

15   "Easter Team Plays Feller Squad Tonight," *Los Angeles Times,* October 25, 1949: Part 4, 4.

16   Michelle Kaufman, "Negro Leaguers Found Respect on Rough Road," *Detroit Free Press,* February 1, 1994: 6D.

17   Associated Press, "Negro Leagues Hurler Cecil Kaiser Dies."

18   Lou Hernández, *The Rise of the Latin American Baseball Leagues, 1947–1961: Cuba, the Dominican Republic, Mexico, Nicaragua, Panama, Puerto Rico and Venezuela* (Jefferson, North Carolina: McFarland, 2011), 244.

19   "1950 Caribbean Series," Baseball-Reference.com, baseball-reference.com/bullpen/1950_Caribbean_Series, accessed November 30, 2016.

20   Negro Leagues Baseball Museum, s.v. "Cecil Kaiser," coe.k-state.edu/annex/nlbemuseum/history/players/kaiser.html, accessed November 30, 2016.

21   Barry Swanton and Jay-Dell Mah, *Black Baseball Players in Canada: A Biographical Dictionary, 1881–1960,* (Jefferson, North Carolina: McFarland, 2009), 99.

22   Kaufman, "Negro Leaguers Found Respect,"6D.

23   Cecil Kaiser Funeral Pamphlet, ancestry.com, accessed November 30, 2016.

24   Associated Press, "Negro Leagues Hurler Cecil Kaiser Dies."

25   "That Old Time Delivery," *Detroit Free Press,* August 29, 1982: 1E.

26   "Congrats," *Detroit Free Press,* July 11, 1990: 4B.

27   Justice B. Hill, "Special Negro Leagues Draft," MLB.com, May 30, 2008, m.mlb.com/news/article/2795840/, accessed December 31, 2016.

28   Susan Harrison Wolffis, "Negro League Player Cecil Kaiser Surrounded by Images from the Past," *Muskegon Chronicle,* January 14, 2011.

LARRY KIMBROUGH

By Chris Rainey

Versatility can be both a blessing and a curse. Larry Kimbrough came to the Negro Leagues with the reputation of being both a switch-hitter and a switch-pitcher. Early in his career he faced the Harrisburg (Pennsylvania) Stars in an exhibition game and held them to two hits until the fourth inning, when they exploded for seven runs. The local paper quipped, "Kimbrough can throw them with either hand … but by the time he found out he wasn't so effective as a right hander, it was too late for him to start twirling from the portside."[1]

Kimbrough was a natural lefty. He explained that when he "was seven or eight, something like that," he had an accident with the family washing machine in which his left arm was pulled through the wringer.[2] The injury required a cast and, during the more than yearlong recuperation, he learned to do everything right-handed. After the cast came off, he struggled to return strength to his left arm. Nursed and guided by his mother, he eventually regained full use of it. As he got older, he realized that he could pitch with either hand and claimed, "I could throw them as hard left-handed as I could right-handed, with a better curveball left-handed."[3]

Lawrence Nathanial Kimbrough was born in Philadelphia on September 23, 1923, to Ercel and Virginia (Johnson) Kimbrough. His parents had married in Virginia, where Ercel worked as a farm laborer. Their first three children, Howard, Edith, and Allen, were born in Virginia before the Kimbroughs joined the Northern migration and settled in Philadelphia in the early 1920s. Ercel became a postal carrier and Virginia worked as a supervisor in a cleaner's. Allen died in February 1923, but Larry was joined by younger siblings Robert, Dorothy, and Dolores.[4] As Larry and Robert grew up, he and Robert spent as much time as possible playing baseball or football on nearby fields. It was not unusual for Virginia to have to track them down to come home for dinner.

Larry graduated from Ben Franklin High School, where he gained prominence as the ace pitcher for the 1941 Ben Franklin team. He pitched a no-hitter against Northeast High School in May 1941. Newspaper reports of the game do not mention it, but Kimbrough claimed to have pitched with both hands in the game.[5] He also tossed a three-hit shut-out that month, and he played shortstop when he was not pitching. It was not unusual for a star athlete to play baseball and run track. A 1945 article about Negro League players in military service lumped Kimbrough with some track stars, indicating that perhaps he had also been a multisport athlete in school.[6]

Ed Bolden, owner of the Negro National League's Philadelphia Stars, worked in the post office with Kimbrough's father. Ercel's insistence and Larry's on-field performances led to the Stars signing him in 1941. In 1942 he played with Judy Johnson's semi-pro Acol Flashes to gain experience; he was added to the Stars' roster late in the season. Negro League record-keeping is haphazard and much has been lost but available statistics credit Kimbrough with one appearance on the mound in 1942.[7] He also made a brief outfield appearance against the New York Black Yankees on September 3.

Dubbed "School Boy" because he came directly from the high-school ranks, Kimbrough was expected to learn the game by watching the veterans. He received training by throwing batting practice and playing in exhibition games. He described himself as 5-feet 10-inches tall and 190 pounds,[8] but some early pictures suggest he was nowhere near that weight in his teens. During high school he was referred to as "little" in a 1941 newspaper article, suggesting that he grew into his 190-pound listing later in his career.[9]

LARRY KIMBROUGH

Larry Kimbrough, who joined the Homestead Grays midway through the 1948 season, became ambidextrous due to an arm injury he suffered as a child and claimed he could pitch equally well with both hands. *(Courtesy of R. D. Retort Enterprises)*

In 1943 the sixth-place Stars' pitching staff was guided by veterans Barney Brown, Ches Buchanan, and manager Homer "Goose" Curry. Together, they earned 14 of the 22 Stars victories that have been verified, which means that Kimbrough saw limited action in league games.[10] Still only 19, he was used in exhibition games by Curry to give him experience. Kimbrough was twice used as a leadoff hitter and out-fielder against the Negro American League Kansas City Monarchs and Satchel Paige. On the mound, he made four starts in his seven appearances and posted a 1-3 record.[11] His lone victory came over the Newark Eagles at Niagara Falls, New York. Kimbrough said he beat Max Manning 4-2 while pitching with both

hands; Negro League historian James Riley lists it as a six-hit, 4-0 victory.[12] Kimbrough also made limited appearances at shortstop, third base, and the outfield, and batted .300.

In August 1943, at 19, Kimbrough enlisted in the Army and served until January 1946. At Fort Indiantown Gap in Pennsylvania he played as a pitcher, infielder, and outfielder for a base team. He was sent to Saipan in June 1945 and spent six months there before returning home to be discharged.

Kimbrough also played for the 444th Port Battalion team while he was stationed at Staten Island, New York. His future wife, Dorothy Suffern, was the daughter of an area baseball promoter. One day, Kimbrough was playing outfield against her father's team, and the two met when Kimbrough, trying to retrieve a long hit, went into the crowd of spectators lining the field. He returned to the ball-park the next day in uniform in the hope she would be there again. Fate was on his side and the romance began.[13] The couple corresponded during his deployment, and they were wed on March 12, 1946. They had four daughters, Dawn, Laura, Roxanne, and Roslyn.

After the Army, Kimbrough returned to the Stars, but he found a glut of pitchers on the team. Barney Brown was still with the squad, and they had added Bill Ricks, Joe "Fireball" Fillmore, Will Harris, and Eddie Jefferson. Kimbrough saw very little action in league games, but he still was paid $350 a month. In 1947 he joined the Richmond Giants in the Negro Carolina League. The following season the Giants became part of the Negro American Association, and 19-year-old Sonny Carroll paced the team's pitching staff. Kimbrough was hampered by a sore arm but did make an impressive appearance against the Homestead Grays, which led to their interest in him.

In August 1948 the Grays acquired Kimbrough's services. Game stories reveal his work in exhibitions, but details of his league appearances prove elusive. He claimed to have "pitched, played outfield, played infield, everything. I did it all."[14] The Grays put on a late-season surge and made the playoffs, eventually defeating the Birmingham Black Barons in the Negro League World Series. Thus, Kimbrough's last experience in professional baseball was as a member of a World Series winner.

After his brief stint with Homestead, Kimbrough joined the ranks of semipro ballplayers. Former teammate Ben Hill sponsored a number of teams. In 1949 Kimbrough played for Hill's Washington Pilots, then joined Hill with the Philadelphia Meteors for a couple of seasons. In 1950 Kimbrough took a job with the post office, but he still harbored dreams of a professional baseball career. He was offered a tryout with the St. Louis Browns, but it was canceled by inclement weather.

In 1953 Kimbrough showcased his talents for the Reading Indians, Cleveland's affiliate in the Class-A Eastern League. He told the scouts he was 22, a gutsy move considering that it had been 12 years since his high-school no-hitter. Throwing right-handed, he fired his fastball, then changed pace with a knuckleball. He recalled, "My curveball was just fair, but I guess it would've gotten better if I'd stayed with it."[15] Former major-league catcher George Susce was in charge of the tryout camp, and he told Kimbrough that he was too old for the Indians to sign.

In 1954 Kimbrough teamed with Henry Miller and Bill Kitts on the pitching staff of the Pittsburgh Crawfords in the Eastern Negro League.[16] The Crawfords and the league continued to play until 1956 but whether or not Kimbrough played with them in 1955-56 is unclear. He had already begun a lengthy career as a baseball and football official in the Philadelphia Public League and Catholic League. He also made it a point to keep alive the memory of the Negro Leagues, especially in the Philadelphia area, and he attended various Cooperstown inductions with fellow Philadelphia Stars players over the years.

In the 1980s and '90s Kimbrough held a membership in the Black Baseball Trailblazers, a Philadelphia-area group that helped to preserve memories of the Negro Leagues. Along with fellow players Bill Cash, Mahlon Duckett, and Gene Benson, he was frequently found at sports collectors conventions in the area. They also visited classrooms to keep the memory of the Negro Leagues alive for future generations. Kimbrough became a member of the Negro League Baseball Players Association and helped to champion their causes.

Kimbrough's involvement in promoting the history and causes of the Negro Leagues led eventually to several accolades being bestowed on him. In 1985 he was honored by the National Association of Black Journalists (NABJ) at its national convention in Philadelphia. In 1990 he was honored at a Philadelphia Phillies game. In 1997 he was inducted into the Negro Baseball Hall of Fame in Kansas City, and in 1998 he was inducted into the Philadelphia Chapter of the Pennsylvania Sports Hall of Fame. In addition to all of his involvement with baseball, he was also an active member of the American Legion.

Kimbrough worked 33 years in the post office. Besides being a popular letter carrier, he served as a union steward. After he retired from the post office, he began an 11-year stint with the Reliance Insurance Company. When death claimed Kimbrough on January 29, 2001, he had seven grandchildren and seven great-grandchildren.

NOTES

1   "1200 Fans Walk to Island Park for Twin Bill," *Harrisburg Telegraph*, June 7, 1943: 12.

2   Brent Kelley, *The Negro League Revisited: Conversations with 66 More Baseball Heroes*, (Jefferson, North Carolina: McFarland and Company, Inc., 2000), 142.

3   Kelley, 144.

4   The 1920 and 1940 censuses were used. Edith appears as Authia in the 1920 census. She is correctly identified from Dolores' obituary in the *Philadelphia Inquirer*, June 3, 1999. In Kimbrough's obituary her name is spelled Edythe.

5   Kelley, 143.

6   *Chicago Defender*, May 12, 1945: 8.

7   seamheads.com/NegroLgs/player.php?playerID=kimbro1lar, accessed March 2, 2017.

8   The description came in Kimbrough's Hall of Fame questionnaire, which he filled out himself.

9   "Franklin Blanks Southeast Catholic," *Philadelphia Inquirer*, April 5, 1941: 22.

10   seamheads.com/NegroLgs/team.php?yearID=1943&teamID=PS&tab=pit, accessed March 2, 2017.

11   seamheads.com/NegroLgs/player.php?playerID=kimbro1lar. Baseball-Reference.com credits Kimbrough with only a 1-1

record in 1943; see baseball-reference.com/register/player. fcgi?id=kimbroooolar, accessed March 2, 2017.

12   James A. Riley, *The Biographical Encyclopedia of the Negro Baseball Leagues* (New York: Carroll & Graf Publishers Inc., 1994), 464; Kelley, 144.

13   Kendall Wilson, "Larry Kimbrough, 77, baseball legend," *Philadelphia Tribune,* February 2, 2001: 6-c.

14   Kelley, 143.

15   Kelley, 146. In the Kelley interview Kimbrough says this was 1952. Colavito was with Reading in 1953. Part of his story was wrong, either the year or his facing Colavito. Dates are easier to confuse than personalities, hence the use of 1953.

16   "Krebs Team Cards Contests with 2 Top Negro League Clubs," *Shamokin* (Pennsylvania) *News-Dispatch,* July 6, 1954: 6-7.

BUCK LEONARD

By Ralph Berger

Negro league fans called him "the black Lou Gehrig," putting Buck Leonard in pretty lofty company. It didn't hurt Buck that he followed Josh Gibson, "the black Babe Ruth," in the Homestead Grays' lineup. Was Buck Leonard the equal of Gehrig as a first baseman and hitter? He probably was a better first baseman than the Iron Horse, having acquired a reputation for being very good around the bag, whereas Lou was essentially adequate. Was he the hitter that Gehrig was? Probably not. Leonard's .328 batting average and .532 slugging percentage (as listed in *The Baseball Encyclopedia*) are impressive, but he's a dozen points behind Gehrig in average and an even hundred short in slugging. More recently, Lawrence Hogan calculates his numbers a bit lower, at .320 and .527. Leonard was an excellent hitter, but Gehrig was in a class almost by himself. Leonard conceded as much when he said, "I considered it an honor to be called the Black Lou Gehrig, but I didn't think I ever measured up to it."[1] Moreover, while Buck often faced exceptional talent, it wasn't always major-league caliber. As men of dignity and universal respect, however, Gehrig and Leonard are, in essence, twins.

Walter "Buck" Leonard's road to the Baseball Hall of Fame was no cakewalk. He had to leave the public school system at age 14 because where he lived there was no school for African American boys at the high school level. For the next 12 years until he was 26, he worked as a mill hand, shoeshine boy, and finally shop worker for the Atlantic Coast Line Railroad, from age 16 "putting brake cylinders on boxcars for a railroad shop."[2]

Buck Leonard was born in Rocky Mount, North Carolina, on September 8, 1907. His father John was a railroad fireman and his mother Emma Leonard (née Sesson) a housewife. Buck Leonard was one of six children, including three sisters (Fanny, Willa, and Lena) and two brothers (Herman and Charlie). His family was religious and attended church every Sunday. Buck wasn't able to go to church as often as he wished while playing baseball, but after his retirement he again became a faithful church-goer every Sunday. Leonard got his nickname "Buck" from his younger brother Charlie. Leonard's parents nicknamed him Buddy, but Charlie had trouble pronouncing Buddy and called him Bucky.

John Leonard died in 1919 from the virulent influenza that came at the end of World War I. After the funeral, Buck's mother told him he would have to get a job after school to help support the family. There were both black and white hosiery mills in the area, and Buck and his oldest sister Fannie went to work at the black mill, working there until the mill closed in 1921. Buck then went to the railroad station and started shining shoes. Since there was no high school for blacks, he finished his schooling at the end of the eighth grade. For the next two years, Buck Leonard shined shoes. There was a black shoeshine stand and a white shoeshine stand, but no one paid attention and shoes were shined at both stands by both blacks and whites. After that he went to work in the shop at the Atlantic Coastline Railroad at age 16.

During the time he was working these various jobs, Leonard was also playing semiprofessional baseball in and around Rocky Mount with the Rocky Mountain Elks and Daughtry's Black Revels, later named the Black Swans. When Leonard was 17, he became the manager of the Black Swans. He initially played the outfield, and then moved to first base. As the manager, he felt first base was more appropriate for him. This position would bring him closer to the umpires in case of bad calls. Leonard's brother Charlie was a pitcher on those teams. Buck lost his job with the railroad in 1932. His only job opportunity during the worldwide Great Depression was in professional baseball. He was hesitant about going

First baseman Buck Leonard, often called the "Black Lou Gehrig," played a Negro League-record 17 seasons with the Homestead Grays. He was elected to the Baseball Hall of Fame in 1972. (*National Baseball Hall of Fame, Cooperstown, New York*)

into professional baseball because at the time he was already 25 years old. Leonard had never given much thought to playing professional baseball full time and considered his engagement in baseball strictly a pastime.

Fortunately, he was approached by Doc Daughtry of the Portsmouth team, who asked if he would like to play for the team at a salary of 15 dollars a week, not bad for those times. Originally named the Portsmouth Firefighters, they were renamed the Black Revels.

The Baltimore Stars, an independent team, came to Portsmouth to play the Black Revels. Leonard played against the Stars, and after the game Ben Taylor, manager of the Stars, asked Leonard how much money he was making playing for Portsmouth. After Leonard told him, Taylor asked him if he

would like to play for the Stars. He told Leonard he wouldn't receive a fixed salary but rather a percentage of the gate. Teammates on the Black Revels told him if he were to go with Baltimore, he would starve to death. Black traveling teams had a hard time scheduling games, but Buck and his brother Charlie signed anyway.

In 1933, with the Baltimore Stars, Leonard was playing right field under manager-first baseman Ben Taylor, who was getting too old to play. Taylor took Leonard under his wing and groomed him to take his place as the first baseman for the Stars. Leonard batted and threw left-handed. He is listed as 5-feet-10 and 185 pounds.

Under Taylor's tutelage Leonard became an excellent first baseman. In 1941, relatively late in Leonard's career, one media source "described four or five sensational stops that were 'way beyond the reach of 99 percent of major-league first basemen.'"[3] Sure-handed, with a strong, accurate arm and acknowledged as a smart player who always made the right play, Leonard was a team man all the way. Jim Riley wrote, "A class guy, he was the best-liked player in the game."[4]

The Stars went bankrupt later in 1933, and Cannonball Dick Redding signed Leonard with the Brooklyn Royal Giants, where Leonard spent the remainder of the 1933 season. In 1934, ex-pitcher Smoky Joe Williams, then tending bar in New York, recommended Leonard to Cumberland (Cum) Posey, owner-manager of the Homestead Grays. The Homestead Grays were situated in an old steel town seven miles outside of Pittsburgh and had been originally formed by a group of black steelworkers known as the Murdock Grays. They played their big games at Forbes Field in Pittsburgh and at Griffith Stadium in Washington, D.C. Leonard said of Posey, "Kind of a quiet guy but he knew baseball. Taught me two or three things I've never forgotten. Taught me how to hit left-handed pitchers, taught me to use an open stance with left-handers. Taught me how to throw the ball when the pitcher's covering first base. And he told me not to try to steal any bases; told me to quit running. I wasn't fast enough to steal bases."[5]

With the Grays, Leonard teamed with catcher Josh Gibson to form a formidable one-two punch called "The Thunder Twins." While teammate Josh Gibson was slugging tape measure home runs, Leonard — batting cleanup — was hitting screaming line drives both off and over the walls.

A thoroughgoing gentleman, Leonard's steady, reliable demeanor earned him the captaincy of the Homestead Grays until they ceased to exist in 1950.

With the Grays, Leonard teamed not only with Josh Gibson but with Vic Harris, Howard Easterling, Cool Papa Bell, and Jud Wilson. From 1937 through 1945, the Grays won nine consecutive championships in the Negro National League, a record possibly unequaled anywhere in professional sports in America. They also won in 1948, when Leonard was 40 years old.

Buck Leonard married Sandra Wroten of Hertford, North Carolina, on New Year's Eve of 1937. Her first husband, a funeral director, had died in 1935. Buck told her he was not going to run a funeral home and had her sell the establishment.[6] Sandra Leonard became a school teacher, and Buck continued to play baseball. Her income from teaching helped keep the family afloat economically, but he also needed to earn money playing winter ball. Married life agreed with Leonard, who had a good 1938 season. In 27 games, he went to bat 99 times, had 33 hits, and scored 21 runs.

In 1942, the Mexican League headed by Jorge Pasquel was luring Negro League stars away from their teams by offering higher salaries. The Homestead Grays lost Josh Gibson to Pasquel's Mexican League. Afraid of losing Leonard to Mexico as well, the Grays paid him $1,000 per game with later increases to stay with the team. At that time, Leonard was called up by his draft board and examined for military duty. According to Lawrence Hogan, he was classified 4F because of a bad back and Josh Gibson was classified 4F due to bad knees. Riley writes that he played in that year's first Negro World Series against the Kansas City Monarchs with a taped broken hand.[7]

The Monarchs swept the Grays in 1942 but won back-to-back World Series against the Birmingham Black Barons in 1943 and 1944, with Leonard batting an even .500 in 1944.

Leonard was now playing baseball year round. He participated in the winter leagues in Puerto Rico, Cuba, and Venezuela between 1935 and 1955. Moreover, in the fall and winter of 1943, Leonard played on Satchel Paige's all-star team against a team of major-league all-stars in California. He batted .500 in eight games. After the eighth game, Commissioner Kenesaw Mountain Landis ordered the major leaguers to stop.

Major-league owners may have tried to sign both Leonard and Gibson to contracts, but they didn't seem to make much of an effort. The first to approach them was Bill Benswanger, president of the Pittsburgh Pirates. Benswanger promised tryouts for the players in 1939, but it became unclear if Cum Posey put a stop to it or Benswanger never followed through with his promise. In 1943, Clark Griffith of the Washington Senators asked Gibson and Leonard if they would like to play in the major leagues, and if they thought they could make it in the majors. They replied in the affirmative to both questions. Griffith told the two that they would hear from him. They never did. Lacking the courage to challenge the system, white owners feared introducing black ballplayers to the major leagues at that time, while black owners of the Negro National League feared it would destroy their league as it eventually did when Jackie Robinson became the first black baseball player to enter the major leagues in the twentieth century. The Negro National League's demise came after the end of the 1948 season.

Leo Durocher, manager of the Brooklyn Dodgers, put the blame squarely on Commissoiner Landis, who he said prevented him from acquiring black players. Leonard hinted at that but did not explicitly state that it was Landis who put pressure on the owners not to sign black players. Landis always said that there was nothing in the white major leagues that stated that blacks were banned; however, there was a Gentlemen's Agreement that owners were loathe to break. As Leonard put it, "I think they believed we could play major league baseball but everyone hated to be the first."[8]

Leonard himself wasn't going to lead the fight. "I wasn't in favor of too much agitating toward opening the doors of white organized baseball, but I let them know that I would be willing to join up in the chance was available. And I told them that if I did get the opportunity I would not desire to socialize with the white players after I was through playing the games and that I would be content to find a respectable hotel for coloreds to stay in. You know, if they don't want you in a place, I don't believe you ought to go there. If they didn't want us in Forbes Field, then I don't think we ought to have gone."[9]

Buck Leonard was a superb hitter and fielder. In the Negro National League, first basemen were often the clowns of the teams. They would make all kinds of contortions and grimaces, anything that would entertain the fans. Not Buck Leonard. "I was strictly business when I was on the ballfield," he later wrote. "I wasn't out there to clown."[10] There was no need for him to act the clown.[11] Leonard was often called the equal or better of such major-league stalwart first basemen as George Sisler and Hal Chase. As a batter, he was described as a terrific hitter, a man who would literally drive pitchers off the mound. Leonard batted fourth in the Grays lineup, following Josh Gibson. Almost every season saw a battle between Leonard and Gibson as to who would wind up with the most homers and runs batted in. Dave Barnhill, a star Negro Leagues pitcher, said, "You could put a fastball in a shotgun and you couldn't shoot it by him."[12] Eddie Gottlieb, an Eastern Booking Agent and former coach of the Philadelphia Warriors of the Basketball Association of America said Leonard "was as smooth a first baseman as I ever saw."[13]

Monte Irvin agreed: "Buck Leonard was the equal of any first baseman who ever lived. If he had gotten the chance to play in the Major Leagues, they might have called Lou Gehrig the white Buck Leonard."[14] For 17 consecutive years Leonard anchored the infield for the Grays at first base. He was voted 12 times to the East-West All-Star Squads. He batted .317 and

stroked three homers in the games. In 1948, at the age of 40, without Josh Gibson, he batted a lusty .395 to win the title. The 1948 Grays were his favorite team. The team featured Luke Easter, Sam Bankhead, Luis Marquez, and Wilmer Fields their ace pitcher. They defeated the Birmingham Black Barons (featuring a young Willie Mays) in the Negro World Series.

After the color line was done away with, Bill Veeck tried to sign Buck Leonard who was then 40 years of age. Leonard declined, believing he was too old and being unwilling to risk embarrassing himself. Said Leonard, "We always believed we could have made the major leagues if baseball hadn't been segregated. I'm not bitter. But it was too late for me. When Jackie Robinson came along, I was 40 years old."[15] In 1953, at the age of 46, Buck Leonard made his only appearance in organized baseball with the Portsmouth Club of the Piedmont League, hitting .333 in 10 games.

Statistics from the Negro National League are on the thin side. John Holway asserts that "Leonard hit over .400 four times and over .390 six times, the last in 1948, when he hit a league leading .391 and tied Luke Easter for the league home run crown. His lifetime batting average was .355 against black big leaguers and .382 against whites."[16] A set of statistics compiled in a project sponsored by the National Baseball Hall of Fame and published in Lawrence Hogan's *Shades of Glory* showed that Leonard had career totals of a batting average of .320, slugging percentage of .527, in 1427 recorded at-bats, with 471 hits, 60 homers, 73 doubles, 26 triples, 257 walks, 352 runs, and 275 RBIs. Jim Riley writes that "following the 1943 season, Leonard was credited with averaging 43 home runs per year for the past eight years."[17] He reports a .341 batting average in league play over the course of his career and a .382 average in exhibition games against major leaguers.[18]

Racism was rampant when it came to finding accommodations for the night. Leonard recalled that it was tough getting a place to sleep at night while on the grinding city tours. Leonard remembers one particular night when the Grays were on their way north from Florida. "We'd come north from Florida and stopped at New Orleans at the Patterson Hotel. We used to call it a chinch parlor. A chinch is what we called bedbugs. As soon as the lights would go out there, the chinches would come out. We used to get newspapers out and spread them on the bed and sleep on top of them. The bedbugs couldn't crawl up on the paper."[19]

Injuries were another problem. Injured players turned to each other because the team had no trainer. If someone had a bad back, he would get another teammate to rub him down. Leonard recalled one time when he was scratched up quite a bit. "I got scratched on my leg. I needed three stitches in my leg and they wouldn't put the three stitches in because I was going to lose some games. I just played until it got well. Now it's got thin skin over it, and it gets inflamed. Had I been in the major leagues, I would have had proper attention."[20] In addition to his playing duties, Leonard assumed the role of traveling

secretary for the Grays and held that position until the team was disbanded in 1950.

Leonard played in the Mexican Leagues during the winters and summers of 1951 through 1955. The first three summers he played with Torreon, in the Main Mexican League, generally considered Triple-A ball, where he batted .322, .335, and .332. The next two years he played with Durango in the Mexican Central League; that league was not considered as good as the main Mexican League. In the winters, he played with Obregon in a Mexican League near the Gulf of California. The next two years he played in Xalapa on a Mexican team. He injured his knee during his last season at Xalapa. A German doctor constructed a knee brace and Leonard went on to become the MVP. After that, Leonard was finished with playing baseball. At 48 years old, his back hurting with arthritis, he decided to hang up his spikes. He went back to Rocky Mount and worked in an

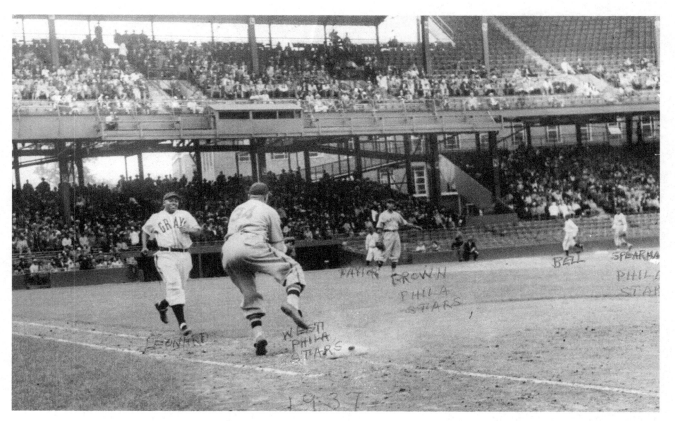

Buck Leonard tries to beat the throw to first base in a 1937 Negro National League game between the Homestead Grays and Philadelphia Stars. (*National Baseball Hall of Fame, Cooperstown, New York*)

automobile garage, where he washed cars and helped out the mechanics.

Later, Leonard worked for 10 years as a truant officer for the Rocky Mount School District and earned a real-estate brokerage license from a correspondence school. He says he also built nine houses from the ground up.[21] He was also an executive with the Rocky Mount team in the Carolina League. Leonard said that his one regret in life was that "I didn't get as much formal education as I would have liked," so he returned to school and earned his high school diploma.[22]

The deeper meaning of the exclusion of blacks from major-league baseball involved opposing forces in ballplayers and the black population as a whole.

W.E. B. DuBois in *The Souls of Black Folk* labeled this dilemma "twoness": "One ever feels his twoness an American and a Negro, two souls, two thoughts, two irreconcilable strivings, two warring ideas in one dark body, whose dogged strength alone keeps it from being torn asunder."[23] Rube Foster, a tall imposing African American star pitcher, lived this dilemma. He wanted to protect the newly formed Negro National League from being controlled by whites but at the same time sought the eventual integration of baseball. An intelligent, introspective man, Leonard surely felt this tension.

In *The New Bill James Historical Abstract*, James ranked Leonard as the best first baseman in the Negro leagues and as the 65th greatest baseball player

Hall of Fame first baseman Buck Leonard kept formidable company with the Homestead Grays. Pictured here, from left to right, are Sam Bankhead, fellow Hall of Famer Josh Gibson, Leonard, Dave Hoskins and Jerry Benjamin. (*National Baseball Hall of Fame, Cooperstown, New York*)

of all time. James regarded Buck Leonard as his most admirable superstar in the Negro Leagues. Leonard was voted as the 47th best player of the century by *The Sporting News*. In addition, Leonard was a finalist for the Major League Baseball All-Century Team.

After the Negro leagues folded, most of the black players who played in it were forgotten. Ted Williams, upon his induction into the Baseball Hall of Fame in 1966, said of Negro players: "Baseball gives every American boy a chance to excel. Not just to be good as anybody else, but to be better. This is the nature of man and the name of the game. I hope someday Satchel Paige and Josh Gibson will be voted into the Hall of Fame as symbols of the great Negro players who are not here only because they weren't given the chance."[24] In time, Leonard and other former stars of the Negro National League contacted Bowie Kuhn, Commissioner of Baseball, and told him they thought it was about time that some of the stars of the Negro Leagues were put up for election to enter the Baseball Hall of Fame. Kuhn listened and promised to see what he could do, but he did not have the clout that Leonard and the others had hoped for, and Leonard would have to wait a while longer before he received a call from the Hall of Fame. In February 1972, when Leonard finally did receive an announcement that he was to be inducted into the National Baseball Hall of Fame, he was both stunned and elated. He was inducted on August 7, 1972. In his speech Leonard told the crowd, "We in the Negro Leagues felt like we were contributing something to baseball too, when we were playing. We played with a round ball and with a round bat and wore baseball uniforms and we thought we were making a contribution to baseball. We loved the game and we liked to play it. But we thought we should have and could have made the major leagues and all of us would have desired to play in the major leagues because we felt and knew that that was the greatest game."[25]

A park near Leonard's home in Rocky Mount stands in his honor, along with a historical marker detailing his accomplishments. There is also a street named in his honor.

On April 4, 1986, Leonard suffered a stroke, which affected his right side. He recuperated to some degree, but the stroke curtailed some of his activities such as attending church every Sunday. On July 7, 1986, 20 years after Sarah's death, he was married to his second wife, Lugenia Fox.

In 1994, Leonard was again honored when he was named honorary captain of the National League team at the All-Star Game at which he said, "I met a whole lot of ballplayers and I had a good time."[26]

Walter Fenner "Buck" Leonard died in his hometown of Rocky Mount on November 27, 1997. He was 90 years of age. He was survived by his second wife Lugenia, sister Lena Cox, stepson Thomas Fox, stepdaughters Florosa Walston, Rose Hunter, and Barbara Fox. Leonard lived a life of accomplishment and left a memory of a life well spent; a good man, a solid citizen, devoutly religious and one hell of a ballplayer. He is buried in The Garden of Gethsemane Cemetery in Rocky Mount.

On Saturday November 1, 2008, a Buck Leonard Exhibit was unveiled in Rocky Mount. The exhibit traces the life of Leonard from his humble beginnings through his ascendance to baseball greatness and also focuses on Leonard's role as a community leader.

SOURCES

In addition to the sources cited in the Notes, the author also consulted:

Clark, Dick, and Larry Lester. *The Negro Leagues Book* (Cleveland: Society for American Baseball Research, 1994).

Holway, John B. *Blackball Stars* (Westport, Connecticut: Meckler Books, 1988).

Riley, James A., *History of Black Baseball and the Negro Baseball Leagues*. Online.

Hogan, Lawrence D. *Shades of Glory* (Washington, DC: National Geographic Society and National Baseball Hall of Fame and Museum, 2006).

Laverro, Thomas. *The Encyclopedia of Negro League Baseball* (New York: Facts on File, 2003).

Light, Jonathan, Fraser. *The Cultural Encyclopedia of Baseball* (Jefferson, North Carolina: McFarland and Company, 1997).

Porter, David, editor. *Biographical Dictionary of American Sports, Baseball* (New York: Greenwood Press, 1987).

Threston, Christopher. Rocky Mountain Telegram.com. "The Integration of Baseball in Philadelphia." Online

Tygiel, Jules. *Past Time: Baseball as History* (New York and London: Oxford University Press, 2000).

NOTES

1   Buck Leonard with James A. Riley, *Buck Leonard, The Black Lou Gehrig: An Autobiography* (New York: Carroll & Graf, 1995), 207.

2   Brian Wilson, MLB.com. http://mlb.mlb.com/mlb/history/mlb_negro_leagues_profile.jsp?player=leonard_buck

3   James A Riley, *The Biographical Encyclopedia of the Negro Baseball Leagues* (New York: Carroll & Graf, 1994, 2002), 476. The "media source" Riley quotes is unknown.

4   Ibid.

5   Editor's note: The exact source of this quotation is uncertain. Ralph Berger's original biography of Leonard, fact-checked and re-edited for this book, contained no endnotes. In his autobiography, Leonard credited Posey as "tops as a teacher of baseball." See *Buck Leonard, The Black Lou Gehrig: An Autobiography*, 36.

6   Ibid., 91.

7   Riley, *Biographical Encyclopedia*, 476.

8   John Holway, *Voices from the Great Black Baseball Leagues* (New York: Dodd, Mead, 1975), 268.

9   *Buck Leonard, The Black Lou Gehrig: An Autobiography*, 100.

10   Ibid., 116.

11   http://baseballhall.org/hof/leonard-buck

12   James A. Riley, Of Monarchs and Black Barons: Essays on Baseball's Negro Leagues (Jefferson, North Carolina: *McFarland & Company*, 2012), 129–132.

13   http://baseballhall.org/hof/leonard-buck

14   Riley, *Of Monarchs and Black Barons*, 129-132.

15   Jean M. White, "Ballpark Figures: The Other League," *Washington Post*, April 25, 1981: B1. There is another quotation widely attributed to Leonard, but which we have been unable to source: "I was not bitter by not being allowed to play in the major leagues. I just said, 'The time has not come.' I only wish I could have played in the big leagues when I was young enough to show what I could do. When an offer was given to me to join up, I was too old and I knew it."

16   John Holway, *Voices from the Great Black Baseball Leagues*, 250.

17   Riley, *Biographical Encyclopedia*, 476.

18   Ibid.

19   *Buck Leonard, The Black Lou Gehrig: An Autobiography*, 104.

20   Holway, *Voices from the Great Black Baseball Leagues*, 260.

21   *Buck Leonard, The Black Lou Gehrig: An Autobiography*, 226-229.

22   Ibid., 263.

23   W. E. B. DuBois, *The Souls of Black Folk*

24   Ted Williams, 1967 induction speech.

25   Buck Leonard, 1972 induction speech.

26   *Buck Leonard, The Black Lou Gehrig*, 262.

LUIS ÁNGEL "CANENA" MÁRQUEZ SÁNCHEZ

By Amy Essington

Luis Márquez was a member of the generation of baseball players who integrated professional baseball in the 1940s and 1950s.
Márquez played in many levels of segregated and integrated baseball including the Puerto
Rican Winter League, the Negro Leagues, the
Mexican Leagues, the minor leagues, and the major
leagues. He integrated the Portland Beavers of the
Pacific Coast League, along with Frank Austin,
in 1949. Two years later, he became only the third
Puerto Rican to play in the major leagues when
he joined the Boston Braves. Although he never
found the success in the majors that he had in other
leagues, Márquez had a 20-year career in professional baseball.

He is the only Puerto Rican with batting titles in
Negro League baseball (1947 Homestead Grays, .417),
Puerto Rican baseball (1953-54 Mayaguez, .333), and
Organized Baseball (1959 Dallas, Triple-A American
Association, .345).

Of Spanish and African heritage, Luis Ángel
"Canena" Márquez Sánchez was born on October
28, 1925, in a house on Calle Mercado in Aguadilla,
Puerto Rico, to Matilde Márquez and Adela Sánchez.
His father left when he was very young, and Adela
married Manuel Acevedo Quinones. Luis was the
oldest of five children, two boys and three girls.
More information about his parents is not known.
In 1944 Marquez played third base for the Puerto
Rican national team in the Amateur World Series
in Venezuela.[1] Aguadilla local Victor Navarro described Márquez as "something else," adding, "He put
up great numbers in the league, but he was a warm,
caring human being."[2] Márquez also exhibited both
a sense of humor and humility when, after missing
a team practice with Mayagüez during the 1945-46
season, he brought manager Joe Buzas "a big local
pineapple, knowing Buzas loved fruit."[3]

The nickname "Canena" was bestowed on Márquez
him by his mother, Adela, a name by which she had
been known. After a truly hot start in a series in the
1944 Amateur World Series in Venezuela, he picked
up the nickname "El Fogón Boricua."[4]

After he finished high school, an 18-year-old
Márquez signed a professional baseball contract
with Mayaguez. During his career, Márquez, who
was quick and had a strong arm, played in both in the
infield and outfield. The 5-foot-10, 174-pound player
threw and batted right-handed. Márquez began his
professional career with the Mayagüez Indios during
the 1944-1945 season. In his first game, Márquez
experienced both high and low points—he raced
from second to home on an infield out, but he also
made two fielding errors.[5] Márquez's career in Puerto
Rican winter ball included time with the Mayagüez
Indios (1944-1946, 1953-1956, 1957-1964), the Aguadilla
Sharks (1946-1951), the San Juan Senators (1952-1953),
and the Ponce Lions (1957-1958, and 1959-60, both
stints as manager).

During his first professional season in Puerto
Rico, Márquez batted .361 and tied with Alfonso
Gerard for 1944-45 Rookie of the Year honors. The
next season, he led the league with 10 triples, tying
the league record, and, during the 1946-47 season, he
set the single-season home run record with 14 round-
trippers, breaking Josh Gibson's record by one.[6]
During the 1953-1954 season, Márquez was the Puerto
Rican Winter League's batting champion with a .333
batting average and was voted Most Valuable Player
as well. He hit two home runs in the 1957 Caribbean
Championship Series.

Over the course of 20 seasons in Puerto Rico,
Márquez played in 4,018 games; scored 768 runs;
registered 1,206 hits which included 235 doubles, 66
triples, and 97 home runs; and batted .300. His totals
of games played, hits, doubles, and runs scored are

all league records. He was inducted into the Puerto Rican Baseball Hall of Fame in October 1991.

After his first season of winter ball in Puerto Rico, Márquez joined the New York Black Yankees in 1945. He then played for the Baltimore Elite Giants and the Homestead Grays of the Negro National League in 1946 and the Grays in 1947 and 1948. In 1947 and 1948, Márquez represented the Grays in both the Chicago and New York games of the Negro Leagues' East-West All-Star Game. In 1947 Márquez led the league in hitting with a .417 batting average, and he had 29 stolen bases. The following season, the second baseman changed positions, moving to the outfield, and also moved to the top of the batting order. James Riley's *Biographical Encyclopedia of the Negro Baseball Leagues* says Marquez had a .274 batting average the year his team won the Negro National

Luis Márquez, a starting outfielder for the 1948 Homestead Grays, is a legend in his native country of Puerto Rico. A bronze statue of Márquez stands outside of the stadium that bears his name in his hometown of Aguadilla. (*National Baseball Hall of Fame, Cooperstown, New York*)

League pennant and the Negro League World Series in 1948. After the Homestead Grays folded in 1949, Márquez's contract was transferred to the Baltimore Elite Giants, now of the Negro American League. By the time his Negro League career concluded, he had posted a .335 career batting average.[7]

The Brooklyn Dodgers' signing of Jackie Robinson on October 23, 1945, initiated the integration of baseball in the United States and allowed Márquez to move from the Negro Leagues into Organized Baseball. Márquez was one of the hundreds of players who participated in the process of integrating the minor and major leagues in the 1940s and '50s. This process included sorting out contracts that may or may not have existed with the teams of the collapsing Negro Leagues.

On February 3, 1949, newspapers reported the purchase of Márquez's contract with the Baltimore Elite Giants by New York Yankees general manager George Weiss.[8] Márquez was the first player of color signed by the Yankees, although he was not the player who ultimately integrated the team. He reported to the Newark Bears, the Yankees' affiliate in the Triple-A International League, at their spring-training camp in Haines City, Florida. Whether the Baltimore Elite Giants or the Homestead Grays owned his contract, however, was in dispute.[9] The Grays still made a claim to Márquez's contract and owner See Posey had offered Bill Veeck of the Cleveland Indians a 120-day option to purchase the contract.

The dispute over Márquez's contract was revealed in the midst of another contract disagreement between the Yankees and Indians. The Yankees accused the Indians of signing Artie Wilson of the Birmingham Black Barons, who was already under contract with them. The commissioner's office mediated the two disputes in the spring of 1949. Commissioner A.B. "Happy" Chandler's decision sent Márquez to the Indians and Wilson to the Yankees. Márquez had been playing with the Newark Bears, the Yankees' affiliate, and Wilson had been playing with the San Diego Padres, the Indians' affiliate. In 18 games in Newark, Márquez had one home run, three stolen bases, and a batting average of .246. Even though his preference was to remain in the Yankees organization, Márquez joined the Indians on May 13, 1949, and was optioned to the Portland Beavers of the Pacific Coast League.[10]

In the United States, Márquez spent most of his baseball career in the minor leagues. He joined the Beavers on May 27, 1949. After he had arrived by plane from New York, he went straight into left field for that night's game.[11] Márquez and his teammate Frank Austin were the first players of color on that team, though Art Pennington of the Chicago Giants later joined the Beavers in July.[12] During the 1949 season, Márquez hit .294 in 132 games and led the team with 32 stolen bases. He returned to Portland in 1950, played 194 games, hit over .300, and again led the club in stolen bases. As one of the players who were at the forefront of the integration of baseball, Márquez faced discrimination on and off the field.[13] Despite the discrimination, he made strong connections in the PCL. In 1957, when the three-time manager of the Portland Beavers, Bill Sweeney, died, Márquez served as an honorary pallbearer.[14]

In 1951 Márquez finally moved up to the major leagues when he was claimed by the Boston Braves in the Rule 5 draft prior to the season.[15] Márquez had joined the Braves one year after Sam Jethroe integrated it, but historian Adrian Burgos has noted that Márquez was the first Afro-Latino player signed by the Braves, and the second one overall (after Minnie Miñoso)[16] His major-league debut came on April 18, 1951, when he entered the game against the New York Giants as a pinch-runner for Jim Wilson.[17] Márquez's first hit, a triple, came on April 19 in the second game of a doubleheader against the New York Giants.[18] His first RBI followed the next day in a 2-for-4 performance against the Philadelphia Phillies; Márquez drove in the first run and scored the second in a 2-1 Braves victory. He scored the winning run on Max Surkont's sacrifice fly after singling, advancing to second base on a sacrifice, and stealing third. Márquez played in 68 games for the Braves in 1951, and he was frequently used as a pinch-runner. He hit only .196 and was successful on only half of his stolen base attempts, going 4-for-8 on the year.

The next season, Márquez returned to the minors, where he played in 136 games for the Milwaukee Brewers of the Triple-A American Association. His batting average was third best in the league at .345, and he had 14 home runs and 99 runs batted in, Márquez's contributions to the Brewers helped the team to win the American Association championship in 1952. During the 1953 season, Márquez played 130 games and batted .292 for another American Association team, the Toledo Sox. With Márquez on the roster, the Sox won the American Association championship and playoffs.

Márquez's performance merited a return to the major leagues in 1954, and he batted .083 in 17 games for the Chicago Cubs; after a trade on June 14, 1954, he hit .111 in 14 games for the Pittsburgh Pirates. He had only one base hit for each of the two teams, and the Pirates released Márquez to Toledo on July 14, 1954. Over the course of his major-league career, Márquez played a total of 99 games for three different teams and finished with a .182 batting average and an on-base percentage of .278. He drove in 11 runs, all during his 1951 season with the Braves.

From 1955 to 1958, Márquez returned to the roster of the Portland Beavers, with a 21-game stint with the Toledo Sox in 1955. In 1956 he represented the Beavers on the Pacific Coast League's All-Star team. During his time as a Beaver, Márquez accepted a Friday the 13th challenge of playing all nine positions in one 1957 game, which he completed by pitching the last three outs of the game.[19]

After his seasons in the Pacific Northwest, Márquez spent two seasons in Texas. In 1959 he was with the Dallas Rangers of the American Association, where he played in 142 games and won the batting championship with a .345 average. The next season he played in 144 games with the Dallas Fort-Worth Rangers of the American Association, batting .264.

In 1961, in Márquez's 17th year as a professional baseball player, he moved down to Single-A ball for the first time, playing in 19 games with the Williamsport Grays of the Eastern League. That season, he also played 18 games with the Dallas Fort-Worth Rangers.

After his final minor-league stints, Márquez moved south of the border for two seasons, and played for the Mexican League's Poza Rica Petroleros in 1962 and 1963. He excelled during his first season in Mexico, batting .357 with 28 doubles, 21 homers, and 91 RBIs in 126 games. His performance was not quite as strong in 1963, but he still hit .314 with 20 home runs and 72 RBIs in his final season.[20]

Márquez's career included three seasons in the Negro Leagues, 12 seasons in the minor leagues, two seasons in major-league baseball, and two seasons in the Mexican Leagues in addition to his years in the Puerto Rican Winter League. As a player, Márquez had a superstition of touching first or third base while trotting in from the outfield at the end of an inning. He later worked as a scout for Montreal Expos in 1969 and 1970, the first two years of the franchise's existence.

Following his short stint as a scout, Márquez worked for the Department of Sports in Aguadilla, and also coached both amateur and professional baseball. A first marriage to Lydia Babilonia was short-lived. He then married Olga Asis Rodríguez, who died in 1974. After her death, Luis went to live with and care for his mother. He and Olga had two children, Wanda and Gloria. In 2017, Wanda worked and gave sports talks at the ballpark that bears her father's name.

At the time of his death, Márquez was working with the Sports and Recreation Department in Aguadilla and in charge of Parque Colón.

His daughter Wanda's husband, Luis Ramos, shot Márquez twice with a handgun when Márquez confronted his son-in-law about the way he treated his daughter.[21] He was shot on the same street where he had been born, Calle Mercado.[22] Márquez was pronounced dead at the hospital in Aguadilla on March 1, 1988. He buried in Monte Cristo Memorial Park in Aguadilla. Reportedly because of a number of police "mistakes" of some sort, Luis Ramos was never convicted of a crime and as of 2017 was free in New York.[23]

The municipal baseball park in Aguadilla, Estadio Luis A. Canena Márquez, is named for the local man who had a 20-year career in professional baseball.[24] A bronze statue of Márquez is located in front of the stadium. Although he did not succeed in the majors, Luis Márquez was part of history as a member of a generation that broke down the racial barriers of professional baseball.

SOURCES

Thanks to Carlos Delgado Sr., Pedro Julio Molinary, and Jorge Colón Delgado for assistance with this biography.

NOTES

1   Thomas E. Van Hyning, *Puerto Rico's Winter League: A History of Major League Baseball's Launching Pad* (Jefferson, North Carolina: McFarland & Company, Inc., 1995), 118.

2   Van Hyning, 119.

3   Van Hyning, 179.

4   Email from Edwin Fernandez Cruz to Bill Nowlin, February 20, 2017. A fogón is a kind of hot stove.

5   "Luis L. Márquez," *1950 Beavers Scrapbook*, Dick Dobbins Collection on the Pacific Coast League, California Historical Society.

6   Van Hyning, 119. The following season (1947-48), Willard Brown, playing for Santurce, shattered the home-run record by hitting 27, which combined the totals from the previous records set by Márquez (14) and Gibson (13).

7   James A. Riley, *The Biographical Encyclopedia of the Negro Baseball Leagues* (New York: Carroll and Graf Publishers, 1994), 513.

8   See, for instance, "Yankees Buy Negro Player," *Oregonian* (Portland), February 3, 1949: 21.

9   "Luis L. Márquez," *1950 Beavers Scrapbook*.

10   Associated Press, "Cleveland Options Marquez to Portland," *Boston Traveler*, May 23, 1949: 32.

11   Al Wolf, "Haney's Comets Take 5th in Row," *Los Angeles Times*, May 28, 1949: B1.

12   Associated Press, "Coast Nine Signs 3rd Negro Player," *Omaha World-Herald*, July 16, 1949: 10.

13   John E. Spalding, *Pacific Coast League Stars: One Hundred of the Best, 1903 to 1957* (John Spalding, 1994), 115. Spalding states, "The Coast League was the scene of many fights between black and white players and Marquez was involved in two altercations in his first year in the league in 1949."

14   "Notables of Baseball at Sweeney Rites," *Los Angeles Times*, April 23, 1957: C1.

15   Al Wolf, "Sportraits," *Los Angeles Times*, January 20, 1951: B2.

16   Adrian Burgos, *Playing America's Game: Baseball, Latinos, and the Color Line* (Los Angeles: University of California Press, 2007), 273.

17   James P. Dawson, "Jethroe's 3-Run Homer in Ninth at Boston Tops Durocher Men, 8-5," *New York Times*, April 19, 1951: 51.

18   "Giants Split with Braves, Losing Wild Second Game in Tenth Inning," *New York Times*, April 20, 1951: 40.

19   "Pacific Coast League," *The Sporting News*, September 25, 1957: 40.

20   Pedro Treto Cisneros, *The Mexican League: Comprehensive Player Statistics, 1937–2001* (Jefferson, North Carolina: McFarland & Company, Inc., 2002), 185.

21   "Asesinan a ex pelotero Luis (Canena) Márquez," *Listen Diario* (February 2, 1988), article in Baseball Hall of Fame Library, player file for Luis Angel Marquez.

22   Email from Edwin Fernandez Cruz.

23   Ibid.

24   skyscrapercity.com/showthread.php?p=91051440.

EUTHUMN (EUDIE) NAPIER

By Tom Hawthorn

Euthumn Napier remembered a bus ride north on April 15, 1947, on which he joined his Homestead Grays teammates in whiling away the hours by talking about the biggest baseball news of the day. Jackie Robinson had started at first base that day for the Brooklyn Dodgers, breaking the modern color barrier.

"We were all thrilled for him," Napier recalled many years later. "We never thought it would happen. It was all we talked about on the bus. To say the least, it was a thrill."[1]

Though it was not yet obvious, Robinson's debut also marked the beginning of the end for the Negro Leagues. Napier, who was 34 at the time, would be too old to have a serious shot at a spot in the majors. He was finally on the cusp of his own starring role with the Grays after serving as a backup to Josh Gibson, who had died just three months before Robinson's first game. Napier, a 5-foot-9, 190-pounder, performed well for the Grays, being named to postseason all-star teams in 1947 and '48. Known as a defensive catcher, Napier backstopped the Pittsburgh Crawfords and the Grays before spending two seasons of Organized Baseball with the Farnham Pirates in the Canadian province of Quebec. He wound up his career playing sandlot baseball in Pittsburgh in his 40s.

In looking back at his career in 1978, Napier expressed resignation at having had to play segregated baseball through the seasons in which he would have been at his physical prime. "I'm not bitter," he said. "I had a lot of fun. You knew they weren't going to let the black man into baseball, so you never gave it a thought. Actually, playing baseball back then, I was making more money than the majority of black people, so I couldn't complain."[2]

His reminiscences of life on the road included anecdotes about how baseball players were not immune from the insults and degradations of Jim Crow rules. Most hotels were forbidden and fountains were reserved for whites. Many restaurants served blacks only from the rear entrance. Once, while he was traveling with the Grays, the team stopped at a gas station in Mississippi to replenish a water supply. They spotted a water fountain next to a cola machine. "We asked the man in charge if we could go over and get some water," Napier recalled. "The man told us he didn't have any water."[3] Another time, a storekeeper in Georgia smashed pop bottles used by the players rather than have them washed and reused by whites.

After Napier's death, his namesake son recounted his father's favorite story about playing in the South. "They were barnstorming and playing an all-white team in Georgia," Euthumn Napier Jr. told the *Pittsburgh Press* in 1983, "and the park didn't have a loudspeaker. The umpire would come up and announce the lineups. He announced the home team like: 'Mr. Smith pitching. Mr. Jones catching.'

"My dad's team had a little pitcher, a guy they called Groundhog. When the guy announced my dad's team, he yelled out, 'Little nigger pitching. Big nigger catching.' My dad, he really laughed about that. See, that would have really made me mad. But he laughed about it. And they went on to kill the team by some outrageous score."[4]

The catcher was known as Eudie or Eddie or Nap or Nape throughout his career, as his uncommon given name proved difficult to master. Authors and sportswriters rendered it incorrectly as Ethan, Ethum, Eutham, Eudis, and Euthumm over the years.

Euthumn Napier was born on a 400-acre farm near the county seat of Milledgeville in Baldwin County, Georgia, on January 3, 1913. He was the youngest of eight boys and one of 12 children to live beyond infancy born to Grace and Horace Napier. The boy was named for a kindly shoemaker who lived nearby. "They'd run out of names," his eldest son quipped in a 2017 interview.[5] The family moved north to Pittsburgh soon after Napier began elementary school, his father giving up farming for laboring work.

Napier made the varsity gridiron team at Allegheny High School and played in three games, which gained him a brief mention in the local African-American daily newspaper. "Allegheny also has two other colored boys on the football team who look to be very promising. They are Euthumn Napier and James Robinson," the *Pittsburgh Courier* reported in 1931. "These boys have done some fine playing, and deserve to be praised and encouraged."[6] The next month, both young men also earned a spot on the roster of the school's basketball team.

After his father died in 1929, not long after the stock-market crash, Napier combined studies with work, as he needed to help support his mother and younger sisters.[7] As a young man, he performed with the Rialto Singers Quartet, part of a theatrical troupe formed as part of a Works Progress Administration (WPA) job-creation program during the Depression. The troupe disbanded in 1936, their final performance conducted for free for unemployed workers and their families at the Labor Temple in Pittsburgh. Napier would later be known as among the better voices on the Pittsburgh Crawfords, as the players sang spirituals and barber-shop songs to pass the time on the long drives between games.

Eudie Napier (at right) with fellow Grays catchers Josh Gibson (left) and Ted "Double Duty" Radcliffe in 1946. In 1949 Napier became one of several 1948 Grays players to play for the Farnham Pirates. (*Noir-Tech Research, Inc.*)

Napier caught, pitched, and sometimes managed the Monarchs team in the second division of the Greater Pittsburgh League, a sandlot circuit. By the start of the 1939 season, he had shown enough skill to be identified as an understudy to Josh Gibson by Cum Posey, owner of the Homestead Grays.

On November 23, 1940, Napier married Leola Beatrice Compton, who was working as a folder at a laundry. They had met in high school, where the young New Orleans-born woman was described in her graduating yearbook as "a pleasant girl with high ambitions."

By the summer of 1944, Napier was sharing catching duties with Jeff Gwynn on a tour by the Pittsburgh Crawfords as they faced the Chicago Brown Bombers in a barnstorming series.

Napier's speed and power impressed a reporter with the *Winnipeg Free Press* when the Crawfords returned to the Manitoba capital in 1945 to face the Honus Wagner All-Stars. In one game, Napier was robbed of a home run when a blow to right field failed to clear the park only because it hit a broadcast booth atop the adjacent hockey rink whose exterior wall also served as the ballpark's fence. Napier was held to a double. Behind the plate, he always raced up the line after a ball was struck to an infielder, reaching "first base to cover up just about as soon as the hitter."[8]

The Grays added Napier to the roster for the 1946 season, though he saw limited service as a backup. Even after the death of the great Josh Gibson at age 35 in January 1947, Napier competed for the starter's role against the likes of Robert Gaston, Gibson's longtime backup, and Victor Sosa, a Cuban import.

With integration coming to provincial baseball, Napier joined a northward migration of some Negro League players to Canada. In 1949, he signed with the Farnham Pirates, a team in the independent Provincial League. The French-language newspaper *La Patrie* scouted him for its readers: "*Il est un frappeur de longue distance*" (He's a long-distance hitter.).[9] The circuit had six teams in Quebec's Eastern Townships region, serving as a great summer entertainment for a French-speaking area with a sizable English-speaking minority. Napier made the all-star game, though he was the goat when the winning run was scored on a passed ball. He was with the club in 1951 when the Provincial League served as a Class-C circuit as he made his debut in Organized Baseball at age 38. Among his teammates was Josh Gibson Jr., the son of the late immortal.

The left-handed-batting Napier hit .285 with 8 home runs in 319 at-bats with Farnham in 1951. He had seen only spot duty with the Grays over several seasons with only 103 plate appearances recorded in parts of four seasons, according to statistics compiled by Baseball-Reference.com. His composite average was .259.

Napier also spent part of the summers in the semiprofessional Major Inter-County League in the neighboring province of Ontario, playing briefly for the Brantford Red Sox and the Guelph Maple Leafs. In winters, he played ball in Puerto Rico (Santurce Cangrejeros), Panama (Chesterfield Smokers), and Venezuela (Cerveza Caracas). By 1954, he was back in the Greater Pittsburgh League, smacking homers for the Bellevue team.

After his playing days ended, Napier found out that his career in the Negro Leagues had brought neither a pension nor an offer for coaching jobs. He worked two janitorial jobs, starting on the overnight shift at the *Pittsburgh Press* from 10 P.M. until 6 A.M. before moving on to sweeping floors at the Joseph Horne's department store from 7 A.M. until 3 P.M. He retired around the date of his 67th birthday in 1980.

Over the years, he stayed in contact with some of his old teammates, including Sam Bankhead, who died in 1976, as well as Willie Pope and Wilmer "Red" Fields.

Napier died of cirrhosis at Suburban General Hospital in the Pittsburgh suburb of Bellevue on March 16, 1983, at the age of 70. He was survived by his wife and by their two adult sons, Euthumn Jr. and Michael. Napier is buried in Union Dale Cemetery in Pittsburgh.

For decades, his woolen Homestead Grays uniform was kept in a cedar chest. More than 20 years after his death, the rare artifact was placed on display at the Senator John Heinz History Center in Pittsburgh, which includes the Western Pennsylvania Sports Museum.

Napier was inducted into the Pennsylvania Sports Hall of Fame, Western Chapter, in 1978. In an appropriate coda for his career, his first name is misspelled as "Eutham" on the plaque.

SOURCES

In addition to the sources cited in the Notes, the author also consulted:

Lester, Larry and Sammy J. Miller. *Black Baseball in Pittsburgh* (Charleston, South Carolina: Arcadia Publishing, 2001).

Ruck, Rob. *Sandlot Seasons: Sport in Black Pittsburgh* (Urbana: University of Illinois Press, 1987).

Swanton, Barry, and Jay-Dell Mah. *Black Baseball Players in Canada: A Biographical Dictionary, 1881–1960* (Jefferson, North Carolina: McFarland & Company, Inc., Publishers, 2009).

Interviews with Michael Napier and Euthumn Napier Jr., September 14, 2016.

NOTES

1   Steve Hecht, "Euthumn Napier Remembers When Only the Ball Was White," *Pittsburgh Post-Gazette*, April 20, 1978: 44.

2   Ibid.

3   Ibid.

4   Tom Wheatley, "A Part of Local Lore Died With Napier," *Pittsburgh Press*, March 30, 1983: 86.

5   Telephone interview with Euthumn Napier Jr., September 14, 2016.

6   Theresa Cutts and Theodore Maddox. "Allegheny High School," *Pittsburgh Courier*, December 5, 1931: 16.

7   In 1978, the *Pittsburgh Post-Gazette* noted offhandedly that Napier played for the Grays under an assumed name while still in high school. If so, the alias was not revealed, and neither of his sons can confirm that this was the case. See "Napier on baseball," *Pittsburgh Post-Gazette*, April 20, 1978: 44.

8   "All-Stars Defeat Crawfords, 7 to 4," *Winnipeg Free Press*, September 5, 1945: 13.

9   "Max Lanier a signé pour les Cubs et Smolko pour Granby dans la ligue Provinciale," *La Patrie* (Montreal), April 8, 1949.

TOM PARKER

By Bill Johnson

Tom Parker, who also answered to the sobriquets of "Big Train" and "Country," enjoyed a long and successful career in professional baseball. He was a pitcher and outfielder not only on the 1948 Homestead Grays, the final Negro League World Series champion, but also for an array of teams both before and after that championship season. Parker's complete life, however, both in and beyond baseball remains untold. The whole story may never be known and, if it were not for his professional excellence at the game, his tale might already have slipped away into the anonymous shadows of the past. The Tom Parker story is one of many case studies in the challenges attached to actively remembering history, and these challenges continue to confront every Negro Leagues researcher.[1]

It is likely that Parker came from Louisiana since all available sources agree that he hailed from the Alexandria area. There are, however, variant listings for his birth year; which can only be narrowed down to the time span between 1910 and 1915. Baseball-reference.com unequivocally states that he was born on February 12, 1912, in Alexandria.[2] James Riley, in his sweeping biographical survey of the Negro leagues, avers that Parker was born "about 1911,"[3] and the archives contained in the Ancestry.com website list two Negro men, both named Tom Parker, who were both from Alexandria, Louisiana, and were born in 1911 and 1912 respectively.[4] The Seamheads.com website simply lists Parker's birth year as 1912.[5] Neither searches of federal cemeteries in Louisiana and surrounding states[6] nor the digitized version of the 1920 US Census shed light on Big Train Parker's birth date; several Tom Parkers fall within those rough parameters.

Parker's life in professional baseball may have begun as early as 1929 or as late as 1931. The Negro Leagues Book[7] and Robert Peterson[8] both state that Parker played for the Memphis Red Sox in 1929, but neither Seamheads.com nor Baseball-Reference.com corroborates that assertion. A review of an array of old issues of the Afro-American, as well as available Memphis newspaper archives, does not produce any reference to Parker playing baseball there in 1929, but such omissions provide no authoritative evidence either. It can be stated with certainty, however, that the 1931 season is the first in Parker's baseball career that can be verified.

According to most sources, including numerous newspaper clippings, Parker was a young pitcher and utility player on the 1931 Indianapolis ABCs. As is the case in so many instances in Parker's life and career, the various biographies diverge. Riley notes that Parker played for the Monroe Monarchs after leaving Indianapolis. The idea that he played for Monroe is interesting; the team, which existed until 1935, actually joined the Negro Southern League for the 1932 season. The Monarchs went 26-22 that year and barnstormed throughout the region, but there is no other corroboration that Parker played for the team.[9] While it would be logical that a Louisiana native would play for a Louisiana team, not even historian John Holway lists Parker as a member of the team.[10]

In 1934 Parker definitely played for the independent New Orleans Crescent Stars. S. Derby Gisclair, via his outstanding website about baseball in Louisiana,[11] found a few extant reports of Parker's achievements, including an early-season account of a game against a Houston team in which the "heavy hitters of the Stars connected in all pinches with 'Big Train' Parker and Wright coming through with home runs with men on base."[12] There exists also an October addendum in which " 'Big Train' Parker and Wright both poled out homers during the opener."[13] While these accounts suggest that Parker played for New Orleans for the entire year, it is also possible that he played games for the Nashville Elite Giants during the same year.[14] This would have been several years before the team relocated to Baltimore, when Nashville was a full member of the second iteration of the Negro National League. His play there is not well documented but—it must again be noted—the mere absence of information does not mean that Parker did not suit up for the squad.

For a brief period of a few years, beginning in 1935, there is widespread agreement on Parker's baseball story. Clearly talented enough to grab the attention of the major black leagues, Parker played for the Homestead Grays until 1939. He actively contributed to a 1937 World Series win by a "combined squad of Grays and Eagles" over a "team of Monarchs and American Giants."[15] Holway notes that "Tom 'Country' Parker of the Grays (in game two) won his own game with a two-run pinch single off Sug Cornelius. Final score: 10-7. There are no other details of the game."[16] Seamheads.com credits Parker with an 11-14 pitching record during his tenure with Homestead, a mark that he complemented with a .321 batting average as an outfielder and occasional shortstop.[17]

Several sources state that Parker joined the Toledo Crawfords for a time in 1939; however, in this instance, there is a lack of corroborative evidence once more. The 1940 season remains a mystery, with no source offering any reference to active participation in baseball, but by June 1941 Parker was again playing with the New Orleans Stars.[18] One newspaper account noted, "In the second game Tom 'Big Train' Parker, recent Star recruit, blanked the Cats *(sic)* with three hits and added to the Floridians' misery by hitting a home run with the bases loaded in the second inning."[19]

A June 1941 article in the *New Orleans Times-Picayune* may shed some light on the winding path of Parker's life, including his whereabouts in 1940. The newspaper reported that "The addition of Tom 'Big Train' Parker, formerly of the New York Black Yankees, to the Star lineup has greatly increased their offensive strength. Parker, with his timely hitting, has won four out of the last nine games."[20] The date of the article and the use of the word "formerly" indicate

Tom "Big Train" Parker was a member of the Birmingham Black Barons in 1945; however, in 1948, he played for the Homestead Grays, who defeated the Black Barons in the last Negro League World Series. (*Negro Leagues Baseball Museum, Kansas City, Missouri*)

that Parker had played most recently for New York, perhaps in either 1940 or 1941, or both; this corroborates Riley's account that Parker played for New York in both 1941 and in 1942. In a major media market like New York, it is improbable, but certainly not impossible, that there was no mention of Parker. The *Times-Picayune* article does validate that New York portion of Parker's itinerant baseball journey, though.

In 1943 Parker played for the independent St. Louis-Harrisburg Stars, arriving as the final piece of a Negro National League controversy. The *Afro-American* shed light on how Parker came to join the Stars:

"Taking a firm stand against the St. Louis-Harrisburg Stars, the only club which has failed to comply with it recent ruling on the transfer of players, the Negro National League, Friday, ordered immediate return of two players from the Stars to the New

York Black Yankees. ... The players, Harry Williams, shortstop and manager, and Jim Starks, first-baseman, were ruled the property of the Black Yankees. George Mitchell, business manager of the St. Louis club, told the NNL that the players declined to leave the club because they had no desire to play with the Yankees. Under the new ruling, the players must report to the Yankees this week, with the New York club pledged to pay them the same salary the St. Louis club has been paying them. A third St. Louis-Harrisburg Stars player, Tom Parker, pitcher and outfielder, was ruled the property of the St. Louis club."[21]

After a half-season of barnstorming, Parker enlisted in the US Army. According to the Center for Negro League Baseball Research, Parker's sole year of service was 1944; he is listed as having been a member of the New York Cubans prior to his enlistment.[22] After his brief tour of duty in the Army, Parker returned to the Birmingham Black Barons for the 1945 season. In Birmingham as an outfielder, he was credited with a .286 batting average, but that did not include his performance in barnstorming games throughout the South.

Pitcher Tom Parker, a member of the 1948 Grays, was a well-traveled player. Here he appears (second from right) with 1942 New York Black Yankees teammates (L-R) Tex Burnett, Harry Williams, and Dan Wilson. (*Noir-Tech Research, Inc.*)

Parker moved to another new environment in 1946, when he joined up with the Boston Blues of the short-lived United States League as player-manager. The USL was the brainchild of former Pittsburgh Crawfords owner Gus Greenlee, who solicited Branch Rickey's involvement to lend greater credibility to the endeavor; however, the league folded in 1946 after less than two full seasons. At the time of the circuit's demise, Parker had the Boston squad in first place.

Forced to relocate yet again due to the failure of the USL, Parker spent 1947 with the Detroit Senators before signing with the Washington Homestead Grays for the 1948 campaign. The *Baltimore Afro-American* reported, "Tom Parker, former Black Yankee and Cuban outfielder, joined the Grays Sunday. Parker is the exchange player in the Jerry Benjamin deal, in which the Cubans acquired the former Grays centerfielder."[23] Parker debuted for the Grays in the season opener, a night game against the Baltimore Elite Giants at Pittsburgh's Forbes Field, and went 1-for 4. He was overshadowed by Luke Easter, who debuted with the Grays by going 3-for-3 with a home run and a double while driving in four runs and scoring twice. Parker was credited with a 7-4 pitching record that year; he also spent some time in the outfield, but he batted only .235 for the season.

The next year, with the Negro Leagues beginning to lose their collective momentum subsequent to Jackie Robinson's major-league debut in 1947 and with age likely beginning to affect his play, Parker joined the Farnham (Quebec) Pirates of the independent Provincial League. While at Farnham, he played against teams like the Drummondville Cubs, the Granby Red Sox, the Sherbrooke Athletics, the St. Hyacinthe Saints, and the St. Jean Braves; however, after one year, Parker hit the road once more.

He remained in Canada, though, and played the 1951-1953 seasons in the Manitoba-Dakota (ManDak) League, a minor-league-level organization that embraced racial integration on the field. Each ManDak team could keep three non-Canadian players on the roster, and the average player could expect to earn between $300 and $1,000 per month.[24] In 1951, with the Elmwood Giants, Parker posted a 5-2 pitching record against competition that included aging stars like Ted "Double Duty" Radcliffe, Willie Wells, and Leon Day, and he batted .429 in 19 games. Parker's numbers dropped off in 1952 as he managed a 5-3 record but hit only .269 for the Winnipeg Giants. During his final year in the circuit, with the Brandon Greys, he posted a 6-4 record and registered a .286 batting average in 20 games.[25]

According to Riley, the 6-foot-1, 230-pound Parker "was a big, robust fastball pitcher with a good curve; he also threw a slider, knuckler, and a change-up with a modicum of success and had a fair drop with average control of his pitches."[26] He also was considered to be a "true gentleman throughout his twenty-one seasons in the Negro Leagues."[27] In spite of exhaustive research efforts by numerous individuals, little else is known about Parker to date. The many unanswered questions about his life may never be satisfactorily answered since Parker and many of his Negro League contemporaries exist now only in snippets of history that have been preserved in newspaper archives. Although such news articles comprise more of a legacy than many people of earlier times enjoy, they are few and they expose a gap in the history of the game. It is unfortunate that Parker's life was not well documented as he was obviously a much-traveled man who likely had many stories to tell about the people he had met and places he had seen.

NOTES

1   The list of scholars interviewed for this essay, all of whom were incredibly helpful but similarly frustrated by an absence of evidence, includes author-historians Jay-Dell Mah and Barry Swanton, Craig Britcher of Pittsburgh's Heinz History Center, Professor Rob Ruck at the University of Pittsburgh, website curator S. Derby Gisclair, the staff of the Negro Leagues Baseball Museum in Kansas City, Missouri, and the staff of the National Baseball Hall of Fame in Cooperstown, New York,

2   See baseball-reference.com/register/player. cgi?id=parker002tom.

3   James Riley, *The Biographical Encyclopedia of the Negro Baseball Leagues* (New York: Carroll & Graf, 2002), 603.

4   interactive.ancestry.com/6061/4300990_00919?pid=8385924 2&backurl=http%3a%2f%2fsearch.ancestry.com%2f%2fcgi-

bin%2fsse.dll%3fdb%3d1920usfedcen%26indiv%3dtry%26h%3d8 3859242&treeid=&personid=&hintid=&usePUB=true.

5   seamheads.com.

6   interment.net/data/us/la/rapides/alexnat/index_npf.htm, and findagrave.com/cgi-bin/fg.cgi?page=gr&GRid=136961025 &ref=acom.

7   Dick Clark and Larry Lester, eds., *The Negro Leagues Book* (Cleveland: Society for American Baseball Research, 1994), 213.

8   Robert Peterson, *Only the Ball Was White* (New York: Oxford University Press, 1970), 370.

9   John Holway, *The Complete Book of Baseball's Negro Leagues: The Other Half of Baseball History* (Fern Park, Florida: Hastings House Publishers, 2001), 292.

10   Ibid.

11   neworleansbaseball.com/articles/html.

12   "Crescent Stars Batter Houston Team 14-1," *New Orleans Times-Picayune*, April 29, 1934: Section 4, 2.

13   "Crescent Stars Trounce Chicago Negro Team, 4-0," *New Orleans Times-Picayune*, October 15, 1934: 13.

14   baseball-reference.com/register/player.cgi?id=parker002tom.

15   Holway, 346.

16   Ibid.

17   seamheads.com/NegroLgs/player.php?ID=1954.

18   "N.O. Stars Will Play Birmingham in Sunday Games," *New Orleans Times-Picayune*, June 8, 1941: Section 4, 2.

19   "N.O. Stars Down Red Caps Twice in Negro A.L. Bill," *New Orleans Times-Picayune*, June 10, 1941: 11.

20   "N.O. St. Louis '9,' Black Barons to Play Here Today," *New Orleans Times-Picayune*, June 15, 1941: Section 4, 4.

21   "NNL Orders Starks and Williams to Yankees," *Afro American*, July 3, 1943: 23.

22   cnlbr.org/Portals/0/RL/Served_in_WWII.htm. No statistics are available for Parker's time with the New York Cubans; however, the fact that he played for them—as well as the New York Black Yankees—is further corroborated by an article in the *Baltimore Afro-American* from May 1, 1948 (see Note 23 below).

23   "Harrismen Launch Season Against Elites, Cubans," *Baltimore Afro-American*, May 1, 1948: 29.

24   Barry Swanton. *The ManDak League* (Jefferson, North Carolina: McFarland and Company, 2006), 5.

25   Swanton, 147.

26   Riley, 603.

27   Ibid.

WILLIE POPE

By Skip Nipper

O n September 19, 1988, the Pittsburgh Pirates paid tribute to the Homestead Grays by hoisting a black-and-white commemorative flag over Three Rivers Stadium. The occasion commemorated an event from 40 years earlier, when the Negro National League's Grays defeated the Birmingham Black Barons, champions of the Negro American League, four games to one in the last Negro League World Series.

The Pirates invited six surviving members of the team to Three Rivers Stadium, and pitcher Willie Pope was one of them. The others were Clarence Bruce, Garnett Blair, Bob Thurman, Wilmer Fields, and Hall of Famer Buck Leonard, who had been inducted into Cooperstown's shrine in 1972.

Pope, who resided in the Library area of Pittsburgh, had retired from the city controller's office the year before, and in 25 years had not told his employer about his baseball career.[1] Once the celebration was held, everyone knew.

The modest, reluctant hero from baseball's past, in an interview with the *Pittsburgh Post-Gazette,* remembered that life in the Negro Leagues was sometimes rough. "It's not real vivid right now, but it was pretty exciting. Traveling was the hardest thing we did," said Pope. "I remember standing on the bus, sleeping while I held on to the overhead rod on a trip all the way from Canada to Louisville. We changed our clothes on the bus."

Of the September 19 ceremony, Pope said, "It's a chance to meet some old friends."[2]

William Lee "Willie" Pope was born in Birmingham, Alabama, on December 24, 1918, the eldest of 11 children of Jackson and Mary Pope. Their father and mother worked as laborers on a farm in Alabama until they moved their young family to Snowden Township, Pennsylvania, near Pittsburgh, in the mid-1920s. Later, they relocated to Library so

his father, who went by Jack, could become a miner. Another of the Pope family's sons, Dave, who was two years younger than Willie, made it to the major leagues and had a four-year career as an outfielder and pinch-hitter for the Cleveland Indians and Baltimore Orioles.

Willie played in the local sandlots and also tried his hand at boxing, fighting as a Golden Gloves heavyweight in Pittsburgh. The day after a tournament bout in December 1937 that lasted 1:56 minutes of the first round, sportswriter Phil Gundelfinger wrote a rave review of his bout: "Nominated for one of the best offenses demonstrated to date must go to William Pope, 197-pound colored boy from the Center Ave. Y.M.C.A., who showed a well-rounded attack in technically knocking out Steve Kovar, 188 pounds. … Pope's rasping left hand is probably the best displayed in the tourney to date."[3]

Three nights later, Pope's fight was stopped at 2:35 of the third round by referee Ernie Sesto, as opponent Mike Cerota had one hand on the ropes and pounded Willie on the head, unable to defend himself. Sesto awarded Pope the victory on a technical knockout for Cerota's illegal blows. The victory gave Pope the heavyweight championship.[4] On March 4, 1938, he lost a decision to Arthur Brown of the Superior Y.M.C.A.

After serving as a technical sergeant in the US Army from 1942 to 1944,[5] Pope joined the Pittsburgh Crawfords, a team that was revived as a member of the United States League in 1945. The original Crawfords franchise had been founded by Pittsburgh black entrepreneur Gus Greenlee in 1931 and had been named after his Crawford Grill; the team had called Forbes Field its home ballpark.

Pope, who stood 6-feet-4 and weighed 247 pounds, was a large presence on the mound. In a game in July 1945 before a crowd of 7,000 at Brooklyn's Ebbets Field, the big right-hander and his Pittsburgh teammates demonstrated why they were leading the league as they won both ends of a three-team doubleheader. According to the *Brooklyn Daily Eagle:*

"In the opener, the Crawfords turned back the Brooklyn Brown Dodgers, 9-4, and then tallied once in the final inning of a seven-inning struggle to break a three-all tie and gain a 4-3 victory over the Chicago Brown Bombers. In the opener, the Crawfords with Willie Pope pitching effectively, had an easy time downing the Brooklyn team. Although he allowed nine hits, Pope was good in the pinches, setting nine batters down on strikes. He issued five walks."[6]

By the end of July, Pope had struck out 146 batters (averaging 17 per game) and had tossed two no-hit, no-run games. Of his nine victories, four were shutouts.[7] His victims included the Chicago Brown Bombers, Philadelphia Hilldales, Detroit Giants, Toledo Cubs, and Knoxville.[8]

In September, the *Brooklyn Daily Eagle*, naming him "Wee Willie," reported that along with his 17 wins, Pope had struck out 211 batters. The newspaper's headline bestowed praise on Pope, reading "Pope, Ace Pitcher, Likened to (Satchel) Paige." The article itself asserted, "Pope is said to be faster than Paige in his prime (Satchel was 39 at the time) and his curves are said to be even sharper."[9]

The next year, 1946, when the team claimed the United States League championship, Pope's brother Dave joined the club, and together they became the battery in several games. The *Pittsburgh Post-Gazette* heralded the younger Pope as a welcome addition to the team, stating, "The addition of a brother battery, Willie Pope, pitcher, and Dave behind the bat, has greatly strengthened the Crawford nine."[10]

At the end of the season, Willie joined Jackie Robinson's All Stars, a team formed to barnstorm in the Midwest and East. The team also played a handful of games in California before disbanding.[11] One of the highlights of Pope's career was when the team beat the Pittsburgh Pirates in an exhibition game at Forbes Field. It was a sweet victory for Willie, as he had asked the Pirates to look at him before Robinson was signed by Brooklyn's general manager, Branch Rickey. Pope remarked, "I was really throwing the ball hard then. I asked them just to give me a look. I had a feeling the barrier would be broken. I could've been the first."[12]

When the Crawfords folded after the 1946 season, Willie was drafted by the Philadelphia Stars,[13] but he signed instead to play for the Homestead Grays. The Grays had been founded in 1912 as an independent team, but had been Negro National League champion from 1939 to 1945.

Josh Gibson died in January 1947, and by April several players were attempting to make the club. Luke Easter was the possible replacement for Gibson, but also joining the 32 others on the preseason roster were Pope, Gabriel Patterson, "Jeep" Johnson, Clarence Bruce, and Maurice Peatros, former Crawfords teammates.[14] Willie amassed only a 6-7 record in 1947; however, in a game against the New York Cubans (who had 22-year-old Minnie Miñoso on the roster) in Washington, he threw a no-hitter.[15]

In 1948 the Grays relied on the services of their previous pitching stars, including R.T. Walker, Pope, Johnny Wright, Frank Thompson, Wilmer Fields, and Cecil Kaiser. The club strengthened the roster by adding two new pitchers, Garnett Bankhead and Willie Smith, before the season.[16] The team won the 1948 Negro National League pennant, and earned the right to face the Birmingham Black Barons in the Negro League World Series. Details of some games of the World Series are incomplete, but Pope hit a two-run triple in Game One, played in Kansas City, that was key to the Grays' 3-2 victory.[17] Homestead went on to defeat Birmingham in five games and win what turned out to be the last Negro League World Series.

In spite of Pope's losing record, the *Pittsburgh Courier* commented positively on his potential, at one point writing, "Wee Willie recently hurled a one-hitter against the champion Newark Eagles. If young Pope will listen to Manager Vic Harris, and work hard on his control, the kid should have a bright future."[18]

The Negro Leagues, however, had begun to decline. After Jackie Robinson played in the 1947 major-league World Series for the Brooklyn Dodgers,

Pitcher Willie Pope (pictured here) and his brother Dave – a future Cleveland Indians outfielder – were teammates on the 1946 Homestead Grays and were reunited in 1949 as members of the Quebec Provincial League's Farnham Pirates. (*Noir-Tech Research, Inc.*)

Negro League teams began to have difficulty drawing crowds. By 1948, the Grays were drawing an average of only 2,000 per game. The club lost nearly $45,000 in the two years Pope was with them, and the team was dissolved after the 1948 World Series victory over Birmingham.[19]

In 1949 Pope played for the Farnham Pirates in Canada's independent Provincial League, where he and his brother Dave were reunited as teammates. (Dave Pope had played in 98 games for Farnham in 1948, hitting .365.) The Provincial League consisted of teams in and around Quebec, and was considered an outlaw league.[20] Former Homestead teammates Clarence Bruce, Eudie Napier, and Tom Parker were also on the team. Season records are unclear, as rosters contained some players with assumed names, especially those who had been suspended by Commissioner A.B. "Happy" Chandler for jumping to the Mexican League. Former major-league players Max Lanier, a St. Louis Cardinals pitcher, and Danny Gardella, outfielder for the New York Giants, were two players who joined the Provincial League when they failed to have their suspensions lifted.[21]

Late in the season, Willie Pope was suspended by manager Joe Krakowski for "insubordination" and was placed up for trade or sale.[22] He remained with Farnham, however, and beat Granby, 3-1, while fanning 15 batters in the first round of the playoffs.[23] Then he came back to win the seventh game in the semifinals against St. Jean.[24] Future major-league star Sal Maglie, who also had been suspended for playing in Mexico, led Drummondville over Farnham to win the playoff championship.

The Provincial League joined Organized Baseball in 1950,[25] and Pope's Farnham team finished in third place under manager Packy Rogers. Pope was 3-5 with a 2.38 ERA.

Pope played winter ball during the 1950-1951 season in Guadalajara, Mexico.[26] In 16 games with Jalisco, he won five, lost eight, and had a 3.94 ERA.[27]

Farnham signed former Negro League legend Sam Bankhead, another of Pope's former Grays teammates, as its player-manager for the 1951 season, but Willie moved to the St. Hyacinthe Saints. His

3.82 ERA was substantially higher than it had been with Farnham the previous season, but he had a winning record at 12-11. The club finished in fifth place, 17½ games behind league champion Sherbrooke Athletiques.

Moving to St. Hyacinthe in 1951, Pope had a 3.82 ERA, substantially higher than it had been with Farnham the previous season, but he had a winning record at 12-11. The club finished in fifth place, 17½ games behind league champion Sherbrooke Athletiques.

At the end of the season, Pope was sold to the Chicago White Sox, along with former Kansas City Monarchs pitcher Connie Johnson.[28] He was assigned to Colorado Springs (Class-A Western League) during spring training in 1952, but the Sky Sox returned him to St. Hyacinthe.[29] It is uncertain whether Pope played in any games while with the Saints, but by May he was back on the Colorado Springs roster.

On May 7 Pope was called on in the eighth inning to quell a rally by the Lincoln A's, and the Sky Sox held on to win 10-6.[30] On May 10 against the Des Moines Bruins, he made his first start and gained his first win of the season, 5-3. For the year, he led the pitching staff with a 3.00 ERA in 23 games, winning 12 games while losing 5.

Returning to Colorado Springs for 1953, Willie started a team-high 30 games and was 16-12 with a 3.38 ERA. He was named to the West roster for the league All-Star game against the East and pitched the final inning in the 6-1 win. On August 1 he won a 1-hour 26-minute complete game over the Lincoln Chiefs, 4-2, for his 11th win.[31] The Sky Sox won the regular-season crown with a 95-59 record but lost to fourth-place Des Moines in the first round of the playoffs.

Pope had a tryout with the White Sox in the spring of 1954,[32] but wound up with the Charleston Senators of the Triple-A American Association. On April 23 he notified the Senators that he had agreed to play for a team in the Dominican Republic that offered him salary plus living expenses for himself and his wife. The Chicago White Sox promised a salary boost of their own, along with a trial with the major-league club, so Pope decided not to leave the Charleston club after all.[33]

For the 1954 season, Pope managed only a 4-11 record with a 5.27 ERA. In Charleston's home preseason opener on April 10, he held Indianapolis to four hits and one run in five innings of a 4-2 loss.[34] On July 1 he ended a two-month victory famine when he gained his fourth win (against 5 losses) by beating Columbus 4-1, allowing only 4 hits.[35]

Pope returned to Colorado Springs in 1955 and fared much better, posting a 13-8 record with a 3.48 ERA. As a left-handed batter, he showed his power at the plate by slamming a grand slam against Wichita on July 9, but he lost the game, 11-7, after losing his pitching control in the sixth inning.[36] On September 1 he endured a bases-loaded, none-out jam in the ninth, securing a 2-1 win at Pueblo.[37]

After the 1955 season, Chicago assigned Pope to the Triple-A International League's Toronto Maple Leafs. For a few weeks in December he played for Estrellas Orientales in the Dominican League.[38] When the White Sox told him they would bring him up during the 1956 season if he would agree first to play for Toronto, he decided to retire.[39]

In 1997 Pope explained why he left the White Sox organization, saying, "They kept telling me they were going to bring me up, kept promising me."[40] Obviously, such promises were never kept.

Once his baseball career was over, Pope owned a restaurant in Pittsburgh and worked as a surveyor for the city. He also ran for ward chairman of the city and managed a baseball team in the Hill District.

"I don't hold any grudges now," Pope told sportswriter Jimmy Dunn in 1997. "We were the best and we knew we were the best. The games were fun, and the guys I played with were great. The travel, along with the bigotry and segregation we faced, was hard to deal with, though."[41]

Pope died in the Veterans Affairs Medical Center in O'Hara Township, a suburb of Pittsburgh, at the age of 91 on June 10, 2010. He was survived by his wife of 59 years, Ethelia, and nine siblings. A memorial service was held at Kingdom Hall East End

Congregation in Penn Hills, and he was buried at the National Cemetery of the Alleghenies in Bridgeville, Pennsylvania.

Acknowledgment

The author wishes to thank Bryan Steverson for sharing his personal notes on Willie Pope.

SOURCES

In addition to the sources cited in the Notes, the author consulted ancestry.com, baseball-reference.com, coe.k-state.edu, newspapers.com, findagrave.com, and the following:

Klima, John. *Willie's Boys: The 1948 Birmingham Black Barons, the Last Negro League World Series, and the Making of a Baseball Legend* (Hoboken, New Jersey: John Wiley & Sons, Inc., 2009).

Plott, William J. *The Negro Southern League: A Baseball History, 1920-1951* (Jefferson, North Carolina: McFarland & Co., 2015).

NOTES

1   Kelly Carter, "Standing Out: Willie Pope Nearly Made It to the Majors," *Pittsburgh Press*, February 27, 1989: 2.

2   Phil Axelrod,"After 40 Years, Grays' Flag Flies High," *Pittsburgh Post-Gazette*, September 7, 1988: 34.

3   Phil Gundelfinger Jr., "Kayoes Mark Novice Bouts," *Pittsburgh Press*, December 4, 1937: 8.

4   Gundelfinger, "New Kensington Mittman Features Novice Tourney," *Pittsburgh Press*, December 7, 1937: 32.

5   Gary Bedingfield, *Baseball in Wartime*, baseballinwartime.com/negro.htm, retrieved February 13, 2017.

6   "Crawfords Too Torrid for Ebbets Rivals," *Brooklyn Daily Eagle*, July 23, 1945: 12.

7   Paul Kurtz, "Play at Pitcairn—Creekers Battle Smilers Tonight," *Pittsburgh Press*, July 28, 1945: 8.

8   "Crawfords Boast Strikeout Star," *Pittsburgh Post-Gazette*, July 28, 1945: 13.

9   "Pope, Ace Pitcher, Likened to Paige," *Brooklyn Daily Eagle*, September 7, 1945: 16.

10   "Crawford, Clippers Play Here Sunday," *Pittsburgh Post-Gazette*, June 14, 1946: 18.

11   "The First Jackie Robinson All-Stars," baseballhistorydaily.com/tag/west-coast-negro-baseball-association, retrieved February 5, 2017.

12   Ed Bouchette, "Memories Golden Here on a Golden Anniversary," *Pittsburgh Post-Gazette*, May 15, 1997: 11.

13   "AL Teams Draft Stars of Clubs Calling It Quits," *Pittsburgh Courier*, February 19, 1949: 11.

14   "Grays Speed Drills in Florida Camps," *Pittsburgh Courier*, April 5, 1947: 15. Some sources render the name as Peatross.

15   Malik Smith, "William 'Willie' Pope - Negro Leagues Pitcher for the Grays, Crawfords," *Pittsburgh Post-Gazette*, June 16, 2010: 13.

16   "Pittsburgh Opener Set for April 29; Outfield Has Power," *Pittsburgh Courier*, April 10, 1948: 15.

17   Rich Emert, "Pittsburgh Was a Special Place in the History of Negro Leagues Baseball," *Pittsburgh Post-Gazette*, July 8, 2001: 37.

18   "Ches" Washington, "Grays Mainstays Top Nats," *Pittsburgh Courier*, September 6, 1947: 14.

19   Daniel Cattau, "Forgotten Champions," *washingtonpost.com/archive/lifestyle/magazine/1990/06/03/forgotten-champions/fa87855d-517c-4cce-bce4-7b3a065b3cfc/?utm_term=.4f39da117447*, retrieved February 19, 2017.

20   "Outlaw League Will Join Organized Baseball," *Winnipeg Tribune*, October 20, 1949: 19.

21   "Baseball Outlaws of Big League Class Spark Quebec Circuit," *Ottawa Journal*, June 3, 1949: 24.

22   Lloyd McGowan, "Tuminelli Tabbed as Most Valuable in Quebec League," *The Sporting News*, August 10, 1949: 38.

23   McGowan, "Brilliant Hurling Features Playoffs in Provincial Loop," *The Sporting News*, September 21, 1949: 17.

24   McGowan, "Sal Maglie Opens Provincial Finals With Shutout Win," *The Sporting News*, October 5, 1949: 52.

25   "Outlaw League Will Join Organized Ball."

26   Robert Retort, *Negro League Legends Pictorial Album* (New Castle, Pennsylvania: Self-published), 246.

27   Pedro Treto Cisneros, *The Mexican League, Comprehensive Player Statistics, 1937-2001* (Jefferson, North Carolina: McFarland & Company, 2002), 477.

28   "Highlights of Lower Minors (Class C)," *The Sporting News*, September 12, 1951: 36.

29   "Western League Notes of Interest," *Greeley* (Colorado) *Daily Tribune*, March 26, 1952: 6.

30   "Home Runs Help Sky Sox Trip Lincoln," *Des Moines Register*, May 8, 1952: 19.

31   "Sky Sox Win, 4-2, In Quick Time," *Des Moines Register*, August 2, 1953: 25.

32   W. Rollo Wilson, "'Our Boys' With New Clubs," *Pittsburgh Courier*, April 3, 1954: 16.

33   "American Association," *The Sporting News*, May 5, 1954: 28.

34   "Tribe Stops Charleston's Bow," *The Sporting News*, April 21, 1954: 29.

35   "American Association," *The Sporting News*, July 14, 1954: 48.

36   "Western League," *The Sporting News*, July 20, 1955: 41.

37   "Western League," *The Sporting News*, September 7, 1955: 33.

38   Alexis Camilo, "Latin Showing Backs Blacks Comeback Bid,"
      The Sporting News, December 14, 1955: 23.

39   Carter, 2.

40   Bouchette, 11.

41   Jimmy Dunn, "He Realized a Dream by Playing for Grays,"
      Pittsburgh Post-Gazette, March 20, 1997: 104.

WILLIE SMITH

By Alan Cohen

According to some references, including the *Pittsburgh Courier* of April 10, 1948, Willie Smith was born on April 15, 1915, in Boswell, Alabama.[1] Or was he? He first appeared in the Negro Leagues with the Newark Eagles in 1938. Or did he? The answers to the two questions are "maybe not" and "probably not," as Homestead's Willie Smith was a pitcher and the man who played for Newark in 1938 was an infielder, although one database shows him having pitched to two batters in one game in 1938.

According to the *Courier*, Smith batted and threw right-handed, was 6-feet-2-inches tall, and tipped the scales at 173 pounds. However, in their pages he was referred to as a young rookie. At age 33, he would have hardly been considered young.

This much is known. Pitcher Willie Smith was acquired by the Homestead Grays prior to the 1948 season, having spent the previous season with the L&N All-Stars in Birmingham, Alabama. The team was a Birmingham Industrial League team sponsored by the Louisville and Nashville Railroad. Perhaps the most renowned of the Industrial League teams in segregated Birmingham were those sponsored by the Tennessee Coal, Iron and Railroad Company (TCI). The TCI team had a center fielder named Cat Mays playing alongside his 16-year-old son Willie, who would play the following season with the Birmingham Black Barons.[2] Spring training had already begun when Smith was signed on March 29, 1948. He joined the Homestead Grays while they were on the road in North Carolina.[3] Being on the road was normal in the Negro Leagues, especially with the Homestead Grays, who played "home" games in Pittsburgh, Washington, and any number of venues in between.

The 1948 season was not Willie Smith's first foray into Negro League baseball. In 1946 he had appeared with the Independent Cincinnati Crescents along-side future Homestead Grays teammate Luke Easter. The 1946 Crescents were managed by Winfield S. Welch and played their home games at Crosley Field. Smith was, according to the *Cincinnati Enquirer*, one of several Smiths on the team, and was said to have been acquired from the Kansas City Monarchs. However, there is no record of his having pitched for the Monarchs.

Records for 1946 are incomplete, but Willie Smith won the second game of a doubleheader against the Clowns on July 7.[4] He pitched the entire six innings of the abbreviated game, surrendering six hits as his team won 6-3.[5] He also pitched in a game at Brooklyn's Dexter Park on July 29, 1946, when Cincinnati took on the New York Black Yankees. He pitched the entire game and came out on the short end of a 4-3 decision, striking out six, walking six, and giving up six hits. The decisive blow was a two-run homer by the Black Yankees' Felix McLaurin.[6] On August 18 Smith shut out the Chicago American Giants in the second game of a doubleheader at Crosley Field.[7] And, of course, in those days the next opponent was a bus ride away. On August 23 the bus stopped at Benton Harbor, Michigan, and the Cincinnati team took on the local American Legion outfit. Smith did the pitching and helped himself with a grand slam in the fourth inning. The homer put the Crescents in the lead, and they went on to win 7-5 as Smith allowed nine hits and struck out four batters.[8]

In 1947, at the beginning of the season, Smith was with the Independent Detroit Wolves, a team about which little is known. He was with the team when it trained in Houston. Or was he? A Willie Smith was with the team, but that Willie Smith hailed from Jackson, Michigan.[9] It appears that the Wolves were headed for the Negro American League but when they had difficulty securing playing dates at Briggs Stadium, they were dropped from the league. The

Wolves were managed by William "Dizzy" Dismukes, a pitching star from the Negro Leagues' early days. It is uncertain how long Smith played for Detroit before he signed on with the L&N squad.

Smith's trail gets a bit cold at this stage of his career, and the next meaningful documentation of his travels has him joining Vic Harris's Homestead Grays in 1948, a team that featured the likes of Luke Easter and Buck Leonard. Prior to the 1948 season, Smith appeared in two exhibition games against Negro National League opponents, defeating the New York Black Yankees and Baltimore Elite Giants.[10]

Smith first took the field in an exhibition game on April 4 in Daytona Beach, Florida. The opponents that day were the Florida Black Cats, and he came into the game in the fourth inning. He pitched six innings, surrendering four hits, as the Grays won 8-4.[11] The Grays broke camp in Daytona Beach on April 9, played exhibitions against the New York Cubans in New Orleans on April 13 and 14, and then headed north.

In the game against the Elite Giants on April 18, as 5,500 fans looked on, Smith pitched the first eight innings at Baltimore's Bugle Field. He scattered nine hits and allowed three runs as he earned the victory in a 5-4 Grays triumph. Two of the Baltimore runs scored on a home run by opposing pitcher Bob Romby, and the other scored on successive doubles by Henry Kimbro and Lester Lockett. Smith left for pinch-hitter Bob Boston in the top of the ninth inning, and Frank Thompson pitched the final stanza for the Grays.[12]

The Grays wrapped up a successful preseason campaign (18-3) on April 30 with a victory over the New Castle (Pennsylvania) Chiefs of the Class-C Mid-Atlantic League. In the 8-0 contest, Smith pitched a complete-game shutout, allowing only five hits, and contributed to the offense with a double in the third inning when the Grays extended their lead to 5-0.[13]

Although there was a "regular season" that included games against Negro National League opponents, the Grays were often involved in exhibition games. Smith appeared in one such contest against

the Bushwicks in Brooklyn. The semipro Bushwicks often played Negro League teams and on June 25 at Dexter Park in Queens, New York, they staged a late rally in which they scored seven runs in the ninth inning while victimizing, among others, Willie Smith. However, the Grays had built up a substantial lead and held on to win the game, 10-8.[14]

Smith got into a handful of league games during the regular season, pitching mostly in relief. On June 20 he entered the second game of a doubleheader against the Philadelphia Stars with two outs in the fourth inning after R. T. Walker had allowed a single and a double and walked three consecutive batters to blow a 2-0 lead. Smith pitched 2⅓ innings before being removed for a pinch-hitter in the sixth inning. The Grays ended up losing the game, 4-2.[15] On June 27 at Griffith Stadium, Smith entered the game in the ninth inning with the Grays trailing 7-2. In a scoreless ninth inning, he registered two outs but allowed a pair of hits. He left the game in favor of Charlie Bell, who retired the final batter.[16]

Smith also appeared in games on consecutive days in July. On July 4, in the first game of a doubleheader against the Newark Eagles in Washington, he pitched the final innings in a 13-4 loss. On July 5 the Grays faced the Baltimore Elite Giants in a doubleheader at Baltimore. The Grays suffered a rare defeat in the second game of the doubleheader, losing 18-6; Smith was one of three Grays pitchers in that game.[17]

Overall, however, Smith saw little action in league games and was more often used in exhibition games. He was handed the ball in an exhibition against the Dormont team from the semipro Greater Pittsburgh League on July 15. He pitched the entire game but came up on the short end as Dormont defeated the Grays 5-4 by scoring two runs in the final inning.[18]

The Homestead Grays and the Negro National League would vanish after the 1948 season. Some of their players joined the ranks of Organized Baseball, where a few advanced to the majors. Others continued to play Negro League baseball. As for Willie Smith, little is known about his life either before or after his years in the sun with the 1946 Cincinnati Crescents and 1948 Homestead Grays.

NOTES

1   "Pittsburgh Opener Set for April 29, Outfield Has Power," *Pittsburgh Courier,* April 10, 1948: 15.

2   James S. Hirsch, *Willie Mays: The Life, The Legend* (New York, Scribner, 2010), 34.

3   "Grays Beat N.C. Stars 6-1; Two New Pitchers Added to Staff," *Pittsburgh Post-Gazette,* March 30, 1948: 14.

4   "Negro Foes Pack Plenty of Talent," *Daily* (Springfield) *Illinois State Journal,* July 10, 1946: 10.

5   "Clowns Split With Crescents," *Chicago Defender,* July 13, 1946: 10.

6   "Black Yanks Trip Cincinnati Nine at Dexter Park," *Brooklyn Daily Eagle,* July 30, 1946: 11.

7   "Crescents Divide with Chicago Club," *Cincinnati Enquirer,* August 19, 1946: 14.

8   "Lafayette Here Sunday Night; Legion Bows to Cincy; Crescents 7-5 Win Fashioned on Three Homers," *News Palladium* (Benton Harbor, Michigan), August 24, 1946: 6.

9   "Detroit Wolves Texas Bound," *Chicago Defender,* March 22, 1947: 11.

10   "Chiefs Sign Two More Players, Prep for Grays Game Friday," *New Castle* (Pennsylvania) *News,* April 28, 1948: 16.

11   "Grays Win Fifth Game in a Row, 8 to 4," *Pittsburgh Post-Gazette,* April 5, 1948: 15.

12   "Elites Play Grays in Washington Sunday," *Baltimore Afro-American,* April 24, 1948: 28.

13   "Grays Blank Chiefs Under Arcs, 8-0: Smith's Hurling Silences Locals, Six Errors Hurt," *New Castle* (Pennsylvania) *News,* May 1, 1948: 14.

14   "Bushwick Nine Bows to Grays in Night Clash," *Brooklyn Daily Eagle,* June 26, 1948: 7.

15   "Grays Lose to Elites, 6-5; Play Cubans," *Baltimore Afro-American,* June 26, 1948: 13.

16   "Elites Make Bid for First Half Title," *Baltimore Afro-American,* July 3, 1948: 13.

17   "Grays Blank Newark After 13-4 Defeat," *Pittsburgh Post-Gazette,* July 5, 1948: 25; "Easter Clouts Three as Grays, Elites Split," *Pittsburgh Post-Gazette,* July 6, 1948: 16.

18   "Dormont Beats Grays," *Pittsburgh Post-Gazette,* July 16, 1948: 18.

FRANK "GROUNDHOG" THOMPSON

By Mike Mattsey

One of the more colorful aspects of baseball history is the wide, imaginative variety of nicknames assigned to the players by their teammates and the media. Some of the sobriquets lend an air of strength and might to the recipients that their birth names might otherwise not. Edwin Snider might not have struck fear in the hearts of opposing pitchers, but Duke kept enemy hurlers awake at night. Some nicknames were disparaging toward their owners: Nick Cullop's ruddy complexion didn't win him sympathy from his compatriots—it earned him the nickname Tomato Face. It is in the latter, less savory, category that one finds Frank Thompson, whose unusual outward appearance earned him the nickname Groundhog. However, Thompson's legacy was far more than a catchy nickname. When he was at the top of his game, the Groundhog competed against best the game had to offer and left them in his wake.

Frank Thompson entered life in October 1918 shortly before the armistice that ended World War I was signed.[1] A circumstance befitting of the nondescript nature of the Groundhog is that even the details of his birth are questionable at best. Census records show no birth records for a man fitting Thompson's background in 1918 in Merryville, Alabama; moreover, Groundhog was said to be from western Louisiana, where he first burst onto the baseball scene. US government records reveal that there was in fact an African-American male named Frank Thompson Jr. born on October 26, 1918, in Merryville, Louisiana—a small town on the border with Texas—to his parents, Frank Sr. and Lillie (née Gordon).[2] Given what is known about Thompson's Louisiana roots, and the records showing a 1918 birth date, it seems that the child born in Louisiana is likely the boy who grew up to be the pitcher known as the Groundhog.

Little is known about Thompson's upbringing in Louisiana. His formal education ended after the fifth grade, a sad but not uncommon reality in the rural Jim Crow South.[3] One thing that is key to Thompson's life is his physical appearance and how others viewed him as a result. According to Hall of Fame great Ted "Double Duty" Radcliffe, Thompson was called Groundhog "because, well, he looked like a groundhog."[4] His Homestead Grays batterymate, Josh Gibson, dubbed Thompson the starting pitcher on his "all-ugly" team due to his chipped tooth, cleft palate, and offset eyes.[5] Amsterdam News columnist Dan Burley described the 5-foot 2, 135-pound pitcher as a "guy… so runty he looked like the tip of a sweet potato sticking out of the ground."[6]

These unflinching remarks about his looks could have crushed the confidence of a lesser man, but in true Napoleonic fashion the diminutive Thompson fought back against those who disparaged him. Future major leaguers Bob Thurman and Luke Easter were Thompson's teammates on the Grays. Easter, who was 14 inches taller than Groundhog and outweighed him by over 100 pounds, threatened the pitcher with a beating after accusing him of cheating at cards. Thurman recounted that Thompson pulled a knife on Easter and threatened, "[I]f you try to hit me, I'll cut you down to my size."[7] There was apparently as much iron in Thompson's words as there was in his blade. Thurman said the result of the confrontation was that "Groundhog made a believer out of Easter."[8]

In a recounting the exploits of Thompson's baseball career, his time with the 1948 Homestead Grays is not a notable period to dwell on. He is credited with one start on the mound that season for the eventual champions, giving up five runs in seven-plus innings in a losing cause. This is not exactly the stuff of legends, but even the best teams have minor players fill small roles to help round out the squad. However, the result of further digging into baseball's archives reveals that Thompson competed with some of the game's greats on equal footing and under conditions that epitomized the overt racism of Jim Crow America.

The Groundhog burst onto the scene in his home state of Louisiana in 1941. The young southpaw had earned enough notoriety for his baseball ability that he was referred to solely by his nickname. "Batteries for Houma in the first game," declared a newspaper article, "will be Ground Hog and Johnson."[9] Thompson's appeal around Louisiana extended to the box office as well. A crowd of over 3,000 came to Kenner in June 1942 to see the home nine defeat Thompson and Houma 7-3. The recap noted that, even in a losing effort, "the mighty Ground Hog … was in there all the way and don't forget that he was as great a hog as ever."[10] Talent like Thompson's was destined for better teams than the Houma Giants, and in

1945 the Groundhog was signed by the Birmingham Black Barons of the Negro American League.

Thompson's debut with the Barons against the New York Cubans in 1945 at the Polo Grounds epitomizes his life on the diamond and perhaps his life in general. When the little left-hander strode to the mound in the first inning, he was greeted by catcalls and derisive laughter from the partisan New York crowd. It was nothing new to Thompson and he knew just how to deal with it. His blazing fastball saw "the roar of laughter based on his unorthodox appearance changed to waves of applause for his pitching skill. … A new star was born."[11]

Black Barons manager W.S. Welch was effusive in his praise for the young hurler. "He's got everything," Welch stated, "a fastball, curve, sinker, control, and poise on the mound. Best of all, he learns fast and is constantly picking up the finer points of the

Diminutive pitcher Frank "Groundhog" Thompson played a minor role with the 1948 Homestead Grays. In 1953 he won 14 games and posted a 2.31 ERA while pitching for his former 1948 foe, the Black Barons. (*Withers Family Trust, Memphis, Tennessee*)

pitching art."[12] An *Amsterdam News* article described Thompson's unique delivery:

"He waves the ball with an Italian flourish, something like an operatic star. There seem to be three distinct motions Thompson uses before tossing the ball plateward. His hand comes in as he grips the ball; his forearm then describes a circular motion with a slight jerk, and there is a momentary pause that looks as if he has committed a balk, but the follow-through completes the arc as the ball rifles across the platter, hitting the catcher's mitt with a resounding plunk!"[13]

Dan Burley predicted that the combination of Thompson's box-office appeal and pitching skill would soon see his annual salary exceed the $40,000 earned by the legendary Satchel Paige.[14] Though this may seem laughable, it serves as evidence that Thompson was seen as somewhat of a phenom in his early days of his career, and it was not the last time he was compared favorably with Paige.

In 1945 Thompson went west with the Black Barons to play in the California Winter League. The CWL was billed as an integrated league that included Negro League stars as well as white players from the major leagues and the Pacific Coast League. The season's final week saw the Birmingham squad matched against the Kansas City Royals, who featured the pitching tandem of Chet Brewer and Paige. The teams split their first two games, making the third tilt the rubber game of the series. The Royals trotted out the legendary Paige to face the upstart Thompson and the Black Barons. The younger Groundhog outdueled the legend that day as he scattered five hits in a comfortable 6-1 complete-game victory for Birmingham.[15] At least for one day, Thompson dominated one of the greatest pitchers in all of baseball, fulfilling some of the promise that the Polo Grounds crowd had seen a few months earlier. Thompson was named to the all-star team of Negro League players that faced off in exhibitions against the white stars of the league that fall, and the *Pittsburgh Courier* named

him to its integrated all-league team for his work that season. The all-star roster was indeed fast company for anyone on it. Jackie Robinson was the shortstop, American League home-run champ Vern Stephens manned one of the outfield spots, and Thompson was named to the pitching staff alongside future Hall of Fame legends Satchel Paige and Bob Feller.[16] Thompson's inclusion on the team served notice to anyone who dared to dismiss his abilities that they did so at their own peril.

Thompson jumped to the Grays in 1946 and pitched sporadically for them over the next three seasons. He failed to live up to the promise he showed in 1945 during his tenure with the Homestead nine, though he did post a 7-3 record in 1947.[17] In 1949 he moved south to join the Memphis Red Sox, for whom he plied his trade for the next three seasons. It was with the Red Sox that Thompson and his teammates experienced an act of overt racism that spoke volumes about the trials and tribulations that African-Americans experienced under Jim Crow. Thompson's teammate Joe Henry recalled a game in which Groundhog's batterymate was Casey Jones, who stood nearly 15 inches taller than the pitcher. A white public-address announcer working the game was announcing the lineups, and told the crowd, "The battery for the Memphis Red Sox tonight will be a big niggah catchin' and a little niggah pitchin'."[18] Though the major leagues were beginning to become integrated by this time, there was no disputing the fact that African-Americans remained a persecuted group throughout the country and particularly in the Jim Crow South.

In 1952 Thompson returned to his original team in Birmingham, where he enjoyed two of his finest seasons in the twilight of his career. He represented the Black Barons in the 1952 East-West All-Star Game and was named the starting pitcher for the East, though he was shelled for six runs in the third inning and chased from the game as the losing pitcher.[19] In 1953 Thompson led the Negro American League with 14 wins and 113 strikeouts while coming in second for the ERA crown with a 2.31 mark.[20] The Negro Leagues no longer had the star power that they had before integrated baseball, but Thompson was dominant against the remaining hitters in the circuit.

After the 1954 season, Thompson's career as a pitcher was over. He no longer appeared in box scores after that date. He seemingly disappeared after that and records of his post-baseball life are virtually non-existent. According to Social Security records, the Groundhog passed away in February 1983 at the age of 64.[21] Frank Thompson may not have been a household name like Satchel Paige or Josh Gibson, but the Groundhog was a fan favorite who could pitch with anyone when he was at his peak.

NOTES

1 Frank Thompson, baseball-reference.com/register/player.cgi?id=thomps009fra.

2 US Social Security Applications and Claims Index, 1936-2007, search.ancestry.com/cgi-bin/sse.dll?indiv=1&db=Numident&h=29484497&tid=&pid=&usePUB=true&_phsrc=ZiA67&_phstart=successSource&usePUBJs=true&rhSource=2442 (Accessed September 10, 2016).

3 Ibid.

4 Kyle P. McNary, *Ted "Double Duty" Radcliffe: 36 Years of Pitching and Catching in Baseball's Negro Leagues* (Minneapolis: McNary Publications, 1994), 190.

5 William J. Plott, *The Negro Southern League: A Baseball History, 1920-1951* (Jefferson, North Carolina: McFarland Publishing, 2014), 148.

6 Dan Burley, *Amsterdam News*, October 13, 1945.

7 Daniel Cattau, "Forgotten Champions," *Washington Post*, June 3, 1990.

8 Ibid.

9 "Flintkotes Meet Houma Giants in 'Header Sunday," *Louisiana Weekly*, June 28, 1941.

10 *Louisiana Weekly*, June 6, 1942.

11 Burley.

12 Negro Leaguer of the Month: February, 2003, http://www.pitchblackbaseball.com/nlotmgroundhog.html, accessed December 23, 2016.

13 Ibid.

14 Burley.

15 William McNeil, *The California Winter League: America's First Integrated Professional Baseball League* (Jefferson, North Carolina: McFarland Publishing, 2002), 148.

16 Ibid.

17 Groundhog Thompson, baseball-reference.com/bullpen/Groundhog_Thompson, accessed December 23, 2016.

18 Brent P. Kelley, *"I Will Never Forget": Interviews With 39 Former Negro League Players* (Jefferson, North Carolina: McFarland Publishing, 2003), 81-82.

19 1952 East-West Game, baseball-reference.com/bullpen/1952_East-West_Game, accessed December 21, 2016.

20 Negro Leaguer of the Month: February 2003.

21 US Social Security Applications and Claims Index, 1936-2007.

BOB THURMAN

By Rick Swaine

Power-hitting Bob Thurman was nick-named "Big Swish" because the free-swinging power-hitter rarely got cheated at the plate. But Thurman, who was a star pitcher as well as a long-ball-hitting outfielder in the Puerto Rican winter league, also earned a nick-name for his hurling. He was dubbed "El Murcaro" or "The Owl" because he always seemed to win the night games that he pitched.

Thurman, who originally signed with the New York Yankees and then spent several years as the property of the Chicago Cubs, was a month shy of his 38th birthday when he made his major-league debut with the Cincinnati Reds on April 14, 1955. His obstacle-strewn path to the big leagues was long and winding with many detours along the way. But when he finally got an opportunity, the former Negro League star developed into one of the most respected pinch-hitters in baseball and established an all-time National League home run record.

Described as broad-shouldered and muscular, Thurman was a left-handed pull hitter who was said to be extremely fast on the bases for a big man. Often referred to as "Big Bob," he's listed as being 6'1" tall and weighing 205 pounds in *The Baseball Encyclopedia*, but during his Negro League career he was reported to be a 6'4", 230-pound giant. His actual size was probably somewhere between the two.

From 1955 until he was released in early 1959, Thurman was one of the most popular players on the Cincinnati Reds. The Reds were an outfit that had been slow to integrate, but made tremendous strides in a short time thanks to the examples set by respected veteran black players like Thurman. Off the field Thurman served as an informal traveling secretary for the Reds' contingent of black players, taking responsibility for arranging accommodations on the road when they couldn't stay with the team and assisting younger players in getting acclimated to the major leagues.

Robert Burns Thurman grew up in Wichita, Kansas. Most sources indicate he was born in Wichita, although nearby Kellyville, Oklahoma is listed as his birthplace in the *Biographical Encyclopedia of the Negro Baseball Leagues*.

Bob was born May 14, 1917, but he trimmed a few years off his age before entering organized baseball. In *The Sporting News* coverage of Thurman's acquisition by the Yankees in 1949, he was reported to be 26 years old. Apparently most of the baseball world bought off on this little fabrication because Thurman's birthday was listed as 5/14/23 by the *Doubleday Official Baseball Encyclopedia*, *Annual Baseball Register*, *Baseball Digest* and even the backs of his baseball cards during his active career.

Somewhere along the line, however, Thurman must have slipped up because the *Macmillan Baseball Encyclopedia* reported his birth date as 5/14/21 and a 1957 Associated Press article mentioned that he was 34 years old in 1955 when he broke in with the Reds. Many years after his retirement Thurman confessed to his real age in a neatly hand-written 1982 letter to the Baseball Hall of Fame as follows:

"Many Baseball clubs like to put players ages back a few years. Mine was put back several times, so much so, that I always use the baseball age. Even when I joined the pension, I didn't think of [using] my correct age. So my real [birth date] is May 14, 1917."

Thurman started his baseball career playing semipro ball with various teams in the Wichita area before entering the U.S. Army at the beginning of World War II. He was stationed in New Guinea and Luzon and saw combat action in the Pacific Theater of Operations. His baseball talent became evident while playing military ball in the Philippines, and when he was discharged in 1945 an offer to play for the Homestead Grays in the Negro National League was waiting for him.

In 1946, Thurman's first season with the Homestead Grays, their roster included some of the greatest names in Negro baseball history. Catcher Josh Gibson, first baseman Buck Leonard, outfielder Cool Papa Bell, infielder Sam Bankhead, pitcher Ted "Double Duty" Radcliffe, outfielder Vic Harris, and third baseman Howard Easterling were some of the veteran stars. In addition, future major leaguers Sam Jones, Dave Hoskins, Luis Marquez, and Dave Pope were also with the Grays. Thurman's mound work was mediocre, but he got some playing time in the outfield and hit .408 with power.

The next year Cool Papa Bell retired and big Bob found himself playing the outfield more than pitching. He handled right field with new recruit Luke Easter in left and league batting champ Luis Marquez in center field. Thurman hit .338 for the 1947 season and showed good power with six homers in 157 at-bats. In 1948 he hit .345 and also posted a 6-4 won/lost record as a regular starting pitcher to help the Grays capture the last Negro National League pennant. They also defeated the Birmingham Black Barons in the World Series that year before their powerhouse squad was dismantled along with the once grand league.

Like most Negro Leaguers, Thurman had to play winter ball to make ends meet. He began playing with the Santurce Crabbers in the Puerto Rican winter league and became a big fan favorite. He led the league with nine homers in the winter of 1947-48 and doubled that total the next winter before reporting to his new employers the Kansas City Monarchs, another fabled Negro League franchise in the newly reorganized Negro American League.

The Monarchs, managed by Buck O'Neill, were still a powerhouse. Listed on their roster were long-time Negro League stars Willard Brown, Booker McDaniels, Nat Peeples, Bonnie Serrell, and Theolic Smith, as well as future big leaguers Elston Howard, Gene Baker, Connie Johnson, Frank Barnes, and Curt Roberts. But with the integration of organized baseball, the Negro Leagues were in their death-throes. The only way they could survive was by selling off their star performers and Thurman's big season in Puerto Rico had attracted the attention of the major leagues.

In his preview of the 1949 East-West All-Star Game clash, Wendell Smith of the *Pittsburgh Courier* wrote, "Another player who seems destined to move up... is Bob Thurman. He is also with Kansas City and many tab him as Josh Gibson's successor when it comes to hitting. Bob is hitting .327 and is a home-run hitter deluxe... Thurman's tootsies are lined with mercury. He's leading both leagues in stolen bases with 12. Formerly a pitcher, he can throw with the best of 'em and is definitely ticketed for the majors."

But Thurman would never play in the East-West classic. On July 29, 1949 it was announced that his contract, along with catcher Earl Taborn's, had been purchased from the Monarchs by the New York Yankees.

Thurman was one of the first black players signed by the Yankees. He was assigned to the Newark Bears of the International League and slammed three homers in his first week in organized baseball, including one tape-measure blast that was said to be the longest hit in the old Newark park in 30 years. In 59 games for the Bears he hit .317 before a hand injury sent him to the sidelines.

But despite his promising freshman campaign, the Yankees disposed of him, transferring his contract to the Chicago Cubs. Thurman spent the 1950 season with Springfield in the International League where his batting average fell to .269 with only 12 homers. He spent the next two years with the San Francisco Seals club of the Pacific Coast League. He hit .274 and .280, respectively, but failed to display the power expected of him. As far as the Cubs were concerned, however, it probably didn't matter how many homers Thurman smashed since they still weren't ready to integrate at the major-league level. During the winter following the 1952 season, Thurman's contract was sold to Charleston of the American Association. But Thurman didn't play for Charleston or any other team in organized baseball for the next two years.

Thurman had continued to play for Santurce in the Puerto Rican winter league after entering organized ball and was one of the biggest names in Latin American baseball. In the early 1950s, the Dominican Republic was in the process of establishing a professional league called the Dominican Summer League. The new league was not affiliated with organized baseball and was able to lure several minor leaguers with generous salary offers. Since Thurman was nearing 36 years of age and going nowhere in the Cubs system, he was receptive to abandoning organized baseball for a more lucrative offer from the Escogido team. He spent two years in the Dominican league, leading the loop in homers and RBIs in 1954 and even pitching occasionally.

When he opted to play in the Dominican Republic, Thurman was suspended from organized baseball. Therefore, when the Caribbean circuit slid under the umbrella of organized baseball in 1955, he was in limbo. Technically he was still under contract to the Cubs, although they didn't really seem to want him. But he proceeded to create a market for his services with his play in the 1954-55 Puerto Rican winter league. He hit .323 and slammed 14 homers for a Santurce team that revered veteran baseball man Don Zimmer, who had been in the game for more than 50 years as a player, manager, and coach, called "the best winter league baseball club ever assembled."

Zimmer, who at the time was the jewel of the Brooklyn system, was the club's shortstop while Thurman played right field and hit 323. Reigning National League Most Valuable Player, Willie Mays, played center field and led the winter league in batting, and young Roberto Clemente, who would join the Pittsburgh Pirates in 1955, hit .344 for fourth place in the league rankings. George Crowe, who'd led the American Association in homers and RBIs and would be a regular for the Milwaukee Braves in 1955, played first base and former Negro League star Bus Clarkson, who topped the Texas with 42 homers in 1954, handled third. Harry Chiti, who would be the Cubs regular catcher the next year, shared backstop duties with future New York Giants receiver Valmy Thomas, and another future major leaguer, Giants

prospect Ron Samford, manned second base. The pitching staff was led by Ruben Gomez, a 17-game-winner for the 1954 World Champion Giants, Sam Jones, who would lead the National League in strikeouts in 1955, and Bill Greason, a Cardinal farmhand and former Negro League standout. And also taking an occasional turn on the mound was 37-year-old left-hander Bob Thurman. Although Thurman was strictly an outfielder in organized baseball, he continued to pitch in the winter leagues. In previous winters he'd been among the top hurlers in the league, but in 1954-55 his services weren't required quite as often on the mound.

Impressed by his winter-league heroics and unaware of his true age, the Cincinnati Reds purchased the rights to Thurman from the Cubs for a reported sum of $2,000. It would turn out to be a terrific investment. Ironically, Thurman's big-league debut occurred on the same day that Elston Howard became

Bob Thurman posted a 6-4 pitching mark and batted .345 as an outfielder with the 1948 Homestead Grays championship team. In 1957 he clouted 16 homers in only 190 at-bats for the Cincinnati Reds. (*Noir-Tech Research, Inc.*)

the first black man to play for Thurman's original organization, the Yankees. During the 1955 season Thurman shared left field with several other players and hit seven homers in only 152 at-bats, though his batting average was only .217. The next year, however, he raised his batting mark to .295 and slammed eight homers in 139 chances at the plate, helping the powerful Reds to tie the all-time major-league home run record of 221 set by the 1947 New York Giants. On August 18, 1956 he slammed three consecutive homers and double against the Milwaukee Braves, enabling the Reds to tie a major-league record with eight homers in the game.

The next season Thurman celebrated his birthday with a home run against the Philadelphia Phillies on May 14, 1957. Unbeknownst to organized baseball at the time, he was the first player to homer on his 40th birthday; and it didn't happen again until Joe Morgan did it in 1983. The 1957 campaign would be Thurman's best season in the major leagues, even though it was interrupted by a trip to the minors. He started the year on fire and was hitting .351 on June 1, but by the end of the month his average had skidded 92 points. On August 2, he was dispatched to Seattle of the Pacific Coast League to make room for Joe Taylor, a younger black outfielder.

Thurman took the demotion in stride. Instead of sulking about it, the irrepressible outfielder told Reds manager Birdie Tebbetts, "I know I'll be back and when I am I'll make you play me."

When Thurman reported to Seattle the next day, after flying all night, the game was already under-way. But Seattle manager Lefty O'Doul asked him to suit up right away. "I may need you to hit one," he cracked. Sure enough, "Big Swish" was needed in the eighth inning and obliged with a pinch homer. He ravaged Pacific Coast League pitching for seven more long ones before being recalled by the Reds later the same month.

The Reds, who missed Thurman's clubhouse presence as much as his big bat, were in a deep slump and the big guy responded by giving them an immediate lift. After flying in from Seattle overnight, he rejoined the Reds in Philadelphia on August 27 and smashed a three-run ninth-inning homer to give the Reds a desperately-needed 5-2 victory.

After two at-bats off the bench on the 30th, Thurman banged a two-run homer off Milwaukee's Lew Burdette in his next start on August 31, but the Reds still suffered their 15th loss in 18 outings. The next day, however, he doubled home a run and added a two-run circuit smash as the Reds beat the Cardinals behind Brooks Lawrence. In total, he hit four home runs and drove in a dozen runs in his first five games back to help get the team back on track. The Reds won 18 of 30 games after the big outfielder's recall to finish the season with 80 victories.

Thurman finished the 1957 campaign with 16 home runs and 40 RBIs in only 190 at-bats for the Reds. At the time, he was the first National Leaguer and only the second player in major league history to slam that many homers in less than 200 at-bats. His home run per at-bat percentage of 8.4% was better than league-leader Duke Snider's 7.9%, although Big Bob didn't have enough plate appearances for official ranking. His eight homers in 104 at-bats with Seattle gave him a personal total of 24 for the year in less than 300 chances at the plate.

Thurman remained with the Reds through the entire 1958 campaign, but hit only .230 with four homers. After a few pinch-hitting appearances early in the 1959 season, he returned to the minor leagues but failed to hit well with either Seattle or Omaha (American Association).

In 1960, the 43-year-old Thurman drifted into the Washington Senators organization and finally reported to Charleston, seven years after the franchise had first tried to acquire his services. He hit .274 with 10 homers for the American Association club. On August 21, Thurman received his first and only opportunity to pitch in organized ball. Charleston starter Jim Kaat had been knocked out of the box and the score was 10-5 when the 43-year-old veteran was summoned from right field to take the mound against Dallas-Fort Worth. Thurman held them scoreless the rest of the way, striking out a trio of batters and giving up a pair of hits in three innings. He also went 3-for-4 at the plate that day. The next year he finally hung up his spikes after 21 games with Charlotte in the South Atlantic League.

Thurman ended his major-league career with a .246 lifetime batting average in 334 major-league games, spread mainly over four seasons. He belted 35 homers and both drove in and scored 106 runs in 663 at-bats. More than one half of his appearances were as a pinch-hitter and he blasted six homers in that role, including four in 1957. In addition, he played 12 winters in the Puerto Rican winter league, 11 with the Santurce Crabbers. He is a member of the Puerto Rican League Hall of Fame and the leagues' all-time home run leader.

Bob Thurman was never considered one of the best players in major-league baseball, although he might have been if he'd gotten an earlier start. But he easily qualifies as one of the most interesting and unusual stories. Despite the fact that he was 38 years of age when he got his first shot at the majors and was used as a pinch-hitter so often, Thurman's career totals equate to approximately 30 homers and 90 runs batted in over a full season.

During his career he was regarded as one of the most dangerous clutch hitters in the game. Reds manager Birdie Tebbetts said, "He's one of the best pinch hitters I have seen in my nearly seventeen years in baseball.....That big boy gets off the bench good and cold, and he just gets hot walking up to the plate."

Like most hitters, however, Thurman was more productive with the bat when playing full time. His career home run percentage was a respectable 3.4 as a pinch hitter, but an extraordinary 6.0 otherwise. To put Thurman's 6.0 figure in perspective, Hank Aaron and Willie Mays, the top two National League home run hitters of the 20th century, both finished their fabulous careers with 6.1 home run percentages.

The accomplishments of "Big Swish" are even more amazing when his age is taken into consideration. There are no other hitters who began their big-league careers at a similar age to compare him to. He may have been the oldest slugger to establish a league home run record, even an obscure one, or set the pace in home run percentage as he did in 1957, until Barry Bonds came along.

The fact that the ancient, veteran slugger was playing baseball year-round when he performed his feats makes them even more remarkable. For most of his career, Thurman would leave for the Caribbean immediately after the season ended in the fall and then report for spring training the following year shortly after the Puerto Rican League season closed. More than one baseball talent evaluator wondered how much Thurman's career in organized ball was harmed by his exhausting schedule.

Then again, there's the fact that Thurman was a two-way performer, at least during the winter. In Puerto Rico he often gave a pretty fair imitation of a young Babe Ruth. For the 1949-50 season his won-lost mark was 5-3 and he hit .353. In 1951-52 and 1952-53 his records of 6-3 and 5-3 put him among the league pitching leaders. In 1953-54 he had a no-hitter going into the seventh inning of a contest, but had to settle for a two-hit shutout. All the while he was consistently among the league home run leaders and finished sixth in batting in 1954-55 and second in 1955-56.

The likeable, hard-working Thurman joined the Minnesota Twins as a scout after his playing days were over, and his first signee was Rudy May, who would pitch in the majors for 16 years. After about a year and a half he returned to the Cincinnati organization to scout for the Reds. In 1970, he moved closer to his Wichita roots when he became a special assignment scout for the Kansas Royals. Later, when the Major League Scouting Bureau was established, he hooked on with them.

Thurman remained physically active after his playing career, keeping close to his playing weight. He had a gym in his house and was an enthusiastic golfer who, by his own admission, worked off a lot of calories searching the woods for his tee shots. He frequently attended old-timer games and reunions, showing off his youthful-looking physique for his envious old buddies.

When he visited Cooperstown at the age of 74 in 1991, Bob Thurman was still working as a senior partner with Marketing Associates in Wichita. He appeared in excellent shape when interviewed for *Sports*

Collectors Digest by Robert Objoski, who more than a decade later would remember him as one of the nicest players he ever talked to. But the big guy fell victim to Alzheimer's disease and died on October 31, 1998 in Wichita at the age of 81, leaving behind Dorothy, his wife of 51 years, and their three children.

Bob Thurman put in a lot of hard work and endured some tough breaks to make the major leagues. Like many former Negro Leaguers he was forced to misrepresent his age to get a chance in organized baseball. "If the Reds knew I was that old, they probably would not have signed me," he said in his 1991 *Sports Collectors Digest* interview.

But old Cincinnati fans are glad that the Reds didn't know—for reasons in addition to Thurman's performance on the field. "Cincinnati wouldn't have signed Johnny Bench without Bob Thurman," said long-time baseball executive Herk Robinson, who was in the Cincinnati front office at the time. He was also instrumental in the signing of Wayne Simpson, Hal McRae, and Gary Nolan among others.

After her husband's death, Dorothy Thurman said, "He never seemed to regret not getting a chance earlier."

But major-league baseball historians regret that we'll never know what kind of career Bob Thurman would have enjoyed, if given an earlier opportunity.

Note

This Bob Thurman biography is an adaptation of a profile in *The Black Stars Who Made Baseball Whole: The Jackie Robinson Generation in the Major Leagues* by Rick Swaine (McFarland 2006).

SOURCES

Boyle, Robert. "The Private World of the Negro Ballplayer," *Sports Illustrated*, March 21, 1960.

Clark, Dick and Larry Lester, *The Negro Leagues Book* (Cleveland: SABR, 1994).

Lester, Larry. *Black Baseball's National Showcase: The East-West All-Star Game 1933-53* (Lincoln: University of Nebraska Press, 2001).

Obojski, Robert. "SCD profiles former Reds outfielder Bob Thurman," *Sports Collectors Digest*, October 11, 1991.

James A. Riley, *The Negro Baseball Leagues: The Biographical Encyclopedia*, Carroll and Graf (1994)

Tygiel, Jules. *Baseball's Great Experiment: Jackie Robinson and His Legacy* (New York: Oxford University Press, 1997).

Young, A. S. "Doc." *Great Negro Baseball Stars* (New York: A. S. Barnes, 1953).

The Sporting News

National Baseball Hall of Fame, miscellaneous clippings from Bob Thurman's file.

BOB TRICE

By Jack V. Morris

O n a sunny but windy and cool September Sunday afternoon in Philadelphia, Bob Trice toed the pitching rubber at Connie Mack Stadium and peered in to the catcher for his signs. With the release of his first pitch, Trice made history. He was the first person of color to play for the Philadelphia Athletics; in fact, he was the first black man ever to play for a Philadelphia major-league baseball team.

Almost a full 6½ years after the Brooklyn Dodgers brought up Jackie Robinson, Trice had forced the Athletics' hand after a spectacular season in the International League. During the 1953 season, Trice posted a 21-10 record with the sixth-place Ottawa A's and was named the International League's Most Valuable Pitcher and Rookie of the Year. Mentored by Sam Bankhead, both with the Homestead Grays and later in Organized Baseball with the Farnham Pirates of the Provincial League, Trice was a fast study. He transitioned from a semipro player who played everywhere on the field to a full-time pitcher. Not a power pitcher, the right-hander used a slider, curve, and changeup to keep batters off balance.[1]

On September 13, as a late-season call up to the Athletics, Trice faced the St. Louis Browns. He lost the game but won his next two starts, including a complete-game win over the Washington Senators. His future appeared bright for the pitching-poor A's.

Seemingly Trice was on his way to fulfilling that promise in 1954. Early in the season, he shut out the defending World Series champion New York Yankees. But on July 11, after losing the first game of a doubleheader, Trice, shockingly, requested to be sent back to Ottawa. His record stood at 7-8 and his seven wins accounted for almost one-quarter of the seventh-place Athletics' wins to that point. Frustrated with a four-game losing streak and having just been shelled in 3⅓ innings in an 18-0 loss to the Boston

Red Sox, he told Art Morrow of the *Philadelphia Inquirer*, "It just wasn't fun anymore; it was work. So I decided to ask to be sent back to Ottawa, where I had a lot of fun last year."[2]

Hindered by a shoulder injury, Trice never rekindled the magic of 1953 in Ottawa. He made it back to Philadelphia out of spring training in 1955 but lasted only four games before he was sent back down to the minors, this time for good.

Robert Lee Trice was born on August 28, 1926, in Newton, Georgia, to Benjamin and Henrietta (Clark) Trice, the second of three boys born to the couple. Sometime after his birth, the family moved to Weirton, West Virginia, in search of work. Benjamin found work in the area's steel mills, where he toiled for the rest of his life. Bob Trice blossomed as an athlete at segregated Dunbar High School, where he captained the football, basketball, and baseball teams.[3] With the country embroiled in World War II, the 17-year-old Trice joined the US Navy on March 30, 1944. While in the Navy, the 6-foot-3, 190-pounder played first base for various base teams.[4]

Discharged from the Navy on May 17, 1946, Trice went home to Weirton, where he joined his father working in a steel mill. According to Trice, he didn't last very long at the mill. "I worked there one day," said Trice, "and that was enough."[5] He continued to play baseball, pitching for a nearby Steubenville, Ohio, semipro team.[6] He also played left field and pitched for the Weirton Negro Stars.[7]

In 1948 Trice caught the eye of the Homestead Grays. He loved to play in the field, but the Grays had different ideas. "I still thought I was a first baseman when I joined the Homestead Grays," said Trice. "They had such a team that the only place a fellow had a chance to break in was as a pitcher. So I started pitching."[8] That's when Sam Bankhead took the youngster under his wing. "(He) taught me about control at Homestead," said Trice.[9]

It wasn't until late in the 1948 season that Trice signed with the Grays, and he ended up playing sparingly. His first known game was in Pittsburgh as the Grays took on the Indianapolis Clowns; he relieved pitcher Ted Alexander in a 4-1 win.[10] Three weeks later he relieved Clarence Evans for 1⅓ innings in an 8-4 win over the Clowns at Griffith Stadium in Washington, which was the Grays' second home after Pittsburgh's Forbes Field.[11]

Trice played more regularly with the Grays in 1949.[12] Homestead had joined the Negro American Association and thoroughly dominated the league in the first half of the season. The Richmond Giants won the second half, setting up a best-of-seven series for the league championship in September. The Grays swept Richmond, four games to none, with Trice picking up the win in Game Two.[13]

Trice began the 1950 season with Homestead, but he was approached by the Farnham Pirates of the Class-C Provincial League midway through the

Bob Trice made the transition from first baseman to pitcher when he joined the Homestead Grays in 1948. In September 1953 he became the first African-American pitcher to play for the Philadelphia Athletics. (*National Baseball Hall of Fame, Cooperstown, New York*)

season. He had been recommended by several of his former Grays teammates who were playing in the Provincial League,[14] and he joined Farnham on July 27, playing third base.[15] After Farnham's season ended, Trice rejoined the Homestead Grays.[16]

Farnham didn't initially pick up Trice's contract for 1951, but Sam Bankhead—who had been named the Pirates manager for the 1951 season—needed pitching help. He signed Trice and used him both as a pitcher and an everyday player. Trice played in 70 games, pitching in 23.[17]

Despite Trice's 7-12 record, George MacDonald, general manager of the St. Hyacinthe A's of the Provincial League, liked what he saw and signed Trice to a contract for 1952.[18] He again played many positions for St. Hyacinthe but excelled at pitching. By season's end, he led the league in winning percentage with a 16-3 mark (.842).

In March 1953 the Ottawa A's of the Triple-A International League signed Trice and three of his teammates, Alfred Pinkston, Joe Taylor, and Hector Lopez. All were players of color.[19] Trice went to spring training with Ottawa, but the Philadelphia Athletics, who owned his rights, fully expected Trice to start the season with Williamsport of the Class-A Eastern League.[20] Pinkston, Taylor, and Lopez all spent time with Williamsport that season, but Trice pitched well enough to start out with Ottawa. "I was sort of jittery when I first got the news that I was heading for the International League because the jump from St. Hyacinthe is a big one," Trice said. "But the chance to eventually make the big time kept me digging all the time."[21]

At the beginning of the season Ottawa used Trice out of the bullpen and as a pinch-hitter,[22] but the team quickly moved him into its starting rotation and he responded with an incredible run. On June 17 he shut out the Montreal Royals, 11-0, on four hits; he also singled and homered, driving in five runs.[23] By July 8 he was tied for the league lead in wins with a 10-5 record.[24] What made Trice's record even more remarkable was the fact that Ottawa wasn't having a good season. Between July 5 and 14 the A's won only four games—Trice was the winning pitcher in three of them.[25] By July 15 Trice was 12-5 for the seventh-place A's.[26]

On July 23 Trice entered a game as a pinch-hitter in the ninth inning. He hit a three-run home run to tie the game, and then came in and pitched the 10th inning to earn the win.[27] Ottawa held a Bob Trice Night during a doubleheader on August 13, and Trice pitched the opener, winning his 16th game of the year with a two-hitter over Springfield, 2-1. Between games he was showered with about 40 gifts and received a surprise appearance by his parents.[28] From August 19 to 25, Trice won three more games, all nine-inning complete games.[29]

By season's end Trice's record stood at 21-10. He led the International League in wins and shutouts (four).[30] Trice was named the IL's Most Valuable Pitcher and Rookie of the Year and was named to the league All-Star team.[31]

Ottawa A's manager Frank Skaff chalked up Trice's success to several different factors. "(He's) one of the best-conditioned athletes I've ever seen," said Skaff. "He helps himself with the bat, and he helps himself on the mound."[32] He added, "He's not afraid of anything, and he doesn't let anything bother him."[33] Trice didn't try to overpower hitters. "I have made up my mind to let the batter hit my pitch," he said. "I pitch to the man's weakness, but not too fine."[34]

The Philadelphia Athletics noticed. On September 8 the A's called him up and quickly announced that Trice would start against the St. Louis Browns in the first game of a doubleheader on Sunday, September 13.[35] A's manager Jimmy Dykes told Trice, "I don't want you to think everything depends on this game. I don't want you to do anything different from what you've been doing."[36] Trice struggled, giving up eight hits and five earned runs in eight innings in a 5-2 loss. One bright spot was the fact that Trice didn't walk a batter—in fact, he never even went to three balls in a count.[37]

In his second start, on September 20, Trice broke through for his first major-league win, over the Washington Senators. He struggled again but won 13-9. Trice went six innings, giving up 10 hits and seven earned runs. Finally, in his last start

of the season, on September 26, Trice found his International League form. He defeated Washington again, 11-2, pitching a complete game and scattering seven hits.

Trice had planned to head south after the season to play winter baseball. But the Athletics told him to not go out of fear that he might hurt his arm after a long season. "The money is fine down there but the real payoff is the majors," said Trice. "And I don't want to risk my chances with the A's because of a sore arm."[38] Instead, Trice joined Jackie Robinson's barnstorming team, which included Al Rosen, Gil Hodges, and Luke Easter. Robinson's team played the Indianapolis Clowns in a series of games throughout the United States.[39]

Philadelphia general manager Arthur Ehlers projected Trice to be the Athletics' fourth or fifth starter for 1954.[40] In December the A's traded for Vic Power, who became the second player of color for Philadelphia. In addition, the A's made former Negro League great Judy Johnson, who had been scouting for Philadelphia, a "special coach" for Trice and Powers to "supervise their activities off, as well as on the field."[41]

Spring training in 1954 didn't begin well for Trice. He was the first Athletic hurt, falling on his left shoulder during a drill.[42] When he got back from his injury, he pitched well and left spring training as the team's fourth starter.[43]

Trice continued to pitch well during the regular season. He won his first four starts, going the route in all four. Most impressively, he shut out the reigning World Series champion Yankees on six hits. On May 1 Ben Phlegar, an Associated Press sportswriter, declared Trice the early favorite for Rookie of the Year.[44]

Trice's calm demeanor on the mound won him many accolades. "I do not believe I have ever seen a more relaxed pitcher in the crisis than he has been," wrote W. Rollo Wilson, a baseball writer for the *Pittsburgh Courier*.[45] "Trice looked like the calmest person in the place," wrote correspondent Art Morrow in *The Sporting News* about Trice's outing against the Yankees.[46] United Press sports writer Carl Lundquist wrote that the "serious Bible-reading pitcher" was buoyed by his faith. "Trice thinks his religion gives him moral inspiration," wrote Lundquist. "But emphasized that 'you've got to work on those hitters, too.'"[47] New A's manager Eddie Joost liked Trice's preparation. "He's a conscientious guy, studies the hitters and gets the ball over the plate," said Joost. "He doesn't overpower you but he had good stuff."[48]

However, Trice's shoulder started to bother him. A lump formed on his shoulder and never went away. After his injury, Trice was unable to completely follow through to throw a fastball. Though he had gotten by through the first four games without throwing one,[49] it didn't take too long for opposing teams to figure this out. Trice's first loss came against the Yankees on May 9, a game in which he lasted but two innings. The next day he lost again when Joost brought him into the game in relief against the Baltimore Orioles in the bottom of the ninth. He gave up two hits before the Orioles won on Sam Mele's walk-off sacrifice fly.

Trice didn't win another game until June 1. After being knocked out of a game early on May 23, he refused to eat his steak dinner on the train ride back home.[50] He hit rock-bottom on July 11 when he was shelled in the first game of a doubleheader against the Boston Red Sox. The Red Sox got to Trice for eight earned runs and 10 hits in just 3⅓ innings. The losses were wearing heavily on Trice. Between games, he shocked Joost and the Athletics management by asking to be sent back to Ottawa.[51]

Trice insisted that even if he had won the game, he would have asked to be sent back. "I planned to make the move anyway," said Trice.[52] "Everything here has been fine and I want to come back," Trice told the *Philadelphia Inquirer*'s Art Morrow. "But right now, I think I'd be better off in Ottawa." His teammates were incredulous. He still led the team in wins despite his woes. "Everybody I talked to says I'm crazy and maybe I am," said Trice. "But I thought about this a long time and I think I am doing the right thing."[53]

Philadelphia obliged Trice and sent him and Ozzie Van Brabant to Ottawa. In return, pitchers Johnny Gray and Charlie Bishop were recalled.[54] Trice tried to rekindle the magic but he never did. He finished

the season at Ottawa with a 4-8 record, though his ERA was a respectable 3.23 and he completed 12 of the 13 games he started.[55] His last game tantalized the Athletics with his potential. He pitched 11 innings of four-hit ball and won the game with a home run.[56] Despite pitching only half a season for the Philadelphia Athletics, Trice was still second on the team in wins.

After the season Trice joined Roy Campanella's barnstorming tour. The team—which included Larry Doby, Monte Irvin, Junior Gilliam, and Don Newcombe—was scheduled to play 33 games from October into November. Trice played well on the tour. On October 12 he pitched a complete-game win against the Birmingham Black Barons in Winston-Salem, North Carolina. Later, in Houston, Trice hit a home run against the Negro American League All-Stars. And on November 6 in Laurel, Mississippi, he pitched a six-hitter against the NAL All-Stars.[57]

In January 1955 Trice signed with the Athletics, who had moved to Kansas City in the offseason.[58] He flashed some of the old magic in spring training. "Trice has been impressive," wrote Ernest Mehl of the *Kansas City Star*.[59] Based on his performance, he made the Athletics roster but as a reliever rather than a starter. He pitched well in his first two appearances but was hammered for four earned runs on five hits in 1⅓ innings of work against the Chicago White Sox. Nine days later, on May 2, he pitched 3⅔ innings against the Washington Senators, giving up five earned runs on six hits. It was his last game in the major leagues.

On May 3, the Athletics sent Trice and infielder Hal Bevan to the Columbus Jets of the International League.[60] Trice continued to struggle at Columbus and, in late July, was sent to the Savannah A's of the Class-A South Atlantic League.[61] With Savannah Trice went 3-5 with a 5.00 ERA. On September 15 Kansas City released Trice outright to Columbus.[62]

In the offseason Trice played with Spur Cola of the Panama winter league. Meanwhile, Columbus sold his contract to the Sacramento Solons of the Pacific Coast League.[63] Toward the end of the winter-league season, Trice left the team to be with his wife, Florence, for the birth of their first child, Henrietta.[64]

On March 3, 1956, Trice signed with Sacramento.[65] But in early April he was sent back to Columbus. From there, Columbus sent him to the Mexico City Reds of the Mexican League.[66]

Trice spent the next three seasons with Mexico City. Both pitching and playing in the outfield, he enjoyed his time in Mexico. "Trice is happy," wrote *The Sporting News* correspondent Miguel A. Calzadilla. "He's having fun pitching, playing in the outfield and hitting."[67] On April 9, 1957, his second child, Robert, was born.[68] He also played winter-league baseball between the 1956 and 1957 seasons, this time with Cerveza Balboa in Panama.[69]

Right before the 1959 season, Trice decided to retire.[70] He went home to Weirton, West Virginia, where he played semipro basketball and worked as a Hancock County property appraiser.[71] Florence and Bob had their third child, Andre, in 1961. In 1967 he opened a bar in Weirton, the After Five Club.[72] He eventually took a job with the Weirton Steel Corporation,[73] and he also became an assistant baseball coach for Weirton Madonna High School in 1971.[74]

On September 16, 1988, at the age of 62, Trice died of pancreatic cancer at the Weirton Medical Center.[75] He was survived by his wife, Florence, and their three children. He is buried in St. Paul Catholic Cemetery in Weirton.

ACKNOWLEDGMENTS

The author would like to thank Negro League experts Scott Simkus and Wayne Stivers for their help.

NOTES

1   Dan Daniel, "Pitcher's Year—With A.L. Out in Front," *The Sporting News*, May 19, 1954: 13.

2   Art Morrow, "Promising A's Hurler (7-8) Wanted Back in Ottawa," *Philadelphia Inquirer*, July 18, 1954: 33.

3   Art Morrow, "A's May Call Up Trice, First Negro to Join Club," *Philadelphia Inquirer*, September 6, 1953: 33.

4   Jack Hand, "Rookie Ace Bob Trice Looks Easy, but Isn't," *Elmira Star-Gazette*, May 10, 1954: 13.

5   Art Morrow, "A's May Call Up Trice."

6   Jack Hand.

7   "Canonsburg Elks Win Double-Header Sunday," *Canonsburg (Pennsylvania) Daily Notes*, July 21, 1947: 8; "Wellsville's Giants Edge Weirton Stars," *East Liverpool (Ohio) Review*, August 1, 1947: 19.

8   Jack Hand.

9   Art Morrow, "A's May Call Up Trice."

10 "Mesa's Miscue Is Costly to Clown," *Chicago Defender*, August 21, 1948: 11.

11 "6,000 Fans Pay Tribute to Grays' Buck Leonard," *Baltimore Afro-American*, September 18, 1948: 7.

12 "'48 NAA Champs Make First Appearance in D.C.," *Baltimore Afro-American*, June 4, 1949: 15; "Homestead Grays Play Ral. Clippers Here Tomorrow," *Beckley (West Virginia) Post-Herald*, June 24, 1949: 12; "Association All-Stars Meet Homestead Grays Today," *Greensboro (North Carolina) Daily News*, August 14, 1949: 6; "Bushwicks Seek Revenge Against Homesteaders," *Brooklyn Daily Eagle*, September 3, 1949: 6.

13 "Grays Twice Nip Richmond in NAA Title Play," *Baltimore Afro-American*, September 10, 1949: 28.

14 Art Morrow, "A's May Call Up Trice."

15 Player card in Trice's Baseball Hall of Fame file; George Beahon, "In This Corner …," *Rochester Democrat & Chronicle*, August 31, 1953: 15.

16 "Bushwicks Host to Grays Sunday," *Brooklyn Daily Eagle*, September 22, 1950: 19.

17 Lionel Hampton, "Show Biz Buzzes," *Pittsburgh Courier*, May 15, 1954: 19; George Beahon, "In This Corner."

18 Lionel Hampton.

19 "Caught on the Fly," *The Sporting News*, March 11, 1953.

20 Art Morrow, "A's May Call Up Trice."

21 Jack Koffman, "Lofty Trice Tops Int Hurlers With 7th-Spot Ottawa," *The Sporting News*, July 22, 1953: 25.

22 "Ottawa," *The Sporting News*, June 17, 1953, 26; Cy Kritzer, "International League," *The Sporting News*, June 24, 1953: 27.

23 "Ottawa."

24 "INT Averages," *The Sporting News*, July 15, 1953: 42.

25 Jack Koffman.

26 Ibid.

27 "Ottawa."

28 "Ottawa," *The Sporting News*, August 26, 1953: 23.

29 Art Morrow, "A's Get Peek at Pair of '53 Farm Prizes," *The Sporting News*, September 23, 1953: 6.

30 Art Morrow, "A's May Call Up Trice"; Art Morrow, "A's Get Peek."

31   Art Morrow, "Trice, Ottawa Hill Ace, First Negro to Join Athletics," *The Sporting News*, September 16, 1953: 5; "Royals Dominate All-Stars; Walker Named Pilot of '53," *The Sporting News*, September 23, 1953: 23.

32   Art Morrow, "A's May Call Up Trice."

33   George Beahon, "In this Corner."

34   Ibid.

35   "A's Call Up Star Negro, Bob Trice," *Richmond Times-Dispatch*, September 9, 1953: 23; "A's Give Rookie Negro Sunday Starting Job," *Rockford Morning Star*, September 9, 1953: B1.

36   Art Morrow, "A's Get Peek."

37   Ibid.

38   Antonio Lutz, "4 Venezuelan Clubs Line Up O.B. Players," *The Sporting News*, October 7, 1953: 22; "Major Flashes," *The Sporting News*, November 4, 1953: 20.

39   "Rosen and Hodges to Appear With Jackie's Barnstormers," *The Sporting News*, October 7, 1953: 24.

40   Art Morrow, "A's in No Spot to Shout Wares, But Will Lend an Ear to Offers," *The Sporting News*, October 28, 1953: 19.

41   Art Morrow, "Salary Fuss? It's News to A's and Gus," *The Sporting News*, February 3, 1954: 23.

42   "Growing Player Casualty Lists Turning Grapefruit League Managers Sour," *Troy (New York) Times Record*, March 3, 1954: 22.

43   Rip Watson, "23 Walks Feature Exhibition Game," *Aberdeen (South Dakota) American-News*, March 22, 1954: 10; Art Morrow, "Fiery Bat Backs Rookie Finigan's Bid for A's Post," *The Sporting News*, April 14, 1954: 23.

44   Ben Phlegar, "Athletics' Bob Trice Is Earliest Candidate for Rookie of Year," *Kingston (New York) Daily Freeman*, May 1, 1954: 6.

45   Lionel Hampton, "Show Biz Buzzes," *Pittsburgh Courier*, May 15, 1954: 19.

46   Art Morrow, "Bob Trice," *The Sporting News*, May 5, 1954: 19.

47   Carl Lundquist, "Bob Trice Beats Tribe For Fourth Pitching Triumph," *Niagara Falls Gazette*, May 5, 1954: 47.

48   Jack Hand, "Rookie Ace Bob Trice Looks Easy, but Isn't," *Elmira Star-Gazette*, May 10, 1954: 13.

49   Lionel Hampton, "Show Biz Buzzes."

50   Art Morrow, "Losses Won't Spur A's Into Panic Moves," *The Sporting News*, June 2, 1954: 12.

51   Art Morrow, "Promising A's Hurler (7-8) Wanted Back in Ottawa," *Philadelphia Inquirer*, July 18, 1954: 33.

52   Ibid.

53   Ibid.

54   Art Morrow, "Bob Trice Requests Return to Minors to 'Have Fun Pitching,'" *The Sporting News*, July 21, 1954: 31.

55   "Ottawa," *The Sporting News*, September 22, 1954: 28.

56   W.S. Coughlin, "Ottawa Scores 4-3 Victory Over Bisons in Extra Inning Game," *Buffalo Courier-Express*, September 3, 1954: 21.

57   "Lopat May Miss Barnstorm Trip; Campy Stays Out," *The Sporting News*, October 6, 1954: 21; Smith Barrier, "Campy's All-Stars, Black Barons Draw Better Than in '53," *The Sporting News*, October 20, 1954: 22; "Campy's Stars 50 Pct. Under their '53 Gate," *The Sporting News*, November 10, 1954: 19; Bill Keefe, "Campy's Tourists Drew 60,231 in 26-Game Trip," *The Sporting News*, November 17, 1954: 18.

58   "DeMaestri Heads 5 A's in Fold," *Dallas Morning News*, January 17, 1955: 22.

59   Ernest Mehl, "Kansas City Athletics," *The Sporting News*, April 13, 1955: 5.

60   "A's Send Bevan, Trice to Columbus," *Philadelphia Inquirer*, May 4, 1955: 39.

61   "Deals of the Week," *The Sporting News*, July 27, 1955: 42.

62   "A's Release Bob Trice to Take on Youngster," *Philadelphia Inquirer*, September 16, 1955: 36; "Deals of the Week," *The Sporting News*, September 28, 1955: 34.

63   Leo J. Eberenz, "Panama Presidential Pitch Will Open League Play, Dec. 1," *The Sporting News*, November 30, 1955: 30; "Solons Buy Trice," *Buffalo Courier-Express*, December 3, 1955: 22.

64   Leo J. Eberenz, "Hec Lopez' 10th Home Run Ties Panama Record," *The Sporting News*, February 8, 1956: 27.

65   Tom Kane, "Solon Officials Count 19 on Unsigned Roster," *Sacramento Bee*, March 3, 1956: 12.

66   "Trice Is Dropped," *Sacramento Bee*, April 12, 1956: 32.

67   Miguel A. Calzadilla, "Trice Having Fun Pitching, Hitting," *The Sporting News*, July 30, 1958: 35.

68   "Weirton General Hospital," *Weirton (West Virginia) Daily Times*, April 9, 1957: 6.

69   Leo J. Eberenz, "Nine Flingers Used in Game — Loop Record," *The Sporting News*, January 23, 1957: 25.

70   Roberto Hernandez, "Tame Tigers Land 4 in Talent Search," *The Sporting News*, May 6, 1959: 33.

71   "Three Exciting Games Forecast in Today's Action," *Weirton Daily Times*, April 3, 1959: 22; "Eight Field Deputies for County Tax Program," *Weirton Daily Times*, September 12, 1961: 14.

72   "Club Chartered," *Weirton Daily Times*, May 1, 1967: 16.

73   "Robert Lee Trice Taken by Death," *Weirton Daily Times*, September 19, 1988: 3.

74   "Wellsburg Is Site for '71 Opener," *Weirton Daily Times*, March 31, 1971: 17.

75   West Virginia Death Certificate in Trice's Baseball Hall of Fame file; "Robert Lee Trice Taken by death."

ROBERT TAYLOR (R.T.) WALKER

By Irv Goldfarb

Robert Taylor Walker was born on August 20, 1914, in Arboa, Florida. For many years, the legend was that his mother had named him after the actor Robert Taylor, but as the motion-picture star was born just three years before Walker and did not make his movie debut until 1934, that particular tale seems implausible. In fact, teammates often teased Walker about his lack of Hollywood movie-star features, with one player (in the nonpolitically-correct world of the times) describing him as looking "like King Kong."[1]

His countenance aside, Walker was a fairly effective right-handed pitcher, described as having "a good fastball and average control."[2] He also utilized a decent curve and drop pitch, the only off-speed deliveries in his repertoire, and was known as an adequate fielder and baserunner.

Walker was originally signed by the St. Louis Stars in 1944. This version of the Stars was not the same one that resided in the Negro National League throughout the 1920s and '30s, but rather an independent team that tangled with the likes of the Atlanta Black Crackers and the Jacksonville Red Caps. Already close to his 29th birthday, Walker started two games for the Stars in 1944, completing them both and tossing a shutout in one.[3]

Since the Stars were an independent franchise, the presidents of both major Negro Leagues agreed that Walker would be a "free agent" at the start of the 1945 campaign, sparking a bidding war between teams eager to sign him. The Homestead Grays made the best offer and Walker became a member of one of the most powerful clubs in professional baseball history.

Though incomplete records make it difficult to know how many appearances spot starters like Walker made, he did have three starts in his first season with Homestead in which he went 1-0 and allowed 12 runs in 23⅔ innings. The highlight of that first year, however, was likely to have been his relief appearance against Honus Wagner's All-Stars in September in which Homestead beat the barnstorming team, 8-7.

On top of his limited success early in his stint with the Grays, his new teammates were no more sympathetic about the pitcher's lack of physical appeal than previous players had been: It was here that slugger Josh Gibson chided Walker about his looks and merrily awarded him a spot on his "all-ugly" team.[4] Nonetheless, Walker's value on the field was underscored by the fact that when the team broke camp in 1946, he was one of only three holdovers (along with Garnett Blair and Dave Hoskins) from the previous season's pitching staff.

That year Walker made two more starts and finished at 2-0, cutting his runs allowed to eight in 24⅔ innings. On June 29, however, the *Pittsburgh Courier* reported that Walker had been released by the Grays (along with infielder Lick Carlisle and pitcher Jim Haynes) to get the team "down to the 20-man roster."[5]

Walker found himself back with Homestead in 1947, however, where he enjoyed his best professional season, starting four times and going 5-1 with three complete games. He gave up 15 runs and struck out 17 batters in 42 innings.

Upon returning to the Grays in 1948, Walker saw limited service, starting only twice and finishing 1-0 while pitching just 20⅓ innings. His career reached its professional summit when the '48 Grays won the final Negro National League pennant, beating the Elite Giants in the league playoffs, and became the champions of the Negro League World Series by defeating the Birmingham Black Barons in five games.

R.T. Walker started and pitched nine innings in Game Five of the World Series. The Grays scored four runs in the top of the 10th inning to claim a 10-6 victory. After Wilmer Fields entered the game in relief and set the Black Barons down in order in the bottom of the 10th, Walker was awarded the win.

R. T. Walker, shown here in 1946, started Game Five of the 1948 Negro League World Series and pitched nine innings to earn the win as the Grays prevailed 10-6 in 10 innings. (*Noir-Tech Research, Inc.*)

Walker and the Homestead Grays had reached the summit of the black baseball world in what became the last Negro League World Series. But both entities soon became footnotes to history. The Negro National League disbanded at the end of 1948, and the Grays played the 1949 season as members of the Negro American Association; after playing the 1950 season as an independent club, the Grays were permanently disbanded prior to the 1951 season. As for Walker, he remained with the team in 1949, but disappeared into history afterward. Information about Walker's origins and his life after his playing career appears to have been lost to the historical record.

SOURCES

In addition to the sources cited in the Notes, the author also consulted Baseball-Reference.com and negroleaguebaseball.com.

NOTES

1 James A. Riley, *The Biographical Encyclopedia of the Negro Baseball Leagues* (New York: Carroll & Graf, 1994), 811.

2 Ibid.

3 It was reported by the *Pittsburgh Courier* on April 1, 1944, that Taylor was sent to the Cleveland Buckeyes of the Negro American League. If this was true, no statistics for Taylor as a member of the Buckeyes exist, nor is there any mention of his playing for Cleveland in any other source.

4 Riley, 811.

5 *Pittsburgh Courier*, June 29, 1946. Riley's *Biographical Encyclopedia* lists Taylor as playing for the Boston Blues at some point during the 1946 season, which conceivably could have been after the Grays' roster cuts. This Blues team was a member of Branch Rickey's short-lived U.S. Baseball League, which did not last the year. But as in the case of Note 3, there are no stats or listings for any time Taylor may have spent with this club.

JOHN WRIGHT

By Niall Adler

John Wright was the "owner of a blazing fast ball and a sharp-breaking curve and plenty of control"[1] and his sinker brought "despair (to) opposing batsmen."[2] To many who saw him, "He dominated batters."[3] Wright will forever be linked in history with Jackie Robinson as the first two players to break the color line in the twentieth century. Wright's story, however, has been lost in history after one year of organized white baseball, while Robinson's career has been widely chronicled.

New Orleans-born Wright cut his teeth in the Negro Leagues beginning in 1937, and had been an ace pitcher for the Indianapolis Crawfords and then the legendary Homestead Grays. As a Navy man stateside, his remarkable pitching caught the attention of the Brooklyn Dodgers and owner Branch Rickey. After Robinson was signed, Wright soon followed, and the duo joined 200 teammates in Daytona Beach in March 1946. *Baltimore Afro-American* writer Sam Lacy said, "Wright doesn't boast the college background that is Jackie's, but he possesses something equally valuable—a level head and the knack of seeing things objectively. He is a realist in a role which demands divorce from sentimentality."[4] Off the field he was affable, quiet, and reserved.[5]

Wright's chief strength as a pitcher was control.[6] However, during his brief and infrequent appearances both in spring training and then with the Montreal Royals, his control failed him. While Robinson excelled, Wright returned to the fading Negro Leagues in 1947, reluctant to talk about his place in history.

Wright grew up in the Jim Crow segregated South. He was born in New Orleans on November 29, 1918, to Louisiana-born parents Richard and Hazel Wright. He had a sister, Isabel, two years older. Richard, at 23, was a railroad laborer, according to the 1920 census.[7]

While Wright was a teen, New Orleans "experienced some of the worst aspects of the Depression."[8]

The area was also forced to recover from the devastating Great Flood of 1927. Wright attended Hoffman and McDonough High Schools and graduated from the latter in 1935.[9] Walter Wright (no relation) remembered one memorable outing: "He was just a kid, about 18 and he struck out the first six batters he faced."[10] In 1934 John's Hoffman team lost the city championship to Wicker High;[11] he had been pitching for Hoffman since 1932.[12]

In 1936 Wright began his pro baseball career with the New Orleans Zulu Social Aid and Pleasure Club. The team was "the Negro carnival organization whose yearly parade is a peak of Mardi Gras."[13] They wore "Mardi Gras hula skirts with black-painted faces and white-painted circles 'round their eyes" and sometimes carried coconuts.[14] A similarly dressed team around the same time, the Jackson Zulu Cannibal Giants, "clowned their way through the game—meanwhile playing excellent ball." That team would fold into the Miami Ethiopian Clowns[15] and eventually become the Indianapolis Clowns one of the longest-surviving black barnstorming teams, owned by Syd Pollock. Wright pitched for the Clowns toward the end of his career.[16]

In March 1937 the Newark Eagles barnstormed through the South[17] and Wright was discovered (and signed) while playing in Louisville.[18] For Wright to get any action, he had to compete with Leon Day, who was second only to Satchel Paige as the Negro League's top arm.[19] He also had to get past a depth chart of Willie Bell, Bob Evans, Terris McDuffie, and Jonas Gaines in the five-man rotation[20] for manager Tex Brunett.

Newark opened the 1937 season on May 18.[21] By early June, the Eagles had lost four league games,[22] but they eventually finished in second place in both the first- and second-half standings. Wright made few appearances: five innings here, two innings there,[23] or a rare start, like one in which he allowed six runs on 12 hits with five strikeouts and no walks against the Pittsburgh Crawfords.[24]

In 1938, again with Newark, Wright once more had to contend with "one of the best pitching staffs in the colored circuit,"[25] Evans, Day, and McDuffie — the "Dizzy Dean of the Negro National League."[26] Despite their stalwart pitching staff, the Eagles finished fifth.[27] Wright pitched more often than he had the previous season, but still was not used consis-

John Wright did not pitch against Birmingham in the third clash between the two teams in 1948; however, he had dominated the Black Barons by pitching two shutouts in Homestead's 1943 World Series triumph. (*John W. Mosley Photograph Collection, Temple University*)

tently. He earned a win in May as a reliever in a 2-1 game on May 8 in which he struck out two in two innings.[28] He pitched in a 14-9 win on June 12 over the Farmers in which he contributed an RBI double at the plate.[29] He took the mound in relief of Day in a 4-1 loss to the Homestead Grays in the nightcap of a June doubleheader.[30] When he did start, his outings were not solid; in one, he eked out a 9-7 win in spite of giving up five runs in the first inning,[31] while another start resulted in a 12-3 loss the New York Black Yankees in August.[32]

In 1939 Newark, which was heavy on pitching, sent Wright to the Toledo Crawfords. At the time, Wright "possessed ... a strong throwing arm, but lacked control."[33] A *Lincoln Evening Journal* article had Wright pitching for the Crawfords in July, but very little else has survived of his 1939 exploits. The Toledo club was managed by Oscar Charleston and had Olympic Gold Medalist Jesse Owens as its owner.[34]

Wright was used sparingly in his first three years of Negro League play. According to the Seamheads. com Negro League Database, Wright was 2-1 in five games against other black teams in 1937, 1-2 in six games in 1938 and 2-3 in five games in 1939. His ERA for those three years, a small sample of his overall record, was 4.30.[35]

During the 1939 offseason, Wright toured California with fellow Negro Leaguers including three all-stars from the previous season, Billy Horne (Chicago American Giants), Billy Wright (Baltimore), and Mule Suttles (Newark). The teams began their trek with the North-South Negro Classic at Pelican Stadium in New Orleans.[36]

In 1940 the Crawfords moved to Indianapolis. The Crawfords played a 54-game spring-training schedule in and around Fort Benning, Georgia, before opening the Negro League season in late May.[37] Owner Jesse Owens would regularly "pull on a pair of long-spiked featherweights" and run exhibitions before Crawfords games. Wright looked to earn his spot in the rotation among veteran "Spoon" Carter, Jimmy Johnson, and Zeke Keyes.[38] More importantly to the bottom line, Owens drew "capacity crowds wherever he has appeared."[39] Owens even outran a motorcycle before 2,000 fans in one of Wright's starts.[40]

Wright's own exploits were catching the *Indianapolis Star's* attention. In May the paper nicknamed him "Sheriff" Wright for the season.[41] Wright had a solid start to 1940, picking up "an impressive victory over the Chicago American Giants in his first local start."[42] He followed with a 1-0, no-hit loss to the St. Louis Stars.[43] A lack of run support continued with back-to-back 1-0 losses in early June.[44] The offense came around in mid-June, as Wright "coasted through the first encounter" of a doubleheader with an eight-hit, 11-6 win over the Lincoln Giants, a group of local amateur Negro players.[45] Wright then turned in a four-hitter against the Kansas City Monarchs.

By the end of June Wright had not allowed more than three runs in any league game and was now considered the Crawfords' ace, finding rhythm with catcher Steel Arm Bell.[46] Wright led a rotation that featured 17-year-old Cannonball Johnson and Jimmy Johnson.[47] In July he returned home to New Orleans to face off against the local New Orleans-St. Louis Stars before a crowd of 15,000[48] as the team's "Sunday starter."[49]

Despite Wright's hurling, the low-scoring Crawfords (39 runs in 23 games) finished in last place in the Negro American League. According to Seamheads.com, Wright was 1-4 against other black teams in 1940, producing an ERA of 1.67 in 43 innings while walking just five and striking out 19. While this is not a complete record, it does provide a good sample of a pitcher with pinpoint control and a low ERA. The legendary Homestead Grays noticed and continued their practice of siphoning off their opponents' best players, of which Wright was now one. He joined the Grays for 1941.

The 1941 season opened on May 10 and 11[50] after spring training in Orlando under manager Vic Harris.[51] The Grays now had to play without Josh Gibson, who jumped to the Mexican League for $6,000.[52] Wright joined a crowded rotation that included Ray Brown, who had gone 18-2 in 1940, left-hander and future Dodgers minor-league team-mate Roy Partlow, and newcomers Terris McDuffie, a future All-Star (from Newark), and Cliff Blackman (from Mobile).[53] Also included was holdover Edsall Walker. Columnist Wendell Smith called them "the best balanced pitching staff in sepia baseball and that in itself makes them the favorites."[54]

The Grays jumped to a 14-6 start by mid-June, and Wright made the most of his opportunities. In one game in which he relieved Hamilton, who was "anything but puzzling," he was "very good" and "never in danger" as he earned the 14-7 win over the Philadelphia Stars. Wright allowed four runs on six hits in the final six innings after the Stars jumped out to a 4-1 lead on Hamilton.[55] His breakout game may have occurred on July 13, at the end of the season's first half, when he pitched a five-hitter with four strikeouts in a 1-0 pitcher's duel against the New York Cubans in a game "marked by fast and glittering fielding and the best pitching seen at the Cricket field in many a year."[56] The Grays won the first half as they were a "championship team of major proportions."[57] They went on to beat the Cubans for the 1941 NNL second-half pennant, but there was no Negro League World Series that season.

Rumblings of blacks playing in the white leagues began to ramp up in early 1940s, when Satchel Paige suggested that a team filled with black players should enter the majors.[58] In 1942 *The Sporting News* raised the issue in an editorial, asserting there was "no good from raising the race issue."[59] The paper noted the benefits of having two games and two leagues and even suggested putting white stars on Negro League teams to "thrust themselves into the limelight as great crusades in the guise of democracy."

Joe Bostic, a sports columnist for the Harlem *People's Voice*, said most were "lukewarm to the idea" and logistical problems such as housing/dining, the "criticism of sometimes-cruel and hot-headed fans" and the majors raiding the Negro Leagues (would lead to) lower quality and less profitable games.[60]

In 1942 Wright was again part of the starting staff of "sharp shooters" along with right-handers Brown, Bill Houston, and Tom Corcoran and lefties Partlow, Lefty Hamilton, and Digger Welmaker. The

Baltimore Afro-American called the Grays "without a doubt, one of the greatest diamond aggregations ever assembled."[61]

No statistics for Wright are available from the 1942 season, but he was part of another Grays championship squad. The Grays and Monarchs met in the first Negro League World Series since 1927 with Partlow and Brown serving as the team's top arms. The Monarchs, behind Paige, took the first three games before "Pitcher Day," an obvious ringer, "fanned a dozen" in a Game Four Grays win, which was later forfeited.[62] The Monarchs swept the series in four games. Two months later, two of the three Grays pitchers considered for the *Pittsburgh Courier* Dream Team, Partlow and Welmaker, were gone, leaving a big hole behind Brown.[63]

January 1943 proved to be a tough month for the Grays. Gibson was diagnosed with a nervous breakdown,[64] the Mexican League grabbed Brown,[65] and manager Harris quit to take a better- paying defense job.[66] There were even questions about whether there would be a Negro National League, as many players joined the military.[67] Eventually things settled down, and a season did take place.

Candy Jim Taylor became the Grays' manager in late January[68] and Wright earned a more prominent role.[69] He established himself in the spring[70] and pitched before ever-rising crowds—6,500 in a doubleheader sweep of the Stars[71] and 9,000 at Griffith Stadium in a sweep of the Elite Giants, when Wright opened the day with a 2-1 five-hitter.[72] In June in Washington, 20,000 fans came out to see Wright win a 10-2 six-hitter over the Monarchs and Satchel Paige.[73] Taylor was "pleased" with his 20-something ace and Wright quickly became "one of the leading moundsmen in the Negro National League."[74]

The "stringbean fireballer with great control and wicked curve" really came into his own. He seemed to "thrive on hard work once he became a ... mainstay of the Pittsburghers' hill corps."[75] By early June Wright had won a half-dozen games and had been "stingy with his hits and runs" following a one-hitter against the Elite Giants.[76] By the middle of the month the team was battling the New York Cubans for first

place as Wright pitched a four-hit shutout of the Cubans to complete a doubleheader sweep and keep the opponent in second.[77] The Grays won the first half and won 45 of 52 games as Gibson, Cool Papa Bell, and Buck Leonard anchored the offense.[78] The Grays had "a lineup loaded with TNT" and a "great pitching staff."[79] By early August, Wright was 13-1 and Ernest Carter was 11-0.[80]

Teams featuring white professionals were no match for the Grays. Wright had a victory over the Army's New Cumberland Reception Center team, which featured a half-dozen major leaguers led by Detroit Tigers outfielder Pat Mullin; he struck out six and allowed four runs.[81] At one point in 1943, New Cumberland was 30-4,[82] with two of those losses coming to the Grays. Wright also defeated the Brooklyn Bushwicks, a top semipro team filled with former major-league players, with a nine-hit, 10-3 win in July.[83]

A crowd of 51,000 saw Wright pitch at Comiskey Park in the 1943 East-West All-Star Game on August 1, in which he gave up the eventual winning run in the fourth inning of a 2-1 West victory while surrendering two hits in two innings.[84]

Regardless of the competition, Wright performed. He later stated that the greatest thrill of his career came when he defeated the Chicago White Sox in 1945. He had also beaten the Brooklyn Dodgers in an exhibition game.[85] In the mid-1940s, Wright was dominant regardless of the foe. Black columnist Ted Yates said that to sell War Bonds, Negro League stars should play a white all-star team at Yankee Stadium to prove they "belong in the same league," which Wright and his Homestead teammates were already showing to be the case.[86]

Wright went 26-4 during the regular season[87] and twice gave the Grays a series lead in the Negro League World series against the Birmingham Black Barons with shutouts. He lost the opener on September 21, giving up two runs in the first inning, as three of the Black Barons' four runs were unearned in a 4-2 Grays loss.[88] At Chicago's Comiskey Park, Wright had a "gilt-edged pitching performance"[89] with a 9-0 five-hit shutout over the Black Barons to give the

Grays a 2-1 Series lead before 6,000 fans.[90] After the Black Barons won Game Four, 11-10, in Columbus, Ohio, Wright put the Grays up, three games to two, with a six-hit shutout in Indianapolis. A five-run seventh led to an 8-0 win.[91] After Birmingham won Game Six 1-0 in 11 innings, controversy ensued prior to Game Seven.

Wright was slated to throw in his native New Orleans in the deciding game, but a mix-up in a wire-service article led to protests by the Grays and the game was eventually played in Montgomery, Alabama. The New Orleans promoter was forced to refund $700 and cancel the game, for which a crowd of 20,000 had been expected.[92] The fiasco started when the Associated Press mistakenly said the game would be played in Montgomery six days earlier, despite assurances by both clubs of a game in New Orleans.[93] After the Grays suggested a nine-game Series, "league officials put their foot flatly down."[94] The Grays prevailed in Montgomery, 8-4. Wright struck out nine and gave up four runs on six hits while walking three in six innings before a crowd of only 4,000.[95]

In October 1943 Wright returned to New Orleans play for the Zulus, opposing a Houma Red Sox pitcher whom the local papers simply listed as "Groundhog."[96] Groundhog Thompson in fact was a future Grays teammate in the late 1940s, and a 1952 Negro League All-Star. Wright also played for the Delta Cubs, as Homestead teammate Joe Spencer and Cleveland's Billy Horne provided his "keystone combination."[97]

After his best season (26-4 and 2-1 in the Negro League World Series), Wright enlisted in the Navy. Along with many Negro League players, 500 white major leaguers and 4,000 minor leaguers served in the armed forces during World War II. Many played baseball stateside to provide entertainment. The Great Lakes Naval Training Station had separate teams that featured white and black stars. The white Great Lakes team had 68 major leaguers at one time or another, including five Hall of Famers.[98]

The all-black Great Lakes Blue Jackets, of which Wright was a part in 1944 and 1945, also featured

Larry Doby, who would become the first black player in the American League, and fellow trail-blazer Chuck Harmon, the first black player for the Cincinnati Reds. In 1944 Wright started 8-2 with an ERA under 3.00 for the Navy team.[99] He later went to Floyd Bennett Field in Brooklyn, and was said to have gone 15-4 with the lowest ERA of any pitcher in armed forces baseball.[100]

In February 1945 color barriers began to fall. New York legislators passed a bill that barred discrimination on the Dodgers, Yankees, Giants, and 13 New York state minor-league teams.[101] Wright, however, was back with the Grays for the Negro League World Series against the Cleveland Buckeyes, though New York's new law would soon play a role in his life and career. Cleveland won all four games, with Wright pitching only the second game of a doubleheader in front of 17,000 fans in Game Two. Wright was the

John Wright poses in the spring training uniform of the 1946 Montreal Royals. Wright was the second African-American player signed by Organized Baseball, joining Jackie Robinson as a member of the Brooklyn Dodgers' Triple-A affiliate. (*National Baseball Hall of Fame, Cooperstown, New York*)

hard-luck 4-2 loser as the Buckeyes tallied two in the seventh and two more in the ninth.[102]

Wright caught the Dodgers' attention while pitching at Ebbets Field in a game between top Negro players in September 1945. In five innings he allowed just two hits and "whipped three fast ones past Ed Slanky" to leave the bases loaded in the first and made an initial impression that would soon lead to Organized Baseball.[103] Dodgers scout Wid Matthews[104] and coach Charlie Dressen, who was at the game,[105] recommended Wright to Rickey. Grays owner Cum Posey saw the impending signing of his players as "thievery."

In October 1945 Rickey signed Jackie Robinson. On January 29, 1946, Wright—who was regarded "as one of the brightest pitching prospects in Negro Baseball"[106]—became the second black player to sign with the Dodgers. Rickey's reasons for signing black players were varied. On the one hand, he saw them as a commodity, once saying that they were "the greatest untapped reservoir of raw material in the history of the game."[107] Rickey also felt guilt because of a 1904 college incident that had occurred when was at Ohio Wesleyan in which a hotel refused to admit the team because it had a black player, Charley Thomas.[108] Signing black players would encourage more black fans to come through the turnstiles, though it did stifle black economic power by weakening the Negro Leagues.[109]

Now 27 years old, Wright weighed 172 pounds and was described as "tall, lean and lanky."[110] His résumé included winning three no-hitters—for the Grays against the Cubans in Youngstown, Ohio; for his Navy team against a naval school; and in Indianapolis against the St. Louis Stars—and losing a fourth when Chin Greene of the St. Louis Stars walked, stole second and third, and scored on a wild pitch. Wright said later, "First of all you want to be the guy who won it and I lost in in spite of the fact I had won three no-hitters and could have won a fourth."[111]

To prepare for the season Wright worked out at Xavier University in New Orleans.[112] Once he arrived in Daytona Beach, Florida, he and Robinson stayed with private families in the black section of town while their white teammates were housed in a hotel.[113] The "debut" of the first black players in Organized Baseball was delayed by two days as bad weather grounded Robinson's plane in New Orleans and Rickey wanted No. 44 (Wright) and No. 36 (Robinson) to begin spring training together.[114]

Rickey was stern with his white players, saying they "must regard them as two more baseball players the same treatments accorded all other players."[115] All the spring-training games for the Montreal Royals, the Dodgers' top farm club, would end up being played in Daytona because of Sanford, Jacksonville, and DeLand barred games with white and black players.[116] The Royals refused to play without their black teammates.[117] Daytona, which was considered to be more progressive and accepting than other Florida cites because of a black middle class, became the team's only option.[118]

The arrival of Robinson and Wright on March 4 was just another day to the white press. The Associated Press talked of the duo going "through the routine practice motions" before seven "uninterested ... spectators."[119] The *Orlando Sentinel* had one paragraph with the caption "Negro Stars Report."[120] For the black press, "(T)he baseball world again vibrated as the announcement flashed across the Nation," Wendell Smith wrote for the *Pittsburgh Courier*.[121]

The mood and attitude toward the first two African-American players in Organized Baseball appeared to change for the better as spring training progressed. The *Baltimore Afro-American* reported:

> "The best example of how the team has warmed up to the pair is shown in the change that has come over the entire camp. During the early days of the training campaign, there was an unmistakable aloofness on the part of several candidates. A majority of these was Southerners. In recent weeks though there has been no noticeable effort on the part of any man in camp to avoid his colored teammates."[122]

Wright concurred, saying of his teammates, "These fellows treat me like a brother and don't think I don't appreciate it." Also, people in Daytona Beach, both black and white, showed him "every courtesy."[123] Baseball Commissioner Happy Chandler watched the right-hander throw.[124]

Bill Mardo of the *Cleveland Call* thought that Wright had a better chance than Robinson to make the big leagues because "The Dodgers are terribly low on good pitchers, and by gosh that Wright is one helluva moundsman."[125] Cuban Stars owner Alex Pompez predicted a 15-win season for Wright in Montreal and tabbed him as the "sleeper" for the Dodgers.[126]

However, things did not go well for Wright. He gave up eight runs on 10 hits in a five-inning intrasquad game, walked four in four innings in another appearance, and was "wilder than an Egyptian Zebra"[127] with four walks and a hit batter in his final Florida appearance. Once the season began, Montreal used him sparingly. With opposing players jeering Robinson in Syracuse, Wright gave up four runs on five hits in 3⅓ innings of relief. Against another hostile crowd in Baltimore, he came on with the bases loaded in the sixth, got out of the jam and did not allow a hit the rest of the way. In spite of this successful performance, he would not be used again.[128] As the *Pittsburgh Courier* wrote, it was a "mystery" that Wright was used in only two road games for Montreal, with the Southern-born manager's response being that "he was not ready yet."[129] Wright was demoted to Three Rivers of the Canadian-American League on May 14.

Despite being lost in the shuffle, Wright never showed resentment for his lack of work and was simply patient.[130] Sam Lacy wrote that Montreal had too many right-handers and that Wright simply "did not have the chance many had hoped he would have nor did he prove any ball of fire when the opportunity presented itself." Don Newcombe, who was with Montreal in spring training, believed that Wright "worked hard and tried, but he was tense."[131]

It was not just the fans or umpires who were against integration in those early days of baseball's Great Experiment, but sometimes his own teammates. Years later Wright told a magazine writer that once, in an exhibition game in Buffalo, "my own catcher (Herman Franks) was tipping off the batters about what pitches I'd be throwing." The umpire brought the team together on the mound, including Robinson, and told (Franks) to knock it off.[132]

Tensions eased in French-speaking Trois-Rivieres (Three Rivers), and Wright rebounded. It was "likely [he] felt at home more than most Americans" because of his hometown New Orleans' French roots.[133] Three Rivers was in seventh place when Wright arrived, but the team ended up winning the league championship. Wright was joined by Negro League right-hander Ray Partlow during the season and "perked up" when the veteran arrived.[134] Wright finished the season at 12-8 with a 4.15 ERA, appearing in 32 games for California-born manager Frenchy Bordagaray, whose background could not have been more different than that of Montreal's skipper, Mississippi-born Clay Hopper.

Wright, however, was released in January 1947 and returned to the Grays.[135] Partlow was released in March.

Not unexpectedly, Branch Rickey's moves led to greater prosperity for other black players. In 1946 the Dodgers had spent a combined $11,310 on salaries for their black players. Robinson ($3,600 for the year), Newcombe ($2,100), and Campanella ($3,110) all remained with the organization in 1947. Pitchers Wright ($2,100) and Partlow ($2,400) did not.[136] Each player had been making more in the Negro Leagues, between $500 and $600 a month, but jumped to Organized Baseball because "there was no future in Negro baseball." By 1953, the top 11 black players in the majors made a combined $238,000.[137]

Integration also accelerated the end of the Negro Leagues. The Negro National League folded after the 1948 season, leaving just the Negro American League, while the Grays held on for one more year as a barnstorming outfit. Attendance fell from 158,000 in 1946 to 48,037 in 1948.[138]

As for Wright, he still had to provide for his family, and that meant playing baseball. In the off-season, he, Partlow, and Campanella played in Puerto Rico, before large crowds that totaled 170,000 in the first four weeks of the season.[139] Once the 1947 season began, there was a sad irony in the fact that Wright had returned to New Orleans to open the Negro League season at Pelican Stadium against the Cubans on April 13 only two days before Robinson broke the color line in Brooklyn.[140] Nonetheless, Wilmer Fields, a teammate with the Grays, said, "John never talked much about his experience with the Dodgers. He was a happy-go-lucky person."[141]

In fact, Wright had said of Rickey, "I couldn't find words to say how swell he really is. He treats Jackie and me as though we were his sons." He also liked Rickey's son, assistant general manager Branch Rickey Jr.[142] Wright and the Grays persevered, but it was an unfortunate fact that they had to play without Josh Gibson, who had died of a stroke during the previous winter.

When Wright was selected for the East-West All-Star Game in late July, he was 7-2, showing some of his old magic.[143] He finished the year 8-4.[144] His team was rolling as well, pushing across a 30-4 record into August.[145] In September 1947 Wright returned to New Orleans for the ninth North-South Negro Classic at Pelican Stadium,[146] a game for which he also had been selected in 1939. The Grays, however, fell short of competing in the Negro League World Series in 1947. In the offseason, Wright and Newcombe pitched for Caracas in the Venezuelan Winter League. Wright pitched well at one point going 2-0-1.[147]

In 1948 the Grays, in what would be their last hurrah in the Negro Leagues, won 10 of their last 11 games—including eight in row—to force a playoff with the Baltimore Elite Giants. They beat the Giants and then defeated the Birmingham Black Barons four games to one in the Negro League World Series. Wright's statistics for 1948 are unavailable, but he did not make an appearance against Birmingham in the Series.

After the 1948 season the Grays and New York Black Yankees disbanded and the Newark Eagles were sold and moved to Houston. Most of the Eagles players decided not to join the club in segregated Texas. Players from the three teams were distributed to other teams by lot. Wright and teammates Tom Parker and Luther Clifford went to the Buckeyes, who had moved from Cleveland to Louisville; however, there is no record of Wright pitching in the Negro Leagues after 1948.[148]

Wright played in the reorganized Mexican League in the 1950s—with the San Luis Potosi Tuneros (1950), the Veracruz Azules (1950), Nuevo Laredo (1951), and Torreon (1951) with former Grays teammate Buck Leonard, who was then 43 years old. In Mexico Wright asked only to pitch on Saturdays so he could see the bullfights on Sundays. The local fans called him "Conejo" (Rabbit) because of his fidgety nature on the mound.[149]

Wright is also listed as playing in the Dominican League from 1952 to 1954 with Leones del Escogido (1952-53), where he went 10-5 with a 2.05 ERA in 1952 and 4-9 with a 1.64 ERA in 1953. With Aguilas Cibaenas (1954) he was 0-7 in 10 games with a 4.95 ERA, bringing his totals in three Dominican seasons to 14-21 with a 2.35 ERA.[150] After his stint in the Dominican Republic, he signed with the Indianapolis Clowns, now a barnstorming team, in August 1954. In his first game, at the age of 36, he shut out the Kansas City Monarchs.[151]

After Wright's baseball career ended, he was employed by National Gypsum as a driver and janitor for the rest of his working life. In his spare time, he enjoyed fishing on Louisiana's bayous. Over the years, Wright was reluctant to grant interviews. When he did sit down to be interviewed by a Canadian journalist in the mid-1980s, the writer described him as very hospitable and a "slim, fit-looking, suave ... (man who) could still step on the mound." By that point, Wright had four children with his wife, Mildred Creecy, 18 grandchildren, and four great-grandchildren. He jokingly told the writer that he had to give up tossing the ball due to "Cousin Arthur" (arthritis).[152] His family knew Wright by the nickname Hoss, but each succeeding generation knew less and less about his exploits in the Negro and Latin leagues as he never talked about baseball with his grandchildren.[153]

Wright died on May 4, 1990. At his funeral, Walter Wright (no relation) said, "I'm sure most of his co-workers at the gypsum plant never even knew he was a ballplayer. And I when I looked over at his casket, I couldn't help wondering how many stories it contained—stories that now would never be told." [154]

NOTES

The author would like to thank Carlis Robinson, John Wright's daughter, for providing information about her father and Ryan Whirty for compiling research that helped with this biography.

1   Chris Lamb, *Blackout: The Untold Story of Jackie Robinson's First Spring* (Lincoln: University of Nebraska Press, 2004), 69.

2   W.M. Akers, "The Forgotten Men Who Broke Baseball's Color Line With Jackie Robinson," Vice Sports, April 15, 2015, sports.vice.com/en_us/article/the-forgotten-men-who-broke-baseballs-color-line-with-jackie-robinson.

3   "New Orleanian John Wright, a Pitcher, Also Signed With Dodgers in 1945, But He Never Made It to the Major Leagues," *New Orleans Times-Picayune*, April 3, 1997.

4   Ryan Whirty, "Second Black Player Signed After Jackie Robinson Never Made His Mark," April 12, 2013, baseballamerica.com/majors/second-black-player-signed-after-jackie-robinson-never-made-his-mark/#iRiGRi7mKX23Y7uI.97.

5   "New Orleanian John Wright."

6   Ibid.

7   Much of the census data, as well as news articles from the *Louisiana Weekly* and *Times-Picayune*, among others was researched and compiled by Ryan Whirty and given to the author.

8   Matthew Reonas, "Great Depression in Louisiana," knowla.org, knowla.org/entry/875/.

9   Dan Burley, "Confidentially Yours," *New York Amsterdam News*, April 27, 1946: 12.

10   "New Orleanian John Wright."

11   "Wright Cops High Point," *Louisiana Weekly*, May 12, 1934.

12   "Wright, New Orleans Baseball Player, to Join Montreal Royals in Mar.," *Louisiana Weekly*, February 9, 1946: 1.

13   Alan Pollock and James A. Riley, *Barnstorming to Heaven: Syd Pollock and His Great Black Teams* (Tuscaloosa: University of Alabama Press, 2006), 261.

14   "New Orleans Zulus Mourn King-Elect," *News Palladium*, November 22, 1939: 2.

15   Raymond Mohl, "Clowning Around: The Miami Ethiopian Clowns and the Cultural Conflict in Black Baseball," *Tequesta: The Journal of the Historical Association of Southern Florida 1*, No. 62 (2002). In the 1930s the Giants regularly traveled to Miami for winter baseball and played the Miami Giants,

relying on Syd Pollock to book them games. In 1937, "possibly by the urging of Pollack," the team was renamed the Ethiopian Clowns." digitalcollections.fiu.edu/tequesta/files/2002/02_1_02.pdf.

16   Pollock and Riley, 27.

17   "NY Black Yanks Set Training Plans," *Pittsburgh Courier*, March 20, 1937: 22.

18   "Second Negro Baseball player Signs Montreal Royals' Contract," *Montreal Gazette*, January 30, 1946: 13.

19   Chester L. Washington,. "Calling All Strikes...," *Pittsburgh Courier*, April 24, 1937: 16.

20   "Eagles Present Strong Line Against Grays," *Pittsburgh Post-Gazette*, June 12, 1937: 17.

21   "Homestead Grays Oppose Newark Eagles Tomorrow," *Morning News*, May 17, 1937: 12.

22   "Colored Teams to Play Friday," *Evening News*, June 5, 1937: 13.

23   "Newark Eagles Fly Away With Double Victory," *Brooklyn Daily Eagle*, July 6, 1937: 20.

24   "Crawfords Defeat Newark Eagles 6-1," *Pennsylvania Gazette and Daily*, August 12, 1937: 11.

25   "Newark Eagles Visit Belmar With Good Pitchers, Hitters," *Asbury Park* (New Jersey) *Press*, June 24, 1938.

26   "Negro Nines Vie Tuesday," *Rochester Democrat and Chronicle*, July 31, 1938: 37.

27   Cum Posey, "Posey's Points," *Pittsburgh Courier*, September 10, 1938: 17.

28   *Brooklyn Eagle*, May 9, 1938: 16.

29   "Eagles Twice Stop Farmers," *Brooklyn Eagle*, June 13, 1938: 14.

30   "Grays Win Two," *Pittsburgh Post-Gazette*, June 6, 1938: 15.

31   Jocko Maxwell, "Eagles Split With Stars," *New York Age*, June 25, 1938: 8.

32   Ibid.

33   Joe Bostic, "Rickey Signs Up Negro Pitcher," *Amsterdam News*, February 2, 1946: 1.

34   "Jesse Owens Coming," *Lincoln* (Nebraska) *Star*, July 6, 1939: 12.

35   In 1939, Wright appeared in a June game for the Camden Giants against Lloyd AC, falling victim to a 19-strikeout performance by Addis Copple. A news article stated afterward that "Wright is no longer with the club." Records were spotty in regard to his complete pitching record. "Copple Fans 19 to Best Newsome Hurling Duel" *Delaware Daily Times*, June 15, 1938: 38. Records are spotty from the period, as the Negro League Baseball Player Association has also listed him with the Atlanta Black Crackers and Pittsburgh Crawfords in 1938 Negro National Players Association Roster. nlbpa.com/the-athletes/wright-john—-needle-nose.

36   "North-South Negro Battle Billed Today," *New Orleans Times Picayune*, October 1, 1939: 2.

37 "Crawfords Are in Form for Negro Loop Openers," *Indianapolis Star*, May 24, 1940: 20.

38 "Negro Stars to Play at Casino," *Monroe* (Louisiana) *News-Star*, April 18, 1940: 9.

39 "Negro Teams to Play Tonight," *Monroe News-Star*, April 24, 1940: 8.

40 "NO Stars Take Two Games From Toledo," *Times Picayune*, July 29, 1940: 13.

41 "Crawfords Will Play Double-Header Sunday," *Indianapolis Star*, May 23, 1940: 19.

42 "St. Louis Stars Play Here Today," *Indianapolis Star*, June 2, 1940: 41.

43 "Crawfords Will Play Cleveland Nine Sunday," *Indianapolis Star*, June 13, 1940: 24.

44 "Crawfords Play Lincoln Giants," *Indianapolis Star*, June 16, 1940: 38.

45 "Crawfords Win, Tie In Twin Bill," *Indianapolis Star*, June 17, 1940: 16.

46 "Crawfords Expect Pitchers' Battle," *Indianapolis Star*, June 28, 1940: 23.

47 "Famous Colored Team and Track Champ Due Here," *Waco Tribune-Herald*, July 14, 1940: 8.

48 "New Orleans Stars Primed for Clash With Toledo Crawfords," *Pittsburgh Courier*, July 27, 1940: 16.

49 "Toledo Crawfords to Play Oilers Tonight," *Indianapolis Star*, August 9, 1940: 16.

50 "Negro Nat'l League to Open Season on May 10 and 11," *New York Age*, March 15, 1941: 11.

51 "Giants to Meet Grays on Sunday," *Orlando-Tennessean*, April 24, 1941: 20.

52 "Homestead Grays Sue Negro Catcher," *Daily Republican*, April 29, 1941: 2.

53 "Grays Begin Here in Baltimore," *Pittsburgh Press*, May 2, 1941: 52.

54 Wendell Smith, "Smitty's Sports Spurts / Good Star," *Pittsburgh Courier*, May 10, 1941: 16.

55 "Homestead Grays' 23-Hit Assault Buries Philly Stars," *Altoona* (Pennsylvania) *Tribune*, Jun 26, 1941: 6.

56 Os Figard, "Homestead Grays Win 1-0 Mound Duel Over NY Cubans," *Altoona Tribune*, July 14, 1941: 6.

57 "Isabella Is Playing Champion Negro Club," *Morning Herald*, July 12, 1941: 6.

58 "Paige's Major Leaguers," *New York Age*, July 26, 1941: 11.

59 *The Sporting News*, August 6, 1942: 4.

60 Ibid.

61 "Grays to Carry Power Nine to Stadium Sunday," *Baltimore Afro-American*, May 19, 1942: 22.

62 "Monarchs Cry 'Ringer' in World Series Loss," *Wilkes-Barre Record*, September 21, 1942: 10.

63 "Kansas City, Homestead Grays Stars Dominate Dream Team," *Pittsburgh Courier*, November 7, 1942: 17.

64 "Famous Catcher Sent to the Hospital," *Pittsburgh Courier*, January 9, 1943: 6.

65 *Pittsburgh Press*, January 11, 1943: 18.

66 Paul Kurtz, "Sports Stew," *Pittsburgh Press*, January 16, 1943: 10.

67 Cum Posey, "Posey's Points," *Pittsburgh Courier*, January 23, 1943: 16.

68 *Pittsburgh Courier*, January 30, 1943: 16.

69 "Grays to Start Training at Akron (O) Park Monday," *Pittsburgh Press*, April 10, 1943.

70 "Homestead Grays Win Double-Header," *Pittsburgh Press*, April 26, 1943: 19.

71 "Grays Defeat Stars 9-3, 8-2," *Pittsburgh Post-Gazette*, May 24, 1943: 16.

72 "Grays Defeat Elites, 2-1, 7-0," *Pittsburgh Post-Gazette*, May 17, 1943: 17.

73 "20,000 See Grays Defeat Monarchs," *Pittsburgh Press*, June 21, 1943: 15.

74 Paul Kurtz, "Grays Pilot Pleased With Pitcher Wright," *Pittsburgh Press*, April 17, 1943: 8.

75 Bostic.

76 "Good Hurlers Boasted," *Cincinnati Enquirer*, June 8, 1943: 20.

77 "Grays Trim Cubans in Double-header," *Pittsburgh Press*, June 13, 1943: 44.

78 "Large Crowd Expected Sunday at Polo Grounds," *New York Age*, July 24, 1943: 11.

79 "Negro Champions at Dexter Sunday" *Brooklyn Daily Eagle*, June 3, 1943: 16.

80 "Heavy Hitters on Army Team," *Pittsburgh Post-Gazette*, August 10, 1943: 13.

81 "Stars Go Down; Face Army Nine" *Evening News*, May 31, 1943: 11.

82 "New Cumberland Bows," *Pottstown* (Pennsylvania) *Mercury*, August 12, 1943: 10.

83 "Lose Again to the Grays," *Brooklyn Eagle*, July 3, 1943: 14.

84 All-Star Box, *Pittsburgh Courier*, August 7, 1943: 19,

85 "Wright, New Orleans Baseball Player, to Join Montreal Royals in Mar.," *Louisiana Weekly*, February 9, 1946: 1.

86 Ted Yates, "I've Been Around," *New York Age*, June 19, 1943: 10.

87 "Grays, Barons Battled for Negro Baseball Championship," *Daily Republican*, October 5, 1943: 1.

88 "Birmingham Wins Opener of Series," *St. Louis Post-Dispatch*, September 22, 1943: 26.

89 "Shutout in Game at Chicago," *Pittsburgh Courier*, October 2, 1943: 16.

90 "Grays Take Series Lead, Whip Barons 9-0 at Chicago," *Louisiana Weekly*, October 2, 1943.

91 "Greys Blank Barons, 8-0," *Indianapolis Star*, September 30, 1943: 13.

92 "Negro World Series Deciding Tilt to Be Played Here Sunday," *Louisiana Weekly*, October 9, 1943.

93 "Canceled: Deciding Game Farce; Weird Schedule of World Series Irks Fans," *Louisiana Weekly*, October 16, 1943.

94 "Grays Are World Champs," *Chicago Defender*, October 16, 1943: 11.

95 Ibid.

96 "Zulus to Play Houma Jax Red Sox in Negro Contest," *Times Picayune*, October 23, 1943.

97 "Delta Cubs Play Houma Sox Today," *Times Picayune*, November 7, 1943: 29.

98 Roger Gogan, *Blue Jackets of Summer* (Ypsilanti, Michigan: Great Lakes Sports Publishing, 2008), foreword.

99 "Great Lakes Colored 9 vs. Red Wings Sunday," *Chicago Daily Herald*, July 21, 1944: 1.

100 Lamb, 103.

101 "NY Bill Would Prevent Color Barriers in Game," *The Sporting News*, February 8, 1945: 17.

102 "Battling Bucks Win 2-1, 4-2 in World Series," *Pittsburgh Courier*, September 22, 1945: 12.

103 Bostic.

104 Ibid.

105 "Grays' Hurler Is Signed by Dodger Farm," *Pittsburgh Post-Gazette*, January 30, 1946: 13.

106 Dan Burley, "Confidentially Yours," *Amsterdam News*, February 2, 1946: 19.

107 Anthony Pratkanis and Marlene Turner, "Mr. Rickey Has His Way," *Across the Board*, July/August 1994.

108 Ibid.

109 Aaron Leibowitz, "On Branch Rickey and the Negro Leagues," Si.com, April 21, 2015, thecauldron.si.com/on-branch-rickey-and-the-negro-leagues-f5bb56cd0dfe#.5wz771axo. "Certainly Robinson's presence in itself challenged white supremacy, and his acceptance was a symbol for the black masses bombarded with falsehoods of physical and mental inferiority," writes Malaika Jabali. "But the other side of integration that is rarely acknowledged goes beyond this symbolism: Robinson's role ultimately was to stifle one of the few institutions of black economic power that, after almost a century, blacks have yet to reach in any athletic league."

110 Dan Burley, "Confidentially Yours," *Amsterdam News*, April 27, 1946: 12.

111 Ibid.

112 "Wright, New Orleans Baseball Player, to Join Montreal Royals in Mar.," *Louisiana Weekly*, February 9, 1946: 1.

113 "Jackie Robinson, First Negro to Crash Organized Baseball in Modern Times, Reports to Brooklyn's Dodgers Today," *Times Daily*, March 1, 1946: 5.

114 Sam Lacy, "Robinson and Wright Arrive at Royals Camp," *Baltimore Afro-American*, March 2, 1946: 18.

115 "Brooks Are Cautioned re Robinson, Wright," *Montreal Gazette*, March 1, 1946: 16.

116 Today in New Orleans History, Associated Press, March 5, 1946, neworleanspast.com/todayinneworleanshistory/november_28.html.

117 Jules Tygiel, *Baseball's Great Experiment: Jackie Robinson and His Legacy* (New York: Oxford University Press, 1997), 115. Montreal club president Hector Racine said, "It will be all or nothing with the Montreal club. Jackie Robinson and John Wright go with the team or there's no game."

118 Andrew Carter, "Spring of 46," *Orlando Sentinel*, March 4, 2006, articles.orlandosentinel.com/2006-03-04/sports/NEWROBINSON04_1_jackie-robinson-sanford-montreal-royals.

119 Today in New Orleans History, Associated Press, March 5, 1946, neworleanspast.com/todayinneworleanshistory/november_28.html.

120 Andrew Carter, "Spring of 46."

121 Whirty, "Second Black Player Signed."

122 "White Mates Remain Loyal to Two Montreal Stars," *Baltimore Afro-American*, April 6, 1946, 31.

123 Dan Burley, "Confidentially Yours," *New York Amsterdam News*, April 27, 1946: 12.

124 Wendell Smith, "The Sports Beat," *Pittsburgh Courier*, March 23, 1946.

125 Today in New Orleans History, Associated Press, March 5, 1946.

126 Tygiel, 118.

127 Ibid.

128 Ibid.

129 "Wright Is Patiently Awaiting Big Chance," *Pittsburgh Courier*, May 11, 1946: 22.

130 Wendell Smith, Wendell "The Sports Beat," *Pittsburgh Courier*, May 11, 1946: 22.

131 Tygiel, 118.

132 Don Bell, "The Wright Stuff," *MVP Magazine*, June 1986: 46.

133 Wendell Smith, "The Sports Beat," *Pittsburgh Courier*, May 11, 1946: 22.

134 Akers, "The Forgotten Men Who Broke Baseball's Color Line With Jackie Robinson."

135 Jim Hall, "Time Out," *Louisiana Weekly*, April 5, 1947.

136 Wendell Smith, "Sports Beat," *Pittsburgh Courier*, January 24, 1953.

137 Ibid.

138 "Yankee Stadium Events Drew 3,101,713 in 1948," *The Sporting News*, January 5, 1949: 18.

139 Santiago Llorens, "Partlow Stars on the Mound, at Plate in Puerto Rico," *The Sporting News*, November 20, 1946.

140 "Homestead Grays Meet NY Cubans," *Times-Picayune*, April 13, 1947: 26.

141 "New Orleanian John Wright."

142 Dan Burley, "Confidentially Yours," *New York Amsterdam News*, April 27, 1946: 12.

143 "50,000 to See 'Dream Game' in Chicago," *Pittsburgh Courier*, July 26, 1947: 14.

144 "Wright, a Pitcher, Also Signed With Dodgers in 1945," *Times-Picayune*, April 13, 1997, files.usgwarchives.net/la/orleans/newspapers/00000344.txt.

145 "Grays Will Play Bronze Thursday," *New Castle* (Pennsylvania) *News*, August 6, 1947: 14.

146 "Ninth Annual North-South Negro Classic Set Sunday," *Times-Picayune*, September 30, 1947: 11.

147 "Around the Hot Stove," *Nashua Telegraph*, January 15, 1948: 17.

148 "AL Teams Draft Stars of Clubs Calling it Quits," *Pittsburgh Courier*, February 19, 1949: 11.

149 Bell, "The Wright Stuff," 46.

150 Dominican League Statistics, history.winterballdata.com/?view_page=player&s_ok=+&season_id=&player_id=4697&team_id=.

151 "Wright Joins Clowns and Beats Monarchs 5-0 in 1st Game," *New York Age*, August 21, 1954: 20.

152 Bell, "The Wright Stuff," 46.

153 Wirty, "Second black player."

154 "New Orleanian John Wright."

VIC HARRIS

By Charlie Fouché

The Homestead Grays were a dominant force in Negro League baseball from 1926 to 1948. While the faces and muscles of this franchise were Hall of Famers Josh Gibson and Buck Leonard, the heart and soul of the Homestead Grays was feisty player-manager Vic Harris, who was known and admired by teammates and opponents alike for his fierce style of play.

Longtime teammate Buck Leonard said of Harris's baserunning style, "He just undressed the opposing infielder—cut the uniform right off his back."[1] Second baseman Dick Seay agreed. "He would cut you in a minute. Cut you and laugh."[2]

Harris earned the nickname Vicious Vic for his reputation for violent behavior, both on and off the field.[3] Harris and teammates Jud Wilson, Oscar Charleston, and Chippy Britt composed a group that became known as "the four big, bad men of black baseball."[4]

Elander Victor Harris was born to William and Frances Harris in Pensacola, Florida, on June 10, 1905. His father was a farmer.[5] Two of his brothers, Bill and Neal, would also play Negro League baseball. He moved with his family to Pittsburgh when he was "nine or ten years old"[6] and soon started to play baseball in with the YMCA team. William Harris brought his family from the agrarian South to the industrial North. Many African American families moved North to find better economic opportunities in the first decades of the twentieth century in a movement known as the great migration. William Harris found a job as a scrap man at a steel factory.[7] Vic Harris attended Pittsburgh's Schenley High School from 1919 to 1922.[8]

Harris caught the eye of Homestead Grays owner Cum Posey, who approached him in 1923 about playing for his team, but Harris joined the Cleveland Tate Stars instead.[9] In his first season in professional baseball, Harris hit .297 as an 18-year-old starting outfielder.

The next year, Harris jumped from the Tate Stars to the Cleveland Browns. As a Brown, Harris hit .229 in 27 games and was second on the team with 14 RBIs. He jumped the Browns to take advantage of the opportunity to play for Negro League pioneer and legend Rube Foster and his Chicago American Giants. In his final 10 games of the 1924 season with Chicago, Harris hit .257. There is no doubt that Foster's leadership style had an impact on the manner by which Harris would later compile his own legendary numbers as a manager.

In 1925, Harris began his long-term service for the Homestead Grays. He recalled, "I stayed with Posey for the rest of my career, except for one year—1934. That's the year I played with Gus Greenlee and the Pittsburgh Crawfords."[10] That "rest of my career" would last 22 years with the Homestead Grays as a player, and from 1935 to 1948 as a player-manager. The only years in which Harris was not associated with the Grays were the 1934 season he spent with the crosstown rival Crawfords and 1943, when he took a job at a defense plant during World War II.[11] Limited records from the 1925 season show Harris hitting .250 (1-for-4) in his first season with the Grays.[12]

Negro League records are scarce for Harris's first few seasons with the Grays. Available statistics show him batting .500 (3-for-6) for 1926, but no statistics for 1927 are to be had. Harris hit .333 for the Grays in 1928. By this time, he had entrenched himself at the top of the Grays lineup, usually batting first or second.[13] Harris was a contact, spray hitter, and this quality made him a good hit-and-run man batting behind a leadoff batter. In 1929 Harris hit a steady .286 for the Grays in 140 at-bats.

The 1930 season was a breakout campaign for Harris. He hit .338, which was third on the team in average, finished second on the team in home runs, and was third in RBIs.

Harris's average dipped to .273 for the 1931 Homestead Grays, a team that notched its place in baseball history via a 143-29-2 record against all levels of competition.[14] Catcher-pitcher Ted "Double Duty" Radcliffe called this team the greatest baseball team of all time, and recalled that the team won 35 games before it suffered its first loss.[15] Baseball scholars have debated whether the 1931 Homestead Grays, 1925 Kansas City Monarchs, or 1935 Pittsburgh Crawfords were the greatest single-season team in Negro League history. More broad-thinking scholars include the 1931 Grays with the 1927 New York Yankees in their discussions of the greatest baseball team of all time. The 1931 Homestead Grays included future Hall of Famers Josh Gibson, Jud Wilson, Oscar Charleston, Willie Foster, and Smokey Joe Williams. The team also included perennial all-stars George Scales, Ted Page, and Double Duty Radcliffe. Harris started and played left field on this great team. With the Great Depression raging, Negro baseball took quite an economic hit. As a result, the 1931 Grays were not affiliated with any league. They were strictly a barn-storming team, which meant that this outstanding lineup did not even have the opportunity to claim a pennant or championship.

In 1932 Homestead joined the East-West League. That year's squad was the first Grays team to win a league championship as it recorded a .614 winning percentage to claim the league pennant. Harris hit

Vic Harris (at left), Homestead's manager in 1948, confers with his future Hall of Fame first baseman Buck Leonard in the Grays' dugout. (*John W. Mosley Photograph Collection, Temple University*)

.333, but the team was so strong that his average was good enough for just fourth on the team.

Harris followed his solid 1932 season by hitting .311 for Homestead in 1933, the first of seven seasons in which he would be selected to participate in the East-West All-Star Game. The annual game was played at Chicago's Comiskey Park (some years a second game was played elsewhere as well) and was the highlight and showcase of every Negro League season. Harris was also named to the East-West Classic in 1934, 1938, 1939, 1942, 1943, and 1947.[16]

The city of Pittsburgh was embroiled in a baseball civil war between Cum Posey of the Homestead Grays and Gus Greenlee of the Pittsburgh Crawfords. Harris left the Grays for the Crawfords for the 1934 season, though he was not the only one. Several Grays jumped to the Crawfords during its eight-year existence in Pittsburgh. Harris hit .339 for the Craws in 1934, which led a team that was stocked with both future Hall of Famers (Josh Gibson, Oscar Charleston, Judy Johnson, Cool Papa Bell, and Satchel Paige) and East-West All-Stars (Rap Dixon, Jimmie Crutchfield, Sam Streeter, and Leroy Matlock among them).

Harris was lured back across town for the 1935 season by an offer he could not refuse. "I went back to the Grays," he recalled, "and Posey made me manager. He had been managing the team until then. He was fiery, and he knew I was fiery, so he made me manager."[17] Harris's first managerial assignment began a career of 15 extremely productive years as a manager and coach. Harris hit .326 and tied for the team lead in home runs for 1935, the season in which he also was selected to his second East-West All-Star team. The Grays recorded a only a 25-35-2 record (.417) in Harris's first season at the helm, but it would be 11 more years before the Homestead Grays had another sub-.500 winning percentage for a season. That winter he played in Puerto Rico for San Juan.

Harris enjoyed a banner year in 1936. Not only did he lead the Grays in batting with a .351 average, but that offseason—on October 14, 1936—Harris married Dorothy Smith, the woman who would remain by his side until the day he died. After the season

Harris also tried his hand at managing in winter ball. For the years 1936-1939, he managed a barnstorming team in the continental United States.[18] He went farther south from 1947 to 1950 to manage Santurce in the Puerto Rican League, where he recorded three straight winning seasons.

The 1937 Negro League season began an unprecedented run of success for the Homestead Grays. From that year through 1945, the Grays won nine consecutive league championships, a record that has never been equaled at any level of professional baseball. Harris did not manage during the 1943 and 1944 seasons because of his work in the defense factory. Negro League legend Candy Jim Taylor was the full-time manager while Harris was doing his bit for the war effort. For those championship years, Harris hit .315 in 1937; .327 in 1938; .264 in 1939; .269 in 1940; .248 in 1941; .264 in 1942; .348 in 1943; .500 in 1944 (10 at-bats); and .333 in 1945 (nine at-bats).

In 1941 Harris was named as a manager for the first time in the East-West Classic, an honor that would again be bestowed upon him in 1942, 1943, 1945, 1946, and 1948. In all, Harris recorded a 4-4 record as a manager in the Classic.[19] His eight games as a manager were twice as many as the runner-up, Oscar Charleston.[20]

Harris came back to the Grays full-time as a manager in 1946. After two sub-.500 seasons in 1946 and 1947, Harris led his 1948 team, a member franchise of the Negro National League, to another pennant, and a 4-games-to-1 victory over the Negro American League's Birmingham Black Barons in the final Negro League World Series.

The NNL disbanded after the 1948 season and the Grays became a member of the Negro American Association, a black minor league, in 1949. By then Negro League baseball teams were losing their best players to the major leagues after Jackie Robinson made it big with the Brooklyn Dodgers in 1947. Harris had foreseen such a fate for the Negro Leagues in 1942, when the integration of major-league baseball had become a hot topic after Brooklyn Dodgers manager Leo Durocher asserted that he would use black players if only the major-league owners and

Commissioner Kenesaw Mountain Landis would allow it. Harris had predicted, "If they take our best boys, we will be but a hollow shell of what we are today."[21]

Harris voiced doubts about whether the integration of Organized Baseball would be a positive development for black ballplayers, saying, "[It] might be a good thing and then again, it might not be."[22] He knew that not every black ballplayer would have a shot at the majors and wondered how the other 75 to 80 percent of Negro League players would survive.[23] Integration had come to pass, however, and Harris's prophecy about its effects on the Negro Leagues was in the process of being fulfilled. Harris signed on as a coach for the Baltimore Elite Giants in 1949. He

As player-manager, "Vicious Vic" Harris led the Grays to nine consecutive pennants (1937-45) and two World Series titles (1943-44); in 1948, as manager only, he piloted the last Negro League World Series championship team. (*National Baseball Hall of Fame, Cooperstown, New York*)

became the skipper of the Birmingham Black Barons in 1950, and posted a 52-25 record in what was his final season as a manager.

Harris retired from professional baseball after the 1950 season. In his retirement, he was the head custodian for the Castaic Union Schools in Castaic, California. He died on February 23, 1978, after an unsuccessful second operation to rid him of cancer.[24] He was survived by Dorothy, his wife of 36 years; a daughter, Judith Victoria Harris; and a son, Ronald Victor Harris.

In evaluating Vic Harris's 27-year career in baseball, several statistics stand out above his peers. On one of the greatest teams of all time, the Homestead Grays, Harris finished his playing career in the top seven of 14 different offensive categories. He finished first on the Grays' all-time list for games played, at-bats, hits, triples, and hit batsmen. He finished second in runs scored, doubles, and bases on balls. He is third on the Grays' list of home runs and runs batted in, fifth in sacrifice hits, sixth in batting average and slugging percentage, and seventh in stolen bases. Add Harris's lifetime .303 batting average,[25] and it is enough to make a person wonder why the National Baseball Hall of Fame has not enshrined him yet.

As impressive as Harris's lifetime totals are as a player, his record as a manager is even more extraordinary. Harris is first on the Grays' list of games won as a manager. His teams won more Negro League titles — eight — than any other manager; the next closest competitors (Candy Jim Taylor, Dick Lundy, Frank Warfield, Dave Malacher, Rube Foster, and Jose Mendez) have three titles each.[26] His lifetime managerial record in the Negro leagues, All-Star games, postseason, and winter leagues stands at 754-352, a .682 winning percentage.[27] Harris was not only the greatest Negro League manager of all times, it can be argued that he may well have been the greatest manager in the history of baseball. If Cooperstown cannot use him in its outfield, surely it can use him as a dugout strategist.

Whether or not Harris was the greatest manager of all time, one thing is certain: He was the manager of the reigning and defending Negro League World

Series champion Homestead Grays, a title he is guaranteed to keep since there never was another Negro League World Series after 1948.

SOURCES

In addition to the sources cited in the Notes, the author also consulted Baseball-Reference.com, the Seamheads.com Negro League Database, the Center for Negro League Baseball Research, and the following:

Clark, Dick, and Larry Lester, eds. *The Negro Leagues Book* (Cleveland: Society for American Baseball Research, 1994).

Hogan, Lawrence D. *Shades of Glory* (Washington: National Geographic, 2006).

Johnson, Earl. "Sports Whirl," n.d.

Lester, Larry, and Sammy J. Miller. *Black America Series: Black Baseball in Pittsburgh* (Charleston, South Carolina: Arcadia Publishing, 2001).

"Obituaries," *The Sporting News*, March 11, 1978.

NOTES

1   Vic Harris and John Holway, "Baseball Old Timers: Vic Harris Managed the Homestead Grays," *Dawn Magazine*, March 8, 1975: 12.

2   Ibid.

3   James Riley, *The Biographical Encyclopedia of the Negro Baseball Leagues* (New York: Carroll and Graf Publishers, Inc., 1994), 360.

4   Karen and Kevin Flynn, "Remembering Vic Harris," dcbaseballhistory.com/2013/08/remembering-vic-harris/.

5   1910 US Census.

6   Harris and Holway: 13.

7   1920 US Census.

8   Merl F. Kleinknecht, "Vic Harris," in David L. Porter, ed., *Biographical Dictionary of American Sports* (Westport, Connecticut: Greenwood Press, 2000).

9   Harris and Holway: 13.

10   Ibid.

11   Brad Snyder, *Beyond the Shadow of the Senators: The Untold Story of the Homestead Grays and the Integration of Baseball* (New York: McGraw-Hill, 2003), 258.

12   baseball-reference.com/register/player.fcgi?id=harris002vic. This appears to reflect incomplete statistics.

13   Riley, 360.

14   Phil S. Dixon, *Phil Dixon's American Baseball Chronicles Great Teams: The 1931 Homestead Grays Volume 1* (Bloomington, Indiana: Xlibris Corporation, 2009), 17.

15   Jon O'Sheal, *Pride and Perseverance: The Story of the Negro Leagues*, A&E Home Video, 2014.

16   Larry Lester, *Black Baseball's National Showcase: The East-West All-Star Game, 1933-1953* (Lincoln: University of Nebraska Press, 2001), 422.

17   Harris and Holway: 13.

18   In 1938 and 1939 he played for and managed the Grays in the American Series in Cuba. In the 1939-40 Cuban Winter League season, he played for the Santa Clara team, but Jose Fernandez was the manager. Jorge S. Figueredo, *Cuban Baseball: A Statistical History, 1878-1961* (Jefferson, North Carolina: McFarland, 2003), 229.

19   Dr. Layton Revel and Luis Munoz, "Forgotten Heroes: Elander Victor 'Vic' Harris" (Carrollton, Texas: Center for Negro League Baseball Research, 2011), 25.

20   Lester, 401.

21   Snyder, 167.

22   Neil Lanctot, *Negro League Baseball: The Rise and Ruin of a Black Institution* (Philadelphia: University of Pennsylvania Press, 2004), 240.

23   Lanctot, 240-41.

24   John Holway, "Negro League Star Harris Dead, Club Won 134 Games in Season," *Washington Post*, February 26, 1978.

25   seamheads.com/NegroLgs/player.php?playerID=harriorvic; baseball-reference.com/register/player.fcgi?id=harris002vic.

26   Revel and Munoz, ii.

27   Ibid.

CUM POSEY

By Brian McKenna

Although his fame rests with his relationship with the great Homestead Grays, Cum Posey was one of the top basketball players of his time. He played at Penn State and Duquesne University and was a major contributor to five Colored Basketball World's Championship teams. He organized, promoted, and managed the Loendi Five, which captured those championships. Posey took the organization skills developed with Loendi and transferred his efforts into baseball and his management of the Homestead Grays.

In 1922 Pittsburgh was invaded by a professional nine run by Dizzy Dismukes. In response Posey converted his part-time semipro outfit into a professional squad. Within a few years they were regularly beating the best clubs in black baseball and numerous college teams, as well as some in organized baseball. Soon, the club signed Oscar Charleston, Josh Gibson, and Judy Johnson and joined the organized black league. The Grays called two major-league stadiums home, Pittsburgh's Forbes Field and Washington's Griffith Stadium. Over the next two decades the Homestead Grays sat atop the world of black baseball, at one time capturing nine pennants in a row.

Cumberland Willis Posey Jr. was born on June 20, 1890 in Homestead, Pennsylvania, a suburb of Pittsburgh in Allegheny County. At the time of his birth the area was known as Harding Station. He was the youngest child of Cumberland and Angelina (Anna) Posey. Cumberland and Angelina were married about 1883 and had three children, Beatrice, Seward (See), and Cumberland. The Posey family was among the richest black families in western Pennsylvania.

As a young man Cumberland Sr. took a job as a deck sweeper on a ferry which ran up and down the Ohio and Little Kanawha Rivers. He eventually studied the mechanics of ship engines which allowed him to seek employment as a riverboat pilot and engineer on the Ohio River, the first African-American licensed as such. He eventually settled in Harding Station and began constructing barges, becoming the proprietor of a large fleet. He expanded his financial portfolio with investments in various coal and coal-related companies and was one of the original investors in the *Pittsburgh Courier*, an African-American newspaper. Eventually, Cumberland Sr. became general manager of the Delta Coal Company and later owned the Preston Coal Company and the Diamond Coal and Coke Company. The latter became the largest black-owned business in Pittsburgh. He also invested in banking and real estate ventures.

Cum Sr. was a leading member of the black community in Pittsburgh. He served as president of the *Courier* and a like position with the prestigious Loendi Social and Literary Club, an exclusive all-black Pittsburgh-based club and the Warren Methodist Episcopal Church. Anna, formerly Anna Stevens, was the daughter of an Ohio Civil War veteran. She became the first African-American to graduate from The Ohio State University and was the first to teach there as well. She was also an artist who decorated her family's walls with her paintings.

See Posey, about three years older than his brother, was an organizer with the Monticello basketball team; he also played with the squad for many years. In baseball he worked as a business manager, traveling secretary, and booking agent for the Homestead Grays, and was associated with the club through much of the period 1920-1951.

Cum Jr. attended local Homestead schools and, like many boys in western Pennsylvania, he played sandlot football, basketball, and baseball. On the gridiron, as a teenager he played for a local amateur club called the Collins Tigers as a fullback, and much later (in 1923) he formed, coached and played for the Homestead Grays football team, which played against local squads.

Meanwhile, in 1909 Posey traveled to Pennsylvania State University to study chemistry and pharmacy. Basketball dominated his thoughts while at Penn State, but poor grades caused him to leave after two years. In 1913 he briefly attended the University of Pittsburgh and in 1915 enrolled at Holy Ghost College, now known as Duquesne University. He did so as a distinct minority—Posey, a light-skinned African-American, standing out in three primarily white colleges.

An extremely quick guard, Posey was one of the top black basketball players of his time. He was one of only a couple of pre-1915 black players who achieved lasting fame. After the spotlight placed on the man with his induction into the National Baseball Hall of Fame in 2006, Posey's resume for induction into the Basketball Hall of Fame at Springfield, Massachusetts, was also reviewed in recent years. He was elected for his basketball accomplishments in 2016. Posey, 5-foot-9 and 140 pounds, copied the style of a local white player named Harry Hough, who was similarly a small, agile, and quick athlete. Posey believed Hough to be the greatest basketball player of the era.

It was in high school that Posey first gained a great deal of attention for his basketball skills. He also started coaching. In 1908 he led Homestead High to the city championship. At Penn State, Posey played basketball for two seasons beginning in 1909, making the varsity squad as a sophomore. In 1909 Posey with his brother See and some friends organized the Monticello (named for a Pittsburgh street) Athletic Association basketball club, also known as the Monticello-Delany Rifles, which played in and around Homestead. The club gained a following outside of Homestead when it defeated Howard University in 1911. The following year they won the Colored Basketball World's Championship. In 1913 the club changed its name to the Loendi Big Five in recognition of its sponsor, the Loendi Social and Literary Club. By this time, it was a professional squad. Posey was the star player and operator, which

included managing, booking, and promoting. Leondi played through 1925, copping the Colored Basketball World's Championship four years in a row from 1920-23.

Posey also played basketball at Holy Ghost in 1915, leading the team in scoring. He performed under the name Charles W. Cumbert to preserve his athletic eligibility. He was also captain of the golf team at Holy Ghost. In 1925 he retired from basketball to concentrate on baseball, though he later formed a Homestead Grays basketball squad in 1927. It defeated the New York Celtics, a club that would win the American Basketball League championship that season.

The Homestead Grays baseball nine was originally formed in 1900 as the Blue Ribbons when a group of teenagers, some of whom worked in local factories and mills, decided to organize to play local white clubs and other company-based nines. Like most amateur and semipro clubs, they played primarily

Cum Posey, who owned the Homestead Grays from 1920 until his death in 1946, was elected to the Baseball Hall of Fame in 2006. (*National Baseball Hall of Fame, Cooperstown, New York*)

on the weekends. Eventually the club became semi-pro and changed its name to the Murdock Grays in 1910. At times they were an integrated squad. White future professionals Ziggy Walsh and Johnny Pearson played for the team. In 1912 the club became the Homestead Grays. Posey, a right-handed thrower and batter, had joined the club the previous year. His quickness made him a natural center fielder. He became captain in 1916 and field manager in 1917. Stemming from his experience with his basketball club, Posey started booking contests for the Grays by 1918 and was consequently named team secretary. In 1920 Posey and local businessman Charlie Walker, a former Grays batboy, purchased the club.

The Grays continued as a semipro outfit until 1922 when the encroachment of Dizzy Dismukes' Keystones into the Pittsburgh area pushed the club to rework its salary structure. The Keystones proved to be the Grays first real competition in Homestead. Dismukes paid his men as professionals, so Posey and Walker decided to do the same. As one of the Grays' players would describe the club's management during the 1920s, Walker was the money behind the club and Posey was the brains.

Posey quickly signed Oscar Owens, Bobby Williams, and Sam Skeeter to kick off the revamped version of the Grays. For the first time Posey also secured use of Forbes Field, home of the Pittsburgh Pirates, in 1922. Over the following winter the

The Homestead Grays' front office. From left to right: Seward Posey, Rufus Jackson, and owner Cum Posey with Russell Bowser. (*Noir-Tech Research, Inc.*)

Eastern Colored League was formed. It was east coast's answer to the predominantly Midwestern Negro National League formed by Rube Foster in 1920. Posey and Walker chose not to participate in the ECL because it would seriously distract from their lucrative barnstorming schedule. Posey later claimed that he spent much of the 1920s being courted by both the NNL and ECL to join their ranks. The Grays, located in Pittsburgh, were desired because geographically they fell in between the two leagues.

By the mid-1920s, the Grays were regularly defeating most of their opponents, including clubs from the black pro leagues, white semipro and professional outfits, Ohio-Pennsylvania League clubs, and postseason barnstorming clubs which often fielded major leaguers. Posey would beef up his lineup against the stronger opponents. The Grays attracted competition from well outside their traditional base for games at Forbes Field. By 1926, they were dominating opponents, posting a 140-13 record, at one point winning 43 consecutive contests. They also won 31 straight in 1927.

The Grays joined the American Negro League, the replacement of the failed ECL, during its only season in 1929. Posey made his last active appearance as a player that year. After the ANL folded, the club grew dramatically in stature, signing such greats as Oscar Charleston, Josh Gibson, and Judy Johnson. Posey capitalized on the unsteady atmosphere at the time of the folding of the ANL to sign Johnson. In 1930 Cum and See Posey were able to lure Gibson from the Pittsburgh Crawfords.

The 1931 Grays are often identified as the top black team of all-time, notching a 163-23 record. In 1932 Posey founded and the Grays joined the East-West League, another one-season venture which collapsed in June that year. The EWL was the first league to merge the eastern and western clubs. When the league failed, Posey initiated a tirade against eastern booking agents, blaming them for the downfall. He also took a firm stance against the Pittsburgh Crawfords in relation to his EWL. Posey naturally wanted the Grays to dominate the Pittsburgh area, but the Crawfords were on the verge of developing

a stranglehold. If the Crawfords wanted to join the EWL, Posey insisted on two outlandish conditions. First, he wanted a five-year contract that allowed the Grays to control the Crawfords' local schedule and their roster and, secondly, he wanted See Posey installed as the Crawfords manager. Crawfords owner Gus Greenlee rejected the ridiculous terms. The tables were turned the following year as Greenlee spearheaded the new Negro National League, a league which would survive past the initial campaign.

At this point the Grays were in a precarious financial plight. The cross-town Crawfords were thus able to lure some of the Grays' top talent including Charleston, Gibson, and Johnson. In 1934 Posey brought in moneyman Rufus "Sonny Man" Jackson, the reputed king of the numbers racket in Homestead, to financially stabilize the Grays. Jackson also owned and leased many of the area's jukeboxes. He served as the club's president and treasurer, but Posey continued to run the day-to-day operations.

With racketeer Jackson aboard the Grays joined the NNL in 1934, a league rife with gambling-based capital. The following year Posey relinquished his field manager responsibilities to Vic Harris after luring him back from the Crawfords. In 1937 Posey was named secretary of the Negro National League. The club moved into Griffith Stadium in Washington D.C. on a more or less a permanent basis in 1940. The Grays remained in the league through 1948, becoming the premier club in the game. They were able to regain Josh Gibson, who teamed with Buck Leonard to solidify the lineup. The club won nine consecutive pennants from 1937-45 and another in '48. This clearly marks them as the leading dynasty in the black baseball history.

Professionally, Posey worked fulltime with the federal postal service at Penn (Railroad) Station in Pittsburgh. After buying into the Grays, he quit the mail job in 1920 to devote himself to basketball and baseball. He also served for years as the athletic director for Homestead High. Through his Homestead Grays Athletic Club, Posey sponsored local baseball, football, basketball and boxing events. He was a member of the Homestead Board of Education from 1931 until his death. Posey furthermore penned a column for the *Pittsburgh Courier*, his father's paper. The column was called "Pointed Paragraphs" from December 1931 to April 1936 and "Posey's Points" from May 1936 until June 1945. He contributed numerous other articles as well, stemming as far back as his early basketball career.

Posey married Ethel Truman, a Pennsylvania native, in 1913. They had four girls. Their oldest daughter Ethel married longtime Grays pitcher Ray Brown at a home plate ceremony on July 4, 1935. Cumberland Posey died at Mercy Hospital from lung cancer on March 28, 1946, at age 55. He had suffered from the disease for more than a year and was confined to a hospital bed for the last three weeks of his life. He was interred at Homestead Cemetery.

Posey left half of the club to his widow though Jackson ran it. After the 1948 season the Grays once again became an independent club. Jackson died on March 6, 1949, from complications after a brain tumor operation. Ethel Posey and Helen Jackson, Rufus's widow, took over administration of the club for a short time. It was then turned over to See Posey, who ultimately disbanded the Grays on May 22, 1951, citing "financial setbacks and the egress of the best Negro talent into organized baseball."

Cum Posey was posthumously elected to the Baseball Hall of Fame in 2006 and the Basketball Hall of Fame in 2016.

SOURCES

Ancestry.com

Chicago Defender

Holway, John. *The Complete Book of Baseball's Negro Leagues: The Other Half of Baseball History* (Fern Park, Florida: Hastings House Publishers, 2001).

Hoopedia.nba.com

Ingham, John N. and Lynne B. Feldman. *African-American Business Leaders* (Westport, Connecticut: Greenwood Press, 1994).

Kirsch, George B., Othello Harris and Claire Elaine Nolte. *Encyclopedia of Ethnicity and Sports in the United States* (Westport, Connecticut: Greenwood Publishing Group, 2000).

New York Amsterdam News

Pittsburgh Courier

Riley, James A. *The Biographical Encyclopedia of the Negro Baseball Leagues* (New York: Carroll and Graf Publishers, 1994).

Ruck, Rob. *Sandlot Seasons: Sport in Black Pittsburgh* (Illinois: University of Illinois Press, 1993).

Washington Post

ETHEL TRUMAN POSEY

By Leslie Heaphy

Ownership in the Negro Leagues was a tough and sometimes precarious job and finances often were the determining factor in whether or not an owner could hang on to a team. In addition to the difficulty of financial stability, female owners had to battle the sexist attitudes of the other owners and society as a whole when they got involved with a team. One of the most respected owners in the Negro Leagues was Cumberland Willis Posey, who owned the successful Homestead Grays for many years, while working with his business partner Rufus "Sonnyman" Jackson, a racketeer, and his brother Seward (See) Posey. After an illness that lasted several months, Posey died in 1946 and left a partnership in the team to his widow, Ethel Posey. His actual 13-word will stated that he left his entire estate, estimated at $3,000, to his widow.[1]

Ethel Posey became a part of the management team, but she did not take an active role in the team. Jackson continued to serve as the Grays' president and brother-in-law Seward Posey retained his position as the business manager. After Jackson died in March 1949 Mrs. Posey and Helen Jackson continued to operate the team before turning it over to See, who did not believe that a woman had any business running the team and wanted to buy her out. Mrs. Posey, wanting to protect her husband's legacy and name, resisted for nearly three years before selling her share.[2]

Ethel Shaw Truman and Cum Posey had been married in 1913, when she was just 20, and they had four daughters, Ethel, Mary, Anne, and Beatrice. Their daughter Ethel married pitcher Ray Brown. While Posey was often on the road with the Grays, Mrs. Posey stayed at home with the girls. That did not mean she did not take an interest in the team or have a role to play. Ethel Posey said that she tended to be the steadying influence on her husband, providing counsel and logic when he often wanted to act too quickly. He consulted her on financial issues in particular, which gave her insights into the running of the club after he died.[3]

After turning over the ballclub to her brother-in-law, Mrs. Posey went to work for the Allegheny County Prothonotary Office until her retirement in 1963. She also served as a member of the Homestead District School Board for 23 years and was a member of the local Samedi Club and the Junior Mothers. In 1984 she moved to Atlanta to be closer to her daughter Beatrice, and she died there due to a heart ailment in 1986. Beatrice moved to New York City, where she spent many years working for the city's Board of Education, before she died in 1998.[4]

In describing Ethel Posey's role with the team, retired *Pittsburgh Courier* city editor Frank Bolden said, "Mrs. Posey was supportive of everything her husband did with the team. You might put her in the same class with any of the wives of well-known baseball magnates."[5] Others saw Mrs. Posey as a mother to many of the young men who moved to the North to play for the Grays. A number of Grays players were from the rural South and had never been to a big city. She helped them find places to live, occasionally cooked meals, and generally watched out for them. When asked about her new role with the ballclub after her husband's death, Mrs. Posey asserted, "I am confident that Mr. Jackson and I will get along together. I am not unfamiliar with the operation of a baseball club and will content myself with being an observer throughout the seasons."[6] Though her role indeed appears to have been that of an observer, Ethel Posey nonetheless belongs to the fairly small group of women who have owned a professional baseball team, white or black.

NOTES

1   *Pittsburgh Press*, April 22, 1946: 11.

2   Brian McKenna, "Cumberland Posey," sabr.bio/posey; *Altoona Mirror,* August 26, 1947; "Widow Takes Club," *Altoona Mirror,* April 12, 1946.

3   *Uniontown* (Pennsylvania) *Morning Herald,* March 29, 1946; *Chester* (Pennsylvania) *Times,* April 11, 1946.

4   *Pittsburgh Post-Gazette,* December 1, 1998: 25.

5   "Ethel T. Posey, Wife of Founder of Grays Team," *Pittsburgh Post-Gazette,* November 27, 1986: C4.

6   "Widow Gets Grays' Share," *Uniontown Morning Herald,* April 12, 1946: 24.

RUFUS "SONNYMAN" JACKSON

By Ralph Carhart

Rufus "Sonnyman" Jackson was born on May 1, 1900, in Columbus, Georgia, to Rufus Jackson Sr. and Rosa Bell Dixon, both Georgia natives.[1] Rosie and her son remained close enough throughout his life that in 1940, when he was already a successful businessman and often-time courthouse visitor, she was still living with her grown son. He had two brothers, Walter and Charles, but nothing is known of Jackson's father or, for that matter, much of Jackson's own life until the mid-1920s. It is a known fact that Rufus never completed the fifth grade, but he still became one of Columbus's wealthiest native sons.[2] That wealth was attained elsewhere, however, as the Jackson family moved from the post-Reconstruction South to the streets of Pittsburgh.

It was there, at 529 East 3rd Avenue in the borough of Homestead, seven miles southeast of the city, where Jackson can be found in the city directory for the first time, in 1927, though his obituary claims he first arrived in 1921. Originally listed as a millworker, by 1929 he would label his profession as the more generic "laborer." In fact, Jackson's real income was already coming from a different business, that of an illegal numbers runner. In April 1929 Jackson was arrested as a part of larger sweep of racketeers by District Attorney Samuel H. Gardner.[3] Accused co-conspirators James Harrison, John Smith, and Jackson were all charged with running a lottery and clearinghouse pool. By May the case had failed to go before the judge four different times that it was on the docket.[4] Jackson ultimately evaded punishment, the first in a long line of narrow misses for a man who often operated on the wrong side of the law.

Jackson's wife was listed as Marie in the 1931 directory, but she either died or simply disappeared from his story forever during that year. In January 1932, he married Helen Mae (maiden name unknown), who was originally from North Carolina. Ten years his junior, Helen ended up being the perfect wife for the mischievous and successful Jackson. She not only became a belle of black society in Homestead, but a tremendous asset in assisting Rufus with all his business endeavors. One time she even admitted to the *Pittsburgh Courier* that she sat at the wheel of the car, ready to speed off on a word from her husband, as he paid off extortionists.[5]

Jackson operated under the cover of the Manhattan Music Company, which he founded in 1931 mainly to provide jukeboxes to the city's restaurants. The endeavor was successful enough that by the end of 1932, he and Helen were accompanying journalist Floyd G. Snelson Jr. on an airplane ride and having the tale retold in the society pages of the *Courier*.[6] Forevermore would Jackson's brushes with fame live in the dual worlds of high-society business and low-life criminal activity. That Christmas, in the "Womans Activities" section of the *Courier*, the Jacksons' Christmas party was celebrated as a jolly affair with "dancing, cards and games, including 'Spin the Bottle.'"[7] When Rufus and Helen sailed to Bermuda in January of 1934, her picture graced the front page as the paper celebrated their "two week's cruise on southern waters and a visit in the exotic islands."[8]

A mere two months later Jackson once again found himself in trouble with the law. He was arrested on numbers charges, along with 16 others, including Pittsburgh gambling kingpin Gus Greenlee. They were apprehended in March at the Belmont, the hotel that served as the headquarters for Greenlee's numbers racket. Greenlee was caught red-handed with his business books on his person when he was arrested. With an audacity that Jackson himself could appreciate, Greenlee never even tried to deny it, telling the judge he was simply "giving work to some of the boys."[9]

Greenlee had made his money as a bootlegger and by the 1930s had an interest in several sports ventures, including partial ownership of the Pittsburgh Crawfords baseball club. He was an important figure in the formation of the Negro National League, the second incarnation of a league by that name, and it was undoubtedly Greenlee who introduced Jackson to Cumberland Willis Posey and brought the young racketeer and entrepreneur into the world of baseball.

Cum Posey was a former ballplayer himself and the owner of the Homestead Grays, having purchased the team in 1920 after serving as their business manager. The Grays were a powerhouse independent team in the late 1920s and early 1930s. They became original members of Greenlee's new league in 1933, but were expelled partway through the season for raiding other clubs' rosters. They were allowed to return as associate members in 1934, but Posey was looking to get the Grays fully back in to the league for the 1935 season. To support that effort, he wanted to build a winner and he needed capital. Jackson, whose own wealth continued to grow, provided that funding. In April 1934 Jackson and Posey, along with their lawyer, Theron B. Hamilton, filed the articles of incorporation for the Homestead Grays Baseball Club, Inc.[10] Posey had the money he needed and Jackson had another legitimate business to serve as a cover for his expanding wealth.

Jackson had yet another brush with the law in May, although this time he was simply a witness. Serving as a poll-watcher during the violent and contentious 1934 election, Jackson would appear before a common pleas court judge to testify that he witnessed "thugs" from Pittsburgh intimidate and assault his local polls overseer, Charles Passafiume.[11] His own involvement with local politics was less than pure, and it is quite likely that Jackson's presence at the polls was not out of altruistic reasons.

It became clear during the Grays' first full season in the NNL that Jackson would be no mere figurehead. He was present when the club was granted league membership in November 1934,[12] and maintained a constant presence with the team, often making executive decisions. Unfortunately for Jackson and

Posey, 1935 was not a glorious start to their NNL membership. Despite having slugging first basemen Buck Leonard—who led the team with a batting average that ranged somewhere between .338 and .386 (depending on the source)—and pitcher Ray Brown (both of whom ultimately were inducted into the Hall of Fame), the Grays finished 25-33 in their first year, which placed them seventh in the eight-team league.

There were few major roster changes for the 1936 season, and the team's mediocre 22-27 record reflected that. By the end of the season, trouble was brewing across the league. Since its inception, the NNL league officers were consistently made up of club owners and higher-ups. The most prominent of these individuals was Greenlee, whose Crawfords had been named league champions the previous two seasons. A small group that included Jackson and Posey, Tom Wilson (owner of the Washington Elite Giants), and, surprisingly, league President Ed Bolden argued that the current system was ripe for corruption and needed to be addressed.[13] The relationship between partners Jackson and Posey, and the man who originally brought them together, Greenlee, started to strain and soon turned into an all-out war that was fought in Pittsburgh's newspaper pages.

In January 1937 Jackson turned the black baseball world upside down when he reacquired Josh Gibson from the Crawfords. Despite the growing acrimony between the men, Greenlee had been under tremendous legal pressure and his numbers business was suffering. He needed money and, in a twist of fate, he was now turning to Jackson for cash. The Grays traded Henry Spearman and Pepper Bassett and, most importantly, paid an additional $2,500 to get Gibson and another future Hall of Famer, Judy Johnson.[14] Johnson, for his part, was stung by the deal and chose not to report to the Grays, instead retiring from the game. But the real catch was Gibson, the biggest draw in all of black baseball and, as Jackson soon discovered, a runaway train barreling his way toward ultimate destruction.

The year 1937 was a combative period in Jackson's life. In March he found himself hospitalized after being cut by a knife wielded by Helen.[15] Although the cause for the injury was listed only as an "accident," it is not unlikely that the same woman who would sit at the wheel of a getaway car might not hesitate to cut a man should he go too far. Jackson also made the papers by fighting off raids on his players from the Dominican Republic. Alerted to the presence of Frederico Nina, a Dominican baseball "mogul," and Luis Mendez, a member of the Dominican consulate, Greenlee and Jackson became part of the sting that led to the two Dominicans' arrests. As contract raiders, the men had been attempting to sign Ernest Carter, a wild power pitcher with the Crawfords.[16] The victory was short-lived, though, as one month later the Grays would lose the mighty Josh Gibson to the Dominican Republic team owned by dictator Rafael Trujillo.

The exodus of players to Trujillo's Dominican Republic hit Greenlee the hardest, though, as Satchel Paige and most of the Crawford stars also abandoned their contracts, which ruined him financially. With the end of Greenlee's reign, Posey became the de facto head of the NNL, and Jackson was now the power behind the most successful team in the game.[17] Life was good for Jackson at this time. The Grays won the NNL title in 1937 and 1938 as they began to cement their legacy. Meanwhile, he and Helen were hosting parties where "everything was piled high, high" for the likes of jazz legend and Homestead native Maxine Sullivan.[18]

Pittsburgh racketeer Rufus "Sonnyman" Jackson (at right) provided Grays' owner Cum Posey with the money he needed to lure many of the Negro Leagues' best players to Homestead in the 1930s and 1940s. (*Noir-Tech Research, Inc.*)

Before long, however, Jackson again found himself in the papers for more dubious reasons. In February 1940 his liquor license was revoked for selling alcohol to minors at his club, the Sky Rocket Grill.[19] He eluded serious punishment for that offense and regained his license just one month later, only to find himself embroiled in one of the highest-profile numbers cases of his career in July. Arrested along with Pittsburgh politician Joe Frank, Jackson and three others were all detained because of a confession by one of Jackson's former men, Julius Swetkuckas.[20] The case took up most of the year, finally resolving itself in November with, perhaps expectedly, a full acquittal for all involved, though Frank would go on to serve time for jury-fixing.[21] Jackson, who was the first man acquitted for lack of evidence in the case, once again evaded punishment for his crimes.

The Grays, meanwhile, began to play some of their home games in Washington in 1940. With the support of Washington Senators owner Clark Griffith, the Grays moved into Griffith Stadium and profited from the growing wealth of the capital's black population. The experiment was a success and Jackson's own wealth continued to expand, as did his influence. In February 1941 he attended the inauguration of President Franklin D. Roosevelt.[22] Later, in August, he sold the house at 529 East 3rd Ave. for $32,000, the equivalent value of $547,000 today after adjusting for inflation. Jackson's success could also be measured by the quality of the team he financed, as the Grays won six consecutive league titles after their part-time move to D.C.

Another legal battle occupied the early part of 1942, when Jackson attempted to move the Sky Rocket Grill from 412 Dixon St. to a new location at 614 Amity St. The new site was just 40 feet from the local Salvation Army headquarters, and the religious organization protested.[23] The license for the property was held in limbo before Jackson's perpetual courtroom luck eventually won the day in April, when Judge James L. O'Toole sided with the tavern. His ruling stated that the success of the Salvation Army was actually a result of being located in "a neighborhood such as this which were fertile fields for its

work," and that the proximity of a bar would only increase their business.[24]

After another successful season for the Grays in 1942, the following year began on a difficult note. In January the papers announced that Gibson had been hospitalized for a nervous breakdown, and his future was uncertain. In addition, World War II was starting to hurt business for the Grays, not only in the size of the crowds they could draw, but even the size of the squads they could put on the field. The team was cut from 22 men in 1942 to just 16 in 1943. Jackson also announced that the Grays would play only weekend baseball instead of their customary five or six games per week.[25] In the end, they managed to play almost as many league games in 1943 as they did the previous year, but by 1944 that number was cut almost in half.

In spite of the economic difficulties created by the war, Jackson's influence continued to grow within the game. In July 1943, in a Pittsburgh police station, Jackson faced down a Mexican consul whom he had accused of attempting to coerce Howard Easterling into breaking his contract.[26] No charges were filed and Easterling remained with the Grays. Jackson also, largely through the words of Posey whose regular column "Posey's Points" appeared in the *Courier*, became a vocal supporter of having a commissioner for Negro League baseball. Posey and Jackson, who had admittedly both capitalized on the incestuous workings of the NNL, also saw that the lack of oversight was jeopardizing the Negro Leagues' long-term viability. While the integration of baseball was still two years away, the schism was coming and the two men knew that without a powerful figure at the head of the sport, overseeing both the NNL and the Negro American League, they would not survive.

The agenda for the NNL's annual meeting in 1944 focused on the fair division of the profits from the East-West Game, the most successful event of the Negro Leagues season. Also discussed were methods for staving off Mexican raiders and how to keep the schedule balanced during the lean economic times. The owners, including Jackson, even addressed their relationship with white baseball, agreeing that it should remain a positive one because of the advantages provided by access to major- and minor-league ballparks.[27] The most conspicuous issue not to be addressed was the idea of clubs losing players to white teams, as the owners all claimed that white baseball personnel had not contacted them.

Jackson and Posey's desire to legitimize the organizational structure of the leagues was likely at the forefront of their decision to sign the first official "World Series Agreement," along with Tom Hayes, the owner of the 1944 NAL champion Birmingham Black Barons. The agreement guaranteed that each team would commit to playing the full series or risk losing a $1,000 deposit that each squad placed as a show of good faith. Dates and cities were agreed to in advance, and both league presidents trumpeted the agreement as evidence that Negro League baseball had finally matured.[28] The 1944 World Series, which was a rematch of the 1943 contest, was quickly won by the Grays in five games. Gibson, whose physical and mental-health troubles continued, still managed to hit a home run in the first game and batted .500 for the Series.

The Grays again dominated the NNL in 1945, winning the pennant over the Baltimore Elite Giants by 5½ games before falling to the Cleveland Buckeyes in the World Series. The loss may have served as a harbinger of dark times to come. At the start of 1946, Jackson and Posey were still appearing on the pages of the *Courier* as well as the white-owned *Pittsburgh Post-Gazette*, emphatically arguing that owners should not be executives within the league. They wanted a limitation on the power of the league presidents and they still vocally advocated, along with *Courier* journalist Wendell Smith, for a commissioner of black baseball. However, it was the headlines on the morning of March 29, 1946, that forever changed the course of the Grays. After a lifelong career that saw him serve as a baseball player, manager, executive, and, ultimately, mogul, Cum Posey died at the age of 55.

Jackson was certainly the wealthier of the two, and he was active in club affairs, but Posey had been the baseball man in their tandem. Posey left half the club to his wife, Ethel, but Jackson took over full control

of the team and it was not long before the Grays became a shadow of their former selves.[29] Gibson, who died the following January, had the worst season of his legendary career in 1946, and the Grays finished in third place behind the Newark Eagles and the New York Cubans. Their reign of dominance was seemingly at an end. As a final insult to that injurious year, in November a grease fire at the Sky Rocket Grill caused $5,000 worth of damage and sent 10 families scurrying into the streets.[30] Jackson could not usher in the new year quickly enough, but little did he know that the 1947 season would sound the death knell for black baseball.

The season began on an optimistic note, with the installation of Rev. John Johnson as the new head of the NNL, a move urged by Jackson.[31] No one noticed this forward step, however, as the full attention of the baseball world, black and white, was focused on Jackie Robinson's inevitable major-league debut. With Robinson's ultimate success, other major-league teams followed the Brooklyn Dodgers' lead and raided the Negro Leagues for their best players. By the end of the 1947 season, both the Cleveland Indians and the St. Louis Browns also had debuted black players. By mid-August Jackson was lamenting the dearth of talented young players in black baseball, which was due largely to the rapidly expanding scouting efforts of teams in Organized Baseball.[32] After another disappointing season that saw the Grays lose the pennant to the New York Cubans, Jackson believed he had to redouble his efforts to build a winner.

Together with Cum Posey's brother, See, Jackson traveled to Cuba in March 1948 in an attempt to mine more talent.[33] Their trip was a flop, as neither of the Cuban stars they brought back with them panned out. Nonetheless, the core team of 1947, whom Jackson had either wisely or luckily signed in their entirety, produced one final year of glory. On the strength of the hot hitting of Buck Leonard, Luke Easter, and Luis Marquez, Jackson saw his club compete throughout the season. They lost out on the first-half title to Baltimore, but won the second half and faced the Elite Giants in the playoffs. After a controversy born from unwillingness on the part of Baltimore to complete a game that was called due to Baltimore's city curfew, the Grays were named the pennant winners of the 1948 NNL season.[34]

The Grays once again faced the Birmingham Black Barons in the World Series and defeated them in five games. With the exception of a 14-1 Grays blowout in Game Four, all of the contests were tight affairs. The final game was deadlocked, 6-6, until a four-run outburst by the Grays in the 10th inning secured the victory and the championship. The 1948 pennant marked the Grays' ninth title since Jackson had bought into the team in 1934, and the World Series victory was their third. It also marked one final moment of triumph as declining attendance and depleted rosters spelled the end for the Negro National League, which folded after the season.

The Grays attempted but failed to arrange an associate membership in the newly expanded NAL for 1949 and instead joined the independent Negro American Association, but that effort was largely spearheaded by See Posey. Jackson had ceased to participate in team operations that winter when it was discovered after the World Series that he had a brain tumor. Doctors at Montefiore Hospital in Pittsburgh attempted to remove the tumor on March 6, but Jackson did not survive the operation. The official cause of death was respiratory failure caused by encephalomalacia, which is a softening of the brain. A banner headline that was spread across the *Pittsburgh Courier*'s March 12 sports pages cried, "Sports World Mourns Passing of Sonnyman."[35] A Homestead icon was gone. Helen outlived her husband by nearly four decades, dying in 1988. Husband and wife are both buried in Homestead Cemetery in the Pittsburgh area.

Jackson's death, coinciding with the demise of the NNL, marked the end of an era in black baseball. While remnants of the Negro Leagues soldiered on for almost another decade, the 1948 Grays were the last truly great black baseball team. Black stars of the future, like Henry Aaron and Ernie Banks, still paid their dues in the Negro Leagues as they played, briefly, for the likes of the Indianapolis Clowns and the Kansas City Monarchs, but the quality of black ball never recovered after integration became a league-wide phenomenon in Organized Baseball. Jackson, who spent his life proving that a black man could be successful (although in his case he had often run afoul of the law to do so), would likely have been torn by the mixed result. Success for individual players ultimately spelled doom for the league. Yet, it is difficult to imagine that a man who enjoyed the good life as much as Jackson would begrudge the march of progress and the glories that it brought.

NOTES

1   Rufus Jackson Death Certificate, State of Pennsylvania.

2   1940 United States Census, accessed at Ancestry.com.

3   "Gardner Lists Many Trials for Next Week," *Pittsburgh Post-Gazette*, April 13, 1929: 1.

4   "Manfredo Put on Trial for Seventh Time," *Pittsburgh Post-Gazette*, May 28, 1929: 13.

5   "Stood By!" *Pittsburgh Courier*, April 6, 1935: 6, First Section.

6   Floyd G. Snelson Jr., "Newsy Newsettes," *Pittsburgh Courier*, November 26, 1932: 6, Second Section.

7   "Holiday Get-togethers," *Pittsburgh Courier*, January 7, 1933: 7, First Section.

8   "In Bermuda," *Pittsburgh Courier*, January 27, 1934: 1, First Section.

9   "Numbers Baron Held for Court," *Pittsburgh Press*, March 5, 1934: 3.

10   "Legal Notices," *Pittsburgh Press*, April 10, 1934: 33.

11   "Polls Quiet Here; Vote Is Cut by Rain," *Pittsburgh Post-Gazette*, May 16, 1934: 2.

12   "Brooklyn Granted N.N. League; Bankhead Goes to Grays in Trade," *Pittsburgh Courier*, November 17, 1934: 5, Second Section.

13   "Owners Ask for Harmony," *Pittsburgh Courier*, October 3, 1936: 5, Second Section.

14   W. Rollo Wilson, "Thru' the Eyes," *Pittsburgh Courier*, January 30, 1937: 4, Second Section.

15   "Flash!" *Pittsburgh Courier*, March 20, 1937: 9.

16   "League Acts to Check Raids," *Pittsburgh Courier*, May 15, 1937: 1.

17   Brad Snyder, *Beyond the Shadow of the Senators* (New York: McGraw Hill, 2003), 51.

18   Julia B. Jones, "'No Highhat, No Divorce, No Blessed Event'; Maxine Sullivan Confides to 'Talk O' Town,'" *Pittsburgh Courier*, December 10, 1938: 13.

19 "Board Revokes Liquor License," *Pittsburgh Post-Gazette*, February 9, 1940: 3.

20 "Numbers Case Goes to Court," *Pittsburgh Press*, July 17, 1940: 2.

21 "Liberty Brief for Numbers Case Suspect," *Pittsburgh Post-Gazette*, November 16, 1940: 4.

22 "At the Inaugural," *Pittsburgh Courier*, February 1, 1941: 9.

23 "Liquor License Hearing Opens," *Pittsburgh Press*, March 20, 1942: 24.

24 "Liquor Board Is Overruled," *Pittsburgh Post-Gazette*, April 23, 1942: 6.

25 Robert Hughey, "Akron Site of Training Camp," *Pittsburgh Courier*, April 3, 1943: 18.

26 Cum Posey, "Posey's Points," *Pittsburgh Courier*, July 24, 1943: 19.

27 "National League Plans Eleventh Annual Meeting," *Pittsburgh Courier*, January 1, 1944: 12.

28 "Plans for 1944 World Series Announced," *Pittsburgh Courier*, September 9, 1944: 12.

29 Brian McKenna, "Cum Posey," SABR BioProject, sabr.org/bioproj/person/ff7b091e.

30 "Fire in Homestead Routs 10 Families," *Pittsburgh Post-Gazette*, November 26, 1946: 13.

31 Wendell Smith, "N.Y. Minister New President of Negro National League," *Pittsburgh Courier*, January 11, 1947: 12.

32 Wendell Smith, "The Sports Beat," *Pittsburgh Courier*, August 2, 1947: 14.

33 "Grays Start Drills Soon," *Pittsburgh Post-Gazette*, February 24, 1948: 15.

34 Snyder, 260.

35 "Sports World Mourns Passing of 'Sonnyman,'" *Pittsburgh Courier*, March 12, 1949: 12.

FORBES FIELD: "THE HOUSE OF THRILLS"

By Curt Smith

Baseball links geography, and rivalry. In 1908, Philadelphia constructed the sport's first concrete and steel double-decked field—Shibe Park. Three hundred miles to the west the Phillies' main foe turned green. That fall Pirates owner Barney Dreyfuss began a search for an idyll that would make his new ballpark *primus inter pares*—in Latin, "first among equals."

Since 1892, the Bucs had inhabited 16,000-seat Exposition Park II. Dreyfuss wanted a larger park in Pittsburgh's future Oakland-Schenley section, three miles from the business district. "There was nothing there but a livery stable and a hot house, with a few cows grazing over the countryside," he said. "A ravine ran through the property [in time, right field]. The first thing necessary to make it suitable for baseball was to level off the entire field."[1]

Critics panned downtown's snub. Oakland's Orchard! Dreyfuss's Folly! Barney smiled. His park would be expandable, accessible by trolley, and far from the smog of mills. Ultimately, the Pirates' hull conjured a soda fountain, stick dams, and unlocked homes. "You had the smell of grass, could park six blocks away, take a walk through the neighborhood," said Bucs 1948-75 announcer Bob Prince of perhaps baseball's most gorgeous-ever park. "'The House of Thrills' it was, and in memory still is."[2]

In 1909, the ravine was filled and building begun on the park named for John Forbes, a British general in the French and Indian War who bivouacked troops in Oakland, captured Fort Duquesne in a crucial battle, and renamed it Fort Pitt. "We shape our buildings," Churchill said," and afterwards our buildings shape us."[3] Racetrack architect Charles Leavitt shaped a vast lawn, irregular shape, and sun-baked infield where players despaired of safety and longevity. Eventually, a visitor scents beauty and memory.

Forbes Field rose at the junction of Bigelow Boulevard, Joncaire Street, the University of Pittsburgh's Cathedral of Learning, and (General Henry) Bouquet (sic Boquet) Street, after a Swiss soldier who helped the British. Later, it was filled by an early-1900s melting pot—Slavs, Poles, Italians, Germans—trooping through southwest Pennsylvania to the flatlands of the Middle West. Thousands remained in Pittsburgh among hills and rivers that split the forest like aorta through the heart. The Roman rhetorician Quintilian wrote, "For it is feeling ... that makes us eloquent."[4] Forbes Field's feeling soon became pleasance and pioneer.

Men worked double shifts to open it on schedule. On June 30, 1909, a throng of 30,388 overflowed the 25,000-seat park. Thousands stood behind a rope barrier, Cubs winning. 3-2. Dreyfuss hymned I told you so. "The formal opening of Forbes Field ... was an historic event," the 1910 Reach *Baseball Guide* wrote: "Words must fail to picture in the mind's eye adequately the splendors of the magnificent pile President Dreyfuss erected as a tribute to the national game, a beneficence to Pittsburgh and an enduring monument to himself. For architectural beauty, imposing size, sold construction, and public comfort and convenience, it has not its superior in the world."[5]

Much later, *Sports Illustrated* hailed the "loveliest setting of any major-league field, with Schenley Park and the ... towering Cathedral of Learning out beyond 12-foot-high left-field wall."[6] Forbes's beauty wore well. Long after its 1970 close, the park was still revered, "never los[ing] its rough Pittsburgh edge," Ron Smith wrote in *The Ballpark Book*, "while retaining its ability to charm even the toughest of baseball souls."[7] Steve Blass, a fine 10-year Pirates pitcher and 1986 announcer, made his Forbes mound inaugural in 1964, "knowing that I was at a ballpark. It smelled of beer and cigars, the field had a vastness to it, yet the seats were almost on it. Forbes was my first love—and *what* a love. When you closed your eyes, you knew this was what baseball was supposed to be. Everything about it was right."[8]

Behind the plate, player and umpire clubhouses underlay the grandstand. Right field abutted Schenley Park. Two decks extended from beyond first base to the left-field line, left- and center-field seats rimming a 12-foot wooden fence. Distances were pitcher-friendly—left to right field, 360, 442, flagpole 462, and 376 feet—as Forbes's first year showed. The '09 Pirates went 110-42, had a 2.07 earned-run average, and beat Detroit in the World Series, Forbes luring more people (81,885) than the total of either of the two prior Series.[9] The yard presaged a franchise more atypical than most. Once two Bucs led off base, the day so dark Christy Mathewson had to approach the catcher to see his signs. A batter lined to right-center field, lightning hitting the ball like a scene from *The Natural*. Red Murray leapt to make a barehanded catch. DeMille could not have staged it better.

No one threw a no-hitter in Forbes's 4,770-game history. By contrast, unassisted triple plays seemed as common as a cold. In 1925, Pirates shortstop Glenn Wright caught Jim Bottomley's liner, stepped on second base to double Jimmy Cooney, and tagged Rogers Hornsby before the Rajah could retouch first. Wright encored as a Cub two years later. "For the unusual, go to Forbes," a saying went. "The impossible, go twice." In 1890, Exposition Park I had hosted baseball's first tripleheader. Thirty years later, Forbes reprised its last three-for-the-price-of-one. By 1920, three teams in each league got money from Series revenue, so the Reds and Pirates played for third place, Cincy winning, 13-4 and 7-3. The Bucs then lost a pointless 6-0 third game, the age clearly treating rules more literally than ours.

In 1912, Chief Wilson hit a still-major-league record 36 triples. Some parks aid homers. Forbes spurred average, defense, and speed. In 1925, Dreyfuss grooved a lollipop to lefties: Two pavilion decks shrank right field to 300 feet. Pitching countered in 1932: A 14½-foot in-play screen topped right field's 9½-foot concrete wall. Left waxed from 360 to 365.

Center field and the flagpole waned to 435 and 457, respectively. Steve Blass was especially stunned by its extremity at night: "I'd look out at center and literally lose track of [5-foot-9] Matty Alou."[10] The backstop was a big-league-high 100 feet behind home plate. In 1923, the batting cage moved from near it to left-center field: in play like the flagpole bottom and light tower cages in left-center, center, and right-center field. Cars and trucks were repainted and sold under the left-field seats. Forbes was special in more ways than size.

Exempla gratia: The Pirates were the first to: use a tarpaulin (1906); put padding on the outfield wall (1930s); host a night All-Star and World Series game (1944 and 1971, respectively); and wear knit uniforms (1970). Two other firsts urbanized to a certain degree then-rural Oakland's Orchard. One happened August 5, 1921, on America's first radio station, KDKA Pittsburgh: baseball's first game on the wireless (Pirates 8, Phillies 5), as announcer Harold Arlin, 26, used a telephone as microphone, sat behind the screen, and chatted as around a pot-bellied stove.

Westinghouse-owned KDKA had debuted on Election Night 1920. "We were looking for programming," Arlin said, "so I went to Forbes and set up shop." Often the transmitter failed, or crowd silenced him. "We didn't know whether we'd talk into a total vacuum or whether somebody would hear us."[11] Like a centerfold, TV leaves little to fantasy. Early radio left all. Fancy retail stores mounted sidewalk speakers. Streets filled with play-by-play, like shopping malls with Muzak. Once Arlin even pinch-spoke for the Sultan of Swat, scheduled to read a speech on KDKA.

"Babe was going on my show," Harold said. "I introduce him and this big, garrulous guy—he can't say a word."

"Babe Ruth froze?" a reporter said.

"Mute," he jabbed. "I read his script on air and now *I'm* Ruth as Babe tries to compose himself, smoking and leaning against the wall. You know something? We pull it off. I sign off and Babe hasn't made a sound."[12]

Forbes Field's remaining first was to house the Negro Leagues' most fabled franchise, the Homestead Grays, whose most famed player was Josh Gibson, the "Black Babe Ruth." The franchise name stemmed from the steel and largely black town across the Monongahela River from Pittsburgh. Founded in 1912, the Grays became a team to which minority players aspired before big-league ball was integrated, playing at Forbes from 1922 through 1948. The owner and manager was Cumberland Posey, who made them a barnstorming magnet—indeed, synonymous with the Negro Leagues—their talent redolent of many teams in the bigs. Gibson was alleged to have hit a fair ball out of Yankee Stadium before Mickey Mantle almost did. Smokey Joe Williams once struck out 25 batters in a 12-inning game. Buck Leonard played the longest—1934-50, hitting .395 at age 41.

Dreyfuss, a close friend of Posey's, rarely missed a Homestead game. Another owner, the Pittsburgh Steelers' Art Rooney, later conceded to "from time to time" financially helping the Grays, so loving baseball that he initially called his football team the Pirates.[13] The July 18, 1930, *Pittsburgh Post-Gazette* wrote how "the famous Homestead Grays and Kansas City Monarchs" played the first night baseball game that evening at Forbes before more than 15,000, helped by floodlights imported from Cleveland, where the two barnstormers played two nights earlier. The paper noted that "six extra lighting towers, owing to the size of our enclosure,"[14] were added—Forbes's outfield yardage perhaps rivaled only by the Polo

The front entrance to Pittsburgh's Forbes Field, which opened on June 30, 1909. The park, which was built to seat 25,000 fans, hosted an overflow crowd of 30,388 on the day of its grand opening. (*Courtesy of Pittsburgh Pirates Baseball Club*)

Grounds, Griffith Stadium, Municipal Stadium, and the Yankees' Big Ballpark in the Bronx.

The mid- to late-1920s Pirates were equally alight. Future Hall of Famer Class of '36 Honus Wagner retired three years before KDKA's debut, but Pie Traynor was a 1920-37 palatine at third base. Bob Prince recalled a local saying of the time: "So and so doubled down the left-field line, and Traynor threw him out."[15] Ten times Max Carey led the NL in stolen bases. In 1925, Kiki Cuyler hit .357. By then, Forbes Field held 41,000 seats, Dreyfuss needing them that fall. The World Series ricocheted. Washington led, three games to one; Pittsburgh won twice; then Walter Johnson yielded 15 hits in the classic final. Some recall Roger Peckinpaugh's eighth-inning home run to give the Senators a 7-6 lead. Others evoke the shortstop's two late-inning muffs to tie the score, then Cuyler fouling off pitch after pitch before doubling to right field to score the last two runs. Pittsburgh won, 9-7, its first title since 1909 and last till 1960. "It's been a long time coming," sang Crosby, Stills, Nash, and Young. Bill Mazeroski would be a long time gone.

It is 423 miles by car from Pittsburgh to Cooperstown, where Hall of Fame plaques hang of 11 Pirates and six Grays, including Dreyfuss and Posey, respectively.[16] The Bucs boast the shrine's sole brothers. In 1927, Lloyd Waner—5-feet-8½-inch "Little Poison"—hit .355. "Big Poison"—brother Paul—led the league in average (.380), RBIs (131), and four other categories. The rightness of things inspired—Pittsburgh in the Series!—except its foil was as great a team as ever lived. The '27 Yankees hit .307, clinched on Labor Day, and outhomered the Pirates, 158-54. Their Classic began on October 5 at Forbes Field. After a workout, says the legend, "[Yankees skipper Miller] Huggins applied psychology," wrote the *New York Times's* George Vecsey. He told "his big men to swing for the fences. Ruth obliged and his cannon shots were followed by barrages" from Lou Gehrig, Bob Meusel, and Tony Lazzeri, tattooing Forbes's power alleys. The Bucs watched, numbed.[17] All presaged a four-game Yankees sweep.

The *Pittsburgh Press* styled the 1930s Bucs "L. Waner, P. Waner, Vaughan [Arky's .385 leading the 1935 NL], and Traynor." On May 25, 1935, a different batter hit his final three home runs—at Forbes. Said Guy Bush, yielding Babe Ruth's No. 713 and 714, the latter the first to clear its 86-foot-high right-field roof: "I'm telling you, it was the longest cockeyed ball I ever saw in my life."[18] Only 16 homers topped the roof, five by Willie Stargell. Inside the Orchard: Chuck Klein's four homers in a 10-inning game, the Bucs taking Forbes's 1940 night debut, and Rip Sewell's eephus pitch baffling the Browns' George McQuinn in the 1944 All-Star Game. Dreyfuss died in 1932. In 1938, new president Bill Benswanger, certain the Bucs would make the Series, ordered a new deck of seats (Crow's Nest) and a press box (with baseball's first elevator) built on the grandstand roof. Glory is fleeting: The Cubs waved the flag. Growing: What Lester Biederman, 1930-69 *Pittsburgh Press* sportswriter, in 1938 termed Forbes's niche as "the perfect ball park. That's what baseball players and fans from all over the country say."[19]

Biederman's article hailed "the Oakland Orchard's picturesque layout" and—the irony was delicious—Forbes's once mocked "location," now deemed "the finest of any [NL] city," lovely and bucolic, next to the University of Pittsburgh, near Carnegie Tech. After 1938's near-miss, the Bucs yearly wailed "wait till next year." For Homestead, almost every year seemed next year. The Grays virtually owned the Negro League National League of Western teams: pennants in 1931, 1948, and each season from 1937 through 1944—nine in a row and 11 total, meriting the term "Yankees of the Negro Leagues." Historian and 1976-79 Bucs announcer Milo Hamilton liked a tall tale of how at Forbes, the Grays trailed by a run, ninth inning, one on, two out, Gibson up. Josh hit a monster that no one could see, let alone catch: Grays win. Next morning the two barnstorming teams arrived in Washington. As players set themselves, Josh in the batter's box, a ball came falling from the sky. A rival outfielder caught it. An umpire yelled at Gibson. "You're out! In Pittsburgh, yesterday!"[20] The Grays also won World Series

An aerial view of the vast expanse of Forbes Field, which *Sports Illustrated* once described as having "the loveliest setting of any major-league field." The stadium served as the Grays' primary home field in Pittsburgh. (*Courtesy of Pittsburgh Pirates Baseball Club*)

in 1943-44 and then 1948, the latter vs. the Negro American League titlist Birmingham Black Barons.

Once "The House of Thrills" hosted a rare two-league doubleheader: Pirates-Phillies and Negro East-West League Grays—Philadelphia Hilldales. A mid-1940s billboard could be spotted, touting: TWI-NITE BASEBALL: PHILADELPHIA STARS V. BIRMINGHAM BARONS AND HOMESTEAD GRAYS V. KANSAS CITY MONARCHS. The Grays' suzerainty ended, like the Negro Leagues', with Jackie Robinson's cracking baseball's color line in 1947, sending black players to the majors. By then, the Grays had begun to play many, then most, of their games in Washington, were renamed the Washington Homestead Grays, and even outdrew the Senators! In the regular season, they moved weekday Pittsburgh dates to nearby West Field in Munhall or Leslie Park in Lawrenceville: Drawing less, they needed cheaper parks to maintain. By 1948, the sole household name of the dynasty was Leonard, some like Cool Papa Bell

and Jud Wilson retired, or like Gibson, dead in 1947 of a stroke. Each welcomed or would have Robinson's same-year revolution, but not its beginning of the Negro Leagues' end.

Despite the Grays' storied history, no player could enter the dressing room of a white-owned field. As bitter to many was the 1948 World Series, no game played at Pittsburgh. Like the Negro Leagues, the Grays collapsed, then failed as an independent, each dissolving in 1951. Lasting are pictures by a 1930s Negro Leagues Pittsburgh Crawfords player and later *Pittsburgh Courier* photographer Charles "Teenie" Harris, whose work magically captured an era come and gone and which became a hit March-September 2014 "Baseball In Pittsburgh" exhibit at Pittsburgh's Carnegie Museum of Art: Gibson, warming up a pitcher; Robert Gaston, swinging, Forbes's stands full; Sam Bankhead, fielding; visitor Satchel Paige, mobbed; a Sunday crowd, dressed to the nines after church.[21] In 2002, the link from

Pittsburgh to Homestead over the Monongahela was renamed the Homestead Grays Bridge.[22] Through 2016, the Pirates wore the Grays' uniform against the Cardinals, Indians, Reds, and Royals. Three of the four existed in the Negro League heyday. The other, Kansas City, won the World Series in 2015, evocative of the Grays at their height.

In the end, the Pirates were too entrenched for Homestead to overcome. In the 1940s, the Bucs erected a bronze and granite Dreyfuss statue near the visitors' exit gate in right-center field. In 1943, it was joined by a wooden US Marine, 32 feet high by 15 feet wide at its feet, standing at parade rest — "there to salute our World War II effort," said Prince. "Maybe the most bizarre in-play object in baseball history."[23] Forbes added objets d'art: a brick and ivied wall from right-center field to the left-field line. A 27-foot-high hand-operated left-field scoreboard listed balls, strikes, outs, scores, and pitching changes. Atop it lay speaker horns and a Western Union (later, Longines) clock. Beyond third base lay bleachers down the line. "This became the look," said Blass, "how people remember her — the scoreboard, brick, the ivy, the short wall in right, the in-play batting cage where no one could hit it — the beauty of the place."[24] A pilgrim also recalled "dipsy-doodle" (curve) and "bases FOB" ("Full of Bucs") and "doozie marooney" (extra-baser). In 1936-55, announcer Rosey Rowswell 10 times braved the second division, loving anything not germane to score.

When a Bucs drive neared the wall, Rowswell shouted, "Get upstairs, Aunt Minnie, and raise the window! Here she [the baseball] comes!" An aide then dropped a pane of glass: to a listener, it meant the window. "That's too bad," Rosey sobbed. "Aunt Minnie tripped over a garden hose! She never made it!" Aunt Minnie debuted in 1938. A year later Rosey and a plump lass by that pseudonym entered Forbes in an Austin car to hype a KDKA-TV exhibit. Few criticized baseball's Empress with No Clothes. Said Prince: "People knew she was fictitious, and didn't care."[25]

Prince's arrival changed Rosey's tack. "Instead of glass — too messy — I had this big dumbwaiter's tray

with bells and nuts and bolts — anything to make noise." On Rowswell's nod, Bob, standing, dropped it. "On radio, it sounded like an earthquake. And Rosey'd say, 'Poor Aunt Minnie. She didn't make it again.'"

Prince quickly picked up the nuts and bolts. "I had to have the tray ready again, just in case the next guy hit one out."[26]

"You got a lot of practice," colleague Jim Woods once said.

"Who wouldn't get practice," Bob said, "with Ralph Kiner around?"[27]

In 1946, slugger Kiner returned from war to lead the National League with 23 home runs. That year Pittsburgh bought another bopper, Hank Greenberg, moved bullpens from foul ground to the base of the scoreboard in left field, strung a chicken-wire fence to left-center field, enclosed the pens, "lopp[ed] 30 feet off home run distances [the line from 365 feet to 335 and the alley from 406 feet to 376]," wrote author Ron Smith, "and dubbed the area 'Greenberg Gardens.'"[28] After one year Hank retired, his Gardens renamed Kiner's Korner, Ralph later saying, "Home run hitters drive the Cadillacs and the banjo hitters have to be content with the Maxwells."[29] Kiner drove to a nonpareil seven straight NL home-run titles, including 1947's 51 and 1949's 54. The long ball didn't win a pennant, but kept the Pirates solvent. In 1948, fourth-place Pittsburgh drew a record 1,517,021. "You didn't dare leave Forbes Field until Kiner's last at-bat," wrote the Post-Gazette's Gene Collier.[30] Then, verdict rendered, half the crowd would leave.

In 1952, Ralph wafted 37 homers. Despite him, the Bucs were last in runs, doubles, triples, home runs, K's, walks, shutouts, ERA, and wins — 42-112. General manager Branch Rickey cut his salary by 25 percent, explaining "We could have finished last without you,"[31] then dealt Kiner the next year to the Cubs, Forbes's inner fence coming down. In 1955, Rickey dedicated an 18-foot, 18,000-pound statue of Wagner in Schenley Park. On May 28, 1956, before 31,221 at home, Dale Long homered in a major-league record eighth straight game. Long got a curtain call—a then-rarity. Even rarer: The '58ers finished second, Danny Murtaugh voted Manager of the Year. In 1959, Dick Stuart became first to clear left-center field's 457-foot mark. Reliever Elroy Face won his 17th straight game. Said Blass: "We won't soon see that again."[32] That was especially true of a year where Tri-Staters in western Pennsylvania, eastern Ohio, and West Virginia celebrated "Beat 'Em Bucs" and an all-time Forbes attendance record of 1,705,828 and a surreal World Series.

Even before October, the Bucs saved their best for last, winning 23 regular-season sets in their final at-bat. MVP shortstop Dick Groat hit a bigs-high .325. Vernon Law went a Cy Young Award-winning 20-9. First basemen Stuart and Rocky Nelson had 30 homers. At second, Bill Mazeroski turned a double play so fast the ball seemed radioactive to his glove. Right fielder Roberto Clemente threw out a league-best 19 runners. On September 25, Pittsburgh clinched its first pennant since 1927. Ten days later the Series began at Forbes. The Pirates thrived on pressure, winning 6-4, 3-2, and 5-2. The Yankees swaggered: 16-3, 10-0, and 12-0. Bobby Richardson set a Series mark for most RBIs in a game (six, Game Three) and Series (12). Whitey Ford threw two shutouts. The Pinstripes outhit (.338-.256), out-homered (10-4), and outscored (55-27) the Bucs. Nova blur: diving stops by Don Hoak and Mazeroski; Mickey Mantle, batting righty, clearing the 436-foot right-center-field mark; Center fielder Bill Virdon's leaping catch off Yogi Berra, saving Game Four.

October 13 broke mild and bright for a Good God Almighty, one frantic play after another, top this final. "We have been blessed again with summer weather," Mel Allen mused on NBC Television. Off-air he asked if Prince wanted a drink. "Don't worry," Bob passed. "I'm just as crazy sober."[33] Game Seven left you feeling like a morning-after binge. Tide: Nelson, first inning. "There's a drive!" said Prince. "Deep into right field! Back she goes! You can kiss that one good-bye!"—Pirates, 2-0. Riptide: The Yankees rallied. Down 4-2, Berra batted in the sixth. "There's a drive hit deep to right field!" Allen said,

calling foul, then amending: "All the way for a home run!"[34]—Yanks, 5-4.

In the eighth inning, behind 7-4, Virdon slapped a one-on grounder to Tony Kubek: an apparent double-play, until the ball likely hit a pebble or spike mark, abruptly bounded up, and hit the Yanks shortstop in the throat. Groat and Clemente singled: 7-6. Hal Smith then drove a two-out and two-on pitch toward the scoreboard. "I don't know—it might be out of here! It is going, going, gone!" said NBC Radio's Chuck Thompson. "Forbes Field is at this moment an outdoor insane asylum!" Pirates, 9-7.[35]

Naturally, in arguably the greatest game of the greatest World Series ever played, New York tied the score, 9-9, in the top half of the ninth inning. In the bottom half, Ralph Terry threw a slider. The left-center-field clock read 3:36 P.M. "There's a drive deep into left field!" said NBC TV's Allen, Berra egressing to the 406-foot sign. "Look out now! That ball is going … going, gone! … Mazeroski hits it over the left-field fence for a home run. And the Pirates win it, 10 to 9, and win the World Series!"[36] Maz's blast became a Baby Boomer touchstone. In Los Angeles, future broadcaster Bob Costas, 8, retired to his room. "I'm sitting there, eyes welling with tears as I take a vow of silence. My plan was not to speak until Opening Day of the '61 season." Reality soon intervened. "But I kept mute for 24 hours—protesting this cosmic curse."[37] In suburban Pittsburgh, Larry Lucchino, 15, was walking home from school. "I was a Pirates fan, and had a radio. When Maz homered, I threw it toward the sky." Aglow, the future president of the Orioles, Padres, and Red Sox raced home: "Really, I was walking on air."[38]

For a long time a hangover shrouded bars, mail routes, and screened-in porches, where one radio after another ferried the Bucs. Five decades later, even a Yankees fan recalls the leaves and splashing hues and spooked-up days that cradled fancy. "We had 'em allll the way!" Prince cried upon a victory. By default, Maz's shot sustained the decade. Blass, his 1964-74 career record 103-76, came to cherish the Forbes Field neighborhood's mom-and-pop patina. Players parked at a gas station, lunched at ex-Pirate Frankie

Gustine's restaurant, "then after a game went to a place named Cum Laude's at the university which was always dark—so we could drink," Steve said. At the park, its pews so near the field you could almost know what the players were like, each bullpen lay down a foul line, pitchers warming next to the crowd. "We knew fans' names, where they went to school, who was getting married, what was going on in their lives." All dreamt of a degree of 1960 *redux*.

It is true that in 1966 Matty Alou won the batting title (.342), Prince coined a hex (the Green Weenie, a hot dog painted green, that locals bought at stores, shook at rivals, and hung on car antennas), and the Bucs barely missed the pennant. It is also true that the 1961-69 Pirates five times flunked the first division, relying on Clemente to grease their creaking gate. The Great One had 3,000 hits, five times led

outfielders in assists, and won a dozen Gold Gloves and four batting titles. His MVP pinnacle was 1966's .317, 29 homers, and 119 RBIs. Clemente ran like Secretariat, hit like Ali vs. Frazier, and treated baseball, Roger Angell later wrote, "as if it were a form of punishment for everyone else on the field."[39] Sadly, he and his team also left Forbes for a very different kind of home.

In 1958, the Pirates sold the House of Thrills to the University of Pittsburgh for $2 million. The college wanted to expand graduate facilities. The Bucs wanted a new multisport stadium. "Amazingly, baseball didn't then grasp what it had—that intimate was better. It wanted something bigger, to accommodate football," said Costas. Prince was personal. "Leaving Forbes Field, they took the players away from the fans. It was unique. So what if girders needed replacing? You

Forbes Field hosted plenty of baseball action. The first night game at the stadium was played on July 18, 1930 when the Homestead Grays and Kansas City Monarchs squared off under portable lights. (*Courtesy of Pittsburgh Pirates Baseball Club*)

could do it, add bleacher seats. They had a way — just not a will."[40] It is likely that no baseball team ever suffered more by leaving one site for another.

Forbes Field closed on June 28, 1970, before 40,918, the Bucs' largest crowd since 1956, in a doubleheader vs. Chicago. "The Cubs won had Forbes's first game [1909]," said Prince. "Now the Buccos returned the favor [winning, 3-2 and 4-1]."[41] Mourners heisted soil, seats, and numbers from the scoreboard. Circular and numb, Three Rivers Stadium took two years to build, cost $55 million, and had Tartan turf, symmetrical distances, a large foul area, and upper deck near the troposphere. A 10-foot inner fence ringed the outfield. Three levels of plastic chairs enclosed the park, including a huge upper deck. Sight lines favored the pro football Steelers. In 1971, Blass threw two complete-game victories and Clemente hit .414 to win an arresting seven-game World Series from Baltimore. Thereafter, the multisport clone's sterility helped football rule the city.

Three Rivers Stadium hosted the Bucs through 2000 — its zenith "being blown up [in February 2001]," said Milo Hamilton — hard to reach, then leave after a game.[42] In turn, it led the Pirates to almost leave Pittsburgh, no longer fitting in its emotional luggage. In 2001, baseball-only $228 million PNC Park opened downtown between the Fort Duquesne and Sixth Street (renamed Roberto Clemente) bridges by the Allegheny River. Designed by a Forbes II Task Force, PNC's brick, steel, terra-cotta-tiled plasters, masonry arches, corner pens, 16 light towers, and flat-green roof evoke the Bucs' longtime dinghy. Like Forbes Field, wall height and distance vary, the farthest seat a big-league-smallest 88 feet from the field. "A lot of people never accepted Three Rivers," said 1994 Bucs announcer Greg Brown. "They've loved this place since Day One — I think like Forbes."[43]

Fire struck the original July 17, 1971, wreckers soon crumpling it. Today part of Forbes's left-field wall stands near PNC. Home plate, in glass, anchors the University of Pittsburgh's Forbes Quadrangle, a large graduate-school classroom and office building. A plaque notes where Maz's homer cleared the wall. A lovely red brick path traces the actual wall itself. Patches of the center field and right-center wall conjure the Waner Brothers and the in-play batting cage. Arriba hovers at Mervix Hall — once right field. You approach the plot on Roberto Clemente Drive. No team in baseball has a window on the past like it.

Each October 13 hundreds flock there, like the curious and devout to Lourdes. "People listen to [NBC Radio's Chuck Thompson and Jack Quinlan announce] Game Seven," said Steve Blass, "remember where they were, talk about why Forbes was special."[44] Prince died in 1985, often returning to a place still pleasant, almost golden. "I'd come by myself, just look around, marvel at what we had."[45] In Schenley Park, memory comes unbidden like a postcard from the past.

SOURCES

In addition to the sources cited in the Notes, the author also consulted:

Books

Vecsey, George. "On Babe Ruth," in Astor, Gerald. *The Baseball Hall of Fame 50th Anniversary Book* (Englewood Cliffs, New Jersey: Prentice Hall, 1988).

Dominik, William J., ed. "The Style Is the Man: Seneca, Tacitus, and Quintilian's Canon," *Roman Eloquence in Society and Literature*, (New York: Routledge, 2003).

Lieb, Fred. *The Pittsburgh Pirates* (New York: G.P. Putnam's Sons, 1948).

Lowry, Philip J. *Green Cathedrals: The Ultimate Celebration of Major and Negro League Ballparks* (New York: Walker and Company, 2006).

Rickey, Branch, and Robert Riger. *The American Diamond* (New York: Simon and Schuster, 1965).

Smith, Boris. *The Churchill Factor: How One Man Made History* (New York: Riverhead Books, 2014).

Smith, Curt. *A Talk in the Park: Nine Decades of Baseball Tales from the Broadcast Booth* (Washington, D.C.: Potomac Books, 2011).

___. *Pull Up a Chair: The Vin Scully Story* (Washington, D.C.: Potomac Books, 2009).

___. *Storied Stadiums: Baseball's History of Its Ballparks* (New York: Carroll & Graf, 2001).

___. *The Voice: Mel Allen's Untold Story* (Guilford, Connecticut: The Lyons Press, 2007).

___. *Voices of the Game: The Acclaimed History of Baseball Radio and Television Broadcasting* (New York: Simon and Schuster, 1992).

___. *Voices of Summer: Ranking Baseball's 101 All-Time Best Announcers* (New York: Carroll & Graf, 2005).

Newspapers

Pittsburgh Courier's Charles "Teenie" Harris photographs, from "Spirit of Community: The Photographs," his 2014 exhibit at Pittsburgh's Carnegie Museum of Art.

Pittsburgh Post-Gazette, July 18, 1930: 15, about baseball's first night game.

Youngstown (Ohio) *Vindicator*, May 23, 1951: 29, about the Grays disbanding.

Pittsburgh Post-Gazette, July 12, 2002, about the bridge between Pittsburgh and Homestead being renamed to honor the Grays.

Magazines

Sports Illustrated, "The Great American Game," April 12, 1956.

Appreciation

As with any baseball book I have written or, in this case, a chapter on beloved Forbes Field, I am indebted to Bill Francis, senior researcher at the National Baseball Hall of Fame and Museum in Cooperstown. Bill is a true professional, and friend.

NOTES

1   Fred Lieb, *The Pittsburgh Pirates* (New York: G.P. Putnam's Sons, 1948), 132.

2   Bob Prince interview with author, August 12, 1978.

3   Boris Johnson, *The Churchill Factor: How One Man Made History* (New York: Riverhead Books, 2014), 135.

4   Marcus Fabius Quintilianus a.k.a. Quintilian, *De Institutione Oratorio* (*c.* 95 AD), Box X, Chapter XII, 15.

5   *Reach Official American League Baseball Guide 1910* (Philadelphia: A.J. Reach Company, 1910), 125.

6   "Baseball Scouting Reports: Pittsburgh Pirates," *Sports Illustrated*, April 15, 1957: 82.

7   Ron Smith, *The Ballpark Book: A Journey Through the Fields of Baseball Magic* (St. Louis: The Sporting News, 2001), 272.

8   Steve Blass interview with author, March 29, 2017.

9   John Thorn, editor. *Total Baseball 2001: The Total Encyclopedia of Major League Baseball* (New York: Total Sports Publishing, 2001), 283, 284, 285.

10   Blass interview.

11   Harold Arlin interview with author, June 10, 1984.

12   Arlin interview.

13   Gene Collier, *Pittsburgh Post-Gazette*, July 18, 2010. Art Rooney Jr., saying of the Pirates' revival, "The Chief [Art Sr.] would have loved this. He loved baseball even more than football."

14   "First Night Baseball Game at Forbes Field," *Pittsburgh Post-Gazette*, July 18, 1930: 13.

15   Prince interview.

16   According to the National Baseball Hall of Fame and Museum, beside the 11 and six men inducted as Pirates and Grays, respectively, 32 and six other Hall players, managers, or executives spent part of their career with Pittsburgh or Homestead, respectively.

17   George Vecsey, "On Babe Ruth." Gerald Astor, *The Baseball Hall of Fame 50th Anniversary Book* (New York: Prentice Hall Press, 1988), 155.

18   Associated Press, "Last Ruth Homers Recalled," March 28, 1974.

19   Lester Biederman, "Forbes Field Rated Top … Gets Perfect Ball Park Tag," *Pittsburgh Press*, June 5, 1938: Sports, 3.

20   Milo Hamilton interview with author: *A Discussion on America's Pastime* at George H.W. Bush Library and Museum, Texas A&M University, October 28, 2011.

21   "Baseball in Pittsburgh" exhibit c/o Carnegie Museum of Art and starring the work of the late photographer Charles "Teenie" Harris.

22   Allison Schlesinger, Associated Press, "Homestead Span Honors Baseball Team," *Pittsburgh Post-Gazette*, July 12, 2002,

23   Prince interview.

24   Blass interview.

25   Prince interview.

26   Prince interview.

27   Prince interview.

28   Ron Smith, *The Ballpark Book: A Journey Through the Fields of Baseball Magic* (St. Louis: The Sporting News, 2001), 273.

29   Edgar Munzel, "Kiner Denies He's Singles Hitter Now," *The Sporting News*: June 16, 1954.

30   Gene Collier, "Gene Therapy: The Skizzler and other Kinerisms," *Pittsburgh Post-Gazette*, April 4, 2003.

31   United Press International, Ralph Kiner acceptance speech, National Baseball Hall of Fame and Museum, August 18, 1975.

32   Blass interview.

33   Prince interview.

34   NBC Television, Mel Allen, Game Seven, World Series, October 13, 1960.

35   NBC Radio, Chuck Thompson, Game Seven, World Series, October 13, 1960.

36   NBC Television, Mel Allen, Game Seven, World Series, October 13, 1960.

37   Bob Costas Interview, Smithsonian Institution, *Voices of The Game* tribute, May 10, 1993.

38   Larry Lucchino interview with author, May 25, 2012.

39   "Clemente Quietly Grew in Stature," Larry Schwartz, ESPN Classic, Sports Century Biography, ESPN.com.

40   Prince interview.

41   Ibid.

42   Hamilton interview.

43   Greg Brown interview with author, March 28, 2017.

44   Blass interview.

45   Prince interview.

GRIFFITH STADIUM

By John R. Schleppi

When the Washington Senators[1] were founded in 1891, they played their games at Boundary Field in Northwest Washington. Boundary Field was named for its location on the northwest boundary line of the District of Columbia at Boundary Line and Seventh Street. The field is labeled on the 1904 Sanborn Fire Insurance Map as "Athletic Fields," bordered on two sides by a "High Wood Fence."[2] The Senators played there until they were dropped by the National League in 1899 when the league contracted. The new American League brought a franchise to Washington, again the Senators, in 1901. They played at the American League Park in Northeast Washington because the National League retained the lease to Boundary Field. The American League Park, located at Florida Avenue NE and Trinidad Avenue, is noted on the same map as "The American League Ball Park," and the map shows the footprint of the stands.[3] After the 1903 AL-NL Peace Agreement,[4] the Senators returned to the Boundary Field location, renamed National Park, and they took the wooden stands from the American League Park to their new home. The National Park's location was now given as Florida Avenue NW (formerly Boundary Line) and Georgia Avenue (formerly Seventh Street).[5]

Boundary Field began as a simple four-sided field. Over the years its dimensions changed, but the playing surface was always large. As early as 1906, it was evident that Boundary Field needed improvement. The *Washington Post's* J. Ed Grillo wrote:

"[T]here is hardly a minor league city today, unless it [is] of the very lowest class, that cannot boast of a better equipped baseball plant than that on which the Nationals have played for the past years. The local so-called park is antiquated and out of date and far from being in keeping with those in other major league cities and it is commendable that the local owners have finally come to this realization and are at least contemplating improvements. As far as the present site is concerned few cities have one better located or more easily accessible, but the days of rough-built frame stands, lacking even ordinary accommodations and with convenient entrances and exits, have long since passed. There are excuses for losing teams, perhaps, but none for such abominable accommodations as the Washington club has furnished its patrons. Men who invested their money in baseball realized years ago that the game had come to stay, and from that time on a most substantial effort to create plants in keeping with the times has been made most everywhere but here in Washington, and it is pleasing to note that there has been an awakening here, even though it is belated."[6]

Finally, in 1910 the club decided to build a new facility.[7] The club's board announced that it was withholding dividends for this investment. The F.J. Osborn Architecture and Engineering firm of Cleveland was selected for the job. Osborn's engineers, with their experience in using steel and concrete in structures, such as bridges, were pioneers in stadium construction and had completed Forbes Field in Pittsburgh in 1909.[8] The plan in Washington was to build stands behind home plate and along first base and third base to seat 15,000 at a cost of $135,000.[9]

On March 17, 1911, a fire destroyed Boundary Field's wooden stands.[10] Spring training had already begun and Opening Day was less than a month away. The Senators' board decided to build the new ballpark on the site and to begin immediately. The *Washington Post* headlines informed the public, "Accommodations for Opening Game Assured—Ban Johnson Here."[11]

Once the remains of the ruined stadium were removed, the new structure rose quickly. The *Washington Evening Star* on April 9 reported, "[D]ay and night the chanting of the negro laborers has been heard in the vicinity. Like Aladdin's Palace the structure rose as if by magic."[12] The playing field was closely aligned with the former one. The left-field line measured 407 feet, right field 328 feet, and center field 421 feet.[13] The center-field line contained a right-angled notch in the fence because homeowners there refused to sell their property to the Senators. The extended left-field foul line proved beneficial when the field was used for football. In addition, home plate was 61 feet from the grandstand, creating a spacious playing area for the catcher.[14] This was a large park compared with other parks of the era.

On Opening Day, April 12, 1911, the stands were completed but uncovered, and ready for a crowd of 16,000 to see the Senators defeat the Boston Red Sox, 8-5.[15] President William Howard Taft threw out the first ball. This tradition had begun two years earlier, on April 14, 1909, in the old ballpark, when Taft was approached by umpire Billy Evans and invited to throw out the first ball to open the season.[16] In previous years, the district commissioner of the District of Columbia had usually done the honors. Eventually a presidential box would be installed in the stadium for the use of future presidents. Calvin Coolidge was the only president to do the honor three times in one season: the Senators' opening game on April 15, 1924, the Olympic Quota Game (a fundraiser for the US Olympic team) on May 19, and the World Series opener on October 4.[17]

Construction continued in earnest whenever the Senators were on the road, and the ballpark was com-

Griffith Stadium in Washington, D.C., was the second home – along with Pittsburgh's Forbes Field – of the Homestead Grays. The Grays regularly outdrew the stadium's usual tenants, the American League's Washington Senators. (*National Baseball Hall of Fame, Cooperstown, New York*)

pleted for the July 25 game against the Detroit Tigers, which the Senators lost, 5-2. The final structure included a double-decked, covered grandstand around the infield and uncovered single decks along both foul lines. The cost was estimated at $125,000.[18] This was considerably less than the $1 million-plus that had been spent to build Forbes Field,[19] although it should be noted that the Senators' new home was a no-frills structure without the substantial façades of Forbes Field, Comiskey Park, and even Cleveland's League Park, which were all built by The Osborn Company.[20]

The following season, 1912, Clark C. Griffith joined the club as player-manager. He had begun his career with the minor-league Milwaukee Brewers in 1888, and afterward had joined the American Association's St. Louis Browns in 1891. He was released by St. Louis that year and went to the Boston Reds, where he was released again in September. In 1892 he went to Tacoma, Washington, in the Pacific Northwest League; when the league folded in August, he moved to Missoula in the Montana State League for the remainder of the season.

The start of the 1893 season found Griffith with Oakland in the California League. The league folded in August. In September he moved to the Chicago Colts of the National League. While with Chicago, where he played through the 1900 season, he attended law school at Northwestern University. Following a longing for the outdoors, he also purchased a ranch in Craig, Montana, in 1899.

With Chicago Griffith had six consecutive seasons (1894-1899) of over 20 wins. This is impressive because he had to adjust to the increase in 1893 of the pitching distance from 55 feet to 60 feet 6 inches.[21] His was one of the best pitching records in late-nineteenth-century baseball.

Griffith was a National Leaguer, but he was not happy with the status of players under their current management arrangement with the reserve clause and salary control. He tried to organize players to challenge the status quo; in fact, he wanted to organize a union. He gained only moderate support from the players, who feared for their jobs if they challenged

the system. Griffith met with his friend Ban Johnson, who wanted to form a new league to address some of these issues. Thus began the American League.

Griffith tried to persuade National Leaguers to jump to the new circuit. For his efforts, he was named player-manager of the American League Chicago White Stockings in 1901 and 1902, and led Chicago to the first AL pennant, in 1901. The AL moved the Baltimore franchise to New York as the New York Highlanders in 1903, and Griffith was their player-manager from 1903 to June 1908. A team in New York City was crucial for the success of any league. Finding that the American League management and administration was little different from the National League, he returned to the NL in December 1908 as manager of the Cincinnati Reds, where he remained through the 1911 season. Ban Johnson drew Griffith back to the American League for the 1912 season as manager of the Senators.

Griffith was always thrifty with money, but in 1912 he purchased a 10 percent interest in the Senators. To raise the funds for the purchase, he "risked everything by mortgaging the Montana ranch he owned with his brother."[22] At the time the club had little going for it talentwise, except for Walter Johnson, but it did have a new ballpark. Even with lesser players, Griffith was still able to take the Senators into the first division several times.

The United States entered World War I in 1917. Griffith, as did many others, believed that military drill for players was patriotic and would prepare them if they were called up for the war effort. On Opening Day, April 25, the players drilled in military formation led by Assistant Secretary of the Navy Franklin D. Roosevelt. In lieu of weapons, the players carried baseball bats.[23] In addition, Griffith raised money to purchase baseball equipment for National Guard camps. He worked out agreements with several sporting-goods companies to supply the equipment.[24]

The next major change to the home of Senators, now known as National Park, came with renovations in 1920s. With improved play on the field and increasing attendance for some visiting teams, such as the New York Yankees and the Cleveland Indians, revenues increased. The stands along the foul lines were given a covered second deck and extended almost the entire length of the foul lines. The second-deck roofs did not connect with the main grandstand because of grading issues. In addition, concrete bleachers were installed behind the left-field fence beyond the stands. These can be seen in a photo of Ty Cobb with the Detroit Tigers sliding into third base in 1924.[25] The distance down the left-field line was 424 feet, the right-field line 326 feet, and center-field (unchanged) 421 feet.[26] This unusual split in the roof line was given a nostalgic nod along the right-field line in Nationals Park, which opened in 2008.

In 1920 Griffith stepped down as manager and devoted himself full-time to administration of the club, with the approval of the Nationals' major investor, William Richardson of Philadelphia. The custom of the era was to name the ballpark after the owner, as in Detroit's Navin Field and Cleveland's Dunn Field. However, although Richardson was the owner, the honor was given to Griffith since he oversaw the operations of the club.

Modifications to the playing area, particularly the relocation of fences, altered the foul lines and center-field distances. In 1926 the left-field line was decreased to 358 feet, the right-field line increased to 328 feet, and center field again remained unchanged. The next alteration came 10 years later, in 1936, when the left-field line was increased to 402 feet, while the right-field line and center-field distance were unaltered. In 1947 the left-field line was increased to 405 feet. The next realignment was in 1950, with the left-field line decreasing to 386 feet. The following year, 1951, the left-field line was increased to 408 feet. In 1955, the right-field line was decreased by 8 feet to 320 feet.[27]

The dimensions proved formidable to hitters. According to baseball-reference.com, "Just two players are known to have hit a fair ball out of Griffith Stadium— Mickey Mantle, who hit the famous '565-foot' blast off Chuck Stobbs in 1953, and Josh Gibson, who reportedly did it twice in the 1940s as a member of the [sometimes] Washington-based Homestead Grays," the Negro League team that

called D.C. its second home (along with Pittsburgh's Forbes Field).[28] However, Larry Doby of the Cleveland Indians is credited with a 500-foot home run in 1949. The *Washington Post* declared of the blast, "When Larry Doby pumped that 500-foot home run over the scoreboard, over the Chesterfield sign and onto the rooftop beyond Griffith's Stadium's right field wall the other night, even Clark Griffith could admire the majesty of the swat."[29]

The field's one anomaly remained: the right-angle notch in the center-field fence, created because a homeowner would not sell the property when the park was renovated in 1920. The scoreboard with its giant National Bohemian beer bottle was in right-center field.[30] Temporary lights were used for boxing and collegiate football, but not for baseball. Permanent light towers were installed for the 1941 season at a cost of $230,000. Shirley Povich of the *Washington Post* commented that "the added cash the night games fetched was permitting (Griffith) to go into the market for better ball players."[31] Washington profited from having night games, especially during the war years, which saw a great increase in government personnel in Washington.

Along with the changes in field dimensions, the ballpark's capacity changed as well. In 1921 it was listed as 32,000; in 1936, 30,171; in 1939, 31,500; in 1940, 29,473; in 1941, 29,613; in 1947, 29,000; in 1948, 25,048; in 1952, 35,000; in 1960, 28,669; in 1961, 27,550.[32] Note that the capacity averaged almost 30,000 until the 5,000-seat increase in 1952. In eight years, by 1960, the capacity had dropped to below 30,000.[33]

Before the age of loudspeakers or radio and TV broadcasting, the lineups for the game were given to the fans at the stadium by a man with a megaphone. At American League Park in 1901, E. Lawrence Phillips made these announcements along both the left- and right-field lines prior to the game. He did this for 28 years before retiring in 1928 but continued to use his megaphone after he purchased a carnival in 1934.[34] A loudspeaker system was introduced in Griffith Stadium on September 1, 1930. It "seemed to make a hit with the fans, especially the early comers who were treated to a musical program before play started."[35]

Other technological advances affected the game in the 1920s. In 1924, "Thousands of Washington baseball fans, unable to obtain tickets for the World Series games because of the limited capacity of the ball park, are listening in on the games by radio. Play by play descriptions of the games are radiocast directly from the ball park. . . ."[36] In this instance, "sport radio's first major star, [Graham] McNamee," broadcast the first of his 12 consecutive World Series.[37] Local radio sales were up 60 percent, but sponsors were concerned that listeners would give up on the poor radio reception and opt for "a first-hand view of the ballgames."[38] The technology continued to improve so that in an article on public-address systems in use in Washington, Fred E. Kunkel reported that the system "is used at Griffith Ball Park picking up any and all sounds desired, in addition to the speaker's voice announcing the progress of the game. Since most of the games played here by the Nationals are broadcast over the radio, the set has to be perfect in every respect. Pickup microphones can be focused in any direction the sound is coming from to catch such details as the batter hitting the ball."[39]

With the emergence of a quality team in the 1920s, the Senators won pennants in 1924, 1925, and 1933, crowned with a World Series victory in seven games in 1924 over the New York Giants. These teams were led by players like Muddy Ruel, Joe Judge, player-manager Bucky Harris, Goose Goslin, and Sam Rice. The pitchers included Tom Zachary, George Mogridge, and Walter Johnson, who was nearing the end of his career. Johnson lost Games One and Five of the 1924 Series, but got credit for the win in Game Seven as a reliever.

After the profitable 1924 season, Griffith purchased land for a home in Washington's diplomatic row at 16th and Decatur Streets.[40] The next year saw the Senators repeat as the AL champions. They lost the World Series to the Pittsburgh Pirates in seven games. Johnson pitched three games, winning Games One and Four, but losing Game Seven. Goslin kept his bat hot with eight hits in the Series.

Walter Johnson retired in 1927. When Washington returned to the World Series in 1933, Joe Cronin was the manager against the New York Giants, who took the Series, four games to one. Earl Whitehill won Washington's only game, Game Three, 4-0. Goslin hit one of only two home runs in the series for the Senators along with teammate Fred Schulte.

The Senators hosted two All-Star Games at Griffith Stadium. In 1937, along with President Franklin Roosevelt, 31,391 people watched as the American League won, 8-3. Second baseman Buddy Myer and the Ferrell brothers (catcher Rick and pitcher Wes) represented the Senators. When the All-Star Game returned in 1956, the National League won, 7-3, with Senators outfielder Roy Sievers pinch-hitting in the ninth.

Although the Senators won only three pennants in Washington, they had many outstanding players. The 1902 AL batting champion was Ed Delahanty, who posted a .376 batting average. Leon Goslin won in 1928 with .379; Buddy Myer in 1935 with .349; and two-time winner Mickey Vernon topped the league in 1946 with .353 and in 1953 with .337. Perhaps the greatest hitting feat came from a Senators shortstop in 1941, when Cecil Travis slipped in between Ted Williams and Joe DiMaggio with a .359 average for the season, second to Williams's .406. After spending four years in the military and even enduring frostbite at one point, Travis returned for three seasons and finished his career in 1947 with a lifetime batting average of .314.

Despite the expansive dimensions of their home field, the Senators had two home-run champions, Roy Sievers in 1957 and Harmon Killebrew in 1959, each with 42 round-trippers. They also boasted several basestealing leaders, starting in 1906 with John Anderson, who stole 39 bases. Clyde Milan stole 88 in 1912 and 75 in 1913. Sam Rice led with 63 stolen bases in 1920. Ben Chapman stole 35 in 1937. From 1939 through 1943, George Case took the honors with 51, 35, 33, 44, and 61, respectively.

In the pitching department, 20-game winners include Bob Groom (1912), Stan Coveleski (1925), General Alvin Crowder (1932, '33), Monte Weaver

(1932), Earl Whitehill (1933), Emil Dutch Leonard (1939), Roger Wolff (1945), and Bob Porterfield (1953). Walter Johnson topped all Senators hurlers with 12 seasons in which he won 20 or more games. On August 2, 1927, in recognition of his accomplishments and to celebrate Johnson's retirement after 20 years with the team, a granite shaft with a bronze tablet was to be placed in the ballpark. Billy Evans, who umpired Johnson's first game, was to umpire the game.[41] However, this did not occur and the monument to Walter Johnson was formally installed at Griffith Stadium in 1946 and dedicated by President Harry S. Truman.[42] The monument is now installed at Walter Johnson High School in Bethesda, Maryland.

Black baseball also had an extended history at Griffith Stadium. Beginning with the Washington Potomacs (Eastern Colored League) in 1924, several teams used Griffith as their home ballpark. The Washington Pilots (East West League) came in 1932, followed by the Washington Elite Giants (Negro National League) in 1936-37 and the Washington Black Senators (Negro National League) in 1938. None of these teams achieved success either on the field or with attendance.[43] The arrival of the Homestead Grays in 1940 changed this circumstance. During Homestead's tenure through 1948 great players graced Griffith Stadium, including James Cool Papa Bell, Ray Brown, Walter Buck Leonard, and Josh Gibson. The Grays won seven of their 10 Negro National League championships in seasons when they split their home games between Pittsburgh and Washington: 1940, '41, '42, '43, '44, '45, and '48. They won the Negro League World Series in 1943, 1944, and 1948, each time against the Birmingham Black Barons of the Negro American League. In 1946 the Grays hosted the East West All-Star Classic, which attracted a crowd of more than 15,000 and netted $7,500 for the Senators, whom the Grays paid for the use of the stadium.[44]

Washington's black population increased during the war years. To reach this fan base, the Grays used their own public-relations man, who highlighted the team's winning ways. There was easy access to Griffith from nearby Ladroit and Shaw neighborhoods that had large black populations, and the Howard University campus was close by as well. Meanwhile, Clark Griffith, in need of fans to fill the ballpark, lifted the ban on interracial games. With the added attraction of Satchel Paige to hurl several games and the Grays' all-star lineup, both the Grays and Griffith profited. The Senators netted $60,000 from the Grays' 11,600 or so fans per game in 1942, almost double the Senators' average for the season. The next year, 1943, was even better, showing a net profit for the ballpark of $100,000 from the Grays, who drew 225,000 in 26 games. Because of the Grays' drawing power that year, Griffith altered the Senators' schedule so that the Grays could host the 1943 Negro League World Series. "It is easy to see Griffith's reluctance to integrate which would potentially lead to the decimation of the Grays," wrote a Griffith biographer.[45] However, no small consideration may have been that this would result in significant loss of revenue for Griffith.

In addition to major-league and Negro League squads, other baseball teams used Griffith Stadium. In 1931, the Hollywood Movie Stars Girls Baseball Team was in Washington to compete against the Pullman Athletic Club. The Washington Post noted, "From all indications, today's game will draw an unprecedented number of fans through the turnstiles to witness a team composed entirely of girls, movie actresses at that, in a baseball game with a rugged group of veteran sandlotters." All redheads were admitted as guests of "Freckles" HooRay of "Our Gang." Griffith donated the use of the stadium for a benefit game for Frank Cinotti.[46] Another charity game, this time to benefit the Metropolitan Police Boys Club, was held on July 12, 1947, and pitted Republican congressmen against Democratic congressmen. Chief Justice Fred Vinson threw out the first ball.[47]

Griffith recognized the value of entertainment for attracting crowds. As an example, he employed two mediocre former Senators, Al Schacht and Nick Altrock, to liven up the game with pantomime routines. In one instance, before a game they mimicked Vincent Richards and Suzanne Lenglen, two well-known tennis players. After the Senators lost to the Athletics, 13-3, the Washington Post reported,

"(Schacht and Altrock) showed better form than many of the Washington players yesterday."[48] In another show, Schacht was "funmaking around the first base," missed a ball, and was "hit in the back of the head and rendered … senseless. Spectators did not know whether Schacht was unconscious or whether he was acting. Several buckets of water thrown by Brownie revived the comedian and he resumed his antics to the great amusement of the crowd."[49] The pair were seen at many festivals at Griffith Stadium and at other ballparks.[50] Besides being a player and comedian, Schacht coached third base for the Senators from 1925 to 1935; he served in World War II and later opened a restaurant in New York City.[51] Altrock remained a favorite of Griffith and coached the Senators into the 1950s.[52] Aside from the entertainment value, some of their antics were used as signals for plays, according to Bob Considine in the *Washington Post*.[53]

Other sporting events and entertainments generated additional revenue for the Senators. Football at the high-school, collegiate and professional levels was played at Griffith. The *Washington Post* reported in November of 1929 that "the strong Emerson Institute will host the Baylor Military Academy, prep school champions of Tennessee."[54] On December 7, 1929, Gonzaga played Devitt for the prep-school championship of Washington.[55] Georgetown University used the ballpark as its home field from 1921 through 1950.[56] George Washington University played there during the 1930s and '40s. Schedule conflicts did arise but were worked out between Georgetown and George Washington. The colleges even scheduled night games at Griffith Stadium in 1930. "After-dinner football in wholesale quantities will be offered Washingtonians," reported the *Washington Post*. "… Seven games will be played under huge floodlights. Teams of Georgetown and George Washington University, and the Marine Corps will participate in

Buck Leonard in action at the plate against the New York Cubans at Griffith Stadium in 1938. In 1948 he batted .395 and tied for the Negro National League lead in home runs. (*National Baseball Hall of Fame, Cooperstown, New York*)

this first attempt of its kind in the city's sports history."[57] The University of Maryland Terrapins played their home games at Griffith Stadium in 1948 while their own campus stadium was under construction.[58] Howard University, located across the street from Griffith Stadium, used the stadium as the Bisons clashed with "their ancient rival, the Lions of Lincoln, in the thirty-fifth rivalry of their turkey day contest" in 1940.[59]

The Boston Redskins (originally the Braves) of the National Football League moved to Washington for the 1937 season and maintained the Redskins name. They met their opponents at Griffith Stadium for 34 seasons (through 1960). The team was moderately successful; however, in 1940 they lost to the Chicago Bears, 73-0, the worst championship loss in NFL history.[60] The football teams contributed an average of $100,000 annually from rental and concessions alone.[61] Griffith also profited from advertising and concessions for revenue. (Tobacco and beer companies sponsored game broadcasts.) In 1940 Griffith Stadium was spruced up with repainted seats (the paint cost $3,000); 150 truckloads of sod were used to repair the damage caused by the Redskins games.[62]

Boxing was prominent among the other sporting events. On July 25, 1938, Al Reid was an 8-5 favorite over Paul "Tennessee") Lee.[63] It rained, and the featherweight match was held the next night at Turner's Arena. (Reid won a unanimous decision.) Rain often plagued events scheduled at Griffith Stadium.[64] Lewis F. Atchison reported on a "lighting system rigged up to indicate the score of the for the fans' enlightenment."[65] A green light appeared over the corner of the boxer who was leading in the match. A 10-round welterweight match featuring Holman Williams and Izzy Jannazzo was held on September 4, 1940; Jannazzo won the decision before a gathering of 2,500. These bouts were held outdoors, in a ring set up on the infield. The Williams-Jannazzo bout had been postponed a week because of rain.[66] When Henry Armstrong, the welterweight champion, fought Phil Furr on September 23, 1940, a crowd of 15,000 and receipts of between $20,000 and $25,000 were expected.[67] Heavyweight champ Joe Louis de-

feated challenger Buddy Baer on May 23, 1941.[68] The rough-and-tumble match was ended at the beginning of the seventh round when Baer's manager stopped the fight. The following year, two other heavyweight contenders, Lee Savold and Tony Musto, finally met after rain forced two postponements.[69] On October 3, 1949, Joe Louis, attempting a comeback, returned to Griffith Stadium for an exhibition match against Abe Gestac.[70] It is estimated that more than 150 boxing matches took place at Griffith Stadium.

Wrestling, another physical, combative sport, also was occasionally featured at Griffith Stadium. Wrestling was a colorful event in 1938, and audience participation was expected. Lewis F. Atchison reported of the Jim Londos-Bobby Bruns match, "[T] is rumored it will be a shooting match. That means only guns, knives and Cyclone Burns shirt will be barred as weapons. It is every man for himself, including the irate customers who inhabit the front row pews."[71] The popular wrestling events continued at Griffith Stadium, bolstered by colorful reporting in the *Washington Post*. For a wrestling card in August 1939, the newspaper commented, "After the culling the ranks of wrestledom—which needless to say are pretty rank—Turner (the promoter) chose the most ferocious of the four wrestling Duseks as the person to break the hindu's celebrated cobra clutch." For this bout between Najo Singh and Ernie Dusek, Turner expected a turnout of 4,000 to 6,000.[72]

During World War II, Griffith Stadium was used to aid the war effort through scrap-metal drives, War Bond sales, and benefit sporting events. The radio personality and singer Kate Smith, a Washington native, appeared for the pregame ceremony before a contest between the Nats and the Norfolk Naval Training Station on May 20, 1943. At home plate she delivered her "notable bond buying speech."[73] Bond buyers received a ticket to the game for each bond purchased in advance. The singer Bing Crosby also was slated to attend the event. During the Korean War, Griffith donated the receipts from the August 10, 1953, game between the Nats and the Red Sox to the Red Cross.[74]

Before the 1960s ballparks were not designed as multipurpose facilities; however, since they were often the largest venue in many cities, they also hosted nonathletic events. Griffith Stadium was a major entertainment center for the capital. It hosted dog races in May 1927. Tiny whippets from across the nation were brought to the city to race for the American Derby title. The weight of the dogs ranged from 10 to 14 pounds.[75] On June 17, 1928, the Masonic Festival highlighted Shrine and Grotto drill teams before a crowd of 8,000.[76] On June 7, 1932, students from the area competed in the Annual Competitive Drill Competition for high school cadet corps.[77] In addition to the drill-team contests, there were also field days. The Colored Elks sponsored one such competition on July 27, 1930, at which events included a fat man race, a tug of war, a sack race, an exhibition drill, a 100-yard race, and baseball; about 2,000 people attended.[78] There was also a "Night of Thrills," an annual circus sponsored by the Masons for the benefit of the Mason and Eastern Star Home. Beginning in 1938, clowns, elephants, and trapeze artists provided annual entertainment.[79]

Griffith Stadium was even used for religious events. On a rainy night in October 1937, 200 people were baptized by immersion by Elder Lightfoot Solomon Michaux. Elder Michaux's church, the Church of God, was across the street from the stadium. For the ceremony, the city Fire Department filled the baptismal tank to a depth of three feet with river water.[80] The Billy Graham National Capital Crusade on June 19-26, 1960, was also held at Griffith Stadium and had an estimated attendance of more than 139,000 over eight days.[81]

Clark Griffith continued to be the administrator for the Senators and Griffith Stadium, but he also worked with his nephew, Calvin Griffith, and Calvin's sister, Thelma Griffith Haynes. Griffith's nephew and niece had been born in Montreal; after their father died, they moved to Washington and adopted the name Griffith.[82] Upon Clark Griffith's death on October 27, 1955, Calvin was elected club president. Clark Griffith left his 52 percent interest in the Senators to Calvin and Thelma, to be shared equally.

The last successful Senators squad was the team that finished in second place in 1945. In 1946, capitalizing on the previous season as well as the postwar return to normalcy, the Nationals drew a record 1,027,216. That was 400,000 more than in 1945 and 200,000 more than in 1947.[83] Calvin Griffith did try to make the experience at the park more enjoyable for the spectators. In 1956, he changed the left-field foul line, which made room for more seating and added a beer garden.[84] However, the ensuing years were marked by declining attendance and the deterioration of the ballpark. Bill DeWitt, president of the St. Louis Browns, declared, "Griffith Stadium is one of the most rundown excuses for a ballpark in the majors."[85] This was harsh criticism from a club spokesman whose own venue, Sportsman's Park, was no palace either.

Calvin Griffith was interested in moving out of Washington because of the deteriorating neighborhood around the ballpark, the racial makeup of the city, and the new competition from the Baltimore Orioles starting in 1954. The American League did not want to lose Washington.

Rumors had circulated as early as the late 1950s about the prospect of a new facility to include the Senators. Finally, after much political maneuvering, the development of a large, dual purpose (baseball-football) stadium began. The proposed location was the end of East Capitol Street near the D.C. Armory.[86] Calvin Griffith had mixed emotions about the prospect of a new stadium in Washington. His reservations were numerous. "Turning to the matter of a stadium in Washington, I feel that the capital of the United States needs one and should have one," Griffith said. "The Washington ballclub would consider playing its games in a new stadium." He was weighing the fact that the club owned the paid-for Griffith Stadium, controlled the concessions, could rent out the facility for added income, and made their own decisions. "We know, on the other hand, that our patrons, who otherwise attend theaters, restaurants, and watch television in the comfort of their home living rooms, have come to expect more and convenient parking, more ample aisle space, roomier seats, more concession stands at our ball park."[87]

Griffith's critics questioned why he listened to offers from other cities. "My answer: I will give that much courtesy to the mayor of any city or his representatives. Besides, the Washington baseball club is a corporation with many stockholders, it is my obligation as their president to listen … to any proposition that would improve the value of their holdings. We are not seeking offers. … We do not invite offers. In fact, we discouraged them."[88]

Despite Griffith's frequent expressions of loyalty to Washington, he was interested in moving the club out of the capital. He became enamored with Minneapolis. He gained permission from the American League to move there in 1961. His reasons for moving were not always clear. However, Nick Coleman of the Minneapolis *Star Tribune* reported that Griffith told the Lions Club of Waseca, Minnesota, "I'll tell you why we came to Minnesota. It was when I found out you only had 15,000 blacks here. Black people don't go to ballgames, but they'll fill up a rassling ring and put up such a chant it'll scare you to death. It's unbelievable. We came here because you've got good, hard-working white people."[89] The American League, fearing congressional backlash against baseball's antitrust exemption, awarded an expansion franchise to Washington also, to be known as the Senators. The Los Angeles Angels entered the American League in the same year, making it a 10-team league. The expansion Senators moved into Griffith Stadium in 1961 for one year. The following season they moved to new D.C. Stadium. After 10 years in Washington, owner Robert Short moved the club to Arlington, Texas, in 1972, where they became the Texas Rangers.

In a fitting tribute, the carillon of the Church of God, across the street from the ballpark stadium, rang out with "Auld Lang Syne" on the last day the Senators played there.[90]

Epilogue

Howard University purchased the Griffith Stadium site for its University Hospital, and the ballpark was demolished in 1965.[91] The location of home plate is marked inside the hospital entrance. A plaque along Georgia Avenue notes the historic ballpark and notable moments in its history.[92] The spring-training site for the Senators, Tinker Field in Orlando, Florida, became the home for 1,000 seats from Griffith Stadium, which remained there until Tinker Field also was demolished in 2015.[93]

SOURCES

In addition to the sources cited in the Notes, the author also consulted Baseball-Reference.com, Baseball-Almanac.com, and a variety of other sources including:

Books, book chapters, book sections

Elston, Gene. *A Stitch in Time: A Baseball Chronology*, 3rd Ed. (Houston: Halcyon Press Inc., 2006).

Lowry, Philip J. *Green Cathedrals: The Ultimate Celebration of Major League and Negro League Ballparks* (New York: Walker & Company, 2006).

Seymour, Harold. *Baseball: The People's Game* (New York: Oxford University Press, 1990).

Snyder, Brad. *Beyond the Shadow of the Senators* (New York: McGraw-Hill, 2003).

Thomas, Henry W. *Walter Johnson: Baseball's Big Train* (Washington: Phenom Press, 1995).

Newspapers and Magazines

Atchison, Lewis F. "New Yorker Rallies After Slow Start," *Washington Post*, July 27, 1938: 16.

"Coast Guards Clash With Marines: Teams Appear Well Matched for Service Title Game," *Washington Post*, November 21, 1929.

"Daisy Belles Play Twin Bill Here Tonight," *Washington Post*, May 5, 1951.

"Display Ad 21—No Title," *Washington Post*, May 24, 1926: 15.

"Girls Teams Play Tonight," *Washington Post*, May 9, 1952.

"G.W.-Ursinus to Attract Notables," *Washington Post*, November 5, 1926.

Johnson, Mrs. Walter Perry, "Loss of Game Was Hard, But 'Luck' at Bat Did It, Says Mrs. Walter Johnson," *Washington Post*, October 5, 1924: 2.

McCannon, Jim. "Famous 'Pebble' Is Forever Lost in Memories of Griffith Stadium," *Washington Post and Times Herald*, March 22, 1964.

"Movie Girls Play Here Tomorrow: Meet Pullman Nine at Stadium in Benefit Day," *Washington Post*, August 8, 1931.

"New Baseball Park: Local Owners Plan Another Home for Nationals," *Washington Post*, January 5, 1910: 8.

"Photo Standalone 1—No Title," *Washington Post*, April 18, 1927: 13.

Weingardt, Richard G. "Frank Osborn: Nation's Pioneer Stadium Designer," *STRUCTURE magazine*, March 2013: 61-63.

Wyatt, Dick. "Virginia, Maryland Clash in Griffith Stadium Tonight," *Washington Post*,

November 4, 1944.

Young, Frank H. "12,000 Fans Cheer Harris, Johnson, Peck, Others as Youth Is Served in Game," *Washington Post*, August 16, 1932: 9.

Online Sources

Bennett, Bryon. "Griffith Stadium and the Site of D.C.'s First National Park," deadballbaseball.com/?p=3073 (deadballbaseball.com/?p=3073), accessed August 20, 2016.

Clem, Andrew. "Clem's Baseball: Our National Pastime and Its 'Green Cathedrals,' Griffith Stadium 1911-1961, andrewclem.com/Baseball/GriffithStadiium.html#Diag (andrewclem.com/Baseball/GriffithStadiium.html#Diag), accessed September 8, 2016.

"Cleveland Architects: Osborn Engineering Company," planning.city.cleveland.oh.us/landmark/arch/pdf/archdetailPrint.php?afil=&archID=189

(http://planning.city.cleveland.oh.us/landmark/arch/pdf/archdetailPrint.php?afil=&archID=189), accessed September 19, 2016.

"Griffith Stadium," ballparksofbaseball.com/ballparks/griffith-stadium/ (ballparksofbaseball.com/ballparks/griffith-stadium/), accessed July 29, 2016.

"Griffith Stadium," projectballpark.org/history/al/griffth.html (Projectballpark.org/history/al/griffith.html), accessed July 29, 2016.

"Griffith Stadium, on Last Legs, Succumbs to Wrecker's Pounding," *Washington Post and Times Herald*, February 12, 1965.

"History," Osborn-eng.com/History (http://Osborn-eng.com/History), accessed July 29, 2016.

"Lease Requirements to Replace Griffith Stadium," ghostsofdc.org/2016/06/29/lease-requirements-replace-griffith-stadium/ (ghostsofdc.org/2016/06/29/lease-requirements-replace-griffith-stadium/), accessed July 7, 2016.

Richard, Paul. "Lights From Griffith Stadium Towers to Shine Again at City Playgrounds," *Washington Post and Times Herald*, May 14, 1966.

"The Info List—Griffith Stadium," theinfolist.com/php/SummaryGet.php?findGo=Griffith Stadium (theinfolist.com/php/SummaryGet.php?findGo=Griffith Stadium), accessed October 19, 2016.

"Tradition," dcgrays.com/tradition-2/ (dcgrays.com/tradition-2/), accessed October 13, 2016.

"Where Was Griffith Stadium? - Ghosts of DC," ghostsofdc.org/image/zoom/Griffith-stadium/15346/view (ghostsofdc.org/image/zoom/Griffith-stadium/15346/view), accessed October 12, 2016.

Other sources

Washington Nationals 2016 Official Media Guide

ebay (ebay.com)

Collections

Baseball Hall of Fame, Griffith Stadium file, courtesy of Cassidy Lent, January 9, 2017.

NOTES

1 ¹The names Senators and Nationals were used interchangeably over the years until the team left Washington in 1965.

2 *Sanborn Fire Insurance Map from Washington, District of Columbia.* Sanborn Map Company,-1916 Vol. 2, 1904—1916, 127.

3 *Sanborn Fire Insurance Map from Washington, District of Columbia.* Sanborn Map Company,-1916 Vol. 2, 1904—1916, 173.

4 "1903 AL-NL Peace Agreement," roadsidephotos.sabr.org/baseball/1903 AL-NL.htm (roadsidephotos.sabr.org/baseball/1903 AL-NL.htm), accessed October 1, 2016.

5 The multiple names in use for the two sites that the Senators/Nationals called home from 1891 through 1964 cause confusion. The primary location, in Northwest Washington at Florida Avenue NW and Georgia Avenue NW, was known as Boundary Field, National Park, or American League Park II. This is near Howard University and where Griffith Stadium was built. The other site used from 1901-1903 was located at Florida Avenue NE and Trinidad Avenue. It was known as American League Park, and then as American League Park I, to distinguish it from American League Park II.

6 J. Ed Grillo, "Sporting Comment," *Washington Post*, January 6, 1910: 8.

7 "Local Owners Plan Another Home for Nationals," *Washington Post*, January 5, 1910: 8.

8 "Cleveland Architects: Osborn Engineering Company," planning.city.cleveland.oh.us/landmark/arch/pdf/archdetailPrint.php?afil=&archID=189 (planning.city.cleveland.oh.us/landmark/arch/pdf/archdetailPrint.php?afil=&archID=189), accessed September 19, 2016.

9 "Play Ball April 12," *Washington Post*, March 18, 1911: 1.

10 Ibid.

11 "Accommodations for Opening Game Assured—-Ban Johnson Here," *Washington Post*, March 20, 1911: 12.

12 "Ready for 'Fans,'" *Washington Sunday Star*, April 9, 1911: 1, 3.

13 "Griffith Stadium," baseball-almanac.com/stadium/st_griff.shtml (baseball-almanac.com/stadium/st_griff.shtml), accessed January 1, 2017.

14 Ibid.

15 "1911 Washington Senators," baseball-almanac.com/teamstats/schedule.php

?y=1911&t=WS1 (baseball-almanac.com/teamstats/schedule. php?y=1911&t=WS1), accessed September 15, 2016.

16 Patrick Mondout, "Taft Becomes First President to Throw First Pitch (4/14/1910)," *Baseball Chronology: The Game Since 1845,*" baseballchronology.com/baseball/Years/1910/April/14-Taft (baseballchronology.com/baseball/Years/1910/April/14-Taft), accessed August 17, 2016.

17 "1924 Washington Senators," baseball-almanac.com/teamstats/schedule.php?y=1924&t=WS1 (baseball-almanac.com/teamstats/schedule.php?y=1924&t=WS1), accessed September 13, 2016; "President to Throw First Ball for Olympic Quota," *Washington Post,* May 17, 1924: 9.

18 "Play Ball April 12," *Washington Post,* March 18, 1911: 1.

19 "Phillies Here First," *Washington Post,* January 25, 1910: 8.

20 "Cleveland Architects: Osborn Engineering Company," planning.city.cleveland.oh.us/landmark/arch/pdf/archdetailPrint.php?afil=&archID=189(planning.city.cleveland.oh.us/landmark/arch/pdf/archdetailPrint.php?afil=&archID=189), accessed September 19, 2016.

21 "National League / Major League Rule Change Timeline: In Chronological Order," baseball-almanac.com/rulechng.shtml (baseball-almanac.com/rulechng.shtml), accessed September 20, 2016.

22 Mike Grahek, "Clark Griffith," sabr.org/bioproj/person/96624988 (sabr.org/bioproj/person/96624988), accessed November 24, 2016.

23 "Franklin D. Roosevelt Opening Baseball Game," gettyimages.com/detail/news-photo/assistant-secretary-of-the-navy-franklin-d-roosevelt-walks-news-photo/514080428#assistant-secretary-of-the-navy-franklin-d-roosevelt-walks-the-out-picture-id514080428 (gettyimages.com/detail/news-photo/assistant-secretary-of-the-navy-franklin-d-roosevelt-walks-news-photo/514080428#assistant-secretary-of-the-navy-frank-lin-d-roosevelt-walks-the-out-picture-id514080428), accessed October 15, 2016.

24 Brian McKenna, *Clark Griffith: Baseball's Statesman* (self-published, 2010), 295.

25 "1924 Detroit Tiger Ty Cobb Safe after Triple Hit Photo Griffith Stadium Baseball," ebay.com/itm/1924-DETROIT-TIGER-TY-COBB-SAFE-AFTER-TRIPLE-HIT-POT-GRIFFITH-STADIUM-BASEBALL-/361584614222 (ebay.com/itm/1924- DETROIT-TIGER-TY-COBB-SAFE-AFTER-TRIPLE-HIT-POT-GRIFFITH-STADIUM-BASEBALL-/361584614222.

26 "Griffith Stadium," baseball-almanac.com/stadium/st_griff.shtml (baseball-almanac.com/stadium/st_griff.shtml), accessed January 1, 2017.

27 Ibid. For diagrams of the field with dimensions and profiles of stands for 1911, 1921, 1954, 1957, and football, see Andrew Clem, "Clem's Baseball: Our National Pastime and Its "Green Cathedrals," Griffith Stadium 1911-1961, andrewclem.com/Baseball/

GriffithStadium.html#Diag (andrewclem.com/Baseball/GriffithStadiium.html#Diag), accessed September 8, 2016.

28 baseball-reference.com/bullpen/Griffith_Stadium, (baseball-reference.com/bullpen/Griffith_Stadium), accessed January 5, 2017.

29 Shirley Povich, "This Morning," *Washington Post,* May 27, 1949: B4.

30 McKenna, 274.

31 Shirley Povich, *The Washington Senators* (New York: G.P. Putnam's & Sons, 1954), 219.

32 "Griffith Stadium," baseball-almanac.com/stadium/st_griff.shtml (baseball-almanac.com/stadium/st_griff.shtml), accessed January 1, 2017.

33 Ibid.

34 Bill McCormick, "Phillips Buys a Circus; Now He Can Bark on His Own Hook," *Washington Post,* April 22, 1934: 17.

35 Frank H. Young, "Centerfielder Must Rest Elbow," *Washington Post,* September 2, 1930, 18.

36 "Thousands of Fans Ticketless, Hear of Series Over Radio," *Washington Post,* October 5, 1924: EA10.

37 Graham McNamee," baseballhall.org/discover/awards/ford-c-frick/2016-candidates/mcnamee-graham (baseballhall.org/discover/awards/ford-c-frick//2016-candidates/mcnamee-graham), accessed November 18, 2016.

38 "Thousands of Fans Ticketless, Hear of Series Over Radio."

39 Fred E. Kunkel, "Capitol's Sound Amplifying Systems Serve Many Purposes," *Washington Post,* June 30, 1935: B9.

40 McKenna, 195.

41 "Tablet Given as Johnson Memorial," *Washington Post,* July 23, 1927: 15.

42 deadballbaseball.com/?p=2283 (deadballbaseball.com/?p=228), accessed January 1, 2017.

43 McKenna, 275.

44 McKenna, 276.

45 Ibid.

46 "Hollywood Girls to Play Baseball at Stadium Today," *Washington Post,* September 1, 1931: 15.

47 "Congressmen Play Baseball Today at Griffith Stadium," *Washington Post,* July 12, 1947: 11.

48 "Washington Clowns Aid Mack's Elephants to Stage 3-Ring Baseball Circus," Photo Standalone 1 — No Title, *Washington Post,* April 18, 1927: 13.

49 "Thomas Halts 3-Run Rally in Ninth," *Washington Post,* August 12, 1929: 9.

50 "Masonic Festival Features Delight Crowd at Stadium," *Washington Post,* June 17, 1928: 2.

51   Al Schacht, *my own particular screwball* (Garden City, New York: Doubleday & Company, 1955), 231-235.

52   "The Manager and His Aides," Washington Nationals yearbook 1953: 7.

53   Bob Considine, "Runs-Hits and Errors," *Washington Post*, January 12, 1933: 10.

54   "Color Added to Emerson Contest," *Washington Post*, November 26, 1929: 20.

55   "Gonzaga to Play Devitt at Griffith Stadium," *Washington Post*, November 30, 1929: 16.

56   "History & Tradition: Stadia Of Georgetown, hoyafootball.com/history/stadia.htm (hoyafootball.com/history/stadia.htm), accessed January 8, 2016.

57   "7 Night Football Contests at Griffith Stadium in Fall," *Washington Post*, May 25, 1930: 20.

58   Jack Walsh, "Terps Play Four Grid Games at Griffith Stadium," *Washington Post*, April 4, 1948: C1.

59   "Howard Meets Lincoln at Griffith Stadium," *Washington Post*, November 21, 1940: 31.

60   Al Hailey, "36,000 See Bears Crush Redskins for Title, 73-0," *Washington Post*, December 9, 1940: 1.

61   McKenna, 275.

62   Al Hailey, "Griffith Stadium Gets Annual Face-Lifting," *Washington Post*, March 29, 1940: 23.

63   Lewis F. Atchison, "Reid Rates an 8-5 Favorite Over Lee in Griffith Stadium Battle," *Washington Post*, July 25, 1938: x13.

64   "Reid Rates": 16.

65   "Reid Rates": x13.

66   "Twice-Postponed Welter Battle Goes on in Griffith Stadium," *Washington Post*, September 4, 1940: 24.

67   "15,000 Expected to See Griffith Stadium Bout," *Washington Post*, September 23, 1940: 17.

68   Tony Neri, "Joe Saw Opening, 'Hit Baer as Matter of Routine' in Sixth," *Washington Post*, May 24, 1941: 15.

69   Tony Neri, "Heavyweight Battle Heads Twice-Postponed Card at Griffith Stadium," *Washington Post*, August 16, 1942: SP2.

70   "Bomber Faces Cestac at Griffith Stadium," *Washington Post*, October 3, 1949: 11.

71   Lewis F. Atchison, "Bruns Meets Londos at Griffith Stadium," *Washington Post*, June 16, 1938: 21.

72   "Nanjo Singh Meets Dusek Thursday in Griffith Stadium," *Washington Post*, August 27, 1939: SP3.

73   Shirley Povich, "Kate Smith, 1st Lady of Radio, to Appear at War Bond Game," *Washington Post*, May 20, 1943: 1.

74   "Red Cross Begins Fund Program in Pro Ball Parks," *Spokane Review*, July 28, 1953.

75   "Tiny Whippet Will Race Here," *Washington Post*, May 17, 1927: 14.

76   "Masonic Festival Features Delight Crowd at Stadium," *Washington Post*, June 17, 1928: 2.

77   "High School Cadet Drills End Today," *Washington Post*, June 7, 1932: 18.

78   "Joint Field Day Held by Colored Elks," *Washington Post*, July 27, 1930: M2.

79   *10th Annual Night of Thrills, May 23, 1947, Souvenir Program, 14th Annual Night of Thrills, June 8, 1948, Souvenir Program, 15th Annual Night of Thrills, June 13, 1952, Souvenir Program, Night of Thrills, June 21st 1940, Souvenir Program, Night of Thrills, June 6, 1941, Souvenir Program.*

80   "200 Baptized By Rain, River and Michaux," *Washington Post*, October 4, 1937: 4.

81   "Billy Graham Predicts Christians' Persecution," *Washington Post*, June 27, 1960: B1.

82   "Thelma Griffith Haynes, 82, Baseball Owner," (obituary), *New York Times*, October 17, 1995.

83   "The Senators: Year By Year (1901-1965)," *The Senators 1966 Yearbook*: 55.

84   "Griffith Stadium," thisgreatgame.com/allparks-griffith-stadium.html (thisgreatgame.com/allparks-griffith-stadium.html), accessed October 1, 2016.

85   Chris Elzey and David K. Wiggins, ed. *DC Sports: The Nation's Capital at Play* (Fayetteville, Arkansas: The University of Arkansas Press, 2015), 30.

86   Brett L. Abrams, *Capital Sporting Grounds: A History of Stadium and Ballpark Construction in Washington, D.C.* (Jefferson, North Carolina: McFarland & Company, Inc., Publishers, 2008), 189-195.

87   Calvin R. Griffith, "Griffith Not Happy With Armory Stadium Site," *Washington Post*, January 15, 1958: A18.

88   Ibid.

89   Howard Sinker, "Recalling Calvin Griffith's Bigoted Outburst in Southern Minnesota," Minneapolis *Star Tribune*, April 2014, startribune.com/recalling-ex-twins-owner-griffith-s-bigoted-outburst/257189521/, accessed on December 8, 2016.

90   Dave Brady, "TV Writes Requiem to Griffith Stadium," *Washington Post*, November 11, 1964, Baseball Hall of Fame, Griffith Stadium file.

91   While in Washington in July 1965, I picked up two bricks from the rubble at Griffith Stadium. They remain proudly in my possession today as bookends.

92   Byron Bennett, "Griffith Stadium and the Site of D.C.'s First National Park," deadballbaseball.com/?=3073 (deadballbaseball.com/?p=3073), accessed August 20, 2016.

93   "Griffith Stadium," thisgreatgame.com/allparks-griffith-stadium.html (thisgreatgame.com/allparks-griffith-stadium.html), accessed October 1, 2016.

MINOR ROLES, MISATTRIBUTIONS, AND MYSTERY MEN:

PLAYERS OMITTED FROM THE ROSTERS AND THE RATIONALE FOR EACH INDIVIDUAL'S OMISSION

By Frederick C. Bush

Attempts to determine the rosters of both the teams featured in this book have turned up players who, based on exhaustive research, were not members of the Black Barons or Grays at all in 1948, or who spent only a brief time with their respective team and contributed little or nothing in league games that counted in the standings. There are also certain cases in which a player is so obscure that it is impossible to unearth any substantial information on him at all. Since different sources often provide somewhat different rosters for each team, an effort has been made to acknowledge those players who appear on some rosters but who have not been covered in this volume.

BIRMINGHAM BLACK BARONS:

Joe Bankhead

Joe Bankhead was born on September 8, 1926, in Empire, Alabama. The fourth of five Bankhead brothers who all played professional baseball, Joe had a brief stint as a pitcher with the Black Barons at the beginning of the 1948 season. He was released in May, at which time he said, "I wasn't given a chance by the Black Barons' management. I wasn't allowed to work a single inning of league play despite the fact we have played 12 games since the season opened."[1]

By June, Bankhead caught on with the Harlem Globe Trotters baseball team, for whom he posted a 5-4 record by the end of the season in early September.[2]

Joe Bankhead died on February 4, 1988, in Empire, Alabama.

Philip Edwards

Philip Edwards is found on the Black Barons' roster only on the Negro Southern League Museum Research Center's website.[3] Edwards was also referred to as a former Black Baron in an article about a June 2014 reunion in Birmingham of Negro League players.[4] Though almost nothing is known about Edwards—including whether or not he is still living—he may have served as a fill-in player on rare occasions when the Black Barons were at home and were short a player due to injury or illness. He did not participate in the World Series against the Homestead Grays.

Clarence "Pijo" King

Clarence Earl "Pijo" King was born on October 9, 1923, in Bessemer, Alabama. He was a two-sport star in baseball and football at Bessemer's Brighton High School. By 1942 King was playing in Birmingham's Industrial League for the Bessemer (U.S. Pipe) Mudcaps. A news article from that year noted, "King, who has yet to learn the art of hitting, is a fielding demon. He bears watching."[5]

King served in the US Army during World War II, and then returned to Birmingham.[6] There is, however, no evidence to support the idea that he was a member of the 1948 Birmingham Black Barons, though he is listed as a member of the team in *The Negro Leagues Book* and on the Negro Southern League Museum Research Center's website.[7] King did play alongside some members of the Black Barons when, as a member of the Birmingham All-Stars, he competed against the Atlanta Black Crackers in a doubleheader

CLARENCE "PIJO" KING

Clarence "Pijo" King was a rookie with the Birmingham Black Barons in 1950. He spent his final season with the Detroit Stars, where his manager was former 1948 Birmingham outfielder Ed Steele. (*Courtesy R. D. Retort Enterprises*)

on May 23, 1948.[8] Perhaps that fact that King played with the All-Stars inadvertently led to his being considered a member of the Black Barons as well.

On April 25, 1950, King was named in a *Birmingham World* article that previewed the Black Barons' coming four-game series at Rickwood Field. According to the *World*, "King, a rookie, seems to have won the utility assignment."[9] This account clearly marks 1950 as King's first season with the Black Barons. The timeline also confirms Bill Greason's recollection that King "played at least part of a season with the Barons."[10] Greason was a pitcher for the Black Barons from 1948 through 1951, but King left Birmingham to play in Canada in 1951; thus, since

King was not a member of the Black Barons in 1948-49, 1950 is the "part of a season" that Greason remembers.

King played for the Brandon Greys of the ManDak League in 1951, split the 1952 season between the Greys and the Black Barons, spent all of 1953 in Brandon, and returned to play in Birmingham in 1954. He finished his career in 1958 with the Detroit Stars, where his manager was Ed Steele, a former Black Barons outfielder from the 1948 team.

Clarence King died on September 11, 1993, in Birmingham, Alabama.

William Morgan

William "Sack" Morgan was a left-handed pitcher who is found on Birmingham's 1948 roster in numerous sources, including *The Biographical Encyclopedia of the Negro Baseball Leagues* and *The Negro Leagues Book*, which provide starting points for many Negro League researchers.[11]

Morgan is mentioned in conjunction with the Black Barons in a May 27, 1948, article in the *Atlanta Daily World*; however, he was named as the starting pitcher for the Atlanta Black Crackers in their coming game against Birmingham.[12] On July 4 Morgan was the starter for the Memphis Red Sox in the first game of a doubleheader against the Black Barons, which Birmingham won, 10-9.[13] Though he competed against Birmingham for two different teams in 1948, there is no verification that he ever played for the Black Barons.

In a tribute to Morgan after his death in September 1989, columnist Chico Renfro wrote, "He pitched his way off the sandlots into the Negro Major Leagues as a member of both the Atlanta Black Crackers and the Memphis Red Sox of the Negro American League."[14] No mention was made of Morgan playing for any other franchise.

Joe Wiley

Joe Wiley (a.k.a. Joe Wiley Jr.) is found on Birmingham's roster on the Negro Southern League Museum Research Center's website and on Baseball-Reference.com; the latter site lists Wiley as 1-for-3 at the plate for the Black Barons in 1948.[15] However, an article about Negro League player Alfred Pinkston, which also can be found on the Negro Southern League Museum's website, mentions Joe Wiley as a "new" acquisition for the New Orleans Creoles that season.[16] The Pinkston article again mentions third baseman Joe Wiley as a returning member of the 1949 Creoles.

New Orleans' preseason acquisition was still with the team late in 1948, as is attested by a *Times-Picayune* article that lists his name in a preview for the Creoles' game against the Newark Eagles on September 16.[17] The source for Baseball-Reference.com's batting line for Wiley is unknown, and no other available information points to Wiley playing elsewhere that year. There remains the slim possibility that he could have played in a single game for Birmingham while on loan to the team; in such a scenario the Black Barons would most likely have been shorthanded while visiting New Orleans to play a game (or series) against the Creoles.

Oddly, on July 5, 1952, a news brief stated, "Joe Wiley, top hitter with the Birmingham Black Barons of Baseball two years ago, has signed to play for the Albuquerque Dukes."[18] The newspaper reported that Wiley was a third baseman and was also "the second Negro player signed for the Duke nine in the past three weeks. The other was Herb Simpson, first baseman."[19]

The report is problematic because Wiley not only did not play for Birmingham in 1948, he also did not play for the team in 1950, which is the year in which, the article alleged, he had been a "top hitter with the Birmingham Black Barons." Herb "Briefcase" Simpson was the first black player signed by the Albuquerque Dukes. In an interview with Negro League historian Brent Kelley, Simpson mentioned, "Later on durin' the season, Albuquerque added another colored and one or two of the other teams had one."[20] However, Simpson did not mention Wiley by name, and Wiley does not appear on Albuquerque's 1948 roster on Baseball-Reference.com; therefore, it is

uncertain whether he was the other player mentioned by Simpson.[21]

Jay Wilson

Jay Wilson is listed as a third baseman and shortstop in *The Negro Leagues Book* and on the Negro Southern League Museum Research Center's website.[22] However, no evidence has been found to confirm that a player named Jay Wilson existed. There is the possibility of a typographical error having occurred in a news account or box score(s), since Artie Wilson played shortstop for the Black Barons in 1948; however, this is mere speculation and cannot be substantiated any more than Jay Wilson's existence can.

HOMESTEAD GRAYS

Garnett Bankhead

Garnett Bankhead was born on June 27, 1928, in Empire, Alabama. He was the youngest of the five baseball-playing Bankhead brothers—behind Fred, Dan, Sam, and Joe—and appears to have spent the first half of the 1948 season with the Grays. The fact that Sam Bankhead was a star shortstop for the Grays no doubt helped Garnett to get his stint with the team.

Garnett Bankhead was listed as a member of the team in numerous news articles, but no mention was made of his pitching in a game. In all likelihood, given the lack of game reports, Bankhead may only have pitched in nonleague games.

On August 14 it was reported that "Garnett Bankhead, Jr. has returned [to Empire, Alabama] from playing ball with the Homestead Grays."[23] No reason was given as to why Bankhead did not finish the season with Homestead, but it is clear that he did not take part in the World Series.

Garnett Bankhead died on September 15, 1991, in Detroit as a result of "a gunshot wound precipitated by an argument."[24] His older brother and former Grays teammate, Sam, had also been killed by a gunshot wound—on July 24, 1976, in Pittsburgh—after drinking too much and fighting with a friend.

William Bell Sr. (a.k.a. Willie Bell)

A 50-year-old pitcher named Willie Bell is listed on the roster of the 1948 Grays on Baseball-Reference.com, and he is credited with having pitched 3⅓ innings that season. The pitcher's name and age indicate that "Willie Bell" must have been William Bell Sr.; however, according to Riley, Bell last played for the Homestead Grays in 1932 and was the manager of the Newark Eagles in 1948.[25]

On August 6, 1948, the *Chicago Defender* reported that "Willie Bell [would be one of] the starting Grays twirlers" in the second game of a doubleheader against the New York Black Yankees at Washington's Griffith Stadium.[26] How the Newark Eagles' manager came to pitch a game for the Grays is unknown, but it appears that he may have logged his 3⅓ innings for Homestead on that day.

There is the possibility, though, that the "Willie Bell" listed in the paper as the starting pitcher against the Black Yankees was actually Willie Pope.

(?) Billings

A player with the last name Billings, whose first name is unknown, is listed on the Grays' roster in *The Negro Leagues Book*.[27] James Riley, in his *Biographical Encyclopedia*, lists Billings as a catcher, but states, "In 1946, the last season before Josh Gibson's death, Billings was one of the Grays' backup catchers."[28] Further research has turned up no evidence of a player named Billings on the 1948 Homestead Grays.

Ben Littles

Outfielder Ben Littles is listed as a member of the Homestead Grays in Riley's *Biographical Encyclopedia*; *The Negro Leagues Book* lists him as a member of both the Grays and the New York Black Yankees in 1948.[29]

In March of that year Littles was listed as one of the Black Yankees' "new faces" in a news article that previewed the team prior to its game against the Atlanta Black Crackers on Opening Day for Atlanta.[30] On July 3 he is found listed in the starting lineup for the Black Yankees in a game against the Kingston Colonials.[31]

Littles was still with New York at the end of the season in September, as the press reported, "The colorful Yankees are led by the fleetest outfield in the Negro league. It includes John Smith, Ben Littles, and Art Hefner."[32] While it is not out of the realm of possibility that Littles may have played for Homestead at some point in 1948, it is difficult to understand when that might have occurred, since news articles that span the course of the season all indicate that he was a member of the New York team.

A. Pope

The Negro Leagues Book lists an outfielder named A. Pope as a member of the Grays in 1948.[33] Further research has turned up no evidence of an A. Pope. Given the proximity of the letters "A" and "W" on a typewriter keyboard, this name was possibly a typographical error for W. Pope. The player in question would then be 1948 Grays pitcher Willie Pope, who sometimes also played in the outfield.

Dave Pope

The exclusion of Dave Pope from the roster of the 1948 Homestead Grays may be controversial to readers with prior knowledge of the 1948 Negro League World Series, since some contemporary news accounts claimed that he participated in some of the series' games. In spite of such reports, the evidence points to Dave's older brother, Willie, as the Pope who played for the Grays in the World Series.

The reasons to believe that Dave Pope was not a member of the 1948 Grays are as follows:

1) In an interview with Brent Kelley, Pope said that he spent only two-thirds of the 1946 season with the Grays before moving to the Pittsburgh Crawfords; he then recalled playing for the Farnham Pirates in Canada's Provincial League in 1948 and 1949 before signing with the Cleveland Indians in 1950.[34]

2) In 1952, much closer to the year in question, Pope told the *Pittsburgh Post-Gazette* that he had lasted only one month with the Grays in 1946 and also mentioned playing in Canada in 1948 and 1949.[35]

3) Dave Pope did not attend the September 10, 1988, ceremony at Pittsburgh's Three Rivers Stadium

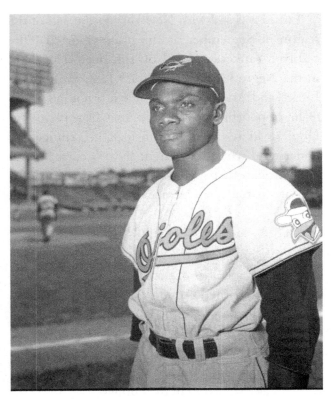

Dave Pope (here with the Baltimore Orioles) played briefly for Homestead in 1946, but news articles about his participation in the 1948 Negro League World Series appear to have confused him with his brother Willie. (*Negro League Baseball Museum, Kansas City, Missouri*)

in which the 1948 Homestead Grays' World Series championship was honored. Willie Pope, who was a Pittsburgh resident, was in attendance. Of course, it is possible that Dave Pope was unable to attend, but he was never named as one of the surviving members of the 1948 Grays, not even in a 1989 *Pittsburgh Press* article about his brother Willie.[36]

4) Lastly, John Klima, author of the book *Willie's Boys*, about the 1948 Birmingham Black Barons, undertook investigative research to put together an accurate account of the 1948 Negro League World Series from the sparse press material that is available. He, too, wanted to be sure that the correct Pope brother was credited for his role in the series. According to Klima, "I know I did a lot of reporting and asked a lot of the players if they were certain it was Willie or Dave and I do remember them all clarifying Willie, because he wasn't as good as Dave.

... One of my questions was to make sure Dave wasn't pretending to be Willie."[37]

Dave Pope did not get to play against Willie Mays in the 1948 Negro League World Series. In the 1954 major-league World Series, however, Pope and the Cleveland Indians were swept by former Birmingham Black Baron Willie Mays and the New York Giants.

Ramon Sosa

The April 10, 1948, edition of the *Pittsburgh Courier* contained the following paragraph about Homestead's catchers for the coming season:

"Behind the bat will be Euthumn Napier and Robert Gaston. To help out, Ramon Sosa was recently obtained from the Mariaona [*sic*] team, a member of the Cuban Winter League. Sosa won the Cuban Batting Championship in 1946 and should prove a lot of help in the Grays bid for the pennant this year."[38]

Riley clearly was familiar with the *Courier*'s article; its content comprises the majority of the entry about Sosa in his *Biographical Encyclopedia*. Sosa is also listed on the Grays' roster in *The Negro Leagues Book*.[39]

In fact, there was a Cuban catcher named Sosa who played for Homestead in 1948, but subsequent news reports referred to him as "Victor" (or simply "Vic") Sosa. One such article in the May 14 edition of the *Harrisburg Evening News* mentioned "Victor Sosa, a Cuban who has been a credit to the Grays this year as a snappy receiver."[40]

The first name "Victor" led to the true identity of Homestead's catcher and exposed some misinformation that had been propagated, perhaps via the Grays' front office. His name was Victoriano Sosa, and he had played for Cuba's Cerro franchise in the 1946 Summer League season, which was his lone season to play in any Cuban league; there is no evidence that he was the batting champion in 1946.[41]

Napier and Gaston received the lion's share of the playing time at catcher, which means that Sosa was likely relegated to playing in nonleague games. The only available statistics show Sosa with an 0-for-3 batting line in 1948; this may have been his only appearance in a league game.[42] It is unknown whether or not Sosa spent the entire season with Homestead.

Author's Note

Throughout this article, and others in this volume, today's researchers have expressed their indebtedness to two pioneering works, both published in 1994. More than 20 years later, both James A. Riley's *The Biographical Encyclopedia of the Negro Baseball Leagues* and Dick Clark and Larry Lester's *The Negro Leagues Book* remain invaluable aids to Negro League researchers. Further research over the past two decades, such as subsequent oral histories, the greater availability of digitized newspapers, and the compilation of more comprehensive databases, have enabled us to present additional, and sometimes different information today.

In spite of modern technology, local libraries and newspaper archive departments are often still the best—and sometimes still the only—way to obtain information about obscure subjects such as lesser-known Negro League players. There remains the possibility that further information about the players discussed in this article may yet be found that would shed light on their lives and careers.

Acknowledgments

The author wishes to thank fellow SABR researchers William J. "Bill" Plott, Margaret Gripshover and Joseph "Jeb" Stewart for uncovering additional information that helped to verify the conclusions reached about Joe Bankhead, William Bell Sr. and Clarence "Pijo" King in this article.

NOTES

1 "Hurler Joe Bankhead Given Release by Black Barons," *Birmingham World*, May, 18, 1948.

2 "Flemings Face Harlem Team Here Next Sunday Afternoon," *Palladium-Item* (Richmond, Indiana), September 5, 1948:11. Owner Abe Saperstein's basketball team was known as the Harlem Globetrotters; however, this news article spelled his baseball team's name as "Globe Trotters."

3 negrosouthernleaguemuseumresearchcenter.org/Portals/0/ Birmingham%20Black%20Barons/Rosters%20-%20 Birmingham%20Black%20Barons-1940-1949.pdf, accessed January 15, 2017.

4 al.com/sports/index.ssf/2014/06/fifth_annual_black_baseball_re.html, accessed January 15, 2017.

5 Emory O. Jackson, "Hits and Bits," *Atlanta Daily World*, August 13, 1942: 5.

6 Larry Powell, *Black Barons of Birmingham: The South's Greatest Negro League Team and Its Players* (Jefferson, North Carolina: McFarland & Company, 2009), 87.

7 Dick Clark and Larry Lester, *The Negro Leagues Book* (Cleveland: Society for American Baseball Research, 1994), 144.

8 "Black Crax, B'ham All-Stars in Doublebill Today: Heated Tilts Set for Poncey Park," *Atlanta Daily World*, May 23, 1948: 7.

9 "Black Barons Set for Series of Games," *Birmingham World*, April, 25, 1950: 4.

10 Bryan Steverson, email to the author, January 13, 2017. Steverson, a Birmingham resident and author of the book *Baseball: A Special Gift from God*, provided research assistance by making inquiries (often of former Black Baron Reverend Bill Greason) about different issues surrounding the 1948 Birmingham team.

11 James A. Riley, *The Biographical Encyclopedia of the Negro Baseball Leagues* (New York: Carroll & Graf Publishers, Inc., 1994), 568; Clark and Lester, 144.

12 "Black Crackers and Black Barons Clash Tonight," *Atlanta Daily World*, May 27, 1948: 5.

13 "Birmingham Black Barons Trip Memphis Red Sox in Twinbill," *Atlanta Daily World*, July 6, 1948: 5.

14 Chico Renfro, "Sports of the World," *Atlanta Daily World*, September 21, 1989: 6.

15 baseball-reference.com/register/player.fcgi?id=wiley-002joe, accessed March 1, 2017.

16 negrosouthernleaguemuseumresearchcenter.org/Portals/0/ Hero/Alfred-Pinkston-Single-Pages-1.pdf, accessed February 24, 2017.

17 "Creoles, Eagles to Meet Tonight," *New Orleans Times-Picayune*, September 16, 1948: 23.

18 "Dukes Sign Second Negro Ball Player," *Albuquerque Journal*, July 5, 1952: 8.

19 Ibid.

20 Brent Kelley, *The Negro Leagues Revisited: Conversations with 66 More Baseball Heroes* (Jefferson, North Carolina: McFarland & Company, Inc., 2000), 152-53.

21 baseball-reference.com/register/team.cgi?id=2ee0006c, accessed February 24, 2017.

22 Clark and Lester, 144.

23 "Empire," *Chicago Defender*, August 14, 1948: 19.

24 Riley, 52.

25 Riley, 74-75.

26 "Grays Oppose Yanks Today," *Chicago Defender*, August 6, 1948: C3.

27 Clark and Lester, 145.

28 Riley, 83.

29 Riley, 486; Clark and Lester, 145.

30 "Black Crackers, Black Yankees Clash Here Sunday: Easter Exhibition Tilt at Poncey Park," *Atlanta Daily World*, March 25, 1948: 5.

31 "Starting Lineups: Colonials vs. Black Yankees," *Kingston* (New York) *Daily Freeman*, July 3, 1948: 7.

32 "Pelicans Meet Black Yankees in Final Game," *Asbury Park* (New Jersey) *Press*, September 2, 1948: 15.

33 Clark and Lester, 145.

34 Kelley, 209.

35 Jimmy Jordan, "Library's Dave Pope Ready to Make Big Bid for Cleveland Indian Berth," *Pittsburgh Post-Gazette,* October 24, 1952: 23.

36 Kelly Carter, "Standing Out: Willie Pope Nearly Made It to the Majors," *Pittsburgh Press*, February 27, 1989: A2.

37 John Klima, email to the author, December 17, 2015.

38 "Pittsburgh Opener Set for April 29; Outfield Has Power," *Pittsburgh Courier*, April 10, 1948: 15.

39 Riley, 731; Clark and Lester, 145.

40 "Cubans to Meet Homestead Here," *Harrisburg Evening News,* May 14, 1948: 24.

41 Jorge S. Figueredo, *Cuban Baseball: A Statistical History, 1878–1961* (Jefferson, North Carolina: McFarland & Company, Inc., 2003), 272-73.

42 baseball-reference.com/register/player.cgi?id=sosa—002ram, accessed January 15, 2017.

THE 1948 EAST-WEST ALL-STAR GAMES

By Thomas E. Kern

Overview

The origins of the Negro League All-Star Game date from 1933 when sportswriters Roy Sparrow of the *Pittsburgh Sun-Telegraph* and Bill Nunn of the *Pittsburgh Courier* championed the idea. Not coincidentally, their brainchild surfaced around the same time as the inaugural major-league All-Star game, which was to be held at Chicago's Comiskey Park in conjunction with the 1933 World's Fair. A series of events guided by Gus Greenlee, owner of the Pittsburgh Crawfords and president of the Negro National League, resulted in a deal with Robert "King" Cole, the owner of the Chicago American Giants, to lease Comiskey Park for the first East-West All-Star Game, to take place on September 10.[1] The 1933 game kicked off an amazing run of contests that paralleled—and sometimes outdrew—the games of their white major-league counterparts. Single all-star games were played through the 1938 season; later, tandem games were played in 1939, 1942, 1946, 1947, 1948, and 1958. Even as the Negro Leagues began their decline in the wake of Organized Baseball's integration, the East-West All Star Game continued to be an annual event until 1962.[2]

According to author Larry Lester, "[T]he span beginning in 1933 and ending in 1953, alpha to omega, Genesis to Revelation, signals the most celebrated period in black baseball history." Then "the demise of the black leagues became predictable, as the younger talented blacks were soon signed into the former white leagues. By the mid-1950s, the [Negro] leagues went from show time to burlesque. They had become a circus. ..."[3] The last Negro League-sanctioned All-Star Game was held in 1961; the final game was played in 1962, the year the Negro American League was shuttered for good.

According to baseball-reference, "thirty-six games were played in the 30 consecutive seasons that the game was active. Twenty-eight games were played at Chicago's Comiskey Park, four at New York's Yankee Stadium, while one each were played at New York's Polo Grounds, Washington's Griffith Stadium, Cleveland's Municipal Stadium and Kansas City's Municipal Stadium. Some of the East-West Games held outside of Comiskey Park were not consistently referred to in the media as the East-West Game—for instance, the eastern matches from 1946-1948 were officially called the 'Dream Game,' though some outlets referred to them as East-West Games."[4]

The 1948 East-West All-Star Games: The Players

On July 31, 1948, the *Chicago Defender* announced the selection of the players for the All-Star Game: three from each team in the two six-team leagues. The *Defender* wrote, "[T]he Negro American League club owners have decided on the players who will represent them in the 16th Annual East v. West game to be played at Comiskey Park, Sunday afternoon [August 22, 1948]. ... A second game between the East and West teams, called the 'Dream Game' will be played in New York that week [August 24, 1948]." Most previous teams were selected by vote of the leagues' fans, but, wrote the *Defender*, "The Negro National League voted against this method, preferring to make their own selections."[5] On August 15 the *Chicago Tribune* printed rosters for the first game, but the game's box score showed additional names that had not been noted by the *Tribune*; additionally, some of the players listed by the paper did not play and may not have appeared at the game at all.[6]

A composite list of players either earmarked by the *Tribune* article to play in the first game or whose names appeared in the box scores of either game follows. Seventeen players were listed in the box scores of both games.

Negro American League Players

Pitchers
- Chet Brewer, Cleveland Buckeyes (game 1)
- Vibert Ernesto Clarke, Cleveland Buckeyes (game 2)
- James "Fireball" Cohen, Indianapolis Clowns (game 2)
- Gentry "Jeep" Jessup, Chicago American Giants (game 1)
- James Lamarque, Kansas City Monarchs (both games)
- Verdel Mathis, Memphis Red Sox (game 1)
- Bill Powell, Birmingham Black Barons (game 1)
- Roberto Enrique Vargas, Chicago American Giants (game 2)

Catchers
- Lloyd "Pepper" Bassett, Birmingham Black Barons (game 2)
- Sam Hairston, Indianapolis Clowns (game 1)
- Quincy Trouppe, Chicago American Giants (both games)

Infielders
- Robert "Bob" Boyd, Memphis Red Sox (both games)
- Lorenzo "Piper" Davis, Birmingham Black Barons (both games)
- Leon Kellman, Cleveland Buckeyes (both games)
- Ray Neil, Indianapolis Clowns (listed by the *Tribune*, but did not appear in game 1)
- Herb Souell, Kansas City Monarchs (both games)
- Arthur Lee "Artie" Wilson, Birmingham Black Barons (both games)

Outfielders
- Willard "Homerun" Brown, Kansas City Monarchs (both games)

- Jose Colas, Memphis Red Sox (Listed in the *Tribune* for game 1, but did not play; played in game 2)
- Willie "Fireman" Grace, Cleveland Buckeyes (Listed in the *Tribune* for game 1, but did not play; played in game 2)
- Samuel "Sam" Hill, Chicago American Giants (both games)
- Cornelius "Neal" or "Shadow" Robinson, Memphis Red Sox (played in game 1, but was not listed by the *Tribune*)

Extra Players
- Ernest "Spoon" Carter, Memphis Red Sox (pinch-runner) (game 2)
- Sam Hairston, Indianapolis Clowns (pinch-hitter) (game 2)
- (The Indianapolis Clowns identified "King Tut" as their third participant. King Tut was the Clowns' "comedian.")
- Manager, Quincy Trouppe, Chicago American Giants

Negro National League Players

Pitchers
- Dave "Impo" Barnhill, New York Cubans (game 2)
- Joe Black, Baltimore Elite Giants (game 2)
- Wilmer Fields, Washington Homestead Grays (played in game 1, but was not listed by the *Tribune*)
- Robert "Schoolboy" Griffith, New York Black Yankees (game 1)
- Rufus "Mississippi" Lewis, Newark Eagles (game 1)
- Max Manning, Newark Eagles (game 2)
- Henry Miller, Philadelphia Stars (game 1)
- Robert Romby, Baltimore Elite Giants (game 1)
- Patricio Scantlebury, New York Cubans (Listed by the *Tribune*, but did not appear in game 1)

Catchers
- William "Ready" Cash, Philadelphia Stars (both games)
- Louis Oliver "Tommy" Louden, New York Cubans (both games)

Infielders
- Frank "Pee Wee" Austin, Philadelphia Stars (both games)
- Thomas "Pee Wee" Butts, Baltimore Elite Giants (game 1)
- George "Big George" Crowe, New York Black Yankees (game 2)
- James "Junior" Gilliam, Baltimore Elite Giants (both games)
- Buck Leonard, Washington Homestead Grays (game 1)
- Orestes "Minnie" Minoso, New York Cubans (both games)

Outfielders
- Lucius "Luke" Easter, Washington Homestead Grays (both games)
- Robert "Bob" Harvey, Newark Eagles (game 1)
- Monte Irvin, Newark Eagles (game 1)
- Lester Lockett, Baltimore Elite Giants (both games)
- Luis Marquez, Washington Homestead Grays (both games)
- James "Seabiscuit" Wilkes, Newark Eagles (game 2)

Extra Players
- Marvin "Hank" Barker, New York Black Yankees (pinch-hitter in game 2)
- Manager, Jose Fernandez, New York Black Yankees; Coaches, Vic Harris, Washington Homestead Grays, and Marvin Barker, New York Black Yankees

Memphis Red Sox pitcher Verdell Mathis stands to the left of Birmingham Black Barons Artie Wilson, Piper Davis, and Bill Powell in the West dugout during the 1948 East-West All-Star Game at Comiskey Park. *(Withers Family Trust, Memphis, Tennessee)*

Game One: Sunday, August 22, 1948, at Comiskey Park, Chicago

Led by the pitching trio of Bill Powell of the Birmingham Black Barons, James LaMarque of the Kansas City Monarchs, and Gentry Jessup of the Chicago American Giants, the West defeated the East in a 3-0 shutout. It was the first time the East had been shut out since the inception of the All-Star Game in 1933. Each of the three West All-Star pitchers hurled three innings, holding the East to a total of three hits, one of which was a double by the 40-year-old Buck Leonard. None of the East's baserunners managed to make it as far as third base. Powell's three shutout innings to start the game gave him the win.

Rufus Lewis started the game well for the East by striking out the side in the first inning. However, he gave up three hits and a walk in the second, allowing the West to score two runs. Willard Brown, a future Hall of Famer who had a cup of coffee in the major leagues with the St. Louis Browns in 1947, opened the frame with a single, which was followed by Bob Boyd's base hit to left field. Neal Robinson drove in Brown with another single; Luke Easter's throw to the plate was wild, and allowed Boyd and Robinson to move to third and second. Quincy Trouppe was intentionally walked to load the bases. Boyd then scored on a groundball to second.. Lewis's poor inning and a lack of run scoring by the East tagged him with the loss.

The damage in the second inning could have been worse, but, as Bill Nunn of the *Pittsburgh Courier* recounted:

"[A]n unusual double play allowed Lewis to escape further damage in this inning. Bill Powell hit a ground ball to James Gilliam on second. Gilliam's throw to the plate was in time to trap Robinson between third and home; He was out when William Cash, the East's catcher, threw to Orestes Minoso at third and the latter made the putout. Minoso then turned and touched Trouppe who was caught off second."[7]

The West's third and final run came in the eighth inning against Robert Griffith of the New York Black Yankees. The *Indianapolis Star* reported, "Piper Davis, West second baseman from Birmingham, opened with a double. Brown singled as Davis stopped at third before scoring on Boyd's fly."[8]

The East's only hits were Junior Gilliam's second-inning single off Powell (Gilliam was thrown out trying to steal second), Leonard's double in the fourth (deflecting off first baseman Boyd's glove), and Minoso's infield single in the sixth. Both of the latter hits were off James LaMarque, the Monarchs' pitcher.

The *Courier's* Nunn wrote, "[F]rom where we sat in the press box row, it appeared to be a very dull game, as the East was able to get only one man as far as second." Nunn may have reconsidered as he watched the ninth inning, noting that "Robinson raced back 365 feet into left center field … and literally climbed the concrete wall as he robbed Minoso of a sure-fire triple."[9] After that gem, Lester Lockett walked, then the game ended when Buck Leonard grounded into a 4-6-3 double play.

Game One Box Score

East	AB	R	H	2B	3B	HR	RBI	E
Marquez (Grays), cf	4	0	0	0	0	0	0	0
Minoso (Cubans), 3b	4	0	1	0	0	0	0	0
Easter (Grays), lf	0	0	0	0	0	0	0	1
Lockett (Elite Giants), lf	2	0	0	0	0	0	0	0
Leonard (Grays), 1b	4	0	1	1	0	0	0	0
Harvey (Eagles), rf	1	0	0	0	0	0	0	0
Irvin (Eagles), rf	2	0	0	0	0	0	0	0
Gilliam (Elite Giants), 2b	3	0	1	0	0	0	0	0
Louden (Cubans), c	3	0	0	0	0	0	0	0
Cash (Stars), c	0	0	0	0	0	0	0	0
Butts (Elite Giants), ss	2	0	0	0	0	0	0	0
Austin (Stars), ss	1	0	0	0	0	0	0	1
Lewis (Eagles), p	1	0	0	0	0	0	0	0
Fields (Grays), p	1	0	0	0	0	0	0	0
Griffith (Black Yankees), p	1	0	0	0	0	0	0	0
Team Totals	29	0	3	1	0	0	0	2

West	AB	R	H	2B	3B	HR	RBI	E
Wilson (Black Barons), ss	3	0	0	0	0	0	0	0
Souell (Monarchs), 3b	4	0	0	0	0	0	0	0
Davis (Black Barons), 2b	3	1	1	1	0	0	0	0
Brown (Monarchs), cf	4	1	2	0	0	0	0	0
Boyd (Red Sox), 1b	4	1	2	0	0	0	1	1
Robinson (Red Sox), lf	3	0	1	0	0	0	1	0
Trouppe (American Giants), c	3	0	0	0	0	0	0	0
Hill (American Giants), rf	3	0	0	0	0	0	1	0
Powell (Black Barons), p	1	0	0	0	0	0	0	0
LaMarque (Monarchs), p	1	0	0	0	0	0	0	0
Jessup (American Giants), p	1	0	1	0	0	0	0	0
Team Totals	30	3	7	1	0	0	3	1

Pitcher	GS	IP	H	R	ER	K	BB	WP	W	L	SV
Lewis	1	3	3	2	2	4	2	0	0	1	0
Fields		3	1	0	0	2	1	0	0	0	0
Griffith		2	3	1	1	2	1	0	0	0	0
Powell	1	3	1	0	0	2	1	1	1	0	0
LaMarque		3	2	0	0	1	0	0	0	0	0
Jessup		3	0	0	0	1	1	0	0	0	1

	1	2	3	4	5	6	7	8	9	R	H	E
East	0	0	0	0	0	0	0	0	0	0	3	2
West	0	2	0	0	0	0	0	1	x	3	7	1

WP: Bill Powell (Birmingham Black Barons). LP: Rufus Lewis (Newark Eagles). LOB: East 4, West 6. Attendance: 42,099. Game time: 2:19.[10]

Game Two: Tuesday, August 24, 1948, at Yankee Stadium, New York

The East-West All-Star Game had its roots in Chicago and Comiskey Park, starting in 1933, and a total of 28 All-Star Games, including the first of two in 1948, had been played there. The game was held at Yankee Stadium twice, first as the second of a two-game series in 1939 and again for the second game in 1948. It was called the Dream Game when it was played in the East. According to the *New York Amsterdam News*, "Alex Pompez, a New York sportsman and owner of the New York Cubans, is chairman of the [Dream Team] committee because he did such a magnificent job last year [at the Polo Grounds] in handling the affair in such a grand manner."[11] Such accolades were afforded to Pompez because the 1947 Dream Game drew 38,402, the best attendance recorded for any East-West game outside of Comiskey Park.

The West scored first in Game Two just as it had in the first game at Comiskey Park. Sam Hill of the Chicago American Giants walked in the top of the third and stole second. Hill took third on a grounder by Vibert Clarke and scored on a single by Artie Wilson of the Birmingham Black Barons.

Held scoreless in Chicago two days earlier, the East squad got on the board in a big way at Yankee Stadium by scoring three runs in the bottom of the third off Vibert Clarke, the eventual losing pitcher.

The annual East-West All-Star Game at Comiskey Park in Chicago, Illinois, was the biggest event of the Negro League season and, during its heyday, attendance at the game was well in excess of 40,000 spectators. (*National Baseball Hall of Fame, Cooperstown, New York*)

Frank Austin of the Philadelphia Stars singled and then came home on the first and only home run of the two 1948 All-Star Games. According to the *New York Times*, Luis Marquez, center fielder of the Homestead Grays, tagged a 330-foot shot into the lower right-field stands to establish a 2-0 East lead. Minnie Minoso of the New York Cubans followed with a double and scored on a single to left field by Lester Lockett of the Baltimore Elite Giants.

The West was to score no more, but as the *Chicago Defender* reported:

"[T]he East added one more in the fourth. George Crowe, New York Black Yankees, singled off Jim Cohen of the Indianapolis Clowns. Herb Souell, Kansas City Monarchs, bobbled Frank Austin's grounder and Crowe went to second. Cash singled Crowe to third and Dave "Impo" Barnhill, New York Cuban hurler who wasn't even with the East nine in the Chicago game, was an infield out, Crowe scoring."[12]

Crowe and Junior Gilliam figured in the final runs scored—two East tallies in the bottom of the eighth—when they both singled and later scored on an error by Cleveland Buckeyes third baseman Leon Kellmann.

The West used four pitchers in the contest, with Clarke throwing three innings and giving up three runs (all earned) to take the loss. He was followed by Jim Cohen of the Clowns (two innings pitched and one run surrendered), Roberto Vargas of the Chicago American Giants (one inning pitched, no runs allowed), and Jim LaMarque of the Monarchs (two innings pitched, two unearned runs given up).

The East threw Max Manning of the Newark Eagles, Dave Barnhill of the New York Cubans, and Joe Black of the Baltimore Elite Giants. Each pitcher tossed three innings, with Manning getting the win.[13]

Before the game the *New York Amsterdam News* had written that the game was expected to draw a crowd of about 40,000.[14] As it turned out, fewer than 18,000 attended, the lowest All-Star Game attendance outside of two games that had been played in Cleveland and Washington.

Game Two Box Score

West	AB	R	H	2B	3B	HR	RBI	E
Wilson (Black Barons), ss	4	0	3	0	0	0	1	0
Souell (Monarchs), 3b	3	0	0	0	0	0	0	1
Carter (Red Sox), pr	0	0	0	0	0	0	0	0
Vargas (American Giants), p	0	0	0	0	0	0	0	0
LaMarque (Monarchs), p	0	0	0	0	0	0	0	0
a) Hairston (Clowns), ph	1	0	0	0	0	0	0	0
Davis (Black Barons), 2b	4	0	0	0	0	0	0	0
Brown (Monarchs), cf	3	0	0	0	0	0	0	0
Boyd (Red Sox), 1b	3	0	0	0	0	0	0	0
Grace (Buckeyes), lf	3	0	1	0	0	0	0	1
Hill (American Giants), rf	2	1	0	0	0	0	0	0
Bassett (Black Barons), c	2	0	0	0	0	0	0	0
Trouppe (American Giants), c	1	0	0	0	0	0	0	0
Clarke (Black Buckeyes), p	1	0	0	0	0	0	0	0
Cohen (Clowns), p	0	0	0	0	0	0	0	0
b) Colas (Red Sox), ph	1	0	1	0	0	0	0	0
Kellman (Buckeyes), 3b	1	0	0	0	0	0	0	1
Team Totals	29	1	5	0	0	0	1	3

a) Batted for Lamarque in 9th
b) Batted for Cohen in 6th

East	AB	R	H	2B	3B	HR	RBI	E
Marquez (Grays), cf-rf	5	1	1	0	0	1	2	0
Minoso (Cubans), 3b	2	1	2	2	0	0	0	0
Lockett (Elite Giants), lf	4	0	1	0	0	0	1	0
Easter (Grays), lf	4	0	0	0	0	0	0	0
Wilkes (Eagles), cf	0	0	0	0	0	0	0	0
Crowe (Black Yankees), 1b	4	2	2	0	0	0	0	0
Gilliam (Elite Giants), 2b	3	1	1	0	0	0	0	0
Austin (Stars), ss	3	0	2	0	0	0	0	0
Cash (Stars), c	3	1	1	0	0	0	0	0
Louden (Cubans), c	1	0	0	0	0	0	0	0
Manning (Eagles), p	0	0	0	0	0	0	0	0
c) Barker (Black Yankees), ph	1	0	0	0	0	0	0	0

Barnhill (Cubans), p	1	0	0	0	0	0	1	0
Black (Elite Giants), p	1	0	0	0	0	0	0	0
Team Totals	32	6	10	2	0	1	4	0

c) Batted for Manning in the 3rd

Pitcher	GS	IP	H	R	ER	K	BB	WP	W	L	SV
Clarke	1	3	4	3	3	1	1	0	0	1	0
Cohen	2	3	1	0	0	1	0	0	0	0
Vargas	1	0	0	0	0	1	0	0	0	0
LaMarque	2	3	2	0	0	2	0	0	0	0
Manning	1	3	1	1	1	2	1	1	0	0	0
Barnhill		3	2	0	0	1	0	0	0	0	0
Black		3	2	0	0	0	0	0	0	0	1

	1	2	3	4	5	6	7	8	9	R	H	E
West	0	0	1	0	0	0	0	0	0	1	5	3
East	0	0	3	1	0	0	0	2	x	6	10	0

WP: Max Manning (Newark Eagles). LP: Vibert Clarke (Cleveland Buckeyes). LOB: West 2, East 7. Attendance: 17,928. Game time: 2:18.[15]

All-Star Players: The Negro League World Series, the Major Leagues, and the Hall of Fame

Players from the Homestead Grays and Birmingham Black Barons, the two teams that ended up in the 1948 Negro League World Series, did not figure all that prominently in either game. The exceptions were two Birmingham players: Game One's winning pitcher, Bill Powell, and Artie Wilson, who went 3-for-4 in the West's Game Two loss. Players from the two eventual World Series teams collected six of the 25 hits in the two games.

Of the 48 players identified either by the *Chicago Tribune* or ultimately appearing in the box score for one or both of the All-Star Games, 15 eventually played in the major leagues. All of them appeared in Game Two; this was the largest single number of Negro Leaguers who became future (or past, when including Willard Brown, who played for the Browns in 1947) major leaguers to play together in a single East-West All-Star Game.[16]

The 15 players and the major-league teams for which they played are:

1. Willard Brown, St. Louis Browns, debuted July 19, 1947 (cut by the Browns and returned to the Kansas City Monarchs after 21 games)
2. Minnie Minoso, Cleveland Indians, April 19, 1949
3. Monte Irvin, New York Giants, July 8, 1949
4. Luke Easter, Cleveland Indians, August 11, 1949
5. Luis Marquez, Boston Braves, April 18, 1951
6. Artie Wilson, New York Giants, April 18, 1951
7. Sam Hairston, Chicago White Sox, July 21, 1951
8. Bob Boyd, Chicago White Sox, September 8, 1951
9. George Crowe, Boston Braves, April 16, 1952
10. Quincy Trouppe, Cleveland Indians, April 30, 1952
11. Joe Black, Brooklyn Dodgers, May 1, 1952
12. Junior Gilliam, Brooklyn Dodgers, April 14, 1953

13. Roberto Vargas, Milwaukee Braves, April 17, 1955

14. Vibert Clarke, Washington Senators, September 4, 1955

15. Pat Scantlebury, Cincinnati Redlegs, April 19, 1956

Three players in the two games were inducted into the National Baseball Hall of Fame: Buck Leonard, Monte Irvin, and Willard Brown.

Conclusion: The Beginning of the End for Negro League Baseball

Though Larry Lester has identified the heyday of the East-West All-Star Games as spanning from their inception in 1933 to the early 1950s, several compelling storylines emerged during and immediately after the 1948 games that affirmed the lesser role the Negro Leagues played relative to major-league baseball and indicated the writing was on the wall for the All-Star Games and the Negro leagues as a whole.

The ticket from the August 24 game made it clear which league had superiority in the pecking order between the Negro and major leagues. On it was written:

"The Colored All-Star Game Dream Game is scheduled to be played on the Night of August 24th. In the event of RAIN it will be played on the Night of August 25th. In the event the Yankee-Chicago game scheduled for the Night of August 23rd is rained out, the game will be played on August 24th, thereby postponing the All-Star Game to the Night of August 25th."[17]

Although not surprising, the casual notation reminds all of the stark inequality of an earlier era, or at least who controlled the pocketbook.

The August 28 edition of the *Chicago Defender* noted:

"Baseball fans and the general public are blaming the slump in the East versus West game attendance to politics and ticket scalping. Last year 48,112 watched the classic.

Sunday 42,099 was the attendance although it was reported a few minutes before as 37,099. Leroy "Satchel" Paige drew 51,000 in the same park on Friday night August 13th. On that night fully 15,000 were unable to get inside the park. Sunday, at the East vs. West game there weren't 15,000 on the outside."

The article went on to assert that the Republican Party took over the pregame ceremonies and kept away droves of Democratic supporters. Exorbitant ticket prices and ticket scalping also drove away cost-conscious fans.[18] As a result, the game's showcase lost its luster.

The *Defender's* Satchel Paige reference spoke to a larger issue facing the Negro Leagues: the beginning of the exodus of its better players to Organized Baseball. In fact, Paige had pitched on Friday, August 20, in Cleveland before 78,383 fans. The *Indianapolis Star* wrote, "Ageless Satchel Paige shut out the Chicago White Sox with three hits last night. ... The fabulous Negro hurler now has won all three of his major league starts and has a season record of five victories and only one loss. A total of 201,829 customers have jammed their way into the stands to watch Paige in his three major league starts."[19]

On September 4, the *Defender* reported:

"[T]he crowd was asked to stand in silent tribute to the late George Herman "Babe" Ruth [Ruth had died on August 16, eight days earlier]. No mention was made of the last Negro baseball men's death — namely Josh Gibson [January 20, 1947], hero of many an East vs. West game; Candy Jim Taylor, manager of the East nine and of the Chicago American Giants [April 3, 1948]; Cum Posey, Homestead Grays and former secretary of the Negro National League [March 28, 1946]. Maybe they didn't amount to much in the eyes of the owners and promoters of the game but baseball fans wondered why."[20]

The lack of respect accorded to the Negro Leagues was only partially mitigated by the slowly increasing number of its players who were afforded an opportunity to play in the minor or major leagues. The breaking of the color barrier brought about conflicted feelings within the African-American community about Negro League baseball, its role, and its future.

In an editorial titled "Don't Let Negro Baseball Die!" a writer for the *Pittsburgh Courier* wrote:

"I pride myself on being a staunch supporter of Satchel Paige, Jackie Robinson, Larry Doby, and Roy Campanella. I'm praying that Don Newcombe, Dan Bankhead, and Sammy Jethro[e] get major league calls next year, but—for God's sake, fans, don't let Negro baseball die! ... The way I see it, Negro fans are doing Negro baseball, future Negro stars and potential major leaguers a great injustice by withdrawing their support. For if the Negro teams are forced to curtail their activities due to inability to meet expenses, the hopes of hundreds of Negro aspirants for major league careers will be doomed. How will major league scouts be able to look over Negro material if there are no Negro teams playing?"[21]

Though Organized Baseball's pilfering of the best black talent resulted in the gradual demise of the Negro Leagues, there is no doubt that baseball's integration made both the nation and its national pastime better entities.

NOTES

1   Cum Posey, "Posey's Points," *Pittsburgh Courier*, August 15, 1942: 16.

2   baseball-reference.com/bullpen/East-West_Game.

3   Larry Lester, *Black Baseball's National Showcase: The East-West All-Star Game, 1933–1953* (Lincoln: University of Nebraska Press, 2001), 375.

4   baseball-reference.com/bullpen/East-West_Game.

5   "West Selects Players for Big Game Aug. 22," *Chicago Defender*, July 31, 1948.

6   "Nines Picked to Compete in Negro Contest," *Chicago Tribune*, August 15, 1948: 62.

7   Bill Nunn Jr., "West Wins 6th Straight over East, 3-0," *Pittsburgh Courier*, August 28, 1948: 10.

8   "West Wins Negro All Star Tilt," *Indianapolis Star*, August 23, 1948: 23.

9   Nunn.

10 Lester, 313.

11 "3rd Annual All Star Game at Stadium," *New York Amsterdam News*, August 14, 1948, quoted in Lester, 314.

12 "Second East versus West Game Draws 17,928," *Chicago Defender*, September 4, 1948, quoted in Lester, 315.

13 Ibid.

14 Swig Garlington, "40,000 Expected at Dream Game," *New York Amsterdam News*, August 21, 1948, quoted in Lester, 314.

15 Lester, 321.

16 Lester, 455-456.

17 Lester, 319.

18 Morgan Holsey, "Scalpers and Politicians Mar East-West Game," *Chicago Defender*, August 28, 1948.

19 "78,382 Fans See Paige Pitch Another Cleveland Shutout," *Indianapolis Star*, August 21, 1948: 16.

20 "Second East versus West Game Draws 17,928."

21 "Don't Let Negro Baseball Die," *Pittsburgh Courier*, September 4, 1948: 10.

THE 1948 NEGRO AMERICAN LEAGUE PLAYOFF SERIES

By Japheth Knopp

Background: Opening Day, May 16, 1948, Kansas City, Missouri

Opening Day in Kansas City was traditionally a highlight of the black social calendar, and 1948 promised to be "the biggest opening in the history of the Kansas City club."[1] A mile-long parade, starting on 18th Street and meandering through the black business district, was planned and featured more than a dozen different groups including a police escort, Kansas State Guard troops, Boy Scouts, local ROTC units, a drum and bugle corps, marching bands, Elks, and the Monarchs Boosters and Band. Also included in the pregame festivities was a "Miss Bathing Beauty" pageant; the winner, Audrey Allen, would represent Kansas City at the annual East/West All-Star Game.[2]

The crowd, which was close to 15,000, were to a person dressed in their Sunday best. For entrance to this spectacle, general admission cost $1 while box seats were $1.50; children got in for 30 cents. The average weekly wage for a black male worker in Kansas City at this time was $23.81 per week, so a trip to the ballpark, especially for the whole family, would have constituted a considerable expenditure.[3]

The procession marched into venerable Blues Stadium and through the outfield, with each group stopping at the flagpole in deep center field. Named after the Yankees' farm club that shared the ballpark, the stadium had been home to the Monarchs since it opened in 1923. Located on Brooklyn Avenue a few blocks off 18th Street, it had originally straddled the dividing line between the black and white sections of town near public transit lines and had attracted spectators from both demographics. By the early 1940s,

however, it was firmly in the black section of town.[4] With the Monarchs being perennial pennant contenders, Municipal Stadium (as the stadium eventually came to be named) hosted several Negro League World Series, including the first one, in 1924. It would also host Game One of the last World Series, though the Monarchs would not be one of the competitors.

Taking on the reigning NAL champion Cleveland Buckeyes to open the season, the Monarchs pulled out a 4-2 victory on the strength of veteran hurler Hilton Smith's two-run complete game. Their first victory secure, the Monarchs seemed poised for yet another pennant run. Speaking with the *Kansas City Call*, manager Buck O'Neil bragged, "The team that wins the Negro American League pennant will have to beat the Monarchs first."[5] His prediction proved to be prophetic. As the summer wore on, the Monarchs once again were one of the premier teams in the league, finishing with a final record of 19-7 for the second half of the season that put them a scant one game ahead of the first-half champion Birmingham Black Barons; they dominated the league in hitting with a .315 team batting average.[6] The Negro American League playoff series was primed to be a spirited contest, and the Monarchs and Black Barons did not disappoint.

Game One
Saturday, September 11, 1948: Birmingham 5, Kansas City 4, at Rickwood Field, Birmingham

It was a particularly hot and muggy evening as 6,000 fans trooped into Rickwood Field to see Game One. The temperature was nearly 90 degrees and it was extremely humid at game time; clouds would begin to roll in as play got underway, bringing

Jim Zapp's homer in the bottom of the ninth inning gave Birmingham a 4-3 victory over the Kansas City Monarchs in Game Three of the Negro American League playoffs at Martin Field in Memphis, Tennessee. (*Courtesy of James Zapp, Jr.*)

the promise of rain and a break in the late-summer swelter.[7] The two teams remained in a scoreless tie until the fifth inning when Piper Davis, Willie Mays, and Artie Wilson each hit singles off Monarchs starter Jim LaMarque in a rally that gave the Black Barons a 3-0 lead. The Monarchs came back against Birmingham starter Bill Powell in their half of the sixth when Elston Howard, Curt Roberts, and Mickey Taborn notched consecutive hits, starting a rally that produced a 3-3 tie.[8]

The score remained tied until the eighth, when Willard Brown came to bat for the Monarchs. Brown, who had posted an excellent season with a .375 batting average (good for fourth in the league), a league-best 18 homers and league-second 68 RBIs, singled, stole second, and scored on Roberts' bloop single to right field, giving the Monarchs a late one-run lead.[9]

The Barons tied the game once more in the bottom of the ninth when Pepper Bassett knocked a double to the outfield and pinch-hitter and relief pitcher Bill Greason singled him home. Greason then threw a scoreless 10th for the Barons.

In the bottom of the 11th, with the bases loaded and two out, rookie standout Willie Mays hit a sharp line drive toward the Monarchs' rookie second baseman, Curt Roberts.[10] Despite a spot-on throw by Roberts to first baseman-manager Buck O'Neil,

Mays was able to beat out the throw and was called safe on a close play. The winning run came around to score and gave the Birmingham squad a 5-4 walk-off victory.[11] The dramatic back-and-forth nature of this opening game set the stage for the rest of the series.

Game Two
Sunday, September 12, 1948:
Birmingham 6, Kansas City 5, at
Rickwood Field, Birmingham

A larger crowd of 8,000 came out for the second game of the series on Sunday afternoon after an overnight storm cooled the area somewhat to a more tolerable and less humid 80 degrees as the game began.[12] As in Game One, the Monarchs were able to take the lead and hold it into the late innings before the Black Barons once again made a comeback to tie the game in the bottom of the ninth and to win it in extra innings, this time on a Piper Davis homer in the bottom of the 10th.[13]

Alonzo Perry, who had had one of the circuit's most successful seasons with a 10-2 record in 18 appearances, started the game for the Black Barons.[14] By September, Perry's side-arm release had begun to take a toll on his elbow, and the Monarchs got to him early.[15] Home runs by Gene Baker (who had hit only one all season) and Willard Brown helped the Monarchs to establish an early lead and knocked Perry out by the end of the third, at which point he had given up three runs.

Pitching for the second game in a row, Bill Greason took over hurling duties from Perry and proceeded to put Birmingham back in the ballgame. Relieving Monarchs starter Ford Smith, who had had a solid year with a 10-5 record and a 2.64 ERA, Greason held the Monarchs to two runs through the ninth inning, which gave his teammates a chance to come back.[16] With Artie Wilson on second and two outs in the bottom of the ninth, Willie Mays, the hero of Game One, smashed a double off the clearly tiring Smith to drive Wilson home and tie the game, 5-5.[17]

After the Monarchs failed to score in the top of the 10th inning, Piper Davis opened the bottom half of the frame by reaching first on an error by Herb Souell and moving to second on a sacrifice by Joe Scott. With Smith still pitching in extra innings and his fastball clearly losing its zip, Bassett ripped the ball into right field, allowing Davis to score from second for the Black Barons' second extra-inning walk-off victory in as many games.[18]

Game Three
Wednesday, September 15, 1948: Birmingham 4, Kansas City 3, at Martin Field, Memphis

After the second game the Monarchs and Black Barons headed north for Kansas City via Memphis, where Game Three was to be played at Martin Field, the home grounds of the Memphis Red Sox and one of the few ballparks owned and exclusively used by a Negro League team. Holding one or more games of a playoff series outside of the team's home cities was not unusual for Negro League teams, nor had it been in the early days of the major leagues.[19] Playing on a neutral field gave other fans an opportunity to see the games; it also gave owners an extra chance to sell tickets.

Traveling through the South in this period posed a frustrating challenge to all African-Americans, who confronted segregated facilities and often-hostile attitudes. For the Monarchs, however, conditions were at least a little better. Unlike most Negro League teams, which either caravaned in cars or rode on segregated and often inadequate trains, the Monarchs owned their own bus, which allowed the group to travel as a unit. Their fame and years of patronizing the same businesses on road trips also allowed them to negotiate with white business owners in the South for the use of facilities that would have been otherwise off-limits.[20] However, as the bus bumped along two-lane Highway 31 into the night, the trip was undoubtedly uncomfortable.[21]

Jim LaMarque, the Monarchs' starting pitcher in Game One, returned to the mound in relief of starter Connie Johnson late in the game to preserve a 3-2 Monarchs lead. LaMarque had come on strong during the second half of the season to replace Hilton Smith atop Kansas City's rotation, finishing first among NAL pitchers with 15 wins against five losses during the regular season.[22] He was also an All-Star selectee and won the second of the two East-West games held that year. While he had the best season of his career in 1948, he encountered considerable bad luck in the playoffs against Birmingham.

With the Monarchs leading 3-2 in the bottom of the ninth, second baseman Curt Roberts, a defensive specialist who was finishing an outstanding rookie season, committed a most unusual throwing error that allowed the Black Barons to score a run and earn their third consecutive walk-off victory—two of them coming in extra innings.[23]

Or, at least, that is how the story ran in the *Kansas City Call*. Reports of exactly how the final run scored differed considerably based on the source. The *Chicago Defender* gave a report similar to the *Call*'s, stating that Jim Zapp hit a home run to tie the game and the winning run came on an error. However, the *Birmingham World* reported a very different set of events, in which Willie Mays hit a double and then came home on a homer by Zapp.[24] None of these stories had bylines, and neither of the teams had reporters traveling with

The Birmingham Black Barons celebrate their Game Three playoff victory in the visitors' locker room at Martin Field in Memphis, Tennessee. Jim Zapp (toward back) is receiving pats on the head for his game-winning homer. *(Withers Family Trust, Memphis, Tennessee)*

them. Nor, for budgetary reasons, did Negro League games generally have official scorers. So reports in the black press frequently conflicted, but not often to this degree. Baseball historian John Klima concluded that the *Call* and the *Defender* articles were written by Dizzy Dismukes, longtime scorekeeper for the Monarchs and occasional freelance writer.[25] Never one to hide his bias, Dismukes would write gleefully in the *Defender* after the Black Barons were routed by the Homestead Grays in Game Three of the World Series. By reporting that Mays reached on an error, he may have been trying to present Birmingham as being lucky rather than simply outperforming his squad. Also, a well-known photo, taken in the Black Barons' locker room immediately after the game, shows teammates surrounding and congratulating Zapp, which adds credence to the hypothesis that he hit the game-winning homer. While exactly how the Barons managed to score the decisive run may forever remain unclear (though Barons players insisted the *World* story, in spite of some inaccuracies, was the closest to the truth), what is certain is that the Black Barons were able to pull from behind to score a walk-off run for the third game in a row. The Monarchs had been ahead in the ninth inning in all three games, yet had lost each one.

Game Four
Sunday, September 19, 1948:
Kansas City 3, Birmingham 1, at
Blues Stadium, Kansas City

To this point, no professional team had ever come back to win a seven-game series after losing the first three.[26] While the black press in Kansas City struck a hopeful note, the team's eventual defeat was almost a foregone conclusion.

The contest was a pitchers' duel most of the way. Pitching for the third time in four games, Jim LaMarque held the Black Barons to a single unearned run in the first inning. The deciding run scored in the eighth when Elston Howard reached on an error by

Birmingham right fielder Ed Steele, was sacrificed to second by Tom Cooper, and scored on a single by the light-hitting catcher Earl "Mickey" Taborn. In his only win of the series, LaMarque aided his own cause when he hit a sacrifice fly in the eighth inning that drove in Baker for a 3-1 lead.

Birmingham's lone run came in a comedy of errors in the top of the first when NAL batting champion Artie Wilson knocked a single into left and hustled to second after Elston Howard unwisely threw to third. The throw was off-line and sailed past Herb Souell, allowing Wilson to advance to third and then scramble home when first baseman Tommy Cooper, backing up Souell at third, overthrew catcher Taborn.[27]

Monarchs third baseman Souell, despite the victory, had a tough game. Both he and Taborn chased after a popup by Joe Scott that was just foul of the third-base line in the first and crashed hard into each other. Souell caught the worst of it, crumpling into a heap and requiring several minutes of attention from Monarchs trainer James "Jew-Baby" Floyd before being able to return to action. In the sixth Souell was squared to bunt, attempting to sacrifice LaMarque to second, when the pitch missed his bat and struck his knee, sending him to the ground in agony for the second time in the game. Home-plate umpire Frank Duncan called him out, prompting manager Buck O'Neil to bolt from the dugout in protest. Both benches cleared while Souell continued to roll on the ground in pain. Duncan stuck to his call over the Monarchs' objections, and Souell eventually limped back to the dugout.[28]

Despite putting the brakes on the Black Barons and avoiding a sweep, the Kansas City club was still down by two games. While they remained in the series, the likelihood of a Monarchs comeback was quite remote. However, with the team back on familiar ground and before their hometown crowd (and, according to Birmingham, with the home umpires favoring them), unlikely outcomes began to seem plausible.

Game Five
Monday, September 20, 1948: Kansas City 3, Birmingham 3 (rain), at Blues Stadium, Kansas City

With intermittent rain sprinkling most of the day and threatening storms, Game Five began Monday night in front of a sparse crowd huddled under umbrellas. Alonzo Perry was back on the mound for Birmingham, pitching effectively through drizzle and mud and allowing three runs on six hits in 5⅓ innings. With the game tied 3-3 after five, the Birmingham club took the lead in the top of the sixth when third baseman Johnny Britton knocked a triple to drive in Artie Wilson. In the bottom half of the frame, the Monarchs had two men on with one out when the heavens opened in a deluge that caused play to be suspended. After a lengthy delay, during which most of the fans filed out of the park, umpires reverted the score to 3-3, as it had been at the end of the fifth inning, and declared the game a tie.[29]

A highly unusual event in baseball at any time, this unlikely outcome posed some problems in a must-win playoff series. The decision was made—over the objections of the Black Barons, who wanted to complete the contest before the next day's game, per league rules—that the game would be officially ruled a tie and would be made up only if necessary. This was not the first instance of alleged preferential treatment for the Monarchs by the officiating staff (and would not be the last), nor did it go unnoticed that former Monarchs pitcher Bullet Joe Rogan was one of the umpires. Dishonestly or not, the Monarchs had survived once again to play another day.

Game Six
Tuesday, September 21, 1948: Kansas City 3, Birmingham 1, at Blues Stadium, Kansas City

Rather than moving back to Birmingham, as had been planned originally, Game Six, as well as Game Seven and an improbable makeup Game Eight (if needed), were rescheduled to be played in Kansas City, as was Game One of the World Series, regardless of which team would be the NAL's representative. Like three of the previous games, this one would be a walk-off victory, this time for the Monarchs.

Birmingham's starting pitcher, Sammy C. Williams, nursed a 4-3 lead going into the bottom of the ninth when Monarchs skipper Buck O'Neil, in an unusual move, sent pitcher Hilton Smith to pinch-hit for pitcher Gene Richardson; presumably, Smith would also take over hurling duties in the case of extra innings. With one on and one out in his first appearance of the series, Smith laced a double to center field, sending Mickey Taborn to third. Hank Thompson then drove them both in with a hit to left. The heroic late-inning appearance proved to be the last in a Hall of Fame career for Smith; the 41-year-old never played professionally again.[30] The Monarchs had come back from being down three games to none in the series to force Game Seven which, due to the tied game, was the equivalent of a Game Six.

Game Seven
Wednesday, September 22: Kansas City 5, Birmingham 3, at Blues Stadium, Kansas City

The Monarchs were once again in a must-win situation as the seventh game began at Blues Stadium. A victory would force a makeup of the rained-out Game Five. If not, the next game played at Blues Stadium would be the first game of the World Series between the Black Barons and the Homestead Grays, who had put away the Baltimore Elite Giants to capture the Negro National League pennant. Following the pattern of the NAL series, Game Seven also turned out to be a barn-burner.

After the Black Barons took a 3-1 lead on a homer by Pepper Bassett in the fourth inning, O'Neil sent Richardson into the game in relief of starter Connie Johnson. Richardson dueled with Birmingham starter Bill Powell and kept the Black Barons from scoring any additional runs. With the score 3-2 heading into the bottom of the ninth, Powell began to show signs of wear, allowing the first two Monarchs batters to reach base. Trying to protect a slender lead, Davis sent Jimmy Newberry to the mound in relief of Powell. Monarchs slugger Hank Thompson promptly belted a home run over the right-field fence, giving the Monarchs a 5-3 walk-off victory that forced a final, winner-take-all game in the series.[31]

Game Eight
Thursday, September 24: Birmingham 5, Kansas City 1, at Blues Stadium, Kansas City

An overused Jim LaMarque took the mound for the Monarchs in the final contest, and received the lead when Kansas City pushed a run across the plate in the bottom of the third. With Gene Baker on third, Hank Thompson's grounder allowed Baker to score. As it turned out, Baker's run was the last one the Monarchs scored in 1948.

As if the series had not had enough strange twists already, fate had one more odd set of circumstances in store. A commotion began in the fifth inning when umpiring crew chief Frank Duncan overruled, from home, first-base umpire Sylvester Vaughn's call that put out the Monarchs' LaMarque at first. This was an extraordinarily unusual move in any game, let alone in the deciding game of a championship series. The game was still a one-run contest at this point, and the Barons walked off the field in frustration at what they felt was consistently bad officiating. But they eventually continued the game under protest, having already voiced displeasure about suspected "home cooking" on the part of the umpiring crew.[32] LaMarque, pitching for the fourth time in eight games and clearly gassed, gave up runs in the fourth, fifth, and eighth innings before being lifted, but by then the damage had been done and the Black Barons won the decisive contest, 5-1, behind a complete-game effort by Bill Greason.[33]

After an unusual and occasionally baffling series, the Birmingham Black Barons had defeated the Kansas City Monarchs, 4-3-1. Five of the officially concluded games ended in walk-off victories for the home team. There were other equally unlikely events: A batter was called out on a hit-by-pitch, a pinch-hitting pitcher produced the decisive run — twice, and an official baseball game ended in a tie. A more unusual set of circumstances is scarcely imaginable.

The first game of the World Series followed the NAL pennant struggle as the Grays came to Kansas City to face the Black Barons. In a spirited, if somewhat less exciting game in front of almost 6,000 fans, the Grays took the first game from the Barons, 3-2. The Grays scored all their runs in the first inning on a slow roller that, by all accounts, should have been an out.[34] It was an omen of things to come.

Author's Note

In regard to some player statistics, it must be noted that significant variances can sometimes be found in different sources. Baseball-Reference.com, for instance, generally tends to include only league games in player statistics, while other sources also add statistics from nonleague games whenever they are available. Every attempt has been made in this article to use the most accurate and comprehensive statistics available.

NOTES

1   "Monarchs to Play First Home Game vs Chicago: Preview May 11; Opener May 16 vs Cleveland Bucks," *Kansas City Call,* May 7, 1948: 8.

2   Janet Bruce, *The Kansas City Monarchs: Champions of Black Baseball* (Lawrence: University of Kansas Press, 1985), 123.

3   Urban League of Kansas City, "Local Survey Made," *Matter of Fact: Newsletter of the Urban League of Kansas City, Missouri.* Vol. I; No. 6, April-May, 1946: 2.

4   Home Owners Loan Corporation, "Security Map of Kansas City, Section D-25." dsl.richmond.edu/panorama/redlining/#loc=16/39.0889/-94.5645&opacity=0.44&city=greater-kansas-citymo&area=D25&adimage=3/71/-120. Accessed October 18, 2016.

5   "Monarchs Win 10 of 12," *Kansas City Call,* May 7, 1948: 8.

6   "Final Negro American League Records—Batting," *Kansas City Call,* October 1, 1948: 9.

7   WeatherSpark, "Historical Weather for Birmingham, Alabama, U.S.A.," weatherspark.com/history/29748/1948/Birmingham-Alabama-United-States (accessed November 17, 2016).

8   "Birmingham Takes Two From Monarchs: Teams Battle for Flag; Barons Win Sunday, 5-4, Saturday 6-5," *Kansas City Call,* September 17, 1948, 8.

9   John Klima, *Willie's Boys: The 1948 Black Barons, the Last Negro Leagues World Series, and the Making of a Baseball Legend* (Hoboken, New Jersey: John Wiley & Sons, 2009), 156.

10   "Monarchs—Barons Playoff Games; First Game," *Kansas City Call,* October 1, 1948: 9.

11   Ibid.

12   WeatherSpark, "Historical Weather for Birmingham, Alabama, U.S.A.," weatherspark.com/history/29748/1948/Birmingham-Alabama-United-States (accessed November 17, 2016).

13   "Monarchs-Barons Playoff Games, Second Game," *Kansas City Call,* October 1, 1948: 9.

14   "Final Negro American League Records—Pitching," *Kansas City Call,* October 1, 1948: 9.

15   Klima, 158.

16   James Riley, *The Biographical Encyclopedia of the Negro Baseball Leagues* (New York: Carroll & Graf, 1994), 725

17   Klima, 158-159.

18   "Monarchs-Barons Playoff Games, Second Game," *Kansas City Call,* October 1, 1948: 9.

19   Peter Golenbock, *The Spirit of St. Louis: A History of the St. Louis Cardinals and Browns* (New York: HarperCollins, 2000), 39.

20   *Baseball.* Netflix. Directed by Ken Burns. Public Broadcasting System, 1994.

21   "Alabama State Road Maps," alabamamaps.ua.edu/historicalmaps/stateroads/ (accessed February 8, 2017).

22   "Final Negro American League Records—Pitching," *Kansas City Call,* October 1, 1948: 9.

23   "Monarchs-Barons Playoff Games; Third Game," *Kansas City Call,* October 1, 1948: 9.

24   Klima, 161.

25   Klima, 162

26   This did not happen until the 2004 ALCS when the Boston Red Sox came back to win four in a row against the New York Yankees.

27   "Barons are Stopped: Monarchs Score First Victory in Playoff Series, 3-1," *Kansas City Times,* September 20, 1948: 17.

28   "Monarchs-Barons Game Notice," *Kansas City Call,* September 24, 1948: 9.

29   "Monarchs-Barons Playoff Games, Fifth Game," *Kansas City Call,* October 1, 1948: 9.

30   Riley, 725.

31   "Monarchs Win on Homer," *Kansas City Times,* September 23, 1948: 17.

32   "Barons Win NAL Pennant; Defeat Kansas City in Playoff: Tense Final Game, Barons Walk Off Field in Protest to Umpire Ruling," *Kansas City Call.* October 1, 1948, 9.

33   "Barons Beat Monarchs 4 Out of 7 for Title," *St. Louis Argus,* October 1, 1948: 17.

34   Ibid.

THE 1948 NEGRO NATIONAL LEAGUE PLAYOFF SERIES

By Steve West

The 1948 Negro National League playoff series between the Homestead Grays and the Baltimore Elite Giants was one of the most controversial series in baseball history. There was controversy that the series was played at all, controversy in the result of one of the games, and controversy in the outcome of the whole series because its final outcome was decided off the field rather than on it.

The league used a split-season format in 1948, with the winner of the first half meeting the winner of the second half in the playoff series. The Elite Giants, with a record of 27-13 to the Grays' 26-13, had won the first-half title by just a half-game. This outcome was even closer than it sounds; on the final day of the half, the two teams had played a doubleheader with the Grays winning the first game to take a half-game lead but then losing the second game to give back the lead and hand the first-half title to the Elite Giants.

The second half was close again, but this time the Grays won by 1½ games, with a 16-7 record to the Elite Giants' 19-13. This outcome was controversial, though; Elite Giants player Frazier Robinson wrote many years later that his team had won the second half as well but somehow was forced into a playoff series instead of being declared outright champion. Why Robinson believed that his team had won the second half is unknown; contemporary newspapers clearly stated that the Grays had won the second half. Robinson said he believed that Grays owner Sonnyman Jackson had complained to the NNL president, Rev. John J. Johnson, and that Johnson had decided to allow a playoff series. Robinson quoted Elite Giants owner Vernon Green as saying "Well, I don't know how they did it, but this is his ruling."[1]

Game One
Tuesday, September 14, 1948: Homestead 6, Baltimore 0, at Bugle Field, Baltimore

With the Grays' usual home field, Griffith Stadium in Washington, unavailable, the entire series was played at Bugle Field in Baltimore, with the two teams alternating as the home team. In Game One the home team was the Elite Giants. The contest was dominated by Tom "Big Train" Parker, who threw a six-hit shutout for the Grays. Parker walked four and struck out five batters, but the Elite Giants never seriously threatened to score; three of their six hits were infield grounders, and they did not advance a runner to second base until the sixth inning. Meanwhile, the Grays hitters chased Elite Giants starter Jonas Gaines in the fourth inning, by which time he had given up three runs in the third and two in the fourth. Bill Byrd finished the game, giving up just a run in the ninth, but the damage had already been done. The big hitting for the Grays came from Luke Easter who, despite three strikeouts, tripled, homered, and had four RBIs. Easter's three-run home run in the third gave the Grays half of their runs, while his triple in the ninth tacked on the final tally. In the fourth Parker singled, Luis Marquez walked, and Sam Bankhead was hit by a pitch to load the bases. Buck Leonard followed with a single to right field to knock in two runs. In the sixth and seventh the Elite Giants loaded the bases, but they failed to score both times and could not bring themselves back into the game.

Game Two
Thursday, September 16, 1948: Homestead 5, Baltimore 3, at Bugle Field, Baltimore

In Game Two it was the Grays' turn to play the home team and bat last. They started quickly, scoring twice in the bottom of the first inning, but the Elite

Giants scored two in the top of the third to tie the score; the runs were the result of an error, a wild pitch, and a hit. The Grays scored twice in the bottom of the third and never looked back, tacking on another run in the fifth while Baltimore was able to reply with just one run in the seventh inning. Joe Black threw a complete game for the Elite Giants in the loss, while Garnett Blair, despite a sore arm, pitched into the seventh inning for the win. Easter continued his solid hitting in the series, getting two hits and scoring three runs for the Grays. The Elite Giants were struggling for anything with their bats, and they did not help themselves when Pee Wee Butts was picked off at second base to kill a late-game rally.

Game Three
Friday, September 17, 1948: Homestead 4, Baltimore 4 (eight innings), at Bugle Field, Baltimore

Friday's Game Three was dominated by events late in the evening and was the most interesting game of the series because of happenings both on and off the field. The early part of the game went back and forth, with the Elite Giants taking a 1-0 lead in the second and the Grays taking a 2-1 lead in the top of the fifth, Baltimore scoring twice in the bottom of the inning to retake the lead, and both teams scoring again until they were tied at 4-4 in the bottom of the eighth.

At that point it was 10:52 P.M., and both Grays manager Vic Harris and umpire Mo Harris, his brother, told chief umpire Ted Lewis that there would not be enough time to finish the game before the 11:15 P.M. baseball curfew. Lewis decided to continue play anyway, stating that an inning could not begin after 11 P.M., but that any inning that started before 11 would be completed.[2] When the Grays came up in the top of the ninth, they quickly scored, and the Elite Giants decided to play for time. They believed that if the game was still going when the curfew time arrived, the score would revert to what it had been at the end of the last completed inning, and the game would end in a tie. The Elite Giants started throwing the ball away, playing slowly, and trying to not get anybody out. Frazier Robinson recalled, "So I threw the ball to

right field instead of throwing to first base and let 'em run. We let 'em run all the runs they wanted to run just so we could prolong the inning into darkness."[3]

By the time 11:15 arrived, the Grays had an 8-4 lead and the bases were loaded. The game was called and the teams left the field, with umpire Lewis resetting the game to the end of the completed eighth inning and restoring the 4-4 tie, which is what newspapers reported the following day. For their part, the Grays thought that the game should have been suspended and finished on Sunday prior to Game Four. Grays owner Sonnyman Jackson argued that Lewis was wrong to restore the tie, and when Lewis denied his appeal, Jackson called the league president, Rev. John J. Johnson, in New York for a ruling. Johnson called Elite Giants owner Vernon Green on Sunday afternoon and told him to resume Game Three before starting Game Four. Green refused; he said it would be unfair to the fans who were coming to the park for Game Four to have to watch the teams complete half an inning of Game Three, which could decide the series and make Game Four meaningless. "I don't intend to abide by this order until a more thorough investigation is made by your office," Green said.[4] Johnson agreed, ordered the teams to play Game Four as scheduled, and said he would come to Baltimore on Monday for a hearing into Game Three.

Game Four
Sunday, September 19, 1948: Baltimore 11, Homestead 3, at Bugle Field, Baltimore

Game Four became a laugher for the Elite Giants as their bats finally woke up. The first four Elite Giants in the batting order each had at least two hits, with Johnny Washington getting two doubles and five RBIs and Lester Lockett a triple and four RBIs. Bill Byrd, who had given up just one run in 5⅓ innings in relief in Game One, continued to pitch well in the series by throwing a complete game in which he held the Grays to five hits.

In a farcical aftermath to Game Four, Grays players took to the bases after the game in the expectation that Game Three would now be resumed. They had left the bases loaded when time was called on Friday night and now resumed their positions, but the Elite Giants players headed to the locker room. After spending some time waiting for the umpires to call the Elite Giants back, the Grays finally left the field.

On Monday, league president Johnson came to Baltimore, stung by criticism that as president of the league he should have been there from the start and harried by Elite Giants owner Green's demand that he appear in person to decide the dispute. After Johnson had heard arguments from both sides, he ruled that Lewis had erred when he allowed the ninth inning to begin. Johnson said Lewis should have known better because he had been an umpire in the city for many years. Johnson also recognized the fact that the Elite Giants players had sought to delay the game so that it would be called a tie. He ruled that the game should be resumed on Friday from the point at which it was suspended, with the Grays leading 8-4 and the bases loaded. If the Elite Giants won, the two teams would play the fifth and deciding game of the series immediately afterward.[5]

Green, presuming that his team could not come back from the four-run deficit, objected to this outcome, saying, "I see no reason why I should ask my fans to pay to see another half-inning of title play."[6] After considering his options, Green decided to forfeit the game. "Our owner said if that's the way it is, let 'em have it. Just give it to 'em. We wouldn't play," said Robinson.[7] The forfeit meant the Grays had won the series three games to none (making Baltimore's Game Four victory meaningless), and were the champions of the Negro National League.

This most unusual series constituted the final events in Negro National League history. The Grays went on to defeat the Negro American League champions, the Birmingham Black Barons, in the World Series, after which the NNL folded in December. Three NNL teams, including the Elite Giants, were accepted into an expanded Negro American League, but the Homestead Grays decided to become members of the Negro American Association (not to be

Members of the 1948 Homestead Grays, Negro National League Champions. (*National Baseball Hall of Fame, Cooperstown, New York*)

confused with the Negro American League) for the 1949 season.

Author's note: As is often the case with memories, Frazier Robinson's book *Catching Dreams* does not match what was reported at the time. The author has chosen to use the contemporary newspaper reports as facts and Robinson's details as color where they reasonably match what happened on the field. Robinson described events in detail, although his facts were often incorrect. For example, he wrote that the series was tied at two games apiece, that the suspended game was the deciding fifth game of the series, and that it had ended in the sixth inning because of darkness as Bugle Field did not have lights. None of those recollections were accurate. He also claimed to have hit a double and a triple in Game Four while the box score for that game shows that he went 0-for-4, and 2-for-12 overall in the series with no extra-base hits.

NOTES

1   Frazier Robinson and Paul Bauer, *Catching Dreams: My Life in the Negro Baseball Leagues* (Syracuse, New York: Syracuse University Press, 1999), 140.

2   "Baltimore 'Stalled'; Grays Awarded Flag," *Pittsburgh Courier*, October 2, 1948: 11.

3   Robinson, 140.

4   "NNL Prexy Called in Playoff Wrangle," *Baltimore Afro-American*, September 21, 1948: 3.

5   "League Upholds Grays' Protest," *Baltimore Sun*, September 21, 1948: 20.

6   "NNL Prexy Called in Playoff Wrangle."

7   Robinson, 141.

THE 1948 NEGRO LEAGUE WORLD SERIES

By Richard J. Puerzer

The 1948 Negro League World Series featured two of the great teams in the history of the Negro Leagues, the Homestead Grays and the Birmingham Black Barons. By the time this series was played in 1948, the performances of Jackie Robinson, Larry Doby, and Satchel Paige in the major leagues had drawn attention, and the talent in the Negro Leagues had begun to thin due to the departure of players to Organized Baseball. The rosters of the Black Barons and Grays had not yet been directly affected, and in spite of the diminishing attention to the Negro Leagues, the teams soldiered on.

Final standings for the first half of the split season in the Negro National League showed that the Baltimore Elite Giants were the champions of the first half of the season with a record of 26-12 that allowed them to squeak past the Grays, who had a record of 25-12. The Homestead Grays were the champions of the second half of the season with a record of 16-7, with the Elite Giants coming in second at 19-13. For the Negro American League, the Birmingham Black Barons earned the first-half championship with a record of 38-14 (a .731 winning percentage), besting the Cleveland Buckeyes, who had a record of 31-21 (.596). In the second half of the season, the Kansas City Monarchs were named as champions with a record of 19-7 (.731), better than the Black Barons record of 17-7 (.708). Following the contentious Negro National League playoffs, won by forfeit by the Grays, and the highly competitive Negro American League playoffs, won in seven tough games by the Black Barons, the Grays faced off against the Black Barons in the World Series.

This incarnation of an annual Negro League World Series, played between the Negro National League and Negro American League champions, had been initiated in 1942. The Homestead Grays

appeared in the World Series every season from 1942 to 1945 and defeated Birmingham to win their two titles in 1943 and 1944. They missed the Series in 1946 and 1947 but now returned in 1948 to face the Black Barons once more in a best-of-seven series to decide the champion of the Negro Leagues for 1948.

Although the entirety of the 1948 Negro League World Series was played in the weeks before the major-league World Series, the press coverage of the games was largely overshadowed by the impending major-league World Series, which featured the Cleveland Indians, starring former Negro Leaguers Larry Doby and Satchel Paige, and the Boston Braves. The African-American press—including the *Pittsburgh Courier*, the *Chicago Defender*, and the *Baltimore Afro American*—did cover the games and run stories for the Negro League World Series, but the papers failed to provide box scores and paid minimal attention to the games. For example, the front page of the October 9 issue of the *Afro American* featured a preview of the major-league World Series written by Sam Lacy.[1] Also, a great deal of press coverage was given to the performances of Jackie Robinson and Roy Campanella with the Brooklyn Dodgers, as well as Don Newcombe in the Dodgers' minor-league system. In fact, the October 9 *Afro American* featured pictures of Newcombe, Sam Jethroe, and Dan Bankhead in anticipation of the Little World Series to be played between the Triple-A Montreal Royals and the St. Paul Saints, both minor-league teams in the Dodgers system.[2] Meanwhile, the game story for Game Four of the Negro League World Series was relegated to the lower half of that page and lacked even a line score. Despite the lack of coverage in the press, the Negro League World Series was an exciting, well-played set of games that featured a number of great players, including future Hall of Famers Willie Mays and Buck Leonard.

Game One

Game One of the World Series was played at Blues Stadium in Kansas City, Missouri, on the afternoon of Sunday, September 26. The Grays played as the home team in the game, in which pitchers Jimmie Newberry of the Black Barons and Ted Alexander of the Grays faced off against each other. It was reported that the third baseman for the Grays in this game and Game Two was Dave Pope, but this was likely a reporting error, as Dave Pope had not played for the Grays since 1946 and definitely played in the Provincial League in Canada in 1948. It is likely that Dave Pope's brother, Willie, or perhaps another player was misidentified as Dave Pope. (The player will be referred to in this account as "the third baseman.")

The Black Barons scored the first run of the game in the second inning. Right fielder Ed Steele walked, advanced to third on left fielder Jim Zapp's single to right field, and scored on first baseman Joe Scott's fly ball to center field. The Grays answered in the bottom of the inning with three runs. Power-hitting center

fielder Bob Thurman led off with a single and catcher Eudie Napier walked. The Grays' third baseman then blasted a triple to right field, scoring Thurman and Napier. Newberry struck out the next two batters, but Grays leadoff hitter Luis Marquez singled to center to score the third baseman. Both pitchers then took control of the game, scattering hits but not allowing any runs for the next five innings. In the top of the eighth, Willie Mays reached first base on a fielder's choice. He advanced to third on a single to right field by Pepper Bassett and scored on a triple by Black Barons player-manager Piper Davis; Bassett was cut down at the plate on the play. The Grays went on to win, 3-2.

Both Newberry and Alexander threw complete games. Despite taking the loss, Newberry pitched well, striking out six, walking just one, and giving up six hits. Alexander struck out four, walked three, and gave up eight hits in gaining the win. It was reported that a crowd of 5,370 attended the game, which was played in 2 hours and 5 minutes. It is curious, and in retrospect disappointing, that this game was the only one in the series documented by a box score.[3]

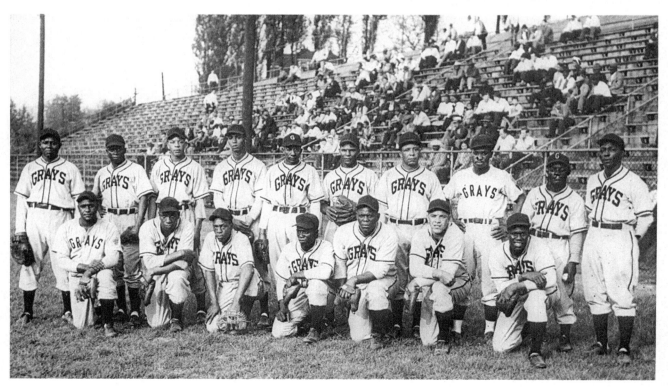

The 1948 Homestead Grays, winners of both the last Negro National League pennant and the last Negro League World Series. (*National Baseball Hall of Fame, Cooperstown, New York*)

Game One Line Score

Black Barons	0	1	0	0	0	0	0	1	0	2	8	1
Grays	0	3	0	0	0	0	0	0	x	3	6	1

Black Barons: Newberry 9 IP; Grays: Alexander 9 IP

Game Two

The second game of the series was played at Birmingham's Rickwood Field on the night of Wednesday, September 29. Grays hurler Bob Thurman faced off against the Black Barons' Bill Powell. The Black Barons scored first, plating two runs in the bottom of the second inning. Piper Davis singled and advanced to second on an error. Ed Steele then reached on a walk, and the bases were loaded after Jim Zapp singled. First baseman Jim Scott followed with a two-run double, scoring Davis and Steele, before Thurman was able to get out of the inning without further damage. In the fifth inning the Grays exploded for five runs. Luis Marquez led off with a single and moved to third on a double by Luke Easter. Next up was Grays slugging first baseman Buck Leonard. The Black Barons apparently chose to pitch around Leonard whenever possible throughout the series, and he was intentionally walked, loading the bases. Wilmer Fields hit into a fielder's choice, erasing Leonard but scoring Marquez. Napier doubled and Easter and Fields scored. The Grays' third baseman followed with a homer over the right-field fence, scoring Napier ahead of him. Newberry was brought in to relieve Powell and closed out the inning, but the damage was already done. In the ninth inning the Black Barons scored one run, but it was not enough to match the Grays, who won, 5–3, putting them up two games to none. It was reported that 4,159 fans were in attendance at the game.[4]

Game Two Line Score

Grays	0	0	0	0	0	5	0	0	0	5	9	2
Black Barons	0	2	0	0	0	0	0	0	1	3	6	0

Grays: Thurman 9 IP; Black Barons: Powell 5⅓ IP, Newberry 3⅔ IP

Game Three

Game Three of the series was played the following night, Thursday, September 30, at Rickwood Field in Birmingham, Alabama. Pitcher Tom Parker started for the Grays against Alonzo Perry of the Black Barons. The Black Barons scored first with a run in the bottom of the third. In the top of the fourth inning, Grays slugger Luke Easter smashed a long home run to tie the game. In the bottom of the inning Parker pulled a muscle and was relieved by R. T. Walker. Walker pitched well until he surrendered two runs in the sixth that gave the Black Barons a 3–1 lead. Walker was relieved by Ted Alexander in the seventh. Meanwhile, Perry put up a strong performance for the Black Barons until he gave up two runs in the eighth inning that tied the game, 3–3. Perry was relieved by Bill Greason, who held the Grays in check in the top of the ninth. In the bottom of the ninth, Greason singled with one out. Artie Wilson flied out and third baseman John Britton walked, bringing up 17-year-old Willie Mays. With two out and two men on base, Mays promptly drove a ball up the middle, reportedly through the pitcher Alexander's legs, to score Greason with the game-winning run. The Black Barons were back in the Series, albeit they were still down two games to one.[5]

Game Three Line Score

Grays	0	0	0	1	0	0	0	2	0	3	9	0
Black Barons	0	0	1	0	0	2	0	0	1	4	10	0

Grays: Parker 3 IP, Walker 3 IP, Alexander 3 IP; Black Barons: Perry 7 IP, Greason 2 IP

Game Four

The Series shifted to New Orleans for Game Four. This game had originally been slated to be played at Rickwood Field, but it was bumped by the Dixie Series, which pitted the Southern Association champion Birmingham Barons against the Texas League champion Fort Worth Cats. Having been displaced by this Double-A championship tilt, the Negro League World Series moved to New Orleans and was played at Pelican Stadium on the afternoon of

Sunday, October 3. The *Birmingham News* reported that Black Barons president Tom Hayes and a large contingent of fans traveled with the team from Birmingham to New Orleans on the day before the game in order to be there to root for their team.

Unfortunately for the Black Barons and their fans, the Grays' offense exploded for their best game in the Series. Wilmer Fields was Homestead's starting pitcher, and Bill Greason took the mound for Birmingham. Greason did not last long; he was one of four pitchers to appear for the Black Barons that day. He was joined by Jehosie Heard, Jimmie Newberry, and Nat Pollard in trying to hold back the Grays. The Grays scored four runs in the second inning, five in the fourth, three in the fifth, and two in the eighth. Four of the five runs scored in the fourth inning were accounted for by a grand slam by the Grays' slugging left fielder, Luke Easter, his second home run of the Series. Fields gave a strong performance to get the win, allowing just one run on seven hits. The Grays scored their 14 runs on 19 hits. By winning the game, they went up three games to one in the best-of-seven Series.[6]

Game Four Line Score

Black Barons	0	0	0	1	0	0	0	0	0	1	7	2
Grays	0	4	0	5	3	0	0	2	x	14	19	1

Black Barons: Greason, Heard, Newberry, Pollard; Grays: Fields 9 IP

Game Five

The series returned to Birmingham's Rickwood Field for Game Five on the night of Tuesday, October 5. R.T. Walker got the start for the Grays and Bill Powell started for the Black Barons. The game was a slugfest, with both teams holding leads twice through the first eight innings. Greason, appearing in his third straight game, relieved Powell in the sixth inning. Going into the ninth trailing 6-5, the Grays scored a run on doubles by Marquez and Easter to tie the game. Then, in the 10th, the Grays scored four runs on three walks, two singles, and a double. The Black Barons eventually brought in Sam Williams to relieve Greason, but the damage was done. The Grays brought in Fields, who had pitched a complete game only two days earlier, to pitch the 10th. Fields closed

The 1948 Birmingham Black Barons, Negro American League Champions. Seventeen-year old outfielder Willie Mays is the player at the far right in the photo. (*National Baseball Hall of Fame, Cooperstown, New York*)

out the game, giving the Grays the win and the Series championship.[7]

Game Five Line Score

Grays	2	0	0	0	0	3	0	0	1	4	10	15	1
Black Barons	0	1	0	1	2	0	0	2	0	0	6	12	4

Grays: Walker 9 IP, Fields 1 IP; Black Barons: Powell 5 IP, Greason 3 IP, Williams 1 IP

After the 1948 Season

The 1948 season was in many ways the last great season for the Negro Leagues. After the season the Negro National League disbanded, with a few teams, including the New York Cubans and Baltimore Elite Giants, merging into the Negro American League Eastern Division. Other teams, including the Grays, continued to barnstorm. Several of the Grays signed major-league contracts; of those, Luke Easter, Luis Marquez, and Bob Thurman went on to play in the majors. In 1949 the Grays defeated the Richmond Giants in the Negro American Association Championship Series, and they hung around through the 1950 season before they disbanded.[8] The Black Barons continued to play in the Negro American League through 1954; however, they also saw an exodus of their players to the major leagues, including Artie Wilson and Bill Greason. The youngest player to appear in the 1948 Negro League World Series, Willie Mays, of course signed with the New York Giants and went on to become one of the greatest players in the history of professional baseball.

SOURCES

In addition to the sources cited in the Notes, the author also consulted:

Clark, Dick, and Larry Lester, eds. *The Negro Leagues Book* (Cleveland: Society For American Baseball Research, 1994).

Fields, Wilmer. *My Life in the Negro Leagues* (McLean, Virginia: Miniver Press, 2013).

Klima, John. *Willie's Boys* (Hoboken, New Jersey: John Wiley and Sons, 2009).

Leonard, Buck, with James A. Riley. *Buck Leonard: The Black Lou Gehrig* (New York: Carroll and Graf, 1995).

NOTES

1 Sam Lacy, "AFRO Picks Indians to Win in 7 Games," *Afro American*, National Edition, October 9, 1948: 1. news.google.com/newspapers?nid=UBnQDr5gPskC&dat=19481009&printsec=frontpage&hl=en.

2 "They'll Play in 'Little World Series,'" *Afro American*, October 9, 1948: 8.

3 For Game One the following references were used: "Grays Score Win in World Series," *Afro American*, October 2, 1948: 9; "National League Champions Clinch Game in Second With 3-Run Rally," *Kansas City Call*, October 1, 1948: n.p.

4 For Game Two the following references were used: "Grays Shade Black Barons By 5-3 Score," *Birmingham Age-Herald*, September 30, 1948: n.p.; "Black Barons Seek Initial Win Tonight," *Birmingham News*, September 30, 1948: n.p.

5 For Game Three the following references were used: "Black Barons Nip Grays, 4-3, for First Series Win," *Birmingham Age-Herald*, October 1, 1948: n.p.; "Black Barons Nip Grays, 4-3," *Birmingham News*, October 1, 1948: n.p.

6 For Game Four the following references were used: "Black Barons, Grays Tangle in N.O. Today," *Birmingham News*, October 3, 1948: n.p.; "Grays Hold 3-1 Lead in Series," *Afro American*, October 9, 1948: 8; "Grays Rout Birmingham in Series," *Pittsburgh Courier*, October 9, 1948: 12; "Homestead Grays Swamp Black Barons, 14-1," *Chicago Defender*, October 9, 1948: 10.

7 For Game Five the following references were used: "Black Barons Take On Grays," *Birmingham News*, October 5, 1948: n.p.; "Grays Nip Black Barons, Win Series," *Birmingham Age-Herald*, October 6, 1948: n.p.; "Grays Blast Black Barons," *Birmingham News*, n.p.; "Grays Win, 10-6 in World Series," *Afro American*, October 16, 1948: 8.

8 "Grays, Giants Clash Monday," *Washington Post*, September 3, 1949: 10.

BASEBALL'S INTEGRATION SPELLS THE END OF THE NEGRO LEAGUES

By Japheth Knopp

t has been asserted that baseball makes an effective metaphor for the history of the United States, reflecting the changing circumstances and values of American society.[1] If such is the case, then the decline and end of the Negro Leagues may provide insights about the changing realities for urban African-Americans in the years after World War II. Shifting political and economic opportunities, and the limits of those opportunities, have had a profound effect on American society, especially for African-Americans, over the course of the last eight decades. The early stages of integration in American society brought with it new hopes for marginalized minority groups; however, it also posed new challenges. Traditionally black-owned enterprises—among them the Negro Leagues—now faced increased competition for black workers and revenue and had difficulties maintaining sustainable businesses, which resulted in the failure of most medium and large-scale black firms during the mid-twentieth century.

For decades, major-league baseball has taken pride in (and rarely failed to publicly point out the fact that) it was a leader in desegregation in the United States, hiring first Jackie Robinson and then numerous other African-American players several years before the civil rights movement began in earnest. However, recent scholarship suggests that this assessment is in error. The traditional narrative of the civil rights movement being mostly restricted to the American South and taking place largely in the 1950s and 1960s has undergone a thorough reassessment. The new paradigm, which views the struggle for civil rights as much lengthier and taking place in Northern urban areas, has altered the understanding of African-American history and has changed the way in which the period of baseball's integration and decline of the Negro Leagues is viewed.[2]

The era of baseball's integration can be reexamined as part of a broader movement toward increased civic, educational, and economic rights that became available to African-Americans in the 1930s and 1940s. Organizations like the Congress of Racial Equality and the National Association for the Advancement of Colored People were extremely active in this period as they pressured political leaders, influenced public sentiment, and used the courts to gain access to better-paying jobs and schools. With the onset of World War II, the nascent civil rights movement was able to harness national rhetoric about combating fascism to push for greater equality on the home front. Activities like the Double V Campaign (for victory against oppression both abroad and at home) and a call for a march on Washington by black leaders helped lead to increased hiring and better wages during the war. However, when wartime industrial production was cut after the end of the war in 1945, black workers once again faced a "last hired, first fired" mentality and an uncertain role in the postwar economy.[3]

Baseball was not unique among professional sports for signing black athletes around this time. The National Football League integrated in 1946 when the Los Angeles Rams, facing mounting public pressure for not hiring black players while playing in a publicly owned and financed stadium, signed Kenny Washington, who had been Robinson's teammate on the UCLA football squad.[4] Horse racing, which had featured a number of black jockeys until around the turn of the twentieth century, had been segregated for decades but featured African-American Jimmy Thompson during the 1948 racing season.[5] Black boxing officials entered the sport for the first time in May 1948 when D. Franklin Chiles served as a ring judge for five bouts at the Chicago Coliseum, including the light-heavyweight championship fight between Enrico Bertola and Jimmy Roberts, and Bill Dody refereed three of the matches.[6] The National Basketball Association was desegregated in 1950 when Earl Lloyd of the Washington Capitals became the first African-American in that circuit. Professional golf and tennis integrated in 1948 and 1950, respectively.[7] Thus, while Robinson's signing to a minor-league contract in October 1945 was the first breach in the color wall of professional sports, it soon became part of a movement in postwar America rather than a singular event.

The famous story of Branch Rickey recruiting Jackie Robinson to become the first black player in the major leagues provides an example of how opportunistic white business leaders were able to profit by the exploitation of newly available black professionals and customers while at the same time present-

ing their actions as affirmative and progressive. This narrative presents Rickey as a stalwart of egalitarianism who, long troubled by the color line in baseball, made the momentous decision to bring black players into the major leagues. Rickey allegedly had been appalled by the treatment of African-Americans, both in baseball specifically and American society more generally, owing to his deeply held religious views and personal experience in seeing the negative effects of discrimination. Supposedly, as a coach for Ohio Wesleyan in 1903, Rickey was traveling with the baseball team when a young black player named Charles Thompson was denied accommodation at the hotel where the team was staying. Seeing how humiliated the young man was, Rickey vowed to fight racial discrimination.[8]

Brooklyn Dodger Jackie Robinson (at left) and Cleveland Indian – and former Homestead Grays outfielder – Luke Easter flank seven-time Negro League All-Star catcher Larry Brown. *(Withers Family Trust, Memphis, Tennessee)*

It is a nice story, but there is serious doubt as to its veracity. Rickey never once, at least publicly, told this story between 1903 and 1945, after which it became one of his favorite and most oft-told anecdotes. There is no evidence to suggest that Rickey was a progressive on the issue of racial integration until it coincided with his self-interest.[9] Indeed, Rickey himself said at the time of the Robinson signing that it was merely a baseball and business decision that would produce results (i.e., wins and increased profits) and that "I will happily bear being a bleeding heart, a do-gooder, and that humanitarian rot."[10] As time passed, the story presented by Rickey and, later, Hollywood evolved into one that presented him as a forward-thinking champion of equality rather than an opportunistic businessman.

Rickey was not the first member of major-league management to advocate the hiring of black players. John McGraw of the New York Giants had lobbied for years during the 1910s and 1920s to integrate baseball and had gone so far as to sign a light-skinned black player whom he attempted to pass off as an American Indian.[11] In 1941, Dodgers manager Leo Durocher had been chastised by Commissioner Kenesaw Mountain Landis for making public comments in which he lamented his inability to sign black players (the official line of baseball was that there was no color barrier and that any team was free to sign any player it chose; it just so happened that none ever hired black players).[12]

The most ambitious attempt to desegregate the game was Bill Veeck's attempt to purchase the Philadelphia Phillies in 1943. Veeck intended to dump most of the perennially awful Phillies roster, and then planned to stock the team with Negro League all-stars.[13] Arrangements had already been made to buy the team and to sign, among others, Satchel Paige, Monte Irvin, and Roy Campanella. When word reached league officials, the sale was voided by National League President Ford Frick; in what was almost certainly an illegal act of collusion, the Phillies then were sold to another bidder at a lower price.[14]

Rickey had been an executive in baseball for more than 30 years before he signed Robinson. He had previously served as the general manager of the St. Louis Browns and St. Louis Cardinals and in neither of those roles had ever so much as hinted at a desire to bring in black players, though St. Louis certainly did not provide an environment that would have welcomed the integration of baseball. Indeed, Sportsman's Park, where both teams played, was the last major-league stadium to desegregate its seating, and it did not do so until Rickey had moved on to Brooklyn.[15] What had been well-known about Rickey in baseball circles for decades, however, was his ability to find new sources of talent that had been untapped by other clubs in order to build championship teams at bargain prices. In St. Louis he had developed what became known as the farm system which provided his teams with a continuous stream of talent and allowed him to keep his players' salaries at below-market prices.[16]

For any manager keen to exploit new pools of talent at minimal prices, using black players in post-war New York was a shrewd move. Brooklyn was likely the most racially and economically diverse of all major-league markets at this time. Also, by not hiring black players, the Dodgers, Yankees, and Giants were all technically breaking New York state law. The Quinn-Ives Act imposed a fine of up to $500 or imprisonment for one year or both for any employer who refused to hire a person based on race.[17] While this law was seldom enforced, and never was applied to professional baseball, there was a groundswell of public support in favor of integration. In New York there were frequent protests of all three major-league teams led by groups like the Congress of Racial Equality that brought out hundreds (and occasionally thousands) of pickets. Local politicians, including Mayor Fiorello LaGuardia, campaigned on the issue.[18] Clearly, Rickey's decision to bring a black player to the Dodgers did not happen in a vacuum.

After Jackie Robinson broke the color line, executives and owners from the Negro Leagues met with their counterparts from the major leagues and proposed a number of options for mergers and cooperation. At first it was suggested that the better clubs with large fan bases from the Negro Leagues, such as the Kansas City Monarchs, be allowed in as expansion franchises.[19] Several of these teams operated in cities that lacked a major-league team, already had large followings, and were perfectly positioned to help the major leagues take advantage of postwar prosperity and newly expendable income. The proposal was unanimously voted down. When this was rejected the possibility of the Negro Leagues becoming a Triple-A minor-league circuit was raised, but this idea also was summarily dismissed.[20] White owners had no interest in cooperating with their black counterparts and made a deliberate choice to put the Negro Leagues out of business after obtaining their best players and wooing away much of their fan base.

The fact that the major leagues wanted only the best Negro League players was due largely to the common practice of using racial quotas; most franchises kept roster spots for African-American players to a minimum (often only two per team). Black players were nearly always signed in even numbers, so that their white teammates would not have to share rooms with them on the road.[21] It was not unusual to see a black player traded or sent to the minors if there were "too many" black players on the squad.[22] Slots for journeymen and utility players were still, for the most part, the territory of white players. The message to black players was clear: produce more than the average white player or lose your roster spot on the team.

Somewhat paradoxically, the years between 1947 and 1950—as Negro League attendance dropped off dramatically due to the loss of star players—were some of the most financially successful for some black teams, among them the Birmingham Black Barons and the Kansas City Monarchs. However, this was due primarily to the sale of players to white-owned teams.[23] The Monarchs were also among the first teams to begin consciously scouting prospects for sale to affiliated white clubs rather than to developing them for their own roster. This had the effect of further distancing an already dwindling fan base. Black

franchises saw their values plummet, with teams that had been worth millions at the close of World War II going out of business by the end of the decade.[24]

To complicate matters further, a number of white teams refused to honor Negro League contracts and pirated players outright without compensating Negro League team owners.[25] Rickey, while gaining esteem among many African-Americans (and earning the animosity of others) for the signing of Robinson, paid the Monarchs nothing for Robinson's contract, stating that Negro League contracts were not in accordance with the National Agreement that governed all affiliated baseball contracts and were therefore void.[26] Teams began to sell their players for a fraction of their market value in order to recoup some of their investment rather than to take a total loss on a player who jumped his contract.[27]

As the 1948 season began, many observers in the black community were reeling from the previous year's dramatic drop in attendance and were uneasy about the future of black baseball. Increased competition from major-league clubs with African-American players was the primary factor involved, though it was certainly not the only one. Radio and, to a limited extent, television were allowing people to experience the game without paying to get into the ballpark; no longer did proximity limit fans' choice of which team to root for as their favorite. New forms of entertainment had become available, especially after the wartime rationing of resources was lifted, and as competition for the black entertainment dollar had increased, Negro League teams already had started to see a decline in attendance in 1947. Now they were fearful about a future in which all the best black players were on major-league teams and were taking their fans with them.

At the same time that attendance at Negro League games was shrinking, patronage of Organized Baseball-affiliated teams was reaching record highs, at least in part due to the new influx of African-American players. The Cleveland Indians, with two black stars in Larry Doby and Satchel Paige, set a new major-league attendance record in 1948 with attendance of 2,620,627. Minor-league teams were also seeing increased fan support, with the Triple-A American Association setting a new record for league attendance that summer.[28] The St. Paul Saints, who finished third in American Association attendance, with 320,483 fans turning out, fielded the league's first black player that season, pitcher Dan Bankhead of the Dodgers organization, who drew large crowds of black fans whenever he pitched.[29] The effects of employing black ballplayers to draw new black fans were instant and profound.

In the now rapidly declining Negro Leagues, the most vocal owner to voice concern about the uncertain financial future of the leagues' teams was Newark Eagles co-owner Effa Manley. In September 1948, she publicly discussed the likelihood of the Eagles being sold or shutting down entirely due to a precipitous drop in revenue since the 1946 season. She blamed the fans for being fickle and said, "Most of our old fans are going to see four men with white teams who played on our teams for years without exciting their present intense interest."[30] Black players were tired of feeling they were being taken for granted by Negro League teams and, now that they had increased options for their services, they began to be vocal about it. Jackie Robinson wrote a piece for *Ebony* in which he roundly criticized black baseball's owners for their low pay, poor accommodations, and generally shoddy treatment of players.[31]

Members of the black press sometimes dealt with these developments in a contradictory nature. John Johnson, the longtime sports editor of the *Kansas City Call*, first used his column to brag about what a monetary success the integration of black players into white leagues had been for their clubs and to poke fun at those who had insisted that any such arrangement would inevitably lead to violence and rioting. Noting the new attendance records that had been set by teams in Organized Baseball since the inclusion of black players, he wrote in early September, "By box office records, Old Gus [Greenlee] is prov-

Birmingham Black Barons outfielder Ed "Stainless" Steele (at left) poses with Brooklyn Dodgers pitcher Joe Black, who had formerly played for the Negro National League's Baltimore Elite Giants. *(Withers Family Trust, Memphis, Tennessee)*

ing that the greatest single new appeal the great old game has come up with in years is the presence and play of Negro players in the Major Leagues."[32] The following week he used his space to attack Manley and her "sob solo for sympathy," saying, "Much of the absenteeism at Negro games is due to the lack of interest due to lack of salesmanship."[33] An ardent supporter of both black baseball and the integration of the major leagues, Johnson appeared to miss the fact that the two entities were fast becoming mutually exclusive. He also took Robinson to task for his remarks, saying, "Pop-offs were as bad as pop-outs," and that while the Negro Leagues had problems, they had given Robinson his start and he ought to have been grateful for that.[34]

As the postwar period continued with a housing boom in suburban areas, African-Americans once again found themselves cut out. Restrictive housing and lending policies like redlining and property covenants keep black residents restricted, at least in practice if no longer by law, to segregated neighborhoods in urban centers. As manufacturing began to follow workers out of the cities, these municipalities now had to provide for public infrastructure with a dwindling tax base, resulting in deep cuts to public amenities. During the 1960s and '70s most of the old, downtown ballparks were demolished in the name of urban renewal with new, cavernous multi-use stadiums built usually away from the city center in acres of parking lots removed from public transit. The numbers of black players making their way to the major leagues has diminished with the lack of access to the game, despite efforts to increase play in the sport among youth.

That the 1948 Negro League World Series was the last played shortly before the collapse of the Negro National League was not an aberration but was part of a growing trend. An organized push for expanded rights and opportunities, particularly in Northern urban areas and during World War II, had helped African-Americans gain ground in American society. However, this was almost always limited and conditional, and it came at the cost of many independent black entrepreneurs. Black baseball struggled on

through the 1950s, but it never approached anything near to the popularity it had enjoyed during its wartime peak. Instead of developing young talent into local stars who stayed with the club throughout their careers, Negro League teams now deliberately scouted players they could sell to the majors. While a number of future stars like, Ernie Banks, and Hank Aaron, played in the Negro Leagues during this period, it was always known that these young men would be with their club only temporarily before moving on. When major-league teams began to scout black players on their own, even this niche began to wane. By the end of the 1950s only a handful of clubs remained in the Negro American League, and even then they played most of their games as barnstorming exhibitions. When the league folded in the early 1960s, its demise went almost unnoticed. The Indianapolis Clowns continued to play as a barnstorming squad into the 1980s, but they were little more than a vestige of the time when Negro League teams were the cornerstone of the African-American community.

NOTES

1 Jules Tygiel, *Past Time: Baseball as History* (Oxford, England: Oxford University Press, 2000), x.

2 The seminal work here is Jaquelyn Dowd Hall's 2005 article "The Long Civil Rights Movement and the Political Uses of the Past," which has led to a paradigm shift in how scholars view the beginnings of racial integration. In this construct, Jackie Robinson and the desegregation of baseball should have been expected as part of a larger pattern of black workers entering formerly exclusive occupations rather than as an aberration.

3 William Sundstrom, "Last Hired, First Fired? Unemployment and Urban Black Workers During the Great Depression," *Journal of Economic History* (Vol. 52, No. 2, June, 1992): 485.

4 Fred Bowen, "Kenny Washington Paved Way for Black Players in NFL," *Washington Post*, February 2014, washingtonpost.com/lifestyle/kidspost/kenny-washington-paved-way-for-black-players-in-nfl/2014/02/19/063ad55e-98c2-11e3-80ac-63a8ba7f7942_story.html?utm_term=.81a6dffc5327 accessed March 24, 2017.

5 "Lone Colored Jockey Rides in Wake of Several Who Made History in the Past," *Kansas City Call*, September 24, 1948: 8.

6 "Chicago Uses First Negro Ring Officials," *Kansas City Call*, May 17, 1948: 9.

7   "Integration Milestones in Pro Sports," espn.go.com/gen/s/2002/0225/1340314.html accessed March 23, 2017.

8   Peter Golenbock, *The Spirit of St. Louis: A History of the St. Louis Cardinals and Browns* (New York: HarperCollins, 2000), 250.

9   Mitchell Nathanson, *A People's History of Baseball* (Chicago: University of Chicago Press, 2012), 81.

10 William Marshall, *Baseball's Pivotal Era, 1945-1951* (Lexington: University Press of Kentucky, 1999), 126.

11 *Baseball.* Netflix. Directed by Ken Burns. PBS, 1994.

12 Lee Lowenfish, *Branch Rickey: Baseball's Ferocious Gentleman* (Lincoln, Nebraska: Bison Books, 2007), 351.

13 Bill Veeck, *Veeck — As in Wreck* (Chicago: University of Chicago Press 1962), 170-171.

14 The main source of this account is found in Veeck's memoirs previously cited and has become a famous story, being recounted elsewhere. However, the validity of this narrative has come under scrutiny. In "A Baseball Myth Exploded: Bill Veeck and the 1943 Sale of the Phillies" in *The National Pastime: A Review of Baseball History 18,* 1998, David Jordan, Larry Gerlach, and John Rossi lay out a compelling argument for this event having been little more than a tall-tale spun by Veeck, who was never one to miss an opportunity for a good story.

15 Nathanson, 80.

16 Golenbock, 83.

17 Irwin Silber, *Press Box Red: The Story of Lester Rodney, the Communist who Helped Break the Color Line in American Sports* (Philadelphia: Temple University Press, 2003), 74.

18 Benjamin Rader, *Baseball: A History of America's Game* (Urbana: University of Illinois Press, 2008), 156.

19 Rob Ruck, *Raceball: How the Major Leagues Colonized the Black and Latin Game* (Boston: Beacon Press 2011), 115.

20 Ruck, 116.

21 Nathanson, 101.

22 Nathanson, 103-104.

23 Janet Bruce, *The Kansas City Monarchs: Champions of Black Baseball* (Lawrence: University of Kansas Press, 1985), 118-119.

24 A comparative example here is the Newark Eagles of the Negro National League who were assessed at $1.5 million in 1945, and the Cleveland Indians, who were sold in 1946 for $2.2 million. The Eagles were sold after the 1948 season and folded after two years in Houston and one in New Orleans.

25 Veeck, 176.

26 Ruck, 118

27 Veeck, 177.

28 "New Record in A.A.: Attendance in the League Reaches 2,235,853, Lane Says," *Kansas City Times,* September 21, 1948: 16.

29 "Many Fail to See Bankhead in K.C. Debut," *Kansas City Call,* September 3, 1948: 8.

30 "May Be Last Year for Newark Eagles," *Kansas City Call,* September 3, 1948: 8.

31 Jackie Robinson, "What's Wrong With Negro Baseball?" *Ebony,* June 12, 1948: 13.

32 John L Johnson, "John L Johnson's Sport Light," *Kansas City Call,* September 3, 1948: 8.

33 Johnson, "John L Johnson's Sport Light," *Kansas City Call,* September 10, 1948: 8.

34 Johnson, "John L Johnson's Sport Light," *Kansas City Call,* May 21, 1948: 8.

THE TRUE STORY OF THE SIGNING OF WILLIE MAYS

By John Klima

At 9:53 on the morning of June 21, 1950, a Western Union telegram arrived at the Memphis office of Tom Hayes, a local businessman who made his fortune in the mortuary business and helped give life to one of the greatest players in baseball history.

Hayes owned the Negro American League's Birmingham Black Barons. Since the 1948 season, several major-league teams had pursued his teen-age center fielder, astounded by the youngster's raw strength, athleticism, and throwing arm.

However, in the initial years following 1947, scouting and acquiring black players remained a foreign endeavor for major-league teams, and a strong lack of trust festered on both sides. The result was the murky underworld of post-integration era baseball, where racial, social, and business lines blurred in an atmosphere baseball had never known. Extracting a player from the Negro Leagues was not simple, especially when it was the beloved son of Birmingham gifted with generational talent.

When the telegram from New York Giants owner Horace Stoneham finally arrived in Hayes's hands, its simple confirmation belied a complex sequence of events that culminated two years of maneuvering and resulted in a historically significant transaction.

"THIS WILL CONFIRM TELEPHONE CONVERSATION TODAY WITH OUR MR. SCHWARZ IN WHICH WE OFFERED TEN THOUSAND DOLLARS FOR THE ASSIGNMENT OF CONTRACT OF PLAYER WILLIE H MAYES JR AND YOU AGREED TO ASSIGN HIS CONTRACT TO THE MINNEAPOLIS BASEBALL CLUB FOR THAT AMOUNT. HORACE C. STONEHAM"

In pencil, Hayes scribbled the words that sent Willie Mays to the world: *Accept your offer of $10,000 for Willie H. Mays Jr.*

The transaction was the conclusion of one of the greatest, yet little known, sagas in baseball history, the true story of how Willie Mays rode the underground railroad between baseball's dying Negro Leagues to his stardom in the major leagues.

A childhood prodigy in baseball-rich Birmingham whose talents were well known locally for years, Mays officially broke into the Negro American League on July 4, 1948, signing a basic contract for $250 a month to play for the Black Barons. He was only 16, a high school student between his sophomore and junior years, but his talent allowed him to compete against men who had been in the league for years.

His guardian and mentor became Black Barons second baseman and manager Lorenzo "Piper" Davis, himself an all-star caliber second baseman who had once been considered a candidate to break major-league baseball's color line.

Davis protected Mays and tutored him on the finer points of the game. Davis also had something most black players in Birmingham did not possess — first-hand experience with what the locals called "White Folks Ball."

Davis gained a national reputation and an instinct for the machinations of player movements in white baseball. He also had years of experience in the northern states, which many southern players lacked. These nuances were completely foreign to young Mays. As important as Davis was to Mays's maturation as a player, he was just as crucial in helping Mays navigate the process of escape through the complex world of black baseball to white. Mays was simply a greenhorn with great gifts; it was up to the community around him to safely deliver him to the world at large.

Davis was established in the black sporting world for his two-sport career as a basketball player for the Harlem Globetrotters as well as his baseball career

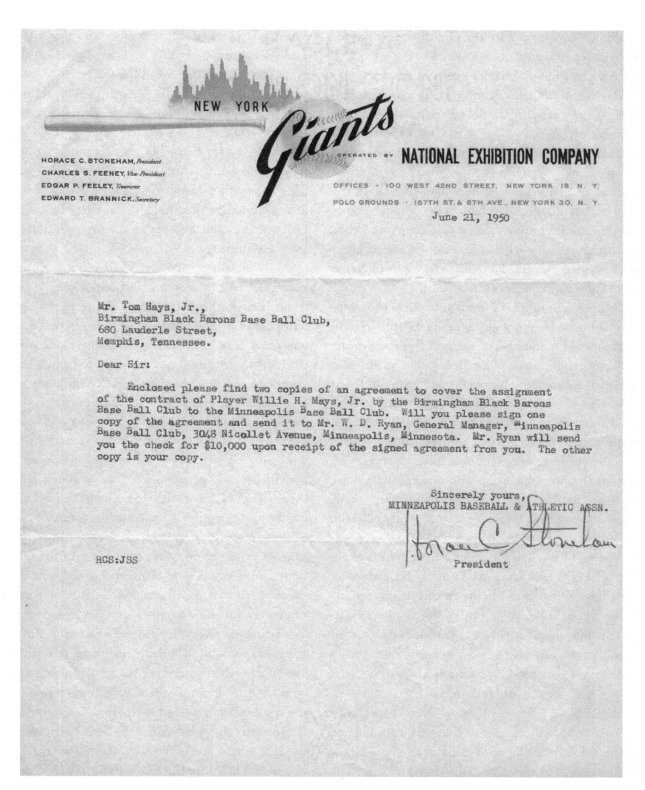

Letter from New York Giants owner Horace Stoneham to Black Barons owner Tom Hayes that accompanied an agreement in which Hayes sold Willie Mays' contract for $10,000. (*Courtesy of Memphis Public Library*)

with the Black Barons during the early 1940s. Mays would not have made it to the Giants were it not for the contacts Piper acquired, which were crucial to shaping the young outfielder's career trajectory.

Davis's former Black Barons manager and Harlem Globetrotters coach, Winfield Welch, was the field manager of the 1948 New York Cubans, owned by the flamboyant and savvy Alex Pompez. One reason Pompez hired Welch was to access the rich talent pipeline that existed in Birmingham thanks for the city's industrial leagues, which fed the Negro Leagues and produced scores of stars, including Piper Davis. These players could help his Cubans win immediately and also give Pompez added inventory to offer the white clubs in the near future.

Pompez, a longtime New York sports promoter who had once been one of Harlem's most successful operators of the "numbers," a gambling racket in the 1930s, was ambitious and intelligent. He dreamed of making the remaining Negro League teams affiliated minor-league teams, so that black and Latin players could be easily scouted and bought by major-league teams at reasonable prices. Pompez's dream was to keep the Negro League model of scouting and development alive in cooperation with major-league clubs, but to do that, he needed the right player to prove his vision and establish his own career in white baseball.

Pompez needed a big score to enhance his reputation. Mays was such a player, and therefore, no single Negro League ballplayer would mean as much to so many lives and affect so many careers as the path of Willie Mays. The first step of Pompez's plan was to see to it that the Giants would see Mays play, not in Birmingham, but on their owvn front yard. So he made sure to let the Giants know when the Black Barons were coming to Harlem.

The first time Mays played at New York's Polo Grounds, not as a member of the New York Giants, but in a doubleheader with the Birmingham Black Barons against Pompez's Cubans, in May 1949.

That day, Pompez sold two of his star players, pitcher Dave Barnhill and third baseman Ray Dandridge, to Giants owner Stoneham and farm czar Carl Hubbell. Barnhill and Dandridge were older players slated for Triple-A rosters, and simply Pompez's warm-up act to Hubbell to prove to the Hall of Fame pitcher that he knew how to evaluate young talent, a key factor in the selling of Mays.

Barnhill described his meeting with Hubbell that day, confirming Hubbell's presence at the Polo Grounds when Mays first played there in 1949, well than a year before Giants territory scout Ed Montague claimed that he happened upon Mays. This means that Montague did not discover Mays, as he claimed for decades. His superior, Hubbell, saw him a year earlier, and began the organization's following process.

Hubbell, the famed screwball pitcher who was then in charge of scouting and minor-league player acquisition for the Giants, had complete power and autonomy for signing and developing players, and he answered only to Stoneham. Signing black players in the early integration years, even to minor-league contracts, was an executive-level decision, not a territory-scout level decision. Pompez understood this division, and used his prestige as owner of Harlem's black ball club that rented the Polo Grounds to build a relationship with his major-league landlords.

Moreover, as a friend and ally of Black Barons owner Tom Hayes in the years when Negro League owners were sharply divided over the future of Negro League baseball, he also had direct knowledge of Hayes's price tag on Mays and access to the owner, both factors which eluded major-league teams interested in Mays. Many times, major-league teams did not even know how to contact Negro League teams.

Meanwhile, Mays continued to develop through 1949 and into 1950. He was no longer a well-kept secret. The Boston Braves made a run at signing Mays before he graduated from high school, but the front office hesitated at the high asking price. A decade later, Braves owner Lou Perini claimed that the Braves had been following Mays since 1945, well before he played for the Black Barons. Bill Maughn, the Braves territory scout, did more legwork than any white scout in Alabama, but lost out when his office paused. Maughn worked with integrity, but he did not understand how the black baseball underground railroad would circumvent his efforts to sign the player.

The Boston Red Sox signed Piper Davis in winter 1949 and sent him to minor-league spring training in 1950; Davis was the first black player signed by the Red Sox organization. Many Birmingham players believed the only reason the Red Sox signed Piper Davis was not because they viewed the beloved Piper as a prospect, but only to gain favor and access to Mays. Davis felt he had been treated poorly and that his performance did not warrant his release a few months later. Many in Birmingham believed that once the Red Sox found their efforts to acquire Mays through Davis insufficient, they cut him. Locals speculated that Hayes would not facilitate a deal for Mays with the Red Sox because a framework deal with Pompez to send Mays to the Giants already existed. His usefulness expired, Piper Davis was released and returned to the Black Barons.

The Birmingham community felt betrayed by the way Davis had been treated in the Red Sox organization. Hayes, in particular, would not reward the Red Sox for mistreating a player which meant much to his city and team. Birmingham did hold grudges and Mays would never become a Boston Red Sox.

The Cleveland Indians knew about Mays at least as early as 1948 because Harlem Globetrotter founder Abe Saperstein was scouting for Bill Veeck in an informal capacity. Veeck tried to sign Black Barons shortstop Artie Wilson after the 1948 season, but in another complex transaction, the deal got mucked up when the Yankees became involved and required Commissioner Chandler to formally award Wilson to the Yankees at a lower price than the Indians offered. This deal soured Hayes on White Folks Ball, and further cemented Mays to the Giants through the trusted connections of Piper Davis and Alex Pompez.

The Yankees and Dodgers were both informed about Mays, but declined to pursue him with intent. Each club had various degrees of information on him, but neither made a serious attempt to sign him.

The Chicago White Sox had a solid inside track thanks to its man on the ground. Former Negro League pitching legend John Donaldson was hired fulltime by the Chicago White Sox in 1949. He was the first fulltime scout dedicated to covering black players. Donaldson wanted Mays but couldn't get his front office to commit, as a series of letters and documents shows.

Mays rewarded Piper Davis's commitment to his growth. Mays played with the Black Barons for the first few months of the 1950 season, and with each game, it became more apparent that he was an impact player whose talents could not be contained to the remnants of the Negro League. Most white teams couldn't understand why Hayes was so reclusive and skeptical, and he gained a poor reputation in white baseball, even though black players said he treated them with integrity and fairness.

The one person Hayes trusted, Pompez, had won the Giants over. Pompez knew as much as he did because of his connections to Piper Davis.

When Mays and the Black Barons returned to play Pompez's Cubans in the Polo Grounds in early June of 1950, Hubbell and Stoneham had one more look at Mays playing a doubleheader. They loved what they saw. He was near major-league ready. They were ready to move once Mays graduated from high school.

Fearful that they would lose him if other teams found out they wanted him, Hubbell tapped power-hitting first baseman Alonzo Perry on the shoulder.

Perry had hit two home runs in the doubleheader and said he thought Hubbell wanted to sign him.

Instead, Hubbell asked him to confirm that Mays was indeed playing center field. Perry related this story to the *Birmingham News* after his playing career, another story that verifies Hubbell was already following Mays and wanted to make sure he had the right player.

Hubbell was looking for potential roommates for Mays, which was a common practice of major-league clubs in the early integration years. Perry would have been such a candidate, and the Giants never considered him a serious prospect. Hubbell, at the top of the chain of command, delegated the task of completing the transaction to Montague, his territory (area) scout, under orders of complete secrecy for the number of clubs pursing Mays. Birmingham players, including pitcher Bill Greason, said that the players knew Perry was a cover story for the Giants to keep their Mays a secret.

Perry, therefore, served as a decoy for Hubbell to dispatch two scouts to Birmingham, Ed Montague and Bill Harris, the following week. There was no such thing as the accidental discovery tale Montague told until it became accepted as fact, a historical fallacy still repeated today. The truth was Ed Montague had not the most to do with the Giants discovering Mays, as he often portrayed, but the least. Montague had no idea what was going on behind the scenes; he told what he thought was the truth; or at least omitted whatever back story he actually knew. It made for a good story for the New York papers, but as in many cases, there is a white history, and there is a black history.

Longtime Giants scout George Genovese confirmed Pompez was sent by Hubbell himself to Birmingham to negotiate with Hayes on behalf of the Giants. Montague's job was simply to come to sign the player; in later years, Montague claimed he alone had stumbled onto Mays when sent to check Perry. That was a scout's tall tale told to the white media in New York City and repeated as fact through the decades, but in truth, a photograph in the *Birmingham News* the weekend Mays was signed shows Montague with several other scouts in Birmingham for a white high school all-star game at Rickwood Field, while the Black Barons were still out of town. Montague didn't just stumble onto Mays, as he claimed. He was waiting for him. He was sent to finish the work arranged by Piper Davis, Alex Pompez, and Carl Hubbell.

In an era where major-league teams raided Negro League teams for their best players, often without fair value, Mays was so important to the Giants that Hayes got the respect he felt he deserved. He wanted to be treated as an equal by major-league owners. He viewed himself as a successful, respectable businessman the same as white owners, and he believed he earned fair acknowledgement. Many white owners

disdained Negro League owners as criminals and hustlers, but the Giants looked past what the rest of white baseball used as excuses to not sign black players. As a result, Hayes got what he wanted. He became the first black owner to receive a telegram from a major-league owner and he got something close to fair market value for the product he was selling.

Hayes had felt disrespected many times by major-league clubs, who he felt tried to buy his best players for below market value. Sometimes, he overpriced his players, perhaps intentionally, in order to keep his team together. His actions indicated that he would rather keep a player and pay him well in the Negro Leagues then sell him to white baseball just so his player could be paid less, play less, and be exploited.

Mays was too talented for the traps that befall other players from Birmingham. When the telegram came to Hayes's office, the owner felt vindicated and bittersweet; the respect he had coveted from the major leagues came at the cost of the best player he would ever sell.

It was a two-part deal: Montague signed Mays to a basic minor-league contract for a $4,000 bonus and Stoneham paid Hayes $10,000 for Mays's contract. Mays bitterly remembered how he never saw any of the $4,000. Genovese speculated that Pompez received a portion to the $4,000 as part of his commission, but most of the money went to Hayes.

That was the final move that made Mays a Giant for life.

The Giants in turn made sure Pompez and Davis were both rewarded for helping them obtain Mays finding creative ways to reward both for their help, another indication that the organization acknowledged that they would have never signed Mays without the help of the two men.

Pompez parlayed his role in the Mays transaction into a job with the Giants and became their key player runner in Latin America, responsible for such players as Juan Marichal, Orlando Cepeda, and the Alou brothers. He worked with George Genovese's brother, Chick. George Genovese said Horace Stoneham felt guilty that Pompez's New

York Cubans eventually went out of business, as did the other Negro League teams. It was a symbolic gesture, but Pompez, over the years, made himself very productive.

When Piper Davis was sold out of Birmingham and to Ottawa in the International League in 1951, the parent club of Ottawa was the New York Giants, who then sold Davis into a favorable situation with the Oakland Oaks, where he became a productive and popular Pacific Coast League player. Davis's strong reputation allowed him to stay in professional baseball for many years as a scout. He would forever remain connected to Willie Mays, but never once would he claim credit for any of his contributions.

For many years after, even when his income was such that he did not need the money, Mays continued to play for Pompez's winter barnstorming tours through the deep south. The connections remained strong. When he was inducted into the Hall of Fame, Mays thanked Piper Davis, and retained fond memories of his beloved '48 Black Barons.

When John Donaldson, the White Sox scoutv, learned that Mays had been bought by the Giants, he knew he would never have the chance to sign a player like Mays again. He wrote to Hayes, "Glad you sold Mays. I wish him the best of luck."

NOTE

This article was adapted by the author from his book *Willlie's Boys: The 1948 Birmingham Black Barons, the Last Negro League World Series, and the Making of a Baseball Legend* (Hoboken, New Jersey: John Wiley & Sons, 2009).

FROM THE NEGRO LEAGUES TO THE QUEBEC PROVINCIAL LEAGUE

By Jack Anderson

Most baseball fans recognize that Jackie Robinson playing for the Montreal Royals of the International League on April 18, 1946, marks the date of the first black player in Organized Baseball outside the Negro Leagues in the twentieth century.

Quebecers were proud that Branch Rickey, the general manager of the Brooklyn Dodgers, had chosen Montreal as the team to take part in "the great experiment" of integrating blacks into a previously all-white professional sport. Rickey has been widely acknowledged as one of the greatest general managers in the history of baseball, and he was not one to make his choices without tremendous consideration. Fewer people know that, only five years later, Rickey would again break new barriers by hiring the first black manager in Organized Baseball, once again in Quebec.

At that time a commonly heard argument was that blacks did not have the ability to play in the major leagues. By signing Jackie Robinson to a minor-league contract with Montreal, Rickey enabled Robinson to prove his ability in the top minor league before the next great step would be made, that of the first black player in the major leagues in the modern era. Rickey had also chosen wisely the venue for Robinson's debut. The mostly French-speaking fans of Quebec were not used to the discrimination shown to blacks in parts of the United States and showed their disapproval of such treatment at every opportunity. Less known, however, is the earlier history of blacks in baseball in Quebec.

In the 1920s there were black players in mixed Montreal baseball leagues, and even an all-black team, managed by former Negro League star George "Chappie" Johnson, who had several former Negro Leaguers on his squad, including Ted Page, Alphonso "Duke" Lattimore, Elias "Country" Brown, Wayne Carr, and Don Perry. Chappie Johnson was the first great Negro League catching star and had a lengthy career from the late 1890s to 1921, and then managed until 1939. Ted Page was an outfielder and first baseman with several Negro League teams, including the 1934 Pittsburgh Crawfords, who included the legendary Cool Papa Bell, Satchel Paige, Josh Gibson, Judy Johnson, and Oscar Charleston. Alphonso Lattimore was a catcher who played in the Negro Leagues from 1929 to 1933, including the Columbus Blue Birds of 1933 under manager William "Dizzy" Dismukes, where one of his teammates was star Ted "Double Duty" Radcliffe. Elias "Country" Brown was a second baseman and third baseman who played in the Negro Leagues from 1918 to 1933. Wayne Carr was a pitcher with nine Negro League teams from 1920 to 1928, and Don Perry was a first baseman with three teams from 1920 to 1927.[1]

By 1935 the Provincial League lost its affiliation with Organized Baseball by signing three black players, pitcher-outfielder Alfred Wilson of Granby, pitcher-infielder Charlie Calvert of the Montreal Jos. Choquette team, and second baseman-catcher Chico Bowden of Sorel. Wilson was a major star, had been signed away from Chappie Johnson's touring team, and went 5-0 with a 3.56 ERA as a pitcher and hit .392 in 72 games. Calvert and Bowden were Canadian-born blacks who had played on various teams for several years before the integration of the Provincial League.[2]

The following year, encouraged by the support given to the three players, Johnson sponsored an all-black team in the Provincial League called the Montreal Black Panthers, with Charlie Calvert as player-manager. The team went 13-16, finishing in fourth place, as it made frequent player changes and used many inexperienced players.

In 1937 the Black Panthers' fortunes deteriorated to a 10-50 record and the team was disbanded, with some of the players signing with local semipro town teams, and others joining barnstorming teams traveling across North America and playing local semipro squads.

By September 1939 Canada was at war in Europe, the borders were closed to casual travel, and there were no more Negro players in the Provincial League. It once more became an affiliated league within Organized Baseball, but it collapsed at the end of the 1940 season, and was not revived until 1947.

Town semipro teams continued to play, particularly in towns near military bases, after the Provincial League disbanded in 1940 and the Canadian-American League followed in 1942. In 1945 Drummondville signed Alfred Wilson, one of the best black players of the wartime leagues.

Branch Rickey did not want Jackie Robinson to room alone, so he added a black journeyman pitcher from the Negro League Homestead Grays, John Wright, to the Royals squad. Wright had an inauspicious time with the Royals in 1946 and was sent down to the Class-C Three Rivers Royals, where he posted a 12-8 record.

The Montreal Royals were not the only Quebec team to have black players in 1946. Wright and Roy Partlow starred with Three Rivers of the Class-C Can-Am league, and the Sherbrooke Canadians of the Class-C Border League, a Pittsburgh farm team, added shortstop Manny McIntyre, a Canadian better known as a hockey player. Wright and Partlow both played for many years in the Negro Leagues, Partlow from 1934 to 1950, and Wright from 1937 to 1954.

In the spring of 1947 Jackie Robinson was promoted to the Brooklyn Dodgers, thereby integrating major-league baseball. The integration of Organized Baseball, although lamentably late in coming, had the unintended effect of weakening the Negro Leagues as major-league teams signed top stars away, often

The 1951 Farnham Pirates of the Quebec Provincial League. Manager Sam Bankhead, formerly of the Homestead Grays, is at center in the front row. (*Courtesy of Center for Negro League Baseball Research*)

without compensating the Negro teams. The Negro National League folded after the 1948 season, and its players were distributed among surviving teams from the remaining Negro Leagues. With most teams in Organized Baseball in the United States, including the minor leagues, still segregated in the late 1940s and fewer positions available in the Negro American League, many black players sought the opportunity to play against white players by coming to Canada. Often they found positions after touring Western Canada with barnstorming squads, while many others opted for Quebec's Provincial League. At least 53 former Negro Leaguers played in the Provincial league between 1948 and 1952.

The Provincial League reached its zenith of popularity in the late 1940s as a Class-C minor league,

After a lengthy playing career, Sam Bankhead earned the distinction of becoming the first African-American manager of a mostly-white team when he took the reins for the Quebec Provincial League's Farnham Pirates in 1951. (*Courtesy of Center for Negro League Baseball Research*)

with many black and Latin players starring in the league along with major leaguers who had been temporarily banished due to their flirtation with Mexican baseball. Playing on the Drummondville team in 1949 were major leaguers Sal Maglie and Max Lanier, young Puerto Rican first baseman Vic Power, and former Negro Leaguer Quincy Trouppe. Among the many former Negro Leaguers who played in the Provincial League in this era were Dave Pope, Buzz Clarkson, Len Hooker, Willie Pope, Lazaro Medina, Maurice Peatros, Clarence Bruce, Nap Gulley, Terris McDuffie, Quincy Barbee, Claro Duany, and Silvio Garcia.

Power had played with Trouppe in the Mexican League before he came to Drummondville, where he hit .345 in 1949 and .334 with 105 runs batted in during the 1950 season. Clarkson was a power-hitting third baseman who had played in the Negro Leagues since 1937 and had a tremendous year with the St. Jean Braves in 1948 with a .401 batting average and 29 home runs. He later reached the majors in 1952 with the Boston Braves at the age of 37.

Garcia was another veteran of the Negro Leagues as well as the Mexican League, and he won the Provincial League's triple crown in 1950 with the Sherbrooke Athletics, hitting .365 with 21 home runs and 116 runs batted in. He never was given the opportunity to play in the majors and retired in 1954 at the age of 40.

Duany was known as the "Puerto Rican Babe Ruth" and had been selected to play in the Negro Leagues' 1947 East-West All-Star game as an outfielder for the New York Cubans. He starred with the Sherbrooke Athletics for three years and reached his high point of a .388 batting average, 23 home runs, and 77 runs batted in for the 1948 season.

Bob Trice, a right-handed pitcher, had played on the Negro Leagues' Homestead Grays before coming to Farnham of the Provincial League in 1950 and 1951. In 1952, while pitching for St. Hyacinthe, he led the league with a 16-3 record. The next year, he led Ottawa of the International League with a 21-10 record before graduating to the big leagues with the Philadelphia Athletics.

In 1951 Branch Rickey, now with the Pittsburgh Pirates, continued his crusade to integrate baseball by naming Sam Bankhead, brother of Dodgers pitcher Dan Bankhead, as manager of Pittsburgh's Class-C farm team in Farnham, Quebec. Sam had been a star shortstop in the Negro Leagues from 1930 to 1950, including eight seasons with the Homestead Grays, and was an inspirational leader on and off the field. His leadership skills led to Bankhead becoming the first black manager in Organized Baseball at Farnham.

Rickey had started his major-league management career in 1914 with the St. Louis Browns before leaving to develop the productive farm system of the St. Louis Cardinals from 1917 to 1942. By the time he left St. Louis for the Dodgers in October 1942, Rickey had developed with his son and right-hand man, Branch Rickey Jr., the finest and largest minor-league farm system. Rickey then replicated this wide-ranging player training and development system throughout the Dodgers organization, reaching a pinnacle of 24 minor-league teams in 1947. With almost 40 years of major-league management experience, Rickey had an unsurpassed network of scouts and former players who funneled leads and prospects to his attention. When he was forced out in Brooklyn and joined the Pittsburgh Pirates in 1951, he greatly increased the budget for scouting and development and tripled the number of scouts, bringing several key former Dodgers staff members to the Pirates. Rickey also used his extensive contacts with the Homestead Grays organization—Homestead being a suburb of Pittsburgh—to bring many promising young black players to his farm team in Farnham once the Provincial League re-entered Organized Baseball in 1950. The Farnham squad, operating first as the Black Sox, then the Pirates beginning in 1951, employed 18 former Negro Leaguers in the period from 1948 to 1952, almost double the number of the second highest team, the Drummondville Cubs, who had 10 black players on their roster in the same period. More than a dozen of Farnham's players had previously played for the Homestead Grays.

Canada, particularly Quebec, has played a major role in the integration of baseball. Most people know of Jackie Robinson's integration of Organized Baseball by way of the Montreal Royals, but the eager acceptance of former Negro League players onto the teams representing the smaller cities of Quebec was also an important factor in removing the color barrier from baseball.

Appendix: Former Negro League players in the Quebec Provincial League, 1948-52

1. Sam Bankhead
P/IF/Mgr., played for seven Negro League teams, 1930-50
1951—Farnham Pirates, player/manager

2. Quincy "Bud" Barbee
OF, 1B, P, played for eight Negro League teams, 1937-49
1949—St. Jean Braves, .342, 26 HR, 86 RBIs/4-1 pitching record
1950—St. Jean Braves, .284, 11 HR, 35 RBIs
1951—Granby Red Sox, .289, 8 HR, 79 RBIs

3. Hiram Alonso Brathwaite
OF/1B—Newark Eagles, Philadelphia Stars, 1944-48
1951—Farnham Pirates, .270, 3 HR, 39 RBIs
1952 -St. Hyacinthe Athletics, .256, 12 HR, 75 RBIs

4. Chet Brewer
P, played for six Negro League teams, 1925-48
1949—St. Jean Braves, 4-2 record

5. Ray Brown
P/OF, played mostly for Homestead Grays, 1930-48
1950—Sherbrooke Athletics, 1-5 record
1951—Sherbrooke Athletics, 11-10, 3.31 ERA, team won title

6. Clarence Bruce
2B, played for Homestead Grays, 1947-48
1949-50—Farnham Pirates, utility infielder

7. Ernest Burke
P, 3B, played for Baltimore Elite Giants, 1947-48
1950—St. Jean Braves, 15-3, 4.34 ERA

1951 — St. Jean Braves, 8-8, 4.92 ERA

8. Luis Cabrera
P, Indianapolis Clowns, 1948
1950 — St. Jean Braves, 7-6, 4.37 ERA
1951 — St. Jean Braves, 2-8, 4.97 ERA

9. Avelino Canizares
SS, Cleveland Buckeyes, 1945
1950 — Sherbrooke Athletics, .294, 0 HR, 37 RBIs

10. James "Buzz" Clarkson
SS/OF/2B, six Negro League teams 1937-50
1948 — St. Jean Braves, .408, 31 HR

11. Johnny Howard Davis
OF/P, Newark/Houston Eagles, 1940-50
1951 — Drummondville Cubs, .347, 31 HR, 116 RBIs

12. Claro Duany
OF, New York Cubans, 1944-47
1948 — Sherbrooke Athletics, .388, 23 HR, 77 RBIs
1949 — Sherbrooke Athletics, .290, 22 HR, 99 RBIs led league
1951 — Sherbrooke Athletics, .337, 23 HR, 84 RBIs

13. Silvio Garcia
SS/3B, New York Cubans, 1940-47
1949 — Sherbrooke Athletics, .315, 4 HR, 76 RBIS
1950 — Sherbrooke Athletics, .365, 21 HR, 116 RBIS
1951 — Sherbrooke Athletics, .346, 12 HR, 82 RBIS

14. Alphonso Gerrard
OF, three Negro League teams 1945-49
1951 — Three Rivers Royals, .337, 1 HR, 55 RBIs
1952 — Granby Phillies, .303, 0 HR, 46 RBIs

15. Stanley "Doc" Glenn
C, Philadelphia Stars, 1943-50
1952 — Quebec Braves, .248, 5 HR, 27 RBIs

16. Napoleon "Nap" Gulley
P/OF, Cleveland Buckeyes/Newark Eagles, 1943-47

1949 — Farnham Black Sox/St. Jean Braves, 0-3 record

17. George Handy
2B/3B, Memphis Red Sox/ Houston Eagles, 1946-49
1950 — St. Hyacinthe Saints, .352, 5 HR, 60 RBIs
1951 — St. Hyacinthe Saints, .333, 13 HR, 72 RBIs

18. Walter Hardy
SS/2B, NY Black Yankees, NY Cubans, KC Monarchs, 1945-50
1950 — St. Jean Braves, .200, 1HR, 9 RBIs
1951 — St. Jean Canadians, .251, 6 HR, 30 RBIs
1952 — St. Jean Canadians, .276, 4 HR, 45 RBIs

19. Lennie Hooker
P, Newark/Houston Eagles, 1940-49
1950 — Drummondville Cubs, 11-6, 2.53 ERA
1951 — Drummondville Cubs, 10-9, 3.79 ERA

20. Clifford "Connie" Johnson P, Indianapolis Crawfords, KC Monarchs, 1940-50
1951 — St. Hyacinthe Saints, 15-14, 3.24 ERA

21. Lester "Buck" Lockett
OF, eight teams in Negro Leagues 1937-50
1951 — Farnham Pirates, .217, 1 HR, 21 RBIs

22. Max Manning
P, Newark/Houston Eagles, 1938-49
1951 — Sherbrooke Athletics, no record available

23. Everett Marcelle
P/OF/C, played for six teams in Negro Leagues, 1939-48
1950 — Farnham Pirates, .272, 7 HR, 42 RBIs

24. Fred McDaniels
OF, played for four teams in Negro Leagues, 1940-51
1952 — record unknown/listed in league registry, 1952-53

25. Terris McDuffie
P/OF, played for 12 teams in Negro Leagues, 1930-45

1948—St. Jean Braves, 19-8, batted .342, 5 HR, 20 RBIs

1949—St. Jean Braves, 12-10, batted .267, 3 HR, 13 RBIs

1951—Sherbrooke Athletics, 6-1, 4.86 ERA

26. Curtis McGowan
P, Memphis Red Sox, 1950
1951—Drummondville Cubs, 2-2, 5.76 ERA

27. Leonardo "Lazarus" Medina
P, Indianapolis Clowns, 1944-46
1949—Drummondville Cubs, 0-1

28. Lee Moody
IF/OF, KC Monarchs, Birmingham Black Barons, 1944-47
1951—Three Rivers Yankees .242, 0 HR, 16 RBIs

29. Eudie Napier
C, Homestead Grays and Pittsburgh Crawfords, 1941-50
1949—Farnham Black Sox, .266, 4 HR, 54 RBIs
1951—Farnham Pirates, .285, 8 HR, 42 RBIs

30. Alex Newkirk
P, New York Black Yankees, New York Cubans, 1946-49
1950—St. Jean Braves, 3-2, 3.54 ERA
1951—St. Jean Braves and Granby, 7-12, 3.67 ERA (combined)

31. Pedro Pages
OF, New York Cubans, 1939 and 1947
1951—Sherbrooke Athletics, .244, 2 HR, 34 RBIs

32. Tom "Big Train" Parker
P, played for 14 teams in Negro Leagues, 1929-48
1949—Farnham Black Sox, 4-5 record

33. Jonathan Clyde Parris
IF, NY Black Yankees, Louisville Buckeyes, Phila. Stars, 1946-49
1951—St. Jean Braves, .294, 16 HR, 44 RBIs

34. Roy Partlow
P/OF, played for four teams in Negro Leagues, 1934-50
1950—Granby Red Sox, 7-2, 1.97 ERA
1951—Granby Red Sox, 8-3, 3.41 ERA

35. Gabe Patterson
OF/P, played for four teams in Negro Leagues, 1941-50
1948—Farnham Black Sox, .365, 9 HR, 28 RBIs

36. Maurice Peatros
1B/OF, Homestead Grays, 1947
1948—Farnham Black Sox, stats not available

37. Alfred Pinkston
1B, Cleveland Buckeyes, 1948
1951—Farnham Pirates, .301, 15 HR, 72 RBIs
1952—St. Hyacinthe Athletics, .360, 30 HR, 121 RBIs, won triple crown

38. Dave Pope
OF, Homestead Grays, 1946
1948—Farnham Black Sox, .361, 23 HR, 72 RBIs
1949—Farnham Black Sox, .306, 19 HR, 77 RBIs

39. Willie Pope
P, Homestead Grays, Pittsburgh Crawfords, 1945-48
1948—Farnham Black Sox, 11-15
1949—Farnham Black Sox, 12-11
1950—Farnham Pirates, 3-5, 2.38 ERA
1951—St. Hyacinthe Saints, 12-11, 3.32 ERA

40. Bill Ricks
P, Philadelphia Stars, 1944-50
1951—Granby Red Sox, 8-8, 4.21 ERA

41. Marshall Riddle
IF, played for five teams in Negro Leagues, 1936-43
1951—Three Rivers Royals, .238, 18 RBIs

42. Wilfredo Salas
P, New York Cubans, 1948

1948—Sherbrooke Athletics, 3-4 record

43. Carlos Santiago
2B/SS, New York Cubans, 1946
1950—Farnham Pirates, .195, 2 HR, 21 RBIs
First black Puerto Rican in Organized Baseball

44. Joe B. Scott
OF, Birmingham Black Barons, Chicago American Giants, 1945-49
1950—Farnham Pirates, .312, 8 HR, 44 RBIs
1951—Farnham/St. Hyacinthe, .264, 4 HR, 38 RBIs

45. John Ford Smith
P, played for five teams in Negro Leagues, 1939-50
1951—Drummondville Cubs, 16-8, 2.97

46. Sylvester "Cy" Snead
P/UT, played for three teams in Negro Leagues, 1939-46
1951—Drummondville/St. Hyacinthe, batted .174 in 31 games

47. Joe Cephus Taylor
C/OF, Chicago American Giants, 1949-51
1951—Farnham Pirates, .360, 10 HR, 29 RBIs
1952—St. Hyacinthe Athletics, .308, 25 HR, 112 RBIs

48. Bob Trice
P, Homestead Grays, 1948-49
1950—Farnham Pirates, 5-3 record
1951—Farnham Pirates, 7-12, 5.15 ERA
1952—St. Hyacinthe A's, 16-3, 3.49 ERA

49. Quincy Trouppe
C, for eight teams in Negro Leagues 1930-49, five-time All-Star
1949—Drummondville Cubs, .282, 5 HR, 30 RBIs

50. Guillermo Vargas
OF, New York Cubans, 1949

1952—Drummondville Cubs, .282, 3 HR, 6 RBIs

51. Roberto Vargas
P, Chicago American Giants, 1948
1949—Drummondville Cubs, 12-9 record

52. Archie Ware
1B, played for six teams in Negro Leagues, 1940-51
1951—Farnham Pirates, .257, 6 HR, 48 RBIs

53. Arstando "Ladd" White
P, Indianapolis Clowns, 1948
1950—Drummondville Cubs, 9-12, 3.77 ERA

SOURCES

In addition to the sources cited in the Notes, the author also consulted:

Carpentier, Patrick, and Paul Foisy, eds. *Baseball au Québec* (St-Hyacinthe, Quebec: Sport et Société, 2009).

Clark, Dick, and Larry Lester, eds. *The Negro Leagues Book* (Cleveland: SABR, 1994).

Heaphy, Leslie A. *The Negro Leagues* (Jefferson, North Carolina: McFarland & Co. Inc., 2003).

Humber, William. *Diamonds of the North* (Toronto: Oxford University Press, 1995).

Lowenfish, Lee. *Branch Rickey: Baseball's Ferocious Gentleman* (Lincoln: University of Nebraska Press, 2007).

Swanton, Barry, and Jay-Dell Mah. *Black Baseball Players in Canada* (Jefferson, North Carolina: McFarland & Co. Inc., 2009).

Trouppe, Quincy. *20 Years Too Soon* (St. Louis: Missouri Historical Society Press, 1977).

Thanks to Christian Trudeau for his assistance in the preparation of this article.

NOTES

1   John Virtue, *South of the Color Barrier* (Jefferson, North Carolina: McFarland, 2008), 48.

2   Christian Trudeau, "Integration in Quebec," Jane Finnan Dorward, ed., *Dominionball* (Cleveland: SABR, 2005), 23.

EPILOGUE: BIRMINGHAM, PITTSBURGH, AND THE NEGRO LEAGUES SINCE 1948

By Frederick C. Bush

To people familiar with the historical relationship between the cities of Pittsburgh, Pennsylvania, and Birmingham, Alabama, it must seem appropriate that the last Negro League World Series, in 1948, was played between teams from those two areas—the Homestead Grays and the Birmingham Black Barons—and inevitable that the Grays would emerge as the victors.[1] Though founded in different centuries (Pittsburgh in 1758 and Birmingham in 1871) and located in different parts of the country, the two cities became powerhouses of their regions as a result of their steel industries and nearby coal-rich areas. In time, Birmingham became the leading manufacturer of foundry iron in the United States, earning the nickname "The Pittsburgh of the South."[2]

In 1907, however, Pittsburgh's US Steel Corporation bought out Birmingham's Tennessee Coal, Iron, and Railroad Company, its largest competitor at that time, in a move that ensured that Pittsburgh would remain the country's leader in the steel industry. When the Great Depression hit in the 1930s, US Steel "started shutting down the mills [in Birmingham] to protect its interests in the North."[3] The effect on Birmingham's economy was so severe that "[t]he city government was on the verge of shutting down by mid-1933" and it took a loan from the First National Bank to keep "the city machinery from grinding to a halt."[4] Birmingham eventually rose from the ashes, but it was clear that there would be only one Pittsburgh in the United States. Toward the end of the twentieth century, Birmingham journalist Paul Hemphill observed, "[V]irtually no new industry, blue-collar or otherwise, had filled in the gap, mainly because U.S. Steel and the local barons didn't want the competition."[5]

In 1948 US Steel still had an open-hearth works facility operating in Homestead, so many of the Grays lived in the shadow of the mills. The same was true for many Black Barons players, who had graduated to the club from Birmingham's industrial leagues. Thus, the competition between the two baseball clubs mirrored the competition between the two cities' primary industry. The teams already had competed for the championship of Negro baseball in both 1943—a hard-fought series won four games to three by the Grays—and 1944, when the Grays needed only five games to prevail. However, by the time of the 1948 Negro League World Series—the third clash in six years between the two teams—the handwriting was on the wall for the demise of the Negro Leagues.

After Jackie Robinson's debut at first base for the Brooklyn Dodgers at Ebbets Field on April 15, 1947, Organized Baseball began to pursue the Negro Leagues' top talents. The result was a rapid decline in the quality of Negro baseball and, as was to be expected, a turning of black fans' attention away from the Negro Leagues and toward the black players who were now taking the field for major-league teams. In 1948 center fielder Larry Doby and pitching legend Satchel Paige helped lead the Cleveland Indians to the World Series title over the Boston Braves, making the Indians franchise the first integrated professional sports team in America to win a championship. Even the black press now devoted most of its attention to the major-league World Series, due to Doby's and Paige's involvement, and included only brief write-ups and line scores (rather than box scores) in its meager coverage of the championship clash between the Grays and the Black Barons.

The integration of Organized Baseball brought hope to those black players who believed they were destined for major-league stardom (including Birmingham's Willie Mays) and sadness to others who knew that they would either toil in obscurity for low wages or have to leave baseball altogether.

Birmingham's Bill Greason, the winning pitcher in the Black Barons' lone victory over the Grays in the 1948 series, summed up the bittersweet feelings of many Negro Leaguers when he said:

"There was a little bit of sadness on the Black Barons that season. We could all sense that something was leaving the game, and a lot of the players who were honest knew that the Negro League wouldn't survive much longer. But Willie [Mays] made us [Black Barons] remember in every game he played why we wanted to play baseball so much in the first place."[6]

Greason's sense of impending doom about the end of the Negro Leagues began to become reality when, shortly after his Black Barons fell to the Grays, the Negro National League, to which Homestead belonged, disbanded. In the absence of competing leagues, it was obvious that no further Negro Leagues World Series would be played.

In spite of Organized Baseball's raid of the best players in black baseball, the full integration of the major leagues did not occur overnight. Initially, an unwritten "two black players per team" quota system was in place for most clubs, and it took until 1959—12 years after Robinson's debut—for every major-league team to have employed at least one black player when the Boston Red Sox added Elijah "Pumpsie" Green to their roster. For every Willie Mays, Henry Aaron, or Ernie Banks who emerged from the remnants of the Negro Leagues into major-league stardom, there were dozens of others who never received a chance equal to that of their white counterparts or who simply were not good enough to make it to the big leagues.

In 1966 Red Sox legend Ted Williams brought attention to the defunct Negro Leagues by using his Hall of Fame induction speech to advocate the inclusion of former Negro League players in base-ball's shrine of the immortals. Williams remarked on the fact that Willie Mays had just surpassed him in career home runs, and added, "I hope that one day Satchel Paige and Josh Gibson will be voted into the Hall of Fame as symbols of the great Negro players who are not here only because they weren't given the chance."[7] Nevertheless, as had been the case with the integration of the sport itself, the integration of its most hallowed halls was a slow process.

In 1969 Bowie Kuhn became the commissioner of baseball, and he appointed a 10-man committee to nominate former Negro League players for induction into the Hall of Fame. As a result, in 1971, Satchel Paige became the first player who had spent the majority of his career in the Negro Leagues to enter the Hall of Fame; many future Negro League inductees would be players who had spent their entire careers in black baseball. However, when Kuhn made the announcement of Paige's election in February 1971, he indicated that Paige would be enshrined in a new Negro wing of the Hall, prompting such an outrage that a once-segregated player would now be a segregated immortal that the idea for a separate wing for Negro Leaguers was scrapped and Paige's bust took its place among those of his baseball peers in Cooperstown, New York, in July of that year.

During the course of the 1970s, baseball historians Robert Peterson and John Holway pioneered Negro League research, but there still appeared to be little interest among most fans and students of the game. Major- and minor-league cities also tended to ignore their former Negro League counterparts. Eventually—on September 11, 1988—the Pittsburgh Pirates became the first franchise to honor its city's Negro League clubs, the Grays and the Pittsburgh Crawfords. Before that evening's game, a flag commemorating the Grays' 1948 championship was raised to fly alongside the Pirates' own championship banners at Three Rivers Stadium. Four members of the 1948 Grays—Clarence Bruce, Buck Leonard, Willie Pope, and Bob Thurman—and six other Negro Leaguers were honored that night. Bruce, speaking at the ceremony, pointed to the Grays' pennant banner and proclaimed, "That means the Grays are a legend. That means we haven't been forgotten."[8]

Two years later, in 1990, the Negro Leagues Baseball Museum was founded in Kansas City, Missouri, by local business leaders, historians, and baseball players. In 1997 the museum moved to its current location at 18th and Vine Streets, a historic African-American district, which it shares with the American Jazz Museum. Visitors to the museum "experience a tour of multi-media displays, museum store, hundreds of photographs, and artifacts dating from the late 1800s through the 1960s."[9]

In his 2007 book *The Soul of Baseball*, a *Kansas City Star* columnist, Joe Posnanski, documented a year he had spent traveling with legendary Kansas City Monarchs player-manager Buck O'Neil, the driving force behind the founding of the museum. Former 1948 Black Baron turned Hall of Fame immortal Willie Mays came to visit the museum one day, but his glaucoma-ravaged eyes would not allow him to step under the bright lights of the center-piece Field of Legends display. Mays told O'Neil, "You know I really don't need to see the museum. I lived it." However, Mays had already seen many of the displays, and they had made such an immense impact that a close friend later phoned O'Neil to tell him that Mays "[had] cried the entire ride back to the hotel."[10]

In addition to the Negro Leagues Baseball Museum, the rediscovery and commemoration of the Negro Leagues were given further impetus by the publication of two landmark books in 1994: James A. Riley's *The Biographical Encyclopedia of the Negro Baseball Leagues*, which provided brief biographical sketches of as many players as Riley could uncover, and Dick Clark and Larry Lester's *The Negro Leagues Book*, which compiled rosters and player statistics and examined the greatest teams and Hall of Famers from black baseball.

Since the mid-1990s, there has been an explosion in research and literature about the Negro Leagues as well as their role in the integration of major-league baseball. Twenty former Negro Leaguers were inducted into the Hall of Fame from 1971 to 1999. The surge of interest in black baseball has brought more attention to its players and has aided in the enshrinement of an additional 15 Negro League players since the turn of the twenty-first century.[11] There were more than 35 Hall of Fame-caliber players in over a half-century of Negro League baseball, of course, though it remains to be seen how many additional players will be selected for induction at Cooperstown.

In 1997 Jackie Robinson's number 42 was universally retired by every major-league team, though the number is worn today by every major leaguer in games played on April 15—Jackie Robinson Day—to commemorate Robinson's first game with the Dodgers. Many major- and minor-league teams throughout the country now also honor their respective city's black baseball heritage, with players often donning throwback uniforms of bygone Negro League teams for one game each year.

In light of America's racial past, however, even attempts to honor the Negro Leagues can sometimes open old wounds or go awry. The Pittsburgh Pirates, the very club to first acknowledge the Negro Leagues, created a display area named Highmark Legacy Square at their current stadium, PNC Park, in 2006. A press release on the team's website stated:

> "The exhibit features life-size bronze statues of former Negro Leagues greats Cool Papa Bell, Oscar Charleston, Josh Gibson, Judy Johnson, Buck Leonard, Satchel Paige, and Smokey Joe Williams. Each statue is accompanied by an interactive kiosk allowing fans to view a personal video and learn about the player's background, Hall of Fame honors, and playing statistics."[12]

In spring of 2015, as the Pirates were experiencing a new era of success, they decided to strip Highmark Legacy Square of its statues in order to accommodate the larger number of fans attending their games. Sean Gibson, president of the Josh Gibson Foundation, which is named after his great-grandfather, suggested relocating the statues to different areas throughout the stadium, but the Pirates decided simply to rid themselves of them, though they did agree to donate them to Gibson's foundation.[13]

The result of the move proved a disaster for the club, which was lambasted by one historian who wrote:

Since 1996, the Friends of Rickwood has held the annual Rickwood Classic in an effort to preserve America's oldest stadium. The 2013 Rickwood Classic honored the 1948 Birmingham Black Barons' NAL championship team. (*From the personal collection of Frederick C. Bush*)

Jimmie Newberry, the ace of the 1948 Birmingham Black Barons' pitching staff, graced the back cover of the program for the 2013 Rickwood Classic, which commemorated the 1948 championship squad. (*From the personal collection of Frederick C. Bush*)

"The Pirates are effectively saying that the Pittsburgh Crawfords and Homestead Grays have nothing to do with the Pirates anymore, and if you want the Crawfords or Grays—or Black history in general—then go to the Forbes Field landmark, the Western Pennsylvania Sports Museum, or the Negro Leagues Baseball Museum."[14]

While the Pirates have taken a step backward, other franchises and cities continue to move forward with tributes to the Negro Leagues.

Most notably, Birmingham—once the most segregated city in the United States and a center of civil rights activism and violence—opened the Negro Southern League Museum in partnership with the Center for Negro League Baseball Research in the summer of 2015. Clayton Sherrod, who has organized reunions of surviving Negro League players at Birmingham's renovated Rickwood Field, believes the museum to be important "not only because of the Negro Leagues but also because of the industrial leagues, which were huge in Birmingham."[15]

Though the founding of the Birmingham museum was a positive development, there was concern on the part of the Kansas City museum that the two entities would compete for the same audience, thus turning the Negro Leagues into a house divided. Dr.

Larry Powell, author of *Black Barons of Birmingham: The South's Greatest Negro League Team and Its Players* and a professor at the University of Alabama at Birmingham, attempted to assuage such fears, saying, "This one [Negro Southern League Museum] doesn't have to be a national museum [as he believes the Kansas City museum has tried to be], but it does need to be a regional museum, one that will attract people from the South."[16]

The Negro Leagues, which would not have had to exist had it not been for Jim Crow, remain an example of African-American entrepreneurship under segregation and were a source of great pride for the black community. The late A. Bartlett Giamatti had been elected commissioner of baseball one week prior to the Pirates' 40-year commemoration of the Grays' championship in 1988. In commenting on the Pittsburgh ceremony, Giamatti pointed out the importance of the Negro Leagues when he stated, "We must never lose sight of our history, insofar as it is ugly, never to repeat it, and insofar as it is glorious, to cherish it."[17]

NOTES

1   Homestead is seven miles southeast of downtown Pittsburgh.

2   Christopher Fullerton, *Every Other Sunday* (Birmingham: R. Boozer Press, 1999), 27.

3   Allen Barra, *Rickwood Field: A Century in America's Oldest Ballpark* (New York: W.W. Norton & Co., 2010), 115.

4   Ibid.

5   Paul Hemphill, *Leaving Birmingham: Notes of a Native Son* (New York: Viking Penguin, 1993), 114.

6   Barra, 156.

7   Paul Dickson, "Celebrating Ted Williams' Historic Call for Inclusion 50 Years Ago This Week," thenationalpastimemuseum.com/article/celebrating-ted-williams-s-historic-call-inclusion-50-years-ago-week, accessed January 6, 2017.

8   "Clarence Bruce, Was Homestead Grays Player" [obituary], *Pittsburgh Post-Gazette*, January 25, 1990.

9   nlbm.com/s/index.cfm.

10 Joe Posnanski, *The Soul of Baseball: A Road Trip through Buck O'Neil's America* (New York: William Morrow, 2007), 34.

11 As of January 2017.

12 Pirates Media Relations, "Pirates unveil Highmark Legacy Square at PNC Park," pittsburgh.pirates.mlb.com/news/press_releases/press_release.jsp?ymd=20060626&content_id=1523995&vkey=pr_pit&fext=.jsp&c_id=pit, accessed January 7, 2017.

13 Josh Howard, "Disappointment in Pittsburgh: How the Pirates Ditched Pittsburgh's Negro Leagues Past," ussporthistory.com/2015/10/12/2902/, accessed January 7, 2017.

14 Ibid.

15 Nick Patterson, "Reclaiming History: More Than a Game, Baseball — Especially the Negro Leagues — Plays a Big Part in Birmingham's Past and Future," weldbham.com/blog/2015/02/03/reclaiming-history-birmingham-black-barons/, accessed January 7, 2017.

16 Ibid.

17 Doron P. Levin, "Pittsburgh Recalls a Neglected Title," *New York Times*, September 12, 1988: C3.

BIBLIOGRAPHY FOR FURTHER RESEARCH

The current volume covers the Negro Leagues during a time of great transition. Many of the players who are profiled in this book also played in Latin America and/or Canada, and several of them eventually made it to the minor or major leagues. Conversely, dark-skinned Latin players were forced to play in the Negro Leagues under segregation in America, so their story is intertwined with the history of African-American players. For readers and researchers who are interested in pursuing this topic further, the editors have provided a bibliography that traces the Negro Leagues from their beginnings to their demise, examines the role of the Latin American and Canadian Leagues in the history of Negro League baseball, and chronicles the early years of integration in the minor and major leagues. Also included is an entry for a book about the first major-league franchise to start nine players of African-American or Latin origin in the same game, the 1971 Pittsburgh Pirates.

BOOKS

Aaron, Hank with Lonnie Wheeler. *I Had a Hammer: The Hank Aaron Story* (New York: HarperCollins, 1991).

Adelson, Bruce. *Brushing Back Jim Crow: The Integration of Minor-League Baseball in the American South* (Charlottesville, Virginia: University Press of Virginia, 1999).

Allen, Maury. *Jackie Robinson: A Life Remembered* (New York: Franklin Watts, 1987).

Alpert, Rebecca T. *Out of Left Field: Jews and Black Baseball* (New York: Oxford University Press, 2011).

Bak, Richard. *Turkey Stearnes and the Detroit Stars* (Detroit: Wayne State University Press, 1995).

Bankes, Jim. *The Pittsburgh Crawfords* (Jefferson, North Carolina: McFarland & Company, Inc., 2001).

Barra, Allen. *Rickwood Field: A Century in America's Oldest Ballpark* (New York: W.W. Norton & Co., 2010).

Bjarkman, Peter C. *Baseball with a Latin Beat: A History of the Latin American Game* (Jefferson, North Carolina: McFarland & Company, Inc., 1994).

_____. *A History of Cuban Baseball, 1864-2006* (Jefferson, North Carolina: McFarland & Company, Inc., 2007).

Brashler, William. *Josh Gibson: A Life in the Negro Leagues* (Chicago: Ivan R. Dee, 2000).

Brioso, Cesar. *Havana Hardball: Spring Training, Jackie Robinson, and the Cuban League* (Gainesville: University Press of Florida, 2015).

Bruce, Janet. *The Kansas City Monarchs: Champions of Black Baseball* (Lawrence: University of Kansas Press, 1985).

Burgos, Adrian. *Cuban Star: How One Negro-League Owner Changed the Face of Baseball* (New York: Hill and Wang, 2011).

_____. *Playing America's Game: Baseball, Latinos, and the Color Line* (Los Angeles: University of California Press, 2007).

Carroll, Brian. *When to Stop the Cheering? The Black Press, the Black Community, and the Integration of Professional Baseball* (New York: Routledge, Taylor, & Francis Group, 2007).

Cash, Bill "Ready" and Al Hunter, Jr. *Thou Shalt Not Steal: The Baseball Life and Times of a Rifle-Armed Negro League Catcher* (Philadelphia: Love Eagle Books, 2012).

Chadwick, Bruce. *When the Game Was Black and White: The Illustrated History of Baseball's Negro Leagues* (New York: Abbeville Press, 1992).

Clark, Dick and Larry Lester. *The Negro Leagues Book* (Cleveland: Society for American Baseball Research, 1994).

Colton, Larry. *Southern League: A True Story of Baseball, Civil Rights, and the Deep South's Most Compelling Pennant Race* (New York: Grand Central Publishing, 2013).

Cottrell, Robert Charles. *The Best Pitcher in Baseball: The Life of Rube Foster, Negro League Giant* (New York: New York University Press, 2001).

_____. *Two Pioneers: How Hank Greenberg and Jackie Robinson Transformed Baseball—And America* (Dulles, Virginia: Potomac Books, 2012).

Debono, Paul. *The Indianapolis ABCs* (Jefferson, North Carolina: McFarland & Company, Inc., 1997).

Dixon, Phil S. *The Negro Baseball Leagues: A Photographic History* (Mattituck, New York: Amereon House, 1992).

_____. *Phil Dixon's American Baseball Chronicles Great Teams: The 1931 Homestead*

Grays, Volume 1 (Bloomington, Indiana: Xlibris Corporation, 2009).

Gonzalez Echevarria, Roberto. *The Pride of Havana: A History of Cuban Baseball* (New York: Oxford University Press, 1999).

Eig, Jonathan. *Opening Day: The Story of Jackie Robinson's First Season* (New York: Simon & Schuster, 2007).

Einstein, Charles. *Willie's Time: Baseball's Golden Age* (Carbondale: Southern Illinois Press, 2004).

Falkner, David. *Great Time Coming: The Life of Jackie Robinson from Baseball to Birmingham* (New York: Simon & Schuster, 1995).

Fields, Wilmer. *My Life in the Negro Leagues: An Autobiography*, reissue with a new introduction (McLean, Virginia: Miniver Press, 2013).

Figueredo, Jorge S. *Cuban Baseball: A Statistical History, 1878-1961* (Jefferson, North Carolina: McFarland & Company, Inc., 2003).

_____. *Who's Who in Cuban Baseball, 1878-1961* (Jefferson, North Carolina: McFarland & Company, Inc., 2007).

Frommer, Harvey. *Rickey and Robinson: The Men Who Broke Baseball's Color Barrier* (Lanham, Maryland: Taylor Trade Publishing, 1982).

Fullerton, Christopher D. *Every Other Sunday: The Story of the Birmingham Black Barons* (Birmingham: R. Boozer Press, 1999).

Gay, Timothy M. *Satch, Dizzy & Rapid Robert: The Wild Saga of Interracial Baseball before Jackie Robinson* (New York: Simon & Schuster, 2010).

Gilbert, Thomas. *Baseball at War: World War II and the Fall of the Color Line* (New York: Franklin Watts, 1997).

Hauser, Christopher. *The Negro Leagues Chronology: Events in Organized Black Baseball, 1920-1948* (Jefferson, North Carolina: McFarland & Company, Inc., Publishers, 2006).

Heaphy, Leslie A. *The Negro Leagues, 1869-1960* (Jefferson, North Carolina: McFarland & Company, Inc., 2003).

Hernández, Lou. *Memories of Winter Ball: Interviews with Players in the Latin American Winter Leagues of the 1950s* (Jefferson, North Carolina: McFarland & Company, Inc., 2013).

_____. *The Rise of the Latin American Baseball Leagues, 1947-1961: Cuba, the Dominican Republic, Mexico, Nicaragua, Panama, Puerto Rico and Venezuela*

(Jefferson, North Carolina: McFarland & Company, Inc., 2011).

Hirsch, James S. *Willie Mays: The Life, the Legend* (New York: Scribner, 2010).

Hoffbeck, Steven R. *Swinging for the Fences: Black Baseball in Minnesota* (St. Paul: Minnesota Historical Society Press, 2005).

Hogan, Lawrence D. *The Forgotten History of African American Baseball* (Santa Barbara, California: Praeger, 2014).

_____. *Shades of Glory: The Negro Leagues and the Story of African-American Baseball* (Washington, D.C.: National Geographic, 2006).

Holway, John B. *Black Diamonds: Life in the Negro Leagues from the Men Who Lived It* (New York: Mecklermedia, 1990).

_____. *Black Giants* (Springfield, Virginia: Lord Fairfax Press, 2010).

_____. *Blackball Stars: Negro League Pioneers* (New York: Carroll & Graf Publishers, 1988).

_____. *Bullet Joe and the Monarchs* (Washington, D.C.: Capital Press, 1984).

_____. *The Complete Book of Baseball's Negro Leagues: The Other Half of Baseball History* (Fern Park, Florida: Hastings House Publishers, 2001).

_____. *Josh and Satch: The Life and Times of Josh Gibson and Satchel Paige* (New York: Meckler Publishing, 1991).

_____. *Voices from the Great Black Baseball Leagues* (Mineola, New York: Dover Publications, Inc., 1975).

Humber, William. *Diamonds of the North* (New York: Oxford University Press, 1995).

Irvin, Monte and James A. Riley. *Nice Guys Finish First: The Autobiography of Monte Irvin* (New York: Carroll & Graf Publishers, Inc., 1996).

Jacobson, Steve. *Carrying Jackie's Torch: The Players Who Integrated Baseball—And America* (Chicago: Lawrence Hill Books, 2007).

Kahn, Roger. *Rickey & Robinson: The True, Untold Story of the Integration of Baseball* (New York: Rodale, 2014).

Kashatus, William C. *Jackie and Campy: The Untold Story of Their Rocky Relationship and the Breaking of Baseball's Color Line* (Lincoln: University of Nebraska Press, 2014).

Kelley, Brent P. *"I Will Never Forget": Interviews with 39 Former Negro League Players* (Jefferson, North Carolina: McFarland & Company, Inc., 2003).

_____. *The Negro Leagues Revisited: Conversations with 66 More Baseball Heroes* (Jefferson, North Carolina: McFarland & Company, Inc., 2000).

_____. *Voices from the Negro Leagues: Conversations with 52 Baseball Standouts* (Jefferson, North Carolina: McFarland & Company, Inc., 1998).

Kirwin, William, ed. *Out of the Shadows: African American Baseball from the Cuban Giants to Jackie Robinson* (Lincoln: University of Nebraska Press, 2005).

Kiser, Brett. *Baseball's War Roster: A Biographical Dictionary of Major and Negro League Players Who Served, 1861 to the Present* (Jefferson, North Carolina: McFarland & Company, Inc., 2012).

Klima, John. *Willie's Boys: The 1948 Birmingham Black Barons, the Last Negro League World Series, and the Making of a Baseball Legend* (Hoboken, New Jersey: Wiley & Sons, Inc., 2009).

Lacy, Sam with Moses J. Newsom. *Fighting for Fairness: The Life Story of Hall of Fame Sportswriter Sam Lacy* (Centreville, Maryland: Tidewater Publishers, 1998).

Lamb, Chris. *Blackout: The Untold Story of Jackie Robinson's First Spring Training* (Lincoln: University of Nebraska Press, 2004).

_____. *Conspiracy of Silence: Sportswriters and the Long Campaign to Desegregate Baseball* (Lincoln: University of Nebraska Press, 2012).

Lanctot, Neil. *Fair Dealing and Clean Playing: The Hilldale Club and the Development of Black Professional Baseball, 1910-1932* (Jefferson, North Carolina: McFarland & Company, Inc., 1994).

_____. *Negro League Baseball: The Rise and Ruin of a Black Institution* (Philadelphia: University of Pennsylvania Press, 2004).

Leonard, Buck with James A. Riley. *Buck Leonard: The Black Lou Gehrig* (New York: Carroll and Graf Publishers, Inc., 1995).

Lester, Larry. *Baseball's First Colored World Series: The 1924 Meeting of the Hilldale Giants and Kansas City Monarchs* (Jefferson, North Carolina: McFarland & Company, Inc., 2006).

_____. *Black Baseball in New York City: An Illustrated History, 1885-1959* (Jefferson, North Carolina: McFarland & Company, Inc., 2017). *Forthcoming in August 2017.

_____. *Black Baseball's National Showcase: The East-West All-Star Game, 1933-1953* (Lincoln: University of Nebraska Press, 2001).

_____. *Rube Foster in His Time: On the Field and in the Papers with Black Baseball's Greatest Visionary* (Jefferson, North Carolina: McFarland & Company, Inc., 2012).

_____ and Sammy J. Miller. *Black Baseball in Kansas City* (Charleston, South Carolina: Arcadia Publishing, 2000).

_____ and Sammy J. Miller. *Black Baseball in Pittsburgh* (Charleston, South Carolina: Arcadia Publishing, 2001).

_____, Sammy J. Miller, and Dick Clark. *Black Baseball in Chicago* (Charleston, South Carolina: Arcadia Publishing, 2000).

_____, Sammy J. Miller, and Dick Clark. *Black Baseball in Detroit* (Charleston, South Carolina: Arcadia Publishing, 2000).

Loverro, Thom. *The Encyclopedia of Negro League Baseball* (New York: Checkmark Books, 2003).

Lowenfish, Lee. *Branch Rickey: Baseball's Ferocious Gentleman* (Lincoln: University of Nebraska Press, 2007).

Luke, Bob. *The Baltimore Elite Giants* (Baltimore: The Johns Hopkins University Press, 2009).

_____. *Integrating the Orioles: Baseball and Race in Baltimore* (Jefferson, North Carolina: McFarland & Company, Inc., 2016).

_____. *The Most Famous Woman in Baseball: Effa Manley and the Negro Leagues* (Lincoln: University of Nebraska Press, 2011).

_____. *Willie Wells: 'El Diablo' of the Negro Leagues* (Austin: University of Texas Press, 2007).

Madden, Bill. *1954: The Year Willie Mays and the First Generation of Black Superstars Changed Major League Baseball Forever* (Boston: Da Capo Press, 2014).

Manley, Effa and Leon Herbert Hardwick. *Negro Baseball before Integration* (Chicago: Adams Press, 1976).

Maraniss, David. *Clemente: The Passion and Grace of Baseball's Last Hero* (New York: Simon & Schuster, 2006).

Markusen, Bruce. *The Team That Changed Baseball: Roberto Clemente and the 1971 Pittsburgh Pirates* (Yardley, Pennsylvania: Westholme Publishing, LLC, 2006).

Marshall, William. *Baseball's Pivotal Era, 1945-1951* (Lexington: University Press of Kentucky, 1999).

Mays, Willie, as told to Charles Einstein. *My Life In and Out of Baseball* (New York: E. P. Dutton & Co., 1972).

_____ with Lou Sahadi. *Say Hey — The Autobiography of Willie Mays* (New York: Simon and Schuster, 1988).

McNary, Kyle. *Black Baseball: A History of African-Americans & the National Game* (New York: Sterling Publishing Company, Inc., 2003).

_____. *Ted "Double Duty" Radcliffe: 36 Years of Pitching and Catching in Baseball's Negro Leagues* (Minneapolis: McNary Publications, 1994).

McNeil, William F. *Black Baseball Out of Season: Pay for Play Outside of the Negro Leagues* (Jefferson, North Carolina: McFarland & Company, Inc., 2007).

_____. *The California Winter League: America's First Integrated Professional Baseball League* (Jefferson, North Carolina: McFarland & Company, Inc., 2002).

Minoso, Minnie. *Just Call Me Minnie: My Six Decades in Baseball* (Champaign, Illinois: Sagamore, 1994).

_____, Fernando Fernandez, and Robert Kleinfelder. *Extra Innings: My Life in Baseball* (Chicago: Regnery Gateway, 1983).

Moffi, Larry and Jonathan Kronstadt. *Crossing the Line: Black Major Leaguers 1947-1959* (Lincoln, Nebraska: University of Nebraska Press, 1994).

Moore, Joseph Thomas. *Larry Doby: The Struggle of the American League's First Black Player* (Mineola, New York, Dover Publications, 2011). *Originally published under the title *Pride against Prejudice: The Biography of Larry Doby* by Greenwood Press, Inc., New York.

Motley, Bob with Byron Motley. *Ruling Over Monarchs, Giants & Stars* (New York: Sports Publishing, 2012).

Nieto, Severo. *Early U.S. Blackball Teams in Cuba: Box Scores, Rosters and Statistics for the American Series, 1900-1945* (Jefferson, North Carolina: McFarland & Company, Inc., 2006).

Nowlin, Bill, ed. *Pumpsie and Progress: The Red Sox, Race and Redemption* (Burlington, Massachusetts: Rounder Books, 2010).

O'Neil, Buck with Steve Wulf and David Conrads. *I Was Right on Time: My Journey from the Negro Leagues to the Majors* (New York: Simon & Schuster, 1996).

Overmeyer, James. *Queen of the Negro Leagues: Effa Manley and the Newark Eagles* (Lanham, Maryland: The Scarecrow Press, Inc., 1998).

Paige, Leroy (Satchel), as told to David Lipman. *Maybe I'll Pitch Forever* (Lincoln: University of Nebraska Press, 1993). *Originally published in 1962.

Peterson, Robert. *Only the Ball Was White: A History of Legendary Black Players and All-Black Professional Teams* (New York: Oxford University Press, 1970).

Plott, William J. *The Negro Southern League: A Baseball History, 1920-1951* (Jefferson, North Carolina: McFarland & Company, Inc., 2014).

Pollock, Alan J. and James A. Riley, ed. *Barnstorming to Heaven: Syd Pollock and His Great Black Teams* (Tuscaloosa: University of Alabama Press, 2006).

Posnanski, Joe. *The Soul of Baseball: A Road Trip through Buck O'Neil's America* (New York: William Morrow, 2007).

Powell, Larry. *Black Barons of Birmingham: The South's Greatest Negro League Team and Its Players* (Jefferson, North Carolina: McFarland & Company, Inc., 2009).

Rampersad, Arnold. *Jackie Robinson: A Biography* (New York: Ballantine Books, 1997).

Reisler, Jim, ed. *Black Writers/Black Baseball: An Anthology of Articles from Black Sportswriters Who Covered the Negro Leagues* (Jefferson, North Carolina, McFarland & Company, Inc., 1994).

Rendle, Ellen. *Judy Johnson: Delaware's Invisible Hero* (Wilmington, Delaware: The Cedar Tree Press, 1994).

Ribowsky, Mark. *A Complete History of the Negro Leagues, 1884-1955* (Secaucus, New Jersey: Carol Publishing, 1997).

_____. *Don't Look Back: Satchel Paige in the Shadows of Baseball* (New York: Simon & Schuster, 1994).

_____. *Josh Gibson: The Power and the Darkness* (Urbana: University of Illinois Press, 2004).

Riley, James A. *The Biographical Encyclopedia of the Negro Baseball Leagues* (New York: Carroll & Graf Publishers, Inc., 1994).

_____. *Dandy, Day, and the Devil* (Cocoa, Florida: TK Publishers, 1987).

_____. *Of Monarchs and Black Barons: Essays on Baseball's Negro Leagues* (Jefferson. North Carolina: McFarland & Company, Inc., 2012).

Robinson, Frazier and Paul Bauer. *Catching Dreams: My Life in the Negro Baseball Leagues* (Syracuse, New York: Syracuse University Press, 1999).

Robinson, Jackie. *Baseball Has Done It* (Brooklyn: Ig Publishing, 2005). *Originally published in 1964.

_____, as told to Alfred Duckett. *I Never Had It Made* (New York: G.P. Putnam's Sons, 1972).

_____, as told to Wendell Smith. *Jackie Robinson: My Own Story* (New York: Allegro Editions, 2013). *Originally published in 1948.

Robinson, Rachel with Lee Daniels. *Jackie Robinson: An Intimate Portrait* (New York: Abrams, 2014).

Rogosin, Donn. *Invisible Men: Life in Baseball's Negro Leagues* (Lincoln: University of Nebraska Press, 1983).

Rowan, Carl T. with Jackie Robinson. *Wait Till Next Year: The Life Story of Jackie Robinson* (New York: Random House, 1960).

Ruck, Rob. *Raceball: How the Major Leagues Colonized the Black and Latin Game* (Boston: Beacon Press, 2011).

_____. *Sandlot Seasons: Sport in Black Pittsburgh* (Urbana: University of Illinois Press, 1987).

_____. *The Tropic of Baseball: Baseball in the Dominican Republic* (Lincoln: University of Nebraska Press, 1991).

Rust, Art, Jr. *Get That Nigger Off the Field: The Oral History of the Negro Leagues* (Los Angeles: Shadow Lawn Press, 1992).

Silber, Irwin. *Press Box Red: The Story of Lester Rodney, the Communist Who Helped Break the Color Line in American Sports* (Philadelphia: Temple University Press, 2003).

Snyder, Brad. *Beyond the Shadow of the Senators: The Untold Story of the Homestead Grays and the Integration of Baseball* (New York: McGraw Hill, 2003).

Spatz, Lyle, ed. *The Team That Forever Changed Baseball and America: The 1947 Brooklyn Dodgers* (Lincoln: University of Nebraska Press, 2012).

Swaine, Rick. *The Black Stars Who Made Baseball Whole: The Jackie Robinson Generation in the Major Leagues, 1947-1959* (Jefferson, North Carolina: McFarland & Company, Inc., 2006).

Swanton, Barry. *The ManDak League: Haven for Former Negro League Ballplayers, 1950-1957* (Jefferson, North Carolina: McFarland and Company, Inc., 2006).

_____ and Jay-Dell Mah. *Black Baseball Players in Canada: A Biographical Dictionary, 1881-1960* (Jefferson, North Carolina: McFarland and Company, Inc., 2009).

Treto Cisneros, Pedro. *The Mexican League: Comprehensive Player Statistics, 1937-2001* (Jefferson, North Carolina: McFarland & Company, Inc., 2002).

Trouppe, Quincy. *20 Years Too Soon: Prelude to Major-League Integrated Baseball* (St. Louis: Missouri Historical Society Press, 1977).

Tye, Larry. *Satchel: The Life and Times of an American Legend* (New York: Random House, 2009).

Tygiel, Jules. *Baseball's Great Experiment: Jackie Robinson and His Legacy*, expanded edition (New York: Oxford University Press, 1997).

_____, ed. *The Jackie Robinson Reader: Perspectives on an American Hero* (New York: Plume, 1997).

_____. *Past Time: Baseball as History* (Oxford: Oxford University Press, 2000).

Van Hyning, Thomas E. *Puerto Rico's Winter League: A History of Major League Baseball's Launching Pad* (Jefferson, North Carolina: McFarland & Company, Inc., 1995).

_____. *The Santurce Crabbers: Sixty Seasons of Puerto Rican Winter League Baseball* (Jefferson, North Carolina: McFarland & Company, Inc., 1999).

Virtue, John. *South of the Color Barrier: How Jorge Pasquel and the Mexican League Pushed Baseball Toward Racial Integration* (Jefferson, North Carolina: McFarland & Company, Inc., 2008).

Ward, Geoffrey and Ken Burns. *Baseball: An Illustrated History* (New York: Alfred A. Knopf, 1994).

White, Frank M. *They Played for the Love of the Game: Untold Stories of Black Baseball in Minnesota* (St. Paul: Minnesota Historical Society Press, 2016).

White, Sol. *Sol White's History of Colored Baseball with other Documents on the Early Black Game, 1886–1936* (Lincoln: University of Nebraska Press, 1996). *Originally published in 1907 with later addenda included in this edition.

Withers, Ernest C. with text by Daniel Wolff. *Negro League Baseball* (New York: Harry N. Abrams, 2005).

Websites and Databases

History of the Negro Leagues:

Agatetype.typepad.com (Negro League & Latin American Baseball History)

Attheplate.com (Western Canada Baseball)

Baseballhall.org (National Baseball Hall of Fame)

CNLBR.org (Center for Negro League Baseball Research)

Homeplatedontmove.wordpress.com (The Negro Leagues Up Close)

NegroSouthernLeagueMuseumResearchCenter.org

NLBPA.com (Negro League Baseball Players Association) *This site is no longer updated.

NLBM.com (Negro Leagues Baseball Museum)

SABR.org (Society for American Baseball Research)

Negro League Statistics:

Baseball-Reference.com

Seamheads.com

Historical Newspapers, Including African-American Newspapers:

Genealogybank.com

News.google.com/newspapers/ (Google News Archive)

Newspapers.com

Paper of Record (Available to SABR members and at some public and university libraries)

ProQuest Historical Newspapers (Available at some public and university libraries)

Genealogy and Public Records:

Ancestry.com

Archives.gov/research/census (U.S. Census Records through 1930)

DVD

Documentary:

Baseball, A Film by Ken Burns. "Inning 5: Shadow Ball, 1930-1940," (1994, PBS Home Video).

The Boys in the Hall, Volume 1. "Larry Doby," (2014, National Baseball Hall of Fame).

The Brooklyn Dodgers: The Original America's Team. "Twilight at Noon: The Jackie Robinson Story," (2005, ESPN).

Jackie Robinson: A Film by Ken Burns, Sarah Burns & David McMahon, (2016, PBS Home Video).

Mr. Kansas City: The Life of Buck O'Neil, (2000, IBT Media).

Only the Ball Was White, (2007, MPI Home Video).

Pitching Man: Satchel Paige Defying Time, (2009, Refocus Digital Media).

Pride and Perseverance: The Story of the Negro Leagues, (2014, Lionsgate).

There Was Always Sun Shining Someplace: Life in the Negro Baseball Leagues, (2003, Refocus Films).

Feature Film:

42: The Jackie Robinson Story, (2013, Warner Brothers).

The Bingo Long Traveling All-Stars and Motor Kings, (2001, Universal). This 1976 film takes a humorous, fictional look at barnstorming during the Negro League era. Though some of the characters and action were inspired by real people and events, the film received mixed reactions from former Negro League players.

The Jackie Robinson Story, (2006, Legend Films). Jackie Robinson portrayed himself in this 1950 film adaptation of his life story.

Soul of the Game, (1996, HBO). A glimpse into the careers of Negro League legends Satchel Paige and Josh Gibson as well as the reaction to Jackie Robinson becoming the player who was chosen to break Organized Baseball's color barrier.

CONTRIBUTORS

NIALL ADLER has been paid to watch sports (and sometimes theatre) since 1998. Everything from diving to swimming, water polo, Aussie Rules, horse racing, hockey, futbol and gridiron, and… baseball on four continents and at two of the top collegiate programs, Long Beach State and Stanford. He's even judged a demolition derby. Educated at the University of San Francisco and farther South in Melbourne, Australia, he's worked some larger events like BCS Bowl Games, the Australian Open, Pan American Games and the Melbourne Cup.

JACK ANDERSON is an Urban Planning graduate of Concordia and McGill Universities in Montreal, Canada, and has worked in the construction supply manufacturing business for 40 years. He has written articles for local and regional history societies and is a life-long baseball aficionado, having grown up a fan of first the Montreal Royals, and then the Montreal Expos. He is an active member of SABR in Quebec, and has a longtime franchise, the Montreal Royals, in the Diamond Mind Historical Baseball simulation league, the Hall of Fame League. He and his wife expect to complete their pilgrimage to every major-league park within the next two years, and then intend to start on the minor-league parks. The Andersons live in Montreal, Canada.

BRIAN BAUGHAN is a freelance editor and writer based in Philadelphia. In 2015 he served as a judge for the CASEY Award, which recognizes the best baseball book of the year. His reviews of baseball books have been published by *Baseball America* and on his own blog, *The Off-Season Reader*. Brian is the also the author of seven books for young readers. More information is available at brianbaughan.com.

RALPH BERGER held a Bachelor of Arts Degree from the University of Pennsylvania and a Master of Public Administration degree from Temple University, and earned a Certificate in Human Resources from the University of Michigan. He wrote over 50 biographies for SABR. He lived with his wife Reina in Huntingdon Valley, Pennsylvania. A lifelong fan of the Fightin' Phillies, he endured as a Philly fan for eons. He hoped to emulate Moe Berg who on his death bed asked, "How did the Mets do today?" by asking, "How did the Phillies do today?" Ralph has died; we do not know if those were his last words.

RICHARD BOGOVICH is the author of *Kid Nichols: A Biography of the Hall of Fame Pitcher* and *The Who: A Who's Who*, both published by McFarland & Co. For SABR he most recently provided biographies of Dewon Brazelton and Freddie Sanchez for *Overcoming Adversity: Baseball's Tony Conigliaro Award* and wrote two chapters for *Baseball's Business: The Winter Meetings*. Earlier he contributed chapters to *Inventing Baseball: The 100 Greatest Games of the Nineteenth Century*. He lives in Rochester, Minnesota.

FREDERICK C. (RICK) BUSH teaches English full-time at Wharton County Junior College in Sugar Land, Texas. Rick has written articles and biographies for numerous SABR books and the SABR website and was also an associate editor for SABR's book about his hometown team, *Dome Sweet Dome: History and Highlights from 35 Years of the Houston Astrodome*. He and his wife Michelle, and their three sons—Michael, Andrew, and Daniel—live in the northwest Houston suburb of Cypress, Texas.

RALPH CARHART is a theatrical production manager and director by trade. He is also an amateur baseball historian with a particular interest in the origins of the game and outsider baseball, including the Negro Leagues and the AAGPBL. He received the 2015 Chairman's Award from the SABR 19th Century Committee and is the head of the 19th Century Baseball Grave Marker Project, spearheading the effort to place stones at the unmarked graves of forgotten pioneers. For the last seven years he has been working on a project he calls "The Hall Ball," in which he is attempting to take a photograph of a single baseball with every member of the Hall of Fame, living and deceased. The ball is pictured in either the hands of the living baseball great, or at the grave of those who are no longer alive. As of this writing he has photographed 298 of the 317 members. To see the photos he's taken so far, visit www.thehall-ball.sportspalooza.com. His research also led to the discovery that Hall of Famer Cristóbal Torriente is not, in fact, buried in his native Cuba as the official record states, but is buried in the same cemetery in Queens where Wee Willie Keeler and Mickey Welch are spending eternity.

ALAN COHEN has been a SABR member since 2011, and is Vice President/Treasurer of the SABR Connecticut Smoky Joe Wood Chapter. He has written more than 35 biographies for SABR's bio-project, has contributed to several SABR books, and has had articles published in *The National Pastime*. He is expanding his research into the Hearst Sandlot Classic (1946-1965), an annual youth All-Star game which launched the careers of 88 major-league players. His initial research appeared in the Fall, 2013 *Baseball Research Journal*. He graduated from Franklin and Marshall College with a degree in history. He has four children and six grandchildren and resides in West Hartford, Connecticut with his wife Frances, one cat and two dogs.

WILLIAM N. DAHLBERG has been a SABR members since 2010. Born in Cooperstown, he grew up in Vermont and found his way to Birmingham, Alabama, where he now lives with his wife, daughter, too many pets, and shelves full of baseball books. He works for Public Radio WBHM, the local NPR affiliate and is also a freelance radio producer and reporter. He graduated from Hiram College with a BA in history and from Dartmouth College with a M.A. in Liberal Studies. He has been a past chair of the Ron Gabriel Award Committee for SABR and presented research from his graduate thesis on baseball in post-war American Occupied Japan at a

SABR 40 in Atlanta. He is an avid Cleveland Indians fan (and drove from Birmingham to Cleveland to attend Games One and Two of the 2016 World Series), a regular attendee at Birmingham Barons games, and believes everyone should make a baseball pilgrimage to Rickwood Field. He can be reached at dahlbergwn@gmail.com

DENNIS D. DEGENHARDT has been a proud SABR member since 1997, thanks to a Christmas gift from his wife Linda. He spent 39 years in the credit union movement and recently retired as President/CEO of Glacier Hills Credit Union. He is doing what he finally wanted to do when he grew up, baseball research and writing because he is proud to call himself a baseball nerd. He also contributed to the SABR publication *From the Braves to the Brewers, Great Games and Exciting History at Milwaukee County Stadium*. In addition, he has been active at the local SABR level serving as the Treasurer of the Ken Keltner Badger State Chapter since 2001.

AMY ESSINGTON is a lecturer at California State University, Fullerton, and Cal Poly Pomona. She is the Executive Director of the Historical Society of Southern California. She completed a Ph.D. at Claremont Graduate University with a dissertation on the integration of the Pacific Coast League. Amy was an intern at the National Baseball Hall of Fame Library and the Smithsonian's National American History Museum.

CHARLES F. FABER was a native of Iowa who lived in Lexington, Kentucky, until his passing in August 2016. He held degrees from Coe College, Columbia University, and the University of Chicago. A retired public school and university teacher and administrator, he contributed to numerous SABR projects, including editing *The 1934 St. Louis Cardinals*. Among his publications are dozens of professional journal articles, encyclopedia entries, and research reports in fields such as school administration, education law, and country music. In addition to textbooks, he wrote 10 books (mostly on baseball) published by McFarland. His last book, co-authored with his grandson Zachariah Webb, was *The Hunt for a Reds October*, published by McFarland in 2015.

DAVE FORRESTER recalls his brother breaking an antique piece of furniture during the seventh game of the 1986 ALCS. Or it might have been himself. David is a nonprofit executive and lifelong Red Sox fan now living in exile with the Seattle Mariners. He joined SABR over a decade ago when his historical research uncovered Allie Moulton, the first person of African American ancestry known to have played in the segregated major leagues.

JAMES FORR is past winner of the McFarland-SABR Baseball Research Award and the co-author (along with David Proctor) of *Pie Traynor: A Baseball Biography*, which was a finalist for the 2010 CASEY Award. He lives in Columbia, Missouri.

CHARLIE FOUCHÉ is a native of Jacksonville, Florida. He received a Bachelor of Science in Journalism from the University of Florida. He has also earned a Master of Divinity, a Doctor of Theology, a Doctor of Christian Education, and a Doctor of Biblical Studies. He has written and edited for several publications, and written several theological works. He teaches in an alternative high school in Dalton, Georgia.

JOSEPH GERARD has been a lifelong Pittsburgh Pirates fan. He grew up hating the Yankees despite being born and raised in Newark, New Jersey—his biggest regret in life is that he was only two years old in 1960. Because of Roberto Clemente, he developed an interest in Latin-American baseball history and has contributed biographies of several Latin players to SABR's BioProject. He lives in New York City with his wife Ann Marie and their two children, Henry and Sophie.

IRV GOLDFARB signed up with SABR in 1999, making the Negro League Committee the first group he joined. He has since contributed to numerous SABR publications, including *Deadball Stars of the AL and NL; The Miracle Has Landed*; and *The Fenway Project*. Irv works for the ABC Television Network

and lives with his wife Mercedes and their furry "kids" Lolo and Consuelo in Union City, New Jersey. All are New York Met fans.

MARGARET M. "PEGGY" GRIPSHOVER is an Associate Professor of Geography at Western Kentucky University. She earned her Ph.D. in Geography at the University of Tennessee and her M.S. and B.S. degrees in Geography from Marshall University. She has been a SABR member since 2006 and combines her love of baseball with her research on race, ethnicity, urban culture, horse racing, and landscapes. Peggy has published articles in the *Baseball Research Journal* and contributed a chapter to *Northsiders: Essays on the History and Culture of the Chicago Cubs*, edited by Gerald R. Wood and Andy Hazucha (McFarland, 2008). She is a native of Cincinnati and lives in Bowling Green, Kentucky, with her husband Thomas L. Bell and their Australian Shepherd, Bella.

TOM HAWTHORN is an author and magazine writer who has contributed to more than a dozen SABR publications. He lives in Victoria, B.C.

LESLIE HEAPHY is an Associate Professor of History at Kent State University at Stark. She is the editor of the national journal *Black Ball* published by McFarland and has written or edited three other books on the Negro Leagues. She is also the editor of the *Encyclopedia of Women in Baseball*.

JAY HURD, a longtime member of SABR, is a librarian and museum educator. He studies and presents on the Negro Leagues and is a regular attendee of the annual Jerry Malloy Negro League Conference. Jay has contributed articles to the SABR BioProject and SABR publications. A fan of the Boston Red Sox, he has recently relocated from Medford, Massachusetts to Bristol, Rhode Island and looks forward to attending meetings of the Lajoie-Chapter of SABR, and to enjoying AAA baseball at McCoy Stadium, the home of the Pawtucket Red Sox.

WILLIAM H. (BILL) JOHNSON and his wife Chris divide their time between Cedar Rapids, Iowa and

Dayton, Ohio. He retired from the US Navy in 2006 after a 24-year career in naval aviation, and currently teaches unmanned aviation systems at Sinclair Community College in Dayton. He has just finished writing *Hal Trosky: A Baseball Biography* (McFarland & Co., 2017), and after two dozen essays for the SABR BioProject, he is now working on a second book, a biography of Negro League star Art "Superman" Pennington. He graduated from the University of California (Berkeley) with a degree in Rhetoric, and has subsequently earned a Master of Arts in Military History from Norwich University and a Masters in Aeronautical Science from Embry-Riddle Aeronautical University.

THOMAS E. KERN was born and raised in Southwest Pennsylvania. Listening to the mellifluous voices of Bob Prince and Jim Woods, how could one not become a lifelong Pirates fan? Tom has been a SABR member dating back to the mid-1980s, and he contributed a biography of Don Robinson to SABR's book about the 1979 Pittsburgh Pirates. He now lives in Washington, DC, and sees the Nationals and Orioles as often as possible. With a love and appreciation for Negro League baseball, Tom wrote a SABR biography of Leon Day after having met him at a baseball card show in the early 1990s, and he has also written a short history of the Homestead Grays for SABR. Tom's day job is in the field of transportation technology.

NORM KING is a retired civil servant from Ottawa, Ontario, Canada. Since joining SABR in 2010, he has written numerous biographies and game summaries, focusing primarily on the Montreal Expos. He was the lead writer and senior editor of *Au jeu/Play Ball: The 50 Greatest Games in the History of the Montreal Expos*, which was SABR's top-selling book of 2016.

JOHN KLIMA wrote *Willie's Boys: The 1948 Birmingham Black Barons, the Last Negro League World Series and the Making of a Baseball Legend*, which was published in 2009. He followed up that book with *Bushville Wins!* in 2012 and *The Game Must Go On* in 2015. A former baseball writer, his story "Deal of the Century," about the Paul Pettit transaction, appeared in the 2007 *Best American Sports Writing*. He has also contributed to several publications, including the *New York Times*. After several years in the baseball media, followed by a stint in the scouting community, which included an invitation to the Major League Scouting Bureau's scout school, he parlayed his writing, research and scouting experiences into a boutique baseball agency called BPR Baseball, which he operates with his wife, Jen. John is currently a fully certified MLBPA Player Agent, along with Jen, who at the time of this writing is one of only nine fully certified female Player Agents in baseball. At the time of their MLBPA certification, John and Jen were the only fully certified husband and wife agent team in baseball.

JAPHETH KNOPP received his Bachelor's and Master's degrees from Missouri State University and is currently in the History Ph.D. program at the University of Missouri. A fan of the Kansas City Royals and Fukuoka Hawks, he has been a member of SABR for a number of years and has previously contributed to the *Baseball Research Journal*. He lives in Columbia, Missouri with his wife Rebecca Wilkinson and their son, Ryphath. He may be contacted at Japheth.knopp@gmail.com.

BOB LEMOINE grew up in South Portland, Maine and has spent most of his life following the Red Sox. He became interested in baseball history as a kid, and a few years spent in Kansas City as an adult gave him a new interest in the history of the Negro Leagues and the great players we have forgotten due to our own ignorance. He lives in Barrington, New Hampshire where he works as a high school librarian. He has contributed to several SABR projects, including co-editing with Bill Nowlin on *Boston's First Nine: the 1871-75 Boston Red Stockings*.

LEN LEVIN, a SABR member since 1977, has been the copyeditor for many SABR publications. A resident of Providence, Rhode Island, he is a retired newspaper editor and adjunct journalism instructor. When he isn't busy editing for SABR, he works part-time editing the opinions of the Rhode Island Supreme Court.

MIKE MATTSEY lives in Sacramento with his wife Maia and his son Otis. He is a long-time fan of the World Series champion Chicago Cubs and is an avid collector of prewar baseball cards and sports memorabilia related to the team. He graduated from Indiana University and holds a Master's degree in history from Indiana State University where he successfully defended a paper examining the role of minor-league baseball in the Progressive Era South. He has written for SABR's BioProject and is currently working on a contribution for a SABR book on Wrigley Field's greatest games.

A Baltimore native, **BRIAN MCKENNA** has contributed over 50 works to SABR's Biography Project. His full-length projects include a biography of Clark Griffith and an analysis of the premature endings of baseball careers. Recently, he researched and wrote the first comprehensive look at the beginning of the sport in Baltimore, 1858-1872. It is available through SABR's Baltimore chapter.

JACK V. MORRIS is the director of a large pharmaceutical company's library. He lives in suburban Philadelphia with his wife and two daughters. His baseball biographies have appeared in numerous books including *The Team That Forever Changed Baseball and America* (1947 Brooklyn Dodgers) and *Scandal on the Southside* (1919 Chicago White Sox). He is not the Jack Morris of World Series fame but, every once in a while, wishes he was.

JUSTIN MURPHY is a newspaper reporter for the *Democrat and Chronicle* in Rochester, New York, where Luke Easter's number 36 is retired by the Rochester Red Wings. He attended the University of Chicago and the S.I. Newhouse School for Public Communications at Syracuse University.

ROB NEYER has written or co-written six books about baseball, and lives in Oregon with his wife and daughter.

SKIP NIPPER is author of *Baseball in Nashville* (2007, Arcadia Publishing), and shares his thoughts on his blog, www.262downright.com, and historical website, www.sulphurdell.com. Born and raised in Nashville, his interest in local baseball is deeply-rooted in his life-long love for the National Game, interlaced with fond memories of Nashville's famous ballpark, Sulphur Dell. A graduate of Memphis State University, Skip serves as secretary of the Nashville Old Timers Baseball Association and chapter leader of the Grantland Rice-Fred Russell (Nashville) chapter of SABR. He and his wife Sheila reside in Mt. Juliet, Tennessee.

BILL NOWLIN took a break from chronologically writing every bio of Boston Red Sox players which wasn't already claimed by others, and contributed three bios to this book. It was a very enriching experience. One of the founders of Rounder Records, he lives in Cambridge, Massachusetts and enjoys researching and writing about baseball people and bluegrass musicians. The University of Nebraska Press is publishing his full-length biography of Red Sox owner Tom Yawkey in 2017.

WILL OSGOOD is a former sports journalist who wrote for Bleacher Report, FanSided, and Cover 32. He graduated from San Diego State University in 2010 with a degree in Communication while minoring in Religious Studies. He is currently pursuing his Master of Divinity degree from Reformed Theological Seminary in Jackson, Mississippi. Will is a die-hard Cubs fan who cannot make up his mind on whether he loves the City of Chicago or New Orleans more.

MARK PANUTHOS is a teacher and coach at the Admiral Farragut Academy in St. Petersburg, Florida, and he also teaches history part-time at St. Petersburg College. Mark lives with his wife and two children in Seminole, Florida.

RICHARD J. PUERZER is an associate professor and chairperson of the Department of Engineering at Hofstra University. He has contributed to a number of SABR Books, including *Mustaches and Mayhem:*

The Oakland Athletics: 1972-1974 (2015) and *The 1986 New York Mets: There Was More Than Game Six (2016)*. His writings on baseball have also appeared in: *Nine: A Journal of Baseball History and Culture, Black Ball, The National Pastime, The Cooperstown Symposium on Baseball and American Culture* proceedings, and *Spitball*.

CHRIS RAINEY now lives in Oxford, Ohio with his wife, Janelle. He spent 35 years as a teacher and coach in Yellow Springs, Ohio. Retirement has afforded him time to work on his Cleveland Indians card and photo collection, as well as write for SABR's BioProject. Specializing in obscure players, he has contributed over 50 biographies to the SABR site.

CARL RIECHERS retired from United Parcel Service in 2012 after 35 years of service. With more free time he became a SABR member that same year. Born and raised in the suburbs of St. Louis, he became a big fan of the Cardinals. He and his wife have three children and he is a proud grandpa of two.

JOHN T. SACCOMAN is a Professor of Mathematics and Computer Science at Seton Hall University in New Jersey. An avid fan of the New York Mets, he team-teaches one of the earliest known Sabermetrics courses there with its founder, Rev. Gabe Costa. They, along with Mike Huber, have co-authored three books published by McFarland: *Understanding Sabermetrics, Practicing Sabermetrics* and *Reasoning with Sabermetrics*. John resides in northern New Jersey with his BoSox-loving wife Mary.

JOHN SCHLEPPI, University of Dayton Professor Emeritus, has worked in sports history for over 50 years. He published *Chicago's Showcase of Basketball: The World Tournament of Professional Basketball and the College All-Star Game*. He founded the Dayton Chapter of SABR and was chair for 15 years.

CURT SMITH, says *USA Today*, is "America's voice of authority on baseball broadcasting." Raised a Yankees fan in Upstate New York, he cried at age 9 when Maz homered in Game Seven. Later, seeing the light, he forever adopted the Boston Red Sox. His 17 books

include the first in-depth history of the Presidency and baseball, *The Presidents and the Pastime*, to be released in spring 2018 by the University of Nebraska Press. Prior books include *Voices of The Game, Pull Up a Chair: The Vin Scully Story*, and his current *George H.W. Bush: Character at the Core*. He also has been privileged to contribute to a number of SABR books, including the 1951 Giants, 1959 White Sox, 1960 Pirates, 1969 Mets, 1972 A's, and 1986 Red Sox. In 1989-93, he wrote more speeches than anyone else for President George H.W. Bush. He is a GateHouse Media and mlblog.com columnist, Associated Press award-winning commentator, and senior lecturer of English at the University of Rochester. He has hosted or keynoted the Great Fenway Park Writers Series, numerous Smithsonian Institution series, and the Cooperstown Symposium on Baseball and American Culture. The former *The Saturday Evening Post* senior editor has written ESPN TV's *Voices of The Game* documentary, created the Franklin Roosevelt Award in Communication at the National Radio Hall of Fame, and been named to the prestigious Judson Welliver Society of former Presidential Speechwriters.

JW STEWART holds a master's degree in history from Sam Houston State University. Currently he teaches American history and lives in Frisco, Texas. He has contributed several baseball articles for EastTexasHistory.org, and can often be found at Frisco Rough Riders games during the summer.

JEB STEWART is a lawyer in Birmingham, Alabama, who enjoys taking his sons (Nolan and Ryan) and his wife Stephanie to the Rickwood Classic each year. He has been a SABR member since 2012, and is a Board Member of the Friends of Rickwood Field. He is a regular contributor to the *Rickwood Times* newspaper and has presented at the annual Southern Association Baseball Conference. He spent most of his youth pitching a tennis ball against his front porch steps, hoping a Yankees scout would happen by and discover him. Although he remains undiscovered, he still has a passion for baseball. He wrote part of the chapters on Piper Davis and Jimmie Newberry in the press box at Rickwood Field.

RICK SWAINE is the author of *Beating the Breaks: Major League Ballplayers Who Overcame Disabilities* (McFarland, 2004). He is a semi-retired CPA who lives near Tallahassee, Florida. A past contributor to various SABR publications, he enjoys writing about baseball's unsung heroes. He teaches a class in baseball history for FSU's Oscher Lifelong Learning Institute and still plays competitive baseball in various leagues and senior tournaments. *Baseball's Comeback Players* (McFarland 2014) is his fourth historical baseball book.

CLARENCE WATKINS is a native of Memphis, Tennessee, and a graduate of Memphis State University. He is a lifelong baseball fan having traveled the southeast for the past 30 years researching the teams of the old Southern Association League. Clarence is the co-founder of the Southern Association Baseball Conference, now in its 14th year. He is a research member of the Negro Southern League Museum in Birmingham, Alabama and on the Board of Directors of the The Friends of Rickwood. Clarence is also a member of SABR. He is the author of *Baseball in Birmingham* and *Baseball in Memphis*. He was a presenter at the 2010 SABR National Convention in Atlanta and the Jerry Malloy Conference in Birmingham. Clarence recently finished his third Arcadia book, *Baseball in Montgomery.*

STEVE WEST loves reading, writing, and analyzing baseball, and has written a number of articles for the SABR BioProject. Steve (a SABR member since 2006), his wife Marian, and son Joshua are die-hard Texas Rangers fans, which is a big reason why he is editing a BioProject book on the 1972 Rangers. By day Steve is owner of a startup travel company in the Dallas area.

DAVE WILKIE grew up in the '70s and '80s in Calgary, Alberta, Canada, idolizing Willie "Stretch" McCovey and the San Francisco Giants. Summers were spent at his Grandparents in the San Francisco Bay Area, where he and his younger brother Wyatt took up residence at Candlestick Park. His obsession with Negro League baseball and its players can be traced to a 1983 mail order purchase of the book, *The All-Time All-Stars of Black Baseball*, by James A. Riley. He now lives in Youngstown, Ohio with his wife, Lillian and their three children, Zachary, Keona, and Monte. He now only sees his beloved Giants once a year when he makes the one-hour drive to Pittsburgh once a year. He's been a SABR member since 2010 and this is his first profile written for SABR's BioProject.

SABR BioProject Team Books

In 2002, the Society for American Baseball Research launched an effort to write and publish biographies of every player, manager, and individual who has made a contribution to baseball. Over the past decade, the BioProject Committee has produced over 6,000 biographical articles. Many have been part of efforts to create theme- or team-oriented books, spearheaded by chapters or other committees of SABR.

THE 1986 BOSTON RED SOX:
THERE WAS MORE THAN GAME SIX
One of a two-book series on the rivals that met in the 1986 World Series, the Boston Red Sox and the New York Mets, including biographies of every player, coach, broadcaster, and other important figures in the top organizations in baseball that year. .
Edited by Leslie Heaphy and Bill Nowlin
$19.95 paperback (ISBN 978-1-943816-19-4)
$9.99 ebook (ISBN 978-1-943816-18-7)
8.5"X11", 420 pages, over 200 photos

THE 1986 NEW YORK METS:
THERE WAS MORE THAN GAME SIX
The other book in the "rivalry" set from the 1986 World Series. This book re-tells the story of that year's classic World Series and this is the story of each of the players, coaches, managers, and broadcasters, their lives in baseball and the way the 1986 season fit into their lives.
Edited by Leslie Heaphy and Bill Nowlin
$19.95 paperback (ISBN 978-1-943816-13-2)
$9.99 ebook (ISBN 978-1-943816-12-5)
8.5"X11", 392 pages, over 100 photos

SCANDAL ON THE SOUTH SIDE:
THE 1919 CHICAGO WHITE SOX
The Black Sox Scandal isn't the only story worth telling about the 1919 Chicago White Sox. The team roster included three future Hall of Famers, a 20-year-old spitballer who would win 300 games in the minors, and even a batboy who later became a celebrity with the "Murderers' Row" New York Yankees. All of their stories are included in Scandal on the South Side with a timeline of the 1919 season.
Edited by Jacob Pomrenke
$19.95 paperback (ISBN 978-1-933599-95-3)
$9.99 ebook (ISBN 978-1-933599-94-6)
8.5"x11", 324 pages, 55 historic photos

WINNING ON THE NORTH SIDE
THE 1929 CHICAGO CUBS
Celebrate the 1929 Chicago Cubs, one of the most exciting teams in baseball history. Future Hall of Famers Hack Wilson, '29 NL MVP Rogers Hornsby, and Kiki Cuyler, along with Riggs Stephenson formed one of the most potent quartets in baseball history. The magical season came to an ignominious end in the World Series and helped craft the future "lovable loser" image of the team.
Edited by Gregory H. Wolf
$19.95 paperback (ISBN 978-1-933599-89-2)
$9.99 ebook (ISBN 978-1-933599-88-5)
8.5"x11", 314 pages, 59 photos

DETROIT THE UNCONQUERABLE:
THE 1935 WORLD CHAMPION TIGERS
Biographies of every player, coach, and broadcaster involved with the 1935 World Champion Detroit Tigers baseball team, written by members of the Society for American Baseball Research. Also includes a season in review and other articles about the 1935 team. Hank Greenberg, Mickey Cochrane, Charlie Gehringer, Schoolboy Rowe, and more.
Edited by Scott Ferkovich
$19.95 paperback (ISBN 9978-1-933599-78-6)
$9.99 ebook (ISBN 978-1-933599-79-3)
8.5"X11", 230 pages, 52 photos

THE TEAM THAT TIME WON'T FORGET:
THE 1951 NEW YORK GIANTS
Because of Bobby Thomson's dramatic "Shot Heard 'Round the World" in the bottom of the ninth of the decisive playoff game against the Brooklyn Dodgers, the team will forever be in baseball public's consciousness. Includes a foreword by Giants outfielder Monte Irvin.
Edited by Bill Nowlin and C. Paul Rogers III
$19.95 paperback (ISBN 978-1-933599-99-1)
$9.99 ebook (ISBN 978-1-933599-98-4)
8.5"X11", 282 pages, 47 photos

A PENNANT FOR THE TWIN CITIES:
THE 1965 MINNESOTA TWINS
This volume celebrates the 1965 Minnesota Twins, who captured the American League pennant in just their fifth season in the Twin Cities. Led by an All-Star cast, from Harmon Killebrew, Tony Oliva, Zoilo Versalles, and Mudcat Grant to Bob Allison, Jim Kaat, Earl Battey, and Jim Perry, the Twins won 102 games, but bowed to the Los Angeles Dodgers and Sandy Koufax in Game Seven
Edited by Gregory H. Wolf
$19.95 paperback (ISBN 978-1-943816-09-5)
$9.99 ebook (ISBN 978-1-943816-08-8)
8.5"X11", 405 pages, over 80 photos

MUSTACHES AND MAYHEM: CHARLIE O'S THREE TIME CHAMPIONS:
THE OAKLAND ATHLETICS: 1972-74
The Oakland Athletics captured major league baseball's crown each year from 1972 through 1974. Led by future Hall of Famers Reggie Jackson, Catfish Hunter and Rollie Fingers, the Athletics were a largely homegrown group who came of age together. Biographies of every player, coach, manager, and broadcaster (and mascot) from 1972 through 1974 are included, along with season recaps.
Edited by Chip Greene
$29.95 paperback (ISBN 978-1-943816-07-1)
$9.99 ebook (ISBN 978-1-943816-06-4)
8.5"X11", 600 pages, almost 100 photos

SABR Members can purchase each book at a significant discount (often 50% off) and receive the ebook editions free as a member benefit. Each book is available in a trade paperback edition as well as ebooks suitable for reading on a home computer or Nook, Kindle, or iPad/tablet.
To learn more about becoming a member of SABR, visit the website: sabr.org/join

THE SABR DIGITAL LIBRARY

The Society for American Baseball Research, the top baseball research organization in the world, disseminates some of the best in baseball history, analysis, and biography through our publishing programs. The SABR Digital Library contains a mix of books old and new, and focuses on a tandem program of paperback and ebook publication, making these materials widely available for both on digital devices and as traditional printed books.

GREATEST GAMES BOOKS

TIGERS BY THE TALE:
GREAT GAMES AT MICHIGAN AND TRUMBULL
For over 100 years, Michigan and Trumbull was the scene of some of the most exciting baseball ever. This book portrays 50 classic games at the corner, spanning the earliest days of Bennett Park until Tiger Stadium's final closing act. From Ty Cobb to Mickey Cochrane, Hank Greenberg to Al Kaline, and Willie Horton to Alan Trammell.
Edited by Scott Ferkovich
$12.95 paperback (ISBN 978-1-943816-21-7)
$6.99 ebook (ISBN 978-1-943816-20-0)
8.5"x11", 160 pages, 22 photos

FROM THE BRAVES TO THE BREWERS: GREAT GAMES AND HISTORY AT MILWAUKEE'S COUNTY STADIUM
The National Pastime provides in-depth articles focused on the geographic region where the national SABR convention is taking place annually. The SABR 45 convention took place in Chicago, and here are 45 articles on baseball in and around the bat-and-ball crazed Windy City: 25 that appeared in the souvenir book of the convention plus another 20 articles available in ebook only.
Edited by Gregory H. Wolf
$19.95 paperback (ISBN 978-1-943816-23-1)
$9.99 ebook (ISBN 978-1-943816-22-4)
8.5"X11", 290 pages, 58 photos

BRAVES FIELD:
MEMORABLE MOMENTS AT BOSTON'S LOST DIAMOND
From its opening on August 18, 1915, to the sudden departure of the Boston Braves to Milwaukee before the 1953 baseball season, Braves Field was home to Boston's National League baseball club and also hosted many other events: from NFL football to championship boxing. The most memorable moments to occur in Braves Field history are portrayed here.
Edited by Bill Nowlin and Bob Brady
$19.95 paperback (ISBN 978-1-933599-93-9)
$9.99 ebook (ISBN 978-1-933599-92-2)
8.5"X11", 282 pages, 182 photos

AU JEU/PLAY BALL: THE 50 GREATEST GAMES IN THE HISTORY OF THE MONTREAL EXPOS
The 50 greatest games in Montreal Expos history. The games described here recount the exploits of the many great players who wore Expos uniforms over the years—Bill Stoneman, Gary Carter, Andre Dawson, Steve Rogers, Pedro Martinez, from the earliest days of the franchise, to the glory years of 1979-1981, the what-might-have-been years of the early 1990s, and the sad, final days.and others.
Edited by Norm King
$12.95 paperback (ISBN 978-1-943816-15-6)
$5.99 ebook (ISBN 978-1-943816-14-9)
8.5"x11", 162 pages, 50 photos

ORIGINAL SABR RESEARCH

CALLING THE GAME:
BASEBALL BROADCASTING FROM 1920 TO THE PRESENT
An exhaustive, meticulously researched history of bringing the national pastime out of the ballparks and into living rooms via the airwaves. Every play-by-play announcer, color commentator, and ex-ballplayer, every broadcast deal, radio station, and TV network. Plus a foreword by "Voice of the Chicago Cubs" Pat Hughes, and an afterword by Jacques Doucet, the "Voice of the Montreal Expos" 1972-2004.
by Stuart Shea
$24.95 paperback (ISBN 978-1-933599-40-3)
$9.99 ebook (ISBN 978-1-933599-41-0)
7"X10", 712 pages, 40 photos

BIOPROJECT BOOKS

WHO'S ON FIRST:
REPLACEMENT PLAYERS IN WORLD WAR II
During World War II, 533 players made the major league debuts. More than 60% of the players in the 1941 Opening Day lineups departed for the service and were replaced by first-times and oldsters. Hod Lisenbee was 46. POW Bert Shepard had an artificial leg, and Pete Gray had only one arm. The 1944 St. Louis Browns had 13 players classified 4-F. These are their stories.
Edited by Marc Z Aaron and Bill Nowlin
$19.95 paperback (ISBN 978-1-933599-91-5)
$9.99 ebook (ISBN 978-1-933599-90-8)
8.5"X11", 422 pages, 67 photos

VAN LINGLE MUNGO:
THE MAN, THE SONG, THE PLAYERS
40 baseball players with intriguing names have been named in renditions of Dave Frishberg's classic 1969 song, Van Lingle Mungo. This book presents biographies of all 40 players and additional information about one of the greatest baseball novelty songs of all time.
Edited by Bill Nowlin
$19.95 paperback (ISBN 978-1-933599-76-2)
$9.99 ebook (ISBN 978-1-933599-77-9)
8.5"X11", 278 pages, 46 photos

NUCLEAR POWERED BASEBALL
Nuclear Powered Baseball tells the stories of each player—past and present—featured in the classic Simpsons episode "Homer at the Bat." Wade Boggs, Ken Griffey Jr., Ozzie Smith, Nap Lajoie, Don Mattingly, and many more. We've also included a few very entertaining takes on the now-famous episode from prominent baseball writers Jonah Keri, Joe Posnanski, Erik Malinowski, and Bradley Woodrum
Edited by Emily Hawks and Bill Nowlin
$19.95 paperback (ISBN 978-1-943816-11-8)
$9.99 ebook (ISBN 978-1-943816-10-1)
8.5"X11", 250 pages

SABR Members can purchase each book at a significant discount (often 50% off) and receive the ebook edtions free as a member benefit. Each book is available in a trade paperback edition as well as ebooks suitable for reading on a home computer or Nook, Kindle, or iPad/tablet.
To learn more about becoming a member of SABR, visit the website: sabr.org/join

SABR BioProject Books

In 2002, the Society for American Baseball Research launched an effort to write and publish biographies of every player, manager, and individual who has made a contribution to baseball. Over the past decade, the BioProject Committee has produced over 2,200 biographical articles. Many have been part of efforts to create theme- or team-oriented books, spearheaded by chapters or other committees of SABR.

THE YEAR OF THE BLUE SNOW:
THE 1964 PHILADELPHIA PHILLIES
Catcher Gus Triandos dubbed the Philadelphia Phillies' 1964 season "the year of the blue snow," a rare thing that happens once in a great while. This book sheds light on lingering questions about the 1964 season—but any book about a team is really about the players. This work offers life stories of all the players and others (managers, coaches, owners, and broadcasters) associated with this star-crossed team, as well as essays of analysis and history.
Edited by Mel Marmer and Bill Nowlin
$19.95 paperback (ISBN 978-1-933599-51-9)
$9.99 ebook (ISBN 978-1-933599-52-6)
8.5"X11", 356 PAGES, over 70 photos

DETROIT TIGERS 1984:
WHAT A START! WHAT A FINISH!
The 1984 Detroit tigers roared out of the gate, winning their first nine games of the season and compiling an eye-popping 35-5 record after the campaign's first 40 games—still the best start ever for any team in major league history. This book brings together biographical profiles of every Tiger from that magical season, plus those of field management, top executives, the broadcasters—even venerable Tiger Stadium and the city itself.
Edited by Mark Pattison and David Raglin
$19.95 paperback (ISBN 978-1-933599-44-1)
$9.99 ebook (ISBN 978-1-933599-45-8)
8.5"x11", 250 pages (Over 230,000 words!)

SWEET '60: THE 1960 PITTSBURGH PIRATES
A portrait of the 1960 team which pulled off one of the biggest upsets of the last 60 years. When Bill Mazeroski's home run left the park to win in Game Seven of the World Series, beating the New York Yankees, David had toppled Goliath. It was a blow that awakened a generation, one that millions of people saw on television, one of TV's first iconic World Series moments.
Edited by Clifton Blue Parker and Bill Nowlin
$19.95 paperback (ISBN 978-1-933599-48-9)
$9.99 ebook (ISBN 978-1-933599-49-6)
8.5"X11", 340 pages, 75 photos

RED SOX BASEBALL IN THE DAYS OF IKE AND ELVIS: THE RED SOX OF THE 1950s
Although the Red Sox spent most of the 1950s far out of contention, the team was filled with fascinating players who captured the heart of their fans. In *Red Sox Baseball*, members of SABR present 46 biographies on players such as Ted Williams and Pumpsie Green as well as season-by-season recaps.
Edited by Mark Armour and Bill Nowlin
$19.95 paperback (ISBN 978-1-933599-24-3)
$9.99 ebook (ISBN 978-1-933599-34-2)
8.5"X11", 372 PAGES, over 100 photos

THE MIRACLE BRAVES OF 1914
BOSTON'S ORIGINAL WORST-TO-FIRST CHAMPIONS
Long before the Red Sox "Impossible Dream" season, Boston's now nearly forgotten "other" team, the 1914 Boston Braves, performed a baseball "miracle" that resounds to this very day. The "Miracle Braves" were Boston's first "worst-to-first" winners of the World Series. Refusing to throw in the towel at the midseason mark, George Stallings engineered a remarkable second-half climb in the standings all the way to first place.
Edited by Bill Nowlin
$19.95 paperback (ISBN 978-1-933599-69-4)
$9.99 ebook (ISBN 978-1-933599-70-0)
8.5"X11", 392 PAGES, over 100 photos

THAR'S JOY IN BRAVELAND!
THE 1957 MILWAUKEE BRAVES
Few teams in baseball history have captured the hearts of their fans like the Milwaukee Braves of the 1950s. During the Braves' 13-year tenure in Milwaukee (1953-1965), they had a winning record every season, won two consecutive NL pennants (1957 and 1958), lost two more in the final week of the season (1956 and 1959), and set big-league attendance records along the way.
Edited by Gregory H. Wolf
$19.95 paperback (ISBN 978-1-933599-71-7)
$9.99 ebook (ISBN 978-1-933599-72-4)
8.5"x11", 330 pages, over 60 photos

NEW CENTURY, NEW TEAM:
THE 1901 BOSTON AMERICANS
The team now known as the Boston Red Sox played its first season in 1901. Boston had a well-established National League team, but the American League went head-to-head with the N.L. in Chicago, Philadelphia, and Boston. Chicago won the American League pennant and Boston finished second, only four games behind.
Edited by Bill Nowlin
$19.95 paperback (ISBN 978-1-933599-58-8)
$9.99 ebook (ISBN 978-1-933599-59-5)
8.5"X11", 268 pages, over 125 photos

CAN HE PLAY?
A LOOK AT BASEBALL SCOUTS AND THEIR PROFESSION
They dig through tons of coal to find a single diamond. Here in the world of scouts, we meet the "King of Weeds," a Ph.D. we call "Baseball's Renaissance Man," a husband-and-wife team, pioneering Latin scouts, and a Japanese-American interned during World War II who became a successful scout—and many, many more.
Edited by Jim Sandoval and Bill Nowlin
$19.95 paperback (ISBN 978-1-933599-23-6)
$9.99 ebook (ISBN 978-1-933599-25-0)
8.5"X11", 200 PAGES, over 100 photos

SABR Members can purchase each book at a significant discount (often 50% off) and receive the ebook editions free as a member benefit. Each book is available in a trade paperback edition as well as ebooks suitable for reading on a home computer or Nook, Kindle, or iPad/tablet.
To learn more about becoming a member of SABR, visit the website: sabr.org/join

THE SABR DIGITAL LIBRARY

The Society for American Baseball Research, the top baseball research organization in the world, disseminates some of the best in baseball history, analysis, and biography through our publishing programs. The SABR Digital Library contains a mix of books old and new, and focuses on a tandem program of paperback and ebook publication, making these materials widely available for both on digital devices and as traditional printed books.

CLASSIC REPRINTS

BASE-BALL: HOW TO BECOME A PLAYER
by John Montgomery Ward
John Montgomery Ward (1860-1925) tossed the second perfect game in major league history and later became the game's best shortstop and a great, inventive manager. His classic handbook on baseball skills and strategy was published in 1888. Illustrated with woodcuts, the book is divided into chapters for each position on the field as well as chapters on the origin of the game, theory and strategy, training, base-running, and batting.
$4.99 ebook (ISBN 978-1-933599-47-2)
$9.95 paperback (ISBN 978-0910137539)
156 PAGES, 4.5"X7" replica edition

BATTING by F. C. Lane
First published in 1925, *Batting* collects the wisdom and insights of over 250 hitters and baseball figures. Lane interviewed extensively and compiled tips and advice on everything from batting stances to beanballs. Legendary baseball figures such as Ty Cobb, Casey Stengel, Cy Young, Walter Johnson, Rogers Hornsby, and Babe Ruth reveal the secrets of such integral and interesting parts of the game as how to choose a bat, the ways to beat a slump, and how to outguess the pitcher.
$14.95 paperback (ISBN 978-0-910137-86-7)
$7.99 ebook (ISBN 978-1-933599-46-5)
240 PAGES, 5"X7"

RUN, RABBIT, RUN
by Walter "Rabbit" Maranville
"Rabbit" Maranville was the Joe Garagiola of Grandpa's day, the baseball comedian of the times. In a twenty-four-year career that began in 1912, Rabbit found a lot of funny situations to laugh at, and no wonder: he caused most of them! The book also includes an introduction by the late Harold Seymour and a historical account of Maranville's life and Hall-of-Fame career by Bob Carroll.
$9.95 paperback (ISBN 978-1-933599-26-7)
$5.99 ebook (ISBN 978-1-933599-27-4)
100 PAGES, 5.5"X8.5", 15 rare photos

MEMORIES OF A BALLPLAYER
by Bill Werber and C. Paul Rogers III
Bill Werber's claim to fame is unique: he was the last living person to have a direct connection to the 1927 Yankees, "Murderers' Row," a team hailed by many as the best of all time. Rich in anecdotes and humor, Memories of a Ballplayer is a clear-eyed memoir of the world of big-league baseball in the 1930s. Werber played with or against some of the most productive hitters of all time, including Babe Ruth, Ted Williams, Lou Gehrig, and Joe DiMaggio.
$14.95 paperback (ISNB 978-0-910137-84-3)
$6.99 ebook (ISBN 978-1-933599-47-2)
250 PAGES, 6"X9"

ORIGINAL SABR RESEARCH

INVENTING BASEBALL: THE 100 GREATEST GAMES OF THE NINETEENTH CENTURY
SABR's Nineteenth Century Committee brings to life the greatest games from the game's early years. From the "prisoner of war" game that took place among captive Union soldiers during the Civil War (immortalized in a famous lithograph), to the first intercollegiate game (Amherst versus Williams), to the first professional no-hitter, the games in this volume span 1833–1900 and detail the athletic exploits of such players as Cap Anson, Moses "Fleetwood" Walker, Charlie Comiskey, and Mike "King" Kelly.
Edited by Bill Felber
$19.95 paperback (ISBN 978-1-933599-42-7)
$9.99 ebook (ISBN 978-1-933599-43-4)
302 PAGES, 8"x10", 200 photos

NINETEENTH CENTURY STARS: 2012 EDITION
First published in 1989, *Nineteenth Century Stars* was SABR's initial attempt to capture the stories of baseball players from before 1900. With a collection of 136 fascinating biographies, SABR has re-released *Nineteenth Century Stars* for 2012 with revised statistics and new form. The 2012 version also includes a preface by **John Thorn.**
Edited by Robert L. Tiemann and Mark Rucker
$19.95 paperback (ISBN 978-1-933599-28-1)
$9.99 ebook (ISBN 978-1-933599-29-8)
300 PAGES, 6"X9"

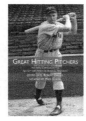

GREAT HITTING PITCHERS
Published in 1979, *Great Hitting Pitchers* was one of SABR's early publications. Edited by SABR founder Bob Davids, the book compiles stories and records about pitchers excelling in the batter's box. Newly updated in 2012 by Mike Cook, *Great Hitting Pitchers* contain tables including data from 1979-2011, corrections to reflect recent records, and a new chapter on recent new members in the club of "great hitting pitchers" like Tom Glavine and Mike Hampton.
Edited by L. Robert Davids
$9.95 paperback (ISBN 978-1-933599-30-4)
$5.99 ebook (ISBN 978-1-933599-31-1)
102 PAGES, 5.5"x8.5"

THE FENWAY PROJECT
Sixty-four SABR members—avid fans, historians, statisticians, and game enthusiasts—recorded their experiences of a single game. Some wrote from inside the Green Monster's manual scoreboard, the Braves clubhouse, or the broadcast booth, while others took in the essence of Fenway from the grandstand or bleachers. The result is a fascinating look at the charms and challenges of Fenway Park, and the allure of being a baseball fan.
Edited by Bill Nowlin and Cecilia Tan
$9.99 ebook (ISBN 978-1-933599-50-2)
175 pages, 100 photos

SABR Members can purchase each book at a significant discount (often 50% off) and receive the ebook editions free as a member benefit. Each book is available in a trade paperback edition as well as ebooks suitable for reading on a home computer or Nook, Kindle, or iPad/tablet.
To learn more about becoming a member of SABR, visit the website: sabr.org/join

Society for American Baseball Research

Cronkite School at ASU
555 N. Central Ave. #416, Phoenix, AZ 85004
602.496.1460 (phone)
SABR.org

Become a SABR member today!

If you're interested in baseball — writing about it, reading about it, talking about it — there's a place for you in the Society for American Baseball Research. Our members include everyone from academics to professional sportswriters to amateur historians and statisticians to students and casual fans who enjoy reading about baseball and occasionally gathering with other members to talk baseball. What unites all SABR members is an interest in the game and joy in learning more about it.

SABR membership is open to any baseball fan; we offer 1-year and 3-year memberships. Here's a list of some of the key benefits you'll receive as a SABR member:

• Receive two editions (spring and fall) of the *Baseball Research Journal,* our flagship publication
• Receive expanded e-book edition of *The National Pastime,* our annual convention journal
• 8-10 new e-books published by the SABR Digital Library, all FREE to members
• "This Week in SABR" e-newsletter, sent to members every Friday
• Join dozens of research committees, from Statistical Analysis to Women in Baseball.
• Join one of 70 regional chapters in the U.S., Canada, Latin America, and abroad
• Participate in online discussion groups
• Ask and answer baseball research questions on the SABR-L e-mail listserv
• Complete archives of *The Sporting News* dating back to 1886 and other research resources
• Promote your research in "This Week in SABR"
• Diamond Dollars Case Competition
• Yoseloff Scholarships

• Discounts on SABR national conferences, including the SABR National Convention, the SABR Analytics Conference, Jerry Malloy Negro League Conference, Frederick Ivor-Campbell 19th Century Conference, and the Arizona Fall League Experience
• Publish your research in peer-reviewed SABR journals
• Collaborate with SABR researchers and experts
• Contribute to Baseball Biography Project or the SABR Games Project
• List your new book in the SABR Bookshelf
• Lead a SABR research committee or chapter
• Networking opportunities at SABR Analytics Conference
• Meet baseball authors and historians at SABR events and chapter meetings
• 50% discounts on paperback versions of SABR e-books
• Discounts with other partners in the baseball community
• SABR research awards

We hope you'll join the most passionate international community of baseball fans at SABR! Check us out online at SABR.org/join.

- - - ✂ -

SABR MEMBERSHIP FORM

	Annual	3-year	Senior	3-yr Sr.	Under 30
Standard:	❏ $65	❏ $175	❏ $45	❏ $129	❏ $45
(International members wishing to be mailed the Baseball Research Journal should add $10/yr for Canada/Mexico or $19/yr for overseas locations.)					
Canada/Mexico:	❏ $75	❏ $205	❏ $55	❏ $159	❏ $55
Overseas:	❏ $84	❏ $232	❏ $64	❏ $186	❏ $55
Senior = 65 or older before Dec. 31 of the current year					

Participate in Our Donor Program!

Support the preservation of baseball research. Designate your gift toward:
❏General Fund ❏Endowment Fund ❏Research Resources ❏_____
❏ I want to maximize the impact of my gift; do not send any donor premiums
❏ I would like this gift to remain anonymous.

Note: Any donation not designated will be placed in the General Fund.
SABR is a 501 (c) (3) not-for-profit organization & donations are tax-deductible to the extent allowed by law.

Name _____

E-mail* _____

Address _____

City _____ ST_____ ZIP_____

Phone _____ Birthday _____

* Your e-mail address on file ensures you will receive the most recent SABR news.

Dues $_____
Donation $_____
Amount Enclosed $_____

Do you work for a matching grant corporation? Call (602) 496-1460 for details.

If you wish to pay by credit card, please contact the SABR office at (602) 496-1460 or visit the SABR Store online at SABR.org/join. We accept Visa, Mastercard & Discover.

Do you wish to receive the *Baseball Research Journal* electronically? ❏ Yes   ❏ No
Our e-books are available in PDF, Kindle, or EPUB (iBooks, iPad, Nook) formats.

Mail to: SABR, Cronkite School at ASU, 555 N. Central Ave. #416, Phoenix, AZ 85004

Made in the USA
Coppell, TX
05 November 2020